Today's real-life careers, real-world activities, and exercises that teach

CAREERS IN CRIMINAL JUSTICE

Transportation Security Officer (TSO)

NATURE OF THE WORK

Employed by the Transportation Security Administration in the government's new Department of Homeland Security, TSOs work at airports where they operate X-ray machines, conducted searches of passengers and luggage, review tickets, and look for suspicious behavior. They must interact courteously with the public as they work in a noisy, stressful environment amid distracting machinery while standing on their feet for three hours at a time. Most importantly, as they pay close attention to people's behavior, clothing, and luggage, they must make effective decisions if crisis situations arise. They must also work irregular hours, including evening and weekend shifts.

REQUIRED QUALIFICATIONS

TSOs must be U.S. citizens or U.S. nationals (citizens of American Samoa or the Commonwealth of Northern Mariana Islands). They must be proficient in English and possess a high [school diploma] or GED. The educational requirement may be [satisfied with at] least one year of full-time work experience in [a job such as] an X-ray technician. They must have correctable [vision of 20]/30 in the best eye for distance vision and cannot be color-blind. They must pass a medical examination that

includes a hearing test and be able to lift and move luggage weighing up to 70 pounds. TSOs must also have good mental abilities for observation, as well as interpersonal skills for dealing with the public in stressful situations.

EARNINGS AND JOB OUTLOOK

Starting salaries range from $23,600 to $35,400 with the possibility of cost-of-living enhancements in certain cities. Although the Transportation Security Administration completed its massive initial hiring campaign when it assumed responsibility for aircraft security after September 11, the employment section of its website continually posts advertisements for more than 200 positions at airports throughout the country. The demands of the job lead to personnel turnover that regularly creates new openings.

MORE INFORMATION

You can obtain additional information about this occupation at the website of the U.S. Transportation Security Administration, listed on the Cole/Smith Criminal Justice in America Companion Website: http://www.thomsonedu.com/criminaljustice/cole.

CHECKPOINT

3. What is the key feature of federalism?

4. What powers does the national government have in the area of criminal justice?

5. What factors have caused federal involvement in criminal justice to expand?

Answers

3. A division of power between a central (national) government and regional (state) governments.

4. Enforcement of federal criminal laws.

5. The expansion of criminal activities across state borders; the war on terrorism.

system A complex whole consisting of interdependent parts whose actions are directed toward goals and are influenced by the environment within which they function.

Crimina[l]

To achieve the[se goals, police, prose]cution, courts[...] sonnel. We mi[...] of professiona[...] works, howeve[...] so, we can use[...] parts whose a[...] which they fu[...]

The crimina[l] police, courts, [...]

A QUESTION OF ETHICS: WRITING ASSIGNMENT

You are a state legislator considering a proposed bill to decrease the mandated prison sentences for crack cocaine to make them equal to those for powder cocaine. You have received a well-documented report demonstrating the disproportionate impact of long crack cocaine sentences on members of minority groups. You have also observed that the law does not impose the same punishments on meth offenders that it imposes on people convicted of selling or possessing crack cocaine.

WRITING ASSIGNMENT

Write an explanation for your position on the proposed bill and include consideration of the following questions. Is evidence of racial disparity a sufficient reason to change sentencing laws? Would it make more sense to increase the sentences for powder cocaine and meth? Alternatively, does crack cocaine have a more harmful effect on society? Do you need any additional information to make your decision about whether to vote for the bill? What considerations would be most important to you?

NEW! *A Question of Ethics: Writing Assignment*—in every chapter

Giving students decision-making, critical-thinking, and writing practice, the *A Question of Ethics* assignment at the end of each chapter places students in the role of decision-maker and enables them to practice defending their decisions in writing—explaining why they are within the framework of the law and consistent with the ethical norms of American society.

REAL-WORLD ACTIVITY: AN APPLICATION

You are a police chief. You receive complaints from citizens that some officers are failing to enforce traffic laws. Reportedly, they merely give warnings to teenage drivers who speed through residential neighborhoods instead of issuing citations that carry fines and license suspension as penalties.

 RESEARCHING THE INTERNET

Go to InfoTrac College Edition. Enter the keyword *traffic enforcement*, then read the article entitled "Police Enforcement of Traffic Laws: A Cost-Benefit Analysis," *FBI Law Enforcement Bulletin*, 1999.

APPLICATION

Say you want to take a strong stand in favor of deterring and punishing dangerous driving by teenagers. How would you make sure that your officers use their discretion to issue traffic citations instead of warnings? Would there be any possible negative consequences from your proposed policies and practices to reduce this aspect of police discretion? Would the benefits outweigh any problems?

NEW! Careers in Criminal Justice Added to every chapter

Showcasing the ever-expanding number of rewarding career opportunities in the criminal justice field, this edition's new *Careers* features give students a real understanding of the nature of the work, required qualifications, earnings and job outlook, and websites where students can get more information. Careers covered include: forensic accountant, FBI special agent, U.S. Border Patrol agent, U.S. Pretrial Services officer, corrections officer, corporate investigator, and probation officer.

Also NEW!
Careers in Criminal Justice Website

Turn to the inside back cover for details on ordering access with new copies of this book.

NEW! *Real-World Activity: An Application*—in every chapter

Through real-life examples provided in these activities, students apply important ideas discussed in the chapter to actual criminal justice practice—and as a result, gain a greater appreciation of the challenges that criminal justice professionals face.

Applied

P-3

Tools that help students apply, compare, reflect, and retain what they learn

▶ **NEW! Compelling real-life vignettes open every chapter**

Showing students—as they begin each chapter—how relevant what they will learn is to the real world of criminal justice, these brief accounts effectively draw students into the material. For example, Chapter 6, "Policing: Contemporary Issues and Challenges," opens with an example of an accidental killing of a child by police during a shootout with an armed man—illustrating the challenges and tragedies associated with policing, and particularly the issue of what constitutes appropriate use of force. In addition, this book includes *Inside the Criminal Justice System and Beyond, Close Up* features, and other real-life examples throughout to show students how theory plays out in practice.

▼ **NEW! *Comparative Perspective* features offer global insights**

Giving students a clearer understanding of the globalization of crime and the need for international cooperation in criminal justice, these new features address Islamic criminal law, police patrol in Japan, pretrial in Russia, and juvenile justice in Norway.

In July 2005, when Los Angeles police officers responded to a midafternoon call about "unknown trouble" at Raul's Auto Sales, they were met by Raul Pena, the owner of the car dealership. The officers could see that Pena had a gun, so they radioed for additional officers. When reinforcements arrived, Pena fired shots at the police. He then emerged from the dealership holding his 19-month-old daughter Susie in his arms as he continued to fire at the police. Pena disappeared inside as police officers surrounded the building (Leovy and Lee, 2005).

During a two-hour standoff, police officers spoke with Pena on the phone in an effort to persuade him to surrender. Pena's teenage stepdaughter emerged from the building as officers exchanged fire with Pena in order to assist her escape. When the officers believed that they had wounded Pena, they rushed into the dealership to discover that he had barricaded himself and his daughter inside a small office. After Pena wounded an officer by firing through the wall of the office, officers broke into the office and engaged in a quick gun battle that left Pena and his daughter dead. Pena fired 40 shots at ... more than 90 (NBC4 News, 2005).

... that the girl suffered from two gunshot wounds, including a shot to the head that ... police officer's weapon (CNN, 2005a). Police administrators reported that the child's ... Meanwhile, Pena's family and community activists angrily complained that the po... worked harder to end the standoff without violence. Police shootings in Los Angeles ... utor's office and the police department's use-of-force board. In this case, the ... nce because the police shooting resulted in the death of an innocent child. ... in this case? Although they knew that any exchange of gunfire would put a small ... nd they had reason to fear Pena could injure or kill additional officers and perhaps

147

70   PART I   CRIME AND THE CRIMINAL JUSTICE SYSTEM

COMPARATIVE PERSPECTIVE

Islamic Criminal Law

The rise of fundamentalist Islamic thought throughout the world has made Americans aware of great cultural differences between American legal traditions and those of the segment of Muslims who seek to have their governments run according to their interpretations of religious rules. Islamic criminal law, in particular, differs significantly from justice as it is administered in the Western democracies. Countries that define their crimes and punishments according to Shari'a, the law of Islam, appear harsh in the eyes of many Americans. Bear in mind, however, that there are different Islamic sects and therefore not all Muslim countries interpret and apply Shari'a in the same way. What are some of the major differences that exist between the American system and the elements of Islamic law described here?

The U.S. State Department, the federal government agency responsible for foreign affairs, publishes annual reports on human rights in countries around the world. The 2004 report on Saudi Arabia provided a glimpse of stark differences between that country's approach to crime and punishment and the approach taken in the United States. According to the *Country Reports on Human Rights Practices* (U.S. Department of State, 2004):

The Government punished criminals according to its interpretation of Shari'a. Punishments included imprisonment, flogging, amputation, and execution by beheading. . . . Authorities punished repeated thievery and other repeated offenses by amputation of the right hand and left foot. . . . [Religious police] reportedly detained young men for offenses including eating in restaurants with young women. . . . Women of many nationalities were detained for actions such as riding in a taxi with a man who was not their relative.

Very few countries actually follow Islamic law to define their crimes and punishments. Although Saudi Arabia and Sudan do, for example, Iran suspended the religion-based use of amputation and execution by stoning in December 2002, although the government can still enforce crimes defined by Islamic law. Pakistan defines some crimes and punishments according ... are rarely enforced, and many prosecutors doubt whether juries will convict people of such offenses, because society has become more tolerant of such commonplace behavior.

other religious punishments. However, in following religious laws, Pakistan can create difficult issues of proof of a crime. As described by one *New York Times* reporter after a Pakistani court overturned a rape conviction in a case that drew international attention and outrage: "In Pakistan, if a woman reports a rape, four Muslim men must generally act as witnesses before she can prove her case. Otherwise, she risks being charged with fornication or adultery—and suffering a public whipping and long imprisonment" (Kristof, 2005). Afghanistan incorporates aspects of Islamic law as demonstrated by the controversy generated in 2005 when a man, who was eventually allowed to leave the country, was threatened with execution by the Afghan justice system for converting from Islam to Christianity (Munadi and Hauser, 2006).

Despite its infrequent use by national governments, Islamic law may be applied in local villages in places such as Pakistan and Afghanistan. In various other countries, including Nigeria and Iraq, advocates are pushing for its use throughout society. Because the use of Islamic law is one focal point for activists seeking to turn these countries into religion-based governments, it is useful to compare the Shari'a with the American approach.

Such practices as stoning for adultery and amputation for theft give Americans the perception that Islamic law is exceptionally harsh. What most Americans do not realize is that there are judicial and evidentiary safeguards within the Shari'a. One reason that the national government of Pakistan has not imposed punishments from the Shari'a is that conviction for these crimes requires the presentation of specific evidence and a higher standard of proof than in nonreligious systems. Islamic criminal law is concerned with (1) the safety of the public from physical attack, insult, and humiliation; (2) the stability of the family; (3) the protection of property against theft, destruction, or unauthorized interference; and (4) the protection ... the Islamic faith against subversion.

Criminal acts are divided into three c ... crimes against God, and punishment is speci ... a compilation of Muhammad's statements ... against others such as those that threaten ... ize the religions of ...

REBELLION

Rebellion is the intentional, forceful overthrow or attempted overthrow of the legitimate leader of the Islamic state.

In the United States, the government can change only through the process of democratic elections. Any effort to use force as the means to overthrow the government will result in criminal prosecution.

DEFAMATION

In addition to false accusations of fornication, this offense includes impugning the legitimacy of a woman's child. Defamation by a husband of his wife leads to divorce and is not subject to punishment.

Defamation under American law can lead to civil lawsuits concerning harmful falsehoods spoken or written about a person that significantly harm that person's reputation.

HIGHWAY ROBBERY

This crime interferes with commerce and creates fear among travelers and is therefore subject to punishment.

Sources: From Nicholas D. Kristof, "When Rapists Walk Free," *New York Times*, March 5, 2005, http://www.nytimes.com; U.S. Department of State, *Country Reports on Human Rights Practices*, 2004, http://www.state.gov; Council of Foreign Relations, "Governing under Sharia," March 14, 2003 (http://www.cfr.org); *Islamic Criminal Law and Procedure: An Introduction*, by M. Lippman, S. McConville, and M. Yerushalmi, 42–43. Copyright © 1988 by Praeger Publishers. Reprinted by permission of Greenwood Publishing Group, Inc., Westport, CT; A. A. Mansour, "Hudud Crimes," in M. C. Bassiouni (ed.), *The Islamic Criminal Justice System*; 195. Copyright © 1982 by Oceana Publications.

▼ ***Checkpoints* embedded throughout every chapter**

Enabling students to review and test themselves *as they progress* through each chapter, *Checkpoints* help students to more effectively review for exams. Answers to the *Checkpoint* questions are now placed immediately beside the questions in order to give students feedback.

CHECKPOINT

	Answers
3. What are the seven principles of criminal law?	→ **3.** Legality, *actus reus*, causation, harm, concurrence, *mens rea*, punishment.
4. What are the defenses in substantive criminal law?	→ **4.** Entrapment, self-defense, necessity, duress (coercion), immaturity, mistake of fact, intoxication, insanity.
5. What are the tests of criminal responsibility used for the insanity defense?	→ **5.** *M'Naghten* Rule (right-from-wrong test), Irresistible Impulse Test, *Durham* Rule, Model Penal Code, Crime Control Act.

Book Companion Website for *Criminal Justice in America*
www.thomsonedu.com/criminaljustice/cole
The site includes:

- Great student resources for every text chapter: multiple-choice quizzes, flash cards, web links, and crossword puzzles.
- *What Americans Think* poll questions that students can answer online and compare their opinions with those of students nationwide, correlated with *What Americans Think* features in this book.
- A direct link to the Wadsworth Criminal Justice Resource Center, which includes U.S. Supreme Court updates, and much more.
- Many instructor tools, such as the Resource Integration Guide, sample syllabus, chapter outlines, and chapter summaries.

WHAT AMERICANS THINK

Percentage of first-year college students who agree with the statement, "There is too much concern in the courts for the rights of criminals."

		Total	Male	Female
1971		48.1%	53.9%	41.1%
1983		68.8%	72.5%	65.2%
1998		72.8%	74.3%	71.5%
2004		56.1%	61.0%	55.7%

Go to http://www.thomsonedu.com/criminaljustice/cole to compare your opinion on this issue with the opinions of other criminal justice students.

Source: Bureau of Justice Statistics, *Sourcebook of Criminal Justice Statistics, 2004* (Washington, DC: U.S. Government Printing Office, 2005), Table 2.92.

Access to ThomsonNOW™—
Available upon request
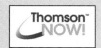
Saves you time with ready-to-go tests, automatic grading, and more. *See the inside front cover of this book for details.*

Web Poll

Do you think there is too much concern in the courts for the rights of criminals?

- ● Yes
- ○ No

Vote Now!
View Results

ExpressPoll

Live Results

Do you think there is too much concern in the courts for the rights of criminals?

Yes	63.63%
No	36.37%

844 responses

This poll reports only the opinions of the actual respondents and is not representative of any group or the public as a whole.

Go Back

This live results summary was created using Perseus ExpressPoll.

InfoTrac® College Edition with InfoMarks®
This extensive, easily searchable database features full-length articles from thousands of academic and popular journals and periodicals. The following print readers include access to InfoTrac College Edition:

Current Perspectives: Readings from InfoTrac College Edition
- *Terrorism and Homeland Security,* Second Edition: 0-495-12994-1
- *Juvenile Justice:* 0-495-12995-X
- *Crisis Management and National Emergency Response:* 0-495-12996-8
- *Racial Profiling:* 0-495-10383-7
- *New Technologies in Criminal Justice:* 0-495-10384-5
- *White-Collar Crime:* 0-495-10385-3

Due to contractual reasons, certain ancillaries are available only in higher education or U.S. domestic markets. Minimum purchases may apply to receive the ancillaries at no charge. For more information, please contact your local Thomson sales representative.

Online Connections

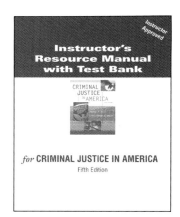

Instructor's Resource Manual with Test Bank
Updated . . . Comprehensive
0-495-38399-6
by Christina DeJong of Michigan State University

- **The comprehensive, completely updated manual** includes learning objectives, detailed chapter outlines, key terms and figures, class discussion exercises, worksheets, lecture suggestions, and a complete *Test Bank*. Also included is a Resource Integration Guide— which will help you make maximum use of the rich supplement package available for this text by integrating media, Internet, video, and other resources into each chapter—and a detailed transition guide to make it easier to change from your current text to *Criminal Justice in America.*

- **Each chapter's test bank** contains approximately 80 multiple-choice, true-false, fill-in-the-blank, and essay questions, which are coded according to difficulty level and *Bloom's Taxonomy;* also included is a full answer key. The *Test Bank* has been carefully reviewed by experienced criminal justice instructors for quality, accuracy, and content coverage. Our *Instructor-Approved* seal, which appears on the front cover, is your assurance that you are working with an assessment and grading resource of the highest caliber.

WebTUTOR ToolBox

WebTutor™ ToolBox available on Blackboard® and WebCT®

Easy and efficient to use, WebTutor™ ToolBox combines course management with content from this text's information-rich Book Companion Website. You can use ToolBox as is—or customize the program with web links, images, and other resources. Contact your Thomson Wadsworth representative for details.

Classroom Activities for Criminal Justice
NEW! A powerful resource for stimulating class participation
0-495-10382-9
This valuable booklet offers instructors the *best-of-the-best* classroom activities for the criminal justice course, including tried-and-true favorites and exciting new projects.

ExamView®
Assessment software with online capabilities
Windows®/Macintosh® 0-495-38400-3

ExamView

Contains all Test Bank questions electronically. Helps you create and customize tests in minutes! You can easily edit and import your own questions and graphics, and edit and maneuver existing questions. ExamView® offers flexible delivery and the ability to test and grade online.

> ### Customize this text for your state . . . and receive a 10% royalty on sales!
>
> ### Thomson State Authoring Program for Criminal Justice
>
> Using our already-developed framework, you'll choose a writing schedule that's convenient for you, and then simply select state-neutral content from our menu, adding your state-specific material. If other faculty in your state wish to purchase your text, we will make it available to them. For each textbook sold (less returns) you will receive a 10% royalty. It's that easy! *Please contact your Thomson representative for details.*

Due to contractual reasons, certain ancillaries are available only in higher education or U.S. domestic markets. Minimum purchases may apply to receive the ancillaries at no charge. For more information, please contact your local Thomson sales representative.

PowerLecture: A Microsoft® PowerPoint® Tool

An easy-to-use, one-stop digital library and presentation tool
0-495-10155-9

Enhance your lectures with the many tools included on this CD-ROM. PowerLecture contains preassembled Microsoft® PowerPoint® images for every chapter, polling/quizzing slides from JoinIn™, textbook art, videos, ExamView® testing software, and a complete *Instructor's Resource Manual* in electronic format. With PowerLecture, you can assemble, edit, and present custom lectures with ease. You can use the material as is or add your own material for a truly customized lecture presentation.

JoinIn™ on TurningPoint®

Tranforms every lecture into an interactive experience
0-495-10157-5

- **Features book-specific content** created especially for use with personal response systems and your choice of several leading keypad systems.

- **With just a click on a hand-held device,** students respond to multiple-choice questions, short polls, interactive exercises and peer review questions. You can take attendance, collect student demographics to better assess student needs, and administer quizzes without collecting paper or grading.

- **NEW! Video clips from current ABC® News stories!** Students view the videos and "click" their responses to onscreen questions. JoinIn on TurningPoint tallies the responses and presents the results on screen.

Please consult your Thomson Wadsworth representative for details or visit www.thomsonedu.com/tlc and select JoinIn on TurningPoint from the drop-down box under "Technology Product."

The Wadsworth Criminal Justice Video Library
www.thomsonedu.com/criminaljustice/media_center

- **ABC® Videos for Criminal Justice—** Current and historic news spanning the following program areas:
  - Introduction to Criminal Justice, Vol. I: 0-495-00113-9
  - Criminology, Vol. I: 0-495-00116-3
  - Corrections, Vol. I: 0-495-00114-7
  - Terrorism, Vol. I: 0-495-00115-5
  - White-Collar Crime: 0-495-00766-8

- ***60 Minutes* DVD—12-minute clips from the CBS® news program**

- **Wadsworth Custom Videos for Criminal Justice**
  - Vol. II on videocassette: 0-534-57335-5 (on DVD: 0-495-18950-2)
  - Vol. III on videocassette: 0-495-12998-4 (on DVD: 0-495-18951-0)

- **Oral History Project Video Series**
  - Volume I, Moments in Time: 0-534-61703-4
  - Volume II, Historical Perspectives: 0-534-61601-1
  - Volume III, Research Methodology in Criminal Justice: 0-534-61602-X

- **Court TV Videos**—One-hour videos presenting seminal and high-profile cases

- **A&E American Justice**—Forty videos to choose from on a variety of criminal justice topics

- **Films for the Humanities**—A selection of nearly 200 criminal justice-related videos

For more information on Wadsworth's Criminal Justice Video Library offerings or to download clip lists and descriptions for videos you already own, please visit **www.thomsonedu.com/criminaljustice/media_center.** This site also lists information about additional media offerings.

Due to contractual reasons, certain ancillaries are available only in higher education or U.S. domestic markets. Minimum purchases may apply to receive the ancillaries at no charge. For more information, please contact your local Thomson sales representative.

Study Guide
Thoroughly updated
0-495-10151-6

The information-packed *Study Guide* has been developed and updated for this edition by Christina DeJong of Michigan State University. Because students learn in different ways, the *Study Guide* includes a variety of pedagogical aids that help them do their best, as well as integrated art and figures from the main text. Each text chapter is outlined and summarized, major terms and figures are defined, and self-tests are provided for review.

NEW! Thomson Audio Study Products
Students simply load these files into their digital music players, and they can review course material while walking to class, driving, working out—whenever it's impossible or inconvenient to read! Available for each chapter of this textbook, these audio files include chapter summaries, key concept reviews, quizzing, and glossary materials. Students can select the chapters they wish to purchase at www.thomsonedu.com.

Wadsworth's Guide to Careers in Criminal Justice, Third Edition
0-495-13038-9

by Caridad Sanchez-Leguelinel, John Jay College of Criminal Justice. Provides a brief introduction to the exciting and diverse field of criminal justice. Students learn about opportunities in law enforcement, courts, and corrections—and how to get those jobs.

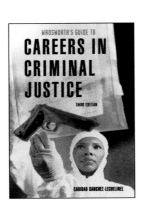

Writing and Communicating for Criminal Justice
0-495-00041-8

Includes articles on writing skills, along with basic grammar review and a survey of verbal communication on the job to give students an introduction to academic, professional, and research writing in criminal justice.

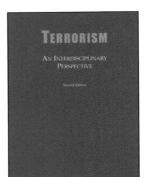

Handbook of Selected Court Cases, Third Edition
0-495-00352-2

Features relevant, seminal Supreme Court cases. An explanatory preface introduces and summarizes relevant general information about court cases to help readers better understand the specific cases discussed.

Terrorism: An Interdisciplinary Perspective, Second Edition
0-534-58202-8

Examines the origins of terrorism in the Middle East, focusing on Osama bin Laden in particular, as well as on issues involving bioterrorism, the role of religion in Middle Eastern terrorism, globalization as it relates to terrorism, and the repercussions of terrorist attacks.

Tools to help with online study— Available packaged with this textbook:

- InfoTrac® College Edition Student Guide for Criminal Justice: 0-534-24719-9

- InfoTrac® College Edition Exercises for Criminal Justice: 0-534-55900-X

- Internet Activities for Criminal Justice, Third Edition: 0-495-10442-6

- The Criminal Justice Internet Investigator, Third Edition: 0-534-56832-7

Due to contractual reasons, certain ancillaries are available only in higher education or U.S. domestic markets. Minimum purchases may apply to receive the ancillaries at no charge. For more information, please contact your local Thomson sales representative.

CRIMINAL JUSTICE
IN AMERICA

About the Authors

George F. Cole (right) is Professor Emeritus of Political Science at the University of Connecticut. A specialist in the administration of criminal justice, he has published extensively on such topics as prosecution, courts, and corrections. George Cole is also co-author with Christopher Smith of *The American System of Criminal Justice,* co-author with Todd Clear and Michael Reisig of *American Corrections,* and co-author with Marc Gertz and Amy Bunger of *The Criminal Justice System: Politics and Policies.* He developed and directed the graduate corrections program at the University of Connecticut and was a Fellow at the National Institute of Justice (1988). Among his other accomplishments, he has been granted two awards under the Fulbright-Hays Program to conduct criminal justice research in England and the former Yugoslavia. In 1995 he was named a Fellow of the Academy of Criminal Justice Sciences for distinguished teaching and research.

Trained as a lawyer and social scientist, Christopher E. Smith, J.D., Ph.D., is Professor of Criminal Justice at Michigan State University, where he teaches courses on criminal justice policy, courts, corrections, and law. In addition to writing more than 80 scholarly articles, he is the author of 20 books, including several other titles with Wadsworth: *Criminal Procedure; Law and Contemporary Corrections; Courts, Politics, and the Judicial Process; The Changing Supreme Court: Constitutional Rights and Liberties* with Thomas R. Hensley and Joyce A. Baugh; *Courts and Public Policy; Politics in Constitutional Law;* and *Courts and the Poor.*

FIFTH EDITION

CRIMINAL JUSTICE
IN AMERICA

GEORGE F. COLE
UNIVERSITY OF CONNECTICUT

CHRISTOPHER E. SMITH
MICHIGAN STATE UNIVERSITY

THOMSON

WADSWORTH

Australia • Brazil • Canada • Mexico • Singapore
Spain • United Kingdom • United States

THOMSON
★
WADSWORTH

Criminal Justice in America,
Fifth Edition
George F. Cole and Christopher E. Smith

Senior Acquisitions Editor, Criminal Justice: Carolyn Henderson Meier
Director of West Coast Softside Acquisitions: Marcus Boggs
Development Editor: Shelley Murphy
Assistant Editor: Rebecca Johnson
Editorial Assistant: Beth McMurray
Technology Project Manager: Amanda Kaufmann
Marketing Manager: Terra Schultz
Marketing Assistant: Emily Elrod
Marketing Communications Manager: Tami Strang
Project Manager, Editorial Production: Jennie Redwitz
Creative Director: Rob Hugel
Art Director: Vernon Boes
Print Buyer: Karen Hunt

Permissions Editor: Bob Kauser
Production Service: Greg Hubit
Text Designer: Diane Beasley
Photo Researcher: Roberta Spieckerman
Copy Editor: Molly Roth
Illustrator: Lotus Art
Cover Designer: Hatty Lee
Cover Images: Top right (eagle): Ron Sanford/Corbis; middle left (police badge): Photodisc Green/Getty Images; bottom middle (gavel): Joe Baraban/Alamy; background (prison): Chris Salvo/Taxi/Getty Images
Compositor: Pre-Press Company, Inc.
Text and Cover Printer: Courier Corporation/Kendallville

Library of Congress Control Number: 2006931158

ISBN-13: 978-0-495-09530-9
ISBN-10: 0-495-09530-3

Thomson Higher Education
10 Davis Drive
Belmont, CA 94002-3098
USA

For more information about our products, contact us at:
Thomson Learning Academic Resource Center
1-800-423-0563

For permission to use material from this text or product, submit a request online at **http://www.thomsonrights.com**
Any additional questions about permissions can be submitted by e-mail to **thomsonrights@thomson.com**

Brief Contents

Contents

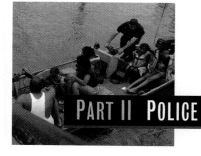

PART II POLICE

4 Police 88

7 Police and Constitutional Law 176

PART III COURTS

8 Courts and Adjudication 200

9 Pretrial Procedures, Plea Bargaining, and the Criminal Trial   228

10 Punishment and Sentencing   256

PART IV   CORRECTIONS

11   Corrections   286

12 Community Corrections: Probation and Intermediate Sanctions   314

13 Incarceration and Prison Society   332

14 Reentry into the Community 362

PART V THE JUVENILE JUSTICE SYSTEM

Boxed Features

Preface

Criminal Justice in America, Fifth Edition, is designed for instructors seeking a textbook that thoroughly introduces students to the dynamics of the American system of criminal justice without overwhelming them. The text is an offspring of *The American System of Criminal Justice*, which has been used by more than half a million students over the course of its eleven editions. But much has changed in the thirty years since the first edition of *The American System of Criminal Justice* was published. And that is exactly why we created *Criminal Justice in America*—a briefer, more applied, student-centered introduction to the American system of criminal justice. In creating the new text, we did not merely drop a few chapters, combine others, and limit the graphic elements to reduce page count, however. We started from scratch. So while *Criminal Justice in America* relies on the research and conceptual framework of the larger text, it is not overly theoretical; throughout the book, examples from today's headlines are used to link the concepts and information to real-life criminal justice situations. And while *Criminal Justice in America* is as interdisciplinary in focus as the comprehensive book, it is less encyclopedic and benefits from added career-based material, international and comparative coverage, skill-building writing exercises, real-world applications, and up-to-the-minute coverage of terrorism, homeland security, cyber crime, and other current topics.

The Approach of This Text

Three key assumptions about the nature of American criminal justice as a discipline and the way the introductory course should be taught run throughout the book.

1. *Criminal justice involves public policies* that are developed within the political framework of the democratic process.
2. *The concept of social system is an essential tool* for explaining and analyzing the way criminal justice is administered and practiced.
3. *American values provide the foundation on which criminal justice is based.*

   With concerns about terrorism and civil liberties at the forefront of the national agenda, basic American values—individual liberty, equality, fairness, and the rule of law—need to be emphasized.

   This book's approach has met with a degree of acceptance and might be called the dominant paradigm in criminal justice education. Criminal justice is interdisciplinary, with criminology, sociology, law, history, psychology, and political science contributing to the field. The three themes of public policy, social system, and American values help to place the research contributions of these disciplines in a context that allows students to understand better the dynamics of criminal justice.

New to the Fifth Edition

This edition encompasses important revisions in content and presentation. Users of the fourth edition will find many significant changes. For example, the chapter

"Police and Constitutional Law" has moved from Chapter 6 to Chapter 7 so that the legal subject matter of that chapter will provide a smooth transition to the courts chapters that follow immediately afterward. In each section of the book, we have added a comparative criminal justice feature that will deepen students' understanding of domestic and international issues by exposing them to such topics as Islamic law and pretrial detention in Russia. There is increased coverage of terrorism, homeland security, and cyber crime, reflecting the growing importance of those subjects in the study of criminal justice. In addition, there is a new emphasis throughout the book on informing students about the variety of careers that exist in the field of criminal justice. Even as some sectors of the American economy face a downturn, criminal justice remains a field with many opportunities, especially as more government resources are directed to issues related to homeland security; as such, within each chapter readers will find a special feature that highlights specific careers, the required qualifications for the career, and the compensation and future job growth for those careers. Each chapter also includes several new writing assignments to help students develop their critical analysis and composition skills, both of which are becoming increasingly important in today's criminal justice workplace.

The rest of this section outlines the major content changes in the book and then examines the new elements in each chapter.

Enhanced Coverage

- **Life Course Theories of Crime Causation** Criminology is not a static field. New explanations for crime causation emerge as research examines additional aspects of American society and the lives of people within social contexts. The coverage of crime causation in Chapter 2 presents the major criminological theories but now adds more attention to life course theories based on the research of Robert Sampson and John Laub. The benefits of their research from longitudinal data can add insights and raise questions concerning existing understandings of crime causation.

- **Cyber Crime** The financial harms caused by rapidly expanding methods of cyber crime are imposing extraordinarily significant costs on governments, businesses, and individuals throughout the world. It is important for students of criminal justice to recognize the extent of these problems and the challenges of addressing forms of criminal behavior that are continuously shifting and adapting. Cyber crime is introduced in Chapter 1 and receives more extensive discussion in Chapter 6.

- **Criminal Justice and Homeland Security** The war on terrorism has brought about changes in the American criminal justice system. The creation of the Department of Homeland Security is reorganizing many law enforcement agencies of the federal government. Private security is playing a much greater role than in the past in protecting people and property. The courts are wrestling over issues of civil liberties and national security. Public policies dealing with terrorists are changing rapidly. Throughout this new edition, we have tried to alert students to the changing dimensions of this aspect of criminal justice.

- **Current Issues in Capital Punishment** Capital punishment remains a key policy controversy within criminal justice. Changes in the Supreme Court's composition present possibilities for future changes, as do legislative actions in light of publicized exonerations. Chapter 10 includes coverage of new material such as the prohibition on execution of juvenile offenders, legal challenges to methods of execution (including lethal injection) and conflicts between the United States and other countries concerning the application of the death penalty to foreign nationals in the American criminal justice system.

Chapter-by-Chapter Changes

- **Chapter 1,** "The Criminal Justice System," opens with a new vignette concerning Martha Stewart's conviction and prison term, a case which beautifully illustrates the various stages of the justice process. This chapter's Careers in Criminal Justice feature presents Transportation Security Officers, an expanding career opportunity within the Department of Homeland Security. The Question of Ethics box near the end of this chapter concerns legislation on differential sentencing for cocaine offenses and now includes a writing assignment. And the Real-World Activity section at the end of the chapter includes a new application to foster students' critical thinking about police discretion.

- **Chapter 2,** "Crime and Justice in America," begins with a new vignette concerning the sentencing of the BTK serial killer in a Wichita, Kansas courtroom, a scene which dramatically illustrates how victims and their families are deeply affected by crime. The Careers in Criminal Justice feature in this chapter highlights the role of forensic accountants in investigating white-collar crime. The expanded coverage of criminology includes life-course research and theories. The Question of Ethics writing assignment considers inconsistent applications of victim compensation, and an application in the Real-World Activity feature focuses on the relationship between public policy and crime causation.

- **Chapter 3,** "Criminal Justice and the Rule of Law," opens with a new vignette describing the murder case of Christopher Pittman, a juvenile who killed his grandparents while being treated with a medically prescribed antidepressant drug that may foster violent or suicidal tendencies, illuminating issues of criminal responsibility and legal defenses. There is a new Comparative Perspective feature that describes some aspects of Islamic criminal law to provide an important focal point for illustrating contrasts with American law. And the new writing assignment in A Question of Ethics focuses on the role of doctors in executions by lethal injection.

- **Chapter 4,** "Police," uses the example of Hurricane Katrina as a new chapter-opening vignette to illustrate the role of police as first responders who face various service and order maintenance challenges in addition to law enforcement duties. We have included new material on the early history of American policing, and expanded coverage of federal agencies today, especially related to the reorganization of agencies as part of the creation of the Department of Homeland Security. The new Careers in Criminal Justice feature in this chapter focuses on FBI special agents. The writing assignment in A Question of Ethics and the application in the Real-World Activity both focus on different aspects of police discretion in light of specific departmental policies.

- **Chapter 5,** "Police Officers and Law Enforcement Operations," has a new opening vignette that discusses the 2005 attack on a Fairfax County, Virginia, police station that resulted in the deaths of two officers, which while illustrating the risks involved in police work also poses questions about why people want to enter law enforcement careers. We follow with an expanded discussion of the qualifications and compensation for various federal, state, and local law enforcement occupations. The new Careers in Criminal Justice feature in this chapter discusses the nature of patrol work and the qualifications required of police patrol officers. The new Comparative Perspective illustrates the role of patrol officers in Japan. The new writing assignment in A Question of Ethics concerns police discretion and opportunities for pretextual traffic stops, and the Real-World Activity application calls for critical analysis of measures for police productivity.

- **Chapter 6,** "Policing: Contemporary Issues and Challenges," opens with the story of police killing a child during a shootout with an armed man barricaded inside a building, an example that illustrates the challenges and tragedies associated with policing as well as quandaries about the appropriate use of force. The chapter now includes expanded coverage of homeland security, cyber crime, and private security. To present another example of private sector occupations that require policing skills, the featured occupation in the new Careers in Criminal Justice for this chapter is corporate investigator. Ethical issues for police who are offered gifts of nominal value is the focus of the new writing assignment in A Question of Ethics, and the application in the Real-World Activity requires critical analysis of potential regulation of private security personnel, a matter of increasing importance for protecting potential terrorism targets in the United States.

■ **Chapter 7,** "Police and Constitutional Law," represents a reorganization of chapters so that legal subject matter will smoothly transition to the subsequent courts chapters. The opening vignette concerns the factual circumstances underlying the Supreme Court's decision in *Maryland v. Pringle* (2003) that approved arresting all occupants of a vehicle when drugs are found in the passenger compartment—an issue of great interest to students. Recent Supreme Court cases have been added as well as a new Careers in Criminal Justice feature on U.S. Border Patrol Agents, one of the fastest-growing occupational opportunities in federal law enforcement. The new writing assignment in A Question of Ethics concerns errors in the administration of *Miranda* warnings and the application in the Real-World Activity requires critical analysis of police discretion in *Terry v. Ohio* stop-and-frisk situations.

■ **Chapter 8,** "Courts and Adjudication," has a new opening vignette about prosecution, describing the case of recording artist Lil' Kim, who was convicted of lying during grand jury testimony in the investigation of a shooting. There is new material on the adversarial system and the functions of courts. The new Careers in Criminal Justice feature focuses on lawyers and discusses them in light of the options to pursue careers as prosecutors, defense attorneys, or judges in the criminal justice system. A prosecutor's dilemma about when there is enough evidence to proceed with a case is the topic for the new writing assignment in A Question of Ethics, and critical analysis of various methods for selecting judges is required in the new end-of-chapter feature Real-World Activity.

■ **Chapter 9,** "Pretrial Procedures, Plea Bargaining, and the Criminal Trial," uses an opening scenario that focuses on the manslaughter trial of former NBA basketball player Jayson Williams. The new Comparative Perspective feature presents a description of the harsh circumstances of pretrial detention in Russia. Careers with the U.S. Marshals are highlighted in the new Careers in Criminal Justice feature. In A Question of Ethics, the writing assignment concerns the guilty plea ceremony and the roles of judges and defense attorneys. And the chapter-concluding application in the Real-World Activity concerns discretion and consistency in setting bail.

■ **Chapter 10,** "Punishment and Sentencing," begins with a new opening vignette on the emotional sentencing hearing for movie actor Tom Sizemore (*Saving Private Ryan*, *Blackhawk Down*) for probation violations after his conviction for domestic violence. In light of the role of substance abuse problems in Sizemore's probation violation, the student is challenged to see the difficulties facing judges in defining appropriate punishments. The new Careers in Criminal Justice feature focuses on U.S. Pretrial Services Officers, an actor in the federal courts whose reports on defendants' behavior during pretrial release supplement presentence reports as part of the sentencing process. There is extensive discussion of new issues affecting capital punishment, including the Supreme Court ruling concerning juvenile offenders, methods of execution, and the implications of international law.

■ **Chapter 11,** "Corrections," opens with a discussion of the problems associated with the expansion of the American prison population and resultant crowding. A new Careers in Criminal Justice feature focuses on corrections officers in jail settings, a source of significant criminal justice job opportunities. Government expenditures on private corrections facilities is the topic addressed in the new writing assignment in A Question of Ethics, and the application in the Real-World Activity feature requires critical analysis of jail design and direction supervision jails.

- **Chapter 12,** "Community Corrections: Probation and Intermediate Sanctions," supplements the extensive discussion of intermediate sanctions with a new Careers in Criminal Justice feature on probation officers. The writing assignment in A Question of Ethics focuses on probation officers' discretion in recommending probation revocation. And the challenges of overwhelming probation caseloads are highlighted in the Real-World Activity.

- **Chapter 13,** "Incarceration and Prison Society," includes a new Careers in Criminal Justice feature on corrections officers at state prisons. The new writing assignment for A Question of Ethics concerns friendly interactions between prisoners and officers and the need for officers to maintain social distance. And in the Real-World Activity feature we challenge students to address the critical problem of HIV/AIDS in prisons.

- **Chapter 14,** "Reentry into the Community," opens with a new vignette describing the release of 20-year-old inmate Angel Coronado from a Texas prison, illustrating some of the problems parolees face when they reenter society. Parole officers are the focus of the new Careers in Criminal Justice feature for this chapter. A parole board's consideration of the possible release of a convicted sex offender is the ethical dilemma presented in Question of Ethics, and the issue of community reaction to a released sex offender moving into a neighborhood is raised in the Real-World Activity feature.

- **Chapter 15,** "Juvenile Justice," provides a new opening vignette discussing an arson case involving three young boys. An interesting new Comparative Perspective examines how the juvenile justice system in Norway deals with youth crime. Students will read about the nature of the work of juvenile probation officers in the new Careers in Criminal Justice feature. The topic of supervision in group homes for youths is considered in the new writing assignment for A Question of Ethics, and the application presented in the Real-World Activity feature concluding Chapter 15 requires critical analysis of efforts to reduce youth homicides and gang violence.

Study and Review Aids

To help students identify and master core concepts, *Criminal Justice in America* provides several study and review aids in each chapter:

- Chapter outlines preview the structure of each chapter.

- Opening vignettes introduce the chapter topic with a high-interest real-life case or illustrative discussion of a major policy issue, enhancing the book's relevancy for today's student.

- *Questions for Inquiry* highlight the chapter's key topics and themes and serve as a roadmap for readers.

- *Checkpoints* throughout each chapter allow students to test themselves on content and get immediate feedback to help them assess their understanding of concepts as they progress through the chapter.

- *Going Online* provides a link to **ThomsonNow** for diagnostic study plans to review each chapter. With ThomsonNow students can identify areas on which to concentrate, master the chapter concepts through interactive exercises, and confirm their proficiency with important concepts through Post-Tests before moving on to the next chapter.

- End-of-chapter *Summaries* and *Questions for Review* reinforce key concepts and provide further checks on learning.

- Key terms and cases are defined throughout the text in the margins of each chapter and can also be located in the Glossary.

Promoting Understanding

Aided by the features just described, diligent students can master the essential content of the introductory course. While such mastery is no small achievement, most instructors aim higher. They want students to complete this course with the ability to take a more thoughtful and critical approach to issues of crime and justice. *Criminal Justice in America*, Fifth Edition, provides several features that help students learn how to think about the field.

- **Close Ups and Other Real-Life Examples** Understanding criminal justice in a purely theoretical way does not give students a balanced understanding of the field. The wealth of examples in this book shows how theory plays out in practice and what the human implications of policies and procedures are. In addition to the many illustrations in the text, the "Close Up" features in each chapter draw on newspaper articles, court decisions, first-person accounts, and other current sources.

- **A Question of Ethics: Writing Assignment** (New to this edition) In the criminal justice system, decisions must be made within the framework of law but also be consistent with the ethical norms of American society. At the end of each chapter, boxes entitled "A Question of Ethics: Writing Assignment" place students in the context of decision makers faced with a problem involving ethics. Students become aware of the many ethical dilemmas that criminal justice personnel must deal with and the types of questions they may have to answer if they assume a role in the system.

- **What Americans Think** Public opinion plays an important role in the policy-making process in a democracy. As such, we present the opinions of Americans on controversial criminal justice issues as collected through surveys.

- **The Policy Debate** This edition includes several important policy issues for student discussion and debate. In each, we describe an issue such as aggressive policing or the death penalty, outline its pros and cons, and then ask students to decide which policy they think the United States should adopt.

- **Careers in Criminal Justice** (New to this edition) The topical focus on career opportunities is primarily intended to help students think about the wide range of occupational possibilities in criminal justice. However, in seeing the nature of the work, the required qualifications, compensation, and future market for specific jobs students will also gain insights about who plays what roles in the criminal justice system. They can see, for example, the qualifications for various positions that can help them understand the potential impact of training, discretion, and motives in the criminal justice system.

- **Real-World Activity: An Application** (New to this edition) Through the real-life examples provided in this feature, students apply important ideas discussed in the chapter to actual criminal justice practice. By thinking about and discussing the issues presented, students gain a greater appreciation of the challenges that criminal justice professionals face.

- **Comparative Perspective** (New to this Edition) The globalization of crime and the need for international cooperation in criminal justice require that students be aware of criminal justice issues and institutions in other countries. Moreover, American students can gain additional perspective and understanding about their own system by contrasting the United States with other countries. Thus we have added a Comparative Perspective feature in each section of the text to present such diverse topics as Islamic criminal law, police patrol in Japan, pretrial detention in Russia, and juvenile justice in Norway.

- **Technology Issues in Criminal Justice** The police, courts, and corrections have been quick to take advantage of technological innovations so as to improve the effectiveness of the system. In each chapter, a technological innovation now being used by a criminal justice agency is described. From the use of nonlethal weapons and patrol car computers to behavior modification and stalker trackers, advances in technology are playing a vital role in the American criminal justice system.

- **Inside the Criminal Justice System and Beyond** Many students have limited first-hand knowledge of what it is like to be "processed" by the criminal justice system. A hallmark of *Criminal Justice in America* is a serialized essay by Chuck Terry titled "Inside the Criminal Justice System and Beyond: One Man's Journey." Each part of the book concludes with a segment of Terry's moving story, providing a rare insider's look at the steps in the criminal justice process.

Supplements

An extensive package of supplemental aids accompanies this edition of *Criminal Justice in America*. They are available to qualified adopters. Please consult your local sales representative for details.

FOR THE INSTRUCTOR

Instructor's Resource Manual

Fully updated and revised by Christina DeJong of Michigan State University, the *Instructor's Resource Manual* for this edition includes learning objectives, detailed chapter outlines, key terms and figures, class discussion exercises, worksheets, lecture suggestions, and a complete test bank. Each chapter's test bank contains approximately 80 multiple-choice, true-false, fill-in-the-blank, and essay questions, which are coded according to difficulty level and Bloom's taxonomy; a full answer key completes the Test Bank. Each question in the Test Bank has been carefully reviewed by experienced criminal justice instructors for quality, accuracy, and content coverage. Our Instructor Approved seal, which appears on the front cover, is our assurance that you are working with an assessment and grading resource of the highest caliber. Also included is a Resource Integration Guide, which will help you make maximum use of the rich supplement package available for this text by integrating media, Internet, video, and other resources into each chapter. Finally, a detailed transition guide is provided to make it easier to change from your current text to *Criminal Justice in America*.

ExamView® Computerized Testing

The comprehensive *Instructor's Resource Manual* described above is backed up by ExamView, a computerized test bank available for IBM-PC compatibles and Macintosh computers. With ExamView you can create, deliver, and customize tests and study guides (both print and online) in minutes. You can easily edit and import your own questions and graphics, change test layouts, and reorganize questions. And using ExamView's complete word processing capabilities, you can enter an unlimited number of new questions or edit existing questions.

JoinIn™ on TurningPoint®

Spark discussion and assess your students' comprehension of chapter concepts with interactive classroom quizzes and background polls developed specifically for use with this edition of *Introduction to Criminal Justice*. Also available are polling/quiz questions that enable you to maximize the educational benefits of the ABC News video clips we custom selected to accompany this textbook. Thomson Wadsworth's exclusive agreement with TurningPoint software lets you run our tailor-made Microsoft® PowerPoint® slides in conjunction with the "clicker" hardware of your choice. Enhance how your students interact with you, your lecture, and each other. *For college and university adopters only. Contact your local Thomson representative to learn more.*

Thomson PowerLecture CD

This instructor resource includes Microsoft® PowerPoint® lecture slides with graphics from the text, making it easy for you to assemble, edit, publish, and present custom lectures for your course. The PowerLecture CD also includes video-based polling and quiz questions that can be used with the JoinIn on TurningPoint personal response system, and integrates ExamView testing software for customizing tests of up to 250 items that can be delivered in print or online. Finally, all of your media teaching resources in one place!

WebTutor™ ToolBox on Blackboard® and WebCT®

A powerful combination: easy-to-use course management tools for whichever program you use (WebCT or Blackboard) with content from this text's rich companion website all in one place. You can use ToolBox as is, from the moment you log on—or, if you prefer, customize the program with web links, images, and other resources.

The Wadsworth Criminal Justice Video Library

So many exciting new videos—so many great ways to enrich your lectures and spark discussion of the material in this text! A list of our unique and expansive video program follows. Or, visit www.thomsonedu.com/criminaljustice/media_center/index.html for a complete, up-to-the-minute list of all of Wadsworth's video offerings—many of which are also available in DVD format—as well as clip lists and running times. The library includes these selections and many others:

- *ABC Videos*: Featuring short, high-interest clips from current news events specially developed for courses in Introduction to Criminal Justice, Criminology, Corrections, Terrorism, and White Collar Crime, these videos are perfect for use as discussion starters or lecture launchers to spark student interest. The brief video clips provide students with a new lens through which to view the past and present, one that will greatly enhance their knowledge and understanding of significant events and open up to them new dimensions in learning. Clips are drawn from such programs as *World News Tonight*, *Good Morning America*, *This Week*, *PrimeTime Live*, *20/20*, and *Nightline*, as well as numerous ABC News specials and material from the Associated Press Television News and British Movietone News collections.

- *The Wadsworth Custom Videos for Criminal Justice*: Produced by Wadsworth and Films for the Humanities, these videos include short (5- to 10-minute) segments that encourage classroom discussion. Topics include white-collar crime, domestic violence, forensics, suicide and the police officer, the court process, the history of corrections, prison society, and juvenile justice.

- *Court TV Videos*: One-hour videos presenting seminal and high-profile cases, such as the interrogation of Michael Crowe and serial killer Ted Bundy, as well as crucial and current issues such as cyber crime, double jeopardy, and the management of the jail on Riker's Island.

- *A&E American Justice*: Forty videos to choose from, on topics such as deadly force, women on death row, juvenile justice, strange defenses, and Alcatraz.

- *Films for the Humanities*: Nearly 200 videos to choose from on a variety of topics such as elder abuse, supermax prisons, suicide and the police officer, the making of an FBI agent, domestic violence, and more.

■ *Oral History Project*: Developed in association with the American Society of Criminology, the Academy of Criminal Justice Society, and the National Institute of Justice, these videos will help you introduce your students to the scholars who have developed the criminal justice discipline. Compiled over the last several years, each video features a set of Guest Lecturers—scholars whose thinking has helped to build the foundation of present ideas in the discipline.

Classroom Activities for Criminal Justice

This valuable booklet, available to adopters of any Wadsworth criminal justice text, offers instructors the best of the best in criminal justice classroom activities. Containing both tried-and-true favorites and exciting new projects, its activities are drawn from across the spectrum of criminal justice subjects, including introduction to criminal justice, criminology, corrections, criminal law, policing, and juvenile justice, and can be customized to fit any course. Novice and seasoned instructors alike will find it a powerful tool to stimulate classroom engagement.

Internet Activities for Criminal Justice, Third Edition

This is the resource that no introductory criminal justice instructor should be without! The user-friendly booklet allows instructors to send their students far beyond the classroom, guiding them online to conduct research and retrieve information. Its URLs and virtual projects, drawn from all foundational criminal justice areas, have been completely revised and expanded for 2008.

The Wadsworth Criminal Justice Resource Center
www.thomsonedu.com/criminaljustice

Designed with the instructor in mind, this web site features information about Thomson Wadsworth's technology and teaching solutions, as well as several features created specifically for today's criminal justice student. Supreme Court updates, timelines, and hot-topic polling can all be used to supplement in-class assignments and discussions. You'll also find a wealth of links to careers and news in criminal justice, book-specific sites, and much more.

FOR THE STUDENT

ThomsonNOW™

This unique, interactive online resource is the most exciting assessment-centered student learning tool ever offered for this course. ThomsonNOW determines each student's unique study needs by having him take a chapter Pre-Test and then offers him a Personalized Study plan that focuses his study time on the concepts he needs to master. Personalized Study includes ABC news clips with questions, career profile videos, concept learning modules with assessments, integrated simulations, interactive diagrams, animations, lectures, topic reviews, an e-book, and more. Once the student has completed her Personalized Study plan, a Post-Test evaluates her improved comprehension of chapter content. At any time the student can view her Pre-/Post-Test scores, and all scores and gradable assignments flow directly into the instructor's grade book.

Study Guide

An extensive student guide has been developed and updated for this edition by Christina DeJong. Because students learn in different ways, the guide includes a variety of pedagogical aids. Each chapter is outlined and summarized, major terms and figures are defined, and worksheets and self-tests are provided.

Thomson Audio Study Products

Students can finally study anytime and anywhere they want using Thomson's Audio Study for *Criminal Justice in America*, Fifth Edition. Our exclusive audio content, which can be downloaded to any mp3 player, includes a review of all key terms and concepts, as well as a summary of the chapter. With this unique supplement, students can quiz themselves on each chapter's vocabulary and key concepts as they go or review important material before tests—even if they don't have their textbook on hand or aren't at their desk.

Companion Website www.thomsonedu.com/criminaljustice/cole

The companion website provides many chapter-specific resources, including chapter outlines, learning objectives, glossary, flash cards, crossword puzzles, web links, and tutorial quizzing.

Careers in Criminal Justice Website www.thomsonedu.com/login

This unique website helps students investigate the criminal justice career choices that are right for them with the help of several important tools:

- *Career Profiles:* Video testimonials from a variety of practicing professionals in the field as well as information on many criminal justice careers, including job descriptions, requirements, training, salary and benefits, and the application process.
- *Interest Assessment:* Self-assessment tool to help students decide which careers suit their personalities and interests.
- *Career Planner:* Résumé-writing tips and worksheets, interviewing techniques, and successful job search strategies.
- *Links for Reference:* Direct links to federal, state, and local agencies where students can get contact information and learn more about current job opportunities.

Wadsworth's Guide to Careers in Criminal Justice, Third Edition

This handy guide, compiled by Caridad Sanchez-Leguelinel of John Jay College of Criminal Justice, give students information on a wide variety of career paths, including requirements, salaries, training, contact information for key agencies, and employment outlooks.

Writing and Communicating for Criminal Justice

This book contains articles on writing skills—along with basic grammar review and a survey of verbal communication on the job—that will give students an introduction to academic, professional, and research writing in criminal justice. The voices of professionals who have used these techniques on the job will help students see the relevance of these skills to their future careers.

Handbook of Selected Supreme Court Cases, Third Edition

This supplementary handbook covers almost 40 landmark cases, each of which includes a full case citation, an introduction, a summary from WestLaw, excerpts from the case, and the decision. The updated edition includes *Hamdi v. Rumsfeld, Roper v. Simmons, Ring v. Arizona, Atkins v. Virginia, Illinois v. Caballes,* and much more.

Current Perspectives: Readings from InfoTrac® College Edition

These readers, designed to give students a deeper taste of special topics in criminal justice, include free access to InfoTrac College Edition. The timely articles are selected by experts in each topic from within InfoTrac College Edition, and are available for free when bundled with the text. Topics include:

- Terrorism and Homeland Security
- Juvenile Justice
- Public Policy and Criminal Justice
- Crisis Management and National Emergency Response
- Racial Profiling
- New Technologies and Criminal Justice
- White-Collar Crime

Terrorism: An Interdisciplinary Perspective

Available for bundling with each copy of *Introduction to Criminal Justice*, Eleventh Edition, this 80-page booklet discusses terrorism in general and the issues surrounding the events of September 11, 2001. This information-packed booklet examines the origins of terrorism in the Middle East, focusing on Osama bin Laden in particular, as well as issues involving bioterrorism, the specific role played by religion in Middle Eastern terrorism, globalization as it relates to terrorism, and the reactions and repercussions of terrorist attacks.

Crime Scenes 2.0: An Interactive Criminal Justice CD-ROM

Recipient of several *New Media Magazine* Invision Awards, this interactive CD-ROM allows your students to take on the roles of investigating officer, lawyer, parole officer, and judge in excitingly realistic scenarios. Available FREE when bundled with every copy of *Criminal Justice in America*, Fifth Edition. An online instructor's manual for the CD-ROM is also available.

Mind of a Killer CD-ROM (*bundle version*)

Voted one of the top 100 CD-ROMs by an annual *PC Magazine* survey, *Mind of a Killer* gives students a chilling glimpse into the realm of serial killers, with over 80 minutes of video *and* 3D simulations, an extensive mapping system, a library, and much more.

Internet Guide for Criminal Justice, Second Edition

Intended for the novice user, this guide provides students with the background and vocabulary necessary to navigate and understand the Web, then provides them with a wealth of criminal justice websites and Internet project ideas.

A Group Effort

No one can be an expert on every aspect of the criminal justice system. Authors need help in covering new developments and ensuring that research findings are correctly interpreted. The many criminal justice students and instructors who have used previous editions of *Criminal Justice in America* have contributed abundantly to this edition. Their comments provided crucial practical feedback. Others gave us their comments personally when we lectured in criminal justice classes around the country.

Others have helped us as well. Chief among them was Senior Acquisitions Editor Carolyn Henderson Meier, who is very supportive of our efforts. Development Editor Shelley Murphy provided invaluable comments as we revised the book. The project has benefited much from the attention of Project Manager Jennie Redwitz, and Christina DeJong was invaluable in helping us develop the supplements. Molly Roth prevented us from committing egregious errors in the use of English. As always, Greg Hubit used his managerial skills to oversee the project from manuscript submission to bound books. Diane Beasley designed the interior of the book. Finally, the following reviewers for this edition contributed valuable comments:

Les Boggess, Fairmont State University

Arnett Gaston, University of Maryland, College Park

Kim Hassell, University of Wisconsin, Milwaukee

John Kavanaugh, Scottsdale Community College

Don Mason, Rio Hondo Community College

Amy Thistlethwaite, Northern Kentucky University

Ultimately, however, the full responsibility for the book is ours alone. We hope you will benefit from it, and we welcome your comments.

George F. Cole
gcole281@earthlink.net

Christopher E. Smith
smithc28@msu.edu

CRIMINAL JUSTICE IN AMERICA

The Criminal Justice System

AP Photo/Louis Lanzano

Martha Stewart, the nationally famous "Domestic Diva," emerged from the federal prison in Alderson, West Virginia, before dawn on March 4, 2005. Her five-month prison sentence, spent scrubbing floors, cleaning offices, and raking leaves, was a far cry from her prior life as a television star and the head of a multimillion-dollar corporation. Even upon release, Stewart remained under the supervision of the criminal justice system, as she was required to spend five additional months wearing an electronic ankle bracelet to monitor her movements and could only leave her home for 48 hours each week in order to work and handle approved errands (Fitzgerald, 2005; "Martha's Prison Time Nearly Over," 2005). Stewart's case helps illustrate many aspects of the criminal justice system. A picture of the system emerges through the ways in which Stewart's wealth positioned her to reduce the risks and burdens experienced by other offenders, and through the procedures and restrictions that affected Stewart in the same manner as anyone else drawn into the justice system.

After her 2004 conviction for obstructing justice and lying to government investigators who examined whether she illegally used inside information to profit from the sale of corporate stock, Stewart became, like millions of her fellow Americans, a convicted criminal. As a wealthy celebrity, Stewart's experience in the criminal justice system differed from that of most other people charged with crimes. She had the money to fight her criminal charges all the way through a complete trial and an appeal rather than enter a guilty plea. She could afford high-priced lawyers who devoted themselves to her defense. Because most defendants are too poor to hire their own attorneys, their fates rest on the efforts of busy and often overworked public defenders. Stewart also differed from most offenders released from prison, because she returned to society with a job, a home, and significant financial assets. Other offenders face tremendous challenges in gaining a foothold in mainstream society when they exit prison with few skills or assets while carrying the stigma of a criminal conviction. These aspects of the Stewart case remind us that a defendant's financial resources are one factor that can affect the path of a specific case. Not all individuals receive identical treatment in the American justice system.

In many other ways, however, Martha Stewart's case illustrates aspects of the criminal justice system that apply with equal force to all people drawn into the process. Law enforcement officials were required to respect her constitutional rights when they sought to obtain her financial records, question her about suspicious activities, and ultimately pursued the prosecution against her. Stewart was tried in the same courthouse, before the same judge, and according to the same court rules as other defendants charged with various federal offenses, ranging from drug trafficking to bank robbery. When she served her prison sentence, Stewart was subject to the same restrictions, regulations, and living conditions as the poor drug offenders and convicted thieves with whom she shared her daily life at the minimum-security prison.

While completing the house arrest and electronic monitoring portion of her sentence after release from prison, Stewart faced frustrations and problems shared by thousands of offenders who either serve their sentences in the community or must experience continued supervision after release from prison. For example, supervised offenders may be sent to prison for either inadvertent or intentional violations of restrictions imposed by the justice system. In Stewart's case, the period of home confinement was extended by three weeks for visiting a yoga class without permission and for the unauthorized use of an off-road vehicle at her home. Although such minor violations rarely cause offenders to be required to complete their sentences in prison, justice system officials could have decided that Stewart

should be sent back to prison ("Martha Stewart's House Arrest Is Extended," 2005). Much like that of other offenders, Martha Stewart's fate rested on the discretionary decisions of individual officials.

The elements of the criminal justice system, including police and courts, operate throughout the United States—in urban and rural areas, in rich and poor neighborhoods. In 2006 the American public received several reminders of the broad reach of the criminal justice system: California Congressman Randy Cunningham went to prison for accepting bribes; I. Lewis Libby, the chief of staff for Vice President Dick Cheney, faced federal prosecution for lying during a criminal investigation; and Tom DeLay, the majority leader in the U.S. House of Representatives, resigned from Congress as he fought criminal charges in Texas concerning illegal campaign contributions. Anyone in the United States, including law-abiding college students, can be drawn into the criminal justice system in a variety of roles: victim, witness, juror, defendant. Thus, all Americans need to gain an understanding of the system, how it operates, and how it affects people's lives.

In this chapter, we examine the goals of the criminal justice system and how American criminal justice operates as a system. Moreover, we shall see how that system's processes are shaped by scarce resources, individual decision makers, and other factors that can lead to divergent treatment for similar criminal cases. In the United States, our history has taught us the importance of knowing that differences in the treatment of suspects, defendants, and offenders may be related to issues of race, ethnicity, and social class and the interaction of these demographic factors with the criminal justice system's processes.

QUESTIONS FOR INQUIRY

- What are the goals of the criminal justice system?
- How is criminal justice pursued in a federal system of government?
- What are the major features of criminal justice as a social system?
- What are the main agencies or operations of criminal justice, and how do they interrelate?
- What is the flow of decision making from arrest to correction and release?
- What are possible causes of racial disparities in the criminal justice system?

The Goals of Criminal Justice

To begin our study of the criminal justice system, we must ask the following: What goals does the system serve? Although these goals may seem straightforward as ideas, saying exactly what they mean in practice can be difficult.

In 1967 the President's Commission on Law Enforcement and Administration of Justice described the criminal justice system as the means that society uses to "enforce the standards of conduct necessary to protect individuals and the community" (U.S. President's Commission, 1967:7). This statement provides the basis of our discussion of the goals of the system. Although there is much debate about the purposes of criminal justice, most people agree that the system has three goals: (1) doing justice, (2) controlling crime, and (3) preventing crime.

DOING JUSTICE

Doing justice is the basis for the rules, procedures, and institutions of the criminal justice system. Without the principle of justice, little difference would exist between criminal justice in the United States and that in authoritarian countries. Fairness is essential. Americans want to have fair laws, and they want to investigate, judge, and punish fairly. Doing justice also requires upholding the rights of individuals and punishing those who violate the law. Thus, the goal of doing justice embodies three principles: (1) offenders will be held fully accountable for their actions, (2) the rights of persons who have contact with the system will be protected, and (3) like offenses will be treated alike and officials will take into account relevant differences among offenders and offenses (DiIulio, 1993:10).

Doing justice successfully is a tall order. We can easily identify situations in which criminal justice agencies and processes fall short of this ideal. In authoritarian political systems, criminal justice clearly serves the interests of those in power, but in a democracy people can try to improve the capacity of their institutions to do justice. Thus, however imperfect they may be, criminal justice institutions and processes can enjoy public support. In a democracy, a system that makes doing justice a key goal is viewed as legitimate and can therefore pursue the secondary goals of controlling and preventing crime.

CONTROLLING CRIME

The criminal justice system is designed to control crime by arresting, prosecuting, convicting, and punishing those who disobey the law. A major constraint on the system, however, is that efforts to control crime must be carried out within the framework of law. Criminal law not only defines what is illegal but also outlines the rights of citizens and the procedures officials must use to achieve the system's goals.

In every city and town, the goal of crime control is actively pursued: Police officers walk a beat, patrol cars race down dark streets, lawyers speak before a judge, probation officers visit clients, and guards patrol the grounds of a prison. Taking action against wrongdoers helps control crime, but the system must also attempt to prevent crimes from happening.

PREVENTING CRIME

Crime can be prevented in various ways. Perhaps most important is the deterrent effect of the actions of police, courts, and corrections. These actions not only punish those who violate the law, they also

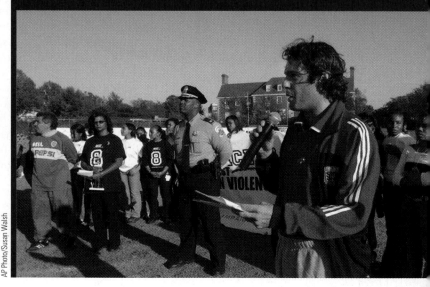

The goals of the criminal justice system cannot be accomplished solely by the police, courts, and corrections. All citizens should take an interest, as shown by this demonstration against gun violence in Washington, D.C.

AP Photo/Susan Walsh

TECHNOLOGY ISSUES IN CRIMINAL JUSTICE

Backscatter X-Ray

The development of new technologies can enhance our capacity to detect and prevent crimes as well as gather evidence of criminal guilt. Traditional crime-fighting technologies such as fingerprints and crime scene photographs have been supplemented by a range of inventions that detect microscopic bits of evidence.

New technologies can also create new dilemmas and problems. For example, they can increase government officials' ability to examine previously private aspects of lives—and bodies. As we consider whether and how to use new devices, we must also consider whether we are sacrificing other important values. Fundamentally, we must ask ourselves whether we are so committed to preventing crime and capturing criminals that we are willing to surrender elements of our privacy and liberty.

An excellent example emerged in 2003 when news reports described the federal Transportation Security Administration (TSA)'s experiments with backscatter X-ray devices to detect whether airline passengers are carrying weapons, bombs, or other contraband. Fully clothed people who are examined with such machines will appear naked in the televison-type monitor while also revealing any objects that they are carrying under their clothes. According to the director of the TSA's security laboratory, "It does basically make you look fat and naked—but you see all this stuff [that is hidden under clothes]." The thought that a government monitor can see the image of someone's unclothed body is likely to make many people uncomfortable.

Indeed, when the TSA began experimenting with the machines at selected airports in 2005, one security expert objected that the devices are too intrusive and described the job of airport screeners as being "paid to go to a peep show." Moreover, he argued that because the low-level X-ray does not penetrate the skin, very overweight people could still hide explosives beneath the folds of their skin.

RESEARCHING THE INTERNET

For an online description of backscatter X-ray devices, go to the corresponding site listed on the Cole/Smith Criminal Justice in America Companion Website: http://www.thomsonedu.com/criminaljustice/cole.

FOR CRITICAL ANALYSIS

If you were boarding an airplane, would you want the security monitor to, in effect, see you naked in order to prevent anyone from carrying weapons on planes? What if such devices could be carried by police officers on the street to detect whether pedestrians were carrying concealed weapons? Should limits be placed on the use of such technologies?

Sources: Leslie Miller, "Airport Screeners May Get X-Ray Eyes" [Associated Press Wire Service], *Lansing State Journal*, June 26, 2003, p. 4A; Office of National Drug Control Policy, "2001 Counterdrug Research and Development Blueprint Update," 2001, Appendix D, http://www.ncjrs.org/ondcppubs/publications; Joe Sharkey, "Airport Screeners Could Get X-Rated X-Ray Views," *New York Times*, May 24, 2005, http://www.nytimes.com.

---

provide examples that will likely keep others from committing wrongful acts. For example, a racing patrol car responding to a crime situation also serves as a warning that law enforcement is at hand. Technological advances also deter crime, but sometimes at a cost to personal liberty; see "Technology Issues in Criminal Justice" for more.

Crime prevention depends on the actions of criminal justice officials and citizens. Unfortunately, many people do not take the simple steps necessary to protect themselves and their property. For example, they leave their homes and cars unlocked, forgo alarm systems, and walk in dangerous areas.

Citizens do not have the authority to enforce the law; society has assigned that responsibility to the criminal justice system. Thus, citizens must rely on the police to stop criminals; they cannot take the law into their own hands. Still, they can and must be actively engaged in preventing crime.

The ways in which American institutions have evolved to achieve the goals of doing justice, controlling crime, and preventing crime lead to a series of choices. Decisions must be made that reflect legal, political, social, and moral values. As we study the system, we need to be aware of the possible conflicts among these values and the implications of choosing one value over another. The tasks assigned to the criminal justice system could be much easier to perform if they were clearly defined so that citizens and officials could act with precise knowledge of their duties.

ThomsonNOW
Improve your grade on the exam with Personalized Study! For reinforcement resources and a mastery check of The Goals of Criminal Justice, go to www.thomsonedu.com/thomsonnow.

CHECKPOINT

Answers

1. What are the three goals of the criminal justice system? ⟶ 1. Doing justice, controlling crime, preventing crime.

2. What is meant by "doing justice"? ⟶ 2. Offenders are held fully accountable for their actions, the rights of persons who have contact with the system will be protected, like offenses will be treated alike, and officials will take into account relevant differences among offenders and offenses.

Criminal Justice in a Federal System

Criminal justice, like other aspects of American government, is based on the concept of **federalism**, in which power is divided between a central (national) government and regional (state) governments. States have a great deal of authority over their own affairs, but the federal government handles matters of national concern. Because of federalism, no single level of government is solely responsible for the administration of criminal justice.

The U.S. government's structure was created in 1789 with the ratification of the U.S. Constitution. The Constitution gave the national government certain powers, including raising an army, coining money, and making treaties with foreign countries. But all other powers, including police power, were retained by the states. No national police force with broad powers may be established in the United States.

The Constitution does not include criminal justice among the federal government's specific powers. However, the United States government is involved in criminal justice in many ways. The Federal Bureau of Investigation (FBI) is a national law enforcement agency. Federal criminal cases are tried in U.S. district courts, which are federal courts, and there are federal prisons throughout the nation. Most criminal justice activity, however, occurs at the state level, and the vast majority of cases are handled by state and local police, state courts, and state correctional agencies.

TWO JUSTICE SYSTEMS

Both the national and state systems of criminal justice enforce laws, try criminal cases, and punish offenders, but their activities differ in scope and purpose. Most criminal laws are written by state legislatures and enforced by state agencies. However, a variety of national criminal laws have been enacted by Congress and are enforced by the FBI, the Drug Enforcement Administration, the Secret Service, and other federal agencies.

Except in the case of federal drug offenses, relatively few offenders break federal criminal laws, compared with the large numbers who break state criminal laws. For example, only small numbers of people violate the federal law against counterfeiting and espionage, whereas large numbers violate state laws against assault, larceny, and drunken driving. Even in the case of drug offenses, which during the 1980s and 1990s swept large numbers of offenders into federal prisons, many drug violators end up in state corrections systems because such crimes violate both state and federal laws.

EXPANSION OF FEDERAL INVOLVEMENT

Since the 1960s the federal government has expanded its role in dealing with crime, a policy area that has traditionally been the responsibility of state and local governments. As Willard Oliver notes, the federal role has become much more active in "legislating criminal activity, expanding [the] federal law enforcement bureaucracy, widening the reach and scope of the federal courts, and building more federal prisons" (Oliver, 2002:1).

The report of the U.S. President's Commission on Law Enforcement and Administration of Justice (1967:613) emphasized the need for greater federal involvement in crime control at the local level and urged that federal grants be directed to the states to support criminal justice initiatives. Since then, Congress has allocated billions of dollars for crime control efforts and passed legislation, national in

> **federalism** A system of government in which power is divided between a central (national) government and regional (state) governments.

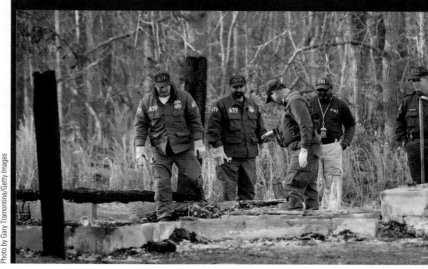

Since 9/11 there has been a major expansion of federal law enforcement involvement in the states and local communities. Here, FBI and ATF investigators look through the remains of the Morning Star Missionary Baptist Church near Boligee, Alabama. Questions were raised initially as to whether terrorists set the blaze.

Photo by Gary Tramontina/Getty Images

scope, to deal with street crime, the "war on drugs," violent crime, terrorism, and juvenile delinquency. Although most criminal justice expenditures and personnel are found at the local level, over the past 40 years the federal government has increased its role in fighting street crime (Oliver, 2002; Scheingold, 1995).

Because many crimes span state borders, we no longer think of some crimes as being committed at a single location within a single state. For example, crime syndicates and gangs deal with drugs, pornography, and gambling on a national level. Thus, Congress expanded the powers of the FBI and other federal agencies to investigate criminal activities that the states had formerly taken responsibility for.

Congress has also passed laws designed to allow the FBI to investigate situations in which local police forces are likely to be less effective. Under the National Stolen Property Act, for example, the FBI may investigate thefts valuing more than $5,000 when the stolen property is likely to have been transported across state lines. As a national agency, the FBI can pursue criminal investigations across state borders better than any state agency can.

Disputes over jurisdiction may occur when an offense violates both state and federal laws. If the FBI and local agencies do not cooperate, they might each seek to catch the same criminals. This can have major implications if the agency that makes the arrest determines the court to which the case is brought. Usually, however, law enforcement officials at all levels of government seek to cooperate and to coordinate their efforts.

After the September 11, 2001 attacks on the World Trade Center and the Pentagon, the FBI and other federal law enforcement agencies focused their resources and efforts on investigating and preventing terrorist threats against the United States. As a result, the role of the FBI as a law enforcement agency has changed. One month after the attacks, 4,000 of the agency's 11,500 agents were dedicating their efforts to the aftermath of September 11. So many FBI agents were switched from their traditional law enforcement activities to antiterror initiatives that some observers claimed that other federal crimes were no longer being vigorously investigated (Kampeas, 2001). For example, the number of FBI agents assigned to drug investigations dropped from 1,400 to 800 between 2001 and 2003 as more agents focused on antiterrorism (New York Times, 2003). An examination of FBI statistics in 2006 found that white-collar crime and drug prosecutions based on FBI investigations declined by more than 40 percent in the years after 2001 (Willing, 2006). The federal government's response to potential threats to national security may ultimately diminish the federal role in traditional law enforcement and thereby effectively transfer responsibility for many criminal investigations to state and local officials.

The reorientation of the FBI's priorities is just one of many changes made in federal criminal justice agencies to address the issues of national security and terrorism. Congress and President Bush sought to increase the government's effectiveness by creating new federal agencies and reorganizing existing agencies. The most significant expansion of the federal government occurred with the creation of a new Department of Homeland Security through the consolidation of border security, intelligence, and emergency response agencies from other departments of government (see Table 1.1). Money invested by the federal government in the Department of Homeland Security created a variety of new career opportunities for people who have studied criminal justice and security issues. For example, the Transportation Security Administration (TSA), a new agency, assumed responsibility for protecting travelers and interstate commerce. Most importantly, federal employees of TSA took over the screening of passengers and their luggage at airports throughout the country. In light of the ease with which the September 11 hijackers brought box cutters on board commercial airliners, there were grave concerns that employees of private security agencies were neither adequately trained nor sufficiently vigilant to protect the traveling public. See "Careers in Criminal Justice" for more on the position of transportation security officer.

Although federal involvement in criminal justice has expanded, laws are enforced and offenders are brought to justice mainly in the states, counties, and cities (see Figure 1.1). As a result, local traditions, values, and practices shape the way criminal justice agencies operate. Local leaders, whether members of the city council or influential

ThomsonNOW·

Improve your grade on the exam with Personalized Study! For reinforcement resources and a mastery check of Criminal Justice in a Federal System, go to www.thomsonedu.com/thomsonnow.

See inside for an illustration of THE CRIMINAL JUSTICE SYSTEM

This brief has muscle!

New CAREERS focus ... Today's HOT topics

REAL-WORLD applications ... WRITING challenges

ALL WITHIN a strong interdisciplinary and policy-based framework!

In this Fifth Edition, George Cole and Christopher Smith have accomplished what many thought impossible to achieve within a brief format ... adding NEW coverage of today's hottest careers, international comparisons, and real-world applications—ALL within a superb interdisciplinary and policy-based framework. We call it the *brief book with muscle*. In fact, it is the **only** concise text for this course that shows students the real-world opportunities of this fast-moving field *while at the same time* giving them a thorough understanding of why public policy and interdisciplinary perspectives are essential to the meaningful study of criminal justice as it is practiced today. This exciting, cutting-edge revision offers you and your students many important advantages:

CURRENT! TODAY'S NEWS AND ISSUES

Homeland security, terrorism, cyber crime, policing challenges, the newest theories on crime causation, and more.
See page P-2.

APPLIED! ENGAGING STUDENTS IN WHAT'S REAL

NEW *Careers in Criminal Justice* features, NEW *Real-World Activities,* NEW chapter openers from today's headlines, NEW *Comparative Perspectives.*
See pages P-3 and P-4.

USER-FRIENDLY! MANY ONLINE TOOLS

Students will love the easy interaction between the book and its many online resources.
See page P-5.

PLUS—A GREAT SELECTION OF TEACHING AND LEARNING TOOLS

Helping you cut the time you spend preparing for and managing your course.
See pages P-6 and P-7. And for more student resources, see page P-8.

THOMSON

WADSWORTH

Preview

ate-breaking developments . . . many topics that draw students into your course!

■ **The growth of cyber crime**—greatly expanded coverage that helps students understand the rapidly expanding methods of cyber criminals and the challenges of addressing their continually shifting and adapting forms of criminal behavior.

■ **Homeland security and its great impact on the criminal justice field**—the increased role of private security, the reorganization of many federal law enforcement agencies, conflicts between national security and civil liberties, and public policies dealing with terrorists.

■ **The latest theories of crime causation**—expanded coverage of life course theories, including Sampson and Laub's research findings.

■ **Expanded coverage of policing,** including recruitment and training.

■ **The latest coverage of courts**—new material on the adversarial system and the function of courts, careers information, and international comparisons.

■ **Current issues in capital punishment**—the prohibition on execution of juvenile offenders and legal challenges to methods of execution.

■ **New and expanded coverage of corrections issues,** such as overcrowding problems and intermediate sanctions.

■ **Current discussion of juvenile justice,** including the nature of the work of juvenile probation officers.

■ **Exceptional coverage of technology issues in criminal justice**—use of nonlethal weapons, patrol car computers, behavior modification, stalker trackers, and more.

> *"One of the best introductory textbooks on the market and the only textbook that I use to teach Introduction to Criminal Justice."*
>
> **Kimberly D. Hassell,**
> **Department of Criminal Justice**
> **University of Wisconsin,**
> **Milwaukee**

---

36   PART I   CRIME AND THE CRIMINAL JUSTICE SYSTEM

Enron founder Ken Lay leaves federal court after he was convicted of all charges in his fraud, conspiracy, and bank fraud trials in Houston. The conviction marked the climax of one of the most notorious corporate scandals in U.S. history. Lay died of a massive heart attack before he was sentenced.

occupational crimes Criminal offenses committed through opportunities created in a legal business or occupation.

organized crime A framework for the perpetuation of criminal acts—usually in fields such as gambling, drugs, and prostitution—providing illegal services that are in great demand.

money laundering In the case of drug offenses, which during

liberty limited by the need to be wary and fearful of actions by people who are drunk or out of control.

Those charged with visible crimes tend to be young men. Further, in many communities, members of minority groups tend to be overrepresented among those arrested and prosecuted for such offenses. Some argue that this is due to the class bias of a society that has singled out visible crimes for priority enforcement. They note that we do not focus as much police and prosecutorial attention on white-collar crimes, such as fraud and other acts committed by office workers and business owners, as we do on street crimes.

OCCUPATIONAL CRIME

Occupational crimes are committed in the context of a legal business or profession. Often viewed as shrewd business practices rather than illegal acts, they are crimes that, if "done right," are never discovered. Such crimes are often committed by respectable, well-to-do people taking advantage of opportunities arising from business dealings. Such crimes impose huge costs on society. Although there are no precise figures on the cost of occupational crime to American society, the Association of Certified Fraud Examiners estimates that occupational fraud may cost American businesses as much as $660 billion annually (ACFE, 2004). By contrast, the FBI calculates that the direct financial losses from street crimes involving the theft of property, such as burglary, robbery, and larceny, are less than $17 billion annually (FBI, 2005a).

ORGANIZED CRIME

Rather than referring to criminal acts per se, the term **organized crime** refers to the framework within which such acts are committed. A crime syndicate has an organizational structure, rules, a division of labor, and the capacity for ruthless violence and for corrupting law enforcement, labor and business leaders, and politicians (Jacobs and Panarella, 1998:160). Organized criminals provide goods and services to millions of people. They engage in any activity that provides a minimum of risk and a maximum of profit. Thus, organized crime involves a network of activities, usually cutting across state and national borders, that range from legitimate businesses to shady deals with labor unions to providing "goods"—such as drugs, sex, and pornography—that cannot be obtained legally. In recent years organized crime has been involved in new services such as commercial arson, illegal disposal of toxic waste. Few organized criminals are arrested and prosecuted.

Justice" to learn more about forensic accountants

1990s swept large numbers of offenders into federal prisons, many drug violators end up in state corrections systems because such crimes violate both state and federal laws.

EXPANSION OF FEDERAL INVOLVEMENT

Since the 1960s the federal government has expanded its role in dealing with crime, a policy area that has traditionally been the responsibility of state and local governments. As Willard Oliver notes, the federal role has become much more active in "legislating criminal activity, expanding [the] federal law enforcement bureaucracy, widening the reach and scope of the federal courts, and building more federal prisons" (Oliver, 2002:1).

The report of the U.S. President's Commission on Law Enforcement and Administration of Justice (1967:613) emphasized the need for greater federal involvement in crime control at the local level and urged that federal grants be directed to the states to support criminal justice initiatives. Since then, Congress has allocated billions of dollars for crime control efforts and passed legislation, national in

Since 9/11 there has been a major expansion of federal law enforcement involvement in the states and local communities. Here, FBI and ATF investigators look through the remains of the Morning Star Missionary Baptist Church near Boligee, Alabama. Questions were raised initially as to whether terrorists set the blaze.

TECHNOLOGY ISSUES IN CRIMINAL JUSTICE

Backscatter X-Ray

The development of new technologies can enhance our capacity to detect and prevent crimes as well as gather evidence of criminal guilt. Traditional crime-fighting technologies such as fingerprints and crime scene photographs have been supplemented by a range of inventions that detect microscopic bits of evidence.

New technologies can also create new dilemmas and problems. For example, they can increase government officials' ability to examine previously private aspects of lives—and bodies. As we consider whether and how to use new devices, we must also consider whether we are sacrificing other important values. Fundamentally, we must ask ourselves whether we are so committed to preventing crime and capturing criminals that we are willing to surrender elements of our privacy and liberty.

An excellent example emerged in 2003 when news reports described the federal Transportation Security Administration (TSA)'s experiments with backscatter X-ray devices to detect whether airline passengers are carrying weapons, bombs, or other contraband. Fully clothed people who are examined with such machines will appear naked in the televison-type monitor while also revealing any objects that they are carrying under their clothes. According to the director of the TSA's security laboratory, "It does basically make you look fat and naked—but you see all this stuff [that is hidden under clothes]." The thought that a government monitor can see the image of someone's unclothed body is likely to make many people uncomfortable.

Indeed, when the TSA began experimenting with the machines at selected airports in 2005, one security expert objected that the devices are too intrusive and described the job of airport screeners as being "paid to go to a peep show." Moreover, he argued that because the low-level X-ray does not penetrate the skin, very overweight people could still hide explosives beneath the folds of their skin.

RESEARCHING THE INTERNET

For an online description of backscatter X-ray devices, go to the corresponding site listed on the Cole/Smith Criminal Justice in America Companion Website: http://www.thomsonedu.com/criminaljustice/cole.

FOR CRITICAL ANALYSIS

If you were boarding an airplane, would you want the security monitor to, in effect, see you naked in order to prevent anyone from carrying weapons on planes? What if such devices could be carried by police officers on the street to detect whether pedestrians are carrying concealed weapons? Should limits be placed on the use of such technologies?

Sources: Leslie Miller, "Airport Screeners May Get X-Ray Eyes" [Associated Press Wire Service], *Lansing State Journal,* June 26, 2003, p. 4A; Office of National Drug Control Policy, "2001 Counterdrug Research and Development Blueprint Update," 2001, Appendix D, http://www.ncjrs.org/ondcppubs/publications; Joe Sharkey, "Airport Screeners Could Get X-Rated X-ray Views," *New York Times,* May 24, 2005, http://www.nytimes.com.

TABLE 1.1   Department of Homeland Security

Congress approved legislation to create a new federal agency dedicated to protecting the United States from terrorism. The legislation merges 22 agencies and nearly 170,000 government workers.

	Agencies Moved to the Department of Homeland Security	Previous Department or Agency
Border and Transportation Security	Immigration and Naturalization Service enforcement functions	Justice Department
	Transportation Security Administration	Transportation Department
	Customs Service	Treasury Department
	Federal Protective Services	General Services Administration
	Animal and Plant Health Inspection Service (parts)	Agriculture Department
Emergency Preparedness and Response	Federal Emergency Management Agency	(Independent agency)
	Chemical, biological, radiological, and nuclear response units	Health and Human Services Department
	Nuclear Incident response teams	Energy Department
	National Domestic Preparedness Office	FBI
	Office of Domestic Preparedness	Justice Department
	Domestic Emergency Support Teams	(From various departments and agencies)
Science and Technology	Civilian biodefense research program	Health and Human Services Department
	Plum Island Animal Disease Center	Agriculture Department
	Lawrence Livermore National Laboratory (parts)	Energy Department
Information Analysis and Infrastructure Protection	National Communications System	Defense Department
	National Infrastructure Protection Center	FBI
	Critical Infrastructure Assurance Office	Commerce Department
	National Infrastructure Simulation and Analysis Center	Energy Department
	Federal Computer Incident Response Center	General Services Administration
Secret Service	Secret Service including presidential protection units	Treasury Department
Coast Guard	Coast Guard	Transportation Department

Source: *New York Times,* November 20, 2002, p. A12.

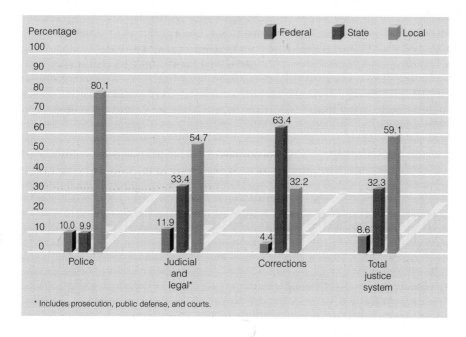

FIGURE 1.1
Percentage (rounded) of criminal justice employees at each level of government, 2001

The administration of criminal justice in the United States is very much a local affair, as these employment figures show. Only in corrections do states employ a greater percentage of workers than do municipalities.

Source: Bureau of Justice Statistics, *Sourcebook of Criminal Justice Statistics, 2003* (Washington, DC: U.S. Government Printing Office, 2004), Table 1.15.

citizens, can help set law enforcement priorities by putting pressure on the police. Will the city's police officers crack down on illegal gambling? Will juvenile offenders be turned over to their parents with stern warnings, or will they be sent to state institutions? The answers to these and other important questions vary from city to city.

CAREERS IN CRIMINAL JUSTICE

Transportation Security Officer (TSO)

NATURE OF THE WORK

Employed by the Transportation Security Administration in the government's new Department of Homeland Security, TSOs work at airports where they operate X-ray machines, conducted searches of passengers and luggage, review tickets, and look for suspicious behavior. They must interact courteously with the public as they work in a noisy, stressful environment amid distracting machinery while standing on their feet for three hours at a time. Most importantly, as they pay close attention to people's behavior, clothing, and luggage, they must make effective decisions if crisis situations arise. They must also work irregular hours, including evening and weekend shifts.

REQUIRED QUALIFICATIONS

TSOs must be U.S. citizens or U.S. nationals (citizens of American Samoa or the Commonwealth of Northern Mariana Islands). They must be proficient in English and possess a high school diploma or GED. The educational requirement may be replaced by at least one year of full-time work experience in security or as an X-ray technician. They must have correctable vision to 20/30 in the best eye for distance vision and cannot be color-blind. They must pass a medical examination that includes a hearing test and be able to lift and move luggage weighing up to 70 pounds. TSOs must also have good mental abilities for observation, as well as interpersonal skills for dealing with the public in stressful situations.

EARNINGS AND JOB OUTLOOK

Starting salaries range from $23,600 to $35,400 with the possibility of cost-of-living enhancements in certain cities. Although the Transportation Security Administration completed its massive initial hiring campaign when it assumed responsibility for aircraft security after September 11, the employment section of its website continually posts advertisements for more than 200 positions at airports throughout the country. The demands of the job lead to personnel turnover that regularly creates new openings.

MORE INFORMATION

You can obtain additional information about this occupation at the website of the U.S. Transportation Security Administration, listed on the Cole/Smith Criminal Justice in America Companion Website: http://www.thomsonedu.com/criminaljustice/cole.

CHECKPOINT

Answers

3. What is the key feature of federalism?

3. A division of power between a central (national) government and regional (state) governments.

4. What powers does the national government have in the area of criminal justice?

4. Enforcement of federal criminal laws.

5. What factors have caused federal involvement in criminal justice to expand?

5. The expansion of criminal activities across state borders; the war on terrorism.

Criminal Justice as a Social System

To achieve the goals of criminal justice, many kinds of organizations—police, prosecution, courts, corrections—have been formed. Each has its own functions and personnel. We might assume that criminal justice is an orderly process in which a variety of professionals act on each case on behalf of society. To know how the system really works, however, we must look beyond its formal organizational structure. In doing so, we can use the concept of a **system:** a complex whole made up of interdependent parts whose actions are directed toward goals and influenced by the environment in which they function.

The criminal justice system comprises several parts or subsystems. The subsystems—police, courts, corrections—have their own goals and needs but are also interdependent.

system A complex whole consisting of interdependent parts whose actions are directed toward goals and are influenced by the environment within which they function.

When one unit changes its policies, practices, or resources, other units will be affected. An increase in the number of people arrested by the police, for example, will affect not only the judicial subsystem but also the probation and correctional subsystems. For criminal justice to achieve its goals, each part must make its own contribution; each must also have some contact with at least one other part of the system.

Although understanding the nature of the entire criminal justice system and its subsystems is important, we must also see how individual actors play their roles. The criminal justice system is made up of a great many people doing specific jobs. Some, such as police officers and judges, are well known to the public. Others, such as bail bondsmen and probation officers, are less well known. A key concept here is exchange, meaning the mutual transfer of resources among individual actors, each of whom has goals that he or she cannot accomplish alone. Each needs to gain the cooperation and assistance of other individuals by helping them achieve their own goals. The concept of exchange allows interpersonal behavior to be seen as the result of individual decisions about the costs and benefits of different courses of action.

Many kinds of exchange relationships exist in the criminal justice system, some more visible than others. Probably the most obvious example is the **plea bargain,** in which the defense attorney and the prosecutor reach an agreement: The defendant agrees to plead guilty in exchange for a reduction of charges or for a lighter sentence. As a result of this exchange, the prosecutor gains a quick, sure conviction; the defendant achieves a shorter sentence, and the defense attorney can move on to the next case. Thus, the cooperation underlying the exchange promotes the goals of each participant.

The concept of exchange serves as a reminder that decisions are the products of interactions among individuals and that the subsystems of the criminal justice system are tied together by the actions of individual decision makers. Figure 1.2 presents selected exchange relationships between a prosecutor and other individuals and agencies involved in the criminal justice process.

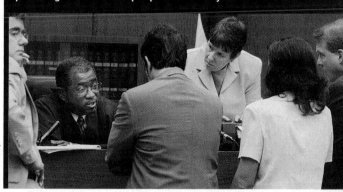

The system perspective emphasizes that criminal justice is made up of parts or subsystems, and police, courts, and corrections. Here, Judge Orlando Hudson confers with prosecutors and defense attorneys in the Durham, North Carolina trial of Michael Peterson, who was charged with murdering his wife, Kathleen. Each participant brings his or her own perspective to the system.

AP/Chuck Liddy

exchange A mutual transfer of resources: a balance of benefits and deficits that flow from behavior based on decisions about the values and costs of alternatives.

plea bargain A defendant's plea of guilty to a criminal charge with the reasonable expectation of receiving some consideration from the state for doing so, usually a reduction of the charge. The defendant's ultimate goal is a penalty lighter than the one formally warranted by the charged offense.

CHECKPOINT

Answers

6. What is a system? — 6. A complex whole made up of interdependent parts whose actions are directed toward goals and influenced by the environment within which they function.

7. What are the subsystems of the criminal justice system? — 7. Police, courts, corrections.

8. What is one example of an exchange relationship? — 8. Plea bargaining.

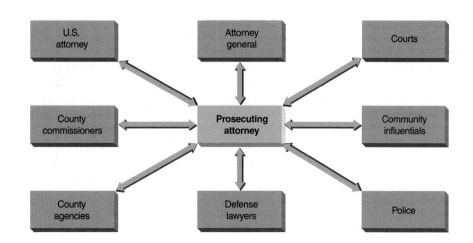

FIGURE 1.2
Exchange relationships between prosecutors and others
The prosecutor's decisions are influenced by relationships with other agencies and members of the community.

discretion The authority to make decisions without reference to specific rules or facts, using instead one's own judgment; allows for individualization and informality in the administration of justice.

Characteristics of the Criminal Justice System

The workings of the criminal justice system have four major characteristics: (1) discretion, (2) resource dependence, (3) sequential tasks, and (4) filtering.

DISCRETION

All levels of the justice process reflect a high degree of **discretion**. This term refers to officials' freedom to act according to their own judgment and conscience (see Table 1.2). For example, police officers decide how to handle a crime situation, prosecutors decide which charges to file, judges decide how long a sentence will be, and parole boards decide when an offender may be released from prison.

The extent of such discretion may seem odd, given that the United States is ruled by law and has created procedures to ensure that decisions are made in accordance with law. However, instead of a mechanical system in which decisions are dominated by law, criminal justice is a system in which actors may take many factors into account and exercise many options as they dispose of a case.

Two arguments are often made to justify discretion in the criminal justice system. First, discretion is needed because the system lacks the resources to treat every case the same way. If every violation of the law were pursued from investigation through trial, the costs would be immense. Second, many officials believe that discretion permits them to achieve greater justice than rigid rules would produce. For more on discretion, see "Real-World Activity" at the end of this chapter.

RESOURCE DEPENDENCE

Criminal justice agencies do not generate their own resources but depend on other agencies for funding. Therefore, actors in the system must cultivate and maintain good relations with those who allocate resources—that is, political decision makers, such as legislators, mayors, and city council members. Some police departments gain revenue through traffic fines and property forfeitures, but these sources cannot sustain their budgets.

Because budget decisions are made by elected officials who seek to please the public, criminal justice officials must also maintain a positive image and good relations with voters. If the police have strong public support, for example, the mayor will be reluctant to reduce the law enforcement budget. Criminal justice officials also seek positive coverage from the news media. Because the media often provide a crucial link between government agencies and the public, criminal justice officials may announce notable achievements while trying to limit publicity about controversial cases and decisions.

SEQUENTIAL TASKS *7 GRAND JURY*

Decisions in the criminal justice system are made in a specific sequence. The police must arrest a person before the case is passed to the prosecutor to determine if charges should be brought. The prosecutor's decisions influence the nature of the court's workload. Officials cannot achieve their goals by acting out of sequence. For example, prosecutors and judges cannot bypass the police by making arrests, and correctional

TABLE 1.2	Who Exercises Discretion?	
Discretion is exercised by various actors throughout the criminal justice system.	
These Criminal Justice Officials...	**Must Often Decide Whether or How to:**
Police	Enforce specific laws
	Investigate specific crimes
	Search people, vicinities, buildings
	Arrest or detain people
Prosecutors	File charges or petitions for adjudication
	Seek indictments
	Drop cases
	Reduce charges
Judges or Magistrates	Set bail or conditions for release
	Accept pleas
	Determine delinquency
	Dismiss charges
	Impose sentence
	Revoke probation
Correctional Officials	Assign to [which] type of correctional facility
	Award privileges
	Punish for infractions of rules
	Determine date and conditions of parole
	Revoke parole

Source: Bureau of Justice Statistics, *Report to the Nation on Crime and Justice,* 2nd ed. (Washington, DC: U.S. Government Printing Office, 1988), 59.

officials cannot punish anyone who has not passed through the earlier stages of the process.

The sequential nature of the system is a key element in the exchange relationships among the justice system's decision makers, who depend on one another to achieve their goals. In other words, the system is highly interdependent in part because it is sequential.

FILTERING

We can see the criminal justice system as a **filtering process**. At each stage some defendants are sent on to the next stage, while others are either released or processed under changed conditions. As shown in Figure 1.3, persons who have been arrested may be filtered out of the system at various points. Note that relatively few suspects who are arrested are then prosecuted, tried, and convicted. Some go free because the police decide that a crime has not been committed or that the evidence is not sound. The prosecutor may decide that justice would be better served by sending the suspect to a substance abuse clinic. Many defendants will plead guilty, the judge may dismiss charges against others, and the jury may acquit a few defendants. Most of the offenders who are actually tried, however, will be convicted. Thus, the criminal justice system is often described as a funnel—many cases enter it, but only a few result in conviction and punishment.

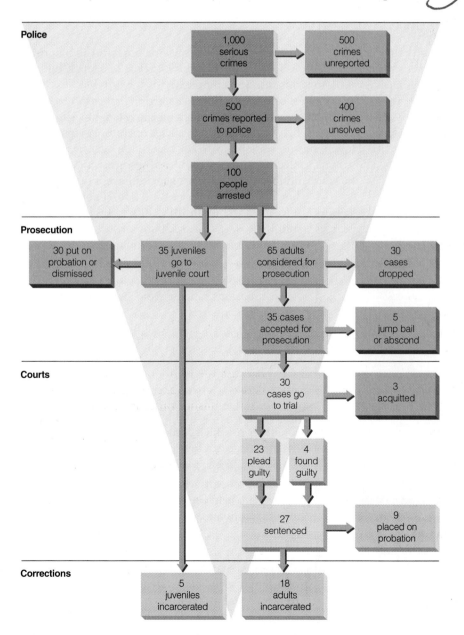

Police

Prosecution

Courts

Corrections

> **filtering process** A screening operation; a process by which criminal justice officials screen out some cases while advancing others to the next level of decision making.

FIGURE 1.3
Criminal justice as a filtering process
Decisions at each point in the system result in some cases being dropped while others are passed to the next point. Are you surprised by the small portion of cases that remain?

Source: Bureau of Justice Statistics, *Sourcebook of Criminal Justice Statistics, 2003* (Washington, DC: U.S. Government Printing Office, 2004), Table 1.15.

To summarize, the criminal justice system is composed of a set of interdependent parts (subsystems). This system has four key attributes: (1) discretion, (2) resource dependence, (3) sequential tasks, and (4) filtering. Using this framework, we look next at the operations of criminal justice agencies and then examine the flow of cases through the system.

CHECKPOINT

Answers

9. What are the major characteristics of the criminal justice system? ⟶ **9.** Discretion, resource dependence, sequential tasks, filtering.

Operations of Criminal Justice Agencies

The criminal justice system has been formed to deal with persons who are accused of violating the criminal law. Its subsystems consist of more than 60,000 public and private agencies with an annual budget of more than $167 billion and more than 2.3 million employees. Here we review the main parts of the criminal justice system and their functions.

POLICE

We usually think of the police as being on the "front line" in controlling crime. The term *police*, however, does not refer to a single agency or type of agency, but to many agencies at each level of government. The complexity of the criminal justice system can be seen in the large number of organizations engaged in law enforcement. There are only 50 federal government law enforcement agencies in the United States, whereas 17,784 state and local law enforcement agencies operate. Forty-nine of these are state agencies (Hawaii has no state police). The remaining agencies are found in counties, cities, and towns, reflecting the fact that local governments dominate the police function. At the state and local levels, these agencies have more than one million full-time employees and a total annual budget that exceeds $58 billion (BJS, 2004f: Table 1.62; Hickman and Reaves, 2006a:iii, 2006b:iii).

Police agencies have four major duties:

1. *Keeping the peace.* This broad and important mandate involves the protection of rights and persons in situations ranging from street-corner brawls to domestic quarrels.

2. *Apprehending violators and combating crime.* This is the task that the public most often associates with police work, although it accounts for only a small portion of police time and resources.

3. *Preventing crime.* By educating the public about the threat of crime and by reducing the number of situations in which crimes are likely to be committed, the police can lower the rate of crime.

4. *Providing social services.* Police officers recover stolen property, direct traffic, give emergency medical aid, help people who have locked themselves out of their homes, and provide other social services.

dual court system A system consisting of a separate judicial structure for each state in addition to a national structure. Each case is tried in a court of the same jurisdiction as that of the law or laws broken.

As part of their law enforcement responsibilities, the police must deal with a wide range of witnesses and victims in emotionally charged situations. Here police officers rescued a child from a day care center where an armed man had sought to hold hostages.

AP Photo/Michael Kim

COURTS

The United States has a **dual court system** that consists of a separate judicial system for each state in addition to a national system. Each system has its own series of courts; the U.S. Supreme Court is responsible for correcting certain errors made in all other court systems. Although the Supreme Court can review cases from both the state and federal courts, it will hear only cases involving federal law or constitutional rights.

With a dual court system, the law may be interpreted differently in various states. Although the wording of laws may be similar, none of the state courts interpret the laws the same way. To some extent, these variations reflect different social and political conditions. The dominant values of citizens and judges may differ from one region to another. Differences in interpretation may also be due to attempts by state courts to solve similar problems by different means. For example, before the Supreme Court ruled that evidence the police obtained in illegal ways should usually be excluded at trials, some states had already established rules barring the use of such evidence.

Courts are responsible for **adjudication**—determining whether or not a defendant is guilty. In so doing, they must use fair procedures that will produce just, reliable decisions. Courts must also impose sentences that are appropriate to the behavior being punished. Certain cases or offenders, such as drug cases or juvenile offenders, may be sent to specialized courts that focus on specific matters.

adjudication The process of determining whether the defendant is guilty.

CORRECTIONS

On any given day, nearly seven million American adults (one of every 34) are under the supervision of state and federal corrections systems. There is no "typical" correctional agency or official. Instead, a variety of agencies and programs are provided by private and public organizations—including federal, state, and local governments—and carried out in many different community and closed settings.

Although the average citizen may equate corrections with prisons, less than 30 percent of convicted offenders are in prisons and jails; the rest are being supervised in the community. Probation and parole have long been important aspects of corrections, as have community-based halfway houses, work release programs, and supervised activities.

The federal government, all the states, most counties, and all but the smallest cities engage in corrections. Nonprofit private organizations such as the Young Men's Christian Association (YMCA) have also contracted with governments to perform correctional services. In recent years, for-profit businesses have also entered into contracts with governments to build and operate correctional institutions.

The police, courts, and corrections are the main agencies of criminal justice. Each is a part, or subsystem, of the criminal justice system. Each is linked to the other two subsystems, and the actions of each affect the others. These effects can be seen as we examine the flow of decision making within the criminal justice system.

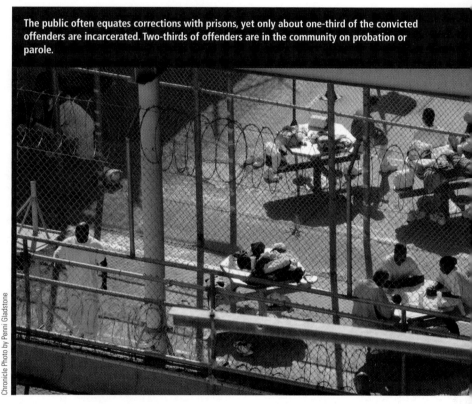

The public often equates corrections with prisons, yet only about one-third of the convicted offenders are incarcerated. Two-thirds of offenders are in the community on probation or parole.

Chronicle Photo by Penni Gladstone

ThomsonNOW™
Improve your grade on the exam with Personalized Study! For reinforcement resources and a mastery check of the Operations of Criminal Justice Agencies, go to www.thomsonedu.com/thomsonnow.

CHECKPOINT

Answers

10. What are the four main duties of police? ⟶ 10. Keeping the peace, apprehending violators and combating crime, preventing crime, providing social services.

11. What is a dual court system? ⟶ 11. A separate judicial system for each state in addition to a national system.

12. What are the major types of state and local correctional facilities and programs? What type of organizations operate them? ⟶ 12. Prisons, jails, probation, parole, intermediate sanctions. Public, nonprofit, and for-profit agencies carry out these programs.

The Flow of Decision Making in the Criminal Justice System

The processing of cases in the criminal justice system involves a series of decisions by police officers, prosecutors, judges, probation officers, wardens, and parole board members. At each stage in the process, they decide whether a case will move on to the next stage or be dropped from the system. Although the flowchart shown in Figure 1.4 appears streamlined, with cases entering at the top and moving swiftly toward the bottom, the actual route taken may be quite long and may involve many detours. At each step, officials have the discretion to decide what happens next. Many cases are filtered out of the system, others are sent to the next decision maker, and still others are dealt with informally.

Moreover, the flowchart does not show the influences of social relations or the political environment. In 2006, a retired FBI agent was charged with providing

FIGURE 1.4

The flow of decision making in the criminal justice system

Each agency is responsible for a part of the decision-making process. Thus the police, prosecution, courts, and corrections are bound together through a series of exchange relationships.

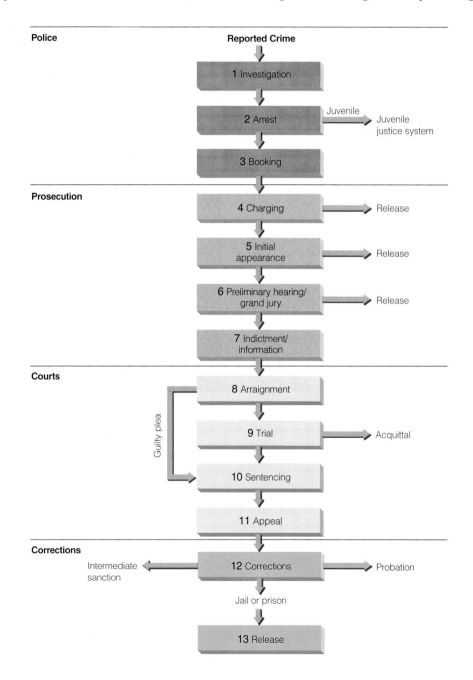

inside information to organized crime figures so that informants could be murdered. It was then discovered that 30 years earlier this agent had been caught illegally selling handguns without a license to undercover agents of the U.S. Bureau of Alcohol, Tobacco, and Firearms. If the FBI agent had been prosecuted for the handgun sales, his career in the FBI would have been over and he never would have ended up in a high-level position that later allegedly allowed him to assist mobsters. However, according to one former federal prosecutor involved in the handgun case in 1976, a high official in the U.S. Justice Department used his discretion to drop the gun charges. According to the former prosecutor, the high official "expressed no other reason not to prosecute the guy except the guy was a cop—and he didn't want to embarrass the [FBI]" (Feuer, 2006). The flowchart does not take into account that someone in authority might exercise discretion unfairly in favor of certain people, including those with wealth or political connections.

Another example shows how social relations and official discretion can create specific situations that make potential prosecutions more difficult. In 2004 Colorado prosecutors dropped rape charges against basketball star Kobe Bryant after the alleged victim changed her mind about her willingness to testify against him (T. R. Reid, 2004). Instead, the alleged victim accepted an undisclosed sum of money from Bryant to settle a lawsuit that she had filed against him (Sarche, 2005). The prosecutors chose not to pursue this case without the victim's cooperation.

On the other hand, prosecutors and judges sometimes do pressure witnesses to testify, sometimes even jailing reluctant witnesses for contempt of court. In 2005, for example, a federal judge sent a news reporter to jail for initially failing to disclose sources concerning an investigation to find the government officials who revealed the identity of a CIA officer. Thus, it is important to recognize that political influence, personal relationships, and specific circumstances may affect how officials' decisions shape the paths and outcomes of individual cases. Might Kobe Bryant have been convicted of rape if prosecutors in Colorado had chosen to exert more pressure on the reluctant witness? Would the victim have been willing to testify if Bryant, a millionaire athlete, had not paid her the money she sought in her lawsuit against him? There is no way to know. Such factors may influence decisions in ways that are not reflected in a simple description of decision-making steps. As we follow the 13 steps of the criminal justice process, bear in mind that the formal procedures do not hold in every case. Discretion, political pressure, and other factors can alter the outcome for different individuals.

STEPS IN THE DECISION-MAKING PROCESS

The criminal justice system consists of 13 steps that cover the stages of law enforcement, adjudication, and corrections. The system looks like an assembly line where decisions are made about *defendants*—persons charged with crimes. As these steps are described, recall the concepts discussed earlier: system, discretion, sequential tasks, filtering, and exchange. Be aware that the terms used for different stages in the process may differ from state to state and that the sequence of the steps differs in some parts of the country. In general, however, the flow of decision making follows this pattern:

1. *Investigation.* The process begins when the police believe that a crime has been committed. At this point an investigation is begun. The police normally depend on a member of the community to report the offense. Except for traffic and public order offenses, it is unusual for the police to observe illegal behavior themselves. Because most crimes have already been committed and offenders have left the scene before the police arrive, the police are at a disadvantage in quickly finding and arresting the offenders.

2. *Arrest.* If the police find enough evidence showing that a particular person has committed a crime, an arrest may be made. An **arrest** involves physically taking a person into custody pending a court proceeding. This action not only restricts the suspect's freedom but is also the first step toward prosecution.

    Under some conditions, arrests may be made on the basis of a **warrant**—a court order issued by a judge authorizing police officers to take certain actions,

arrest The physical taking of a person into custody on the grounds that there is reason to believe that he or she has committed a criminal offense. Police may use only reasonable physical force in making an arrest. The purpose of the arrest is to hold the accused for a court proceeding.

warrant A court order authorizing police officers to take certain actions, for example, to arrest suspects or to search premises.

such as arresting suspects or searching premises. In practice, most arrests are made without warrants. In some states, police officers may issue a summons or citation that orders a person to appear in court on a certain date. This avoids the need to hold the suspect physically until decisions are made about the case.

3. *Booking.* After an arrest the suspect is usually transported to a police station for booking, in which a record is made of the arrest. When booked, the suspect may be fingerprinted, photographed, questioned, and placed in a lineup to be identified by the victim or witnesses. Before being questioned, all suspects in custody must also be warned that they have the right to counsel, that they may remain silent, and that any statement they make may be used against them later. Bail may be set so that the suspect learns what amount of money must be paid or what other conditions must be met to gain release from custody until the case is processed.

4. *Charging.* Prosecuting attorneys are the key link between the police and the courts. They must consider the facts of the case and decide whether there is reasonable cause to believe that an offense was committed and that the suspect committed the offense. The decision to charge is crucial because it sets in motion the adjudication of the case.

5. *Initial appearance.* Within a reasonable time after arrest, the suspect must be brought before a judge. At this point, suspects are given formal notice of the charge(s) for which they are being held, advised of their rights, and, if approved by the judge, given a chance to post bail. At this stage, the judge decides whether there is enough evidence to hold the suspect for further criminal processing. If enough evidence has not been produced, the judge will dismiss the case.

   The purpose of bail is to permit the accused to be released while awaiting trial and to ensure that he or she will show up in court at the appointed time. Bail requires the accused to provide or arrange a surety (or pledge), usually in the form of money or a bond. The amount of bail is based mainly on the judge's view of the seriousness of the crime and the defendant's prior criminal record. Suspects may also be released on their own recognizance (also known as ROR)—a promise to appear in court at a later date without the posting of bail. In a few cases bail may be denied and the accused held because he or she is viewed as a threat to the community.

6. *Preliminary hearing/grand jury.* After suspects have been arrested, booked, and brought to court to be informed of the charges against them and advised of their rights, a decision must be made as to whether there is enough evidence to proceed. The preliminary hearing, used in about half the states, allows a judge to decide whether there is probable cause to believe that a crime has been committed and that the accused person committed it. If the judge does not find probable cause, the case is dismissed. If there is enough evidence, the accused is bound over for arraignment on an **information**—a document charging a person with a specific crime.

   In the federal system and in some states, the prosecutor appears before a grand jury, which decides whether there is enough evidence to file an **indictment** or "true bill" charging the suspect with a specific crime. The preliminary hearing and grand jury are designed to prevent hasty and malicious prosecutions, to protect persons from mistakenly being humiliated in public, and to decide whether there are grounds for prosecution.

7. *Indictment/information.* If the preliminary hearing leads to an information or the grand jury vote leads to an indictment, the prosecutor prepares the formal charging document and presents it to the court.

8. *Arraignment.* The accused person appears in court to hear the indictment or information read by a judge and to enter a plea. Accused persons may plead guilty or not guilty, or in some states, stand mute. If the accused pleads guilty, the judge must decide whether the plea is made voluntarily and whether the person has full knowledge of the consequences. When a guilty plea is accepted as "knowing" and voluntary, there is no need for a trial and the judge imposes a sentence.

information A document charging an individual with a specific crime. It is prepared by a prosecuting attorney and presented to a court at a preliminary hearing.

indictment A document returned by a grand jury as a "true bill" charging an individual with a specific crime on the basis of a determination of probable cause as presented by a prosecuting attorney.

Plea bargaining may take place at any time in the criminal justice process, but it is likely to be completed before or after arraignment. Very few criminal cases proceed to trial. Most move from the entry of the guilty plea to the sentencing phase.

9. *Trial.* For the small percentage of defendants who plead not guilty, the right to a trial by an impartial jury is guaranteed by the Sixth Amendment if the charges are serious enough to warrant incarceration for more than six months. In many jurisdictions, lesser charges do not entail a right to a jury trial. Most trials are summary or bench trials; that is, they are conducted without a jury. Because the defendant pleads guilty in most criminal cases, only about 10 to 15 percent of cases go to trial and only about 5 percent are heard by juries. Whether a criminal trial is held before a judge alone or before a judge and jury, the procedures are similar and are set out by state law and Supreme Court rulings. A defendant shall be found guilty only if the evidence proves beyond a reasonable doubt that he or she committed the offense.

10. *Sentencing.* Judges are responsible for imposing sentences. The intent is to make the sentence suitable to the offender and the offense within the limits set by the law. Although criminal codes place limits on sentences, the judge still has leeway. Among the judge's options are a suspended sentence, probation, imprisonment, or other sanctions such as fines and community service.

11. *Appeal.* Defendants who are found guilty may appeal convictions to a higher court. An appeal may be based on the claim that the trial court failed to follow the proper procedures or that constitutional rights were violated by the actions of police, prosecutors, defense attorneys, or judges. The number of appeals is small compared with the total number of convictions; further, in about 80 percent of appeals, trial judges and other officials are ruled to have acted properly. Even defendants who win appeals do not go free right away. Normally the defendant is given a second trial, which may result in an acquittal, a second conviction, or a plea bargain to lesser charges.

12. *Corrections.* The court's sentence is carried out by the correctional subsystem. Probation, intermediate sanctions such as fines and community service, and incarceration are the sanctions most often imposed. Probation allows offenders to serve their sentences in the community under supervision. Youthful offenders, first offenders, and those convicted of minor violations are most likely to be sentenced to probation rather than incarceration. The conditions of probation may require offenders to observe certain rules—to be employed, maintain an orderly life, or attend school—and to report to their supervising officer from time to time. If these requirements are not met, the judge may revoke the probation and impose a prison sentence.

Many new types of sanctions have been used in recent years. These intermediate sanctions are more restrictive than probation but less restrictive than incarceration. They include fines, intensive supervision probation, boot camp, home confinement, and community service.

Whatever the reasons used to justify them, prisons exist mainly to separate criminals from the rest of society. Those convicted of misdemeanors usually serve their time in city or county jails, whereas felons serve time in state prisons. Isolation from the community is one of the most painful aspects of incarceration. Not only are letters and visits restricted, but supervision and censorship are ever present. In order to maintain security, prison officials make unannounced searches of inmates and subject them to strict discipline.

13. *Release.* Release may occur when the offender has served the full sentence imposed by the court, but most offenders are returned to the community under the supervision of a parole officer. Parole continues for the duration of the sentence or for a period specified by law. Parole may be revoked and the offender returned to prison if the conditions of parole are not met or if the parolee commits another crime.

To see the criminal justice process in action, read the story of Christopher Jones, who was arrested, charged, and convicted of serious crimes arising from the police investigation of a series of robberies. The story is located just after this chapter.

THE CRIMINAL JUSTICE WEDDING CAKE

Although the flowchart shown in Figure 1.4 is helpful, recall that not all cases are treated equally. The process applied to a given case, as well as its outcome, is shaped by many factors, including the importance of the case to decision makers, the seriousness of the charge, and the defendant's resources.

Some cases are highly visible either because of the notoriety of the defendant or victim or because of the shocking nature of the crime. At the other extreme are "run-of-the-mill cases" involving unknown persons charged with minor crimes.

As shown in Figure 1.5, the criminal justice process can be compared to a wedding cake. This model shows clearly how different cases receive different kinds of treatment in the justice process.

Layer 1 of the "cake" consists of "celebrated" cases that are highly unusual, receive much public attention, result in a jury trial, and often drag on through many appeals. These cases embody the ideal of an adversary system of justice in which each side actively fights against the other, either because the defendant faces a stiff sentence or because the defendant has the financial resources to pay for a strong defense. The child molestation trial of pop star Michael Jackson in 2005 and the 2006 trial of Enron Corporation executives for financial misdeeds are of this type. Not all cases in Layer 1 receive national attention. From time to time, local crimes, especially cases of murder and rape, are treated in this way.

These cases serve as morality plays. The carefully crafted arguments of the prosecution and defense are seen as expressing key issues in our society or tragic flaws in individuals. Too often, however, the public concludes that all criminal cases follow this model.

Layer 2 consists of **felonies** that are considered serious by officials. Here we see violent crimes committed by persons with long criminal records against victims unknown to them. Police and prosecutors speak of serious felonies as "heavy" cases that should result in "tough" sentences. In such cases the defendant has little reason to plead guilty and the defense attorney must prepare for trial.

Layer 3 also consists of felonies, but the crimes and the offenders are seen as less important than those in Layer 2. The offenses may be the same as in Layer 2, but the

felonies Serious crimes usually carrying a penalty of death or incarceration for more than one year.

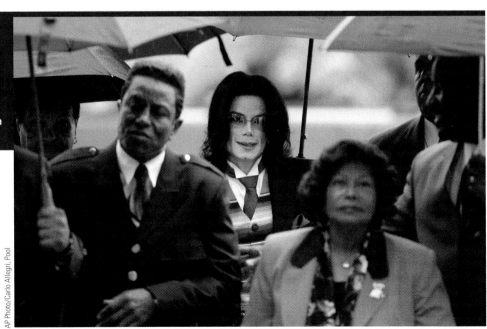

The trial of singer Michael Jackson on child molestation charges had all of the earmarks of a Layer 1 case. These cases embody the ideal of the adversary system, in which each side actively fights against the other. Like morality plays, Layer 1 cases concern key issues in society and tragic flaws in individuals.

AP Photo/Carlo Allegri, Pool

offender may have no record, and the victim may have had a prior relationship with the accused. The main goal of criminal justice officials is to dispose of such cases quickly. For this reason, many are filtered out of the system, often through plea bargaining.

Layer 4 is made up of **misdemeanors**. About 90 percent of all cases fall into this category. They concern such offenses as public drunkenness, shoplifting, prostitution, disturbing the peace, and traffic violations. Looked on as the "garbage" of the system, these cases are handled by the lower courts, where speed is essential. Prosecutors use their discretion to reduce charges or recommend probation as a way to encourage defendants to plead guilty quickly. Trials are rare, processes are informal, and fines, probation, or short jail sentences result.

The wedding cake model is a useful way of viewing the criminal justice system. Cases are not treated equally; some are seen as very important, others as merely part of a large caseload that must be processed. When one knows the nature of a case, one can predict fairly well how it will be handled and what its outcome will be.

CRIME CONTROL VERSUS DUE PROCESS

Models are simplified representations that illustrate important aspects of a system. As we saw in discussing the wedding cake model, they permit generalized statements and comparisons even though no one model necessarily portrays precisely the complex reality of specific situations. We now look at two more models to expand our picture of how the criminal justice system really operates.

In one of the most important contributions to systematic thought about the administration of justice, Herbert Packer (1968) described two competing models of the administration of criminal justice: the **crime control model** and the **due process model**. These are opposing ways of looking at the goals and procedures of the criminal justice system. The crime control model is much like an assembly line, whereas the due process model is like an obstacle course.

In reality, no one official or agency functions according to one model or the other. Elements of both models are found throughout the system. However, the two models reveal key tensions within the criminal justice process, as well as the gap between how the system is described and the way most cases are actually processed. Table 1.3 presents the major elements of each model.

Crime Control: Order as a Value   The crime control model assumes that every effort must be made to repress crime. It emphasizes efficiency and the capacity to catch, try, convict, and punish a high proportion of offenders; it also stresses speed and finality. This model places the goal of controlling crime uppermost, putting less emphasis on protecting individuals' rights. As Packer points out, in order to achieve liberty for all citizens, the crime control model calls for efficiency in screening suspects, determining guilt, and applying sanctions to the convicted. Because of high rates of crime and the limited resources of law enforcement, speed and finality are necessary. All these elements depend on informality, uniformity, and few challenges by defense attorneys or defendants.

FIGURE 1.5
The criminal justice wedding cake
This figure shows that different cases are treated in different ways. Only a very few cases are played out as "high drama"; most are handled through plea bargaining and dismissals.

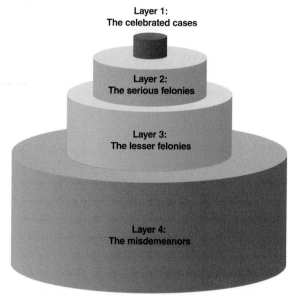

Source: Drawn from Samuel Walker, *Sense and Nonsense about Crime and Drugs,* 4th ed. (Belmont, CA: Wadsworth, 1998), 30–37.

misdemeanors Offenses less serious than felonies and usually punishable by incarceration of no more than a year, probation, or intermediate sanction.

crime control model A model of the criminal justice system that assumes freedom is so important that every effort must be made to repress crime; it emphasizes efficiency, speed, finality, and the capacity to apprehend, try, convict, and dispose of a high proportion of offenders.

due process model A model of the criminal justice system that assumes freedom is so important that every effort must be made to ensure that criminal justice decisions are based on reliable information; it emphasizes the adversarial process, the rights of defendants, and formal decision-making procedures.

TABLE 1.3	Due Process and Crime Control Models Compared				
What other comparisons can be made between the two models?					
	Goal	**Value**	**Process**	**Major Decision Point**	**Basis of Decision Making**
Due Process Model	Preserve individual liberties	Reliability	Adversarial	Courtroom	Law
Crime Control Model	Repress crime	Efficiency	Administrative	Police, pretrial processes	Discretion

In this model, police and prosecutors decide early on how likely the suspect is to be found guilty. If a case is unlikely to end in conviction, the prosecutor may drop the charges. At each stage, from arrest to preliminary hearing, arraignment, and trial, established procedures are used to determine whether the accused should be passed on to the next stage. Instead of stressing the combative aspects of the courtroom, this model promotes bargaining between the state and the accused. Nearly all cases are disposed of through such bargaining, and they typically end with the defendant pleading guilty. Packer's description of this model as an assembly-line process conveys the idea of quick, efficient decisions by actors at fixed stations that turn out the intended product—guilty pleas and closed cases.

Due Process: Law as a Value   If the crime control model looks like an assembly line, the due process model looks more like an obstacle course. This model assumes that freedom is so important that every effort must be made to ensure that criminal justice decisions are based on reliable information. It stresses the adversarial process, the rights of defendants, and formal decision-making procedures. For example, because people are poor observers of disturbing events, police and prosecutors may be wrong in presuming a defendant to be guilty. Thus, the people should be labeled as criminals only on the basis of conclusive evidence. To reduce error, the government must be forced to prove beyond a reasonable doubt that the defendant is guilty of the crime. Therefore, the process must give the defense every opportunity to show that the evidence is not conclusive, and the outcome must be decided by an impartial judge and jury. According to Packer, the assumption that the defendant is innocent until proved guilty has a far-reaching impact on the criminal justice system.

In the due process model, the state must prove that the person is guilty of the crime as charged. Prosecutors must prove their cases while obeying rules dealing with such matters as the admissibility of evidence and respect for defendants' constitutional rights. Forcing the state to prove its case in a trial protects citizens from wrongful convictions. Thus, the due process model emphasizes particular aspects of the goal of doing justice. It protects the rights of individuals and reserves punishment for those who unquestionably deserve it. These values are stressed even though some guilty defendants may go free because the evidence against them is not conclusive enough. By contrast, the crime control model values efficient case processing and punishment over the possibility that innocent people might be swept up in the process.

ThomsonNOW
Improve your grade on the exam with Personalized Study! For reinforcement resources and a mastery check of The Flow of Decision Making in the Criminal Justice System, go to www.thomsonedu.com/thomsonnow.

CHECKPOINT

13. What are the steps of the criminal justice process?

14. What is the purpose of the wedding cake model?

15. What are the main features of the crime control model and the due process model?

Answers

13. (1) Investigation, (2) arrest, (3) booking, (4) charging, (5) initial appearance, (6) preliminary hearing/grand jury, (7) indictment/information, (8) arraignment, (9) trial, (10) sentencing, (11) appeal, (12) corrections, (13) release.

14. To show that not all cases are treated equally.

15. Crime control: Every effort must be made to repress crime through efficiency, speed, and finality. Due process: Every effort must be made to ensure that criminal justice decisions are based on reliable information; it stresses the adversarial process, the rights of defendants, and formal decision-making procedures.

Crime and Justice in a Multicultural Society

One important aspect of American values is the principle of equal treatment. This value is prominently displayed in important national documents such as the Declaration of Independence and the Fourteenth Amendment to the Constitution, which guarantees the right to "equal protection." Critics of the criminal justice system argue that discretionary decisions and other factors produce racial discrimination. Discrimination calls into question the country's success in fulfilling the values that it claims to regard as supremely important. As such, it is good to look closely at whether or not discrimination exists in various criminal justice settings.

DISPARITY AND DISCRIMINATION

African Americans, Hispanics, and other minorities are subjected to the criminal justice system at much higher rates than are the white majority (T. H. Cohen and Reaves, 2006; Cole, 1999:4-5; Engel and Calnon, 2004; J. Hagan and Peterson, 1995:14). For example:

- African Americans account for 43 percent of felony defendants in the nation's 75 largest counties despite comprising only 15 percent of the population of those counties.

- A study of traffic stops found that, despite the greater likelihood of white drivers carrying drugs or guns, Hispanic drivers were 3.6 times more likely to be searched and 2.3 times more likely to be arrested by the police.

- The per capita incarceration rate for African Americans is seven times greater than that for whites.

- Since 1980 the proportion of Hispanics among all inmates in U.S. prisons has risen from 7.7 percent to 18.5 percent.

- About one-third of all male African Americans in their twenties are under criminal justice supervision.

- Among men aged 25–29, 8.4 percent of African Americans are in prison or jail, compared with 2.5 percent of Hispanics and about 1.2 percent of whites.

- The rate of unfounded arrests of Hispanics in California is double that of whites.

- Among 100,000 African American men aged 15–19, 68 will die as the result of a homicide involving a gun, compared with about 6 among 100,000 white men in the same age group.

- The robbery victimization rate for African Americans is 150 percent of that for whites, and they are victimized by rapes and aggravated assaults at rates that similarly exceed those for whites.

- The crime victimization rate is 260 per 1,000 Hispanic households versus 144 per 1,000 non-Hispanic households.

- The violent crime victimization rate for Native Americans is more than twice the rate for the nation.

The experiences of minority group members with the criminal justice system may contribute to differences in their views about the system's fulfillment of the goal of

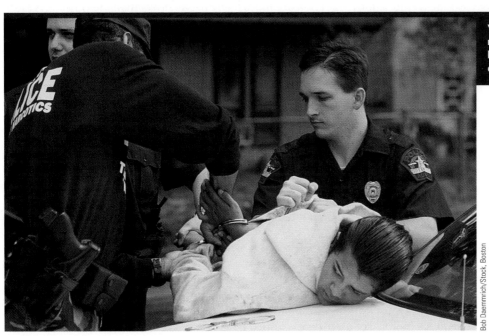

Young African American and Hispanic men contend that they are always being hassled by the police. Is this racism, or effective police work?

Bob Daemmrich/Stock, Boston

equal treatment (Lundman and Kaufman, 2003). See "What Americans Think" for more on this.

A central question is whether racial and ethnic disparities like those just listed are the result of discrimination (Mann, 1993:vii–xiv; Wilbanks, 1987). A **disparity** is simply a difference between groups. Such differences can often be explained by legitimate factors. For example, the fact that 18- to 24-year-old men are arrested out of proportion to their numbers in the general population is a disparity explained by the fact that they commit more crime. It is not thought to be the result of public policy of singling out young men for arrest. **Discrimination** occurs when groups are differentially treated without regard to their behavior or qualifications, for example, if people of color are routinely sentenced to prison regardless of their criminal history. Thus, a disparity could be the result of either fair or unfair practices.

EXPLAINING DISPARITIES

Racial disparities in criminal justice are often explained in one of three ways: (1) people of color commit more crimes, (2) the criminal justice system is racist, with the result that people of color are treated more harshly, or (3) the criminal justice system expresses the racism found in society as a whole. We consider each of these views in turn.

Explanation 1: People of Color Commit More Crimes

Nobody denies that the proportion of minorities arrested and placed under correctional supervision (probation, jail, prison, parole) is greater than their proportion to the general population. However, people disagree over whether racial bias is responsible for the disparity.

Disparities in arrests and sentences might be due to legitimate factors. For example, prosecutors and judges are supposed to take into account differences between serious and petty offenses, and between repeat and first-time offenders. It follows that more people of color will end up in the courts and prisons if they are more likely to commit more serious crimes and have more serious prior records than do whites (S. Walker, Spohn, and DeLeone, 2003).

But why would minorities commit more crimes? The most extreme argument is that they are more predisposed to criminality. This assumes that people of color are a "criminal class." The available evidence does not support this view. Behavior that violates criminal laws is prevalent throughout all segments of society. Indeed, nearly every adult American has committed an act for which he or she could be jailed. For example, studies of illicit drug use find that young adults, men, whites, and those with less than a high school education are more likely to use drugs than are others. As General Barry McCaffrey, the former director of the U.S. Office of National Drug Control Policy, has said, "The typical drug user is not poor and unemployed" (*New York Times*, September 9, 1999:A14). The 2004 *National Survey on Drug Use and Health* found that the percentage of white teens who used illicit drugs was higher than that of African American and Hispanic teens, but lower than that of Native Americans (U.S. Department of Health and Human Services, 2005). Furthermore, self-report studies, in which people are asked to report on their own criminal behavior, have shown that nearly everyone has committed a crime, although most are never caught. Indeed, both President George W. Bush and Vice President Dick Cheney have had drunken-driving convictions; further, in secretly taped conversations released in 2005, President Bush indicated that he had used marijuana and said, "I haven't denied anything" with respect to questions about whether he had used cocaine (Kirkpatrick, 2005).

Many of these kinds of crimes are difficult to detect or are low priorities for law enforcement agencies. In other instances, affluent perpetrators are better positioned to gain dismissals because of their status within the community, social networks, or access to high-quality legal representation.

In evaluating theories about possible links between race and crime, we must be aware that many commentators may be focusing only on crimes that resulted in prosecutions. Such limitations can distort an accurate understanding of this important issue. Race itself is not a cause of criminal behavior. Instead, any apparent associations

disparity A difference between groups that may either be explained by legitimate factors or indicate discrimination.

discrimination Differential treatment of individuals or groups based on race, ethnicity, gender, sexual orientation, or economic status, instead of on their behavior or qualifications.

WHAT AMERICANS THINK

Question: "Do you think that African Americans' civil rights are being respected by the country's criminal justice system?"

Non-Hispanic Whites

Yes, being respected 69%

No opinion 4%

No, not being respected 27%

African Americans

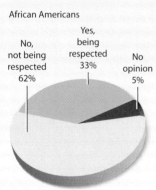

No, not being respected 62%

Yes, being respected 33%

No opinion 5%

Go to http://www.thomsonedu.com/criminaljustice/cole to compare your opinion on this issue with the opinions of other criminal justice students.

Source: National telephone survey of adults conducted by the Gallup Organization, June 3–9, 2002. Data supplied by the Roper Center for Public Opinion Research, University of Connecticut.

between crime and race relate only to subcategories of people within racial and ethnic groups, such as poor, young men, as well as certain categories of crimes that are commonly investigated and prosecuted. Research links crime to social contexts, not to race (Bruce, 2003).

Crime problems evolve and change over time. Identity theft and computer crime, for example, cause economic losses in the billions of dollars, yet no one has claimed a link between these crimes and race. Even if we look at developments affecting "street crimes," we can see that factors other than race appear to create the contexts for criminal behavior. For example, one of the most significant crime problems to hit the United States at the dawn of the twenty-first century is the "meth crisis": the spread of highly addictive methamphetamine that can be "cooked" in homemade labs using over-the-counter medicines and readily available chemicals. Americans use this inexpensive, dangerous drug more often than crack cocaine or heroin. Moreover, the "crisis has spread among white, often poor, usually rural Americans . . . [and] is rampant in small communities" (Bonne, 2001). According to U.S. Senator Tom Harkin, meth addiction accounts for up to 50 percent of thefts and burglaries in Iowa, as addicts try to support their habits, and methamphetamine played a role in the crimes of 26 percent of that state's prison population (Harkin, 2005).

The link between crime and economic disadvantage is significant (McNulty and Bellair, 2003). The meth crisis has spread among poor whites in rural areas and small towns. Other kinds of crime prevail among the poor in urban areas. Further, minority groups suffer greatly from poverty and unemployment. If poor people seek to steal, it is likely to be through means available, whether they be burglaries at farmhouses or carjacking and shoplifting in urban areas. These sorts of crimes receive more attention from police than do crimes such as tax cheating, employee theft, and illegal stock transactions, which are associated with economic advantage. In light of the associations between race and poverty and between economic status and criminal opportunities, it is not surprising to find Native Americans, Hispanics, and African Americans to be overrepresented among perpetrators of certain categories of crimes, especially those that are the focus of police attention (Beckett, Nyrop, and Pfingst, 2006).

Explanation 2: The Criminal Justice System Is Racist   Racial disparities may result if people who commit similar offenses are treated differently by decision makers in the criminal justice system because of their race or ethnicity. In this view, the fact that people of color are arrested more often than whites does not mean that they are more crime prone. For example, although only 13 percent of monthly drug users are African American, these same people represent 35 percent of those arrested for drug possession, 55 percent of convictions, and 74 percent of prison sentences (Butterfield, 1995). One study found that the police make unfounded arrests of African Americans four times as often as of whites (Donziger, 1996:109). *Racial profiling,* as described in the Close Up box, is an example of what many people believe is a racist activity by police. Evidence of its existence has led to new laws and policies that require police to keep records about their traffic-law enforcement patterns (Engel, Calnon, and Bernard, 2002).

Despite efforts to monitor and prevent such activities, evidence that some police officers use race as the basis for stopping, searching, and arresting individuals persists. A 2005 study of Texas law enforcement agencies reported, for example, that the Houston Police Department searched 12 percent of African American drivers and 9 percent of Hispanic drivers stopped by its officers but searched only 3.7 percent of white drivers who were pulled over (Steward and Totman, 2005). A national study of traffic stops found that the odds of being searched were 50 percent higher for black drivers and 42 percent higher for Hispanic drivers than for white drivers (Durose, Schmitt, and Langan, 2005; Engel and Calnon, 2004).

Is the criminal justice system racist? The arrest rate of minority citizens is greater than their offense rates justify. According to data from the Bureau of Justice Statistics for 2002, victims of violent crimes identified their assailants as African Americans in 23 percent of cases, yet African Americans comprised 38 percent of suspects arrested

CLOSE UP

Racial Profiling

Most people of all races and ethnic groups are never convicted of a crime, but stereotypes can work to brand all members of some groups with suspicion. These stereotypes are bad enough in the culture at large, but they also work their way into law enforcement through the use of criminal profiles, putting an undue burden on innocent members of these groups. Moreover, such actions produce stark collisions with important American values that we claim to hold dear, especially the values of equal treatment and fairness.

Many people of color, including well-known actors, prominent scholars, and successful doctors, can provide examples of being stopped and searched without justification. The evidence of profiling is not merely based on individuals' stories, however. Research has documented evidence of differential treatment. One study in Maryland found that African American motorists constituted 17 percent of the motorists and 17.5 percent of the speeders. But African American motorists were subjected to 77 percent of the automobile searches made by the police looking for contraband. The evidence of racial profiling in the criminal justice system is not limited to traffic enforcement. A study by the U.S. Government Accountability Office, the research agency that provides reports to Congress, discovered that African American women returning from abroad were nine times as likely as white women to be subjected to X-ray searches at airports, even though white women were found to be carrying illegal contraband twice as often as African American women were.

Racial profiling need not be limited to African Americans. Hispanics in many locations claim that they are targeted by police who assume that they are illegal immigrants or involved in drug trafficking. Since the tragic hijackings on September 11, many Muslims and other people of Middle Eastern and Asian ancestry claim that they are subjected to groundless suspicion and questioning by the police and airport security officials as part of the war on terrorism.

Determining when and how the police should use race to assess suspects and situations involves a complicated balancing of public safety and civil liberties. Law enforcement experts insist that effective police work depends on quick analysis and that skin color is one factor among many— like dress and demeanor—that officers must consider. But minority leaders say that racial profiling is based on the presumption that African Americans and Hispanics are linked to crime or that Arab Americans might be linked to terrorism. This has led to the humiliation and physical abuse of innocent citizens. As a result, some police agencies have attempted to develop specific policies to steer their officers away from improper use of race and ethnicity as factors in their decisions to make stops and conduct searches.

RESEARCHING THE INTERNET

See one public interest legal group's reports on racial profiling throughout the United States at the ACLU website listed on the Cole/Smith Criminal Justice in America Companion Website: http://www.thomsonedu.com/criminaljustice/cole.

FOR CRITICAL ANALYSIS

Is there any effective way to prevent criminal justice officials from using stereotypes as part of the suspicions that lead them to stop and investigate specific people? What impact does racial profiling have on people who believe that they have been subjected to it?

Sources: Drawn from Jennifer Loven, "Black Women Searched More Often," Associated Press Wire Service, April 10, 2000; Frederick Schauer, *Profiles, Probabilities, and Stereotypes* (Cambridge, MA: Harvard University Press, 2003); Christopher Stone, "Race, Crime, and the Administration of Justice," National Institute of Justice Journal, April 1999, pp. 24-32; U.S. General Accounting Office, *U.S. Customs Service: Better Targeting of Airline Passengers for Personal Searches Could Produce Better Results* (Washington, DC: U.S. Government Printing Office, March 2000).

for violent crimes (BJS, 2004f). A study of 150,000 cases in Connecticut found that on average an African American or Hispanic man must pay double the bail that would be paid by a white man for the same offense (Donziger, 1996:111). Further, research has found that judges' discretion in sentencing produces longer sentences for African Americans in some jurisdictions, even when studies control for other factors (Bushway and Piehl, 2001). Research finds that Hispanic defendants are at risk of receiving sentences severer than those of other offenders (Steffensmeier and Demuth, 2001). These conclusions do not mean that every minority defendant is treated in a disadvantageous manner when compared with the treatment of white defendants. Instead, the existence, nature, and extent of discrimination can vary from community to community (Britt, 2000). Thus, racial discrimination may be limited to specific types of cases, circumstances, and defendants (S. Walker, Spohn, and DeLeone, 2003).

Explanation 3: America Is a Racist Society   Some people claim that the criminal justice system is racist because it is embedded in a racist society. In fact, some accuse the system of being a tool of a racist society.

Evidence of racism exists in the way society asks the criminal justice system to operate. For example, federal sentencing guidelines punish users of crack cocaine much more harshly than users of powder cocaine, even though the drugs are chemically almost identical. The key difference is that whites tend to use powder, whereas people of color in the inner cities tend to use crack. State and federal legislators emphasized lengthy prison sentences during the perceived "crack crisis" of the late twentieth century. By contrast, government responses to the meth crisis of the early twenty-first century placed greater emphasis on prevention, such as limiting sales of over-the-counter medications used to manufacture meth, as well as treatment. For example, the Drug Policy Report of Iowa, a state hard hit by meth problems, says, "More treatment and related resources need to be targeted to meth-addicted offenders. It is only by reducing the demand for meth and other drugs that we can hope to break the cycle of addiction" (Governor's Office on Drug Control Policy, 2006). Some observers suspect that the less punitive orientation toward meth offenders, who are predominantly white, may reflect race-based attitudes that perceive crack offenders, many of whom have been African American, as less worthy of rehabilitation. (See "A Question of Ethics" at the end of the chapter.)

Other evidence of racism in American society shows up in the stereotyping of offenders. That race-based stereotyping affects police actions can be seen in cases of African American and Hispanic professionals who were falsely arrested when the police were looking for a person of color and these individuals happened to be "out of place." Judge Claude Coleman was handcuffed and dragged through crowds of shoppers in Short Hills, New Jersey, while protesting his innocence; Princeton University philosopher Cornel West was stopped on false cocaine charges while driving across Massachusetts; and law student Brian Roberts was pulled over by the police as he drove in an affluent St. Louis neighborhood on his way to interview a judge for a class project (Tonry, 1995:51).

If people of color are overrepresented in the justice system because of racism in society, the solution may seem a bit daunting. Nobody knows how to quickly rid a society of biased policies, practices, and attitudes.

ThomsonNOW
Improve your grade on the exam with Personalized Study! For reinforcement resources and a mastery check of Crime and Justice in a Multicultural Society, go to www.thomsonedu.com/thomsonnow.

CHECKPOINT

Answers

16. What is meant by racial or ethnic disparities in criminal justice? ⟶ **16.** That racial and ethnic minorities are subjected to the criminal justice system at much higher rates than are the white majority.

17. What three alternative explanations are put forward to account for such disparities? ⟶ **17.** Minorities commit more crime; the criminal justice system is racist; America is a racist society.

A QUESTION OF ETHICS: WRITING ASSIGNMENT

You are a state legislator considering a proposed bill to decrease the mandated prison sentences for crack cocaine to make them equal to those for powder cocaine. You have received a well-documented report demonstrating the disproportionate impact of long crack cocaine sentences on members of minority groups. You have also observed that the law does not impose the same punishments on meth offenders that it imposes on people convicted of selling or possessing crack cocaine.

WRITING ASSIGNMENT

Write an explanation for your position on the proposed bill and include consideration of the following questions. Is evidence of racial disparity a sufficient reason to change sentencing laws? Would it make more sense to increase the sentences for powder cocaine and meth? Alternatively, does crack cocaine have a more harmful effect on society? Do you need any additional information to make your decision about whether to vote for the bill? What considerations would be most important to you?

REAL-WORLD ACTIVITY: AN APPLICATION

You are a police chief. You receive complaints from citizens that some officers are failing to enforce traffic laws. Reportedly, they merely give warnings to teenage drivers who speed through residential neighborhoods instead of issuing citations that carry fines and license suspension as penalties.

RESEARCHING THE INTERNET

Go to InfoTrac College Edition. Enter the keyword *traffic enforcement,* then read the article entitled "Police Enforcement of Traffic Laws: A Cost-Benefit Analysis," *FBI Law Enforcement Bulletin,* 1999.

APPLICATION

Say you want to take a strong stand in favor of deterring and punishing dangerous driving by teenagers. How would you make sure that your officers use their discretion to issue traffic citations instead of warnings? Would there be any possible negative consequences from your proposed policies and practices to reduce this aspect of police discretion? Would the benefits outweigh any problems?

SUMMARY

- The three goals of the criminal justice system are doing justice, controlling crime, and preventing crime.

- Both the national and state systems of criminal justice enforce laws, try cases, and punish offenders.

- Criminal justice is a system made up of several parts or subsystems—police, courts, and corrections.

- Exchange is a key concept in the analysis of criminal justice processes.

- Four major characteristics of the criminal justice system are discretion, resource dependence, sequential tasks, and filtering.

- The processing of cases in the criminal justice system involves a series of decisions by police officers, prosecutors, judges, probation officers, wardens, and parole board members.

- The criminal justice system consists of 13 steps that cover the stages of law enforcement, adjudication, and corrections.

- The four-layered criminal justice wedding cake model shows that not all cases are treated equally.

- The crime control model and the due process model are two ways of looking at the goals and procedures of the criminal justice system.

- Analysts explain the disproportionate impact of the criminal justice system on minorities through competing arguments about the criminal behavior of different groups' members and racism affecting American society and the criminal justice system.

QUESTIONS FOR REVIEW

1. What are the goals of the criminal justice system?

2. What is a system? How is the administration of criminal justice a system?

3. Why is the criminal justice wedding cake more realistic than a linear model depicting the criminal justice system?

4. What are the major elements of Packer's crime control model and due process model?

5. What evidence exists concerning the impact of the criminal justice system on members of racial minority groups?

KEY TERMS AND CASES

adjudication (p. 15)
arrest (p. 17)
crime control model (p. 21)
discretion (p. 12)
discrimination (p. 24)
disparity (p. 24)

dual court system (p. 14)
due process model (p. 21)
exchange (p. 11)
federalism (p. 7)
felonies(p. 20)
filtering process (p. 13)

indictment (p. 18)
information (p. 18)
misdemeanors (p. 21)
plea bargain (p. 11)
system (p. 10)
warrant (p. 17)

GOING ONLINE

Maximize your study time by using ThomsonNOW's diagnostic study plan to help you review this chapter. The Study Plan will

- Help you identify areas on which you should concentrate

- Provide interactive exercises to help you master the chapter concepts

- Provide a posttest to confirm you are ready to move on to the next chapter

THE CRIMINAL JUSTICE PROCESS

The State of Michigan versus
Christopher Jones

In October 1998, police in Battle Creek, Michigan, investigated a string of six robberies that occurred in a ten-day period. People were assaulted during some of the robberies. One victim was beaten so badly with a power tool that he required extensive reconstructive surgery for his face and skull. The police received an anonymous tip on their Silent Observer hotline, which led them to put together a *photo lineup*—an array of photographs of local men who had criminal records. Based on the tip and photographs identified by the victims, the police began to search for two men who were well known to them, Christopher Jones and his cousin Fred Brown.

Arrest

Jones was a 31-year-old African American. A dozen years of struggle with cocaine addiction had cost him his marriage and several jobs. He had a criminal record stretching back several years, including attempted larceny and attempts at breaking and entering. Thus, he had a record of stealing to support his drug habit. He had spent time on probation and done a short stretch in a minimum-security prison and a boot camp. But he had never been caught with drugs or been accused of an act of violence.

Fearing that Jones would be injured or killed by the police if he tried to run or resist arrest, his parents called the police and told them he was holed up in the bedroom of their home. At approximately 10:00 P.M. on October 28, as officers surrounded the house, the family opened the door and showed the officers the way to the bedroom. Jones surrendered peacefully and was led to the waiting police car in handcuffs.

At the police station, a detective with whom Jones was acquainted read him his *Miranda* rights and then informed him that he was looking at the possibility of a life sentence in prison unless he helped the police by providing information about Brown. Jones said he did not want to talk to the police, and he asked for an attorney. The police thus ceased questioning Jones, and he was taken to the jail.

Booking

At the jail, Jones was strip-searched, given a bright orange jumpsuit to wear, and photographed and fingerprinted. He was told that he would be arraigned the next morning. That night he slept on the floor of the overcrowded *holding cell*—a large cell where people are placed immediately upon arrest.

Arraignment

The next morning, Jones was taken to a room for video arraignment. A two-way camera system permitted Jones to see the district courtroom in the neighboring courthouse. At the same time, the judge and others could view him on a television screen. The judge informed Jones that he was being charged with breaking and entering, armed robbery, and assault with intent to commit murder. The final charge alone could draw a life sentence. Under Michigan law, these charges can be filed directly by the prosecutor without being presented to a grand jury for indictment, as is true in federal courts and some other states. The judge set bail at $200,000.

At a second video arraignment several days later, Jones was informed that he faced seven additional counts of assault with intent to commit

[handwritten: unless waived]

murder, armed robbery, unarmed robbery, and home invasion for four other robberies. Bond was set at $200,000 for each alleged robbery. Thus, he faced ten felony charges for the five robberies, and his total bail was $1 million.

Unable to make bail, Jones was held in the Calhoun County Jail to await his day in court. Eventually he would spend nine months in the jail before all of the charges against him were processed.

Defense Attorney

Under state court procedures, Jones was supposed to have a preliminary hearing within two weeks of his arraignment. At the preliminary hearing the district judge would determine whether enough evidence had been gathered to justify sending Jones's case up to the Calhoun County Circuit Court, which handled felony trials.

Jones received a letter informing him of the name of the private attorney appointed by the court to represent him, but he did not meet the attorney until he was taken to court for his preliminary hearing. Minutes before the hearing, the attorney, David Gilbert, introduced himself to Jones. Jones wanted to delay any preliminary hearing until a lineup could be held to test the victims' identifications of him as a robber. According to Jones, Gilbert said they must proceed with the preliminary hearing for the armed robbery case in which the victim was beaten with the power tool, because a witness had traveled from another state to testify. Preliminary hearings on the four additional robbery cases were postponed, but the out-of-town witness's testimony led the district judge to conclude that sufficient evidence existed to move that case to the circuit court on an armed robbery charge.

Lineup

Jones waited for weeks for the lineup to be scheduled. When he was taken to his rescheduled preliminary hearing, his attorney complained to the judge that the lineup had never been conducted. The judge ordered that the lineup be held as soon as possible.

At the lineup Jones and five other men stood in front of a one-way mirror. One by one, the victims of each of the six robberies looked at the men and attempted to determine if any were their assailant. At the end of each identification, one of the men was asked to step forward. Because he was asked to step forward only twice, Jones guessed that he was picked out by two of the victims.

Jones's defense attorney was unable to attend the lineup. Another attorney arrived and informed Jones that he would take Gilbert's place. Although Jones protested that the other men in the lineup were much shorter and older, he was disappointed that the substitute attorney was not more active in objecting that the other men looked too different from Jones to adequately test the victims' ability to make an accurate identification. He later discovered that his substitute attorney had just entered private practice after serving as an assistant prosecutor at Jones's first preliminary hearing.

Preliminary Hearing

At the next preliminary hearing, the victims of the four additional robberies testified. Because they focused mainly on Brown as the perpetrator of the assaults and robberies, the defense attorney argued that many of the charges against Jones should be dropped. However, the judge determined

THE CRIMINAL JUSTICE PROCESS (CONTINUED)

that the victims' testimony provided enough evidence to send most of the charges against Jones to the circuit court.

Plea Bargaining

Jones waited for weeks in jail without hearing much from his attorney. Although he did not know it, the prosecutor was formulating a plea agreement and communicating to the defense attorney the terms under which some charges would be dropped in exchange for a guilty plea from Jones. A few minutes before a hearing on the proposed plea agreement, Gilbert told Jones that the prosecutor had offered to drop all of the other charges if Jones would plead guilty to one count of unarmed robbery for the incident in which the victim was seriously injured by the power tool wielded by Brown, and one count of home invasion for another robbery. Jones did not want to accept the deal, because he claimed he was not even present at the robbery for which he was being asked to plead guilty to home invasion. According to Jones, the attorney insisted that this was an excellent deal compared with all of the other charges that the prosecutor could pursue. Jones still resisted.

In the courtroom, Judge James Kingsley read aloud the offer, but Jones refused to enter a guilty plea. Like the defense attorney, the judge told Jones that this was a favorable offer compared with the other more serious charges that the prosecutor could still pursue. Jones again declined.

As he sat in the holding area outside of the courtroom, Jones worried that he was making a mistake by turning down the plea offer. He wondered if he could end up with a life sentence if one of the victims identified him by mistake as having done a crime that was committed by Brown. When his attorney came to see him, he told Gilbert that he had changed his mind. They went right back into the courtroom and told the judge that he was ready to enter a guilty plea. As they prepared to plead guilty, the prosecutor said that as part of the agreement Jones would be expected to provide information about the other robberies and to testify against Brown. The defense attorney protested that this was not part of the plea agreement. Jones told the judge that he could not provide information about the home invasion to which he was about to plead guilty because he was not present at that robbery and had no knowledge of what occurred. Judge Kingsley declared that he would not accept a guilty plea when the defendant claimed to have no knowledge of the crime.

After the hearing, discussions about a plea agreement were renewed. Jones agreed to take a polygraph test so that the prosecutor could find out which robberies he knew about. Jones hoped to show prosecutors that his involvement with Brown was limited, but no test was ever administered.

Scheduled Trial and Plea Agreement

Jones waited in jail for several more weeks. When Gilbert came to visit him, Jones was informed that the armed robbery trial was scheduled for the following day. In addition, the prosecutor's plea offer had changed. Brown had pleaded guilty to armed robbery and assault with intent less than murder and was facing a sentence of 25 to 50 years in prison. Because of Brown's guilty plea, the prosecutor no longer needed Jones as a witness against Brown. Thus the prosecutor no longer offered robbery and home invasion pleas. He now wanted Jones to plead to the same charges as Brown in exchange for dropping the other pending charges. According to Jones, Gilbert claimed that the prosecutor would be very angry if he did not take the plea, and the attorney encouraged Jones to accept the plea by arguing that the prosecutor would otherwise pursue all of the other charges, which could bring a life sentence if Jones refused to plead guilty.

The next day, Jones was given his personal clothes to wear instead of the orange jail jumpsuit, because he was going to court for trial rather than a hearing. Prior to entering court the next day, Jones says Gilbert again

encouraged him to accept the plea agreement in order to avoid a possible life sentence after trial. According to Jones, Gilbert said that the guilty plea could be withdrawn if the probation office's sentencing recommendation was too high. Because he did not want to risk a life sentence, and believed he could later withdraw the plea, Jones decided to accept the offer.

With his attorney's advice, he entered a plea of "no contest" to the two charges. A "no contest" plea is treated the same way as a guilty plea for punishment purposes.

Before taking the plea, Judge Kingsley informed Jones that by entering the plea he would be waiving his right to a trial, including his right to question witnesses and to have the prosecutor prove his guilt beyond a reasonable doubt. Judge Kingsley then read the charges of armed robbery and assault with intent to do great bodily harm and asked, "What do you plead?" Jones replied, "No contest." Then the judge asked a series of questions.

Judge Kingsley:	"Mr. Jones, has anyone promised you anything other than the plea bargain to get you to enter this plea?"
Jones:	"No."
Judge Kingsley:	"Has anyone threatened you or forced you or compelled you to enter the plea?"
Jones:	"No."
Judge Kingsley:	"Are you entering this plea of your own free will?"
Jones:	"Yes."

The judge reminded Jones that there had been no final agreement on what the ultimate sentence would be and gave Jones one last opportunity to change his mind about pleading "no contest." Jones repeated his desire to enter the plea, so the plea was accepted.

Immediately after the hearing Jones had second thoughts. According to Jones, "I was feeling uneasy about being pressured [by my attorney] to take the plea offer . . . [so I decided] to write to the Judge and tell him about the pressures my attorney put upon me as well as [the attorney] telling me I had a right to withdraw my plea. So I wrote the Judge that night." Jones knew he was guilty of stealing things in one robbery, but he had been unarmed.

When Gilbert learned that Jones had written the letter, he asked the judge to permit him to withdraw as Jones's attorney. Judge Kingsley initially refused. However, when Jones spoke in open court at his sentencing hearing about his criticisms of Gilbert, as well as his complaints about the prosecutor's handling of the lineup and the failure to administer the polygraph test, the judge decided to appoint a new defense attorney, Virginia Cairns, to handle sentencing at a rescheduled hearing.

Presentence Investigation

Probation officers are responsible for conducting presentence investigations, in which they review offenders' records and interview the offenders about their education, work history, drug use, and family background before making recommendations to the judge about an appropriate punishment. During his interview, Jones learned that there were errors in his record that indicated he had three prior convictions instead of just the two that he actually had. When the errors were eventually corrected, the presentence report prepared by the probation office ultimately recommended 5 to 25 years for armed robbery and 4 to 7 years for assault.

Sentencing

Although arrested in October 1998, Jones was not sentenced until July 1999. At the hearing Judge Kingsley asked Jones if he would like to make a statement. Jones faced the judge as he spoke, glancing at his family and at the victim when he referred to them.

First and foremost, I would like to say what happened to the victim was a tragedy. I showed great remorse for that. He is in my prayers along with his family. Even though, your Honor, I'm not making any excuses for what I'm saying here today, the injuries the victim sustained were not at the hands of myself nor did I actually rob this victim. I was present, your Honor, as I told you once before, yes, I was. And it's a wrong. Again I'm not making any kind of excuse whatsoever. . . .

Your Honor, I would just like to say that drugs has clouded my memory, and my choices in the past. I really made some wrong decisions. Only times I've gotten into trouble were because of my drug use. . . . One of the worst decisions I really made was my involvement of being around the codefendant Fred Brown. That bothers me to this day because actually we didn't even get along. Because of my drug use again I chose to be around him.

Jones also talked about his positive record as a high school student and athlete, his work with the jail minister, and his desire to talk to young people about his experiences to steer them away from drugs.

Attorney Cairns spoke next. She called the court's attention to several errors in the presentence report that recommended Jones serve 5–25 years for armed robbery and 4–7 years for assault. She emphasized letters of support from Jones's family, which she had encouraged them to write to the judge, describing his positive qualities and prospects for successful rehabilitation. She argued that Jones should receive a less severe sentence than that imposed on Brown.

Next, the victim spoke about his injuries and how his $40,000 worth of medical bills had driven him to bankruptcy.

I went from having perfect vision to not being able to read out of my left eye. I got steel plates in my head. . . . They left me to die that morning. He took the keys to my car. . . . So today it's true, I don't think Mr. Jones should be sentenced same as Brown. That's who I want—I want to see him sentenced to the maximum. He's the one that crushed my skull with a drill. But Jones did hit me several times while Mr. Brown held me there to begin with. It's true that I did hit him with a hammer to get them off me. But he still was there. He still had the chance of not leaving me without keys to my car so I could get to a hospital. He still had the choice to stop at least and phone on the way and say there's someone that could possibly be dead, but he didn't. . . . You don't treat a human being like that. And if you do you serve time and pretty much to the maximum. I don't ask the Court for twenty-five years. That's a pretty long time to serve. And I do ask the Court to look at fifteen to twenty. I'd be happy. Thank you.

Gary Brand, the assistant prosecutor, rose and recommended a 20-year sentence and noted that Jones should be responsible for $35,000 in restitution to the victim and to the state for medical expenses and lost income.

Judge Kingsley then addressed Jones. He acknowledged that Jones's drug problem had led to his criminal activity. He also noted that Jones's family support was much stronger than that of most defendants. He chas-

tised Jones for falling into drugs when life was tougher after enjoying a successful high school career. Judge Kingsley then proceeded to announce his sentencing decision.

You are not in my view as culpable as Mr. Brown. I agree with [the victim] that you were there. When I read your letter, Mr. Jones, I was a bit disturbed by your unwillingness to confront the reality of where you found yourself with Mr. Brown. You were not a passive observer to everything that went on in my view. You were not as active a participant as Mr. Brown. . . . What I'm going to do, Mr. Jones, is as follows: Taking everything into consideration as it relates to the armed robbery count, it is the sentence of the Court that you spend a term of not less than twelve years nor more than twenty-five years with the Michigan Department of Corrections. I will give you credit for the [261 days] you have already served.

The judge also ordered payment of $35,000 in restitution as a condition of parole. He concluded the hearing by informing Jones of his right to file an application for a leave to appeal.

Prison

After spending a few more weeks in jail awaiting transfer, Christopher Jones was sent to the state correctional classification center at Jackson for evaluation to determine to which of Michigan's 40 prisons he would be sent.

Prison security classifications range from Level I for minimum to Level VI for "supermaximum," high security. Jones was initially assigned to a Level IV prison. Because Jones was a high school graduate who had previously attended a community college, he was one of the most highly educated prisoners in his institution. After working as the head clerk of the prison library in one prison, he was transferred to another prison, where he earned a certificate in substance abuse counseling. He taught classes on substance abuse and addiction for other prisoners before he was transferred to a lower-security institution. He hopes that he can contribute to his own personal development while doing productive work that might help him eventually earn parole.

RESEARCHING THE INTERNET

The Jones case illustrates the important role of the defense attorney. Read the U.S. Supreme Court's decision about the attorney's responsibilities for presenting a strong defense. Go to the link for "Cases and Codes" at the Findlaw website and search for the case of *Wiggins v. Smith* (2003). To reach this site, go to the Cole/Smith Criminal Justice in America Companion Website: http://www.thomsonedu.com/criminaljustice/cole.

FOR CRITICAL ANALYSIS

Were any aspects of the processes and decisions in the Jones case unfair or improper? Did the outcome of the case achieve "justice"?

Sources: Calhoun County Circuit Court transcripts for plea hearing, May 20, 1999, and sentencing hearing, July 16, 1999; T. Christenson, "Two Charged in Violent Robberies," *Battle Creek Inquirer*, October 30, 1998, p. 1A; interview with Christopher Jones, St. Louis Correctional Facility, St. Louis, Michigan, October 19, 1999; letters to Christopher Smith from Christopher Jones, October and November 1999.

2

Crime and Justice in America

In the hushed courtroom in Wichita, Kansas, family members of murder victims rose and, one after another, expressed their feelings to the judge, the murderer, and courtroom audience. On that August day in 2005, the emotion and anger of the family members fueled their harsh statements (CNN, 2005b):

"This man needs to be thrown in a deep, dark hole and left to rot."

"[A]ll of his victims will be waiting with God and watching him as he burns in hell."

"[He is] a walking cesspool [and] social sewage."

"[I wish his mother had] aborted his demon soul."

"I'd just like for him to suffer for the rest of his life."

Convicted serial killer Dennis Rader cried as he heard these statements. When it was his turn to speak, he apologized to the families of his victims. Years earlier, while calling himself "BTK" for bind, torture, and kill, Rader had taunted the police and news media through letters and packages as he terrorized Wichita by escaping detection as

he murdered ten people between 1974 and 1991. When he sought to taunt the police again in 2005, they were able to identify and capture him by tracing a computer disk back to him (CNN, 2005b). After the announcement of his arrest, the public was shocked to learn that the BTK killer was a family man, a Boy Scout leader, and the president of the Lutheran church council. As he faced the victims' families in the courtroom and awaited the official announcement of his 175-year prison sentence, Rader expressed hope for eventual forgiveness by God.

The dramatic scene in the Wichita courtroom illustrated a tragic reality of criminal justice: Victims and their families are deeply affected by crime. They can experience losses of money and property, painful injuries, and even the violent end of their lives. Moreover, surviving victims and their families can suffer lingering harms that affect their lifestyles and freedom, such as persistent fear that keeps them locked in their homes, expensive medical treatments, and psychological scars.

In order to understand the criminal justice system, we must understand the nature of crime and all of the people affected by it. Chapter 1 introduced you to decision makers in the system, such as police and prosecutors, as well as processes for handling criminal cases. Here you will consider other key individuals: criminal offenders and their victims. You will also examine the nature and extent of crime—the key elements that effectively tell us how many offenders and victims may cause or be affected by crime in a given year.

Although it is easy to understand the hurt and anger experienced by crime victims, a complete understanding of victimization requires a broad examination of the varied and complex consequences of crime. By contrast, understanding why a criminal offender inflicts harm on victims is not always so easy. Why would someone stalk and kill numerous strangers? Radar said that he killed people in order to fulfill his bizarre sexual fantasies (CNN, 2005c). For the average person, such feelings are presumably quite difficult to understand. Whether or not Radar's assessment of himself was accurate, his motives and actions clearly differed a great deal from those of other criminal offenders, such as a teenager who steals a candy bar from a store. We can imagine some possible motives for the teenager's action— hunger, thrill seeking, selfishness—but can we truly know why particular crimes are committed? The identification of the underlying causes of crime has long posed a difficult challenge for scholars and law enforcement officials. Because the puzzle of criminal behavior is so potentially important for the design of policies and programs to curb crime, scholars have grappled with the issue for centuries.

In this chapter, we examine the complex issue of crime. Specifically, we examine the nature and extent of crime, including the causes and consequences of criminal activity. We shall see that the importance of victims is emphasized more frequently by both scholars and justice system officials. We shall also see that there is no clear agreement about what causes people to commit crimes.

QUESTIONS FOR INQUIRY

- What are the major types of crimes in the United States?
- How much crime is there, and how is crime measured?
- Who are the victims of crime?
- What are the major theories about the causes of crime?

Defining Crime

SUBSTANTIVE LAW

Why does the law label some types of behavior as criminal and not others? For example, why is it a crime to use marijuana when it is legal to drink alcohol, a substance that also has serious intoxicating, addictive, and harmful health affects?

The criminal law is defined by elected representatives in state legislatures and Congress, who make choices about the behaviors that the government will punish. Some of these choices reflect broad agreement in society that certain actions, such as rape and murder, are so harmful that they must be punished. Such crimes have traditionally been called *mala in se*—wrong in themselves.

However, for other criminal laws, legislatures make decisions even though people in society may disagree about the harmfulness of certain acts. These crimes are called *mala prohibita*—they are crimes because they are prohibited by the government and not because they are wrong in themselves. Everyone does not agree, for example, that gambling, prostitution, and drug use should be punished.

mala in se Offenses that are wrong by their very nature.

mala prohibita Offenses prohibited by law but not wrong in themselves.

The definitions of crimes do not necessarily remain fixed over time. Legislators can change the definitions as society's values change. For example, lotteries and casino gambling were illegal in most states during the first half of the twentieth century. In the second half of the century, however, states decided that they could profit from gambling; they began to sponsor state lotteries and, over time, approve various forms of casino gambling. Presumably, the moral value and social risks from gambling did not change over the decades. Instead, attitudes toward gambling changed and legislators enacted laws to reflect those changes in public policy.

Changes in the definitions of crimes can also occur when court decisions declare that the criminalization of specific actions violates people's constitutional rights. Court decisions ended the criminalization of early-term abortions (*Roe v. Wade*, 1973) and private sexual conduct between adult homosexuals (*Lawrence v. Texas*, 2003).   *GA case 1986*

CHECKPOINT

1. What is the difference between *mala in se* offenses and *mala prohibita* offenses? ➡

Answers

1. *Mala in se*—offenses that are wrong in themselves (murder, rape, assault).
Mala prohibita—acts that are crimes because they are prohibited (gambling, drug use).

Types of Crime

Crimes can be classified in various ways. As we have seen, scholars often use the distinction between *mala in se* and *mala prohibita*. Crimes can also be classified as either felonies or misdemeanors, depending on whether the prescribed punishment is more or less than one year in prison. A third scheme classifies crimes by the nature of the act. This approach has traditionally yielded five types of crime: visible crime, occupational crime, organized crime, victimless crime, and political crime. Each type has its own level of risk and reward, each arouses varying degrees of public disapproval, and each is committed by a certain kind of offender. New types of crime emerge as society changes. Cyber crimes committed through the use of computers and the Internet are becoming a major global problem.

VISIBLE CRIME

Visible crime, often called "street crime" or "ordinary crime," ranges from shoplifting to homicide. For offenders, such crimes are the least profitable and, because they are visible, the hardest to hide. These are the acts that the public regards as "criminal." The majority of law enforcement resources are employed to deal with them. We can divide visible crimes into three categories: violent crimes, property crimes, and public order crimes.

visible crime An offense against persons or property, committed primarily by members of the lower class. Often referred to as "street crime" or "ordinary crime," this type of offense is the one most upsetting to the public.

Violent Crimes   Acts against people in which death or physical injury results are *violent crimes*. These include criminal homicide, assault, rape, and robbery. The criminal justice system treats them as the most serious offenses and punishes them accordingly. Although the public is most fearful of violence by strangers, many of these offenses are committed by people who know their victim.

Property Crimes   *Property crime*s are acts that threaten property held by individuals or by the state. Many types of crimes fall under this category, including theft, larceny, shoplifting, embezzlement, and burglary. Some property offenders are amateurs who occasionally commit these crimes because of situational factors such as financial need or peer pressure. In contrast, professional criminals make a significant portion of their livelihood from committing property offenses.

Public Order Crimes   Acts that threaten the general well-being of society and challenge accepted moral principles are defined as *public order crimes*. They include public drunkenness, aggressive panhandling, vandalism, and disorderly conduct. Although the police tend to treat these behaviors as minor offenses, some scholars argue that this type of disorderly behavior instills fear in citizens, leads to more-serious crimes, and hastens urban decay (Kelling and Coles, 1996). The definition and enforcement of such behaviors as crimes highlight the tensions between different interpretations of American values. Many people see such behavior as simply representing the liberty that adults enjoy in a free society to engage in offensive and self-destructive behavior that causes no concrete harm to other people. By contrast, other people see their own

Enron founder Ken Lay leaves federal court after he was convicted of all charges in his fraud, conspiracy, and bank fraud trials in Houston. The conviction marked the climax of one of the most notorious corporate scandals in U.S. history. Lay died of a massive heart attack before he was sentenced.

REUTERS/Richard Carson/Landov

liberty limited by the need to be wary and fearful of actions by people who are drunk or out of control.

Those charged with visible crimes tend to be young men. Further, in many communities, members of minority groups tend to be overrepresented among those arrested and prosecuted for such offenses. Some argue that this is due to the class bias of a society that has singled out visible crimes for priority enforcement. They note that we do not focus as much police and prosecutorial attention on white-collar crimes, such as fraud and other acts committed by office workers and business owners, as we do on street crimes.

OCCUPATIONAL CRIME

occupational crimes Criminal offenses committed through opportunities created in a legal business or occupation.

Occupational crimes are committed in the context of a legal business or profession. Often viewed as shrewd business practices rather than illegal acts, they are crimes that, if "done right," are never discovered. Such crimes are often committed by respectable, well-to-do people taking advantage of opportunities arising from business dealings. Such crimes impose huge costs on society. Although there are no precise figures on the cost of occupational crime to American society, the Association of Certified Fraud Examiners estimates that occupational fraud may cost American businesses as much as $660 billion annually (ACFE, 2004). By contrast, the FBI calculates that the direct financial losses from street crimes involving the theft of property, such as burglary, robbery, and larceny, are less than $17 billion annually (FBI, 2005a).

ORGANIZED CRIME

organized crime A framework for the perpetuation of criminal acts—usually in fields such as gambling, drugs, and prostitution—providing illegal services that are in great demand.

Rather than referring to criminal acts per se, the term **organized crime** refers to the framework within which such acts are committed. A crime syndicate has an organizational structure, rules, a division of labor, and the capacity for ruthless violence and for corrupting law enforcement, labor and business leaders, and politicians (Jacobs and Panarella, 1998:160). Organized criminals provide goods and services to millions of people. They engage in any activity that provides a minimum of risk and a maximum of profit. Thus, organized crime involves a network of activities, usually cutting across state and national borders, that range from legitimate businesses to shady deals with labor unions to providing "goods"—such as drugs, sex, and pornography—that cannot be obtained legally. In recent years organized crime has been involved in new services such as commercial arson, illegal disposal of toxic wastes, and **money laundering.** Few organized criminals are arrested and prosecuted. See "Careers in Criminal Justice" to learn more about forensic accountants, who fight financial crime committed by individuals or organized criminals.

money laundering Moving the proceeds of criminal activities through a maze of businesses, banks, and brokerage accounts so as to disguise their origin.

Although the public often associates organized crime with Italian Americans—indeed, the federal government indicted 73 members of the Genovese New York crime "family" in 2001 (Worth, 2001)—other ethnic groups have dominated at various times. Thirty-five years ago, one scholar noted the strangeness of America's "ladder of social mobility," in which each new immigrant group uses organized crime as one of the first rungs of the climb (Bell, 1967:150). However, debate about this notion continues, because not all immigrant groups have engaged in organized crime (Kenney and Finckenauer, 1995:38).

Over the last few decades, law enforcement efforts have greatly weakened the Italian American Mafia. An aging leadership, lack of interest by younger family members, and pressures from new immigrant groups have also contributed to the fall of the Mafia. Today African Americans, Hispanics, Russians, and Asians have

CAREERS IN CRIMINAL JUSTICE

Forensic Accountant—Law Enforcement, Business

NATURE OF THE WORK

Forensic accountants investigate and interpret financial crimes such as securities fraud and embezzlement. They must analyze complex financial transactions to seek to reveal money laundering by organized crime organizations. According to the U.S. Department of Labor, "Forensic accountants combine their knowledge of accounting and finance and investigative techniques in order to determine whether [financial] activity is illegal" (Bureau of Labor Statistics, 2005). They may also focus on homeland security and terrorism issues by analyzing entities that secretly seek to funnel money to terrorist organizations. The FBI, state attorneys general, and other law enforcement agencies may also employ them to fight occupational crime. Finally, they may be employed by corporations and local governments that seek to detect illegal activity, such as embezzlement, by their own employees or by the employees of contractors or business partners.

REQUIRED QUALIFICATIONS

Forensic accountants and related positions that provide oversight over financial records and transactions, such as auditors within businesses, generally must possess a college degree in accounting or a related field. Professional certification can enhance credentials and job opportunities such as qualification as a Certified Public Accountant (CPA) or a Certified Fraud Examiner (CFE). Students in criminal justice programs are increasingly enhancing their skills and qualifications by adding coursework in accounting, computer science, or foreign languages in order to make themselves more attractive and valuable to agencies that deal with occupational crime, organized crime, cyber crime, or terrorism.

EARNINGS AND JOB OUTLOOK

The employment of accountants and auditors is expected to grow faster than average for all occupations through the year 2014. With the increased attention of law enforcement agencies on financial crimes as well as tracing the funding of terrorist organizations, opportunities for specialists in forensic accounting may expand even faster. Working conditions involve working in office settings and traveling to the locations of financial records in order to conduct investigations. The median annual salary of accountants and auditors was $51,000 in 2004. Starting salaries for accountants with bachelor's degrees averaged $43,200 in 2005. Starting salaries in government agencies was less than $30,000. Accountants and auditors in the federal government eventually average more than $74,000 per year.

MORE INFORMATION

Career information is available at the website of the Association of Certified Fraud Examiners, listed on the Cole/Smith Criminal Justice in America Companion Website: http://www.thomsonedu.com/criminaljustice/cole.

---

formed organized crime groups. Drug dealing has brought Colombian and Mexican crime groups to U.S. shores, and Vietnamese-, Chinese-, and Japanese-led groups have formed in California. Because these new groups do not fit the Mafia pattern, law enforcement agencies have had to find new ways to deal with them (Kleinknecht, 1996).

Just as multinational corporations have emerged during the past 20 years, organized crime has also developed global networks. Increasingly transnational criminal groups "live and operate in a borderless world" (Zagaris, 1998:1402). In the aftermath of the events of September 11, American law enforcement and intelligence officials increased their efforts to monitor and thwart international organizations that seek to attack the United States and its citizens. Many of these organizations use criminal activities, such as drug smuggling and stolen credit card numbers, to fund their efforts.

CRIMES WITHOUT VICTIMS

Crimes without victims involve a willing and private exchange of goods or services that are in strong demand but illegal—in other words, offenses against morality.

crimes without victims Offenses involving a willing and private exchange of illegal goods or services that are in strong demand. Participants do not feel they are being harmed, but these crimes are prosecuted on the ground that society as a whole is being injured.

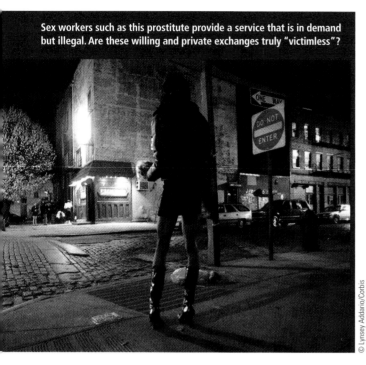

Sex workers such as this prostitute provide a service that is in demand but illegal. Are these willing and private exchanges truly "victimless"?

© Lynsey Addario/Corbis

Examples include prostitution, gambling, and drug sales and use. These are called "victimless" crimes because those involved do not feel that they are being harmed. Prosecution for these offenses is justified on the ground that society as a whole is harmed because the moral fabric of the community is threatened. However, using the law to enforce moral standards is costly. The system is swamped by these cases, which often require the use of police informers and thus open the door for payoffs and other kinds of corruption.

The war on drugs is the most obvious example of policies against one type of victimless crime. Possession and sale of drugs—marijuana, heroin, cocaine, opium, amphetamines—have been illegal in the United States for over a hundred years. Especially during the past 40 years, all levels of government have applied extensive resources to enforce these laws and punish offenders.

The crime-fighting duties of police patrol officers typically focus on visible crimes and crimes without victims. As we shall see in later chapters, police officers also fulfill other functions, such as order maintenance and public service.

POLITICAL CRIME

political crime An act, usually done for ideological purposes, that constitutes a threat against the state (such as treason, sedition, or espionage); also describes a criminal act by the state.

Political crime refers to criminal acts either by the government or against the government that are carried out for ideological purposes (F. E. Hagan, 1997:2). Political criminals believe they are following a morality that is above the law. Examples include James Kopp—arrested for the murder of Dr. Barnett Slepian near Buffalo, New York, and other doctors who performed abortions—and Eric Rudolph, convicted for the bombing of abortion clinics in Atlanta and Birmingham and the pipe bomb explosion at the Atlanta Olympics. Similarly, shocking acts of violence that are labeled as terrorism, including the 1995 bombing of the Federal Building in Oklahoma City by Timothy McVeigh and the 2001 attacks on the World Trade Center and Pentagon, spring from political motivations.

In some authoritarian states, merely criticizing the government is a crime that can lead to prosecution and imprisonment. In Western democracies today, there are few political crimes other than treason, which is rare. Many illegal acts, such as the World Trade Center and Oklahoma City bombings, can be traced to political motives, but they are prosecuted as visible crimes under laws against bombing, arson, and murder rather than as political crimes per se.

CYBER CRIME

cyber crimes Offenses that involve the use of one or more computers.

Cyber crimes involve the use of computers and the Internet to commit acts against people, property, public order, or morality. Thus, cyber criminals have learned "new ways to do old tricks." Some use computers to steal information, resources, or funds. Others use the Internet to disseminate child pornography, to advertise sexual services, or to stalk the unsuspecting. The more sophisticated "hackers" create and distribute viruses designed to destroy computer programs or gain control of computers from unsuspecting individuals. In 2003 a man in Great Britain was acquitted of child pornography charges when he argued successfully that an unknown individual had used a virus to hijack his computer and use it to download and disseminate child pornography (Schwartz, 2003).

The global nature of the Internet presents new challenges to the criminal justice system. For example, through electronic financial networks that link much of the world, money launderers in Moscow can simply tap on their computer keyboard and send their money digitally to New York. A few more keystrokes and the money can be sent to a private account in Antigua, where it will be shielded from the prying eyes of government agencies. In another example, stolen credit card numbers are sold on the Internet, primarily by dealers based in states that were formerly part of the Soviet Union. Computer hackers steal large numbers of credit card numbers from the computer systems of legitimate businesses and sell the numbers in large quantities to dealers who sell them throughout the world via "members-only" websites. Credit card fraud costs online merchants more than $1 billion each year (Richtel, 2002).

Law enforcement officials have developed new methods for investigating computer crime. These new methods can themselves raise issues about the limits of government authority and individuals' right to privacy, such as concerns arising from the increased capacity to monitor email communications and eavesdrop on cell phone calls. In addition, since 9/11 the federal government has asserted that it has the authority to intercept communications concerning foreign threats without providing evidence of wrongdoing in order to obtain a warrant. Thus, if the government has suspicions about threats to homeland security, the government monitors calls, including overseas calls originating from Americans within the United States, without obtaining permission from a judge or informing the individual that the calls have been intercepted (Lichtblau and Risen, 2006). Government monitoring of individuals' behavior as

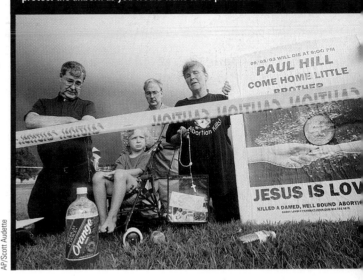

Calling him a martyr, supporters of "right to life" advocate Paul Hill pray outside of the Florida State Prison prior to his execution for the slaying of abortionist Dr. John Britton and his bodyguard. Hill, defiant even as he was strapped to a gurney, said "May God help you to protect the unborn as you would want to be protected."

AP/Scott Audette

TECHNOLOGY ISSUES IN CRIMINAL JUSTICE

Database Utilization

Computer technology permits law enforcement officials to gather, store, and analyze data. In minutes, or even seconds, computers can sort through data with the effectiveness that spares a user from spending hours combing through papers stored in a filing cabinet. For example, New York City detectives solved an armed robbery case in 2005 by taking a witness's description of the robber's tattoo and running it through the police department's computerized tattoo database. Very quickly, the detectives identified a suspect, showed his mug shot to the robbery victim, and tracked him down to make the arrest. The New York Police Department's database contains records on criminal complaints, warrants, 911 calls, individuals' criminal and parole records, and other kinds of property and public records.

DNA databases have been useful in identifying suspects when computers can match DNA test results with samples stored in a database. Questions arise, however, about who should be required to submit DNA samples to be stored in government computer records. Forty-three states require convicted felons to submit DNA samples, but New York would like to expand its database to include samples from people convicted of misdemeanors. Louisiana's law requires DNA samples from everyone arrested, even if they are not convicted of a crime, yet the state does not have sufficient funds to take and test the samples as required by its own law.

What other problems might arise? Could a massive database lead to misidentification of suspects if, for example, hairs or other DNA sources are left at a location before a crime later takes place there?

In May 2006 a controversy emerged when three major phone networks supplied information to the federal government so that it could develop a database of phone calls made within the United States, even those by people not suspected of wrongdoing. The federal government wanted to use the database to identify any suspicious patterns of phone calls. However, complaints about keeping records on innocent Americans who have done nothing suspicious led members of Congress to criticize the program and President Bush to hold an unscheduled press conference to defend the database. Clearly, many people do not trust the government to keep accurate records and use those records properly.

RESEARCHING THE INTERNET

Go to the website of the federal government's National Security Agency (NSA) and read about the responsibilities, objectives, and technical capacity of the NSA. This site is listed on the Cole/Smith Criminal Justice in America Companion Website: http://www.thomsonedu.com/criminaljustice/cole.

FOR CRITICAL ANALYSIS

If a member of Congress proposed that all Americans submit a DNA sample to a national criminal investigation database, how would you react? Do you see any potential risks or problems from databases and their utilization? Is there a clash between the government's acquisition and use of information and Americans' right to privacy?

Sources: Diane Cardwell, "New York State Draws Nearer to Collecting DNA in All Crimes," *New York Times,* May 4, 2006, http://www.nytimes.com; Leslie Cauley, "NSA Has Massive Database of Americans' Phone Calls," *USA Today,* May 11, 2006, http://www.usatoday.com; Tom Hays, "NYC Real Time Crime Center Tracks Suspects," *Washington Post,* May 10, 2006, http://www.washingtonpost.com; John O'Neil, "Bush Says U.S. Spying Is Not Widespread," May 11, 2006, http://www.nytimes.com.

CLOSE UP

Hate Crimes: A New Category of Personal Violence

Black churches are set afire in the Southeast; the home of the mayor of West Hartford, Connecticut, is defaced by swastikas and anti-Semitic graffiti; gay Wyoming student Matthew Shepard is murdered; a black woman in Maryland is beaten and doused with lighter fluid in a race-based attack. These are just a few of the more than 7,500 hate crimes reported to the police each year. The U.S. Department of Justice said that threats, assaults, and acts of vandalism against Arab Americans and people of South Asian ancestry increased in the months following the events of September 11. Crimes based on the victims' ethnicity may become more diversified as Americans react to their anger and fear about the threat of terrorism from foreign organizations.

Hate crimes have been added to the penal codes of 46 states and the District of Columbia. The FBI's annual report on hate crimes defined them as bias-motivated offenses that target people for their race, religion, sexual orientation, ethnicity, or disability (FBI, 2005a). Some states also include crimes based on gender discrimination. The laws also make it a crime to vandalize religious buildings and cemeteries or to intimidate another person out of bias. Although the Ku Klux Klan, the World Church of the Creator, and Nazi-style "skinhead" groups represent the most visible perpetrators, most hate crimes are committed by individuals acting alone.

Hate crime laws have been challenged on the ground that they violate the right of free speech. Some argue that racial and religious slurs must be allowed on this basis. In response, supporters of hate crime laws say that limits must be placed on freedom of speech and that some words are so hateful that they fall outside the free speech protection of the First Amendment.

The U.S. Supreme Court has considered the constitutionality of such laws in two cases. In *R.A.V. v. City of St. Paul* (1992), the Court ruled unconstitutional a law that singled out only certain "race-baiting" words. However, in *Wisconsin v. Mitchell* (1993), it upheld a law providing for a severer sentence in cases in which the offender "intentionally selects the person against whom the crime [is committed] because of the race, religion, color, disability, sexual orientation, national origin or ancestry of that person." By asking, "Do you all feel hyped up to move on some white people?" and by calling out, "There goes a white boy; go get him," the defendant had incited a group of young black men, who had just seen the film *Mississippi Burning,* to assault a young white man. The Court said that the penalty was appropriate because the conduct was "thought to inflict greater individual and societal harm." It rejected the argument that the law would have a "chilling effect" on free speech. In a later case on a related issue, the Supreme Court decided that states can make it a crime to burn a cross with an intent to intimidate people. They rejected the argument that cross burning, a traditional ritual act by the Ku Klux Klan, a white supremacist organization with a violent history, constituted a protected form of free expression (*Virginia v. Black,* 2003).

In a society that is becoming more diverse, hate crimes arguably hurt not only their victims but the social fabric itself. Democracy depends on people sharing common ideals and working together. Under this view, when groups are pitted against one another, the entire community suffers.

RESEARCHING THE INTERNET

To see the American Psychological Association's analysis of hate crimes, go to the corresponding site listed on the Cole/Smith Criminal Justice in America Companion Website: http://www.thomsonedu.com/criminaljustice/cole.

FOR CRITICAL ANALYSIS

Is criminal law the way to attack the problem of expressions of racial hatred?

Sources: Drawn from Federal Bureau of Investigation, *Hate Crime Statistics, 2004* (Washington, DC: U.S. Department of Justice, 2005); J. Jacobs, "Should Hate Be a Crime?" *The Public Interest,* Fall 1993, pp. 1–14; C. Newton, "Crimes against Arabs, South Asians Up," *Washington Post,* June 26, 2002, http://www.washingtonpost.com.

ThomsonNOW

Improve your grade on the exam with Personalized Study! For reinforcement resources and a mastery check of Types of Crime, go to www.thomsonedu.com/thomsonnow.

well as the accumulation of data in government computers raises concerns about whether such investigative techniques threaten Americans' privacy rights. "Technology Issues in Criminal Justice" on page 39 presents a closer look at the benefits and potential abuses of such programs.

Which of these main types of crime is of greatest concern to you? If you are like most people, it is visible crime. Thus, as a nation, we devote most of our criminal justice resources to dealing with such crimes. To develop policies to address these crimes, however, we need to know more about the amount of crime and all the types of crimes that occur in the United States. One of the most disturbing crimes, which has gained much attention lately, is hate crime; see the Close Up box for more.

CHECKPOINT

Answers

2. What are the six main types of crime? ————————▶ **2.** Visible crime, occupational crime, organized crime, crime without victims, political crime, cyber crime.

3. What is the function of organized crime? ————————▶ **3.** Organized crime usually provides goods and services that are in high demand but are illegal.

4. What is meant by the term *crimes without victims?* ————————▶ **4.** These are crimes against morality in which the people involved do not believe that they have been victimized.

How Much Crime Is There?

Many Americans believe that the crime rate is rising, even though it has generally declined since the 1980s (see "What Americans Think"). For example, the rate of violent crime decreased by 57 percent from 1993 to 2004, including a 9 percent drop from the period 2001–2002 to the period 2003–2004. According to the Bureau of Justice Statistics, "violent and property crimes rates in 2004 remain at the lowest levels since the [national victimization] survey's inception in 1973" (Catalano, 2005).

In June 2006 the FBI released preliminary crime statistics for 2005. The initial analysis showed a 2.5 percent increase in violent crime. Although rape and property crimes declined, murders and robberies increased. The most notable increases were for robberies in cities with populations between 500,000 and 1 million and for murders in cities with populations from 250,000 to 500,000 (FBI, 2006a). Scholars and law enforcement officials will watch reports for subsequent years very closely to see if the results for 2005 indicate one unusual year or the beginning of an upward trend. The important point is that these figures represent a very modest one-year increase and crime rates still remain low compared with the rates from two decades ago.

One of the frustrations in studying criminal justice is the lack of accurate means of knowing the amount of crime. Surveys reveal that much more crime occurs than is reported to the police. This is referred to as the **dark figure of crime.**

Most homicides and auto thefts are reported to the police. In the case of a homicide, a body must be accounted for, and insurance companies require a police report before they will pay for a stolen car. But about 43 percent of rape victims do not report the attack; almost 56 percent of victims of simple assault do not do so. Figure 2.1 shows the percentage of victimizations not reported to the police.

Until 1972, the only crimes counted by government were those that were known to the police and that made their way into the Federal Bureau of Investigation's Uniform Crime Reports (UCR). Since then the Department of Justice has sponsored the National Crime Victimization Surveys (NCVS), which survey the public to find out how much victimization has occurred. One might hope that the data from these two sources would give us a clear picture of the amount of crime, crime trends, and the characteristics of offenders. However, the picture is blurred, perhaps even distorted, because of differences in the way crime is measured by the UCR and the NCVS.

THE UNIFORM CRIME REPORTS

Issued each year by the FBI, the **Uniform Crime Reports (UCR)** are a statistical summary of crimes reported to the police. At the urging of the International Association of Chiefs of Police, Congress in 1930 authorized this system for compiling crime data (Rosen, 1995). The UCR data come from a voluntary national network of some 16,000 local, state, and federal law enforcement agencies, policing 98 percent of the U.S. population.

With the sharp drop in crime in recent years, new pressures have been placed on police executives to show that their cities are following the national trend. Some officials have even falsified their crime statistics as promotions, pay raises, and department budgets have become increasingly dependent on positive data. For example, an audit of the Atlanta police released in 2004 found that they had underreported crimes as part of an effort to make the city appear safer when it was competing to be the host city for the 1996 Summer Olympics (Niesse, 2004). In 2005 leaders of police unions in New York City alleged that officers were pressured to report felonies as merely misdemeanors in order to help the city show favorable results (Moses, 2005). Because the FBI relies on reports from local police departments, the UCR are inaccurate when agencies underreport crime.

The UCR use standard definitions to ensure uniform data on the 29 types of crimes listed in Table 2.1. For 8 major crimes—Part I (Index Offenses)—the data

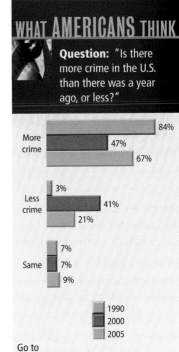

WHAT AMERICANS THINK

Question: "Is there more crime in the U.S. than there was a year ago, or less?"

More crime — 84% / 47% / 67%

Less crime — 3% / 41% / 21%

Same — 7% / 7% / 9%

- 1990
- 2000
- 2005

Go to http://www.thomsonedu.com/criminaljustice/cole to compare your opinion on this issue with the opinions of other criminal justice students.

Source: Gallup Poll, national survey of adults, reported February 3, 2006, as adapted by Bureau of Justice Statistics, *Sourcebook of Criminal Justice Statistics, 2005* (Washington, DC: U.S. Government Printing Office, 2006), Table 2.33.2005.

dark figure of crime A metaphor that emphasizes the dangerous dimension of crime that is never reported to the police.

Uniform Crime Reports (UCR) An annually published statistical summary of crimes reported to the police, based on voluntary reports to the FBI by local, state, and federal law enforcement agencies.

FIGURE 2.1

Percentage of victimizations *not* reported to the police

Why do some people not report crimes to the police? What can be done to encourage reporting?

Source: Bureau of Justice Statistics, *Sourcebook of Criminal Justice Statistics, 2002* (Washington, DC: U.S. Government Printing Office, 2003), Table 3.36.

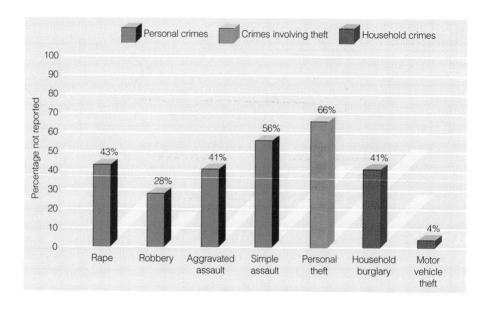

TABLE 2.1   Uniform Crime Reports Offenses

The UCR present data on 8 index offenses and 21 other crimes for which there is less information. A limitation of the UCR is that they tabulate only crimes that are reported to the police.

Part I (Index Offenses)	Part II (Other Offenses)
1. Criminal homicide	9. Simple assaults
2. Forcible rape	10. Forgery and counterfeiting
3. Robbery	11. Fraud
4. Aggravated assault	12. Embezzlement
5. Burglary	13. Buying, receiving, or possessing stolen property
6. Larceny/theft	14. Vandalism
7. Auto theft	15. Weapons (carrying, possession, etc.)
8. Arson	16. Prostitution and commercialized vice
	17. Sex offenses
	18. Violation of narcotic drug laws
	19. Gambling
	20. Offenses against the family and children
	21. Driving under the influence
	22. Violation of liquor laws
	23. Drunkenness
	24. Disorderly conduct
	25. Vagrancy
	26. All other offenses (excluding traffic)
	27. Suspicion
	28. Curfew and loitering (juvenile)
	29. Juvenile runaways

Source: Federal Bureau of Investigation, *Crime in the United States, 2000* (Washington, DC: U.S. Government Printing Office, 2001).

show factors such as age, race, and number of reported crimes solved. For the other 21 crimes—Part II (Other Offenses)—the data are less complete.

The UCR provide a useful but incomplete picture of crime levels. Because they cover only reported crimes, these reports do not include data on crimes for which people failed to call the police. Also, the UCR do not measure occupational crimes and other offenses that are not included in the 29 types covered. And because reporting is voluntary, police departments may not take the time to make complete and careful reports.

In response to criticisms of the UCR, the FBI has made some changes in the program that are now being implemented nationwide. Some offenses have been redefined, and police agencies are being asked to report more details about crime events. Using the **National Incident-Based Reporting System (NIBRS)**, police agencies are to report all crimes committed during an incident, not just the most serious one, as well as data on offenders, victims, and the places where they interact. While the UCR now count incidents and arrests for the 8 index offenses and count arrests for other crimes, the NIBRS provides detailed incident data on 46 offenses in 22 crime categories. The NIBRS distinguishes between attempted and completed crimes as well.

THE NATIONAL CRIME VICTIMIZATION SURVEYS

A second source of crime data is the **National Crime Victimization Surveys (NCVS)**. Since 1972 the Census Bureau has done surveys to find out the extent and nature of crime victimization. Thus, data have been gathered on unreported as well as reported crimes. Interviews are conducted twice each year with a national probability sample of approximately 76,000 people in 43,000 households. The same people are interviewed twice a year for three years and asked if they have been victimized in the last six months.

Each person is asked a set of "screening" questions (for example, did anyone beat you up, attack you, or hit you with something such as a rock or a bottle?) to determine whether he or she has been victimized. The person is then asked questions designed to elicit specific facts about the event, the offender, and any financial losses or physical disabilities caused by the crime.

Besides the household interviews, surveys are carried out in the nation's 26 largest cities; separate studies are done to find out about the victimization of businesses. These data allow us to estimate how many crimes have occurred, learn more about the offenders, and note demographic patterns. The results show that for the crimes measured (rape, robbery, assault, burglary, theft) there were 24 million victimizations in 2004 (down from 43 million in 1973) (Catalano, 2005). This level is much higher than the number of crimes actually reported to the police suggests.

Although the NCVS provide a more complete picture of the nature and extent of crime than do the UCR, they too have flaws. Because the surveys are done by government employees, the people interviewed are unlikely to report crimes in which they or members of their family took part. They also may not want to admit that a family member engages in crime, or they may be too embarrassed to admit that they have allowed themselves to be victimized more than once. In addition, the survey covers a limited range of crimes and the relatively small sample of interviewees may lead to erroneous conclusions about crime trends for an entire country of nearly 300 million people (Mosher, Miethe and Phillips, 2002).

The NCVS are also imperfect because they depend on the victim's *perception* of an event. The theft of a child's lunch money by a bully may be reported as a crime by one person but not mentioned by another. People may say that their property was stolen when in fact they lost it. Moreover, people's memories of dates may fade, and they may misreport the year in which a crime occurred even though they remember the event itself clearly. In 1993 the Bureau of Justice Statistics made some changes in the NCVS to improve their accuracy and detail.

The next time you hear or read about crime rates, take into account the source of the data and its possible limitations. Table 2.2 compares the Uniform Crime Reports and the National Crime Victimization Surveys.

TRENDS IN CRIME

Experts agree that, contrary to public opinion and the claims of politicians, crime rates have not been steadily rising. The NCVS show that the victimization rate peaked in 1981 and has declined since then. The greatest declines are in property crimes, but crimes of violence have also dropped, especially since 1993. The violent crime victimization rate fell by 57 percent from 1993 through 2004. Property crimes also saw steep declines over the same period with a 49 percent drop in household burglaries and a 54 percent drop in motor vehicle thefts (Catalano, 2005). The UCR

National Incident-Based Reporting System (NIBRS) A reporting system in which the police describe each offense in a crime incident, together with data describing the offender, victim, and property.

National Crime Victimization Surveys (NCVS) Interviews of samples of the U.S. population conducted by the Bureau of Justice Statistics to determine the number and types of criminal victimizations and thus the extent of unreported as well as reported crime.

[handwritten margin notes: 60,000 households / 130,000 people]

TABLE 2.2   The UCR and the NCVS

Compare the data sources. Remember that the UCR tabulate only crimes reported to the police, whereas the NCVS are based on interviews with victims.

	Uniform Crime Reports	National Crime Victimization Survey
Offenses Measured	Homicide Rape Robbery (personal and commercial) Assault (aggravated) Burglary (commercial and household) Larceny (commercial and household) Motor vehicle theft Arson	Rape Robbery (personal) Assault (aggravated and simple) Household burglary Larceny (personal and household) Motor vehicle theft
Scope	Crimes reported to the police in most jurisdictions; considerable flexibility in developing small-area data	Crimes both reported and not reported to police; all data are for the nation as a whole; some data are available for a few large geographic areas
Collection Method	Police department reports to Federal Bureau of Investigation	Survey interviews: periodically measures the total number of crimes committed by asking a national sample of 43,000 households representing 76,000 people over the age of 12 about their experiences as victims of crime during a specific period
Kinds of Information	In addition to offense counts, provides information on crime clearances, persons arrested, persons charged, law enforcement officers killed and assaulted, and characteristics of homicide victims	Provides details about victims (such as age, race, sex, education, income, and whether the victim and offender were related) and about crimes (such as time and place of occurrence, whether or not reported to police, use of weapons, occurrence of injury, and economic consequences)
Sponsor	Department of Justice's Federal Bureau of Investigation	Department of Justice's Bureau of Justice Statistics

show similar results, revealing a rapid rise in crime rates beginning in 1964 and continuing until 1980, when the rates began to level off or decline. The overall crime rate rose slightly in 2001 because of an increase in property crimes, but it subsequently resumed modest annual declines (BJS, 2004f: Table 3.106.2003).

Figure 2.2 displays four measures of violent crime, adjusted for changes made in the NCVS in 1992. The top two measures are based on the victimization survey; crimes recorded by the police and arrests are from the UCR and are presented below these. Remember that the differences in the trends indicated by the NCVS and the UCR are explained in part by the different data sources and different populations on which their tabulations are based.

What explains the drop in both violent and property crime well below the 1973 levels? Among the reasons given by analysts are the aging of the baby boom population, the increased use of security systems, aggressive police efforts to keep handguns off the streets, and the dramatic decline in the use of crack cocaine. Other factors may include the booming economy of the 1990s and the quadrupling of the number of people incarcerated since 1970. Let us look more closely at two factors—age and crack cocaine—as a means of assessing future crime levels.

Age   Changes in the age makeup of the population are a key factor in the analysis of crime trends. It has long been known that men aged 16 to 24 are the most crime-prone group. The rise in crime in the 1970s has been blamed on the post–World War II baby boom. By the 1970s the "boomers" had entered the high-risk crime group of 16- to 24-year-olds. They made up a much larger portion of the U.S. population than ever before. Between 40 and 50 percent of the total arrests during that decade could have been expected as a result of the growth in the total population and in the size of the crime-prone age group. Likewise, the decline in most crime rates that began during the 1980s has been attributed to the maturing of the post–World War II generation. During the 1990s the 16- to 24-year age cohort was smaller than it had been at any victimized by crime in a subsequent year (Menard, 2000). Research also shows that members of certain demographic groups are more likely to be victimized than others. Puzzling over this fact, victimologists have come up with several answers (Karmen, 2001:87). One explanation is that demographic factors (age, gender, income) affect lifestyle—people's routine activities, such as work, home life, and recreation. Lifestyles, in turn, affect people's exposure to dangerous places, times, and people (Varano et al., 2004). Thus, differences in lifestyles lead to varying degrees of exposure to risks (R. F. Meier and Miethe, 1993:466). Figure 2.3 shows the links among the factors used in the lifestyle-exposure model of personal victimization. Using this model, think of people whose lifestyle includes going to nightclubs in a "shady" part of town. Such people run the risk of being robbed if they walk alone through a dark high-crime area at two in the morning to their luxury car. By contrast, older individuals who watch television at night in their small-town home have a very low chance of being robbed. But these cases do not tell the entire story. What other factors make victims more vulnerable than nonvictims?

Men, Youths, Nonwhites   The lifestyle-exposure model and survey data shed light on the links between personal characteristics and the chance that one will become a victim. Figure 2.4 shows the influence of gender, age, and race on the risk of being victimized by a violent crime, such as rape, robbery, or assault. If we apply these findings to the lifestyle-exposure model, we might suggest that male African American teenagers are most likely to be victimized because of where they live (urban, high-crime areas), how they may spend their time (on the streets late at night), and the people with whom they may associate (violence-prone youths) (Lauritsen, Laub, and Sampson, 1992). Lifestyle factors may also explain why elderly white women are least likely to be victimized by a violent crime. Perhaps it is because they do not go out at night, do not associate with people who are prone to crime, carry few valuables, and take precautions such as locking their doors. Thus, lifestyle choices directly affect the chances of victimization.

Race is a key factor in exposure to crime. African Americans and other minorities are more likely than whites to be raped, robbed, and assaulted. The rate of violent crime victimization for whites is 21 per 1,000 people, compared with 26 per 1,000 for African Americans. For Hispanics, the rate is only 18 per 1,000 (Catalano, 2005). White Americans are fearful of being victimized by African American strangers (Skogan, 1995:59). However, most violent crime is intraracial: More than two-thirds of victims are of the same race as the attacker (BJS, 2006: Table 42). These numbers simply reflect that African Americans and whites often live in separate neighborhoods. Most of their daily contacts are with people who share their demographic characteristics. And, most

> According to the lifestyle-exposure model, demographic factors (age, gender, income) and exposure to dangerous places, times, and people influence the probability of being victimized.

AP Photo/Kevork Djansezian

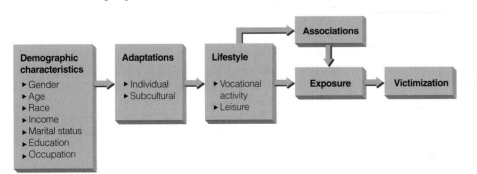

Demographic characteristics
▸ Gender
▸ Age
▸ Race
▸ Income
▸ Marital status
▸ Education
▸ Occupation

Adaptations
▸ Individual
▸ Subcultural

Lifestyle
▸ Vocational activity
▸ Leisure

Associations

Exposure

Victimization

FIGURE 2.3
Lifestyle-exposure model of victimization
Demographic and subcultural factors determine personal lifestyles, which in turn influence exposure to victimization.

Source: Adapted with permission from Robert F. Meier and Terance D. Miethe, "Understanding Theories of Criminal Victimization," in *Crime and Justice: A Review of Research*, ed. Michael Tonry (Chicago: University of Chicago Press, 1993), 467.

FIGURE 2.4
Victimization rates for violent crimes
Male African American teenagers aged 12–15 have the highest victimization rate for violent crimes. Why are they more likely than other age, gender, and racial groups to be robbed or assaulted?

Source: Bureau of Justice Statistics, *Criminal Victimization in the United States—Statistical Tables* (Washington, DC: U.S. Department of Justice, 2004), Table 10—Violent Crimes, 2003 (see also http://www.ojp.usdoj.gov/bjs/).

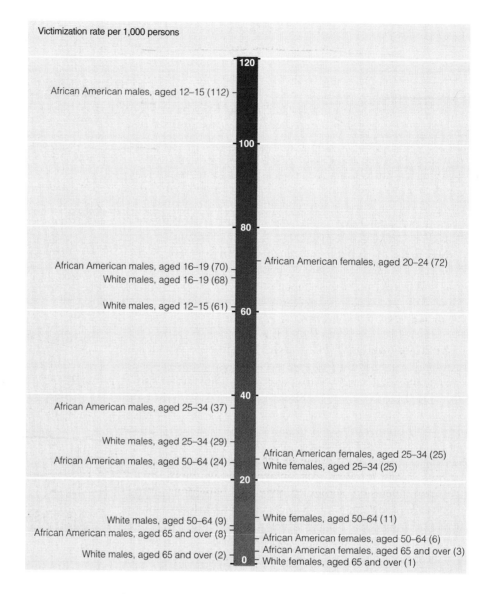

importantly, African American neighborhoods are much more likely to experience what scholars call "high levels of socioeconomic disadvantage" with respect to unemployment, quality of schools, quality of housing, and other factors associated with income and wealth (Lauritsen and White, 2001:53). These factors are often associated with higher levels of street crime, although obviously other kinds of crime, such as occupational crime and computer crime, occur in other settings.

Low-Income City Dwellers   Income is also closely linked to exposure to crime. Americans with incomes below $15,000 annually experienced a victimization rate in excess of 38 violent crimes per 1,000 people. By contrast, those with incomes in excess of $75,000 experienced only 17 violent crimes per 1,000 people (Catalano, 2005). Economic factors largely determine where people live, work, and seek recreation. For low-income people, these choices are limited. Some have to live in crime-prone areas, lack security devices to protect their homes, cannot avoid contact with people who are prone to crime, or cannot spend their leisure time in safe areas. Poor people and minorities have a greater risk of being victimized, because they are likely to live in inner-city zones with high rates of street crime. People with higher incomes have more lifestyle-exposure choices open to them and can avoid risky situations (R. F. Meier and Miethe, 1993:468).

Living in a city is, in fact, a key factor in victimization. Violent crime occurs mainly in large cities, where the violent crime and personal theft victimization rate is

29 per 1,000 people, compared with 18 per 1,000 in suburbs and 20 per 1,000 in rural areas. Urban households are also more prone to property victimization, with victimization rates more than 50 percent higher than those in suburbs and rural areas (Catalano, 2005).

In the inner cities, where drug dealing and drug use have been significant and visible problems, murder rates are higher than elsewhere. Like their killers, most of the victims tend to be young African Americans. The national homicide rate among African American men aged 18 to 24 is 102 for every 100,000 of the same group, about eight times that for white men in the same age bracket (BJS, 2004f: Table 3.126). But this does not tell the whole story, because homicide rates differ by city and state. In some cities and states, the gaps between rates for African Americans and whites are even greater. Further, we cannot conclude that crime rates will be high in all poor urban areas. There is more crime in some poor areas than in others. Many factors besides poverty—such as the physical condition of the neighborhood, the residents' attitudes toward society and the law, the extent of opportunities for crime, and social control by families and government—can affect the crime rate of a given area.

ACQUAINTANCES AND STRANGERS

The frightening image of crime in the minds of many Americans is the familiar scene played out in many movies and television shows in which a dangerous stranger grabs a victim on a dark street or breaks into a home at night. Many crimes are committed by strangers against people they have never seen before. However, most Americans do not realize the extent to which violent crimes occur among acquaintances, friends, and even relatives. In 2004, for example, female victims of violent crimes were victimized by strangers in only 34 percent of those crimes; acquaintances, spouses, boyfriends, or relatives committed two-thirds of the violent crimes against female victims. Although only 48 percent of male victims suffered violent crimes at the hands of acquaintances and relatives, that figure still constitutes a significant percentage of violent crimes (Catalano, 2005).

Victims tend to suffer different kinds of crimes, depending on whether strangers or nonstrangers are the perpetrators. Most robberies are committed by strangers to the victim, but sexual assault victims are more likely to be victimized by someone they know. These differences reflect, in part, the contexts in which these crimes occur. In robberies, valuables are taken from an individual by force and then the robber typically runs away. Thus, the scenario fits situations in which the robber hopes to escape without being caught or identified. This result is much more difficult for a robber who is known to the victim. By contrast, sexual assaults often take place in isolated or private locations. People are most likely to place themselves in isolated or private locations, such as inside a house or apartment, with someone they know.

Courtesy of Community Coalition on Family Violence, Knoxville TN.

Although fear of violent victimization by strangers is prevalent among the American public, most violence against women is prepetrated by those with whom they are initimate—husbands, boyfriends, lovers.

He says he loves me

He says he is sorry

He says it won't happen again

People may be reluctant to report crimes committed by relatives, such as the theft of their own valuables by a relative with a substance abuse problem. They may be upset about losing their valuables, but they do not want to see their son, daughter, or cousin arrested and sent to prison. If the perpetrators of such crimes know that their relatives will not report them, they may feel encouraged to victimize these people further in order to support a drug habit. Thus, the prior relationships among people may facilitate some crimes and keep victims from seeking police assistance.

The lifestyle-exposure model helps us understand some of the factors that increase or decrease the risk of being victimized, but what is the impact of crime on the nation and on individuals? We turn to this question in the next section.

THE IMPACT OF CRIME

Crime affects not only the victim but all members of society. We all pay for crime through higher taxes, higher prices, and fear. These factors impinge on key American values such as individual liberty and protection of private property and personal wealth.

Costs of Crime   Crime has many kinds of costs: (1) the economic costs—lost property, lower productivity, and medical expenses, (2) the psychological and emotional costs—pain, trauma, and lost quality of life, (3) the costs of operating the criminal justice system.

A Justice Department study from the mid-1990s estimated the total annual cost of tangible losses from crime (medical expenses, damaged or lost property, work time) at $105 billion. The intangible costs (pain, trauma, lost quality of life) to victims were estimated at $450 billion (NIJ, 1996). Operating the criminal justice system costs taxpayers more than $167 billion a year to pay for police, courts, and corrections (BJS, 2004f). Government costs also increased in the aftermath of the September 11 tragedy as more money was spent on airport security, border patrols, and counterterrorism activities. These figures do not include the costs of occupational and organized crime to consumers. Businesses' losses from hackers' attacks on their computers stood at $600 million in 2003 (McGuire, 2004). Overall losses from economic crimes alone were estimated to be $200 billion in 2000, and private businesses spent more than $103 billion on consultants, services, and products to combat these economic crimes (Security Industry Association, 2000). In addition, individual citizens who install locks and alarms or employ guards and security patrols incur crime-related costs.

Fear of Crime   One impact of crime is fear. Fear limits freedom. Because they are fearful, many people limit their activities to "safe" areas at "safe" times. Fear also creates anxieties that affect physiological and psychological well-being. Ironically, the very people who have the least chance of being victimized, such as women and the elderly, are often the most fearful (Miethe, 1995:14). Not all Americans experience the same fears (Lee and Ulmer, 2000), but some of the population adjust their daily activities to prevent being victimized. Since 1965, public opinion polls have asked Americans whether they "feel more uneasy" or "fear to walk the streets at night" (see "What Americans Think").

From 1972 to 1993, more than 40 percent of respondents indicated that fear of crime limited their freedom. Coinciding with the declining crimes rates during the 1990s, the percentage of respondents who were fearful of walking near their homes dropped to 30 percent in 2001. In subsequent years, the percentage moved up but remained below 40 percent. Thus, a significant segment of the American public remains fearful despite the significant drop in crime rates over the past 20 years.

Although crime rates are down, Americans' fears seem to exceed actual victimization risks. As we have seen, people do not have a clear picture of the true risk of crime in their lives. They gain perceptions about crime from talk at their workplace and from politicians' statements and campaign promises. Their views about crime also seem to be shaped more by what they see on television than by reality (Chiricos, Padgett, and Gertz, 2000). Although fewer than 8 percent of victimizations are due to violent crime, such crimes are the ones most frequently reported by the media.

WHAT AMERICANS THINK

Question: "Is there any area right around here—that is, within a mile—where you would be afraid to walk alone at night?"

Yes 38%

No 62%

10 20 30 40 50 60 70 80

Go to http://www.thomsonedu.com/criminaljustice/cole to compare your opinion on this issue with the opinions of other criminal justice students.

Source: Bureau of Justice Statistics, *Sourcebook of Criminal Justice Statistics, 2005* (Washington, DC: U.S. Government Printing Office, 2005), Table 2.37.2005.

THE EXPERIENCE OF VICTIMS WITHIN THE CRIMINAL JUSTICE SYSTEM

After a crime has occurred, the victim is often forgotten. Victims may have suffered physical, psychological, and economic losses, yet the criminal justice system focuses on finding and prosecuting the offender.

Too often the system is not sensitive to the needs of victims. For example, defense attorneys may ask them hostile questions and attempt to paint them, rather than the defendant, as having caused the crime to occur. Similarly, whereas victims are a key source of evidence, the police may question them closely—and in a hostile fashion—to find out if they are telling the truth. Often the victim never hears the outcome of a case. Sometimes a victim comes face-to-face with the assailant who is out on bail or on probation. This can be quite a shock, especially if the victim assumed that the offender was in prison.

Victims may be forced to miss work and lose pay in order to appear at judicial proceedings. They may be summoned to court again and again, only to learn that the arraignment or trial has been postponed. Any recovered property may be held by the court for months as the case winds its way through the system. In short, after cases have been completed, victims may feel that they have been victimized twice, once by the offender and once by the criminal justice system.

During the past three decades, justice agencies have become more sensitive to the interests of crime victims. This has happened partly because victims often are the only witnesses to the crime and their help is needed. Many victims are not willing to provide such help if it involves economic and emotional costs. Some research indicates that victims are more likely to cooperate with the prosecutor if victims assistance workers meet with them to provide comfort as well as information about how the court system operates (Dawson and Dinovitzer, 2001).

Various laws adopted in recent years provide funds to counsel victims and give financial compensation for injuries, although victims often do not receive enough timely information to take advantage of these programs (Sims, Yost, and Abbott, 2005). In addition, victims' rights statutes in many states permit crime victims to speak at sentencing and parole hearings and receive information about any impending release of the offender who victimized them. The Justice for All Act passed by Congress in 2004 mandates such rights for victims in criminal cases processed in the federal courts. A Crime Victims' Bill of Rights has been proposed as a new amendment to the U.S. Constitution, but it has not been approved.

Victims' assistance laws raise questions about which individuals or family members can receive benefits as "victims" (Trulson, 2005). Questions about fairness may arise if some individuals receive different benefits than do other people. Read "A Question of Ethics" at the end of the chapter to consider whether the families of crime victims in general are treated fairly when compared with the families of 9/11 victims.

THE ROLE OF VICTIMS IN CRIME

Victimologists study the role victims play in some crimes. Researchers have found that many victims behave in ways that facilitate the acts committed against them. This does not mean that it is the victim's fault that the crime occurred. It means instead that the victim's behavior may have led to the crime through consent, provocation, enticement, risk taking, or carelessness with property.

What do studies tell us about these situations? First, some people do not take proper precautions to protect themselves. For example, they leave keys in their cars or fail to lock their doors and windows at night. They seem to lack the "common sense" of understanding the price of living safely in modern society. Second, some victims provoke or entice another person to commit a crime. Arguing with a stranger at a bar can lead to criminal assaults. Third, some victims of nonstrangers are not willing to help with the investigation and prosecution. These behaviors do not excuse criminal acts, but they do force us to think about other aspects of the crime situation.

ThomsonNOW

Improve your grade on the exam with Personalized Study! For reinforcement resources and a mastery check of Crime Victimization, go to www.thomsonedu.com/thomsonnow.

Answers

7. What are the main elements of the lifestyle-exposure model? ⟶ 7. Demographic characteristics, adaptations, lifestyle, associations, exposure.

8. What are some of the impacts of crime? ⟶ 8. Fear, financial costs, emotional costs, lifestyle restrictions.

9. Why do some crime victims feel mistreated by the criminal justice system? ⟶ 9. The system focuses on finding and punishing the offender; police and lawyers often question victims closely, in an unsympathetic manner; victims do not always receive assistance that covers their medical expenses and other losses.

Causes of Crime

Whenever news of a crime hits the headlines, whether the crime is a grisly murder or a complex bank fraud, the first question is, "Why did he (or she) do it?" Do people commit crimes because they are poor, greedy, mentally ill, or just plain stupid? Do any of these explanations apply to Dennis Rader, the serial killer discussed at the beginning of the chapter? What about Martha Stewart, whose case was discussed in Chapter 1?

Various theories about the root causes of criminal behavior have been developed, and scholarly research regularly tests these theories. If proven to explain the causes of crime, these theories could provide the basis for new public policies aimed at preventing crime.

Criminology is concerned mainly with learning about criminal behavior, the nature of offenders, and how crime can be prevented. Research focuses mainly on the offender. Fewer questions are asked about how factors such as the economy, government policy, family, and education affect crime (Messner and Rosenfeld, 1994:45–47). In this section we look at the two major schools of criminological thought—classical and positivist. We then review biological, psychological, sociological, and life course theories of the causes of criminal behavior.

CLASSICAL AND POSITIVIST THEORIES

Two major schools of criminological thought are the classical and positivist schools. Each was pioneered by scholars who were influenced by the dominant intellectual ideas of their times.

The Classical School   Until the eighteenth century, most Europeans explained criminal behavior in supernatural terms. Those who did wrong were "possessed" by the devil. Some Christians believed that all humanity had fallen with Adam and had remained in a state of total depravity ever since. Indictments often began, "[John Doe], not having the fear of God before his eyes but being moved and seduced by the instigation of the devil, did commit [a certain crime]." Before the eighteenth century, defendants had few rights. The accused had little chance to put forth a defense, confessions were obtained through torture, and the penalty for most offenses was physical punishment or death.

In 1764 Cesare Beccaria published his *Essays on Crime and Punishments*. This was the first attempt to explain crime in secular, or worldly, terms, as opposed to religious terms. The book also pointed to injustices in the administration of criminal laws. Beccaria's ideas prompted reformers to try to make criminal law and procedures more rational and consistent. From this movement came **classical criminology**, whose main principles are as follows:

1. Criminal behavior is rational, and most people have the potential to engage in such behavior.

2. People may choose to commit a crime after weighing the costs and benefits of their actions.

3. Fear of punishment is what keeps most people in check. Therefore, the severity, certainty, and speed of punishment affects of the level of crime.

classical criminology A school of criminology that views behavior as stemming from free will, demands responsibility and accountability of all perpetrators, and stresses the need for punishments severe enough to deter others.

4. The punishment should fit the crime rather than the person who committed it.

5. The criminal justice system must be predictable, with laws and punishments known to the public.

Classical ideas declined in the nineteenth century, partly because of the rise of science and partly because its principles did not take into account differences among individuals or the way the crime was committed.

Neoclassical Criminology   After remaining dormant for almost a hundred years, classical ideas took on new life in the 1980s, when America became more conservative. Some scholars argue that crimes may result from the rational choice of people who have weighed the benefits to be gained from the crime against the costs of being caught and punished. But they also recognize that criminal law must take account of differences among individuals. To a large extent, sentencing reform, criticisms of rehabilitation, and greater use of incarceration stem from a renewed interest in classical ideas. However, the positivist school of thought is what has dominated American criminology since the start of the twentieth century.

Positivist Criminology   By the middle of the nineteenth century, as the scientific method began to take hold, the ideas of the classical school seemed old-fashioned. Instead, **positivist criminology** used science to study the body, mind, and environment of the offender. Science could help reveal why offenders committed crimes and how they could be rehabilitated. Here are the key features of this approach:

1. Human behavior is controlled by physical, mental, and social factors, not by free will.

2. Criminals are different from noncriminals.

3. Science can be used to discover the causes of crime and to treat deviants.

Understanding the main theories of crime causation is important because they affect how laws are enforced, guilt is determined, and crimes are punished. As we describe each of the theories, consider its implications for crime policies. For example, if biological theories are viewed as sound, then the authorities might try to identify potential offenders through genetic analysis and then segregate or supervise them. On the other hand, the acceptance of sociological theories might lead to efforts to end poverty, improve education, and provide job training.

positivist criminology A school of criminology that views behavior as stemming from social, biological, and psychological factors. It argues that punishment should be tailored to the individual needs of the offender.

BIOLOGICAL EXPLANATIONS

The medical training of Cesare Lombroso (1836–1909) led him to suppose that physical traits distinguish criminals from law-abiding citizens. He believed that some people are at a more primitive state of evolution and hence are born criminal. These "throwbacks" have trouble adjusting to modern society. Lombroso's ideas can be summarized as follows (Lombroso, 1912/1968):

1. Certain people are **criminogenic,** that is, they are born criminals.

2. They have primitive physical traits such as strong canine teeth, huge jaws, and high cheekbones.

3. These traits are acquired through heredity or through alcoholism, epilepsy, or syphilis.

criminogenic Having factors thought to bring about criminal behavior in an individual.

Early biological studies traced the generations of specific families to count how many people in each violated criminal laws. These early studies may no longer seem credible to us, but they were taken seriously in their time and affected criminal justice for decades. For example, many states passed laws that required repeat offenders to be sterilized. It was assumed that crime could be controlled if criminal traits were not passed from parents to children. Not until 1942 did the U.S. Supreme Court declare required sterilization unconstitutional (*Skinner v. Oklahoma*).

Although **biological explanations** of crime were ignored or condemned as racist after World War II, they have attracted renewed interest. *Crime and Human Nature,* by James Wilson and Richard Herrnstein (1985), reviews the research on

biological explanations Explanations of crime that emphasize physiological and neurological factors that may predispose a person to commit crimes.

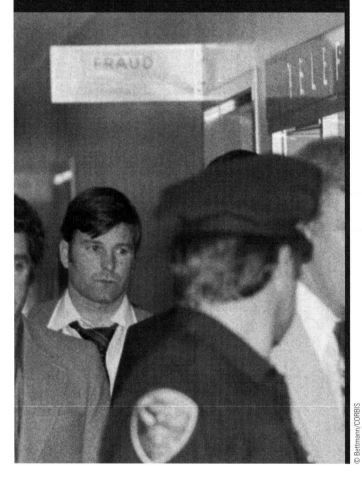

Dan White (far left), a former San Francisco police officer and city supervisor, was tried for killing Mayor George Moscone and Supervisor Harvey Milk. During the 1979 trial a psychiatrist testified that White suffered from depression brought on, in part, by overindulging in Twinkies and Coca-Cola. The unpopularity of the eventual manslaughter verdict and lighter sentence (which set off riots) gave rise to the belief that White's lawyers successfully used the "Twinkie defense."

this subject. Unlike the early positivists, the authors do not claim that any one factor explains criminality. Instead, they argue that biological factors predispose some individuals to a crime. Genetic makeup, body type, and IQ may outweigh social factors as predictors of criminality. The findings of research on nutrition, neurology, genetics, and endocrinology give some support to the view that these factors may contribute to violent behavior in some people (Brennan, Mednick, and Volavka, 1995:65). Other researchers have identified physiological factors associated with antisocial behavior, an association they see as a step toward considering a possible link between biology and offending (Cauffman, Steinberg, and Piquero, 2005).

These new findings have given biological explanations a renewed influence and have reduced the dominance of sociological and psychological explanations. Scientists are doing further research to see if they can find biological factors that make some people prone to violence and criminality (Fishbein, 1990:27). For example, a study published in 2002 found that a single gene can help predict which abused children will become violent or antisocial adults. Abused children with a specific gene identified in the study were twice as likely as other abused children to commit acts of violence (Hathaway, 2002). Other studies examine the role of nutrition, such as consumption of fish rich in omega-3 being associated with lower levels of hostility in young adults (Iribarren et al., 2004), and the impact of environmental lead, such as lead-based paint, on brain development and behavior (University of Pittsburgh Medical Center, 2005). These findings behind biology and behavior do not necessarily purport to seek a single explanation for crime. They merely demonstrate an increased recognition that biological factors influence certain kinds of behavior in some offenders.

© Bettmann/CORBIS

PSYCHOLOGICAL EXPLANATIONS

psychological explanations
Explanations of crime that emphasize mental processes and behavior.

People have often viewed criminal behavior as being caused by a mental condition, a personality disturbance, or limited intellect. **Psychological explanations** of crime center on these ideas.

Sigmund Freud (1856–1939), now seen as one of the foremost thinkers of the twentieth century, proposed a psychoanalytic theory that crime is caused by unconscious forces and drives. Freud also claimed that early childhood experiences had major effects on personality development. Freud's followers expanded his theory, saying that the personality is made up of three parts: the id, ego, and superego. The id controls drives that are primarily sexual, the ego relates desires to behavior, and the superego (often referred to as the conscience) judges actions as either right or wrong. Psychoanalytic theory explains criminal behavior as resulting from either an undeveloped or an overdeveloped superego. For example, a person who commits a violent sex crime is thought to have an undeveloped superego, because the urges cannot be controlled. Alternatively, a person with an overdeveloped superego may suffer from guilt and anxiety. To reduce the guilt, the person may commit a crime, knowing that punishment will follow. To ensure punishment, the offender will unconsciously leave clues at the crime scene. Psychoanalysts say this occurred in the famous Loeb-Leopold murder of Bobby Franks in 1924 (Regoli and Hewitt, 1994).

Psychiatrists have linked criminal behavior to such concepts as innate impulses, psychic conflict, and repression of personality. Such explanations propose that crime is a behavior that stems from abnormal urges and desires. Although the psychological approach takes many different forms, all are based on the idea that early personality development is a key factor in later behavior. The terms *psychopath, sociopath,* and *antisocial personality* refer to a person who is unable to control impulses, cannot learn from experience, and does not feel emotions, such as love. This kind of person is viewed as psychologically abnormal and may become a crazed killer or sex fiend.

Psychological theories have been widely criticized. Some critics point to the fact that it is hard to measure emotional factors and to identify people thought to be prone to crime. Others note the wide range of sometimes contradictory theories that take a psychological approach to crime.

SOCIOLOGICAL EXPLANATIONS

In contrast to psychological approaches, **sociological explanations** focus on the way that belonging to social groups shapes people's behavior. Sociologists believe that criminality is not inborn but caused by external factors. Thus, sociological theories of crime assume that contact with the social world, as well as such factors as race, age, gender, and income, mold the offender's personality and actions.

In the 1920s a group of researchers at the University of Chicago looked closely at aspects of urban life that seemed to be linked to crime: poverty, bad housing, broken families, and the problems faced by new immigrants. They found high levels of crime in those neighborhoods that had many opportunities for delinquent behavior and few legitimate means of earning a living.

From a sociological perspective, criminals are made, not born. Among the many theories stressing the influence of societal forces on criminal behavior, three types deserve special mention: social structure theories, social process theories, and social conflict theories.

Social Structure Theories **Social structure theories** suggest that criminal behavior is related to social class. People in various social classes have quite different amounts of wealth, status, and power. Those in the lower class suffer from poverty, poor education, bad housing, and lack of political power. Therefore, members of the lower class, especially the younger members, are the most likely to engage in crime. Crime thus is created by the structure of society.

The sociologist Robert Merton drew from theories about the role of social change and urbanization on crime. He stressed that social change often leads to a state of **anomie,** in which the rules or norms that guide behavior have weakened or disappeared. People may become anomic when the rules are unclear or they cannot achieve their goals. Under such conditions, antisocial or deviant behavior may result.

It is said, for example, that U.S. society highly values success but makes it impossible for some of its members to succeed. It follows that those who are caught in this trap may use crime as a way out. Theorists believe that this type of situation has led some ethnic groups into organized crime. Others argue that social disorganization brings about conditions in which, among other things, family structure breaks down, alcohol or drug abuse becomes more common, and criminal behavior increases. They assert that poverty must be ended and the social structure reformed if crime is to be reduced (Sampson and Wilson, 1995).

Contemporary theorists have drawn from social structure concepts and Merton's anomie theory to develop certain theories of crime causation. Prominent among modern approaches is the general theory of strain. According to this approach, negative relationships can lead to negative emotions. These emotions, particularly anger, are expressed through crime and delinquency. Strain is produced by the failure to achieve valued goals, which may particularly affect poor people in a society that values financial success. Strain is also produced by negative experiences, including unemployment, child abuse, criminal victimization, and family problems, which also tend to prevail in

sociological explanations
Explanations of crime that emphasize as causes of criminal behavior the social conditions that bear on the individual.

social structure theories
Theories that blame crime on the existence of a powerless lower class that lives with poverty and deprivation and often turns to crime in response.

anomie A breakdown or disappearance of the rules of social behavior.

poor communities. Under this theory, those who cannot cope with negative experiences may be predisposed to criminal behavior (Liska and Messner, 1999:36–37).

As these ideas have become more refined, they have also been used to explain white-collar crime. To achieve even higher levels of success in a structure that values ever-increasing wealth, individuals may break rules and violate laws in order to enhance their personal success. Poverty relative to others' wealth is what causes crime. Thus, structure theories have been used to explain the behavior of corporate leaders who manipulate stock prices and take other actions to add to their wealth despite already being millionaires (Liska and Messner, 1999:37).

Social Process Theories Despite such arguments, many criminologists believe that the social structure approach does not adequately explain criminality by middle-class and affluent people. More importantly, they fear that a focus on social structure erroneously emphasizes crime as primarily a problem of the poor. **Social process theories,** which date from the 1930s but did not gain recognition until the 1960s and 1970s, assume that any person, regardless of education, class, or upbringing, has the potential to become a criminal. However, some people are likely to commit criminal acts because of the circumstances of their lives. Thus, these theories try to explain the processes by which certain people become criminals.

There are three main types of social process theories: learning theories, control theories, and labeling theories.

Learning theories hold that criminal activity is learned behavior. Through social relations, some people learn how to be a criminal and acquire the values associated with that way of life. This view assumes that people imitate and learn from one another. Thus family members and peers are viewed as major influences on a person's development.

In 1939 Edwin Sutherland proposed a type of learning theory called the **theory of differential association,** which states that behavior is learned through interactions with others, especially family members (Sutherland, 1947). Criminal behavior occurs when a person encounters others who are more favorable to crime than opposed to it. If a boy grows up in a family in which, say, an older brother is involved in crime, he is likely to learn criminal behavior. If people in the family, neighborhood, and gang believe that illegal activity is nothing to be ashamed of, this belief increases the chance that the young person will engage in crime.

Control theories hold that social links keep people in line with accepted norms (Gottfredson and Hirschi, 1990; Hirschi, 1969). In other words, all members of society have the potential to commit crime, but most are restrained by their ties to family, church, school, and peer groups. Thus, sensitivity to the opinion of others, commitment to a conventional lifestyle, and belief in the standards or values shared by friends all influence a person to abide by the law. A person who lacks one or more of these influences may engage in crime.

Finally, **labeling theories** stress the social process through which certain acts and people are labeled as deviant. As Howard Becker noted, society creates deviance—and, hence, criminality—"by making the rules whose infraction constitutes deviance, and by applying those rules to particular people and labeling them outsiders" (Becker, 1963).

According to labeling theories, social control agencies, such as the police, courts, and corrections, are created to label certain people as outside the normal, law-abiding community. When they have been labeled, those people come to believe that the label is true. They take on a deviant identity and start acting in deviant ways. Labeling theory suggests the justice system creates criminals by labeling people in order to serve its own bureaucratic and political ends. Those who support this view call for decriminalization of drug use, gambling, and prostitution.

Social Conflict Theories In the mid-1960s, the reigning biological, psychological, and sociological explanations of criminal behavior were challenged by **social conflict theories.** These theories assume that criminal law and the justice system are designed

---

social process theories Theories that see criminality as normal behavior. Everyone has the potential to become a criminal, depending on (1) the influences that impel one toward or away from crime and (2) how one is regarded by others.

learning theories Theories that see criminal behavior as learned, just as legal behavior is learned.

theory of differential association The theory that people become criminals because they encounter more influences that view criminal behavior as normal and acceptable than influences that are hostile to criminal behavior.

control theories Theories holding that criminal behavior occurs when the bonds that tie an individual to society are broken or weakened.

labeling theories Theories emphasizing that the causes of criminal behavior are not found in the individual but in the social process that labels certain acts as deviant or criminal.

social conflict theories Theories that assume criminal law and the criminal justice system are primarily a means of controlling the poor and the have-nots.

mainly to control the poor. The rich commit as many crimes as do the poor, it is argued, but the poor are more likely to be caught and punished. Those in power use the law to impose their version of morality on society in order to protect their property and safety. They also use their power to change the definitions of crime to cover acts they view as threatening.

There are different types of social conflict theories. One type, proposed by critical, radical, or Marxist criminologists, holds that the class structure causes certain groups to be labeled as deviant. In this view, "deviance is a status imputed to groups who share certain structural characteristics (e.g., powerlessness)" (Spitzer, 1975:639). Thus, the criminal law is aimed at the behavior of specific groups or classes. One result is that the poor are deeply hostile toward the social order, and this hostility is one factor in criminal behavior. Moreover, when the status quo is threatened, legal definitions of crime are changed in order to trap those who challenge the system. For example, vagrancy laws have been used to arrest labor union organizers, civil rights workers, and peace activists when those in power believed that their interests were threatened by these groups.

Like other theories about the causes of criminal behavior, sociological theories have been criticized. Critics argue that these theories are imprecise, unsupported by evidence, and based on ideology. Even so, sociological theories have served as the basis for many attempts to prevent crime and rehabilitate offenders.

LIFE COURSE THEORIES

Life course theories seek to identify factors that shape criminal careers, in order to explain when and why offenders begin to commit crimes and to see what factors lead individuals to stop their participation in crimes. Studies in this area often try to follow individuals from childhood through adulthood in order to identify the factors associated with beginning, avoiding, continuing, or ceasing criminal behavior. Criminal careers often begin at an early age; people who eventually become involved with crime often exhibit disruptive behavior, lack family support, and experiment with drinking and drugs as youths. Some theorists discuss *pathways* into crime, which may begin with minor habits of lying and stealing that lead to more serious offenses. However, pathways into crime are not identical for all kinds of offenders (Maxwell and Maxwell, 2000). For example, those youths who engage in bullying and fighting may begin a pathway toward different kinds of crimes than do those who start out using drugs.

As identified by life course theorists, the factors that can impact criminal career overlap with factors discussed in psychological, social structure, and social process theories, such as unemployment, failure in school, impulsiveness, and unstable families. In other words, life course theorists' ideas about factors associated with criminal behavior are consistent with factors identified in other theories. However, these theorists study criminal behavior from a broader perspective.

The research of Robert Sampson and John Laub is among the most influential in examining the life course and criminal careers (Laub and Sampson, 2003; Sampson and Laub, 1993). They reanalyzed and built on the famous studies of Sheldon and Eleanor Glueck that had followed the lives of 1,000 Boston-area boys from 1940 through the 1960s (Glueck and Glueck, 1950). Sampson and Laub gathered data on the same men in the 1990s, by which time the surviving "boys" from the original study were senior citizens.

Based on their research, Sampson and Laub discuss informal and formal social controls over the life course. Unlike some researchers, who see youthful criminality as setting behavior patterns that continue into adulthood, Sampson and Laub emphasize *turning points* in life that move individuals away from criminal careers. For example, their study showed that military service, employment, and marriage served as particularly important factors leading away from criminal careers. By contrast, incarceration and alcohol abuse were associated with continued lawbreaking.

Life course explanations do not seek to identify a single or primary factor as the cause of criminal behavior. Instead, they try to identify and evaluate the timing, interaction, and results of complex factors that affect people's lives.

life course theories Theories that identify factors affecting the start, duration, nature, and end of criminal behavior over the life of an offender.

WOMEN AND CRIME

Theories about causes of crime are almost all based on observations of men. This is understandable, because men commit far more crimes than do women. It also reflects the fact that until recently most criminologists were men. Only in the past few decades has research focused on women and crime. Although they have raised new questions, scholars in this field base their research on the theories just described (Daly, 1998).

Except in the case of so-called "female" crimes such as prostitution and shoplifting, before the 1970s little research was done on female offenders, who then accounted for fewer than 10 percent of arrests. It was assumed that women had a nurturing and dependent nature that kept most of them from committing serious crimes. Those who did commit crimes were labeled as "bad" or "fallen" women. Unlike male criminals, then, female criminals were usually viewed as moral offenders. Such viewpoints raised the possibility that women offenders were treated differently than men by police, prosecutors, and judges.

Today criminologists are looking more closely at female offenders (Daly and Chesney-Lind, 1988:497). Two books published in 1975, Freda Adler's *Sisters in Crime: The Rise of the New Female Criminal* and Rita Simon's *Women and Crime*, led to a new view of gender and crime. Both books looked at increases in female crimes, but they reached different conclusions.

Adler stressed the impact of the women's movement. She believed that as the roles of women changed, their criminality would be more like that of men. As she noted, "When we did not permit women to swim at the beaches, the female drowning rate was quite low. When women were not permitted to work as bank tellers or presidents, the female embezzlement rate was low" (F. Adler, 1975:31). In other words, as women and men become more equal, gender differences decrease.

According to Simon, because of recent changes, women now have greater freedom, are less likely to be victimized and oppressed by men, and are less likely to be dependent on them. Simon placed less emphasis than Adler did on the women's movement and more on changes in the job market. She argued that with new opportunities for women, the number of business-related and property crimes committed by women would likely rise (R. Simon, 1975:19).

But has female criminality really changed? From 1960 to 1990 the female share of all arrests rose from 10 percent to 20 percent. This shift was most evident among women under 18 and older women. For both age groups the greatest increase was for larceny/theft—for older women, this mainly took the form of fraud and forgery (Daly, 1998:88). From 1995 to 2004, arrests of men declined by 27 percent, apparently in conjunction with falling crime rates. By contrast, arrests of women increased by more than 9 percent over the same period, so that women constituted 24 percent of suspects arrested in 2004. Although arrests of men declined over that period for every serious offense except drug abuse, women experienced jumps in arrests for drug abuse, assault, and embezzlement. For many crimes, women remain minor players. Women make up a relatively small percentage of arrestees for all types of crime except larceny/theft, fraud, embezzlement, and, among juveniles, being runaways (FBI, 2005a).

To what extent has the lawbreaking behavior of women changed? It appears that the increases in arrests for embezzlement and fraud may indicate that expanding job opportunities have created new opportunities for criminal behavior, just as several scholars predicted. We must also consider that some increases in arrests and prosecutions may stem from police and prosecutors treating women in

Laura Morris and her attorney listen to Judge John Ross during Morris's arraignment in Bellefontaine, Ohio, on charges of using her four children to shoplift and then selling the items on eBay. The number of women arrested has increased during the past decade, with larceny/theft the most frequent Index Crime charged.

the same manner as they treat men rather than treating women in a paternalistic manner by reducing or dropping charges.

ASSESSING THEORIES OF CRIMINALITY

Scholars have presented evidence to support aspects of each theory of crime (see Table 2.3). This does not mean, however, that the strength of supporting evidence is the same for each theory. In addition, some research may provide evidence for more than one theory. For example, research about the impact of neighborhoods may have implications for both social structure and social process theories (Kurbrin and Stewart, 2006). When criminologists theorize that a recent rise in murders among young people in Boston is attributable, in part, to a "street culture" in which lethal violence is used to preserve reputations and respect (Llana, 2006), does that reflect social structure, social processes, or some other theory? As yet, no theory is accurate enough to predict criminality or establish a specific cause for an offender's behavior. See "Real-World Activity" at the end of this chapter for more on the policy implications of theory.

The theories are limited in other ways as well. They tend to focus on visible crimes and the poor. They have less to say about upper-class or organized crime. Most of the theories also focus on male behavior. What is missing, and truly needed,

TABLE 2.3	Major Theories of Criminality and Their Policy Implications

Scholars and the public support various types of policies. We know little about the real causes of crime, but note how many people think they have the answers!

Theory	Major Premise	Policy Implications	Policy Implementation
Biological	Genetic, biochemical, or neurological defects cause some people to commit crime.	Identification and treatment or control of persons with crime-producing biological factors. Selective incapacitation, intensive supervision. *STERILIZATION*	1 Use of drugs to inhibit biological urges of sex offenders. 2 Use of controlled diet to reduce levels of antisocial behavior caused by biochemical imbalances. 3 Identification of neurological defects through CAT scans. Use of drugs to suppress violent impulses. 4 Special education for those with learning disabilities.
Psychological	Personality and learning factors cause some people to commit crime.	Treatment of those with personality disorders to achieve mental health. Those whose illegal behavior stems from learning should have their behavior punished so they will realize that crime is not rewarded.	1 Psychotherapy and counseling to treat personality disorders. 2 Behavior modification strategies, such as electric shock and other negative impulses, to change learned behavior. 3 Counseling to enhance moral development. 4 Intensive individual and group therapies.
Social Structure	Crime is the result of underlying social conditions such as poverty, inequality, and unemployment.	Actions taken to reform social conditions that breed crime. *RESTRICT ADVERTISIN.*	1 Education and job-training programs. 2 Urban redevelopment to improve housing, education, and health care. 3 Community development to provide economic opportunities.
Social Process	Crime is normal learned behavior and is subject to either social control or labeling effects.	Individuals to be treated in groups, with emphasis on building conventional bonds and avoiding stigmatization.	1 Youth programs that emphasize positive role models. 2 Community organizing to establish neighborhood institutions and bonds that emphasize following society's norms. 3 Programs designed to promote family stability.
Social Conflict	Criminal definitions and punishments are used by some groups to control other groups.	Fundamental changes in the political and social systems to reduce class conflict.	1 Development of programs to remove injustice in society. 2 Provision of resources to assist women, minorities, and the poor in dealing with the criminal justice system and other government agencies. 3 Modification of criminal justice to deal similarly with crimes committed by upper-class members and crimes committed by lower-class members.
Life Course	Offenders have criminal careers that often begin with pathways into youth crime but can change and end through turning points in life.	Foster positive turning points such as marriage and stable employment.	1 Policies to reduce entry pathways associated with youth incarceration and substance abuse. 2 Policies to promote educational success, full employment, successful marriages, and stable families.

is a theory that merges these disparate ideas about the causes of crime. Once we have a complete and testable account of what causes crime, we can develop better policies to deal with it.

CHECKPOINT

		Answers
10.	What were the main assumptions of the classical school of criminology?	10. Criminal behavior is rational, and the fear of punishment keeps people from committing crimes.
11.	What are the different kinds of sociological theories?	11. Social structure theories; social process theories; social conflict theories.
12.	What are potential turning points for criminal careers in life course theories?	12. Military service, employment, marriage.

A QUESTION OF ETHICS: WRITING ASSIGNMENT

Imagine the following scenarios: Two women, who live in different cities, arise early one morning to prepare to leave for their jobs at different insurance companies. As single parents, they both bear the responsibility of providing financial support as well as parental guidance to their children. After one woman parks in the underground garage next to her office building, an unfamiliar man sneaks up behind her, places a handgun against her face, and demands her purse and the keys to her car. Because she is startled and frightened, she drops her keys and reflexively bends to retrieve them. When she moves, the gun goes off and she is killed. In the other city, the woman is sitting at her desk in her office tower when suddenly her entire office suite bursts into flames in an explosion. She is killed instantly. The date is September 11, 2001. One woman has been killed in a parking garage in the Midwest and the other has died in the hijackers' attack on the World Trade Center in New York City.

In the aftermath of the September 11 tragedy, Congress enacted legislation to compensate victims with financial awards that exceed those of victim compensation programs and instead match the kinds of significant awards that someone might win in a wrongful death lawsuit. Thus, the family of the woman killed at the World Trade Center would be eligible for significant financial support from the federal government to replace the income that she would have provided for her family. By contrast, the family of the woman killed in the parking garage would receive very little. If the state's law provided for compensation, it would probably be a modest amount that might not even cover the cost of the funeral. Both women were killed during sudden attacks by strangers. Both women left behind children who had relied on them for financial support as well as emotional support and parental guidance.

WRITING ASSIGNMENT

Is it ethical for the federal government to provide financial support for one victim's family but not for the other? Are there any persuasive reasons to treat the two families differently? Imagine that you are the advisor to a commission that must propose a policy concerning compensation for future crime victims as well as future victims of terrorist attacks. Write a memo explaining how you would treat these two groups for purposes of government compensation. Be sure to explain the reasons for your recommendation.

REAL-WORLD ACTIVITY: AN APPLICATION

You are the advisor to a governor who wants to develop public policies that address the root causes of crime. The governor wants to learn about different criminological theories and their connection to possible policy choices.

RESEARCHING THE INTERNET

Go to InfoTrac College Edition. Enter the keyword *crime rates,* then read the editorial in the *Record* (Stockton, California) entitled "How to Arrest High Crime Rates," February 3, 2006.

APPLICATION

Which suggestions, if any, in the editorial are connected to a specific theory of criminality? In making recommendations to the governor, can you draw from the editorial's suggestions in discussing theories of criminality? Make a list of your own public policy recommendations. Which of these would fit with a biological theory of crime? Which would follow from a psychological theory of crime? Which would you make if the governor adopted various sociological theories of crime? Would any recommendations facilitate "turning points" or block "pathways into crime" under life course theories?

SUMMARY

- There are six broad categories of crime: visible crime, occupational crime, organized crime, crimes without victims, political crime, and cyber crime.

- The amount of crime is difficult to measure. The Uniform Crime Reports and the National Crime Victimization Surveys are the best sources of crime data.

- Crime rates are affected by changes in social conditions, including demographic trends and unemployment rates.

- Young male residents of lower-income communities are among those most likely to be victimized by crime.

- Because of the connection between race and social status in the United States, African Americans are more frequently victimized by crime than are whites.

- A significant percentage of crimes, especially those against women, are committed by acquaintances and relatives of victims.

- Because of the financial and other costs it produces, crime significantly affects all of society.

- Government agencies have begun to be more sensitive to the needs of crime victims. Thus, there are now programs in many places to provide services and compensation.

- Scholars have begun to study the role that victims may play in facilitating crimes.

- The classical school of criminology emphasized reform—of criminal law, procedures, and punishments.

- The rise of science led to the positivist school, which viewed behavior as stemming from social, biological, and psychological factors.

- Positivist criminology has dominated the study of criminal behavior since the beginning of the twentieth century.

- Biological theories of crime claim that physiological and neurological factors may predispose a person to commit crimes.

- Psychological theories of crime propose that mental processes and behavior hold the key to understanding the causes of crime.

- Sociological theories of crime emphasize as causes of criminal behavior the social conditions that bear on the individual. Three types of sociological theory are social structure theories, social process theories, and social conflict theories.

- Life course theories consider pathways into crime and turning points, such as marriage, employment, and military service, that move individuals away from criminal careers.

- The criminality of women has only recently been studied. Some argue that, as society increasingly treats women and men as equals, the number of crimes committed by women will increase.

- Theories of criminality are criticized for focusing too exclusively on lower-class and male perpetrators.

QUESTIONS FOR REVIEW

1. What are the six types of crimes?

2. What are the positive and negative attributes of the two major sources of crime data?

3. Who is most likely to be victimized by crime?

4. What are the costs of crime?

5. How does the criminal justice system treat victims?

6. What are the major theories of criminality?

7. What have scholars learned about the criminal behavior of women?

KEY TERMS AND CASES

anomie (p. 55)
biological explanations (p. 53)
classical criminology (p. 52)
control theories (p. 56)
crimes without victims (p. 37)
criminogenic (p. 53)
cyber crimes (p. 38)
dark figure of crime (p. 41)
labeling theories (p. 56)
learning theories (p. 56)
life course theories (p. 57)

mala in se (p. 34)
mala prohibita (p. 34)
money laundering (p. 36)
National Crime Victimization Surveys (NCVS) (p. 43)
National Incident-Based Reporting System (NIBRS) (p. 43)
occupational crimes (p. 36)
organized crime (p. 36)
political crime (p. 38)
positivist criminology (p. 53)

psychological explanations (p. 54)
social conflict theories (p. 56)
social process theories (p. 56)
social structure theories (p. 55)
sociological explanations (p. 55)
theory of differential association (p. 56)
Uniform Crime Reports (UCR) (p. 41)
victimology (p. 45)
visible crime (p. 35)

GOING ONLINE

ThomsonNOW™

Maximize your study time by using ThomsonNOW's diagnostic study plan to help you review this chapter. The Study Plan will

- Help you identify areas on which you should concentrate

- Provide interactive exercises to help you master the chapter concepts

- Provide a posttest to confirm you are ready to move on to the next chapter

3

Criminal Justice and the Rule of Law

Twelve-year-old Christopher Pittman carried a shotgun into his grandparents' bedroom and fired two blasts, killing them as they slept. Unlike homicide cases in which the police must identify a suspect, there was no question that Pittman pulled the trigger on that tragic night in 2001. He confessed to the police. Did Pittman's action and confession guarantee that he would be found guilty and punished for killing his grandparents? No. Criminal law in the United States does not treat every harmful act and every perpetrator in the same manner, even in cases in which victims have been killed. Circumstances can arise that pose questions about whether all offenders of a given type are equally responsible and equally deserving of punishment. Christopher Pittman's case raised just such issues (Dewan and Meier, 2005).

Although Pittman was only 12 at the time of the killings, local prosecutors decided to try him as an adult. If convicted as an adult, he faced the possibility of life in prison rather than a juvenile detention sentence that would see him released in under ten years. To place a child so young on trial as an adult, even for murder, is quite unusual. Were the charges against Pittman appropriate? Can a person so young really understand and be held responsible the way an adult can be? Although American law has traditionally not treated juveniles as fully accountable for their actions, in recent years many states have permitted youths to be treated as adults when accused of serious offenses (B. Meier, 2004).

Pittman's case was further complicated by his prescription for an antidepressant drug. He came to live with his grandparents after he had been abandoned by his mother and experienced conflicts with his father. He had previously run away from home, threatened to kill himself, and spent time in a treatment center. During treatment, doctors prescribed an antidepressant drug that some researchers believed could contribute to suicidal thoughts, violence, and a lack of self-control. Because of the risk of suicide, the laws of Great Britain forbid prescribing this drug for patients under age 18.

Further, this drug had been challenged in American courts, including a case in California in which a jury found a man to be not guilty of attempted murder, because the antidepressant medication affected his behavior and made him "involuntarily intoxicated" (Redfern, 2004).

Based on the controversy surrounding the drug's potentially harmful effects, Pittman's attorneys argued that he, too, should be acquitted due to "involuntary intoxication." Under traditional criminal law, if someone became intoxicated through no fault of his or her own, such as unknowingly drinking alcohol that had been poured into a fruit drink, that person would not be held legally responsible for behaviors caused by a level of intoxication that caused him or her to lose the ability to distinguish right from wrong.

In the end, a South Carolina jury convicted Pittman of murder, and he was sentenced to 30 years in prison (Dewan and Meier, 2005). Did the case produce justice? Should someone so young have **legal responsibility** for criminal acts in the same manner as an adult? Do we really understand how prescription medications affect people's behavior, especially when such drugs are given to youths? We inevitably confront such difficult questions when we write our criminal laws and apply them to new situations in a changing world.

A primary function of criminal law is to define those behaviors that are labeled criminal and thus worthy of punishment. The law must also identify whether there are any exceptional circumstances, such as "involuntary intoxication," that will excuse otherwise punishable behavior. An additional primary function of criminal law is to describe the procedures to be followed under the U.S. adversarial system by those responsible for law enforcement, adjudication, and corrections.

In previous chapters, we saw how criminal justice operates as a system influenced by political and social forces; now we turn to a third ingredient of our analysis—law. This chapter explores the two main aspects of criminal law: substantive criminal law and the law of criminal procedure.

QUESTIONS FOR INQUIRY

- How does substantive criminal law define a crime and the legal responsibility of the accused?
- How has the United States Supreme Court interpreted the criminal justice amendments to the Constitution?

Foundations of Criminal Law

legal responsibility The accountability of an individual for a crime because of the perpetrator's behavior and the circumstances of the illegal act.

Like most Americans, you are probably aware that law and legal procedures are key elements of the criminal justice system. Americans are fond of saying that "we have a government of laws, not of men (and women)." According to our American values, we do not have a system based on the decisions of a king or dictator. In the United States even our most powerful leaders have to make decisions within limits imposed by law. The government can seek to punish only people who violate defined laws, and their guilt has to be determined through procedures established by law. Since the tragic events of September 11, however, some commentators have expressed fears that the federal government has moved away from traditional constitutional values by jailing suspected terrorists without charging them with crimes or presenting evidence to prove their involvement in wrongdoing (Turley, 2002). Thus, we find ourselves entering a new era in which the government's actions against terrorism clash with traditional American values and functions of law.

Laws tell citizens what they can and cannot do. Laws also tell government officials when they can seek to punish citizens for violations and how they must go about it. Government officials, including the President of the United States, who take actions according to their own preferences run the risk that judges will order them to take different actions that comply with the law. Government officials are expected to follow and enforce the law. Thus, in a democracy, laws are a major tool to prevent government officials from seizing too much power or using power improperly.

Criminal law is only one category of law. Peoples' lives and actions are also affected by **civil law**, which governs business deals, contracts, real estate, and the like. For example, if you damage other people's property or harm them in an accident, they may sue you to pay for the damage or harm. By contrast, the key feature of criminal law is the government's power to punish people for damage they have done to society.

Among the two categories of criminal law, **substantive criminal law** defines actions that may be punished by the government. It also defines the punishments for such offenses. Often called the "penal code," substantive law answers the question, "What is illegal?" Elected officials in Congress, state legislatures, and city councils write the substantive criminal laws. These legislators decide which kinds of behaviors are so harmful that they deserve to be punished. They also decide whether each violation should be punished by imprisonment, a fine, probation, or another kind of punishment. When questions arise about the meaning of substantive criminal laws, judges interpret the laws by seeking to fulfill the legislators' intentions.

By contrast, **procedural criminal law** defines the rules that govern how the laws will be enforced. It protects the constitutional rights of defendants and provides the rules that officials must follow in all areas of the criminal justice system. Many aspects of procedural criminal law are defined by legislatures, such as how bail will be set and which kind of preliminary hearing will take place before a trial. However, the U.S. Supreme Court and state supreme courts also play a key role in defining procedural criminal law. These courts define the meaning of constitutional rights in the U.S. Constitution and in state constitutions. Their interpretations of constitutional provisions create rules on such issues as when and how police officers can question suspects and when defendants can receive advice from their attorneys.

civil law Law regulating the relationships between or among individuals, usually involving property, contracts, or business disputes.

substantive criminal law Law that defines acts that are subject to punishment and specifies the punishments for such offenses.

procedural criminal law Law defining the procedures that criminal justice officials must follow in enforcement, adjudication, and corrections.

ThomsonNOW

Improve your grade on the exam with Personalized Study! For reinforcement resources and a mastery check of Foundations of Criminal Law, go to www.thomsonedu.com/thomsonnow.

CHECKPOINT

Answers

1. What is contained in a state's penal code? ⟶ 1. Penal codes contain substantive criminal law that defines crimes and also punishments for those crimes.

2. What is the purpose of procedural criminal law? ⟶ 2. Procedural criminal law specifies the defendants' rights and tells justice system officials how they can investigate and process cases.

Substantive Criminal Law

Substantive criminal law defines acts that are subject to punishment and specifies the punishments. It is based on the doctrine that no one may be convicted of or punished for an offense unless the offense has been defined by the law. In short, people must know in advance what is required of them. Thus, no act can be regarded as illegal until it has been defined as punishable under the criminal law. While this sounds like a simple notion, the language of law is often confusing and ambiguous. As a result, judges must become involved in interpreting the law so that the meaning intended by the legislature can be understood.

SEVEN PRINCIPLES OF CRIMINAL LAW

The major principles of Western criminal law were summarized in a single statement by legal scholar Jerome Hall (1947). To convict a defendant of a crime, prosecutors must prove that all seven principles have been fulfilled (see Figure 3.1).

1. *Legality.* There must be a law that defines the specific action as a crime. Offensive and harmful behavior is not illegal unless it has been prohibited by law before it was committed. The U.S. Constitution forbids *ex post facto laws,* or laws written and applied after the fact. Thus, when the legislature defines a new

The Draconian Code, promulgated in classical Greece in the seventh century B.C.E., is one of the earliest substantive criminal laws. It defined acts that were illegal and specified punishments for each offense.

Archive Photos

inchoate offense Conduct that is criminal even though the harm that the law seeks to prevent has not been done but merely planned or attempted.

FIGURE 3.1

The seven principles of criminal law

These principles of Western law are the basis for defining acts as criminal and the conditions required for successful prosecution.

A crime is	
1 legally proscribed	(legality)
2 human conduct	(actus reus)
3 causative	(causation)
4 of a given harm	(harm)
5 which conduct coincides	(concurrence)
6 with a blameworthy frame of mind	(mens rea)
7 and is subject to punishment	(punishment)

crime, people can be prosecuted only for violations that occur after the new law has been passed.

2. *Actus reus.* Criminal laws are aimed at human acts, including acts that a person failed to undertake. The U.S. Supreme Court has ruled that people may not be convicted of a crime simply because of their status. Under this *actus reus* requirement, for a crime to occur there must be an act of either commission or omission by the accused. In *Robinson v. California* (1962), for example, the Supreme Court struck down a California law that made it a crime to be addicted to drugs. States can prosecute people for using, possessing, selling, or transporting drugs when they catch them performing these acts, but states cannot prosecute them for the mere status of being addicted to drugs.

3. *Causation.* For a crime to have been committed, there must be a causal relationship between an act and the harm suffered. In Ohio, for example, a prosecutor tried to convict a burglary suspect on a manslaughter charge when a victim, asleep in his house, was killed by a stray bullet as officers fired at the unarmed, fleeing suspect. The burglar was acquitted on the homicide charge because his actions in committing the burglary and running away from the police were not the direct cause of the victim's death (Bandy, 1991).

4. *Harm.* To be a crime, an act must cause harm to some legally protected value. The harm can be to a person, property, or some other object that a legislature deems valuable enough to deserve protection through the government's power to punish. This principle is often questioned by those who feel that they are not committing a crime, because they may be causing harm only to themselves. Laws that require motorcyclists to wear helmets have been challenged on this ground. Such laws, however, have been written because legislatures see enough forms of harm to require protective laws. These forms of harm include injuries to helmetless riders, tragedy and loss for families of injured cyclists, and the medical costs imposed on society for head injuries that could have been prevented.

An act can be deemed criminal if it could do harm that the law seeks to prevent; this is called an **inchoate offense.** Thus, the criminal law includes conspiracies and attempts, even when the lawbreaker does not complete the intended crime. For example, people can be prosecuted for planning to murder someone or hiring a "hit man" to kill someone. The potential for grave harm from such acts justifies the application of the government's power to punish.

5. *Concurrence.* For an act to be considered a crime, the intent and the act must be present at the same time (J. Hall, 1947:85). Let us imagine that Joe is planning to murder his archenemy, Bill. He spends days planning how he will abduct Bill and carry out the murder. While driving home from work one day, Joe accidentally hits and kills a jogger who suddenly—and foolishly—runs across the busy street without looking. The jogger turns out to be Bill. Although Joe had planned to kill Bill, he is not guilty of murder, because the accidental killing was not connected to Joe's intent to carry out a killing.

6. *Mens rea.* The commission of an act is not a crime unless it is accompanied by a guilty state of mind. This concept is related to intent. It seeks to distinguish between harm-causing accidents, which generally are not subject to criminal punishment, and harm-causing crimes, in which some level of intent is present. Certain crimes require a specific level of intent; examples include first-degree murder, which is normally a planned, intentional killing, and larceny, which involves the intent to deprive an owner of his or her property permanently and unlawfully. Later in this chapter we examine several defenses, such as necessity and insanity, that can be used to assert that a person did not have **mens rea**—"guilty mind" or blameworthy state of mind—and hence should not be held responsible for a criminal offense. The element of *mens rea* becomes problematic when there are questions about an offender's capacity to understand or plan harmful activities, as when the perpetrator is mentally ill or a child.

Exceptions to the concept of *mens rea* are strict liability offenses involving health and safety, in which it is not necessary to show intent. Legislatures have criminalized certain kinds of offenses in order to protect the public. For example, a business owner may be held responsible for violations of a toxic waste law whether or not the owner actually knew that his employees were dumping polluting substances into a river. Other laws may apply strict liability to the sale of alcoholic beverages to minors. The purpose of such laws is to put pressure on business owners to make sure that their employees obey regulations designed to protect the health and safety of the public. Courts often limit the application of such laws to situations in which recklessness or indifference is present.

7. *Punishment.* There must be a provision in the law calling for punishment of those found guilty of violating the law. The punishment is enforced by the government and may carry with it social stigma, a criminal record, loss of freedom, and loss of rights.

The seven principles of substantive criminal law allow authorities to define certain acts as being against the law and provide the accused with a basis for mounting a defense against the charges. During a criminal trial, defense attorneys will often try to show that one of the seven elements either is unproven or can be explained in a way that is acceptable under the law.

mens rea "Guilty mind" or blameworthy state of mind, necessary for legal responsibility for a criminal offense; criminal intent, as distinguished from innocent intent.

ELEMENTS OF A CRIME

Legislatures define certain acts as crimes when they fulfill the seven principles just outlined under certain "attendant circumstances" while the offender has a certain state of mind. These three factors—the act (*actus reus*), the attendant circumstances, and the state of mind (*mens rea*)—are together called the *elements* of a crime. They can be seen in the following section from a state penal code:

Section 3502. Burglary 1 Offense defined: A person is guilty of burglary if he enters a building or occupied structure, or separately secured or occupied portion thereof, with intent to commit a crime therein, unless the premises are at the time open to the public or the actor is licensed or privileged to enter.

The elements of burglary are, therefore, entering a building or occupied structure (*actus reus*) with the intent to commit a crime therein (*mens rea*) at a time when the premises are not open to the public and the actor is not invited or otherwise entitled to enter (attendant circumstances). For an act to be a burglary, all three elements must be present.

STATUTORY DEFINITIONS OF CRIMES

Federal and state penal codes often define criminal acts somewhat differently. To find out how a state defines an offense, one must read its penal code; this will give a general idea of which acts are illegal. To understand the court's interpretations of the code, one must analyze the judicial opinions that have sought to clarify the law.

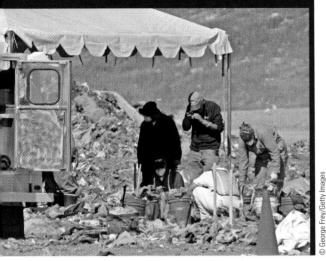

Salt Lake City investigators photograph a human body believed to be a murder victim. Police must find the perpetrator, and prosecutors must convince a jury that the crime fits the definition of criminal homicide as outlined in the penal code.

© George Frey/Getty Images

The classification of criminal acts becomes complicated when statutes divide related acts, such as taking a person's life, into different offenses. For example, the definition of criminal homicide has been subdivided into degrees of murder and voluntary and involuntary manslaughter. In addition, some states have created new categories, such as reckless homicide, negligent homicide, and vehicular homicide. Each of these definitions involves slight variations in the *actus reus* and the *mens rea*. Table 3.1 defines these offenses according to the Uniform Crime Reports, which count murder and nonnegligent manslaughter as index offenses.

In legal language, the phrase *malice aforethought* is used to distinguish murder from manslaughter. This phrase indicates that the crime of murder is a deliberate, premeditated, and willful killing of another human being. Most states extend the definition of murder to these two circumstances: (1) defendants knew their behavior had a strong chance of causing death, showed indifference to life, and thus recklessly engaged in conduct that caused death or (2) defendants' behavior caused death while they were committing a felony. Mitigating circumstances, such as "the heat of passion" or extreme provocation, would reduce the offense to manslaughter, because the requirement of malice aforethought would be absent or reduced. Similarly, manslaughter would include a death resulting from an attempt to defend oneself that was not fully excused as self-defense. It might also include a death resulting from recklessness or negligence.

The definitions of crimes and required proof in the American system differ from those in other systems. The definitions of crimes and punishments reflect the values of a particular system of justice. An act committed in one country may not be a crime, yet if that same act were committed elsewhere, it might be punished harshly. The Comparative Perspective on traditional Islamic criminal law provides examples

---

TABLE 3.1   Definitions of Offenses in the Uniform Crime Reports (Part I)

The exact descriptions of offenses differ from one state to another, but these UCR definitions provide a national standard that helps us distinguish among criminal acts.

1 **Criminal homicide:**

   a. Murder and nonnegligent manslaughter: the willful (nonnegligent) killing of one human being by another. Deaths caused by negligence, attempts to kill, assaults to kill, suicides, accidental deaths and justifiable homicides are excluded. Justifiable homicides are limited to (1) the killing of a felon by a law enforcement officer in the line of duty and (2) the killing of a felon by a private citizen.

   b. Manslaughter by negligence: the killing of another person through gross negligence. Excludes traffic fatalities. While manslaughter by negligence is a Part I crime, it is not included in the Crime Index.

2 **Forcible rape:**

   The carnal knowledge of a female forcibly and against her will. Included are rapes by force and attempts or assaults to rape. Statutory offenses (no force used—victim under age of consent) are excluded.

3 **Robbery:**

   The taking or attempting to take anything of value from the care, custody, or control of a person or persons by force or threat of force of violence and/or by putting the victim in fear.

4 **Aggravated assault:**

   An unlawful attack by one person upon another for the purpose of inflicting severe or aggravated bodily injury. This type of assault usually is accompanied by the use of a weapon or by means likely to produce death or great bodily harm. Simple assaults are excluded.

5 **Burglary—breaking or entering:**

   The unlawful entry of a structure to commit a felony or a theft. Attempted forcible entry is included.

6 **Larceny/theft (except motor vehicle theft):**

   The unlawful taking, carrying, leading, or riding away of property from the possession or constructive possession of another. Examples are thefts of bicycles or automobile accessories, shoplifting, pocket picking, or the stealing of any property or article that is not taken by force and violence or by fraud. Attempted larcenies are included. Embezzlement, "con" games, forgery, worthless checks, and so on, are excluded.

7 **Motor vehicle theft:**

   The theft or attempted theft of a motor vehicle. A motor vehicle is self-propelled and runs on the surface and not on rails. Specifically excluded from this category are motorboats, construction equipment, airplanes, and farming equipment.

8 **Arson:**

   Any willful or malicious burning or attempt to burn, with or without intent to defraud, a dwelling house, a public building, a motor vehicle or an aircraft, the personal property of another, and so on.

Source: Federal Bureau of Investigation, *Crime in the United States, 2001* (Washington, DC: U.S. Government Printing Office, 2002).

of approaches that differ from those in the United States. These traditional approaches are not advocated by all Muslims and are not followed in all countries in which Muslims constitute a majority of the population. However, these approaches operate in several locations around the world and they are advocated by many fundamentalists who seek to have their interpretation of Islam control law and government.

RESPONSIBILITY FOR CRIMINAL ACTS

entrapment The defense that the individual was induced by the police to commit the criminal act.

Of the seven principles of criminal law, *mens rea* is crucial in establishing responsibility for the act. To obtain a conviction, the prosecution must show that the offender not only committed the illegal act but also did so in a state of mind that makes it appropriate to hold him or her responsible for the act. In 2002, two Florida brothers pleaded guilty and accepted eight-year prison sentences for killing their sleeping father with a baseball bat when they were 12 and 13 years of age, despite their mother's claim that they did not understand the charges and the plea agreement (Kaczor, 2002). Were these young boys old enough to plan their crimes and understand the consequences of their actions? Is a child capable of forming the same intent to commit a crime that an adult can form? The analysis of *mens rea* is difficult because the court must inquire into the defendant's mental state at the time the offense was committed. It is not easy to know what someone was thinking when he or she performed an act.

Although many defendants admit that they committed the harmful act, they may still plead not guilty. They may do so not only because they know that the state must prove them guilty but also because they—or their attorneys—believe that *mens rea* was not present. Accidents are the clearest examples of such situations: The defendant argues that it was an accident that the pedestrian suddenly crossed into the path of the car.

The absence of *mens rea,* as we have seen, does not guarantee a verdict of not guilty in every case. In most cases, however, it relieves defendants of responsibility for acts that would be labeled criminal if they had been intentional. Besides the defense of accidents, there are eight defenses based on lack of criminal intent: entrapment, self-defense, necessity, duress, immaturity, mistake of fact, intoxication, and insanity.

Entrapment   Entrapment is a defense that can be used to show lack of intent. The law excuses a defendant when it is shown that government agents have induced the person to commit the offense. That does not mean the police may not use undercover agents to set a trap for criminals, nor does it mean the police may not provide ordinary opportunities for the commission of a crime. But the entrapment defense may be used when the police have acted so as to encourage the criminal act.

Entrapment raises tough questions for judges, who must decide whether the police went too far toward making a crime occur that otherwise would not have happened (D. D. Camp, 1993). The key question is the predisposition of the defendant. In 1992 the Supreme Court stressed that the prosecutor must show beyond a reasonable doubt that a defendant was predisposed to break the law before he or she was approached by government agents. The Court's decision invalidated the conviction of a Nebraska farmer who purchased child pornography after receiving multiple solicitation letters from law enforcement officials pretending to be pen pals and bookstore operators (*United States v. Jacobson*).

While suffering from paranoid schizophrenia, Eric Clark shot and killed a Flagstaff, Arizona, police officer during a routine traffic stop. He was found incompetent to stand trial and spent the next three years in a mental hospital. After receiving treatment, he was deemed competent and he pleaded not guilty by reason of insanity. However, Arizona law does not allow a defendant to present evidence of diminished mental capacity with criminal intent. A defendant must request a verdict of "guilty except insane" and must then show that at the time of the crime he did not know his conduct was wrong. Clark was convicted and received a life sentence. He appealed his conviction to the U.S. Supreme Court on the ground that Arizona had not provided him with due process. In a 2006 decision the Court upheld the Arizona law.

AP Photo/Arizona Daily Sun/Greg Bryan

COMPARATIVE PERSPECTIVE

Islamic Criminal Law

*T*he rise of fundamentalist Islamic thought throughout the world has made Americans aware of great cultural differences between American legal traditions and those of the segment of Muslims who seek to have their governments run according to their interpretations of religious rules. Islamic criminal law, in particular, differs significantly from justice as it is administered in the Western democracies. Countries that define their crimes and punishments according to Shari'a, *the law of Islam, appear harsh in the eyes of many Americans. Bear in mind, however, that there are different Islamic sects and therefore not all Muslim countries interpret and apply* Shari'a *in the same way. What are some of the major differences that exist between the American system and the elements of Islamic law described here?*

The U.S. State Department, the federal government agency responsible for foreign affairs, publishes annual reports on human rights in countries around the world. The 2004 report on Saudi Arabia provided a glimpse of stark differences between that country's approach to crime and punishment and the approach taken in the United States. According to the *Country Reports on Human Rights Practices* (U.S. Department of State, 2004):

> The Government punished criminals according to its interpretation of *Shari'a.* Punishments included imprisonment, flogging, amputation, and execution by beheading. . . . Authorities punished repeated thievery and other repeated offenses by amputation of the right hand and left foot. . . . [Religious police] reportedly detained young men for offenses including eating in restaurants with young women. . . . Women of many nationalities were detained for actions such as riding in a taxi with a man who was not their relative.

Very few countries actually follow Islamic law to define their crimes and punishments. Although Saudi Arabia and Sudan do, for example, Iran suspended the religion-based use of amputation and execution by stoning in December 2002, although the government can still enforce crimes defined by Islamic law. Pakistan defines some crimes and punishments according to the *Shari'a*, but over the past 20 years it has only used ordinary punishments, such as imprisonment, rather than amputation and

other religious punishments. However, in following religious laws, Pakistan can create difficult issues of proof of a crime. As described by one *New York Times* reporter after a Pakistani court overturned a rape conviction in a case that drew international attention and outrage: "In Pakistan, if a woman reports a rape, four Muslim men must generally act as witnesses before she can prove her case. Otherwise, she risks being charged with fornication or adultery—and suffering a public whipping and long imprisonment" (Kristof, 2005). Afghanistan incorporates aspects of Islamic law as demonstrated by the controversy generated in 2005 when a man, who was eventually allowed to leave the country, was threatened with execution by the Afghan justice system for converting from Islam to Christianity (Munadi and Hauser, 2006).

Despite its infrequent use by national governments, Islamic law may be applied in local villages in places such as Pakistan and Afghanistan. In various other countries, including Nigeria and Iraq, advocates are pushing for its use throughout society. Because the use of Islamic law is one focal point for activists seeking to turn these countries into religion-based governments, it is useful to compare the *Shari'a* with the American approach.

Such practices as stoning for adultery and amputation for theft give Americans the perception that Islamic law is exceptionally harsh. What most Americans do not realize is that there are judicial and evidentiary safeguards within the *Shari'a.* One reason that the national government of Pakistan has not imposed punishments from the *Shari'a* is that conviction for these crimes requires the presentation of specific evidence and a higher standard of proof than in nonreligious systems. Islamic criminal law is concerned with (1) the safety of the public from physical attack, insult, and humiliation; (2) the stability of the family; (3) the protection of property against theft, destruction, or unauthorized interference; and (4) the protection of the government and the Islamic faith against subversion.

Criminal acts are divided into three categories. *Hudud* offenses are crimes against God, and punishment is specified in the Koran and the Sunna, a compilation of Muhammad's statements. *Quesas* and *Tesars* are crimes against others such as those that threaten a family's livelihood, including physical assault and murder, which are punishable by retaliation—"the return of life for a life in case of murder." As shown here for the seven *Hudud*

Self-Defense   A person who feels that he or she is in immediate danger of being harmed by another person may ward off the attack in *self-defense*. The laws of most states also recognize the right to defend others from attack, to protect property, and to prevent a crime. For example, in August 2002, T. J. Duckett, an African American player on the Atlanta Falcons professional football team, was attacked by three white men who also yelled racial slurs at him as he walked toward his car after a concert. After Duckett lost a tooth and suffered a cut that required four stitches when he was struck with a bottle in the surprise attack, the 250-pound running back defended himself. He knocked one attacker unconscious and caused a second attacker to be hospitalized with injuries. The third attacker ran away when their intended victim fought back against them. The attackers received the most serious injuries, yet they faced criminal charges because Duckett was entitled to defend himself with reasonable force against an unprovoked criminal assault (Winkeljohn, 2002).

The level of force used in self-defense cannot exceed the person's reasonable perception of the threat. Thus, a person may be justified in shooting a robber who is holding a gun to her head and threatening to kill her, but homeowners generally are offenses, the Koran defines the crime, specifies the elements of proof required, and sets the punishment.

THEFT

Theft is the taking of property belonging to another, the value of which is equal to or exceeds a prescribed amount, usually set at ten dirhams or about 75 cents. The property must be taken from the custody of another person in a secret manner, and the thief must obtain full possession of the property. "Custody" requires that the property should have been under guard or in a place of safekeeping.

By contrast, American criminal law focuses on ownership rather than custody, so that stealing something left in the open, including items sitting unattended in public places, clearly falls under laws against theft if the offender intends to take items known to be owned by others.

EXTRAMARITAL SEXUAL ACTIVITY

Sexual relations outside marriage are believed to undermine marriage and lead to family conflict, jealousy, divorce, litigation, and the spread of disease.

Some American states continue to criminalize adultery and premarital cohabitation through old laws that remain on the books. However, these laws are rarely enforced, and many prosecutors doubt whether juries will convict people of such offenses, because society has become more tolerant of such commonplace behavior.

DEFAMATION

In addition to false accusations of fornication, this offense includes impugning the legitimacy of a woman's child. Defamation by a husband of his wife leads to divorce and is not subject to punishment.

Defamation under American law can lead to civil lawsuits concerning harmful falsehoods spoken or written about a person that significantly harm that person's reputation.

HIGHWAY ROBBERY

This crime interferes with commerce and creates fear among travelers and is therefore subject to punishment.

American robbery statutes typically apply in all contexts and do not focus on travelers. The primary exception is "carjacking" statutes enacted by Congress and state legislatures in response to highly publicized incidents of drivers being killed and injured by robbers who forcibly stole their vehicles as they sat at traffic lights or stop signs.

USE OF ALCOHOL

Drinking wine and other intoxicating beverages is prohibited because it brings about indolence and inattention to religious duties.

By contrast, alcoholic beverages are legal in the United States, subject to regulations concerning the legal drinking age and criminal statutes concerning the operation of vehicles while a person is under the influence of alcohol.

APOSTASY

This is the voluntary renunciation of Islam. The offense is committed by any Muslim who converts to another faith, worships idols, or rejects any of the tenets of Islam.

In the United States, the First Amendment protections for freedom of religion and freedom of speech permit people to change religions and to criticize the religions of others without fear of criminal prosecution.

REBELLION

Rebellion is the intentional, forceful overthrow or attempted overthrow of the legitimate leader of the Islamic state.

In the United States, the government can change only through the process of democratic elections. Any effort to use force as the means to overthrow the government will result in criminal prosecution.

Sources: From Nicholas D. Kristof, "When Rapists Walk Free," *New York Times*, March 5, 2005, http://www.nytimes.com; U.S. Department of State, *Country Reports on Human Rights Practices*, 2004, http://www.state.gov; Council of Foreign Relations, "Governing under *Sharia*," March 14, 2003 (http://www.cfr.org); *Islamic Criminal Law and Procedure: An Introduction*, by M. Lippman, S. McConville, and M. Yerushalmi, 42–43. Copyright © 1988 by Praeger Publishers. Reprinted by permission of Greenwood Publishing Group, Inc., Westport, CT; A. A. Mansour, "Hudud Crimes," in M. C. Bassiouni (ed.), *The Islamic Criminal Justice System*, 195. Copyright © 1982 by Oceana Publications.

not justified in shooting an unarmed burglar who has left the house and is running across the lawn. See "Real-World Activity" at the end of the chapter for more on self-defense.

Necessity   Unlike self-defense, in which a defendant feels that he or she must harm an aggressor to ward off an attack, the *necessity* defense is used when people break the law in order to save themselves or prevent some greater harm. A person who speeds through a red light to get an injured child to the hospital or breaks into a building to seek refuge from a hurricane could claim to be violating the law out of necessity.

The English case *The Queen v. Dudley and Stephens* (1884) is a famous example of necessity. After their ship sank, four sailors were adrift in the ocean without food or water. Twenty days later, two of the sailors, Thomas Dudley and Edwin Stephens, killed the youngest sailor, the cabin boy, and ate his flesh. Four days later they were rescued by a passing ship. When they returned to England, they were tried and convicted for murder because the court did not accept their claim of necessity. However, their sentences were later reduced from the death penalty to six months in prison.

Duress (Coercion)   The defense of *duress* arises when someone commits a crime because he or she is coerced by another person. During a bank robbery, for instance, if an armed robber forces one of the bank's customers at gunpoint to drive the getaway car, the customer would be able to claim duress. However, courts generally are not willing to accept this defense if people do not try to escape from the situation.

Immaturity   Anglo American law excuses criminal acts by children under age seven on the grounds of their *immaturity* and lack of responsibility for their actions—*mens rea* is not present. Common law has presumed that children aged 7–14 are not liable for their criminal acts; however, prosecutors have been able to present evidence of a child's mental capacity to form *mens rea*. Juries can assume the presence of a guilty mind if it can be shown, for example, that the child hid evidence or tried to bribe a witness. As a child grows older, the assumption of immaturity weakens. Since the development of juvenile courts in the 1890s, children above age seven generally have not been tried by the same rules as adults. In some situations, however, children may be tried as adults—if, for example, they are repeat offenders or are charged with a particularly heinous crime. Because of the public's concerns about violent crimes by young people, in the 1990s it became increasingly common to see prosecutors seek to hold children responsible for serious crimes in the same manner that adults are held responsible. For example, in Cincinnati a 14-year-old boy was tried as an adult for murder after shooting a man during a robbery. Upon conviction, the judge ordered that the boy serve at least 27 years of his life sentence before being eligible for possible release on parole (Kettler, 2005).

Mistake of Fact   The courts have generally upheld the view that ignorance of the law is no excuse for committing an illegal act. But what if there is a *mistake of fact?* If an accused person has made a mistake on some crucial fact, that may serve as a defense (Christopher, 1994). For example, suppose some teenagers ask your permission to grow sunflowers in a vacant lot behind your home. You help them weed the garden and water the plants. Then it turns out that they are growing marijuana. You were not aware of this because you have no idea what a marijuana plant looks like. Should you be convicted for growing an illegal drug on your property? The answer depends on the specific degree of knowledge and intent that the prosecution must prove for that offense. The success of such a defense may also depend on the extent to which jurors understand and sympathize with your mistake.

Intoxication   The law does not relieve an individual of responsibility for acts performed while voluntarily intoxicated. There are, however, cases in which *intoxication* can be used as a defense, as when a person has been tricked into consuming a substance without knowing that it may cause intoxication. Christopher Pittman's attorney attempted unsuccessfully to use this defense by arguing that the boy's prescribed antidepressant drugs caused his violent behavior. Other complex cases arise in which the defendant must be shown to have had a specific, rather than a general, intent to commit a crime. For example, people may claim that they were too drunk to realize that they had left a restaurant without paying the bill. Drunkenness can also be used as a mitigating factor to reduce the seriousness of a charge.

In 1996 the U.S. Supreme Court narrowly approved a Montana law that barred the use of evidence of intoxication, even for defendants who claimed that their condition prevented them from forming the specific intent necessary to be guilty of a crime (*Montana v. Egelhoff*). Thus, states may enact laws that prevent the use of an intoxication defense.

Insanity   The defense of *insanity* has been a subject of heated debate. It is available in all but four states (Idaho, Montana, Nevada, and Utah). The public believes that many criminals "escape" punishment through the skillful use of psychiatric testimony. Yet, only about 1 percent of incarcerated offenders are held in mental hospitals because they were found "not guilty by reason of insanity." The insanity defense is rare and is generally used only in serious cases or where there is no other valid defense.

Over time, U.S. courts have used five tests of criminal responsibility involving insanity: the *M'Naghten* Rule, the Irresistible Impulse Test, the *Durham* Rule, the *Model Penal Code*'s Substantial Capacity Test, and the test defined in the federal Comprehensive Crime Control Act of 1984. These tests are summarized in Table 3.2.

M'NAGHTEN RULE More than a dozen states use the *M'Naghten* Rule, which was developed in England in 1843. In that year Daniel M'Naghten was acquitted of killing Edward Drummond, a man he had thought was Sir Robert Peel, the prime minister of Great Britain. M'Naghten claimed that he had been delusional at the time of the killing. The British court developed a standard for determining criminal responsibility known as the "right-from-wrong test." It asks whether "at the time of the committing of the act, the party accused was laboring under such a defect of reason, from disease of the mind, as not to know the nature and quality of the act he was doing, or if he did know it that he did not know he was doing what was wrong" (*M'Naghten's Case*, 1843).

IRRESISTIBLE IMPULSE TEST Four states supplemented the *M'Naghten* Rule with the Irresistible Impulse Test. Because psychiatrists argued that some people can feel compelled by their mental illness to commit criminal actions even though they recognize the wrongfulness of their conduct, the Irresistible Impulse Test was designed to bring the *M'Naghten* Rule in line with modern psychiatry. This test excuses defendants when a mental disease was controlling their behavior even though they knew that what they were doing was wrong.

THE *DURHAM* RULE The *Durham* Rule, originally developed in New Hampshire in 1871, was adopted by the Circuit Court of Appeals for the District of Columbia in 1954 in the case of *Durham v. United States*. Under this rule, the accused is not criminally responsible "if an unlawful act is the product of mental disease or mental defect."

MODEL PENAL CODE'S SUBSTANTIAL CAPACITY TEST It was argued that the *Durham* Rule offered no useful definition of "mental disease or defect." By 1972 (*United States v. Brawner*) the federal courts had overturned the *Durham* Rule in favor of a modified version of a test proposed in the *Model Penal Code* (a penal code developed by the American Bar Association as a model of what "should" be). By 1982 all federal courts and about half of the state courts had adopted the *Model Penal Code*'s Substantial Capacity Test, which states that a person is not responsible for criminal conduct "if at the time of such conduct as a result of mental disease or defect he lacks substantial capacity either to appreciate the criminality [wrongfulness] of his conduct or to conform his conduct to the requirements of law." The Substantial

TABLE 3.2   Insanity Defense Standards

The standards for the insanity defense have evolved over time.

Test	Legal Standard Because of Mental Illness	Final Burden of Proof	Who Bears Burden of Proof
M'Naghten (1843)	"Didn't know what he was doing or didn't know it was wrong."	Varies from proof by a balance of probabilities on the defense to proof beyond a reasonable doubt on the prosecutor	
Irresistible Impulse (1897)	"Could not control his conduct."		
Durham (1954)	"The criminal act was caused by his mental illness."	Beyond a reasonable doubt	Prosecutor
Model Penal Code (1972)	"Lacks substantial capacity to appreciate the wrongfulness of his conduct or to control it."	Beyond a reasonable doubt	Prosecutor
Present federal law	"Lacks capacity to appreciate the wrongfulness of his conduct."	Clear and convincing evidence	Defense

Source: National Institute of Justice, *Crime File*, "Insanity Defense," a film prepared by Norval Morris (Washington, DC: U.S. Government Printing Office, n.d.).

CLOSE UP

The Insanity Defense and Its Aftermath

Defendants who are judged not guilty by reason of insanity are typically committed to mental hospitals. If medical experts subsequently determine that they are not a danger to themselves or the community, they may be released. New York law provides the opportunity for a jury trial if a person acquitted through the insanity defense wants to challenge a judge's decision to extend the length of confinement in a mental hospital. In April 1999 Albert Fentress, a former school teacher, sought such a jury trial. Twenty years earlier, he had tortured, killed, and cannibalized a teenager but had been found not guilty by reason of insanity. The jury listened to four expert witnesses, presented by the prosecution, who asserted that Fentress had not changed during two decades in the hospital. They also listened to four expert witnesses, including doctors from the state's psychiatric facility, who said that Fentress no longer posed a danger to society. How can jurors drawn from among average citizens in the general public know which set of experts presented the most accurate diagnosis? In the end, the jury voted 5 to 1 that although Fentress was still mentally ill, he no longer needed to be confined to the hospital.

Undoubtedly, many members of the public would be shocked to think that someone, such as Fentress, who has committed an outrageous, gruesome murder could be released to walk freely among the rest of us in society. Many members of the public were probably equally shocked in 1999 when John Hinckley, Jr., the man who shot President Ronald Reagan in 1981, was granted permission to take supervised outings away from the mental hospital where he had been confined after successfully presenting an insanity defense. Some states have sought to prevent the release of mentally ill violent offenders by enacting statutes that permit the state to hold such people in mental hospitals after they have finished serving prison sentences. In 1997 the U.S. Supreme Court approved the use of such laws for people diagnosed as "sexually violent predators" (*Kansas v. Hendricks*). However, such laws apply only to people who are convicted of crimes, not to those found not guilty by reason of insanity.

An insanity acquittal does not always lead to more-lenient treatment for people committed to mental hospitals. In Virginia, for example, one-quarter of the 239 people confined to mental hospitals after asserting the insanity defense were only accused of misdemeanors. Thus, if they had been convicted, they would have served a jail sentence of one year or less. Instead, some of them may serve much longer commitments in the hospital. A man named Leroy Turner has spent more than 13 years in Virginia's Central State Hospital after having been found not guilty by reason of insanity for the misdemeanor charge of breaking a window.

Judges, politicians, and the public periodically show great concern about how the insanity defense works in practice. In the aftermath of public outcry about the impending release of Albert Fentress in New York, a state judge overturned the jury's release decision and kept Fentress in the mental hospital.

RESEARCHING THE INTERNET

To read a detailed discussion of the insanity defense and case examples, go to the corresponding site listed on the Cole/Smith Criminal Justice in America Companion Website: http://www.thomsonedu.com/criminaljustice/cole.

FOR CRITICAL ANALYSIS

Do these examples raise questions about society's commitment to the insanity defense? If there are so many problems, then why do we keep the insanity defense? What would you do about this issue?

Sources: Drawn from John Flesher, "Testimony: Defendant Thought Victim Was Antichrist," *Lansing State Journal*, June 25, 1999, p. 3D; David M. Halbfinger, "Verdict in Cannibalism Case Is Set Aside," *New York Times*, June 11, 1999; "In Virginia, Insanity Plea Can Bring Long Incarceration," *Washington Post*, June 21, 1999, p. B3; Charlie LeDuff, "Jury Decides Hospitalized Killer in Cannibalism Case Can Go Free," *New York Times*, April 22, 1999; "Man Gets Life Sentence in Killing," *Lansing State Journal*, August 4, 1999, p. 3B; Bill Miller, "Judges Let Stand Hinckley Ruling; St. Elizabeth's Officials Have Right to Decide on Day Trips," *Washington Post*, April 28, 1999, p. A7.

Capacity Test broadens and modifies the *M'Naghten* and Irresistible Impulse rules. By stressing "substantial capacity," the test does not require that a defendant be unable to distinguish right from wrong.

COMPREHENSIVE CRIME CONTROL ACT   The Comprehensive Crime Control Act of 1984 changed the federal rules on the insanity defense by limiting it to those who are unable, as a result of severe mental disease or defect, to understand the nature or wrongfulness of their acts. This change means that the Irresistible Impulse Test cannot be used in the federal courts. It also shifts the burden of proof from the prosecutor to the defendant, who has to prove his or her insanity. Further, the act creates a new procedure whereby a person who is found not guilty only by reason of insanity must be committed to a mental hospital until he or she no longer poses a danger to society. These rules apply only in federal courts, but they are spreading to the states.

All of the insanity tests are difficult to apply. Moreover, as the Close Up box shows, there are significant difficulties in deciding what to do with someone who has been found not guilty by reason of insanity. It is even possible that jurors' fears about seeing the offender turned loose might affect their decisions about whether the person was legally insane at the time of the crime.

John Hinckley's attempt to assassinate President Ronald Reagan in 1981 reopened the debate on the insanity defense. Television news footage showed that Hinckley had shot the president. Yet, with the help of psychiatrists, Hinckley's

ThomsonNOW

Improve your grade on the exam with Personalized Study! For reinforcement resources and a mastery check of Substantive Criminal Law, go to www.thomsonedu.com/thomsonnow.

lawyers were able to counteract the prosecution's efforts to persuade the jury that Hinckley was sane. When Hinckley was acquitted, the public was outraged, and several states acted to limit or abolish the insanity defense. Twelve states introduced the defense of "guilty but mentally ill" (Klofas and Yandrasits, 1989:424). This defense allows a jury to find the accused guilty but requires that he or she be given psychiatric treatment while in prison (L. A. Callahan et al., 1992).

CHECKPOINT

Answers

3. What are the seven principles of criminal law? ⟶ **3.** Legality, *actus reus,* causation, harm, concurrence, *mens rea,* punishment.

4. What are the defenses in substantive criminal law? ⟶ **4.** Entrapment, self-defense, necessity, duress (coercion), immaturity, mistake of fact, intoxication, insanity.

5. What are the tests of criminal responsibility used for the insanity defense? ⟶ **5.** *M'Naghten* Rule (right-from-wrong test), Irresistible Impulse Test, *Durham* Rule, *Model Penal Code,* Crime Control Act.

Procedural Criminal Law

Procedural law defines how the state must process cases. According to procedural due process, accused persons must be tried in accordance with legal procedures. The procedures include providing the rights granted by the Constitution to criminal defendants. As we saw in Chapter 1, the due process model is based on the premise that freedom is so valuable that efforts must be made to prevent erroneous decisions that would deprive an innocent person of his or her freedom. Rights are not only intended to prevent the innocent from being wrongly convicted. They also seek to prevent unfair police and prosecution practices aimed at guilty people, such as conducting improper searches, using violence to pressure people to confess, and denying defendants a fair trial.

The importance of procedural law has been evident throughout history. U.S. history contains many examples of police officers and prosecutors harassing and victimizing those who lack political power, including poor people, racial and ethnic minorities, and unpopular religious groups. The development of procedural safeguards through the decisions of the U.S. Supreme Court has helped protect citizens from such actions. In these decisions, the Supreme Court may favor guilty people by ordering new trials or may even release them from custody because of the weight it places on protecting procedural rights and preventing police misconduct.

Individual rights and the protection against improper deprivations of liberty represent central elements of American values. Americans expect that their rights will be protected. At the same time, however, the protection of rights for the criminally accused can clash with competing American values that emphasize the control of crime as an important component of protecting all citizens' freedom of movement and sense of security. Because the rules of procedural criminal law can sometimes lead to the release of guilty people, some observers believe that it is weighted too heavily in favor of American values emphasizing individual rights rather than equally valid American values that emphasize the protection of the community.

Public opinion does not always support the decisions by the Supreme Court and other courts that uphold the rights of criminal defendants and convicted offenders. Many Americans would prefer if other goals for society, such as stopping drugs and ensuring that guilty people are punished, took a higher priority over the protection of rights. Such opinions raise questions about Americans' commitment to the rights described in the Bill of Rights. Public opinion data indicate that most first-year college students believe that courts have placed too much emphasis on the rights of criminal defendants. Moreover, this sentiment has grown over the past 30 years. In addition, although male and female students' support for rights differed in 1971, there is little difference between the two groups today (see "What Americans Think"). Do you agree that there are too many rights? Can you identify specific rights that give too much protection to criminal defendants? Would there be any risks from reducing the rights available in the criminal justice process?

Percentage of first-year college students who agree with the statement, "There is too much concern in the courts for the rights of criminals."

1971	Total	48.1%
	Male	53.9%
	Female	41.1%
1983		68.8%
		72.5%
		65.2%
1998		72.8%
		74.3%
		71.5%
2004		56.1%
		61.0%
		55.7%

0   20   40   60   80   100

Go to http://www.thomsonedu.com/criminaljustice/cole to compare your opinion on this issue with the opinions of other criminal justice students.

Source: Bureau of Justice Statistics, *Sourcebook of Criminal Justice Statistics, 2004* (Washington, DC: U.S. Government Printing Office, 2005), Table 2.92.

The Magna Carta, signed by England's King John in 1215, is the first written guarantee of due process. It established the principle that people must be arrested and tried according to the processes outlined in the law.

Time Life Pictures/Mansell//Getty Images

Unlike substantive criminal law, which is defined by legislatures through statutes, procedural criminal law is defined by courts through judicial rulings. Judges interpret the provisions of the U.S. Constitution and state constitutions, and those interpretations establish the procedures that government officials must follow. Because it has the authority to review cases from state supreme courts as well as from federal courts, the U.S. Supreme Court has played a major role in defining procedural criminal law. The Supreme Court's influence stems from its power to define the meaning of the U.S. Constitution, especially the Bill of Rights—the first ten amendments to the Constitution, which list legal protections against actions of the government. Although public opinion may clash with Supreme Court rulings, the Supreme Court can make independent decisions because its members cannot be removed from office by the voters but only through impeachment for misconduct.

THE BILL OF RIGHTS AND THE FOURTEENTH AMENDMENT

The U.S. Constitution contained few references to criminal justice when it was ratified in 1788–1789. Because many people were concerned that the document did not set forth the rights of individuals in enough detail, ten amendments were added in 1791. These first ten amendments are known as the **Bill of Rights.** As you read the Bill of Rights, included here, note how many amendments focus on criminal justice. Although a number of amendments have implications for criminal justice, four amendments directly concern procedural criminal law. The Fourth Amendment bars unreasonable searches and seizures. The Fifth Amendment outlines basic due process rights in criminal cases. For example, consistent with the assumption that the state must prove the defendant's guilt, protection against **self-incrimination** means that persons cannot be forced to respond to questions whose answers may reveal that they have committed a crime. The protection against **double jeopardy** means that a person may be subjected to only one prosecution or punishment for a single offense within the same jurisdiction. The Sixth Amendment provides for the right to a speedy, fair, and public trial by an impartial jury, as well as the right to counsel. The Eighth Amendment bars excessive bail, excessive fines, and cruel and unusual punishment.

Bill of Rights The first ten amendments added to the U.S. Constitution to provide specific rights for individuals, including criminal justice rights concerning searches, trials, and punishments.

self-incrimination The act of exposing oneself to prosecution by being forced to respond to questions whose answers may reveal that one has committed a crime. The Fifth Amendment protects defendants against self-incrimination.

double jeopardy The subjecting of a person to prosecution more than once in the same jurisdiction for the same offense; prohibited by the Fifth Amendment.

Here are the Bill of Rights and the Fourteenth Amendment of the United States Constitution. The first ten were ratified on December 15, 1791; the Fourteenth Amendment was ratified on July 28, 1868. Refer back to these texts in the sections that follow.

First Amendment: Congress shall make no law respecting an establishment of religion, or prohibiting the free exercise thereof; or abridging the freedom of speech, or of the press; or the right of the people peaceably to assemble, and to petition the Government for redress of grievances.

Second Amendment: A well regulated Militia, being necessary for the security of a free State, the right of the people to keep and bear Arms, shall not be infringed.

Third Amendment: No Soldier shall, in time of peace, be quartered in any house, without the consent of the Owner, nor in time of war, but in a manner to be prescribed by law.

Fourth Amendment: The right of the people to be secure in their persons, houses, papers, and effects, against unreasonable searches and seizures, shall not be violated, and no Warrants shall issue, but upon probable cause, supported by Oath or affirmation, and particularly describing the place to be searched, and the persons or things to be seized.

Fifth Amendment: No person shall be held to answer for a capital or otherwise infamous crime, unless on a presentment or indictment of a Grand Jury, except in cases arising in the land or naval forces, or in the Militia, when in actual service in time of War or public danger; nor shall any person be subject for the same offence to be twice put in jeopardy of life or limb; nor shall be compelled in any criminal case to be a witness against himself, nor be deprived of life, liberty, or property, without due process of law; nor shall private property be taken for public use, without just compensation.

Sixth Amendment: In all criminal prosecutions, the accused shall enjoy the right to a speedy and public trial, by an impartial jury of the State and district wherein the crime shall have been committed, which district shall have been previously ascertained by law, and to be informed of the nature and cause of the accusation; to be confronted with the witnesses against him; to have compulsory process for obtaining witnesses in his favor, and to have the Assistance of Counsel for his defense.

Seventh Amendment: In Suits at common law, where the value in controversy shall exceed twenty dollars, the right of trial by jury shall be preserved, and no fact tried by a jury, shall be otherwise re-examined in any Court of the United States, than according to the rules of the common law.

Eighth Amendment: Excessive bail shall not be required, nor excessive fines imposed, nor cruel and unusual punishments inflicted.

Ninth Amendment: The enumeration in the Constitution, of certain rights, shall not be construed to deny or disparage others retained by the people.

Tenth Amendment: The powers not delegated to the United States by the Constitution, nor prohibited by it to the States, are reserved to the States respectively, or to the people.

Fourteenth Amendment: Section 1. All persons born or naturalized in the United States, and subject to the jurisdiction thereof, are citizens of the United States and of the State wherein they reside. No State shall make or enforce any law which shall abridge the privileges or immunities of citizens of the United States; nor shall any State deprive any person of life, liberty, or property, without due process of law; nor deny to any person within its jurisdiction the equal protection of the laws. . . .

Section 5. The Congress shall have the power to enforce, by appropriate legislation, the provisions of this article.

For most of American history the Bill of Rights did not apply to most criminal cases, because it was designed to protect people from abusive actions by the federal government. It did not seek to protect people from state and local officials, who handled nearly all criminal cases. This view was upheld by the U.S. Supreme Court in the

Barron v. Baltimore (1833) The protections of the Bill of Rights apply only to actions of the federal government.

1833 case of *Barron v. Baltimore.* However, as we shall see shortly, this view gradually changed in the late nineteenth and early twentieth centuries.

THE FOURTEENTH AMENDMENT AND DUE PROCESS

After the Civil War, three amendments were added to the Constitution. These amendments were designed to protect individuals' rights against infringement by state and local government officials. The Thirteenth Amendment abolished slavery and the Fifteenth Amendment attempted to prohibit racial discrimination in voting; these had little impact on criminal justice. However, the Fourteenth Amendment, ratified in 1868, profoundly affected it by barring states from violating people's right to due process of law. It says that "no State shall . . . deprive any person of life, liberty, or property without due process of law; nor deny to any person within its jurisdiction the equal protection of the laws." These rights to due process and equal protection served as a basis for protecting individuals from abusive actions by local criminal justice officials. However, the terms *due process* and *equal protection* are so vague that it was left to the U.S. Supreme Court to decide if and how these new rights applied to the criminal justice process.

Powell v. Alabama (1932) An attorney must be provided to a poor defendant facing the death penalty.

For example, in *Powell v. Alabama* (1932), the Supreme Court ruled that the due process clause required courts to provide attorneys for poor defendants facing the death penalty. This decision stemmed from a notorious case in Alabama in which nine African American men, known as the "Scottsboro boys," were quickly convicted and condemned to death for allegedly raping two white women, even though one of the alleged victims later admitted that she had lied about the rape (Goodman, 1994).

In these early cases, the justices had not developed clear rules for deciding which specific rights applied to state and local officials as components of the due process clause of the Fourteenth Amendment. They implied that procedures must meet a standard of **fundamental fairness.** In essence, the justices simply reacted against brutal situations that shocked their consciences. In doing so, they showed the importance of procedural criminal law in protecting individuals from abusive and unjust actions by government officials.

fundamental fairness A legal doctrine supporting the idea that so long as a state's conduct maintains basic standards of fairness, the Constitution has not been violated.

THE DUE PROCESS REVOLUTION

From the 1930s to the 1960s, the fundamental fairness doctrine was supported by a majority of the Supreme Court justices. It was applied on a case-by-case basis, not always consistently. After Earl Warren became chief justice in 1953, he led the Supreme Court in a revolution that changed the meaning and scope of constitutional rights. Instead of requiring state and local officials merely to uphold fundamental fairness, the Court began to require them to abide by the specific provisions of the Bill of Rights. Through the process of incorporation, the Supreme Court during the Warren Court era declared that elements of the Fourth, Fifth, Sixth, Eighth, and other amendments were part of the due process clause of the Fourteenth Amendment. Previously, states could design their own procedures so long as those procedures passed the fairness test. Under Warren's leadership, however, the Supreme Court's new approach imposed detailed procedural standards on the police and courts.

incorporation The extension of the due process clause of the Fourteenth Amendment to make binding on state governments the rights guaranteed in the first ten amendments to the U.S. Constitution (the Bill of Rights).

As it applied more and more constitutional rights against the states, the Court made decisions that favored the interests of many criminal defendants. These defendants had their convictions overturned and received new trials because the Court believed that it was more important to protect the values underlying criminal procedure than single-mindedly to seek convictions of criminal offenders. In the eyes of many legal scholars, the Warren Court's decisions made criminal justice processes consistent with the American values of liberty, rights, and limited government authority.

To critics, however, these decisions made the community more vulnerable to crime and thereby harmed American values by diminishing the overall sense of liberty and security in society. Warren and the other justices were strongly criticized by politicians, police chiefs, and members of the public. These critics believed that the Warren Court was rewriting constitutional law in a manner that gave too many legal protections to criminals who harm society. In addition, Warren and his colleagues were criticized for ignoring established precedents that defined rights in a limited fashion.

From 1962 to 1972 the Supreme Court, under Chief Justices Earl Warren (1953–1969) and Warren Burger (1969–1986), applied most criminal justice rights in the U.S. Constitution against the states. By the end of this period, the process of incorporation was nearly complete. Criminal justice officials at all levels—federal, state, and local—were obligated to respect the constitutional rights of suspects and defendants.

THE FOURTH AMENDMENT: PROTECTION AGAINST UNREASONABLE SEARCHES AND SEIZURES

The Fourth Amendment limits the ability of law enforcement officers to search a person or property in order to obtain evidence of criminal activity. It also limits the ability of the police to detain a person without justification (Perkins and Jamieson, 1995). When police take an individual into custody or prevent an individual from leaving a location, such detentions are considered to be "seizures" under the Fourth Amendment. As we shall examine in greater detail in Chapter 7, the Fourth Amendment does not prevent the police from conducting searches or making arrests; it merely protects people's privacy by barring "unreasonable" searches and arrests. It is up to the Supreme Court to define the situations in which a search or seizure is reasonable or unreasonable.

The use of bomb-sniffing dogs checking luggage at airports has become prevalent. Heightened security is an inconvenience to many but is believed to be a necessary precaution by most Americans. Is there a Fourth Amendment right to resist these procedures?

Joel Nito/AFP/Getty Images

The justices also face challenges in defining such words as *searches* and *seizures*. For example, in 2005 the Supreme Court ruled that no issues concerning Fourth Amendment rights arose when a K-9 officer had a trained police dog sniff the exterior of a vehicle that was stopped for a traffic violation. The dog indicated to the officer that the car's trunk contained marijuana, and that discovery led to a criminal conviction. However, unlike a *search,* for which officers must have proper justifications, the use of the dog did not require any justification, because the dog's scent-based examination of the vehicle's exterior did not invade the driver's right to privacy (*Illinois v. Caballes*). Because different Supreme Court justices do not always agree on the Constitution's meaning, the definitions of these words and the rules for police searches can change as the makeup of the Court changes.

The wording of the Fourth Amendment makes clear that the authors of the Bill of Rights did not believe that law enforcement officials should have the power to pursue criminals at all costs. The Fourth Amendment's protections apply to suspects as well as law-abiding citizens. Police officers are supposed to follow the rules for obtaining search warrants, and they are not permitted to conduct unreasonable searches even when trying to catch dangerous criminals. As we shall see in Chapter 7, improper searches that lead to the discovery of criminal evidence can lead judges to bar police and prosecutors from using that evidence to prove the suspect's guilt. Thus, police officers need to be knowledgeable about the rules for searches and seizures and to follow those rules carefully in conducting criminal investigations.

Police face challenges in attempting to respect Fourth Amendment rights while also actively seeking to prevent crimes and catch offenders. Officers may be tempted to go too far in investigating crimes without an adequate basis for suspicion and thereby violate Fourth Amendment rights. The discussion of racial profiling in Chapter 1 illustrates one aspect of the risk that officers will, by conducting stops and searches without an appropriate basis, use their authority in ways that collide with the Fourth Amendment.

THE FIFTH AMENDMENT: PROTECTION AGAINST SELF-INCRIMINATION AND DOUBLE JEOPARDY

The Fifth Amendment clearly states some key rights related to the investigation and prosecution of criminal suspects. For example, the protection against compelled self-incrimination seeks to prevent authorities from pressuring people into acting as witnesses against themselves. "Technology Issues in Criminal Justice" explores how certain devices that detect truth in people may raise questions of self-incrimination. Presumably, this right also helps to protect against torture or other rough treatment when police officers question criminal suspects. In Chapter 7, we shall discuss the Fifth Amendment rules that guide officers in questioning criminal suspects. The right against double jeopardy seeks to keep prosecutors from putting defendants on trial over and over again in repeated efforts to convict them of the same offense. One of the rights in the Fifth Amendment, the entitlement to indictment by a grand jury before being prosecuted for a serious crime, applies only in federal courts. This is one of the few rights in the Bill of Rights that the Supreme Court never applied to the states. A **grand jury** is a body of citizens drawn from the community to hear evidence from the prosecutor in order to determine whether there is a sufficient basis to move forward with a criminal prosecution. Some states use grand juries by their own choice; they are not required to do so by the Fifth Amendment. Other states simply permit prosecutors to file charges directly against criminal suspects.

grand jury Body of citizens drawn from the community to hear evidence presented by the prosecutor in order to decide whether enough evidence existed to file charges against a defendant.

Because of the limit imposed by the Fifth Amendment, a person charged with a criminal act may be subjected to only one prosecution or punishment for that offense in the same jurisdiction. As interpreted by the Supreme Court, however, the right against double jeopardy does not prevent a person from facing two trials or receiving two sanctions from the government for the same criminal acts (Henning, 1993; Hickey, 1995; Lear, 1995). Because a single criminal act may violate both state and federal laws, for example, a person may be tried in both courts. Thus, when Los Angeles police officers were acquitted of assault charges in a state court after they had been video-taped beating motorist Rodney King, they were convicted in a federal court for violating King's civil rights. The Supreme Court further refined the meaning of double jeopardy in 1996 by ruling that prosecutors could employ both property forfeiture and criminal charges against someone who grew marijuana at his home. The Court did not see this as double jeopardy, because the property forfeiture was not a "punishment" (*United States v. Ursery*). In yet another case, the Supreme Court permitted Alabama to pursue kidnapping and murder charges against a man who had already been convicted for the same murder in Georgia, because the victim was kidnapped in one state

TECHNOLOGY ISSUES IN CRIMINAL JUSTICE

Detecting Guilt

The Fifth Amendment includes protection against compelled self-incrimination. However, judicial decisions interpreting this right focus on the Amendment as a barrier to using people's own words against them in court. But what if new technologies enable law enforcement officials to accurately read people's bodies to determine if they are telling the truth? Polygraph machines, often called "lie detectors," have been in use for decades. They evaluate people's heart rates as they respond to a series of questions. Because of concerns that these devices will wrongly indicate that naturally nervous people are liars, and because effective liars may fool the machines, polygraph results are typically not considered reliable enough to be presented in court as evidence in a criminal case. Scientists are developing new techniques, however, that may be more accurate than polygraphs.

One device being tested monitors people's brain waves as specific words and pictures are flashed on a screen. In theory, if the person shows a brain-wave response to words or pictures that would only be familiar to the witness or perpetrator of a crime, then law enforcement officials could take a giant step toward solving the crime. Another device uses a thermal-imaging camera to detect whether people are blushing when a specific question is posed. A common physiological response when people lie is that blood rushes to the area of the face around the eye. Unlike traditional polygraph devices, the camera can be used "on the spot" without hooking the subject up to any monitoring devices and therefore might be used on the street or at an airport.

RESEARCHING THE INTERNET

To read about the use of thermal imaging to detect deception, see the corresponding site listed on the Cole/Smith Criminal Justice in America Companion Website: http://www.thomsonedu.com/criminaljustice/cole.

FOR CRITICAL ANALYSIS

Are there any problems with the development of thermal-imaging or similar devices? Would the use of such devices by law enforcement officials violate the Fifth Amendment?

Sources: "Catching Red-Faced Liars," *ABC News,* January 2, 2002, http://abcnews.go.com (see also William J. Broad, "Polygraph Is Poor Tool for Screening Employees, Panel Says," *New York Times,* October 8, 2002); "Taking a Byte out of Crime," *Time,* October 21, 2002, p. 39; Richard Willing, "Terrorism Lends Urgency to Hunt for Better Lie Detector," *USA Today,* November 4, http://www.usatoday.com.

and killed in the other (*Heath v. Alabama*, 1985). Thus, the protection against double jeopardy does not prevent two different trials based on the same criminal acts as long as the trials are in different jurisdictions and based on different charges, a violation of the Georgia murder law being a different charge than a violation of the Alabama murder law even when both charges concern the same killing.

THE SIXTH AMENDMENT: THE RIGHT TO COUNSEL AND A FAIR TRIAL

The Sixth Amendment includes several provisions dealing with fairness in a criminal prosecution. These include the rights to counsel, to a speedy and public trial, and to an impartial jury.

The Right to Counsel   Although the right to counsel in a criminal case had prevailed in federal courts since 1938, not until the Supreme Court's landmark decision in *Gideon v. Wainwright* (1963) was this requirement made binding on the states. Many states already provided attorneys, but in this ruling the Court forced all of the states to meet Sixth Amendment standards. In previous cases, the Court, applying the doctrine of fundamental fairness, had ruled that states must provide poor people with counsel only when this was required by the special circumstances of the case. A defense attorney had to be provided when conviction could lead to the death penalty, when the issues were complex, or when a poor defendant was either very young or mentally handicapped.

Although the Gideon ruling directly affected only states that did not provide poor defendants with attorneys, it set in motion a series of cases that affected all the states by deciding how the right to counsel would be applied in various situations. Beginning in 1963, the Court extended the right to counsel to preliminary hearings, initial appeals, postindictment identification lineups, and children in juvenile court proceedings. Later, however, the Burger Court declared that attorneys need not be provided for discretionary appeals or for trials in which the only punishment is a fine (*Ross v. Moffitt*, 1974; *Scott v. Illinois*, 1979).

Because defense attorneys are an important component of a legal process that uses an adversarial system to pursue the truth and protect rights, defendants' conversations and communications with attorneys are secret. Prosecutors are not entitled to know what defendants tell their attorneys, even if they admit their guilt. As part of the effort to combat terrorism, however, the federal government proposed that it gain the authority to monitor conversations between jailed defendants and their attorneys. Do you think such a proposal improperly weakens Sixth Amendment rights? See "What Americans Think" to compare your view with those of others in the United States.

The Right to a Speedy and Public Trial   The nation's founders were aware that, in other countries, accused people might often languish in jail awaiting trial and often were convicted in secret proceedings. At the time of the American Revolution, the right to a speedy and public trial was recognized in the common law and included in the constitutions of six of the original states. But the word *speedy* is vague, and the Supreme Court has recognized that the interest of quick processes may conflict with other interests of society (such as the need to collect evidence) as well as with interests of the defendant (such as the need for time to prepare a defense).

The right to a public trial is intended to protect the accused against arbitrary conviction. The Constitution assumes that judges and juries will act in accordance with the law if they must listen to evidence and announce their decisions in public. Again, the Supreme Court has recognized that there may be cases in which the need for a public trial must be balanced against other concerns. For example, the right to a public trial does not mean that *all* members of the public have the right to attend the trial. The courtroom's seating capacity and the interests of a fair trial, free of outbursts from the audience, may be considered. In hearings on sex crimes when the victim or witness is a minor, courts have barred the public in order to spare the child embarrassment. In some states, trials have become even more public than the authors of the Sixth Amendment ever imagined, because court proceedings are televised—some are even carried on national cable systems through COURT-TV.

FELONIES

Gideon v. Wainwright (1963)
Indigent defendants have a right to counsel when charged with serious crimes for which they could face six or more months of incarceration.

WHAT **AMERICANS** THINK

Question: "Until now, in criminal cases of all kinds, conversations between attorneys and their clients who are in jail have been private. Now, the government wants to be able to listen in on conversations between attorneys and their clients. Do you think this is a good idea or a bad idea?"

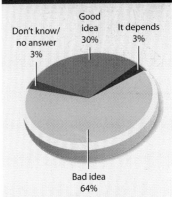

Don't know/ no answer 3%
Good idea 30%
It depends 3%
Bad idea 64%

Go to http://www.thomsonedu.com/ criminaljustice/cole to compare your opinion on this issue with the opinions of other criminal justice students.

Source: Survey based on telephone interviews of a national adult sample conducted December 7–10, 2001, by CBS News/*New York Times*. Data Provided by the Roper Center for Public Opinion Research, University of Connecticut.

The Right to an Impartial Jury   The right to a jury trial was well established in the American colonies at the time of the Revolution. In their charters, most of the colonies guaranteed trial by jury, and it was referred to in the First Continental Congress's debates in 1774, the Declaration of Independence, the constitutions of the thirteen original states, and the Sixth Amendment to the U.S. Constitution. Juries allow citizens to play a role in courts' decision making and to prevent prosecutions in cases in which there is not enough evidence.

Several Supreme Court decisions have dealt with the composition of juries. The Court has held that the amendment requires selection procedures that create a jury pool made up of a cross section of the community. Most scholars believe that an impartial jury can best be achieved by drawing jurors at random from the broadest possible base (Hans and Vidmar, 1986; Levine, 1992). The jury is expected to represent the community, and the extent to which it does so is a central concern of jury administration (C. E. Smith, 1994).

THE EIGHTH AMENDMENT: PROTECTION AGAINST EXCESSIVE BAIL, EXCESSIVE FINES, AND CRUEL AND UNUSUAL PUNISHMENT

Although it is the briefest of the amendments, the Eighth Amendment deals with the rights of defendants during the pretrial (bail) and correctional (fines, punishment) phases of the criminal justice system.

Release on Bail   The purpose of bail is to allow for the release of the accused while he or she is awaiting trial. The Eighth Amendment does not require that all defendants be released on bail, only that the amount of bail not be excessive. Many states do not allow bail for those charged with some offenses, such as murder, and there seem to be few limits on the amounts that can be required. In 1987 the Supreme Court, in *United States v. Salerno and Cafero,* upheld provisions of the Bail Reform Act of 1984 that allow federal judges to detain without bail suspects who are considered dangerous to the public.

Excessive Fines   The Supreme Court ruled in 1993 that the forfeiture of property related to a criminal case can be analyzed for possible violation of the Excessive Fines Clause (*Austin v. United States*). In 1998 the Court declared for the first time that a forfeiture constituted an impermissible excessive fine. In that case, a man failed to comply with the federal law requiring that travelers report if they are taking $10,000 or more in cash outside the country (C. E. Smith, 1999). There is no law against transporting any amount of cash. The law only concerns filing a report to the government concerning the transport of money. When one traveler at a Los Angeles airport failed to report the money detected in his suitcase by a cash-sniffing dog trained to identify people who might be transporting money for drug dealers, he was forced to forfeit all $357,000 that he carried in his luggage. Because there was no evidence that the money was obtained illegally and because the usual punishment for the offense would only be a fine of $5,000, a slim five-member majority on the Supreme Court ruled that the forfeiture of all the traveler's money constituted an excessive fine (*United States v. Bajakajian,* 1998). It remains to be seen whether the Court's recent interest in violations of the excessive fines clause will limit law enforcement agencies' practices in forcing criminal defendants to forfeit cash and property.

Cruel and Unusual Punishment   The nation's founders were concerned about the barbaric punishments that had been inflicted in seventeenth- and eighteenth-century Europe, where offenders were sometimes burned alive or stoned to death—hence the ban on "cruel and unusual punishment." The Warren Court set the standard for judging issues of cruel and unusual punishment in a case dealing with a former soldier who was deprived of U.S. citizenship for deserting his post during World War II (*Trop v. Dulles,* 1958). Chief Justice Earl Warren declared that judges must use the values of contemporary society to determine whether a specific punishment is cruel and unusual.

Through the use of this test, punishments may be declared unconstitutional for being either disproportionate to the offense or comparable to a form of torture through

Lethal injection is thought to be the most humane way of carrying out the death penalty. Because of cases where the procedure was "botched," some claim that the method is cruel and unusual punishment in violation of the Eighth Amendment.

Courtesy of California Dept. of Corrections and Rehabilitation

the infliction of physical or psychological pain. In recent years the Supreme Court has seldom regarded punishments other than the death penalty as disproportionate to any crime for which a legislature chooses to mandate it. The Court reinforced this view in 2003 by endorsing California's sentences of 25 years to life for offenders convicted of three felonies, even in a case when the third offense was merely shoplifting some children's videos from K-Mart (*Lockyer v. Andrade*, 2003).

3 STRIKES

The Court's test has been used in death penalty cases, but the justices have strongly disagreed over the values of American society on this issue. For example, only Justices William Brennan, Thurgood Marshall, and Harry Blackmun felt that the death penalty violates the Eighth Amendment's ban on cruel and unusual punishments. These three justices all retired from the Supreme Court during the 1990s. The Supreme Court's decisions in death penalty cases are extensively discussed in Chapter 10. (See "A Question of Ethics" at the end of this chapter for a further discussion of capital punishment.)

Since the 1950s the rights of defendants in state criminal trials have greatly expanded. The Supreme Court has incorporated most portions of the Fourth, Fifth, Sixth, and Eighth Amendments. Figure 3.2 shows the amendments that protect defendants at various stages of the criminal justice process.

ThomsonNOW

Improve your grade on the exam with Personalized Study! For reinforcement resources and a mastery check of Procedural Criminal Law, go to www.thomsonedu.com/thomsonnow.

CHECKPOINT

Answers

6. What is incorporation? ──────────────▶ **6.** Taking a right from the Bill of Rights and applying it against state and local officials by making it a component of the due process clause of the Fourteenth Amendment.

7. Which Supreme Court era made the most significant expansion in the ──▶ **7.** Warren Court. definitions of constitutional rights for criminal defendants?

8. What are the main criminal justice rights set forth in the Fourth, Fifth, ──▶ **8.** Fourth: The protection against unreasonable searches and seizures; Fifth: The right Sixth, and Eighth Amendments? against compelled self-incrimination and against double jeopardy (also the right to due process); Sixth: The right to counsel, to a speedy and fair trial, to a jury trial (also to confrontation and compulsory process); Eighth: The right to protection against excessive bail, excessive fines, and cruel and unusual punishments.

FIGURE 3.2
Protections of constitutional rights
The Bill of Rights and the Fourteenth Amendment protect defendants during various phases of the criminal justice process.

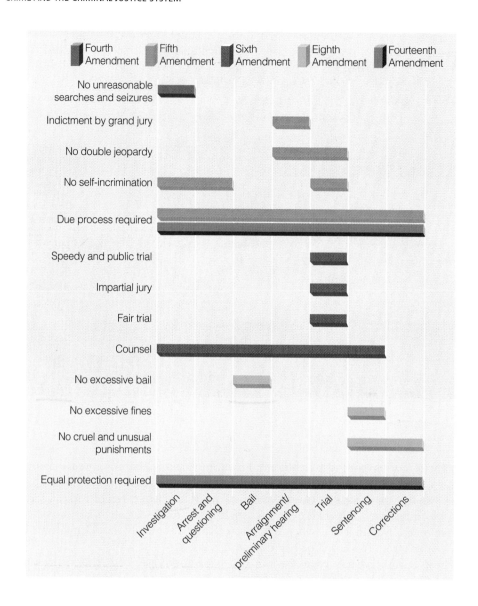

Constitutional Rights and Criminal Justice Professionals

As a result of the Supreme Court's decisions, people in all states now enjoy the same minimum protections against illegal searches, improper police interrogations, and other violations of constitutional rights. In response to these decisions, police, prosecution, and correctional offices have had to develop policies and guidelines to inform criminal justice professionals about what they are and are not permitted to do while investigating, prosecuting, and punishing criminal offenders.

If you were a police officer, prosecutor, or correctional officer, how would you feel about the Supreme Court's decisions defining rights that benefit criminal defendants? Although you would recognize the desirability of upholding constitutional rights in order to maintain democratic freedoms, you might also feel frustrated when court decisions excluded relevant evidence, especially if such exclusion led to the release of a guilty offender. In addition, you would be concerned about whether the Supreme Court's decisions give you clear guidance about what to do. You would not want to make an unintentional error that prevents an offender from being properly convicted of a crime.

Many people question whether the Supreme Court has struck the proper balance between the protection of constitutional rights and the ability of criminal justice officials to punish offenders (C. E. Smith and Baugh, 2000). Some people believe that criminal defendants' rights are too broad. Others believe that the Supreme Court favors law enforcement at the expense of constitutional rights. These debates are likely to continue even though the Supreme Court has moved consistently in one direction during the past two decades. In cases affecting criminal justice, the contemporary Supreme Court endorses the actions of police officers and prosecutors in more than two-thirds of cases (C. E. Smith, 2003).

In 2005 President George W. Bush appointed two new justices to the Supreme Court, Chief Justice John Roberts and Justice Samuel Alito. Based on their prior decisions as federal appellate judges, both of the new appointees are expected to reinforce the Court's support for broader police authority and more narrowly defined rights for criminal suspects and defendants. Observers predict that several aging justices may retire in the near future, especially Justices John Paul Stevens and Ruth Bader Ginsburg, who were, respectively, 86 and 73 years old in 2006. Future directions in Supreme Court decisions concerning rights in the criminal justice process will depend on which president is in office when additional retirements occur and who this president selects to fill these influential judicial positions.

A QUESTION OF ETHICS: WRITING ASSIGNMENT

In 2006, states faced numerous legal challenges from defense attorneys about whether lethal injection provides a humane means of execution. A majority of justices on the Supreme Court have decided that the death penalty does not violate the Constitution. However, courts have blocked specific means of execution, such as the gas chamber, because they produced prolonged, excruciating pain that judges regard as violating the Eighth Amendment prohibition on cruel and unusual punishments. In executions by lethal injection, states typically use a combination of three drugs that, if administered improperly, merely paralyze the condemned convict without actually rendering him or her unconscious. This leads to the individual experiencing excruciating pain as a burning sensation in the veins and a slow process of suffocation. A medical study on postexecution examinations reported that as many as 43 percent of offenders executed in six states may have been subject to an excruciating death because of improperly administered or inadequate dosages of the drugs. Because of the infliction of needless pain, many states ban the use of these same drugs when veterinarians euthanize animals (put them "to sleep").

As a result of the issues surrounding lethal injection, many doctors have refused to participate in executions. Indeed, the American Medical Association regards it as a violation of doctors' ethical obligations and the oath to "do no harm," if physicians participate in executions. On the other hand, lethal injections are more likely to be botched if carried out by technicians and correctional officers who struggle to insert needles into proper veins and administer the drugs with appropriate dosages and timing.

WRITING ASSIGNMENT

If you were a doctor employed by a state's department of corrections, how would you respond if you were asked to participate in an execution? Is there an ethical dilemma when trained healers intentionally kill condemned offenders in a procedure that is legal under most states' laws and the U.S. Constitution? Write a memo to the department of corrections as if you were a doctor responding to a request to administer the lethal injections for an execution.

Sources: Diane Jennings, "Lethal Injection Challenges Mount," *Dallas Morning News,* April 30, 2006, http://www.dallasnews.com; Nathan Thornburgh, "Legal Objection," *Time,* March 6, 2006, http://www.time.com.

REAL-WORLD ACTIVITY: AN APPLICATION

An elderly man approaches a 20-year-old, male college student on a dark street as the student walks home from a convenience store, sipping iced tea from a small glass bottle. With one hand jammed inside his coat pocket, the gray-haired senior citizen says to the student, "Give me your wallet right now or else you're going to get hurt." The student immediately strikes the man in the head with the bottle and runs to his apartment to call 911. When the police come to the door, they tell the student that the man died from head injuries and that he had a long criminal record for robberies and burglaries—but that he had no weapon in his pocket. If the student is charged with manslaughter and his attorney argues that he acted in self-defense, should he be acquitted of the crime? Did he use excessive force under the circumstances? If you were on the jury, what would you decide?

 ### RESEARCHING THE INTERNET

Go to InfoTrac College Edition. Enter the keyword *self defense trial,* then read the article entitled "Witness Describes Fatal Beating at Akron Bar," *Akron Beacon Journal,* February 9, 2006.

APPLICATION

Compare the Akron case with the foregoing example. Did either individual use too much force? As a juror in such a case, how would you know if a self-defense action crossed the line to become a criminal assault?

SUMMARY

- Criminal law is divided into two parts: substantive law, which defines offenses and penalties, and procedural law, which defines individuals' rights and the processes that criminal justice officials must follow in handling cases.

- Substantive criminal law involves seven important elements that must exist and be demonstrated by the prosecution in order to obtain a conviction: legality, *actus reus,* causation, harm, concurrence, *mens rea,* and punishment.

- The *mens rea* element, concerning intent or state of mind, can vary with different offenses, such as various degrees of murder.

- The values and goals of criminal law can differ according to a society's values, as illustrated by those countries that follow elements of religion-based Islamic law.

- Criminal law provides opportunities to present several defenses based on lack of criminal intent: entrapment, self-defense, necessity, duress (coercion), immaturity, mistake of fact, intoxication, and insanity.

- Standards for the insanity defense vary by jurisdiction, with various state and federal courts using several different tests: *M'Naghten* Rule, Irresistible Impulse Test,

Durham Rule, *Model Penal Code,* and Comprehensive Crime Control Act.

- The provisions of the Bill of Rights were not made applicable to state and local officials by the U.S. Supreme Court until the mid-twentieth century, when the Court incorporated most of the Bill of Rights' specific provisions into the due process clause of the Fourteenth Amendment.

- The Fourth Amendment's prohibition on unreasonable searches and seizures seeks to impose limits on police authority to intrude on people's expectations of privacy with respect to their bodies, homes, and property.

- The Fifth Amendment provides protections against compelled self-incrimination and double jeopardy.

- The Sixth Amendment includes the right to counsel, the right to a speedy and public trial, and the right to an impartial jury.

- The Eighth Amendment includes protections against excessive bail, excessive fines, and cruel and unusual punishments. Only a few Supreme Court justices have viewed the death penalty as a violation of the prohibition on cruel and unusual punishments.

QUESTIONS FOR REVIEW

1. What are the two major divisions within criminal law?

2. What are the seven principles of criminal law theory?

3. What is meant by *mens rea?* Give examples of defenses that may be used by defendants in which they deny that *mens rea* existed when the crime was committed.

4. What is meant by the incorporation of rights into the Fourteenth Amendment of the U.S. Constitution?

5. What rights are contained in the Fourth Amendment?

6. What rights are contained in the Fifth Amendment?

7. What rights are contained in the Sixth Amendment?

8. What rights are contained in the Eighth Amendment?

KEY TERMS AND CASES

Bill of Rights (p. 76)
civil law (p. 65)
double jeopardy (p. 76)
entrapment (p. 69)
fundamental fairness (p. 78)
grand jury (p. 80)

inchoate offense (p. 66)
incorporation (p. 78)
legal responsibility (p. 64)
mens rea (p. 67)
procedural criminal law (p. 65)
self-incrimination (p. 76)

substantive criminal law (p. 65)
Barron v. Baltimore (1833) (p. 78)
Gideon v. Wainwright (1963) (p. 81)
Powell v. Alabama (1932) (p. 78)

GOING ONLINE

ThomsonNOW™

Maximize your study time by using ThomsonNOW's diagnostic study plan to help you review this chapter. The Study Plan will

- Help you identify areas on which you should concentrate

- Provide interactive exercises to help you master the chapter concepts

- Provide a posttest to confirm you are ready to move on to the next chapter

INSIDE THE CRIMINAL JUSTICE SYSTEM AND BEYOND: ONE MAN'S JOURNEY

Written by Chuck Terry

My Affair with Heroin

Seldom do we have the opportunity to view the criminal justice system through the eyes of a person who has experienced it. Chuck Terry is most unusual in that, after more than 20 years of heroin addiction, 12 of them incarcerated, he has "beaten the habit" and gained a Ph.D. and is now an assistant professor of criminal justice. The vivid chronicles of his journey, which conclude each part of this book, provide rare insights into the workings of "the system." His reflections should be thoughtfully considered by all students of criminal justice.

Tight handcuffs. Loud cellblocks. Racial tension. No women, kids, or pets. Violence. Road dogs (close friends). Iron bars. Concrete beds. Hate. Guard towers. Getting booked. Count times. Food lines. Parole boards. Judges. Degradation. District attorneys. Death. Cops. A.M.'s and P.M.'s—year in and year out. Monotony. Withdrawals. Preliminary hearings. The need to show no pain—ever. Release dates. Parole officers. Alienation. Hopelessness. Determinate sentencing. A guard on the way out of prison: "See you when you get back, Terry. Guys like you are job security for guys like me." A lot to deal with for a white, California-raised kid from middle-class suburbia. A lot for anybody.

From my first arrest in 1970 to my last discharge from parole in 1992, I became intimately familiar with all the components of the criminal justice system. Over the course of this twenty-plus-year "career," which included spending over twelve years inside state (prisons) and county (jails) "correctional" facilities for drug-related crimes, I experienced almost everything the system has to offer—except the death penalty or a sentence of life without possibility of parole.

These experiences have taught me that the way "criminals" are dealt with in America is anything but "fair" or "just." Rather, their fate is determined by who they are and how they are seen by system actors such as judges and prosecutors and by the general public. It is important to note that this "seeing" varies dramatically and is relative to an ever-changing social, economic, political, and historical context.

Crime today is politicized and a main focus of media attention. The "threat" posed by "criminals" is used to generate fear and legitimate spending millions on more police, more prisons, and more mechanisms of social control. The reasons for this are complex and controversial. But it hasn't always been like this.

I was a kid in the 1960s, when the civil rights movement, protests against the Vietnam War, and an antiestablishment-oriented "counterculture" were in full swing. Instead of bombarding the public with visions of low-level street crime, the nightly news sent us images from the war, urban riots, and people getting beaten by police for participating in nonviolent sit-ins. Governmental policies and social inequality rather than addicts and "juvenile predators" were seen as "criminal" by a significant portion of the population. Rules and rule enforcers (like racial segregation policies, drug laws, government officials) were the targets of attention. In defiance of "the way things were," we grew our hair, spoke out against social norms, and got high.

My own drug use began in 1967 and escalated over time. Initially, I used whatever was available: alcohol, marijuana, reds, yellows, whites, LSD. In 1969 I used heroin for the first time.

Now, how could any sane person try heroin? Doesn't everyone know it's a "bad" thing to do? Though it was scary, I rationalized it as being OK. After all, I knew several people who used it. They seemed to be fine. Everything I had been told about all the other drugs I used had proved to be a lie; we were told that if we smoked pot we'd lie down on train tracks, and if we took LSD we'd jump out of tall buildings and lose our minds. So one night at a party I gave it a shot. Or, I should say, I stuck my arm out and a friend gave me a shot.

Turning points. Crossroads. Where do we go from here? The first thing I thought when I felt the effects of heroin was, "I can't believe I've been doing anything in life other than trying to use this stuff all the time." For the next twenty-plus years I did just that. Heroin made me feel "normal," like I fit, belonged, was not out of place. It is a powerfully enticing drug: Many first-time users instantly fall in love with it. I was one of those people. It provided me with a clear purpose in life and, though I didn't know it at first, a future that would involve spending a lot of time inside the various worlds of the criminal justice system.

Once I began using illegal drugs, I started seeing anyone affiliated with any type of legal authority as a potential enemy—especially police, whose job (in my mind) was to "catch" or "arrest" me. This distrustful outlook became magnified once I began using heroin. After all, heroin users are seen as "real" criminals.

The people in my life changed as my heroin habit took hold. Where I used to have friends who were about my age and white, now I frequently hung out with older people who were often a different color, brown or black. Their images remain. A 40-year-old hooker fixing (injecting narcotics), sores all over her body, pushing scabs on her arms out of the way with the needle in a desperate attempt to find a vein. A 65-year-old, jaundiced-eyed black man welcoming me into his home to share the joys of addiction. Trips into ethnic neighborhoods to buy dope where few, if any, white people were seen. Nodding. Throwing up. People getting arrested, disappearing, overdosing, dying. As my social circle changed, so did the way I saw the world and myself. Without realizing it I was "becoming" what society calls "criminal."

My love of heroin took me down a road that included many unplanned pit stops. I was investigated, arrested, booked more times than I care to recall. I appeared more than once at a preliminary hearing, still going through withdrawal—looking sickly and feeling weak as I interacted with bailiffs, public defenders, judges, and other prisoners. The road took me through cramped cell blocks, courtroom holding tanks, and jailhouse chow halls—to places where I witnessed alcoholics suffering from the DTs, epileptics and diabetics going into convulsions from a lack of medication, people jammed into cells with bullets still in their bodies, and more. From four different prison commitments came years behind walls, isolated from the world. My love of heroin took me down a path where I was either on the run, locked up, or on probation or parole for more than twenty years. The pieces that conclude each part of this book are scenes from that journey.

[handwritten annotations:]

I take essue.
- P.O JUVENILE — REHAB- TREATMENT
- PRETRIAL SERVICES
PRESUMPTION OF INNOCENCE
CONFIDENTIALTY
LEAST RESTRICTIVE CONSTITU

4

Police

Hurricane Katrina roared ashore along the Gulf Coast in August 2005 with winds over 160 miles per hour pushing 20-foot walls of water across coastal lands. The hurricane devastated areas of Mississippi, Alabama, and Louisiana, including the near-destruction of New Orleans. Including its aftermath, the most significant hurricane in the country's history killed 1,600 people and caused $75 billion in damage.

For most Americans, Hurricane Katrina brought this devastation into their living rooms from afar, through the televised images of hungry, desperate people, left with only the clothes on their backs, stranded on rooftops and in shelters while they waited for slow-developing assistance from government officials. By contrast, the police officers serving in Gulf Coast communities found themselves in the middle of a catastrophic disaster to which they had to respond immediately.

When emergencies occur, police officers are "first re-sponders." Along with firefighters and emergency medical technicians, law enforcement officers are expected to rush to the scene, restore order, and assist in rescue operations. While other citizens fled or waited for assistance, it fell to local police departments to organize immediate responses to the hurricane, even though they had often lost access to police vehicles and working communications equipment. Police officers in various communities risked their lives in rising floodwaters to rescue the elderly, handicapped, and children. Officers used creativity to "hot-wire" boats for use in rescues, set up feeding stations for hungry people, and administer first aid. They also faced difficult challenges in attempting to coordinate efforts with state and federal agencies that often blocked access to available supplies (Jenkins, 2005).

In the face of an unprecedented crisis, not all officers put their professional responsibilities first. Police are, after all, human beings who can succumb to fear, greed, and so forth. In New Orleans, for example, some officers deserted the city and others participated in looting. However, many officers who remained on the job, often for 24-hour-shifts, performed heroically in dealing with looters, performing rescues, and foraging for supplies without any vehicles, resources, or backup (Baum, 2006).

The uniformed men and women who patrol the streets are the most visible presence of government in the United States. They are joined by thousands of plainclothes officers who share various law enforcement responsibilities. Whether they are members of the local or state police, sheriff's departments, or federal agencies, the more than 700,000 sworn officers in the country play key roles in U.S. society. Citizens look to them to perform a wide range of functions: crime prevention, law enforcement, order maintenance, and community service. However, the public's expectations of the police are not always clear. Citizens also form judgments about the police, and those judgments strongly affect the way the police function.

In a free society the police are required to maintain order. In performing this task, police officers receive a great deal of authority. Using their powers to arrest, search, detain, and use force, they can interfere with the freedom of any citizen. If they abuse such powers, they can threaten the basic values of a stable, democratic society.

In this chapter we examine several aspects of policing. A brief history of the police precedes discussions of the organization, functions, and policies of law enforcement.

QUESTIONS FOR INQUIRY

- How has policing evolved in the United States?
- What are the main types of police agencies?
- What are the functions of the police?
- How are the police organized?
- What influences police policy and styles of policing?
- How do police officers balance actions, decision making, and discretion?
- What role does the link between the police and the community play in preventing crime?

The Development of Police in the United States

Law and order is not a new concept; it has been a subject of debate since the first police force was formed in London in 1829. Looking back even farther, we find that the Magna Carta of 1215 placed limits on constables and bailiffs. Reading between the lines of that historic document reveals that the modern problems of police abuse, maintenance of order, and the rule of law also existed in thirteenth-century England. Further, current remedies—recruiting better-qualified people to serve as police, stiffening the penalties for official misconduct, creating a civilian board of control—were suggested even then to ensure that order was kept in accordance with the rule of law.

THE ENGLISH ROOTS OF THE AMERICAN POLICE

The roots of American policing lie in the English legal tradition. Three major aspects of American policing evolved from that tradition: (1) limited authority, (2) local control, and (3) fragmented organization. Like the British police, but unlike police in continental Europe, the police in the United States have limited authority; their powers and duties are specifically defined by law. England, like the United States, has no national police force; instead, 43 regional authorities are headed by elected commissioners who appoint the chief constable. Above these local authorities is the home secretary of the national government, which provides funding and can intervene in cases of police corruption, mismanagement, and discipline. In the United States, policing is fragmented: There are many types of agencies—constable, county sheriff, city police, FBI—each with its own special jurisdiction and responsibilities.

Systems for protecting citizens and property existed before the thirteenth century. The **frankpledge** system required that groups of ten families, called *tithings*, agree to uphold the law, keep order, and bring violators to a court. By custom, every male person above the age of 12 was part of the system. When a man became aware that a crime had occurred, he was obliged to raise a "hue and cry" and to join others in his tithing to track down the offender. The tithing was fined if members did not perform their duties.

Over time, England developed a system in which individuals were chosen within each community to take charge of catching criminals. The Statute of Winchester, enacted in 1285, set up a parish constable-watch system. Members of the community were still required to pursue criminals, just as they had been under the frankpledge system, but now a constable supervised those efforts. The constable was a man chosen from the parish to serve without pay as its law enforcement officer for one year. The constable had the power to call the entire community into action if a serious disturbance arose. Watchmen, who were appointed to help the constable, spent most of their time patrolling the town at night to ensure that "all's well" and to enforce the criminal law. They were also responsible for lighting street lamps and putting out fires.

Not until the eighteenth century did an organized police force evolve in England. With the growth of commerce and industry, cities expanded while farming declined as the main source of employment and the focus of community life. In the larger cities, these changes produced social disorder.

In the mid-eighteenth century, the novelist Henry Fielding and his brother, Sir John Fielding, led efforts to improve law enforcement in London. They wrote newspaper articles to inform the public about crime, and they published flyers describing known offenders. After Henry Fielding became a magistrate in 1748, he organized a small group of "thief-takers" to pursue and arrest lawbreakers. The government was so impressed with Fielding's Bow Street Amateur Volunteer Force (known as the Bow Street Runners) that it paid the participants and attempted to form similar groups in other parts of London.

After Henry Fielding's death in 1754, these efforts declined. As time went by, however, many saw that the government needed to assert itself in enforcing laws and maintaining order. London, with its unruly mobs, had become an especially dangerous place. In the early 1800s several attempts were made to create a centralized police force for London. While people saw the need for social order, some feared that a police force would threaten the freedom of citizens and lead to tyranny. Finally, in 1829 Sir Robert Peel, home secretary in the British Cabinet, pushed Parliament to pass the Metropolitan Police Act, which created the London police force.

This agency was organized like a military unit, with a thousand-man force commanded by two magistrates, later called "commissioners." The officers were called "bobbies" after Sir Robert Peel. In the British system, cabinet members who oversee government departments are chosen from the elected members of Parliament. Thus, because it was supervised by Peel, the first police force was under the control of democratically elected officials.

Under Peel's direction, the police had a four-part mandate:

1. To prevent crime without using repressive force and to avoid having to call on the military to control riots and other disturbances

2. To maintain public order by nonviolent means, using force only as a last resort to obtain compliance

3. To reduce conflict between the police and the public

4. To show efficiency through the absence of crime and disorder rather than through visible police actions (Manning, 1977:82)

In effect, this meant keeping a low profile while maintaining order. Because of fears that a national force would threaten civil liberties, political leaders made every effort to focus police activities at the local level. These concerns were transported to the United States.

POLICING IN THE UNITED STATES

As with other institutions and areas of public policy, the development of formal police organizations reflected the social conditions, politics, and problems of different eras of American history. The United States drew from England's experience but implemented policing in its own way.

The Colonial Era and the Early Republic   As settlers arrived in North America from Europe and eventually moved westward from the East Coast, they relied on each other for assistance and protection in all matters, from weather disasters to conflicts with Native Americans. They also needed to protect themselves and their neighbors from those who might cause harm through theft or other crimes.

Along the East Coast, the colonists drew from their experiences in England by adopting the English offices of constable, sheriff, and night watchman as the first positions with law enforcement responsibilities. Boston's watch system began before 1640. Such systems served to warn of dangers ranging from fires to crime. Each male citizen was required to be a member of the watch, but paid watchmen could be hired as replacements. Although the watch system originally operated at night, cities eventually began to have daytime watches, too. Over time, cities began to hire paid, uniformed watchmen to deal with public danger and crime (S. Walker, 1999).

In the South, slave patrols developed as organized forces to prevent slave revolts and catch runaway slaves. These patrols had full power to break into the homes of slaves who were suspected of keeping arms, to physically punish those who did not obey their orders, and to arrest runaways and return them to their masters. Under the watch system in northern cities, watchmen reacted to calls for help. By contrast, the mobility of slave patrols positioned them to operate in a proactive manner by looking for African Americans whom whites feared would disrupt society, especially the economic system of slavery. Samuel Walker (1999) describes the slave patrols as a distinctly American form of law enforcement and the first modern police force in the United States.

Beginning in the 1830s and continuing periodically for several decades, many American cities experienced violent riots. Ethnic conflicts, election controversies, hostility toward nonslave blacks and abolitionists, mob actions against banks during economic declines, and violence in settling questions of morality, such as the use of alcohol—all these factors contributed to fears that a stable democracy would not survive. The militia was called in to quell large-scale conflicts, because constables and watchmen proved ineffective in restoring order (Uchida, 2005). These disorders, along with perceptions of increased problems with serious crimes, helped push city governments to consider the creation of professional police forces.

American policing is often described in terms of three historical periods: the political era (1840–1920), the professional model era (1920–1970), and the community policing era (1970–present) (Kelling and Moore, 1988). This description has been criticized because it applies only to the urban areas of the Northeast and does not take into account the very different development of the police in rural areas of the South and West. Still, it remains a useful framework for exploring the organization of the police, the focus of police work, and the strategies employed by police (H. Williams and Murphy, 1990).

The Political Era: 1840–1920   The period from 1840 to 1920 is called the *political era* because of the close ties that were formed between the police and local political leaders at that time. In many cities the police seemed to work for the mayor's political party rather than for the citizens. This relationship served both groups in that the political "machines" recruited and maintained the police while the police helped the machine leaders get out the vote for favored candidates. Ranks in the police force were often for sale to the highest bidder, and many officers took payoffs for not enforcing laws on drinking, gambling, and prostitution (S. Walker, 1999:26).

In the United States, as in England, the growth of cities led to pressures to modernize law enforcement. Around 1840 the large cities began to create police forces. In

1845 New York City established the first full-time, paid police force. Boston and Philadelphia were the first to add a daytime police force to supplement the night watchmen; other cities—Chicago, Cincinnati, New Orleans—quickly followed.

By 1850 most major cities had created police departments organized on the English model. A chief, appointed by the mayor and city council, headed each department. The city was divided into precincts, with full-time, paid patrolmen assigned to each. Early police forces sought to prevent crimes and keep order through the use of foot patrols. The officer on the beat dealt with crime, disorder, and other problems as they arose.

In addition to foot patrols, the police performed service functions, such as caring for derelicts, operating soup kitchens, regulating public health, and handling medical and social emergencies. In cities across the country, the police provided beds and food for homeless people. In station houses, overnight "lodgers" might sleep on the floor or sometimes in clean bunkrooms (Monkkonen, 1981:127). Because they were the only government agency that had close contact with life on the streets of the city, the police became general public servants as well as crime control officers. These close links with the community and service to it earned them the citizens' support (Monkkonen, 1992:554).

Police developed differently in the South because of the existence of slavery and the agrarian nature of that region. As noted previously, the first organized police agencies with full-time officers developed in cities with large numbers of slaves (Charleston, New Orleans, Richmond, and Savannah), where white owners feared slave uprisings (Rousey, 1984:41).

Westward expansion in the United States produced conditions quite different from those in either the urban East or the agricultural South. The frontier was settled before order could be established. Thus, those who wanted to maintain law and order often had to take matters into their own hands by forming vigilante groups.

One of the first official positions created in rural areas was that of sheriff. Although the sheriff had duties similar to those of the "shire reeves" of seventeenth-century England, the American sheriff was elected and had broad powers to enforce the law. As elected officers, sheriffs had close ties to local politics. They also depended on the men of the community for assistance. This is how the *posse comitatus* (Latin for "power of the county"), borrowed from fifteenth-century Europe, came into being. Local men above age 15 were required to respond to the sheriff's call for assistance, forming a body known as a posse.

After the Civil War, the federal government appointed U.S. marshals to help enforce the law in the western territories. Some of the best-known folk heroes of American policing were U.S. Marshals Wyatt Earp, Bat Masterson, and Wild Bill Hickok, who tried to bring law and order to the "Wild West" (Calhoun, 1990). While some marshals did extensive law enforcement work, most had mainly judicial duties, such as keeping order in the courtroom and holding prisoners for trial.

During the twentieth century, all parts of the country became increasingly urban. This change blurred some of the regional differences that had helped define policing in the past. In addition, growing criticism of the influence of politics on the police led to efforts to reform the nature and organization of the police. Specifically, reformers sought to make police more professional and to reduce their ties to local politics.

During the political era, the officer on a neighborhood beat dealt with crime and disorder as it arose. Police also performed various social services, such as providing beds and food for the homeless.

Culver Pictures

During the professional era, the police saw themselves as crime fighters. Yet many inner-city residents saw them as a well-armed occupying force rather than as public servants who might be looked to for help.

Photo by David McNew/Getty Images

The Professional Model Era: 1920–1970   American policing was greatly influenced by the Progressive movement. The Progressives were mainly upper middle-class, educated Americans with two goals: more efficient government and more government services to assist the less fortunate. A related goal was to reduce the influence of party politics and patronage (favoritism in handing out jobs) on government. The Progressives saw a need for professional law enforcement officials who would use modern technology to benefit society as a whole, not just local politicians.

The key to the Progressives' concept of professional law enforcement is found in their slogan, "The police have to get out of politics, and politics has to get out of the police." August Vollmer, the chief of police of Berkeley, California, from 1909 to 1932, was a leading advocate of professional policing. He initiated the use of motorcycle units, handwriting analysis, and fingerprinting. With other police reformers, such as Leonhard Fuld, Raymond Fosdick, Bruce Smith, and O. W. Wilson, he urged that the police be made into a professional force, a nonpartisan agency of government committed to public service. This model of professional policing has six elements:

1. The force should stay out of politics.
2. Members should be well trained, well disciplined, and tightly organized.
3. Laws should be enforced equally.
4. The force should use new technology.
5. Personnel procedures should be based on merit.
6. The main task of the police should be fighting crime.

Refocusing attention on crime control and away from maintaining order probably did more than anything else to change the nature of American policing. The narrow focus on crime fighting broke many of the ties that the police had formed with the communities they served. By the end of World War I, police departments had greatly reduced their involvement in social services. Instead, for the most part, cops became crime fighters.

O. W. Wilson, a student of Vollmer, was another leading advocate of professionalism. He earned a degree in criminology at the University of California in 1924 and became chief of police in Wichita, Kansas, in 1928. By reorganizing the department and fighting police corruption, he came to national attention. He promoted the use of motorized patrols, efficient radio communication, and rapid response. He believed that one-officer patrols were the best way to use personnel and that the two-way radio, which allowed for supervision by commanders, made officers more efficient (Reiss, 1992:51). He rotated assignments so that officers on patrol would not become too familiar with people in the community (and thus prone to corruption). In 1960 Wilson became the superintendent of the Chicago Police Department with a mandate to end corruption there.

The new emphasis on professionalism spurred the formation of the International Association of Chiefs of Police (IACP) in 1902 and the Fraternal Order of Police (FOP) in 1915. Both organizations promoted training standards, the use of new technologies, and a code of ethics.

By the 1930s the police were using new technologies and methods to combat serious crimes. Officers became more effective against crimes such as murder, rape, and robbery—an important factor in gaining citizen support. By contrast, efforts to control victimless offenses and to maintain order often aroused citizen opposition. "The clean, bureaucratic model of policing put forth by the reformers could be sustained only if the scope of police responsibility was narrowed to 'crime fighting'" (Moore and Kelling, 1983:55).

In the 1960s the civil rights and antiwar movements, urban riots, and rising crime rates challenged many of the assumptions of the professional model. In their attempts to maintain order during public demonstrations, the police in many cities seemed to be concerned mainly with maintaining the status quo. Thus, police officers found themselves enforcing laws that tended to discriminate against African Americans and the poor. The number of low-income racial minorities living in the inner cities was growing, and the professional style kept the police isolated from the communities they served. In the eyes of many inner-city residents, the police were an occupying army keeping them at the bottom of society, not public servants helping all citizens.

Although the police continued to portray themselves as crime fighters, citizens became aware that the police often were not effective in this role. Crime rates rose for many offenses, and the police could not change the perception that the quality of urban life was declining.

The Community Policing Era: 1970–Present   Beginning in the 1970s, calls were heard for a move away from the crime-fighting focus and toward greater emphasis on keeping order and providing services to the community. Research studies revealed the complex nature of police work and the extent to which day-to-day practices deviated from the professional ideal. The research also questioned the effectiveness of the police in catching and deterring criminals.

Three findings of this research are especially noteworthy:

1. Increasing the number of patrol officers in a neighborhood had little effect on the crime rate.

2. Rapid response to calls for service did not greatly increase the arrest rate.

3. Improving the percentage of crimes solved is difficult.

Such findings undermined acceptance of the professional crime-fighter model (Moore, 1992:99). Critics argued that the professional style isolated the police from the community and reduced their knowledge about the neighborhoods they served, especially when police patrolled in cars. Use of the patrol car prevented personal contacts with citizens. Instead, it was argued, police should get out of their cars and spend more time meeting and helping residents. This would permit the police to help people with a range of problems and in some cases to prevent problems from arising or growing worse. For example, if the police know about conflicts between people in a neighborhood, they can try to mediate and perhaps prevent the conflict from growing into a criminal assault or other serious problem. Reformers hoped that closer contact with citizens would not only permit the police to help them in new ways but would also make citizens feel safer, knowing that the police were available and interested in their problems.

In a provocative article titled "Broken Windows: The Police and Neighborhood Safety," James Q. Wilson and George L. Kelling argued that policing should work more on "little problems" such as maintaining order, providing services to those in need, and adopting strategies to reduce the fear of crime (1982: 29). They based their approach on three assumptions:

1. Neighborhood disorder creates fear. Areas with street people, youth gangs, prostitution, and drunks are high-crime areas.

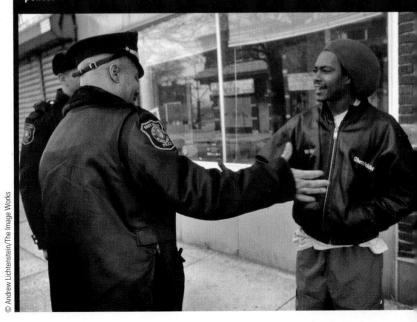

Community policing encourages personal contact between officers and citizens'. How do such contacts affect citizens' expectations about relationships with police?

© Andrew Lichtenstein/The Image Works

2. Just as broken windows are a signal that nobody cares and can lead to worse vandalism, untended disorderly behavior is a signal that the community does not care. This also leads to worse disorder and crime.

3. If the police are to deal with disorder and thus reduce fear and crime, they must rely on citizens for assistance.

Advocates of the community policing approach urge greater use of <u>foot patrols</u> so that officers will become known to citizens, who in turn will cooperate with the police. They believe that through attention to little problems, the police may not only reduce disorder and fear but also improve public attitudes toward policing. When citizens respond positively to police efforts, the police will have "improved bases of community and political support, which in turn can be exploited to gain further cooperation from citizens in a wide variety of activities" (Kelling, 1985:299).

Closely related to the community policing concept is <u>problem-oriented</u> policing. Herman Goldstein, the originator of this approach, argued that instead of focusing on crime and disorder, the police should identify the underlying causes of such problems as noisy teenagers, battered spouses, and abandoned buildings used as drug houses. In doing so they could reduce disorder and fear of crime (Goldstein, 1979:236). Closer contacts between the police and the community might then reduce the hostility that has developed between officers and residents in many urban neighborhoods (Sparrow, Moore, and Kennedy, 1990).

In *Fixing Broken Windows*, written in response to the Wilson and Kelling article, George L. Kelling and Catherine Coles (1996) call for strategies to restore order and reduce crime in public spaces in U.S. communities. In Baltimore, New York, San Francisco, and Seattle, police are paying greater attention to "quality-of-life crimes" by arresting subway fare-beaters, rousting loiterers and panhandlers from parks, and aggressively dealing with those who are obstructing sidewalks, harassing others, and soliciting. By handling these "little crimes," the police not only help restore order but also often prevent worse crimes. In New York, for example, searching fare-beaters often yielded weapons, questioning a street vendor selling hot merchandise led to a fence specializing in stolen weapons, and arresting a person for urinating in a park resulted in discovery of a cache of weapons.

Although reformers argue for a greater focus on order maintenance and service, they do not call for an end to the crime-fighting role. Instead, they want a shift of emphasis. The police should pay more attention to community needs and seek to understand the problems underlying crime, disorder, and incivility. These proposals have been adopted by police executives in many cities and by influential organizations such as the Police Foundation and the Police Executive Research Forum. The federal government created the Office of Community Oriented Policing Services, more commonly known as the "COPS Office," which provided grants for hiring new officers and developing community policing programs. Between 1995 and 2003, the COPS Office supplied nearly $7 billion to 13,000 state and local agencies to hire 118,000 new officers and implement training and other programs (Uchida, 2005).

The call for a new focus for the police has not gone unchallenged (Reichers and Roberg, 1990:105). Critics question whether the professional model really ever isolated police from community residents (S. Walker, 1984:88). Carl Klockars doubts that the police will give higher priority to maintaining order and wonders whether Americans want their police to be something other than crime fighters (1985:300). Others wonder whether the opportunity to receive federal money and hire new officers led departments to use the language of community policing in portraying their activities even though they never fully adopted the new methods.

HOMELAND SECURITY: THE NEXT ERA OF POLICING?

The events of 9/11 made homeland security and antiterrorism efforts among the highest priorities for the U.S. government. As we shall see in Chapter 6, this event shifted the federal government's funding priorities for law enforcement and led to a reorganization of federal agencies. According to Craig Uchida, "Priorities for training, equipment, strategies, and funding have transformed policing once again—this time focusing on homeland security" (2005:38). Instead of focusing funds on community policing, federal money moved toward supplying emergency preparedness training, hazardous materials gear, equipment for detecting bombs and other weapons of mass destruction, and the collection of intelligence data. In public comments, a few police officials have made reference to "terrorist-oriented policing," but how such a concept or emphasis would be defined at the local level is not clear (Kerlikowske, 2004). Some observers believe that a shift toward homeland security may appeal to traditionalists in law enforcement who prefer to see themselves as heroically catching "bad guys" rather than solving problems within neighborhoods.

Community policing will not disappear. Many police executives remain committed to its purposes and principles. However, federal agencies have clearly made homeland security their top priority, and federal funding for local police departments has shifted as well. Further development of a focus on homeland security throughout policing may depend on whether American cities suffer additional terror attacks.

Whichever approach the police take—professional, crime fighting, or community policing—it must be carried out through bureaucratic structure. We therefore turn to a discussion of police organization in the United States.

ThomsonNOW
Improve your grade on the exam with Personalized Study! For reinforcement resources and a mastery check of The Development of Police in the United States, go to www.thomsonedu.com/thomsonnow.

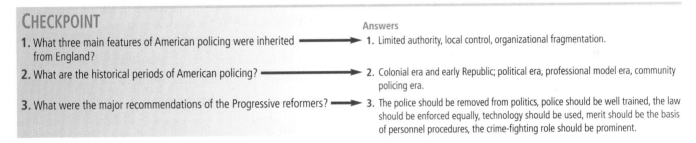

CHECKPOINT

Answers

1. What three main features of American policing were inherited ⟶ 1. Limited authority, local control, organizational fragmentation.
   from England?

2. What are the historical periods of American policing? ⟶ 2. Colonial era and early Republic; political era, professional model era, community policing era.

3. What were the major recommendations of the Progressive reformers? ⟶ 3. The police should be removed from politics, police should be well trained, the law should be enforced equally, technology should be used, merit should be the basis of personnel procedures, the crime-fighting role should be prominent.

Law Enforcement Agencies

As discussed in Chapter 1, the United States has a federal system of government with separate national and state structures, each with authority over certain functions. Police agencies at the national, state, county, and municipal levels are responsible for carrying out four functions: (1) enforcing the law, (2) maintaining order, (3) preventing crime, and (4) providing services to the community. They employ a total of more than one million sworn and unsworn personnel. Nearly 800,000 full-time sworn officers serve in state and local agencies, and an additional 88,000 sworn officers operate in federal agencies. Police agencies include the following (BJS, 2005e):

- 12,666 municipal police departments
- 3,070 sheriff's departments
- 49 state police departments (all states except Hawaii)
- 135 Native American tribal police agencies
- 30 federal agencies that employ 100 or more full-time officers authorized to carry firearms and make arrests

In addition, there are 1,376 special police agencies (jurisdictions limited to transit systems, parks, schools, and so on) as well as additional federal agencies each with fewer than 100 officers.

This list shows both the _fragmentation_ and the _local orientation_ of American police. Seventy percent of expenditures for policing occur at the local level. Each level of the system has different responsibilities, either for different kinds of crimes, such as the federal authority over counterfeiting, or for different geographic areas, such as state police authority over major highways. The broadest authority tends to lie with local units.

FEDERAL AGENCIES

Federal law enforcement agencies are part of the executive branch of the national government. They investigate a specific set of crimes defined by Congress. Recent federal efforts against drug trafficking, organized crime, insider stock trading, and terrorism have attracted attention to these agencies, even though they handle relatively few crimes and employ only 88,496 full-time officers authorized to make arrests.

The FBI   The Federal Bureau of Investigation (FBI) is an investigative agency within the U.S. Department of Justice (DOJ) with the power to investigate all federal crimes not placed under the jurisdiction of other agencies. Established as the Bureau of Investigation in 1908, it came to national prominence under J. Edgar Hoover, its director from 1924 until his death in 1972. Hoover made major changes in the bureau (renamed the Federal Bureau of Investigation in 1935) to increase its professionalism. He sought to remove political factors from the selection of agents, established the national fingerprint filing system, and oversaw the development of the Uniform Crime Reporting System. Although Hoover has been criticized for many things, such as FBI spying on civil rights and antiwar activists during the 1960s, his role in improving police work and the FBI's effectiveness is widely recognized.

Within the United States, the FBI's 12,346 special agents work out of 56 field offices and 400 additional satellite offices known as "resident agencies." In 2002 the FBI announced a new list of priorities that describes its work:

1. Protect the United States from terrorist attack.
2. Protect the United States against foreign intelligence operations and espionage.
3. Protect the United States against cyber-based attacks and high-technology crimes.
4. Combat public corruption at all levels.
5. Protect civil rights.
6. Combat transnational and national criminal organizations and enterprises.
7. Combat major white-collar crime.
8. Combat significant violent crime.
9. Support federal, state, county, municipal, and international partners.
10. Upgrade technology to successfully perform the FBI's mission.

As indicated by this list, the FBI has significant responsibilities for fighting terrorism and espionage against the United States. In addition, it continues its traditional mission of enforcing federal laws, such as those aimed at organized crime, corporate crime, corrupt government officials, and violators of civil rights laws. The bureau also provides valuable assistance to state and local law enforcement through its crime laboratory, training programs, and databases of fingerprints, stolen vehicles, and missing persons. With the growth of cyber crime, the FBI has become a leader in using technology to counteract crime as well as to prevent terrorism and espionage.

Specialization in Federal Law Enforcement   The FBI is the federal government's general law enforcement agency. By contrast, other federal agencies enforce specific laws. Elsewhere within the Department of Justice is the semiautonomous Drug Enforcement Administration (DEA) which investigates the importation and sale of controlled drugs. The Internal Revenue Service (IRS) pursues violations of tax laws, and the Bureau of Alcohol, Tobacco, Firearms, and Explosives (ATF) deals with alcohol, tobacco, gun control, and bombings.

Some other agencies of the executive branch, such as the National Parks Service, have police powers related to their specific duties. The park officers need to enforce law and maintain order to protect people and property at national parks. In addition, few people realize that some law enforcement officers in federal agencies focus on noncriminal justice policies. For example, special agents in the U.S. Department of Education investigate student loan fraud, and similar officers in the U.S. Department of Health and Human Services investigate fraud in Medicare and Medicaid programs.

The war on terrorism has greatly expanded the work of federal law enforcement agencies. Here, Mohammed Hossain walks out of a federal building after federal and local police raided a mosque in Albany, New York. Hossain was arrested after being approached by an FBI informant and asked to launder money to be used for a terrorist attack.

© Syracuse Newspapers/Dennis Nett/ The Image Works

FEDERAL AGENCIES AFTER SEPTEMBER 11

The aftermath of 9/11 has brought expansion, redirection, and reorganization, especially among federal law enforcement agencies. The creation of the Department of Homeland Security, the reordering of crime control policies away from street crime and drugs to international and domestic terrorism, and the great increase in federal money to pursue the war against terrorism are greatly affecting law enforcement at all levels of government.

Specifically, in 2004 the President requested a budgetary allocation of $36.2 billion to the new Department of Homeland Security to "develop and coordinate the implementation of a comprehensive national strategy to secure the United States from terrorist threats or attacks" (Gorman, 2003). As described in Chapter 1, the Department of Homeland Security is comprised of agencies that moved from other departments as well as newly created agencies.

Within the Department of Homeland Security, many agencies are responsible for criminal justice matters. These agencies include the following:

1. *National Cyber Security Division of the Directorate for Preparedness.* Responsible for preventing and addressing computer-based attacks on U.S. computer systems

2. *Transportation Security Administration.* As discussed in Chapter 1, responsible for security at airports as well as travel safety for passenger trains and ships

3. *Customs and Border Protection.* Responsible for the protection of borders and prevention of smuggling

4. *U.S. Secret Service.* Responsible for the personal security of the president and vice president as well as the investigation of financial crimes, including counterfeiting

5. *U.S. Coast Guard.* Responsible for the nation's ports and waterways, including the interception of drugs and other illegal items smugglers transport by boat

The federal government's emphasis on antiterrorism also affects agencies that have remained outside the Department of Homeland Security. The FBI has an increased budget and a restructuring plan in place to "increase the emphasis in counterterrorism, counterintelligence, cyber crimes, and relations with state and local law enforcement" (Oliver, 2002:1). This new thrust in policy shifts the focus of the FBI from the investigation of local street crimes to cases of international and domestic terrorism. FBI Director Robert Mueller has acknowledged that, following 9/11, many criminal investigations had to be set aside as many agents directed their attention toward Al-Qaida and anthrax cases. Further, the bureau has come to rely on state and local law enforcement to fill the gaps where the FBI could not respond to matters, such as bank robberies, that are crimes under both federal and state laws.

Although crime has historically been a state and local issue in this country, the "federalization" of crime has been a mainstay of American criminal justice policy since the 1960s. With the events of 9/11 the role of federal law enforcement agencies is apparently being reoriented to focus more on international and domestic terrorism and less on local street crimes. This may mean that state and local police will pursue their crime control policies with less support from federal agencies and fewer overlapping activities.

Antiterrorism efforts also increase the importance of federal agencies' activities abroad. The FBI and other agencies established offices in foreign countries in order to work more closely with other governments' officials who battle international crime organizations, computer crime, drug trafficking, and smuggling of illegal immigrants (Nadelmann, 1993). The contacts and international coordination developed for these anticrime activities must be expanded to enhance federal agencies' antiterrorism activities. See "Careers in Criminal Justice" for an overview of the job of an FBI special agent.

STATE AGENCIES

Each state has a police agency. Hawaii's has the unusual name of "Sheriff's Division." In about half of the states, state police agencies carry out a wide range of law

CAREERS IN CRIMINAL JUSTICE

FBI Special Agent

NATURE OF THE WORK

FBI special agents conduct investigations and enforce criminal laws to advance the agency's responsibilities for antiterrorism, counterintelligence, and law enforcement for federal offenses, such as bank robbery, public corruption, kidnapping, and fraud. Special agents must be prepared to travel and work long, irregular hours. As armed, plainclothes officers, they may face danger in investigating and apprehending suspects. They must coordinate their activities with state and local law enforcement officials as well as agents from other federal agencies. They assist federal prosecutors in preparing cases and often testify in court in criminal cases.

REQUIRED QUALIFICATIONS

Applicants must possess a four-year college degree, be aged 23 to 36, and be a U.S. citizen or a citizen of the Northern Mariana Islands. They must meet vision and hearing requirements, have a valid driver's license, and be in excellent physical condition. In selecting special agents, the FBI currently favors candidates who possess additional needed skills and education, such as knowledge of accounting, computer science, law, chemistry, or certain foreign languages (for example, Arabic, Farsi, Russian, Chinese, or Korean). Applicants must also pass a background investigation, drug test, and polygraph

test. Applicants can be disqualified for a felony or major misdemeanor conviction.

EARNINGS AND JOB OUTLOOK

Special agents enter federal service as GS-10 employees with a base pay of $42,548 a year but averaging over $53,000 because of bonuses for overtime work. Supervisory and management personnel can earn over $100,000 annually. The U.S. Department of Labor predicts that investigatory law enforcement positions will increase as fast as other jobs in the labor market. Because of new budget allocations to combat terrorism, certain other jobs in the FBI are currently increasing at a greater rate. In particular, the FBI has recently sought to add several hundred intelligence analysts with computer, foreign language, or other expertise to organize and analyze information. Intelligence analysts work in FBI offices and do not conduct field investigations, which are the responsibility of special agents.

MORE INFORMATION

Information about employment opportunities and job requirements can be found at the FBI's website, listed on the Cole/Smith Criminal Justice in America Companion Website: http://www.thomsonedu.com/criminaljustice/cole.

enforcement tasks. The others have state highway patrols with limited authority, primarily over enforcing traffic laws. The American reluctance to centralize police power has generally kept state police forces from replacing local ones.

All state forces regulate traffic on main highways, and two-thirds of the states have also given them general police powers. In only about a dozen populous states—such as Massachusetts, Michigan, New Jersey, New York, and Pennsylvania—can these forces perform law enforcement tasks across the state. For the most part, they operate only in areas where no other form of police protection exists or where local officers ask for their help. In many states, for example, the crime lab is run by the state police as a means of assisting local law enforcement agencies.

COUNTY AGENCIES

Sheriffs are found in almost every one of the 3,100 U.S. counties (except those in Alaska), which employ 174,000 full-time sworn officers (Hickman and Reaves, 2006b:iii). Sheriffs' departments are responsible for policing rural areas, but over time, especially in the Northeast, many of their criminal justice functions have been assumed by the state or local police. In parts of the South and West, however, the sheriff's department is a well-organized force. In 33 states, sheriffs are elected and hold the position of chief law enforcement officer in the county. Even when well organized, however, the sheriff's office may lack jurisdiction over cities and towns. In these situations, the sheriff and his or her deputies patrol unincorporated parts of the county or small towns that do not have police forces of their own.

In addition to performing law enforcement tasks, the sheriff often serves as an officer of the court; sheriffs may operate jails, serve court orders, and provide the bailiffs who maintain order in courtrooms. In many counties, law enforcement mixes with politics because sheriffs appoint their political supporters as deputies and bailiffs. In other places, such as Los Angeles County and Oregon's Multnomah County, the sheriff's department is staffed by professionals who are hired through competitive civil service processes.

NATIVE AMERICAN TRIBAL POLICE

Through treaties with the United States, Native American tribes are separate, sovereign nations and have a significant degree of legal autonomy. They have the power to enforce tribal criminal laws against everyone on their lands, including non-Native Americans (Mentzer, 1996). Traditionally, Native American reservations have been policed either by federal officers of the Bureau of Indian Affairs (BIA) or by their own tribal police. The 20 largest tribal police forces employ a combined total of 1,100 sworn officers. The largest tribal police force with 321 sworn officers is the Navajo Nation Department of Law Enforcement in Arizona, which has jurisdiction over 170,000 people on a land area covering nearly 22,000 square miles (BJS, 2004f: Table 1.63).

MUNICIPAL AGENCIES

The police departments of cities and towns have general law enforcement authority. City police forces range in size from more than 40,000 full-time sworn officers in the New York City Police Department to only one sworn officer in hundreds of small towns. Sworn personnel are officers with the power to make arrests. There are 452,000 full-time sworn municipal police officers nationwide (Hickman and Reaves, 2006a:iii). The six largest departments—New York City, Chicago, Los Angeles, Houston, Philadelphia, and Detroit—provide law enforcement services to less than 8 percent of the U.S. population, yet they face 23 percent of all violent crime. These big-city departments hire 19 percent of all police employees (BJS, 2002e:10).

In a metropolitan area composed of a central city and many suburbs, policing is usually divided among agencies at all levels of government, giving rise to conflicts between jurisdictions that may interfere with efficient use of police resources. The city and each suburb buy their own equipment and deploy their officers without coordinating with those of nearby jurisdictions. In some areas with large populations, agreements have been made to enhance cooperation among jurisdictions.

ThomsonNOW

Improve your grade on the exam with Personalized Study! For reinforcement resources and a mastery check of Law Enforcement Agencies, go to www.thomsonedu.com/thomsonnow.

Police Functions

The police are expected to maintain order, enforce the law, and prevent crime. However, they perform other tasks as well, many of them having little to do with crime and justice and more to do with community service. They direct traffic, handle accidents and illnesses, stop noisy parties, find missing persons, enforce licensing regulations, provide ambulance services, take disturbed people into protective custody, and so on. The list is long and varies from place to place. Some researchers have suggested that the police have more in common with social service agencies than with the criminal justice system.

How did the police gain such broad responsibilities? In many places the police are the only public agency that is available 7 days a week, 24 hours a day to respond to calls for help. They are also best able to investigate many kinds of problems. Moreover, the power to use force when necessary allows them to intervene in problematic situations.

The functions of the police can be classified into three groups: (1) order maintenance, (2) law enforcement, and (3) service. Police agencies divide their resources among these functions on the basis of community need, citizen requests, and departmental policy.

ORDER MAINTENANCE

order maintenance The police function of preventing behavior that disturbs or threatens to disturb the public peace or that involves face-to-face conflict among two or more people. In such situations the police exercise discretion in deciding whether a law has been broken.

The **order maintenance** function is a broad mandate to prevent behavior that either disturbs or threatens to disturb the peace or involves face-to-face conflict among two or more people. A domestic quarrel, a noisy drunk, loud music in the night, a beggar on the street, a tavern brawl—all are forms of disorder that may require action by the police.

Unlike most laws that define specific acts as illegal, laws regulating disorderly conduct deal with ambiguous situations that different police officers could view in different ways. For many crimes, determining when the law has been broken is easy. On the other hand, order maintenance requires officers to decide not only whether a law has been broken but also whether any action should be taken and, if so, who should be blamed. In a bar fight, for example, the officer must decide who started the fight, whether an arrest should be made for assault, and whether to arrest other people besides those who started the conflict.

Officers often must make judgments in order maintenance situations. They may be required to help people in trouble, manage crowds, supervise various kinds of services, and help people who are not fully accountable for what they do. The officers have a high degree of discretion and control over how such situations will develop. Patrol officers are not subject to direct control. They have the power to arrest, but they may also decide not to make an arrest. The order maintenance function is made more complex by the fact that the patrol officer is normally expected to "handle" a situation rather than to enforce the law, usually in an emotionally charged atmosphere. In controlling a crowd outside a rock concert, for example, the arrest of an unruly person may restore order by removing a troublemaker and also serving as a warning to others that they could be arrested if they do not cooperate. However, an arrest may cause the crowd to become hostile toward the officers, making things worse. Officers cannot always predict precisely how their discretionary decisions will promote or hinder order maintenance.

Read "Real-World Activity" at the end of the chapter to consider the challenges of handling unpredictable, dangerous situations.

LAW ENFORCEMENT

The **law enforcement** function applies to situations in which the law has been violated and the offender needs to be identified or located and then apprehended. Police officers who focus on law enforcement serve in specialized branches such as the vice squad and the burglary detail. Although the patrol officer may be the first officer at the scene of a crime, in serious cases a detective usually prepares the case for prosecution by bringing together all the evidence for the prosecuting attorney. When the offender is identified but not located, the detective conducts the search. If the offender is not identified, the detective must analyze clues to find out who committed the crime.

The police often portray themselves as enforcers of the law, but many factors interfere with how effectively they can do so. For example, when a property crime is committed, the perpetrator usually has some time to get away. This limits the ability of the police to identify, locate, and arrest the suspect. Burglaries, for instance, usually occur when people are away from home. The crime may not be discovered until hours or days have passed. The effectiveness of the police is also reduced when assault or robbery victims cannot identify the offender. Victims often delay in calling the police, reducing the chances that a suspect will be apprehended.

SERVICE

Police perform a broad range of services, especially for lower-income citizens, that are not related to crime. This kind of **service**—providing first aid, rescuing animals, helping the disoriented, and so on—has become a major police function. Crime prevention has also become a major component of police services to the community. Through education and community organizing, the police can help the public take steps to prevent crime.

It may appear that valuable resources are being inappropriately diverted from law enforcement to services. However, performing service functions can help police control crime. Through the service function, officers gain knowledge about the community, and citizens come to trust the police. Checking the security of buildings clearly helps prevent crime, but other activities—dealing with runaways, drunks, and public quarrels—may help solve problems before they lead to criminal behavior.

IMPLEMENTING THE MANDATE

Although most citizens depend most heavily on the order maintenance and service functions of the police, the public acts as though law enforcement—the catching of lawbreakers—is the most important function. According to public opinion polls, the crime-fighter image of the police is firmly rooted in citizens' minds and is the main reason that recruits give for joining the force.

Public support for budgets is greatest when the crime-fighting function is stressed. This emphasis can be seen in the organization of big-city departments. The officers who perform this function, such as detectives, enjoy high status. The focus on crime leads to the creation of special units to deal with homicide, burglary, and auto theft. All other tasks fall to the patrol division. In some departments, this pattern creates morale problems because extra resources are allocated and prestige devoted to a function that is concerned with a small percentage of the problems brought to the police. In essence, police are public servants who keep the peace, but their organization reinforces their own law enforcement image and the public's focus on crime fighting.

But do the police prevent crime? David Bayley claims that they do not. He says that "the experts know it, the police know it, but the public does not know it" (1994:3).

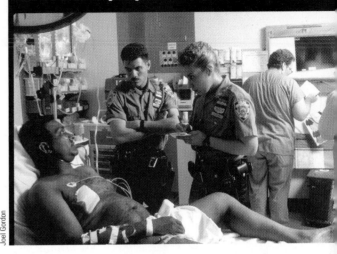

The law enforcement function requires the police to identify and apprehend the person guilty of committing a crime. By questioning this gunshot victim, officers may obtain information vital to achieving this goal.

Joel Gordon

law enforcement The police function of controlling crime by intervening in situations in which the law has clearly been violated and the police need to identify and apprehend the guilty person.

service The police function of providing assistance to the public, usually in matters unrelated to crime.

ThomsonNOW
Improve your grade on the exam with Personalized Study! For reinforcement resources and a mastery check of Police Functions, go to www.thomsonedu.com/thomsonnow.

He bases this claim on two facts. First, no link has been found between the number of police officers and crime rates. Second, the main strategies used by modern police have little or no effect on crime. Those strategies are street patrolling by uniformed officers, rapid response to emergency calls, and expert investigation of crime by detectives. Bayley says that the police believe these strategies are essential to protecting public safety, yet no evidence exists that they achieve this goal (1994:5).

CHECKPOINT

Answers

7. What is the order maintenance function? What are officers expected to do in situations where they must maintain order?

➤ 7. Police have a broad mandate to prevent behavior that either disturbs or threatens to disturb the peace or involves face-to-face conflict among two or more people. Officers are expected to "handle" the situation.

8. How do law enforcement situations compare with order maintenance situations?

➤ 8. The police in order maintenance situations must first determine if a law has been broken. In law enforcement situations, that fact is already known; thus, officers must only find and apprehend the offender.

Organization of the Police

Most police agencies follow a military model of organization, with a structure of ranks and responsibilities. But police departments are also bureaucracies designed to achieve objectives efficiently. *Bureaucracies* are characterized by a division of labor, a chain of command with clear lines of authority, and rules to guide the activities of staff. Police organization differs somewhat from place to place depending on the size of jurisdiction, the characteristics of the population, and the nature of the local crime problems. However, all sizeable departments have the basic characteristics of a bureaucracy.

BUREAUCRATIC ELEMENTS

The police department in Phoenix, Arizona, reveals the elements of bureaucracy in a typical urban police force. Figure 4.1 shows the Phoenix Police Department's organizational chart, which we refer to in the following discussion.

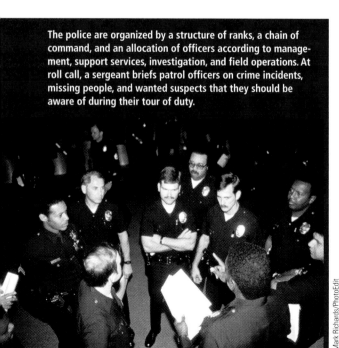

The police are organized by a structure of ranks, a chain of command, and an allocation of officers according to management, support services, investigation, and field operations. At roll call, a sergeant briefs patrol officers on crime incidents, missing people, and wanted suspects that they should be aware of during their tour of duty.

Mark Richards/PhotoEdit

Division of Labor   The Phoenix department is divided into four divisions, marked in Figure 4.1 by different colors: Headquarters, Management and Support Services, Investigations, and Field Operations (patrol). Within the Management and Support Services division and the Investigations Division, authority is further delegated to bureaus and units that have special functions (for example, property management, training, laboratory, organized crime). The Field Operations Divisions are further divided into geographic units for patrol in precincts and into specialized units to deal, for example, with traffic or special projects.

The bureaucratic organization of an urban police department such as Phoenix's allows the allocation of resources and the supervision of personnel, taking into account the needs and problems of each district.

Chain and Unity of Command   The military character of police departments is illustrated by the chain of command according to ranks—officer, commander, sergeant, lieutenant, captain, major, and chief. These make clear the powers and duties of officers at each level. Each officer has an immediate supervisor who holds authority over and responsibility for the actions of those below. Relationships between superiors and subordinates emphasize discipline, control, and accountability. These values help officers mobilize resources.

FIGURE 4.1
Organization of the Phoenix, Arizona, Police Department
This is a typical structure. Note the major divisions of headquarters, management, support services, investigations, and field operations (patrol). Specialized and geographic divisions are found within these divisions.

Source: City of Phoenix, Arizona, Police Department, *Annual Report,* 1990.

They also help protect important legal rights; if police officers are accountable to their superiors, they are less likely to abuse their authority by needlessly interfering with the freedom and rights of citizens.

OPERATIONAL UNITS

All but the smallest police departments assign officers to operational units that focus on specific functions: patrol, investigation, traffic, vice, and juvenile. These units perform the basic tasks of crime prevention and control. The patrol and investigation (detective) units form the core of the modern department. The patrol unit handles a wide range of functions, including preventing crime, catching suspects, mediating quarrels, helping the ill, and giving aid at accidents. The investigation unit identifies, apprehends, and collects evidence against lawbreakers who commit serious crimes.

Because of their overlapping duties, the separation of patrol and investigation can cause problems. Whereas the investigation unit usually focuses on murder, rape, and major robberies, the patrol unit has joint responsibility for investigating those crimes but is also solely responsible for investigating the more numerous lesser crimes.

The extent to which departments create special units may depend on the size of the city. Many departments have traffic units, but only those in mid-size to large cities also have vice and juvenile units. As a result of the war on drugs, some cities have special units working only on this problem. Large departments usually have an internal affairs section to investigate charges of corruption against officers as well as other problems associated with the staff and officers. All special units depend on the patrol officers for information and assistance.

THE POLICE BUREAUCRACY AND THE CRIMINAL JUSTICE SYSTEM

The police play an important role as a bureaucracy within the broader criminal justice system. Three issues arise in the organizational context within which the police operate.

First, the police are the gateway through which information and individuals enter the justice system. Police have the discretion to determine which suspects will be arrested and moved into the system. Cases that are sent to the prosecutor for charging and then to the courts for adjudication begin with an officer's decision that there is probable cause for an arrest. The ultimate success of the prosecution depends on the care taken by the officer in making the arrest and collecting evidence. To a large extent the outcome of the case hinges on the officer's judgment and evidence-gathering activities.

Second, police administration is influenced by the fact that the outcome of a case is largely in the hands of others. The police bring suspects into the criminal justice process, but they cannot control the decisions of prosecutors and judges. In some cases, the police officers feel that their efforts have been wasted. For example, the prosecutor sometimes agrees to a plea bargain that does not, in the eyes of the officer, adequately punish the offender. The potential for conflict between police and other decision makers in the system is increased by the difference in social status between police officers, who often do not have college degrees, and lawyers and judges, who have graduate degrees.

Third, as part of a bureaucracy, police officers are expected to observe rules and follow the orders of superiors while at the same time making independent, discretionary judgments. They must stay within the chain of command yet also make choices in response to events on the streets. To understand the impact of these factors on police behavior, let us examine two aspects of their daily work—organizational response and productivity.

ThomsonNOW™
Improve your grade on the exam with Personalized Study! For reinforcement resources and a mastery check of the Organization of the Police, go to www.thomsonedu.com/thomsonnow.

CHECKPOINT

Answers

9. What are three characteristics of a bureaucracy? ⟶ 9. Division of labor, chain and unity of command, rules and procedures.

10. What are the five operational units of all but the smallest police ⟶ 10. Patrol, investigation, traffic, vice, juvenile.
departments?

Police Policy

The police cannot enforce every law and catch every lawbreaker. Legal rules limit the ways officers can investigate and pursue offenders. For example, the constitutional ban on unreasonable searches and seizures prevents police from investigating many crimes without a search warrant.

Because the police have limited resources, they cannot have officers on every street at all times of the day and night. This means that police executives must develop policies regarding how the members of their department will implement their mandate (W. Hicks, 2003). These policies guide officers as to which offenses will receive the most attention and which tactics will be used—for example, which neighborhoods to patrol and whether to patrol in cars or on foot. These policies also determine which people will be caught committing crimes and brought into the criminal justice system for prosecution and punishment. Changes in policy—such as increasing the size of the night patrol or tolerating prostitution and other public order offenses—affect the amount of crime that gets official attention and affect the system's ability to deal with offenders. Policies with regard to high-speed pursuit, a controversial tactic in most departments, are discussed in the Close Up box.

Police policies may reflect the preferences and values of police executives. However, choices about policies are also influenced by politics, public pressure, and social context. American cities differ in government, economic, and racial and ethnic characteristics as well as in their degree of urbanization. These factors can affect the style of policing expected by the community. In a classic study, James Q. Wilson found that citizen expectations regarding police behavior affect departments through the political process; specifically, chiefs who run their departments in ways that antagonize the community are not likely to stay in office very long. Wilson's key finding was that a city's political culture, which reflects its socioeconomic characteristics and its government organization, had a major impact on the style of policing found there. Wilson further described three different styles of policing—the watchman, legalistic, and service styles (Wilson, 1968).

CLOSE UP

ALLENTOWN
+4 & OLD

High-Speed Pursuit

The suspect's pickup truck barreled across the Bridgeport, Connecticut, city line with a Trumbull police cruiser in hot pursuit. When the driver of the truck lost control, it slammed into a parked station wagon with two women inside. One, a mother of three, later died, and her sister was hospitalized for seven months. The truck continued on its way. Instead of stopping to assist the injured, the officer continued the pursuit.

Trumbull police say the pursuing officer followed departmental procedures. The suspect had broken into a house and stolen a microwave oven and other household goods. Critics say that the officer was so intent on making his collar that he never noticed others on the street.

National Highway and Traffic Safety Administration data show that about four hundred people die annually in police chases nationwide. About 1 to 3 percent of pursuits result in death. In Metro-Dade County, Florida, researchers found that 20 percent of pursuits resulted in injuries and 41 percent in accidents. Only 35 percent of pursuits were initiated to catch suspected felons, with nearly half for traffic violators.

Critics have called for strict rules banning high-speed chases, arguing that the risk to public safety is too great. Police organizations say that officers cannot be constrained too tightly or they will not be able to catch suspects. However, public pressure to restrict high-speed chases has come from accident victims and their families who, since 1980, have filed an increasing number of civil lawsuits. When a bicyclist was killed by a motorist being pursued by police in Kansas City in 2003, a citizens' committee worked with the police department to develop a restrictive policy and training program for pursuits.

Many states now require police departments to have written policies governing high-speed chases. Some departments have banned them completely.

Others have guidelines requiring officers to consider such factors as driving conditions, the seriousness of the crime, and the danger the suspect poses to the community, before pursuing a suspect. Courts have consulted such departmental policies in considering the liability of officers for damages resulting from high-speed chases.

As in so much of police work, guidelines may exist, but it is still the officer, acting alone, who must analyze the situation and exercise discretion in a highly emotional environment.

RESEARCHING THE INTERNET

To read more about police pursuit driving, read a 2004 report written for San Francisco's government officials that includes descriptions of differences in training and discretionary decision making authority for police officers in different cities. You can find the report at the corresponding website listed on the Cole/Smith Criminal Justice in America Companion Website: http://www.thomsonedu.com/criminaljustice/cole.

FOR CRITICAL ANALYSIS

Should police simply let traffic violators and suspects in nonviolent crime cases escape because of a reluctance to engage in chases? Are there any new technologies that could be developed to address the problems associated with high-speed chases?

Sources: Geoffrey P. Alpert, "Pursuit Driving: Planning Policies and Action from Agency, Officer, and Public Information," *Police Forum* 7 (January 1997): 3; Hartford Courant, September 12, 1997, p. 1; "Bicyclists Request for Changes in KCMO Police Pursuit Policies Pays Off," *Missouri Bicycle News,* November 17, 2004, http://mobikefed.org/2004/11/bicyclists-request-for-changes-in-kcmo-php.

Departments with a *watchman* style stress order maintenance. Patrol officers may ignore minor violations of the law, especially those involving traffic and juveniles, as long as there is order. The police exercise discretion and deal with many infractions in an informal way. Officers make arrests only for flagrant violations and when order cannot be maintained. The broad discretion exercised by officers can produce discrimination when officers do not treat members of different racial and ethnic groups in the same way.

In departments with a *legalistic* style, police work is marked by professionalism and an emphasis on law enforcement. Officers are expected to detain a high proportion of juvenile offenders, act vigorously against illicit enterprises, issue traffic tickets, and make a large number of misdemeanor arrests. They act as if there is a single standard of community conduct—that prescribed by the law—rather than different standards for juveniles, minorities, drunks, and other groups. Thus, although officers do not discriminate in making arrests and issuing citations, the strict enforcement of laws, including traffic laws, can seem overly harsh to some groups in the community.

Suburban middle-class communities often experience a *service* style. Residents feel that they deserve individual treatment and expect the police to provide service. Burglaries and assaults are taken seriously, whereas minor infractions tend to be dealt with by informal means such as stern warnings. The police are expected to deal with the misdeeds of local residents in a personal, nonpublic way so as to avoid embarrassment. See "A Question of Ethics" at the end of the chapter for a look at how policing styles can affect ethical decisions "down at the station."

In all cases, before officers investigate crimes or make arrests, each police chief decides on policies that will govern the level and type of enforcement in the community. Given that the police are the entry point to the criminal justice system, the decisions made by police officials affect all segments of the system. Just as community expectations shape decisions about enforcement goals and the allocation of police resources, they also shape the cases that will be handled by prosecutors and correctional officials.

CHECKPOINT

11. What are the characteristics of the watchman style of policing? ⟶

12. What is the key feature of the legalistic style of policing? ⟶

13. Where are you likely to find the service style of policing? ⟶

Answers

11. Emphasis on order maintenance, extensive use of discretion, and differential treatment of racial and ethnic groups.

12. Professionalism and using a single standard of law enforcement throughout the community.

13. Suburban middle-class communities.

Police Actions

We have seen how the police are organized and which three functions of policing—law enforcement, order maintenance, and service—compose their mandate. We have also recognized that police officers must be guided by policies developed by their superiors as to how policing is to be implemented. Police officers' actions and effectiveness also depend on the resources available to them, as illustrated by the example of computers in patrol cars (see "Technology Issues in Criminal Justice"). In the next section we look at the everyday actions of the police as they deal with citizens in often highly discretionary ways. We then discuss domestic violence, to show how the police respond to serious problems.

ENCOUNTERS BETWEEN POLICE AND CITIZENS

To carry out their mission, the police must have the public's confidence, because they depend on the public to help them identify crime and carry out investigations (see "What Americans Think"). Each year one in five Americans has face-to-face contact with law enforcement officers. A third of these contacts involve people seeking help or offering assistance. Another third involve witnessing or reporting a crime. A little less than a third say that the police initiated the contact.

TECHNOLOGY ISSUES IN CRIMINAL JUSTICE

Computers in Patrol Cars

A technological innovation that has improved police efficiency is the use of computers inside patrol cars. Computer programs permit officers to type information about traffic violations, crime suspects, and investigations directly into central computers without filling out numerous, separate forms by hand.

Officers can also gain quick access to information about automobile license plates and pending warrants. For example, new computer technology tested by the officers in the Texas Department of Public Safety reduced the time required for an officer to process a drunken driving arrest from four hours to less than one hour. A study of the Washington State Police found that officers with laptop computers in their cars were able to ticket twice as many speeders and three times as many drunken drivers as were officers who filled out paperwork by hand. The computer-connected officers also made more felony and misdemeanor arrests, presumably because paperwork absorbed less of their time.

The increase in efficiency gained through the use of computers may give police administrators greater flexibility in deciding how to deploy officers on patrol. However, the new technology has its costs and consequences. Patrol car computers can require increased time and money for training officers as well as raise safety issues if the computers become dangerous projectiles within the vehicles during high-speed pursuits or collisions. In addition, because local police departments are under the control of local governments that do not possess equal resources, some departments cannot afford to purchase computers for patrol cars. These departments—and the citizens that they serve—will not enjoy the same benefits from available technology.

RESEARCHING THE INTERNET

You can read a detailed online description of the capabilities of computers in East Hanover, New Jersey, patrol cars at the corresponding site listed on the Cole/Smith Criminal Justice in America Companion Website: http://www.thomsonedu.com/criminaljustice/cole.

FOR CRITICAL ANALYSIS

Would having a central authority that could distribute the same amount of money, and therefore technology, be good for law enforcement? Or does retaining local control outweigh the inequality in access to technology that different police departments experience?

Sources: Ricardo Alonso-Zaldivar, "Police Officers Face New Hazard: Assault by Airbag," *Los Angeles Times*, August 7, 2002, p. 24; Julie Garner, "Laptop Network in Cruisers Makes Dramatic Difference," September 10, 1999, http://www.apbnews.com [MSNBC]; Lois Pilant, "Going Mobile in Law Enforcement Technology," *National Institute of Justice Journal*, January 1998, pp. 11–16.

Although most people are willing to help the police, factors such as fear and self-interest keep some from cooperating. Many people who avoid calling the police do so because they think it is not worth the effort and cost. They do not want to spend time filling out forms at the station, appearing as a witness, or confronting a neighbor or relative in court. In some low-income neighborhoods, citizens are reluctant to assist the police, because their past experience has shown that contact with law enforcement "only brings trouble." Without information about a crime, the police may decide not to pursue an investigation. Clearly, then, citizens have some control over the work of the police through their decisions to call or not to call them.

Officers learn that developing and maintaining effective communication with people is essential to doing their job. As Officer Marcus Laffey of the New York Police Department says, "If you can talk a good game as a cop, you're halfway there." He says that police use of "confrontation and force, of roundhouse punches and high speed chases" makes the movies and the news, but "what you say and how you say it come into play far more than anything you do with your stick or your gun, and can even prevent the need for them" (Laffey, 1998:38).

Citizens expect the police to act both effectively and fairly—in ways consistent with American values. Departmental policy often affects fairness in encounters between citizens and police. When should the patrol officer frisk a suspect? When should a deal be made with the addict-informer? Which disputes should be mediated on the spot, and which left to more formal procedures? Surprisingly, these conflicts between fairness and policy are seldom decided by heads of departments but fall largely to the discretion of the officer on the scene. In many situations, the department has little control over the actions of individual officers.

POLICE DISCRETION

Police officers have the power to deprive people of their liberty, to arrest them, to take them into custody, and to use force to control them. In carrying out their

Until the 1970s most citizens and criminal justice agencies viewed domestic violence as a "private" matter best settled within the family. Today, the majority of calls to the police involve family disturbances. In many cities, police provide assistance to victims of domestic violence.

6. PRIOR RECORD
7. ATTITUDE OF VICTIM

© Viviane Moos/CORBIS

Who cares if you've been battered?

Victim Services does. And we'll help. Call our 24-hour hotline.

VICTIM SERVICES
212-577-7777

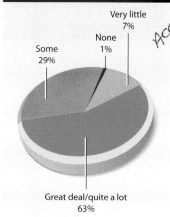

professional responsibilities, officers are expected to exercise *discretion*—to make choices in often ambiguous situations as to how and when to apply the law. Discretion can involve ignoring minor violations of the law or holding some violators to rule-book standards. It can mean arresting a disorderly person or taking that person home. In the final analysis, the officer on the scene must define the situation, decide how to handle it, and determine whether and how the law should be applied. Five factors are especially important:

1. *The nature of the crime.* The less serious a crime is to the public, the more freedom officers have to ignore it.

2. *The relationship between the alleged criminal and the victim.* The closer the personal relationship, the more variable the use of discretion. Family squabbles may not be as grave as they appear, and police are wary of making arrests, because a spouse may later decide not to press charges.

3. *The relationship between the police and the criminal or victim.* A polite complainant will be taken more seriously than a hostile one. Similarly, a suspect who shows respect to an officer is less likely to be arrested than one who does not.

4. *Race/ethnicity, age, gender, class.* Although contested by many criminal justice officials, some research shows that officers are more likely to strictly enforce the law against young, minority, poor men while being more lenient to the elderly, to whites, and to affluent women.

5. *Departmental policy.* The policies of the police chief and city officials promote more or less discretion.

DOMESTIC VIOLENCE

How the police deal with domestic violence can show the links between police–citizen encounters, the exercise of discretion, and actions taken (or not taken) by officers. Domestic violence, also called "battering" and "spouse abuse," is assaultive behavior involving adults who are married or who have a prior or an ongoing intimate relationship.

Violence by an intimate (spouse, ex-spouse, girlfriend, ex-boyfriend, and so forth) accounts for about 20 percent of all violence experienced by female victims, compared with 3 percent for male victims (BJS, 2002c). The highest rates of nonlethal violence by an intimate are among African American women, women aged 16 to 24, women in households in the lowest income categories (less than $10,000), and women residing in urban areas. A National Crime Victimization Survey estimated that during any one year, 900,000 women aged 12 or older had been victims of violence by an intimate. The survey also found that 30 percent of all female murder victims were killed by an intimate (BJS, 2000d:1, 10).

From the viewpoint of most police departments, domestic violence used to be seen as a "no-win" situation in which officers responding to calls for help were often set upon by one or both disputants. If an arrest was made, the police found that the victim often refused to cooperate with a prosecution. In addition, entering a home to deal with an emotion-laden incident was thought to be more dangerous than investigating "real" crimes. Many officers believed that trying to deal with family disputes was a leading cause of officer deaths and injury. However, this belief has been challenged by researchers who have found that domestic violence cases are no more dangerous to officers than are other incidents (Garner and Clemmer, 1986; Stanford and Mowry, 1990).

Police response to domestic violence involves a highly charged, uncertain, and possibly dangerous encounter with citizens in which officers must exercise discretion. In such a situation, how does an officer maintain order and enforce the law in accordance with the criminal law, departmental policies, and the needs of the victim? In the past, most police departments advised officers to try to calm the parties and refer them to social service agencies rather than arrest the attacker.

Prodded by the women's movement, police departments began to rethink this policy of leniency when research in Minneapolis found that abusive spouses who are arrested and jailed briefly are much less likely to commit acts of domestic violence again (Sherman and Berk, 1984:261). Although studies in other cities (Charlotte, Milwaukee, and Omaha) did not produce similar results (Ho, 2000), the research led some departments to order officers to make an arrest in every case in which evidence of an assault existed (Sherman et al., 1991:821). In many states, policies have been changed as a result of lawsuits by injured women who claimed that the police ignored evidence of assaults and in effect allowed the spouse to inflict serious injuries (Robinson, 2000). In addition, there is a growing sense that domestic violence can no longer be left to the discretion of individual patrol officers. Today, 23 states and the District of Columbia now require the arrest without a warrant of suspects in violent incidents, even if the officer did not witness the crime but has probable cause to believe that the suspect committed it (Hoctor, 1997). Most large departments and police academies have programs to educate officers about domestic violence.

Even though we can point to policy changes imposed to deal with domestic violence, the fact remains that the officer in the field is the one who must handle these situations. Each context may be different, both in terms of the officer's perceptions about what occurred and with respect to the victim's desire to see the abuser arrested and punished (Hirschel and Hutchinson, 2003). As with most law enforcement situations, laws, guidelines, and training can help; however, as is often true in police work, in the end the discretion of the officer inevitably determines what actions will be taken.

ThomsonNOW
Improve your grade on the exam with Personalized Study! For reinforcement resources and a mastery check of Police Actions, go to www.thomsonedu.com/thomsonnow

CHECKPOINT

Answers

14. Why do patrol officers have so much discretion? ⟶ **14.** They deal with citizens, often in private, and are charged with maintaining order and enforcing laws. Many of these laws are ambiguous and deal with situations in which the participants' conduct is in dispute.

15. Why have police in the past failed to make arrests in domestic violence situations? ⟶ **15.** Officers are often set upon by both parties, the victim is often uncooperative, and intervention is thought to be dangerous.

Police and the Community

The work of a police officer in a U.S. city can be very difficult, involving hours of boring, routine work interrupted by short spurts of dangerous crime fighting. Although police work has always been frustrating and dangerous, officers today must deal with situations ranging from helping the homeless to dealing with domestic violence to confronting shoot-outs at drug deals gone sour. Yet police actions are sometimes mishandled by officers or misinterpreted by the public, making some people critical of the police.

SPECIAL POPULATIONS

Urban police forces must deal with a complex population. City streets contain growing numbers of people suffering from mental illness, homelessness, alcoholism, drug addiction, or serious medical conditions such as acquired immune deficiency syndrome (AIDS) (Hails and Borum, 2003). In addition, they may find youthful runaways and children victimized by their parents' neglect. Several factors have contributed to increasing numbers of "problem" people on the streets. These factors include overcrowded jails, cutbacks in public assistance, and the closing of many psychiatric institutions, which must then release mental health patients. Most of these "problem" people do not commit crimes, but their presence disturbs many of their fellow citizens and thus they may contribute to fear of crime and disorder.

Patrol officers cooperate with social service agencies in helping individuals and responding to requests for order maintenance. The police must walk a fine line when requiring a person to enter a homeless shelter, obtain medical assistance, or be taken to a mental health unit (McCoy, 1986; Melekian, 1990). Police departments have developed various techniques for dealing with special populations. In some cities, mobile units are equipped with restraining devices, mace, and medical equipment to handle disturbed people.

Clearly, dealing with special populations is a major problem for police in most cities. Each community must develop policies so that officers will know when and how they are to intervene when a person may not have broken the law but is upsetting residents. Inevitably, police officers will make mistakes in some situations. For instance, their interactions with troubled people sometimes lead to tragic consequences, such as using lethal force against deaf or mentally ill people whose actions are misperceived as threatening. In 2003 a controversy erupted in Denver after police shot a legally blind, mentally handicapped teenager who was holding a knife (Felch, 2003).

POLICING IN A MULTICULTURAL SOCIETY

Carrying out the complex tasks of policing efficiently and according to the law is a tough assignment even when the police have the support and cooperation of the public. But policing in a multicultural society like the United States presents further challenges.

In the last half century, the racial and ethnic composition of the United States has changed. During the mid-twentieth century, many African Americans moved from rural areas of the South to northern cities. In recent years, immigrants from Central and South America have become the fastest-growing minority group in many cities. Latinos are now the largest minority population in the nation. Immigrants from Eastern Europe, Russia, the Middle East, and Asia have entered the country in greater numbers than before. Policing requires trust, understanding, and cooperation between officers and the public. People must be willing to call for help and provide information about wrongdoing. But in a multicultural society, relations between the police and minorities are complicated by stereotypes, cultural variations,

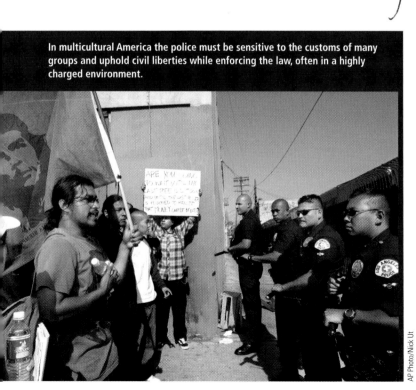

In multicultural America the police must be sensitive to the customs of many groups and uphold civil liberties while enforcing the law, often in a highly charged environment.

AP Photo/Nick Ut

and language differences. Most of these immigrants come from countries with cultural traditions and laws that differ from those in the United States. These traditions may be unfamiliar to American police officers. Further, some immigrants cannot communicate easily in English. Lack of familiarity, difficulties in communicating, and excessive suspicion can create risks that officers will violate the American value of equal treatment of all people (C. E. Smith, McCall, and Perez McCluskey, 2005).

Like other Americans who have limited personal experience or familiarity with people from different backgrounds, officers may attribute undesirable traits to members of minority groups. Treating people according to stereotypes, rather than as individuals, creates tensions that harden negative attitudes. Racial profiling, as discussed in Chapter 1, can contribute to mistrust and conflict.

Public opinion surveys have shown that race and ethnicity play a key role in determining people's attitudes toward the police. As seen in "What Americans Think," questions of fair treatment by the police differ among racial groups. Young, low-income, racial-minority men carry the most negative attitudes toward the police (S. Walker, Spohn, and DeLeone, 2003). Inner-city neighborhoods—the areas that need and want effective policing—often significantly distrust the police; citizens may therefore fail to report crimes and refuse to cooperate with the police. Encounters between officers and members of these communities are often hostile and sometimes lead to large-scale disorders. For example, in April 2001 three nights of violent protests erupted in Cincinnati, Ohio, after a police officer shot and killed an unarmed African American teenager whom police sought for outstanding misdemeanor and traffic violations.

Race is not the only factor affecting attitudes toward the police. Attitudes also stem from negative personal experience with the police, a factor associated with race. In some neighborhoods, such experience may contribute to people's unhappiness with the overall quality of life and a lack of cooperation between the public and the police. Thus, police actions and policies clearly have a significant effect on the attitudes some citizens have about the fairness of the larger political community.

Why do some urban residents resent the police? John DiIulio argues that this resentment stems from permissive law enforcement and police abuse of power (DiIulio, 1993:3). The police are perceived as failing to give protection and services to minority neighborhoods and as abusing residents physically or verbally. Thus, urban ghetto dwellers may think of the police as an army of occupation, and the police may think of themselves as combat soldiers. As noted by Jerome Skolnick and James Fyfe, the military organization of the police and the war on crime can lead to violence against inner-city residents, whom the police see as the enemy (1993:160). All aspects of officers' responsibilities, including service, order maintenance, and crime control, can suffer when police officers and the communities that they serve lack cooperation and trust.

COMMUNITY CRIME PREVENTION

There is a growing awareness that the police cannot control crime and disorder on their own. Social control requires involvement by all members of the community. Community crime prevention can be enhanced if government agencies and neighborhood organizations cooperate. Across the country, community programs to help the police have proliferated (Zhao et al., 2002). We now look at several such approaches.

More than six million Americans belong to citizen crime-watch groups, which often have direct ties to police departments. Many communities also use the Crime Stoppers Program to enlist public help in solving crimes. Television and radio stations present the "unsolved crime of the week," and cash rewards are given for information that leads to conviction of the offender. Although these programs help solve some crimes, the number solved is still small compared with the total number of crimes committed.

Research on 40 neighborhoods in six cities shows that while crime prevention efforts and voluntary community groups have seen some success in more affluent neighborhoods, such efforts and groups are less likely to be found in poor neighborhoods

Question: "Do you think the police in your community treat all races fairly or do they tend to treat one or more of these groups unfairly?"

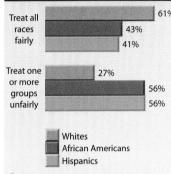

Treat all races fairly — 61%, 43%, 41%

Treat one or more groups unfairly — 27%, 56%, 56%

■ Whites
■ African Americans
■ Hispanics

Go to
http://www.thomsonedu.com/
criminaljustice/cole to compare your
opinion on this issue with the opinions
of other criminal justice students.

Source: Bureau of Justice Statistics, *Sourcebook of Criminal Justice Statistics, 2002* (Washington, DC: U.S. Government Printing Office, 2003), Table 2.24.

with high levels of disorder. In such areas, "residents typically are deeply suspicious of one another, report only a weak sense of community, perceive they have low levels of personal influence on neighborhood events, and feel that it is their neighbors, not 'outsiders,' whom they must watch with care" (Skogan, 1990:130). Scholars say that the citizens of a community must take responsibility for maintaining civil and safe social conditions. Experience has shown that "while police might be able to retake a neighborhood from aggressive drug dealers, police could not hold a neighborhood without significant commitment and actual assistance from private citizens" (Kelling and Coles, 1996:248).

CHECKPOINT

Answers

16. What "special populations" pose challenges for policing? ⟶ 16. Runaways and neglected children; people who suffer from homelessness, drug addiction, mental illness, or alcoholism.

17. What factors make policing in a multicultural society difficult? ⟶ 17. Stereotyping, cultural differences, language differences.

18. How are citizen watch groups and similar programs helpful to the police? ⟶ 18. They assist the police by reporting incidents and providing information.

A QUESTION OF ETHICS: WRITING ASSIGNMENT

Officer Jorge Perez jumped at the chance to move from the mid-size city where he began his career to the wealthiest suburb of a large city. He received better pay and benefits while gaining the opportunity to move his children to the state's most respected school system.

During his first month on the job, he caught three teenagers tossing five mailboxes filled with mail into a dumpster. He arrested the youths and took them to the station while ignoring their protests that they were merely pulling pranks on friends from school. At the station, he handcuffed them to a bench in the booking area and began to gather the proper forms to process the arrests.

Another officer walked through the booking area and asked Officer Perez what the teenagers had done.

"They stole mailboxes, so it's destruction of property plus potential federal charges for interfering with the mail, since there were letters inside the mailboxes." The other officer pulled him aside and whispered.

"Whoa, buddy. We handle things differently around here. I'll help you out. Let's call their parents quickly and get them out of here before the captain sees what's going on."

"What are you talking about? They need to learn a lesson. They committed a crime."

"You don't understand. These are rich kids whose parents will raise a ruckus if they're charged with anything. Give them a warning and let the parents pay for the damage. You might be in trouble already just for bringing them down to the station in handcuffs."

WRITING ASSIGNMENT

What should Officer Perez do? Would it be wrong to set the youths free without pursuing any charges? Do the ethics of police behavior depend on the style of policing used in a specific community? Write a memo that explains your views on the proper course of action for Officer Perez.

REAL-WORLD ACTIVITY: AN APPLICATION

On a Saturday night, a man runs into the street and flags down Officer Susette Johnson's patrol car. He points excitedly toward the door of Sam's Bar and shouts, "Some guys are about to start fighting in there."

Officer Johnson parks her car and hurries into the bar, where she sees two men standing chin-to-chin as they yell threats at each other. A crowd of bar patrons has gathered around them. One of the men sees her as she pushes through the crowd.

"Hey, arrest this dude. He's been threatening me."

The other man glances at Johnson and says sternly, "Step off, cop lady. This guy put his hands on my girlfriend and I'm not letting anybody diss me and my lady like that."

Several men in the crowd can be heard saying, "That's right" and nodding in agreement at this statement.

RESEARCHING THE INTERNET

Go to InfoTrac College Edition. Enter the keyword *police discretion* and read the article entitled "Court Backs Town in Lawsuit over Domestic Violence," *Washington Post,* 2005, to learn something about whether police officers are always at risk of lawsuits for failing a citizen's request to make an arrest.

APPLICATION

What should Officer Johnson do to handle this situation? Could her actions make a bad situation even worse? Could someone seek to have the officer punished in some way for declining to make an arrest? Should an officer have complete discretion in such situations, or should the officer's decisions be directed by specific policies?

SUMMARY

- The police in the United States owe their roots to early nineteenth-century developments in policing in England.

- Like their English counterparts, the American police have limited authority, are under local control, and are organizationally fragmented.

- The three distinctive eras of policing after the founding of the United States are the political era (1840–1920), the professional model era (1920–1970), and the community policing era (1970–present).

- In the U.S. federal system of government, police agencies are found at the national, state, county, and municipal levels.

- The functions of the police are order maintenance, law enforcement, and service.

- Police executives develop policies on how they will allocate their resources according to one of three styles: the watchman, legalistic, or service styles.

- Discretion is a major factor in police actions and decisions.

- Patrol officers exercise the greatest amount of discretion.

- The problem of domestic violence illustrates the links among police encounters with citizens, their exercise of discretion, and the actions they take.

- Police face challenges in dealing with special populations, such as the mentally ill and homeless, who need social services yet often attract the attention of police because they disturb or offend other citizens.

- Policing in a multicultural society requires an appreciation of the attitudes, customs, and languages of minority group members.

- For police to be effective, they must maintain their connection with the community.

QUESTIONS FOR REVIEW

1. What principles borrowed from England still underlie policing in the United States?

2. What are the three eras of policing in the United States in the nineteenth century and later, and what are the characteristics of each?

3. What are the functions of the police?

4. How are the police organized?

5. How do communities influence police policy and police styles?

6. How does the problem of domestic violence illustrate basic elements of police action?

7. What problems do officers face in policing a multicultural society?

KEY TERMS

frankpledge (p. 91)
law enforcement (p. 103)
order maintenance (p. 102)
service (p. 103)

GOING ONLINE

ThomsonNOW™

Maximize your study time by using ThomsonNOW's diagnostic study plan to help you review this chapter. The Study Plan will

- Help you identify areas on which you should concentrate

- Provide interactive exercises to help you master the chapter concepts

- Provide a posttest to confirm you are ready to move on to the next chapter

Police Officers and Law Enforcement Operations

Shortly before 4:00 P.M. on April 8, 2006, Officer Michael Garbarino, aged 53, sat in a cruiser in the parking lot at his Fairfax County, Virginia, police station. Having reached the end of his shift, he had removed his protective vest and uniform prior to completing final tasks before leaving for home. Without warning, a man dressed in camouflage walked into the parking lot carrying an AK-47, a hunting rifle, and five handguns. He fired 12 rounds into the cruiser. Five bullets struck Garbarino, but the officer managed to radio for help. Just as the shooting began, Detective Vicky Armel, aged 40, was leaving the back door of the police station to investigate a reported carjacking—one that in fact, had been committed by the gun-toting assailant, who had used the stolen vehicle to drive to the parking lot. The man turned and fired on Detective Armel. Although mortally wounded, she managed to return fire and wound the attacker (Jackman, 2006).

At the sound of the gunshots, two additional officers rushed from the building just as a third officer arrived at

work in his own car. Their training and sense of duty led them to react courageously in a moment of extreme danger. All three officers exchanged gunfire with the attacker until one of their shots killed him (Jackman and Barr, 2006).

The assailant was 18-year-old Michael Kennedy, a teenager with psychiatric problems who had escaped from a mental health facility and committed another carjacking only two weeks earlier. Kennedy's unexplained rampage left two veteran officers dead. Detective Armel died shortly after arriving at the hospital, and Officer Garbarino died from his wounds a few days later. These tragic events shocked the entire community. Fellow police officers in the Fairfax department were equally stunned. Their department had never before had any officers shot and killed in the line of duty (Jackman and Barr, 2006).

Officer Garbarino and Detective Armel had no way to predict the lethal danger that they would face that afternoon. Who could know that an escaped mental patient would choose that moment to launch a violent assault against police officers in a quiet community? Yet, as veteran police officers, they were constantly aware of the possibility that their jobs might someday place them in extreme danger. This is a reality that all law enforcement officers in the United States face daily. For most officers, the possibility of facing violence on any given day is remote. Indeed, many officers serve their entire careers without firing a shot while on duty. Despite the low probability of violence as they spend many hours responding to requests for service, directing traffic, and patrolling quiet neighborhoods, police officers know that the possibility of danger exists.

Who would choose a career that might entail life-threatening danger? What attracts people to a public service career that brings them into situations of conflict? How do officers' careers affect their lives and their families? These are important questions. So, too, are questions of how police departments organize training and work assignments in order to accomplish their responsibilities, including their responses to crime and dangerous situations.

In this chapter, we examine the recruitment and training of police. We also focus on the actual work of the police as they pursue suspects, prevent crimes, and otherwise serve the public. The police must be organized so that their patrol efforts can be coordinated, investigations carried out, arrests made, evidence gathered, and violators prosecuted. They also must be prepared to respond to emergencies, including situations that may place them in danger. All of these tasks must be accomplished in ways that still permit officers to fulfill their other important functions, maintaining order and providing needed services for the citizens in a community.

QUESTIONS FOR INQUIRY

- What people become police officers, and how do they learn their jobs?
- What is the police officer's "working personality?"
- What two factors affect police response?
- What are the main functions of police patrol, investigation, and special operations units?
- What patrol strategies do police departments employ?

Who Are the Police?

As they walk or drive on patrol, police officers never know what they might encounter around the next corner. What if they encounter an armed fugitive who surprises them with gunfire? Who would want to face such risks? What motivates someone to choose such a career? These questions are important because they help determine which people will be granted the authority to carry firearms and make discretionary decisions about arrests, searches, and even ending the lives of other human beings by pulling the trigger during the stressful, fast-moving events that confront police officers.

According to research, the biggest attraction of a career in policing is the variety of tasks that fill an officer's day. Instead of sitting in an office doing repetitive tasks, police officers are out on the streets doing a variety of activities that may change from day to day. Other factors that attract people to a career in policing are the opportunity to take on important responsibilities, an interest in serving the public, the possibility of adventure, and the prospect of having job security (Slater and Reiser, 1988).

Because policing is such an important occupation, society would obviously benefit from recruiting its most thoughtful, athletic, and dedicated citizens as police officers. Happily, many such individuals are attracted to this field. Yet many other people who would make fine law enforcement officers turn to other occupations because policing is such a difficult job. The modest salaries, significant job stress, and moments of danger involved in police work can deter some individuals from choosing this public service occupation.

RECRUITMENT

How can departments recruit well-rounded, dedicated public servants who will represent the diversity of contemporary America? Moreover, how can law enforcement agencies make sure that each individual is qualified to handle the wide array of responsibilities facing police officers? All agencies use a list of requirements concerning education, physical abilities, and background record in accepting applications. Some federal agencies, including the FBI and Drug Enforcement Administration, seek additional skills, such as expertise in computers and accounting or fluency in a foreign language. A typical list of basic requirements for a career in law enforcement includes the following (if you are interested in working for a particular agency, check for that agency's specific requirements):

■ Be a U.S. citizen.

■ Meet age requirements. The minimum age is normally 21, although some federal agencies place the minimum at 23. The maximum age for hiring in federal agencies ranges from 36 (FBI and DEA) to 39 (Border Patrol), depending on the agency.

■ Have a high school diploma. Increasingly, state and local agencies require some college coursework (four-year college degree required for some federal agencies such as the FBI and DEA).

■ Possess a valid driver's license.

■ Have a healthy weight in proportion to height, body frame, and age.

■ Pass a medical health examination, including a hearing test—reliance on a hearing aid can result in disqualification.

■ Be in excellent physical condition. Recruits are typically required to pass a physical fitness exam administered by the agency or as part of law enforcement certification program in a police training academy. For example, the U.S. Border Patrol requires 20 push-ups in one minute; 25 sit-ups in one minute; 30 steps-per-minute up and down at a one-foot step for five minutes; a 1.5 mile run in 13 minutes; a 220-yard dash in 46 seconds; and a timed obstacle course.

■ Be able to lift and carry moderately heavy objects (45 to 60 pounds).

■ Have vision correctable to 20/20 and uncorrected vision of at least 20/200; some agencies require normal color vision (the DEA, for example).

■ Pass a background investigation, including an arrest record and a credit check. Prior felony or serious misdemeanor convictions can disqualify an applicant, as can a misdemeanor conviction for domestic violence.

■ Pass a polygraph examination (lie detector test).

■ Take a urinalysis drug test. Often, recruits are also required to respond to written or interview questions about any prior use of illegal drugs.

■ Take a written test to demonstrate literacy, basic math skills, and reasoning ability. Knowledge of law and other subjects is also sometimes tested.

In addition, agencies increasingly require recruits to undergo psychological evaluations, because each officer will ultimately make important discretionary decisions, including those that determine life and death in stressful situations (Langworthy, Hughes, and Sanders, 1995:26).

Candidates for state and local enforcement positions must often obtain a certification for their state's law enforcement training agency, such as the Michigan Commission on Law Enforcement Standards. Many small towns and counties cannot afford to send their officer-applicants to a police academy program for this certification. Thus, they advertise job vacancies with the requirement that applicants have already obtained certification by attending a police academy, such as the 12- to 22-week non-degree classes offered through the criminal justice programs at many colleges. Paying to attend police academy programs imposes an extra expense on many individuals who seek a career in law enforcement. However, some of these programs can fulfill some of the requirements for associate's or bachelor's degrees in criminal justice, depending on the college offering the program. Larger cities are more likely either to pay for their selected candidates to attend a police academy or to run their own academies to train their new hires. State police agencies also typically run their own training academies for new hires. The U.S. Marine Corps Base at Quantico, Virginia, is home to the training academies for new special agents in the DEA (16-week program) and the FBI (17-week program). New agents in the U.S. Secret Service, the ATF, and other federal law enforcement agencies attend 11-week training academies at the primary Federal Law Enforcement Training Center (FLETC) in Glynco, Georgia. These agencies subsequently provide new agents with additional specialized training, sometimes at the other FLETC training centers in Artesia, New Mexico; Charleston, South Carolina; and Cheltenham, Maryland.

Which agencies are the most attractive to people seeking careers in law enforcement? One factor in attracting recruits is the compensation that departments offer. In 2003 the average starting salary in local police departments was $35,162 per year; the average maximum salary for regular patrol officers was $48,733, a level that typically takes seven years to attain (BJS, 2004f). In the larger cities, with a population of 50,000 or more, salaries tend to be higher. Further, because supervisory personnel make higher salaries, many officers seek promotions to detective, sergeant, captain, and other ranks. The average annual salary for city police chiefs nationwide was $68,212; chiefs in cities with populations of 50,000 or more averaged over $100,000 per year (BJS, 2004f: Table 1.70). Poor, rural counties may have a more difficult time competing for applicants. Such departments may recruit outstanding officers who want to live in a particular rural community, but more attractive compensation packages in other agencies may also lure rural officers away.

Federal agencies, which offer higher salaries and better benefits than do many local departments, often attract large numbers of applicants. These positions also require higher levels of education and experience than do many local law enforcement agencies. Starting salaries for Border Patrol Agents are $34,966 per year (GS-5 level: four-year degree or one year of relevant professional experience) or $39,797 (GS-7 level: one year of graduate school or one year of law enforcement experience). FBI special agents begin at $43,441 (GS-10: four-year degree and special skill or law enforcement experience).

As indicated by these examples, federal agencies typically look for college graduates. By contrast, only 1 percent of local police departments require a four-year college degree, whereas 8 percent of departments require a two-year degree, and an additional 6 percent expect some college coursework (Hickman and Reaves, 2003). The number of departments requiring college classes for officers is steadily growing. Even those departments that require only a high school diploma often prefer candidates with college coursework and encourage their officers to seek additional education. The idea that college-educated officers would make more effective officers helped to spur the creation of the federal Police Corps program that provided training and financial incentives for college graduates to work as local police officers (Gest, 2001). Although some researchers found that a college education makes little difference for police performance, other scholars have concluded that it reduces disciplinary problems and citizens' complaints while it improves report writing and other aspects of performance (Krimmel, 1996; Lersch and Kunzman, 2001). See Table 5.1 for examples of educational requirements and starting salaries for a variety of law enforcement positions.

THE CHANGING PROFILE OF THE POLICE

For most of the nation's history, almost all police officers were white men. Today, women and minorities represent a growing percentage of police departments in many areas. The Equal Employment Opportunity Act of 1972 bars state and local governments from discriminating in their hiring practices. Pressured by state and federal agencies as well as by lawsuits, most city police forces have mounted campaigns to recruit more minority and female officers (Martin, 1991). Since the 1970s the percentage of minority group members and women working as police has doubled.

TABLE 5.1 Educational Requirements and Starting Salaries in Law Enforcement Careers (Selected Examples)			
Position	**Agency**	**Education Required**	**Starting Salary**
Local			
Police Officer	New York City Police Dept.	2 years college or 2 years military service	$32,700
Police Officer	Alamogorodo, NM, Police Dept.	HS diploma and state law enforcement certification	$26,000–$30,000
Deputy Sheriff	St. Mary's County, MD, Sheriff's Dept.	HS diploma	$37,731
Deputy Sheriff	Cumberland County, NC, Sheriff's Dept.	HS diploma	$28,806
State			
Trooper	Tennessee Highway Patrol	HS diploma	$30,528
Highway Patrol Officer	California Highway Patrol	HS diploma	$50,952
Federal (minimum salaries listed; higher salaries come with more education and skills)			
Border Patrol Agent	U.S. Customs and Border Protection	4-year college degree or substantial work experience	$34,966
Special Agent	U.S. Secret Service	4-year college degree or substantial work experience	$34,966
Federal Air Marshal	Transportation Security Administration	4-year college degree or substantial work experience	$36,400

Sources: Websites of individual law enforcement agencies.

More than 22 percent of officers nationwide belong to minority groups (see Figure 5.1). The percentage is even larger—38 percent—in big-city police departments (Reaves and Hickman, 2002).

Minority Police Officers   Before the 1970s many police departments did not hire non-whites. As this practice declined, the makeup of police departments changed, especially in large cities. A study of the nation's 62 local police departments serving a population of 250,000 or more found that from 1990 to 2000 the percentage of African American officers rose to 20 percent of the force, Hispanics rose to 14 percent, and Asian/Pacific Islander/Native Americans to 3.2 percent (Reaves and Hickman, 2002). The fact that minority officers constitute 38 percent of these departments represents a dramatic change in staff composition over the past two decades.

As population and political power shift toward minorities in some U.S. cities, the makeup of their police forces reflects this change. Three-quarters of Detroit's population is now African American, as is about 63 percent of the city's police officers. In El Paso and San Antonio, Texas, which have large Hispanic populations, 72 percent and 42 percent of their police departments are Hispanic, respectively. The extent to which the police reflect the racial composition of a city is believed to affect police–community relations and thus the quality of law enforcement. A survey of Detroit residents found that African Americans held more favorable attitudes toward the police than did whites. As researchers note, "In Detroit, the people who perform the police function are not alien to African Americans; instead they represent an indigenous force" (Frank et al., 1996:332).

Women on the Force   Women have been police officers since 1905, when Lola Baldwin became an officer in Portland, Oregon. However, the number of women officers remained small for most of the twentieth century because of the belief that policing was "men's work." This attitude changed as the result of federal and state laws against employment discrimination as well as court decisions enforcing those laws. Court decisions opened up police work for women by prohibiting job assignments by gender; changing

FIGURE 5.1

The changing profile of the American police officer

Today about one in ten officers is female and one in five belongs to a racial or ethnic minority.

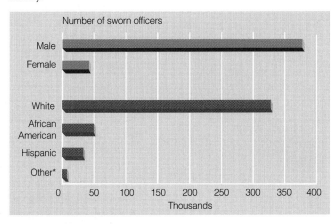

*Includes Asian, Pacific Islander, Native American, and Native Alaskan.

Source: Brian A. Reaves and Andrew L. Goldberg, *Local Police Departments, 1997* (Washington, DC: Bureau of Justice Statistics, U.S. Government Printing Office, 2000), 3.

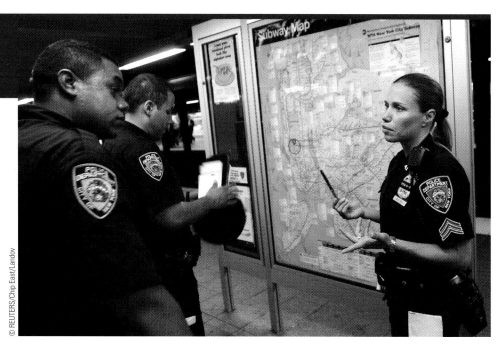

Police are no longer exclusively made up of white males. Women and minorities now represent an increasing portion of the force, especially in urban areas.

© REUTERS/Chip East/Landov

minimum height, weight, and physical fitness requirements; and insisting that departments develop job classification and promotion criteria that were nondiscriminatory (*Blake v. Los Angeles*, 1979; *Griggs v. Duke Power Company*, 1971).

The percentage of female officers has risen from 1.5 percent of sworn officers in 1970 to about 10 percent today (Reaves and Goldberg, 2000). Interestingly, the larger the department, the higher the proportion of women as sworn officers. In cities of more than 250,000, women make up 16 percent of officers (Reaves and Hickman, 2002). In some police departments, such as Detroit's, more than 20 percent of officers are women (S. Walker and Turner, 1992). By contrast, women make up only 2 to 5 percent of officers, on average, in cities with fewer than 50,000 inhabitants (Reaves and Goldberg, 2000). A study of 800 police departments by the International Association of Chiefs of Police (IACP) found that almost 20 percent of the departments surveyed had no women officers, and of the nation's 17,000 departments, only 123 had women serving as chiefs (IACP, 1998:5).

Many male officers were upset by the entry of women into what they viewed as a male world. They complained that if their patrol partner was a woman, they could not be sure of her ability to provide necessary physical help in times of danger. The challenges for female officers from minority groups may be even more difficult if they perceive others as doubting their qualifications and ability because of their race as well as their gender (Dodge and Pogrebin, 2001).

The IACP survey found that 25 percent of top law enforcement officials expressed concerns that female officers could not handle physical conflicts (IACP, 1998:23). However, although some male police officers still question whether women can handle dangerous situations and physical confrontations, most policewomen have easily met the expectations of their superiors. Further, studies done by the Police Foundation and other researchers have found that, in general, male and female officers perform in similar ways. Alissa Worden's research found few differences in the ways male and female officers viewed "their role, their clientele, or their departments" (Worden, 1993:203). Research has also found that most citizens have positive things to say about the work of policewomen (Bloch and Anderson, 1974; Grennan, 1987; Sichel, 1978; Worden, 1993). Some researchers believe that women have generally superior performance in avoiding excessive use of force and interviewing crime victims, especially in cases of sexual assault and domestic violence (Prussel and Lonsway, 2001). Rape victims sometimes specifically request to be interviewed by a female officer, so gender diversity on a police force may be valuable in investigating specific types of crimes or dealing with certain kinds of victims and witnesses (Jordan, 2002). Despite these findings, women still have trouble breaking into police work. Cultural expectations of women often conflict with ideas about the proper behavior of officers.

According to Susan Martin, the statistics on women in policing provide both "good news and bad news . . . because the steady numerical and proportional gains [are counterbalanced] by the concentrate[ion] of women at the bottom of the police hierarchy" (Martin, 2005:352). In a few cities, such as Atlanta, Georgia, and Portland, Oregon, a small number of women have risen to the top ranks of police departments. Elsewhere, employment discrimination lawsuits have helped open promotional opportunities for women. In many other departments, however, few women have gained supervisory jobs. Thus, male administrators are usually the ones who must identify and combat any remaining barriers to the recruitment, retention, and promotion of female officers (Lord and Friday, 2003; S. Walker and Turner, 1992).

TRAINING

The performance of the police is not based solely on the types of people recruited; it is also shaped by their training. As mentioned previously, aspiring officers may be required to pay for their own police academy training if they are not hired by departments that pay for or provide the training. Police academy training courses range from two-week sessions that stress the handling of weapons to academic four-month programs followed by fieldwork. Recruits hear lectures on social relations, receive foreign-language training, and learn emergency medical treatment.

Much of police training is on the job. Working with a senior officer, "rookies" are socialized into the police subculture.

Michael Nagle/The New York Times/Redux

Formal training is needed to gain an understanding of legal rules, weapons use, and other aspects of the job. However, the police officer's job also demands social skills that cannot be learned from a lecture or a book. Much of the most important training of police officers takes place during a probationary period when new officers work with and learn from experienced ones. When new officers finish their classroom training and arrive for their first day of patrol duty, experienced officers may say, "Now, I want you to forget all that stuff you learned at the academy. You really learn your job on the streets." Many departments require newcomers to ride with an experienced training officer for a certain number of weeks or months before they can patrol on their own.

The process of **socialization**—in which members learn the symbols, beliefs, and values of a group or subculture—includes learning the informal rather than the rule-book ways of law enforcement. New officers must learn how to look "productive," how to take shortcuts in filling out forms, how to keep themselves safe in dangerous situations, how to analyze conflicts so as to maintain order, and a host of other bits of wisdom, norms, and folklore that define the subculture of a particular department. Recruits learn that loyalty to other officers, esprit de corps, and respect for police authority are highly valued.

In police work, the success of the group depends on the cooperation of its members. All patrol officers are under direct supervision, and their performance is measured by their contribution to the group's work. Besides supervisors, the officers' colleagues also evaluate and influence them. Officers within a department may develop strong, shared views on the best way to "handle" various situations. How officers use their personal skills and judgment can mean the difference between defusing

socialization The process by which the rules, symbols, and values of a group or subculture are learned by its members.

a conflict and making it worse so that it endangers citizens and other officers. In tackling their "impossible mandate," new recruits must learn the ways of the world from the other officers, who depend on them and on whom they depend.

The Police Subculture

subculture The symbols, beliefs, values, and attitudes shared by members of a subgroup of the larger society.

A **subculture** is made up of the symbols, beliefs, values, and attitudes shared by members of a subgroup within the larger society. The subculture of the police helps define the "cop's world" and each officer's role in it. Like the subculture of any occupational group that sees itself as distinctive, police develop shared values that affect their view of human behavior and their role in society. As we just saw, the recruit learns the norms and values of the police subculture through a process of socialization. This begins at the training academy but really takes hold on the job through interactions with experienced officers. The characteristics of a subculture are not static, though; they change as new members join the group and as the surrounding environment changes. For example, the composition of the police has changed dramatically during the past 30 years in terms of race, gender, and education. We should thus expect these "new officers" to bring different attitudes and cultural values to the police subculture (S. Walker, 1999:332).

There are four key issues in our understanding of the police subculture: the concept of the "working personality," the role of police morality, the isolation of the police, and the stress involved in police work.

THE WORKING PERSONALITY

working personality A set of emotional and behavioral characteristics developed by members of an occupational group in response to the work situation and environmental influences.

Social scientists have demonstrated that there is a relationship between one's occupational environment and the way one interprets events. The police subculture produces a **working personality**—that is, a set of emotional and behavioral characteristics developed by members of an occupational group in response to the work situation and environmental influences. The working personality of the police thus influences the way officers view and interpret their occupational world.

Two elements of police work define the working personality of the police: (1) the threat of danger and (2) the need to establish and maintain one's authority (Skolnick, 1966:44).

Danger   Because they often face dangerous situations, officers are keenly aware of clues in people's behavior or in specific situations that indicate that violence and law-breaking may be about to happen. As they drive the streets, they notice things that seem amiss—a broken window, a person hiding something under a coat—anything that looks suspicious. As sworn officers, they are never off duty. People who know that they are officers will call on them for help at any time, day or night.

Throughout the socialization process, experienced officers warn recruits to be suspicious and cautious. Rookies are told about officers who were killed while trying to settle a family squabble or writing a traffic ticket. The message is clear: Even minor offenses can escalate into extreme danger. Constantly pressured to recognize signs

The occupational environment and working personality are so interlocked that they greatly influence the daily experience of the police.

Bob Daemmrich/The Image Works

of crime and be alert to potential violence, officers may become suspicious of everyone, everywhere. Thus, police officers are in a constant state of "high alert," always on the lookout and never letting down their guard.

Being surrounded by risks creates tension in officers' lives. They may feel constantly on edge and worried about possible attack. This concern with danger may affect their interactions with citizens and suspects. Citizens who come into contact with them may see their caution and suspicion as hostile, and such suspicion may generate hostile reactions from suspects. As a result, many on-the-street interrogations and arrests can lead to confrontations.

Authority   The second aspect of the working personality is the need to exert authority. Unlike doctors, psychiatrists, lawyers, and other professionals whose clients recognize and defer to their authority, police officers must establish authority through their actions. The officer's uniform, badge, gun, and nightstick symbolize his or her position and power, but the officer's demeanor and behavior are what determine whether people will defer.

Victims are glad to see the police when they are performing their law enforcement function (Hawdon and Ryan, 2003), but the order maintenance function puts pressure on officers' authority. If they try too hard to exert authority in the face of hostile reactions, officers may cross the line and use excessive force.

Researchers have studied expressions of disrespect by officers toward members of the public and vice versa (Reisig et al., 2004). One finding indicates that police officers' own expressions of disrespect in encounters with citizens, such as name-calling and other kinds of derogatory statements, occur most often when those citizens had already shown disrespect to the officers (Mastrofski, Reisig, and McCluskey, 2002).

In sum, working personality and occupational environment are closely linked and constantly affect the daily work of the police. Procedural rules and the structure of policing are overshadowed by the need to exert authority in the face of potential danger in many contexts in which citizens are angry, disrespectful, or uncooperative.

POLICE MORALITY

In his field observations of Los Angeles patrol officers, Steve Herbert found a high sense of morality in the law enforcement subculture. He believes that three aspects of modern policing create dilemmas that their morality helps to overcome. These dilemmas include (1) the contradiction between the goal of preventing crime and the officers' inability to do so, (2) the fact that officers must use their discretion to "handle" situations in ways that do not strictly follow procedures, and (3) "the fact that they invariably act against at least one citizen's interest, often with recourse to coercive force that can maim or kill" (Herbert, 1996:799).

Herbert believes that justifying their actions in moral terms, such as upholding the law, protecting society, and chasing "bad guys," helps officers lessen the dilemmas of their work. Thus, they may condone use of force as necessary for ridding "evil from otherwise peaceable streets." It is the price we pay to cleanse society of the "punks," "crazies," or "terrorists." But police morality can also be applauded: Officers work long hours and are genuinely motivated to help people and improve their lives, often placing themselves at risk. Yet, to the extent that police morality crudely categorizes individuals and justifies insensitive treatment of some community members, it contributes to police–citizen tensions.

POLICE ISOLATION

Police officers' suspicion of and isolation from the public may stem in part from their belief that the public is hostile to them. Many officers feel that people look on them with suspicion, in part because they have the authority to use force to gain compliance. Public opinion polls have found that a majority of people have a high opinion of the police. However, as shown in "What Americans Think," people have different opinions regarding the police officers' ethical standards.

WHAT AMERICANS THINK

Question: "Please tell me how you would rate the honesty and ethical standards of the police—very high, high, average, low, or very low?"

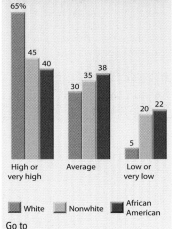

■ White   ■ Nonwhite   ■ African American

Go to http://www.thomsonedu.com/criminaljustice/cole to compare your opinion on this issue with the opinions of other criminal justice students.

Note: Nonwhite includes African American respondents.

Source: Bureau of Justice Statistics, *Sourcebook of Criminal Justice, 2005* (Washington, DC: U.S. Government Printing Office, 2006), Table 2.21.2005.

Police officers' isolation from the public is made worse by the fact that many officers interact with the public mainly in moments of conflict, emotion, and crisis. Victims of crimes and accidents are often too hurt or distraught to thank the police. Citizens who are told to stop some activity when the police are trying to keep order may become angry at the police. Even something as minor as telling someone to turn down the volume on a stereo can make the police the "bad guy" in the eyes of people who believe that the officer's authority limits personal freedom.

Ironically, these problems may be worst in poor neighborhoods, where effective policing is needed most. There, pervasive mistrust of the police may keep citizens from reporting crimes and cooperating with investigations. Because they believe that the public is hostile to them and that the nature of their work makes the situation worse, the police tend to separate themselves from the public and to form strong in-group ties.

One result of the demands placed on the police is that officers often cannot separate their job from other aspects of their lives. From the time they receive badges and guns, they must always carry these symbols of the position—the "tools of the trade"—and be prepared to use them. Their obligation to remain vigilant even when off duty and to work at odd hours reinforces the values shared with other officers. Strengthening this bond is officers' tendency to socialize mainly with their families and other officers.

JOB STRESS

The work environment and police subculture contribute to the stress felt by officers. This stress can affect not only the way officers treat the citizens they encounter but also the officer's health (Anderson, Litzenberger, and Plecas, 2002). Stress also affects how officers interact with each other (Haarr and Morash, 1999). Scholars have also found that work environment, work–family conflict, and individual coping mechanisms are the most significant predictors of stress for individual officers (Zhao et al., 2003).

Police officers are always on alert, sometimes face grave danger, and feel unappreciated by a public they perceive to be hostile. Thus, that their physical and mental health suffers at times is not surprising. In fact, the American Institute of Stress states that policing is one of the ten most stress-producing jobs (*Newsweek,* April 25, 1988:43). The effects of stress are compounded by the long hours many officers work, including double shifts that deprive them of sleep and make them work under conditions of severe fatigue (Vila and Kenney, 2002). The stress of police work may help explain why officer suicide poses a problem for some law enforcement agencies (Hackett and Violanti, 2003).

In 2002 many Americans were shocked when a Nebraska state trooper killed himself after botching a background check on a man who later participated in killing five people during a bank robbery. When checking the serial number of a gun that he found on the man during a traffic stop, the trooper inadvertently typed the wrong numbers into the computer and failed to discover that the gun was stolen. Apparently, he blamed himself because he believed that the homicides would have been prevented if he had arrested the man after doing a proper background check (Lorentzen, 2002). Because of their important duties and self-image as guardians of society, some police officers suffer severe stress when they cannot prevent tragic crimes from occurring. Only since the late 1970s have law enforcement officials become fully aware of the stress-related harms experienced by officers (Lumb and Breazeale, 2003).

Psychologists have identified four kinds of stress that officers face and the factors that cause each (Cullen et al., 1985):

1. *External stress.* This is produced by real threats and dangers, such as the need to enter a dark and unfamiliar building, respond to "man with a gun" alarms, and chase lawbreakers at high speeds.

2. *Organizational stress.* This is produced by the nature of work in a paramilitary structure: constant adjustment to changing schedules, irregular work hours, and detailed rules and procedures.

3. *Personal stress.* This can be caused by an officer's racial or gender status among peers, which can create problems in getting along with other officers and adjusting to group-held values that differ from one's own. Social isolation and perceptions of bias also contribute to personal stress.

4. *Operational stress.* This reflects the total effect of dealing with thieves, derelicts, and the mentally ill; being lied to so often that all citizens become suspect; being required to face danger to protect a public that seems hostile; and always knowing that one may be held legally liable for one's actions.

Some departments now have programs centering on stress prevention, group counseling, liability insurance, and family involvement. Many states have more liberal disability and retirement rules for police than for other public employees, because their jobs are more stressful (Goolkasian, Geddes, and DeJong, 1989).

As we have seen, police officers face special pressures that can affect their interactions with the public and even harm their physical and mental health. How would you react to the prospect of facing danger and being on the lookout for crime at every moment, even when you were not actually working? It seems understandable that police officers become a close-knit group, yet their isolation from society may decrease their understanding of other people. It may also strengthen their belief that the public is ungrateful and hostile. As a result, officers' actions toward members of the public may be hostile, gruff, or even violent.

ThomsonNOW
Improve your grade on the exam with Personalized Study! For reinforcement resources and a mastery check of The Police Subculture, go to www.thomsonedu.com/thomsonnow.

CHECKPOINT

Answers

4. What are the two key aspects of the police officer's working personality? ➡ **4.** Danger, authority.

5. What are the four types of stress felt by the police? ➡ **5.** External stress, organizational stress, personal stress, operational stress.

Police Response and Action

In a free society, people do not want police on every street corner asking them what they are doing. Thus, the police are mainly **reactive** (responding to citizen calls for service) rather than **proactive** (initiating actions in the absence of citizen requests). Studies of police work show that 81 percent of actions result from citizen telephone calls, 5 percent are initiated by citizens who approach an officer, and only 14 percent are initiated in the field by an officer. These facts affect the way departments are organized and the way the police respond to incidents.

Because they are mainly reactive, the police usually arrive at the scene only after the crime has been committed and the perpetrator has fled. This means that the police are hampered by the time lapse and sometimes by inaccurate information given by witnesses. For example, a mugging may happen so quickly that victims and witnesses cannot accurately describe what happened. In about a third of cases in which police are called, no one is present when the police arrive on the scene.

Citizens have come to expect that the police will respond quickly to every call, whether it requires immediate attention or can be handled in a more routine manner. This expectation has produced **incident-driven policing**, in which calls for service are the primary instigators of action. Studies have shown, though, that less than 30 percent of calls to the police involve criminal law enforcement—most calls concern order maintenance and service (S. Walker, 1999:80). To a large extent, then, reports by victims and observers define the boundaries of policing.

The police do use proactive strategies such as surveillance and undercover work to combat some crimes. When addressing crimes without victims, for example, they must rely on informers, stakeouts, wiretapping, stings, and raids. Because of the current focus on drug offenses, police resources in many cities have been assigned to proactive efforts to apprehend people who use or sell illegal drugs.

reactive Occurring in response, such as police activity in response to notification that a crime has been committed.

proactive Acting in anticipation, such as an active search for potential offenders that is initiated by the police without waiting for a crime to be reported. Arrests for crimes without victims are usually proactive.

incident-driven policing Policing in which calls for service are the primary instigators of action.

New high-tech tools, connected to high-speed wireless communications, have become widely available to officers in the field. Here, Officer Mike Frome of Portland, Oregon, uses a mobile device that can scan a person's fingerprints and compare them with others in a database.

John Klicker/The New York Times/Redux

ORGANIZATIONAL RESPONSE

The organization of the police bureaucracy influences how the police respond to citizens' calls. Factors that affect the response process include the separation of police into various functional groups (patrol, vice, investigation, and so on), the quasi-military command system, and the techniques used to induce patrol officers to respond in desired ways.

Police departments are being reshaped by new communications technology, which has tended to centralize decision making. The core of the department is the communications center, where commands are given to send officers into action.

Patrol officers are expected to be in constant touch with headquarters and must report each of their actions. Two-way radios, cell phones, and computers are the primary means by which administrators monitor the decisions of officers in the field. In the past, patrol officers might have administered on-the-spot justice to a mischievous juvenile, but now they must file a report, take the youth into custody, and start formal proceedings. Because officers must contact headquarters by radio or computer with reports about each incident, headquarters is

---

CLOSE UP

Holding the 911 Line

It's a new day. I walk down to the basement of the public-safety building, pass through a secured entrance and walk slowly down a long, quiet corridor. My stomach tightens a bit as I approach a final locked door. . . . I'm in the Phoenix Police Communications Center, known as "911." . . .

It's 0800 hours. I take a deep breath, say a little prayer and hope that I don't make any mistakes that might get me on the 6 o'clock news. This will be my not-so-happy home for the next 10 hours.

"911, what is your emergency?" It's my first call of the day. The woman is crying but calm. She has tried to wake her elderly husband. With the push of a button I connect her to the fire department. They ask if she wants to attempt CPR, but she says, "No, he's cold and blue . . . I'm sure he's dead." I leave the sobbing widow in the hands of the fire dispatcher. I'm feeling sad, but I just move on. I have more incoming calls to take. It's busy this morning. The orange lights in each corner of the room are shining brightly, a constant reminder that nonemergency calls have been holding more than 90 seconds. My phone console appears to be glowing, covered with blinking red lights. It's almost hypnotic, like when you sit in the dark and stare at a lit Christmas tree, or gaze into a flickering fireplace. But then I remember that each light represents a person—a person with a problem, someone in crisis.

A loud bell is ringing. It means an emergency call is trying to get through but the lines are jammed. All operators are already on a call. I quickly put my caller on hold. He's just reporting a burglary that occurred over the weekend. . . .

"911, what is your emergency?" This one's serious. A bad traffic accident, head-on collision. "Yes, sir, we'll get right out there." I get officers started and advise the fire department. Now everyone in the vicinity of the accident is calling. "Yes, ma'am, we're on the way." "We'll be out shortly, sir, thanks for calling." My supervisor comes out of his office to advise us of something. He always looks serious, but this time it's different. He looks worried and upset. He tells us that two of our detectives were involved in the

collision. He doesn't know who they are or how badly they're injured. My heart stops momentarily because my husband is a detective. I quickly call the office and confirm that he is safe. I'm relieved but still stunned. . . . But there's not much time for sentiment. There are more calls to take, more decisions to make and more pressures needing attention. . . .

"911, what is your emergency?" It's just a boy on a phone getting his kicks by calling me vulgar names. He hangs up before I have a chance to educate him on correct 911 usage. We get a lot of trivial calls, pranksters, hang-ups, citizens complaining to us about a noncrime situation, something they should handle themselves. People call us because they don't know where to turn. Everyone must be treated fairly and with respect. It's a difficult balance to maintain.

My supervisor again comes out to advise us. His face shows a sadness I've never seen in him. "The officers were killed in the accident." A quietness descends over the room. I suppose the bells are still ringing and the lights flashing but I don't hear or see them. The typing stops; talking ceases. I just want to get out of here and cry, but I have to stay and do my job. I have to keep going. I can break down on my long drive home tonight; for now I have phones to answer, people to help.

RESEARCHING THE INTERNET

Many police departments try to educate the public about when it is appropriate to dial 911. For an online example of such guidance, see the site listed on the Cole/Smith Criminal Justice in America Companion Website: http://www.thomsonedu.com/criminaljustice/cole.

FOR CRITICAL ANALYSIS

What skills are needed by a 911 operator? How should such operators be trained? What kinds of errors might be made by 911 operators and how would those errors occur?

Source: Tracy Lorenzano, "Holding the 911 Line," *Newsweek*, June 20, 1994, p. 10. Copyright © 1994 by Newsweek, Inc. All rights reserved. Reprinted by permission.

better able to guide officers' discretion and ensure that they comply with departmental policies. Although most large cities and state police agencies have acquired computers for their patrol cars, it often takes longer for small towns and rural sheriff's departments to receive funding from their local governments to purchase new technology.

Most residents in urban and suburban areas can call 911 to report a crime or obtain help or information. The 911 system has brought a flood of calls to police departments—many not directly related to police responsibilities. In Baltimore a "311 system" has been implemented to help reduce the number of nonemergency calls, estimated as 40 percent of the total calls. Residents have been urged to call 311 when they need assistance that does not require the immediate dispatch of an officer. Recent studies found that this innovation reduced calls to 911 and resulted in extremely high public support (Mazerolle et al., 2003; *New York Times*, October 10, 1997, p. A12). The Close Up box examines the emotionally draining work of a 911 operator.

To improve efficiency, police departments use a **differential response** system that assigns priorities to calls for service. This system assumes that it is not always necessary to rush a patrol car to the scene when a call is received. The appropriate response depends on several factors—such as whether the incident is in progress, has just occurred, or occurred some time ago, as well as whether anyone is or could be hurt. A dispatcher receives the calls and asks for certain facts. The dispatcher may (1) send a sworn officer to the scene right away, (2) give the call a lower rank so that the response by an officer is delayed, (3) send someone other than a sworn officer, or (4) refer the caller to another agency.

Some experts criticize centralized communications and decision making. Many advocates of community policing believe that certain technologies tend to isolate the police from citizens. Community policing strategies attempt to enhance interaction and cooperation between officers and citizens (Morash and Ford, 2002). Widespread use of motorized patrols has meant that residents get only a glimpse of officers as they cruise through their neighborhoods. Community-oriented policing attempts to overcome some of the negative aspects of centralized response.

PRODUCTIVITY

Police response and action in part depend on departmental productivity. A recent innovation in productivity management has brought major changes to police operations. New York's Compstat program emphasizes precinct-level accountability for crime reduction. This program has inspired similar approaches in police departments in Baltimore, New Orleans, Indianapolis, and other cities. Through twice-weekly briefings before their peers and senior executives, precinct commanders must explain the results of their efforts to reduce crime. In the Compstat approach, they are held responsible for the success of crime control efforts in their precincts as indicated by crime statistics (Weisburd et al., 2003). Essential to this management strategy is timely, accurate information. Computer systems have been developed to put up-to-date crime data into the hands of managers at all levels (Willis, Mastrofski, and Weisburd, 2004). This allows discussion of department-wide strategies and puts pressure on low producers (Sherman, 1998:430; Silverman, 1999). The Compstat approach has raised questions as to how police work should be measured. It has also raised questions about whether measures of performance based on data tend to move departments away from community policing by emphasizing a centralized hierarchy focused on accountability and control (Walsh and Vito, 2004).

Quantifying police work is difficult in part because of the wide range of duties and day-to-day tasks of officers. In the past, the crime rate and the clearance rate have been used as measures of "good" policing. A lower crime rate might be cited as evidence of an effective department, but critics note that factors other than policing affect this measure. Like other public agencies, the police departments and the citizens in a community have trouble gauging the quantity and quality of police officers' work (see "What Americans Think").

differential response A patrol strategy that assigns priorities to calls for service and chooses the appropriate response.

WHAT **AMERICANS** THINK

Question: "How would you rate the police in your community on the following?"

	Excellent/pretty good	Only fair/poor
Responding quickly to calls for help and assistance	68	28
Preventing crime	65	31
Solving crime	61	33

Go to http://www.thomsonedu.com/criminaljustice/cole to compare your opinion on this issue with the opinions of other criminal justice students.

Note: Percentages do not add to 100, because some respondents declined to answer specific questions.

Source: Bureau of Justice Statistics, *Sourcebook of Criminal Justice Statistics, 2002* (Washington, DC: U.S. Government Printing Office, 2003), Table 2.23

clearance rate The percentage of crimes known to the police that they believe they have solved through an arrest; a statistic used to measure a police department's productivity.

The **clearance rate**—the percentage of crimes known to police that they believe they have solved through an arrest—is a basic measure of police performance. The clearance rate varies by type of offense. In reactive situations this rate can be low. For example, the police may learn about a burglary hours or even days after it has occurred; the clearance rate for such crimes is only about 13 percent. Police have much more success in handling violent crimes, in which victims often know their assailants; the clearance rate is 46 percent (BJS, 2005e).

In proactive situations, the police are not responding to the call of a crime victim; rather, they seek out crimes. Hence, at least in theory, arrests for prostitution, gambling, and drug selling have a clearance rate of 100 percent, because every crime known to the police is matched with an arrest.

These measures of police productivity are sometimes supplemented by other data, such as the numbers of traffic citations issued, illegally parked cars ticketed, and suspects stopped for questioning, as well as the value of stolen goods recovered. These additional ways of counting work done reflect the fact that an officer may work hard for many hours but have no arrests to show for his or her efforts. Yet, society may benefit even more when officers spend their time in activities that are hard to measure, such as calming disputes, becoming acquainted with people in the neighborhood, and providing services to those in need. Some research indicates that officers who engage in activities that produce higher levels of measurable productivity, such as issuing citations or making arrests, also receive higher numbers of citizen complaints about alleged misconduct (Lersch, 2002). See "Real-World Activity" at the end of this chapter for more on police productivity.

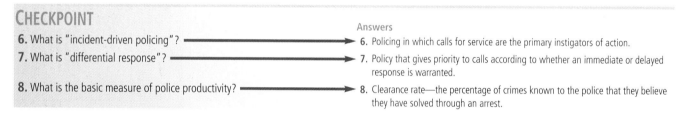

CHECKPOINT

6. What is "incident-driven policing"? ⟶

7. What is "differential response"? ⟶

8. What is the basic measure of police productivity? ⟶

Answers

6. Policing in which calls for service are the primary instigators of action.

7. Policy that gives priority to calls according to whether an immediate or delayed response is warranted.

8. Clearance rate—the percentage of crimes known to the police that they believe they have solved through an arrest.

Delivery of Police Services

In service bureaucracies like the police, a distinction is often made between line and staff functions. **Line functions** are those that directly involve field operations: patrol, investigation, traffic control, vice and juvenile crimes, and so on. By contrast, *staff functions* supplement or support the line functions. Staff functions are based in the chief's office and the support or services bureau, as well as in the staff inspection bureau. An efficient department maintains an appropriate balance between line and staff duties.

line functions Police components that directly perform field operations and carry out the basic functions of patrol, investigation, traffic, vice, juvenile, and so on.

PATROL FUNCTIONS

Patrol is often called the backbone of police operations. The word *patrol* is derived from a French word, *patrouiller*, which once meant "to tramp about in the mud." This is an apt description of a function that one expert has described as "arduous, tiring, difficult, and performed in conditions other than ideal" (Chapman, 1970:ix). For most Americans, "policing" is the familiar sight of a uniformed and armed patrol officer, on call 24 hours a day.

Every local police department has a patrol unit. Even in large departments, patrol officers account for up to two-thirds of all **sworn officers**—those who have taken an oath and received the powers to make arrests and use necessary force in accordance with their duties. In small communities, police operations are not specialized, and the patrol force is the department. As we have seen, the patrol officer must be prepared for any imaginable situation and must perform many duties.

Television portrays patrol officers as always on the go—rushing from one incident to another and making several arrests in a single shift. A patrol officer may indeed be

sworn officers Police employees who have taken an oath and been given powers by the state to make arrests and use necessary force, in accordance with their duties.

called to deal with a robbery in progress or to help rescue people from a burning building. However, the patrol officer's life is not always so exciting, often involving routine and even boring tasks such as directing traffic at accident scenes and road construction sites.

Most officers, on most shifts, do not make even one arrest (Bayley, 1994:20). To better understand patrol work, note in Figure 5.2 how the police of Wilmington, Delaware, allocate time to various activities.

The patrol function has three parts: answering calls for help, maintaining a police presence, and probing suspicious circumstances. Patrol officers are well suited to answering calls, because they usually are near the scene and can move quickly to provide help or catch a suspect. At other times, they engage in **preventive patrol**—that is, making the police presence known in an effort to deter crime and to make officers available to respond quickly to calls. Whether walking the streets or cruising in a car, the patrol officer is on the lookout for suspicious people and behavior. With experience, officers come to trust their own ability to spot signs of suspicious activity that merit stopping people on the street for questioning.

When officers earn the trust and respect of the residents of the neighborhoods they patrol, people become much more willing to provide information about crimes and suspicious activities. Effective work by patrol officers can also help reduce citizens' fear of crime and foster a sense of security.

Patrol officers' duties sound fairly straightforward, yet these officers often find themselves in complex situations requiring sound judgments and careful actions. As the first to arrive at a crime scene, the officer must comfort and give aid to victims, identify and question witnesses, control crowds, and gather evidence. These roles call for creativity and good communication skills.

Because the patrol officer has the most direct contact with the public, the patrol officer's actions in large part determine the image of the police and their relations with the community. Moreover, successful investigations and prosecutions often depend on patrol officers' actions in questioning witnesses and gathering evidence after a crime. Think of the variety of events that come to the attention of patrol officers. How would you handle them?

Patrol officers often find themselves in complex situations requiring sound judgments and careful actions. How would you interpret this picture? What is the problem? What actions are the officers taking?

AP Photo/Erik S. Lesser

preventive patrol Making the police presence known, to deter crime and to make officers available to respond quickly to calls.

FIGURE 5.2
Time allocated to patrol activities by the police of Wilmington, Delaware
The time spent on each activity was calculated from records for each police car unit. Note the range of activities and the time spent on each.

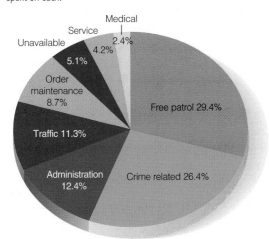

Medical 2.4%
Service 4.2%
Unavailable 5.1%
Order maintenance 8.7%
Traffic 11.3%
Administration 12.4%
Crime related 26.4%
Free patrol 29.4%

Free patrol: park and walk

Crime related: officer in trouble, suspicious person/vehicle, crime in progress, alarm, investigate crime not in progress, serve warrant/subpoena, assist other police

Administration: meal break, report writing, firearms training, police vehicle maintenance, at headquarters, court related

Traffic: accident investigation, parking problems, motor vehicle driving problems, traffic control, fire emergency

Order maintenance: order maintenance in progress, animal complaint, noise complaint

Service: service related

Medical: medical emergency, at local hospital

Source: Jack R. Greene and Carl B. Klockars, "What Police Do," in *Thinking about Police,* 2nd ed., ed. Carl B. Klockars and Stephen D. Mastrofski (New York: McGraw-Hill, 1991), 279.

Because the patrol officer's job involves the most contact with the public, the best-qualified officers should be chosen to perform it. However, because of the low status of patrol assignments, many officers seek higher-status positions such as that of detective. A key challenge facing policing is to grant to patrol officers a status that reflects their importance to society and the criminal justice system. See "Careers in Criminal Justice" to learn more about a patrol officer's job.

INVESTIGATION

All cities with a population of more than 250,000, and 90 percent of smaller cities, have officers called *detectives*, who are assigned to investigative duties. Detectives make up 15 percent of police personnel. Compared with patrol officers, they enjoy a higher status in the department: Their pay is higher, their hours are more flexible, and they are supervised less closely. Detectives do not wear uniforms, and their work is considered more interesting than that of patrol officers. In addition, they engage solely in law enforcement rather than in order maintenance or service work; hence, their activities conform more closely to the image of the police as crime fighters.

Within federal law enforcement agencies, the work of special agents is similar to that of detectives. In agencies such as the FBI, DEA, and Secret Service, special agents are plainclothes officers who focus on investigations. One key difference between federal special agents and detectives in local departments is that federal agents are more likely to be proactive in initiating investigations to prevent terrorism, drug trafficking,

CAREERS IN CRIMINAL JUSTICE

Patrol Officer

NATURE OF THE WORK

Police officers with patrol duties are employed by cities and towns as well as state police agencies and county sheriff's departments. Additional opportunities come from colleges and universities, some public school districts, and special jurisdictions such as national, state, and county parks. The federal government employs uniformed officers to patrol federal property in Washington, D.C., and elsewhere throughout the country.

Police work can be stressful and potentially dangerous. Police must respond to medical emergencies and public disorder situations as well as reported crimes. Officers must possess good interpersonal communication skills to handle encounters with citizens who are angry, injured, or filled with despair. Officers work outdoors and patrol an assigned area, always on the lookout for suspicious activity and people in need of assistance.

REQUIRED QUALIFICATIONS

Applicants must be U.S. citizens and meet age requirements, typically facing a maximum entry age of 36 to 40. A high school diploma or GED is typically required, although an increasing number of departments seek officers with a college education. Officers must be in good physical condition, including acceptable eyesight and hearing. They must pass a background investigation and drug tests. Often they must also pass a polygraph examination and psychological testing. Officers must also obtain certification through a police training academy, sometimes at their own expense. Some agencies will pay to send their own hired candidates through training.

EARNINGS AND JOB OUTLOOK

Starting salaries vary by agency but are typically around $35,000 per year. Small towns and rural counties often have lower salaries. The U.S. Department of Labor expects employment opportunities to grow as fast as the average for all occupations. Although public demand for public safety services will continue, limited government budgets may hinder the rate of job growth.

MORE INFORMATION

Information about job opportunities for police and detectives can be found in the federal government's online *Occupational Outlook Handbook* at the site listed on the Cole/Smith Criminal Justice in America Companion Website: http://www.thomsonedu.com/criminaljustice/cole. Additional information about specific jobs can be found at the websites of specific government agencies, including the sites of city and county governments.

and other crimes. Local detectives are typically reactive, responding to crimes already discovered.

Detectives typically become involved after a crime has been reported and a patrol officer has done a preliminary investigation. The job of detectives is mainly to talk to people—victims, suspects, witnesses—to find out what happened. On the basis of this information, detectives develop theories about who committed the crime; they then set out to gather the evidence that will lead to arrest and prosecution.

In performing an investigation, detectives depend not only on their own experience but also on technical experts. Much of the information they need comes from criminal files, lab technicians, and forensic scientists. Many small departments turn to the state crime laboratory or the FBI for such information. Often depicted as working alone, detectives in fact operate as part of a team.

Although detectives focus on serious crimes, they are not the only ones who investigate such crimes. Patrol, traffic, vice, and juvenile units may also be involved. In small towns and rural areas, patrol officers must conduct investigations, because police departments are too small to have separate detective bureaus. In urban areas, because they are likely to be the first police to arrive at the scene of a crime, patrol officers must do much of the initial investigative work. As we have seen, the patrol unit's investigation can be crucial. Successful prosecution of many kinds of cases, including robbery, larceny, and burglary, is closely linked to the speed with which a suspect is arrested. If patrol officers cannot obtain information from victims and witnesses right away, their odds of arresting and prosecuting the suspect greatly decrease.

Apprehension   The discovery that a crime has been committed sets off a chain of events leading to the capture of a suspect and the gathering of the evidence needed to convict that person. It may also lead to several dead ends, such as a lack of clues pointing to a suspect or a lack of evidence to link the suspect to the crime.

The process of catching a suspect has three stages: detection of a crime, preliminary investigation, and follow-up investigation. Depending on the outcome of the investigation, these three steps may be followed by a fourth: clearance and arrest. As shown in Figure 5.3, these actions are designed to use criminal justice resources to arrest a suspect and assemble enough evidence to support a charge.

Forensic Techniques   American police have long relied on science in gathering, identifying, and analyzing evidence. The public has become increasingly aware of the wide range of scientific testing techniques used for law enforcement purposes, through the television drama *CSI* (crime scene investigation) and its spin-offs. Scientific analysis of fingerprints, blood, semen, hair, textiles, soil, weapons, and other materials has helped the police identify criminals. All states and many large cities have forensic labs. However, this does not guarantee that the latest tests can be applied to all pieces of evidence. Not all labs have the same technical machinery and personnel. In addition, some police departments, especially those in small towns and rural areas, have little access to crime labs and other technology (Hickman and Reaves, 2001).

Forensic scientists who work in such labs often have graduate degrees in science. There are three primary areas of forensic science in which these scientists may have received their training. A background in biological sciences is necessary to examine blood, hair, and DNA samples. Scientists who test bomb residue, textiles, and other materials typically have training in chemistry. Forensic anthropologists examine bone fragments and skeletal remains.

The technological weapons employed to investigate many kinds of crimes include DNA "fingerprinting." This technique identifies people through their distinctive gene patterns (also called genotypic features). DNA, or deoxyribonucleic acid, is the basic component of all chromosomes; all the cells in an individual's body, including those in skin, blood, organs, and semen, contain the same unique type of DNA. The characteristics of certain segments of DNA vary from person to person and thus form a genetic "fingerprint." Analysts can therefore analyze DNA from, say, samples of hair and compare them with those of suspects. Use of the DNA technique has been hampered by the limited number of labs equipped to perform DNA analysis. Many labs have a

FIGURE 5.3

The apprehension process

Apprehension of a felony suspect results from a sequence of actions by patrol officers and detectives. Coordination of these efforts is key to solving major crimes.

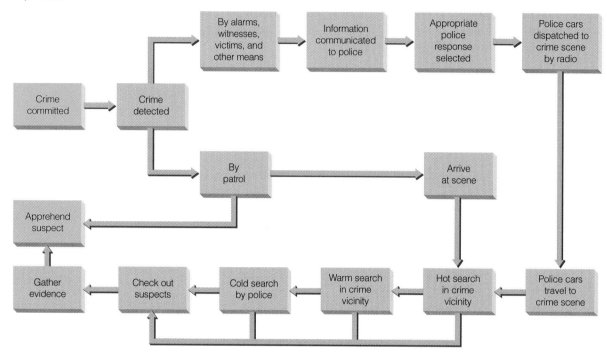

backlog of cases, especially because of the need to test and record samples from offenders whose DNA must be added to databases.

DNA testing has played a role in thousands of convictions, particularly in sexual contact and abuse cases. It has also been responsible for the release from prison of an increasing number of people after testing has shown that they could not have committed the crimes for which they were imprisoned (Connors et al., 1996:2). Read "Technology Issues in Criminal Justice" to explore issues related to DNA testing in criminal investigations.

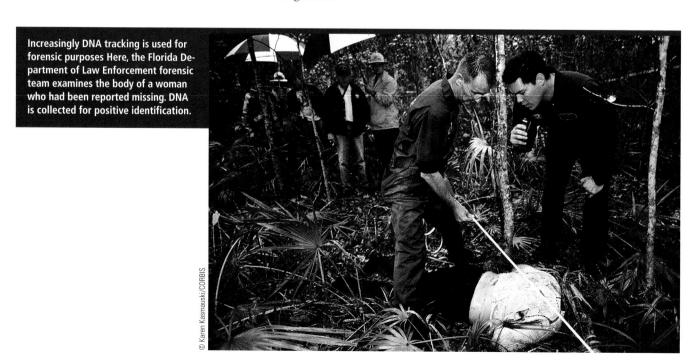

Increasingly DNA tracking is used for forensic purposes Here, the Florida Department of Law Enforcement forensic team examines the body of a woman who had been reported missing. DNA is collected for positive identification.

© Karen Kasmauski/CORBIS

TECHNOLOGY ISSUES IN CRIMINAL JUSTICE

DNA Testing

Many states and the federal government are building a national database of DNA records that is maintained by the FBI. Known as CODIS, which stands for Combined DNA Index System, the program began in 1990 as a pilot project serving a few state and local laboratories. CODIS has now grown to include 137 laboratories in 47 states and the District of Columbia.

In the federal corrections system, the Bureau of Prisons obtains DNA through blood samples from offenders convicted of murder, sex offenses, robbery, kidnapping, and burglary. Under federal law, offenders can be convicted of a misdemeanor for refusing to contribute a requested blood sample. By taking samples from people convicted of specific crimes in the state and federal systems, officials hope that CODIS will enable them to close unsolved crimes that involve DNA evidence.

Some officials argue that samples should be taken from everyone arrested, whether or not they are ever convicted of the crime for which they were arrested. There are concerns that many unsolved rapes and murders would be cleared by making CODIS include as many people as possible. Critics view the expansion of CODIS as a threat to personal privacy and as placing people unnecessarily at risk if there are computer or laboratory errors in analyzing the data. Several forensic labs have been closed or had contracts canceled with law enforcement agencies when it was discovered that they made numerous errors in testing and reaching conclusions about evidence samples.

An example of the use of a DNA database to solve crimes comes from Florida. A Ft. Lauderdale detective searching old cases noticed an unsolved 1986 murder in which a trail of blood leading away from the victim indicated the attacker had been wounded. A single droplet stored for more than a decade matched the DNA of a convicted sex offender, Scott Edward Williams. Williams was in custody but was scheduled to be released. When confronted with the evidence, he confessed and committed suicide a week later.

RESEARCHING THE INTERNET

To learn more about the CODIS program, see the website listed on the Cole/Smith Criminal Justice in America Companion Website: http://www.thomsonedu.com/criminaljustice/cole.

FOR CRITICAL ANALYSIS

Is there a risk that the database could be misused? Forensic scientists in several agencies have been caught giving false or unsupported testimony about DNA evidence. How can agencies guard against such problems?

Sources: Nancy Beatty Gregoire, "Federal Probation Joins the World of DNA Collection," *Federal Probation* 66 (June 2002): 30–32; Adam Liptak, "Prosecutions Are a Focus in Houston DNA Scandal," *New York Times*, June 9, 2003, http://www.nytimes.com; *Newsweek*, November 16, 1998, p. 69; Gretchen Ruethling, "Illinois State Police Cancels Forensic Lab's Contract, Citing Errors," *New York Times*, August 20, 2005, http://www.nytimes.com; John Solomon, "New Allegations Target DNA, Bullet Analysis at FBI Lab" [Associated Press Wire Service], *Lansing State Journal*, April 16, 2003, p. 3A; Gerald J. Turetsky, "Take DNA When You Can," *New York Times*, April 9, 2006, http://www.nytimes.com.

Research on Investigation   The results of several studies raise questions about the value of investigations and the role detectives play in apprehension. This research suggests that the police attach too much importance to investigation as a means of solving crimes and shows that most crimes are cleared because of arrests made by the patrol force at or near the scene. Response time is key to apprehension, as is the information given by the victim or witnesses.

A classic study of 153 large police departments found that a crucial factor in solving crimes was identification of the perpetrator by the victim or witnesses. Of those cases that were not solved right away but were cleared later, most were cleared by routine procedures such as fingerprint searches, tips from informants, and mug-shot "show-ups." The report found that actions by the investigative staff mattered in very few cases. In sum, about 30 percent of the crimes were cleared by on-scene arrests and another 50 percent through identification by victims or witnesses when the police arrived. Thus, only about 20 percent could have been solved by detective work. Even among this group, however, the study found that most crimes "were also solved by patrol officers, members of the public who spontaneously provide[d] further information, or routine investigative practices" (Greenwood, Chaiken, and Petersilia, 1977:227).

Does this research show that detectives are not important? No. Some cases are weak, with little evidence; some are strong, with a lot of evidence. Police need not devote a great deal of effort in these polar cases. However, the many cases with moderate evidence do require additional effort by detectives; as one researcher found, this "is extremely important with respect to subsequent making of follow-up arrests" (Bayley, 1998:149). This was confirmed by a study of a Midwestern department's follow-up investigations of burglary and robbery (Brandl and Frank, 1994:163).

SPECIAL OPERATIONS

Patrol and investigation are the two largest and most important units in a police department. In metropolitan areas, however, special units are set up to deal with specific types of problems. The most common of such units concern traffic, vice, juveniles, and SWAT (strategic weapons and tactics) teams. Some cities also have units to deal with organized crime and drugs. Even with special units in place, however, patrol officers and investigators continue to deal with the same problems.

Traffic Traffic regulation is a major job of the police. On average, 7 percent of officers are assigned to traffic units (Bayley, 1994:94). The police regulate the flow of vehicles, investigate accidents, and enforce traffic laws. This work may not seem to have much to do with crime fighting or order maintenance, but in fact it does. Besides helping to maintain order, enforcement of traffic laws educates the public by promoting safe driving habits and provides a visible service to the community.

Traffic work is mostly proactive and permits officers to use broad discretion about whom to stop and whether to issue a citation. Traffic duty can also help the police catch criminals. In enforcing traffic laws, patrol officers can stop cars and question drivers. Stolen property and suspects linked to other criminal acts are often found this way. Most departments can now automatically check license numbers against lists of wanted vehicles and suspects. See "A Question of Ethics" at the end of this chapter for more on this topic.

Vice Enforcement of vice laws depends on proactive police work, which often involves the use of undercover agents and informers. Most big-city police departments have a vice unit. Strict enforcement of these laws requires that officers receive wide discretion. They often must engage in degrading activities, such as posing as prostitutes or drug dealers, in order to catch lawbreakers. The special nature of vice work requires members of the unit to be well trained in the legal procedures required for arrests to lead to convictions.

The potential for corruption in this type of police work presents some administrative problems. Undercover officers are in a position to blackmail gamblers and drug dealers and may also be offered bribes. In addition, officers must be transferred when their identities become known.

The growth of undercover work and electronic surveillance, common in vice patrols, troubles critics who favor more open policing. They fear that the use of these tactics violates civil liberties and increases government intrusion into the private lives of citizens, whether or not those citizens commit crimes.

Drug Law Enforcement Many large cities have a bureau to enforce drug laws. These agencies may include task forces that deal with organized crime or with gangs involved in drug dealing. Other groups may use sting operations to arrest drug sellers on the street; still others may provide drug education in the community.

Drug enforcement sometimes reflects the goal of *aggressive patrol,* or assigning resources so as to get the largest number of arrests and to stop street dealing. Police executives believe that they must show dealers and the community that drug laws are enforced.

The police have used various strategies to attack drug dealing. One of these involves code or building inspections of houses and buildings used by drug dealers. Those that do not meet city standards can be boarded up in order to rid the neighborhood of dealers. Streets on which drugs are dealt openly can be flooded with officers who engage in proactive stops and questioning. There are risks, however, that drug dealers will simply move their operations to new locations.

Although arrests for drug sale or possession have increased dramatically, some observers believe that this is not the best way to deal with the problem. Many public officials argue that drugs should be viewed as a public health problem rather than as a crime problem. Critics of current policies believe that society would benefit more if more resources were devoted to drug treatment programs, which can get some people to stop using drugs, than from police actions that fill prisons without doing much to reduce drug use.

CHECKPOINT

Answers

9. What are the three parts of the patrol function? ➔ 9. Answering calls for assistance, maintaining a police presence, probing suspicious circumstances.

10. What are the four steps in the apprehension process? ➔ 10. (1) Detection of crime, (2) preliminary investigation, (3) follow-up investigation, (4) clearance and arrest.

11. What are three kinds of special operations units that police departments often employ? ➔ 11. Traffic, vice, narcotics.

Issues in Patrolling

In the last 30 years much research has been done on police methods of assigning tasks to patrol officers, deploying them, and communicating with them. Although their conclusions have been mixed, these studies have caused experts to rethink some aspects of patrolling. However, even when researchers agree on which patrol practices are the most effective, those practices often run counter to the desires of departmental personnel. For example, foot patrol may be key to some community policing strategies, but many officers would rather remain in squad cars than walk the pavement. Police administrators therefore must deal with many issues in order to develop and implement effective patrol strategies.

ASSIGNMENT OF PATROL PERSONNEL

In the past it has been assumed that patrol officers should be assigned where and when they will be most effective in preventing crime, keeping order, and serving the public. For the police administrator, the question has been, "Where should the officers be sent, when, and in what numbers?" There are no guidelines to answer this question, and most assignments seem to be based on the notion that patrols should be concentrated in "problem" neighborhoods or in areas where crime rates and calls for service are high. Thus, the assignment of officers is based on factors such as crime statistics, 911 calls, degree of urbanization, pressures from business and community groups, ethnic composition, and socioeconomic conditions. Experimentation with different strategies in various cities has led to numerous choices for police leaders. In addition, research on these strategies sheds light on the strengths and weaknesses of various options. We shall examine several options in greater detail: (1) preventive patrol, (2) hot spots, (3) rapid response time, (4) foot versus motorized patrol, (5) one-person versus two-person patrol units, (6) aggressive patrol, and (7) community policing.

Preventive Patrol   Preventive patrol has long been thought to help deter crime. Many have argued that a patrol officer's moving through an area will keep criminals from carrying out illegal acts. In 1974 this assumption was tested in Kansas City, Missouri. The surprising results shook the theoretical foundations of American policing (Sherman and Weisburd, 1995).

In the Kansas City Preventive Patrol Experiment, a 15-beat area was divided into three sections, each with similar crime rates, population characteristics, income levels, and numbers of calls to the police. In one area, labeled "reactive," all preventive patrol was withdrawn, and the police entered only in response to citizens' calls for service. In another section, labeled "proactive," preventive patrol was raised to as much as four times the normal level; all other services were provided at the same levels as before. The third section was used as a control, with the usual level of services, including preventive patrol, maintained. After observing events in the three sections for a year, the researchers concluded that the changes in patrol strategies had had no major effects on the amount of crime reported, the amount of crime as measured by citizen surveys, or citizens' fear of crime (Kelling et al., 1974). Neither a decrease nor an increase in patrol activity had any apparent effect on crime.

Despite contradictory findings of other studies using similar research methods, the Kansas City finding "remains the most influential test of the general deterrent

Community policing [handwritten margin note]

effects of patrol on crime" (Sherman and Weisburd, 1995:626). Because of this study, many departments have shifted their focus from law enforcement to maintaining order and serving the public. Some have argued that if the police cannot prevent crime by changing their patrol tactics, they may serve society better by focusing patrol activities on other functions while fighting crime as best they can.

Hot Spots   In the past, patrols were organized by "beats." It was assumed that crime can happen anywhere, and the entire beat must be patrolled at all times. Research shows, however, that crime is not spread evenly over all times and places. Instead, direct-contact predatory crimes, such as muggings and robberies, occur when three elements converge: motivated offenders, suitable targets, and the absence of anyone who could prevent the violation. This means that resources should be focused on *hot spots*, places where crimes are likely to occur (L. E. Cohen and Felson, 1979:589).

In a study of crime in Minneapolis, researchers found that a small number of hot spots—3 percent of streets and intersections—produced 50 percent of calls to the police. By analyzing the places from which calls were made, administrators could identify those that produced the most crime (Sherman, Gartin, and Buerger, 1989:27).

With this knowledge, administrators can assign officers to **directed patrol**—a proactive strategy designed to direct resources to known high-crime areas. Research indicates that directed patrol activities focused on suspicious activities and locations can reduce violent gun crime (McGarrell et al., 2001). However, the extra police pressure may simply cause lawbreakers to move to another neighborhood.

directed patrol A proactive form of patrolling that directs resources to known high-crime areas.

Rapid Response Time   Most departments are organized so that calls for help come to a central section that dispatches the nearest officers by radio to the site of the incident. Because most citizens have access to phones, most cities have 911 systems, and because most officers are in squad cars linked to headquarters by two-way radios, cell phones, and computers, police can respond quickly to calls. But are response times short enough to catch offenders?

Several studies have measured the impact of police response time on the ability of officers to intercept a crime in progress and arrest the criminal. In a classic study, William Spelman and Dale Brown (1984) found that the police succeeded in only 29 of 1,000 cases. It made little difference whether they arrived 2 minutes or 20 minutes after the call. What did matter, however, was how soon the police were called. Figure 5.4 presents these findings.

Although delayed arrival of the police is often due to slowness in calling, it seems unlikely that arrest rates would be improved merely by educating the public about their key role in stopping crime. As Spelman and Brown (1984) point out, three types of decision-making delays slow the process of calling the police:

1. *Ambiguity delays.* Some people find the situation ambiguous and are not sure whether the police should be called. They might see an event but not know whether it is a robbery or two young men "horsing around."

2. *Coping delays.* Other people are so busy coping—taking care of the victim or directing traffic—that they cannot leave the scene to call the police.

3. *Conflict delays.* Still other people must first resolve conflicts before they call the police. For example, they may call someone else for advice about whether to call the police.

Besides these delays, communication problems can slow response. For example, a telephone may not be available or the dispatcher may not be able to handle the incoming call because she or he is dealing with other problems.

The proliferation of cell phones among the American public has increased people's immediate access to phones when emergencies occur. One-third of 911 calls nationwide come from cell phones. Emergency systems in some counties are being upgraded to enable 911 operators to trace the location of cell phone calls, so that accident or crime victims who do not know their precise location can be found (Purser, B. 2005. "Houston County, Georgia E-911 Able to Pinpoint Cell Phones." *Macon (GA)*

Telegraph, February 10, p. 6). However, with dropped calls and bad connections, cell phones can create their own problems.

Although delay is a major factor in decreasing probability of arrest in certain types of cases, reducing delay would only slightly increase overall arrest rates. In about three-quarters of crime calls, the police are reactive, in that the crimes (burglary, larceny, and the like) are discovered long after have they have occurred. A much smaller portion are "involvement" crimes (robbery, rape, assault) that victims know about right away and for which they can call the police promptly (Spelman and Brown, 1984:4). In addition, the danger created by high-speed response may outweigh any possible increase in effectiveness (Sherman, 1995:334).

Foot versus Motorized Patrol
One of the most frequent citizen requests is for officers to be put back on the beat. This was the main form of police patrol until the 1930s, when motorized patrol came to be viewed as more effective. Of the 195 million Americans served by local police departments, 85 percent are served by a department that uses some amount of foot patrol, bicycle patrol, or both (Hickman and Reaves, 2001; Reaves and Hart, 2000). However, departments typically use these strategies only in selected neighborhoods or districts with a high business or population density. Most patrolling is still conducted in cars, accounting for 94 percent of patrol time in large cities (Reaves, 1992). With advances in communications technologies and onboard computers, patrol officers have direct links to headquarters and to criminal information databases. Now the police can be quickly sent where needed, with crucial information in their possession.

On the other hand, many citizens and some researchers claim that patrol officers in squad cars have become remote from the people they protect and less aware of their needs. By contrast, officers on foot stay close to the daily life of the neighborhood. They detect criminal activity and apprehend lawbreakers more easily than do car patrols. Further, patrol officers who are known to citizens are less likely to be viewed as symbols of oppression by poor or minority residents (Hawdon and Ryan, 2003).

Although studies have shown that foot patrols are costly and do not greatly reduce crime, they do make citizens less fearful, increase satisfaction with the police, and give officers a greater appreciation of neighborhood values (M. Cohen, Miller, and Rossman, 1990; Kelling, 1991). In terms of the cost and benefit, foot patrols are effective in high-density urban neighborhoods and business districts.

One-Person versus Two-Person Patrol Units
The debate over one-person versus two-person patrol units has raged in police circles for years. Officers and their union leaders support the two-person squad car. They claim that police are safer and more effective when two officers work together in dangerous or difficult situations.

FIGURE 5.4
Probability of arrest as a function of elapsed time after crime
The probability of arrest declines sharply when the police are not called within seconds. What does this imply for patrol policies?

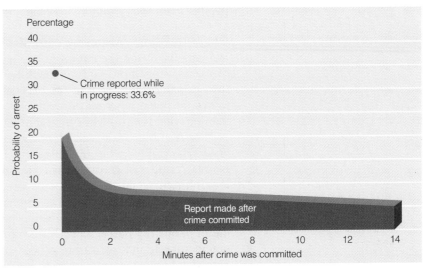

Crime reported while in progress: 33.6%

Report made after crime committed

Minutes after crime was committed

Source: William G. Spelman and Dale K. Brown, *Calling the Police: Citizen Reporting of Serious Crime* (Washington, DC: Police Executive Research Forum, 1984), 65. Reprinted by permission.

Many citizens and researchers advocate the use of foot (or bike) patrol of neighborhoods. Advocates say that officers on foot stay close to the daily life of the community, are supported by the residents, and can more easily prevent and detect criminal activity. What arguments might the advocates of motorized patrol make?

© Royalty-Free/Corbis

However, police administrators contend that the one-person squad car is much more cost-effective and permits them to deploy more cars on each shift. With more cars to deploy, each can be assigned to a smaller area and response time can be decreased. They also contend that an officer working alone is more alert and attentive because he or she cannot be distracted by idle conversation with a colleague.

Aggressive Patrol   **Aggressive patrol** is a proactive strategy designed to maximize police activity in the community. It takes many forms, such as "sting" operations, firearms confiscation, raids on crack houses, programs that encourage citizens to list their valuables, and the tracking of high-risk parolees. Some have argued that the effect of the police on crime depends less on how many officers are deployed in an area than on what they do while they are there.

The zero-tolerance policing of the 1990s in New York City is an example of aggressive patrol linked to the "broken windows" theory introduced in Chapter 4. As you will recall, this theory asserts "that if not firmly suppressed, disorderly behavior in public will frighten citizens and attract predatory criminals, thus leading to more serious crime problems" (Greene, 1999:172). Thus, the police should focus on minor, public order crimes such as aggressive panhandling, graffiti, prostitution, and urinating in public. By putting more police on the streets, decentralizing authority to the precinct level, and instituting officer accountability, the zero-tolerance policy was judged to be a major factor in reducing New York City's crime rate (Silverman, 1999).

Aggressive policing has also been applied as part of the war on drugs, with police officers stopping many vehicles and frisking pedestrians on certain streets. In Detroit, aggressive, zero-tolerance police practices reduced gang-related crime in targeted precincts (Bynum and Varano, 2002). Police departments also use aggressive patrol strategies to track high-risk parolees and apprehend them if they commit new offenses.

The most cost-effective of the aggressive patrol strategies seem to be those that encourage officers to carry out more field questioning and traffic stops. To implement such a strategy, the department must recruit certain kinds of officers, train them, and devise requirements and reward systems (traffic ticket quotas, required numbers of field interrogations, chances for promotion) that will encourage them to carry out the intended strategy.

Recent research raises questions about whether the "broken windows" approach actually reduces crime. Several studies present new analyses of data that challenge claims that aggressive policing is what caused crime reduction during the 1990s (Harcourt and Ludwig, 2006). Moreover, the "broken windows" approach might actually lead to citizen hostility. In some urban neighborhoods there are rumblings that aggressive patrol has gone too far and is straining police relations with young African Americans and Hispanics. This issue centers on balancing the rights of individuals against the community's interest in maintaining order (Kolbert, 1999:50). "Put another way, it's whose son is being hassled" (Reibstein, 1997:66). See "The Policy Debate" for more on the pros and cons of aggressive enforcement.

aggressive patrol A patrol strategy designed to maximize the number of police interventions and observations in the community.

Community Policing   To a great extent, community policing has been seen as the solution to problems with the crime-fighter stance that prevailed during the professional era (Murphy, 1992). Community policing consists of attempts by the police to involve residents in making their own neighborhoods safer. Based on the belief that citizens are often concerned about local disorder as well as crime in general, this strategy emphasizes cooperation between the police and citizens in identifying community needs and determining the best ways to meet them (Moore, 1992).

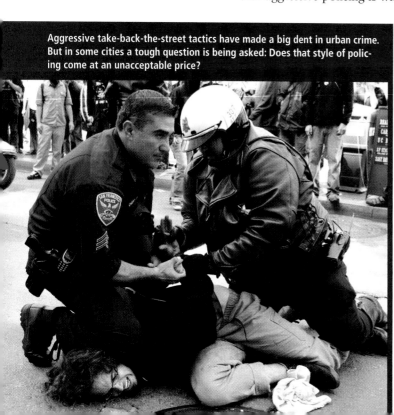
Aggressive take-back-the-street tactics have made a big dent in urban crime. But in some cities a tough question is being asked: Does that style of policing come at an unacceptable price?

THE POLICY DEBATE

Should the Police Aggressively Enforce Public Order Laws?

The police in many cities are now paying greater attention to public order offenses. Officials believe that these "little crimes" can lead to more serious offenses. They say the police must deal with public order offenses in an aggressive, proactive manner to prevent crime.

Research has shown that high levels of disorder are linked to high levels of crime, and that disorder often leads to community decline, as fearful residents move, property values drop, and businesses close. In some cities a policy of zero tolerance for public order offenses has been instituted. Community crime-fighting initiatives can reduce disorderly behavior, fear, and urban decay. And the lives of citizens are improved.

Newer research raises questions about the "broken windows" theory. This research says the police should encourage the development of collective efficacy in neighborhoods. As described by Sampson and Raudenbush (2001:5–6),

Informally mobilizing a neighborhood cleanup, for example, would reduce physical disorder while building collective efficacy by creating and strengthening social ties and increasing awareness of residents' commitment to their neighborhood. . . . By contrast, a police-led crackdown on disorder would probably produce a very different response by residents.

For Aggressively Enforcing Public Order Laws

Supporters of a focus on public order offenses argue that this initiative is necessary to reduce residents' fears and prevent more serious crimes. Research, they say, has shown that using community policing to deal effectively with public order offenses is the best way to control crime and make urban areas more livable. Through aggressive foot patrol, order can be restored and maintained.

The arguments for aggressively enforcing public order laws are these:

- Enforcing public order laws reduces serious crime, residents' fears, and urban decay.

- When the police deal with low-level offenders, they learn about those who have committed serious offenses.

- Officers walking through a neighborhood become familiar with the residents and gain their cooperation and assistance when serious crime erupts.

- Police action on public order offenses encourages citizens to uphold neighborhood standards for behavior in public spaces.

Against Aggressively Enforcing Public Order Laws

Enforcing the law and improving the quality of urban life may seem to be positive goals for any community. However, some officers say they have enough to do just dealing with the "bad guys," and they should not divert resources to lesser offenses. Further, recent research challenges the idea that reducing disorder in a neighborhood through police enforcement will produce a decline in serious crime. Recent research suggests that police should encourage community-building projects to empower neighborhood residents rather than swooping in to enforce every small rule. Civil libertarians say the new policies targeting public order offenses are designed to harass the poor, the homeless, and the mentally ill—the people society has pushed into the streets. They emphasize that some officers misuse force in enforcing these policies.

The arguments against aggressive enforcement of public order laws are these:

- Police resources and tactics should be focused on fighting serious crime.

- The link among disorder, fear, and crime has been challenged by recent research.

- Aggressive police tactics against people using public spaces are attacks on the poor and other social outcasts.

- The civil liberties of the poor are infringed when the police aggressively enforce public order laws.

What Should U.S. Policy Be?

How would the American people react if greater police resources were allocated to deal with public order offenses? Some have argued that by aggressively dealing with disorder, the police reduce residents' fear and prevent more serious crimes. Others see this new emphasis as targeting primarily the weak—the poor and the outcasts of society. Civil liberties are trampled in the process.

RESEARCHING THE INTERNET

To read research that challenges the assumptions of aggressive policing and the "broken windows" theory, see the corresponding website listed on the Cole/Smith Criminal Justice in America Companion Website: http://www.thomsonedu.com/criminaljustice/cole.

FOR CRITICAL THINKING

Does aggressive enforcement of public order laws reduce crime or does it interfere with citizens' personal freedom and generate animosity toward the police?

Community policing has four components (Skolnick and Bayley, 1986):

1. Community-based crime prevention

2. Changing the focus of patrol activities to nonemergency services

3. Making the police more accountable to the public

4. Decentralizing decision-making to include residents

As indicated by these four components, community policing requires a major shift in the philosophy of policing. In particular, police officials must view citizens as customers to be served and partners in the pursuit of social goals rather than as a population to be watched, controlled, and served reactively (Morash et al., 2002). Although crime control may remain a priority in community policing, the change in emphasis can strengthen police effectiveness for order maintenance and service (Zhao et al., 2003).

Departments that view themselves as emphasizing community policing do not necessarily have identical patrol strategies and initiatives (Thurman, Zhao, and Giacomazzi, 2001). Some departments emphasize identifying and solving problems related to disorder and crime. Other departments work mainly on strengthening local neighborhoods. A department's emphasis can affect which activities become the focus of officers' working hours.

Organizational factors can also affect the implementation of community policing (E. J. Williams, 2003). For example, community policing could be carried out by patrol officers assigned to walk neighborhood beats so that they can get to know residents better. It could entail creating police ministations in the community and police-sponsored programs for youth and the elderly. Police departments could also survey citizens to find out about their problems and needs (Reisig, 2002). The common element in community policing programs is a high level of interaction between officers and citizens and the involvement of citizens in identifying problems and solving them.

A central feature of community policing for many departments is **problem-oriented policing,** a strategy that seeks to find out what is causing citizens to call for help (Goldstein, 1990). The police seek to identify, analyze, and respond to the conditions underlying the events that prompt people to call the police (DeJong, Mastrofski, and Parks, 2001). Knowing those conditions, officers can enlist community agencies and residents to help resolve them (Braga, 1999). Recent research indicates that problem-solving approaches can impact homicide rates (Chermak and McGarrell, 2004). Police using this approach do not just fight crime (M. D. White et al., 2003); they address a broad array of other problems that affect the quality of life in the community.

Community policing has spread across the country and gained a great deal of support from citizens, legislators, and Congress (Bayley, 1994; Zhao, Schneider, and Thurman, 2003). This support can be seen in the emphasis on community policing in the Violent Crime Control and Law Enforcement Act passed by Congress in 1994. Portions of the act call for increases in the number of officers assigned to community policing and for the development of new community policing programs.

As with any reform, change might not come easily (Schafer, 2002). Police chiefs and midlevel managers, accustomed to dealing with problems according to established procedures, may feel that their authority decreases when responsibility shifts to precinct commanders and officers on the streets (Alley, Bonello, and Schafer, 2002). Another problem with implementing community policing is that it does not reduce costs; it requires either additional funds or redistribution within existing budgets. Measuring the success of this approach in reducing fear of crime, solving underlying problems, maintaining order, and serving the community is also difficult. In addition, there is the debate about how far the police should extend their role beyond crime fighting to remedying other social problems. Finally, police officers may resist committing themselves to daily activities that emphasize roles other than the crime-fighting role that may have attracted them to a career in law enforcement (Mastrofski, Willis, and Snipes, 2002; Williams, 2003).

THE FUTURE OF PATROL

Preventive patrol and rapid response to calls for help have been the hallmarks of policing in the United States for the past half century. However, research done in the past 30 years has raised many questions about which patrol strategies police should employ. The rise of community policing has shifted law enforcement toward problems that affect the quality of life of residents. Police forces need to use patrol tactics that fit the needs of the neighborhood. Neighborhoods with crime hot spots may require different strategies than do neighborhoods where residents are concerned mainly with order maintenance. Many researchers believe that traditional patrol efforts have focused too narrowly on crime control, neglecting the order maintenance and service activities for which police departments were originally formed. Critics have urged the police to

problem-oriented policing
An approach to policing in which officers routinely seek to identify, analyze, and respond to the circumstances underlying the incidents that prompt citizens to call the police.

become more community oriented and return to the first principle of policing: "to remain in close and frequent contact with citizens" (H. Williams and Pate, 1987). To see this policy in action, we look to Japan, where most patrolling is done on foot, as described in the Comparative Perspective box.

How the national effort to combat terrorism will affect local police patrol operations remains uncertain. Since the attacks of September 11, state and local police have assumed greater responsibility for investigating bank robberies and other federal crimes as the FBI and other federal agencies devote significant attention to catching people connected with terrorist organizations. In addition, even local police officers must be

ThomsonNOW™

Improve your grade on the exam with Personalized Study! For reinforcement resources and a mastery check of patrolling, go to www.thomsonedu.com/thomsonnow.

COMPARATIVE PERSPECTIVE

Patrol in Japan

Many community policing strategies now being used in the United States have been the tradition in Japan for many years. Patrol officers walking through their assigned neighborhoods and working out of local offices are a hallmark of Japanese policing.

Japanese policemen are addressed by the public as Omawari-san—Mr. Walkabout. This is an accurate reflection of what the public sees the police doing most of the time. Foot patrolling is done out of *kobans* [mini police stations in urban neighborhoods], usually for periods of an hour. Patrols are more common at night, when officers work in pairs. . . . Patrolmen amble at a ruminative pace that allows thorough observation. . . . Patrolling by automobile, which is much less common than foot patrolling, can be frustrating too. Due to the narrow congested streets of Japanese cities . . . patrol cars are forced to move at a snail's pace. . . .

Patrolling is by no means a matter of high adventure. For the most part it consists of watching and occasionally answering questions. Patrolmen rarely discover genuine emergencies; the chance of coincidence between patrolmen and sudden need are simply too great. Patrolling does not reduce reaction time or particularly enhance availability. What patrolling does is to demonstrate the existence of authority, correct minor inconveniences . . . such as illegally parked cars . . . and generate trust through the establishment of familiar personal relations with a neighborhood's inhabitants. On patrol, policemen are alert for different kinds of problems in different places. In a residential area they watch for people who appear out of place or furtive. In public parks they give attention to loitering males. Around major railroad stations they look for runaway adolescents, lured by the glamour of a big city, who could be victimized by criminal elements. They also watch for *teyhaishi* . . . labor contractors . . . who pick up and sell unskilled laborers to construction companies. In a neighborhood of bars and cabarets, patrolmen stare suspiciously at stylishly dressed women standing unescorted on street corners. They determine whether wheeled carts piled with food or cheap souvenirs are blocking pedestrian thoroughfares. Throughout every city they pay particular attention to illegally parked cars and cars that have been left with their doors unlocked. . . .

When a Japanese policeman is out on patrol he makes a special point of talking to people about themselves, their purposes, and their behavior. These conversations may be innocent or investigatory. The law provides that policemen may stop and question people only if there is reasonable ground for suspecting they have committed or are about to commit a crime or have information about a crime. Nevertheless, standard procedure on patrol is

to stop and question anyone whenever the policeman thinks it may be useful. One reason for doing so is to discover wanted persons. And the tactic has proved very effective; 40 percent of criminals wanted by the police have been discovered by patrolmen on the street. Not only do officers learn to question people adroitly on the street, they become adept at getting people to agree to come to the *koban* so that more extended, less public inquiries can be made. People are under no obligation to do so, any more than they are to stop and answer questions. The key to success with these tactics is to be compelling without being coercive. This in turn depends on two factors: the manner of the police officer and a thorough knowledge of minor laws. The first reduces hostility, the second provides pretexts for opening conversations justifiably. People who park illegally, ride bicycles without a light, or fail to wear helmets when riding a motorcycle are inviting officers to stop them and ask probing questions. The importance with which the police view on-street interrogation is indicated by the fact that prefectural and national contests are held each year to give recognition to officers who are best at it. . . . Senior officers continually impress upon new recruits the importance of learning to ask questions in inoffensive ways so that innocent people are not affronted and unpleasant scenes can be avoided. . . .

The most striking aspect of the variety of situations confronted by policemen is their compelling, unforced naturalness. The police see masses of utterly ordinary people who have been enmeshed in situations that are tediously complex and meaningful only to the persons immediately involved. The outcomes are of no interest to the community at large; the newspapers will not notice if matters are sorted out or not; superior officers have no way of recording the effort patrolmen expend in trying to be helpful; and the people themselves are incapable by and large of permanently escaping their predicaments. Policemen are responsible for tending these individuals, for showing that they appreciate—even when they are tired, hurried, bored, and preoccupied—the minute ways in which each person is unique. It is perhaps, the greatest service they render.

RESEARCHING THE INTERNET

To learn more about policing in Japan, see the English-language website of Japan's National Police Agency, listed on the Cole/Smith Criminal Justice in America Companion Website: http://www.thomsonedu .com/criminaljustice/cole.

Source: David H. Bayley, *Forces of Order: Police Behavior in Japan and the United States* (Berkeley: University of California Press, 1979), 33–34, 37, 41, 51–52. Copyright © 1976 The Regents of the University of California. Reprinted by permission.

ready to spot suspicious activities that might relate to terrorist activity. They are the first responders in a bombing or other form of attack. Obviously, federal law enforcement officials must work closely with local police in order to be effective. Yet many local police chiefs have criticized the FBI for failing to share important information about local suspects (Bowers, 2002). The new concerns will not alter traditional police responsibilities for crime fighting, order maintenance, and service, but they will provide an additional consideration as police administrators plan how to train and deploy their personnel.

CHECKPOINT

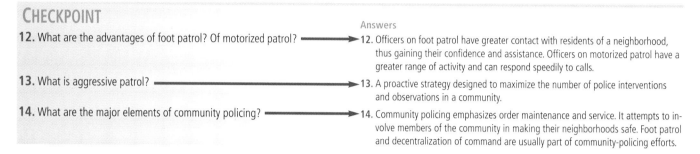

Answers

12. What are the advantages of foot patrol? Of motorized patrol? ➤ 12. Officers on foot patrol have greater contact with residents of a neighborhood, thus gaining their confidence and assistance. Officers on motorized patrol have a greater range of activity and can respond speedily to calls.

13. What is aggressive patrol? ➤ 13. A proactive strategy designed to maximize the number of police interventions and observations in a community.

14. What are the major elements of community policing? ➤ 14. Community policing emphasizes order maintenance and service. It attempts to involve members of the community in making their neighborhoods safe. Foot patrol and decentralization of command are usually part of community-policing efforts.

A QUESTION OF ETHICS: WRITING ASSIGNMENT

You are a police officer on road patrol. The previous day there was a report that a man wearing a blue baseball cap and driving a light-colored car attempted to abduct a girl. You are driving behind a silver car, and it appears that the driver is wearing a dark baseball cap. When the car changes lanes, a blinding glare in your eyes from the sun glinting off the silver car makes it difficult to see if the driver used his turn signal. You are curious about whether this driver is connected to the attempted abduction.

WRITING ASSIGNMENT

Would you stop the vehicle? What would be the reason for the stop? Could you make a stop for failure to signal a lane change? Write out what you would say if you were in a private conversation with a new police officer who came to you to seek advice about what to do in such situations.

REAL-WORLD ACTIVITY: AN APPLICATION

You are the new police chief in a city that has traditionally measured police officers' productivity by counting the number of arrests made and traffic citations issued by each officer. You must decide how productivity should be measured for officers in your department.

RESEARCHING THE INTERNET

Go to InfoTrac College Edition. Use the keyword *police productivity*. Read an article entitled "Police Practice: Productivity Analysis for Basic Police Patrol Activities," by Roy H. Herndon, III, *FBI Law Enforcement Bulletin,* May 2005.

APPLICATION

After reading the article, write a memo that addresses the following questions: Will you continue to rely on the current productivity measures of your department, or will you introduce new measures? Would the current measures pose any problems? What alternative measures might be used? Is it important to have measures of productivity or are there other ways to evaluate the performance and effectiveness of patrol officers?

SUMMARY

- To meet current and future challenges, the police must recruit and train individuals who will uphold the law and receive citizen support.

- Improvements have been made during the past quarter-century in recruiting more women, racial and ethnic minorities, and well-educated people as police officers.

- Police officers work in an environment greatly influenced by their subculture.

- The concept of the working personality helps us understand the influence of the police subculture on how individual officers see their world.

- The isolation of the police strengthens bonds among officers but can also add to job stress.

- Police services are delivered through the work of the patrol, investigation, and special operations units.

- The patrol function has three components: answering calls for assistance, maintaining a police presence, and probing suspicious circumstances.

- The investigation function is the responsibility of detectives working in close coordination with patrol officers.

- The felony apprehension process is a sequence of actions that includes crime detection, preliminary investigation, follow-up investigation, clearance, and arrest.

- Large departments usually have specialized units dealing with traffic, drugs, and vice.

- Police administrators must make choices about possible patrol strategies, which include directed patrol, foot patrol, and aggressive patrol.

- Community policing seeks to involve citizens in identifying problems and working with police officers to prevent disorder and crime.

QUESTIONS FOR REVIEW

1. How do recruitment and training practices affect policing?

2. What is meant by the police subculture, and how does it influence an officer's work?

3. What factors in the police officer's working personality influence an officer's work?

4. What is the purpose of patrol? How is it carried out?

5. Why do detectives have so much prestige on the force?

6. What has research shown about the effectiveness of patrol?

KEY TERMS

aggressive patrol (p. 140)
clearance rate (p. 130)
differential response (p. 129)
directed patrol (p. 138)
incident-driven policing (p. 127)

line functions (p. 130)
preventive patrol (p. 131)
proactive (p. 127)
problem-oriented policing (p. 142)
reactive (p. 127)

socialization (p. 123)
subculture (p. 124)
sworn officers (p. 130)
working personality (p. 124)

GOING ONLINE

ThomsonNOW™

Maximize your study time by using ThomsonNOW's diagnostic study plan to help you review this chapter. The Study Plan will

- Help you identify areas on which you should concentrate

- Provide interactive exercises to help you master the chapter concepts

- Provide a posttest to confirm you are ready to move on to the next chapter

6

Policing: Contemporary Issues and Challenges

Police Abuse of Power
Use of Force
Corruption

Civic Accountability
Internal Affairs Units
Civilian Review Boards
Standards and Accreditation
Civil Liability Suits

Policing and New Technology
Cyber Crime
Investigative Tools
Weapons Technology

Homeland Security
Preparing for Threats
New Laws and Controversies

Security Management and Private Policing
Functions of Security Management and Private Policing
Private Employment of Public Police
The Public–Private Interface
Recruitment and Training

In July 2005, when Los Angeles police officers responded to a midafternoon call about "unknown trouble" at Raul's Auto Sales, they were met by Raul Pena, the owner of the car dealership. The officers could see that Pena had a gun, so they radioed for additional officers. When reinforcements arrived, Pena fired shots at the police. He then emerged from the dealership holding his 19-month-old daughter Susie in his arms as he continued to fire at the police. Pena disappeared inside as police officers surrounded the building (Leovy and Lee, 2005).

During a two-hour standoff, police officers spoke with Pena on the phone in an effort to persuade him to surrender. Pena's teenage stepdaughter emerged from the building as officers exchanged fire with Pena in order to assist her escape. When the officers believed that they had wounded Pena, they rushed into the dealership only to discover that he had barricaded himself and his daughter inside a small office. After Pena wounded an officer by firing through the wall of the office, officers broke into the office and engaged in a quick gun battle that left Pena and his daughter dead. Pena fired 40 shots at the police; 11 officers returned fire with more than 90 (NBC4 News, 2005).

A subsequent investigation revealed that the girl suffered from two gunshot wounds, including a shot to the head that killed her. The fatal shot was fired by a police officer's weapon (CNN, 2005a). Police administrators reported that the child's death devastated the officers involved. Meanwhile, Pena's family and community activists angrily complained that the police should have been more patient and worked harder to end the standoff without violence. Police shootings in Los Angeles trigger investigations by both the prosecutor's office and the police department's use-of-force board. In this case, the investigation assumed additional importance because the police shooting resulted in the death of an innocent child.

Did the police use force appropriately in this case? Although they knew that any exchange of gunfire would put a small child at risk, one officer was wounded and they had reason to fear Pena could injure or kill additional officers and perhaps

147

even his own daughter. On the other hand, could they have taken more time for engage in additional negotiations? Could they have used tear gas or another less-lethal weapon in order to capture Pena? These kinds of difficult questions regularly arise because highly publicized incidents of allegedly inappropriate uses of force by police capture the public's attention each year. For example, in 2005, 13 deputies in the Los Angeles County Sheriff's Department were suspended from duty after firing 120 shots at an unarmed car driver whom they mistakenly believed had been involved in a shooting. The driver was wounded four times, and many bullets smashed through the windows and walls of homes in the residential neighborhood where the shooting occurred (Associated Press, 2005).

When issues of excessive force or corruption affect the police, they can strain the bonds that connect the police to the community that they serve and rely on for information, assistance, and support. These bonds are often fragile, especially when racial, gender, or class bias comes into play. How can we make sure that those with authority do not misuse their power?

In this chapter we discuss several new developments and continuing issues about police and their role in society. We look at troubling issues that arise when police abuse their power. We also examine how technological changes have given police new abilities to investigate criminal activity and how these technologies raise questions about the role of police and the preservation of rights. Related to these issues are the expansion of police activities concerning homeland security and their impact on police and society. In addition, we consider the growing importance of private-sector policing, which falls under the title of security management, a growing industry that increasingly affects police operations and requires cooperation between public agencies and private corporations.

For each topic, questions emerge about the role of police in a democratic society. Any police shooting or other use of force that injures a citizen raises concerns that officers may have disregarded the rights guaranteed to people under the U.S. Constitution. Constitutional issues also arise in less stark forms with respect to other issues. For example, technological developments and the shifting emphasis toward homeland security raise concerns about surveillance and searches of citizens who have done nothing wrong. In a democratic society, police must act within legal guidelines, remain under the control of elected officials, and be accountable for their actions. These principles can be violated when law enforcement personnel exhibit unethical and illegal behavior. Problems also arise if legislators permit police powers to expand too far because of public fear, a situation that some critics believe is developing with respect to certain aspects of security policies.

QUESTIONS FOR INQUIRY

- In what ways do the police abuse their power, and how can this abuse be controlled?
- What methods can be used to make police more accountable to citizens?
- What new technologies have assisted police investigations, and how might they affect citizens' rights?
- What issues and problems emerge from law enforcement agencies' increased attention to homeland security?
- What policing and related activities does private-sector security management undertake?

Police Abuse of Power

The controversy surrounding the police use of force against Raul Pena and his young daughter is not unique. The videotaped beating of Rodney King by Los Angeles police officers drew worldwide attention in 1991 and eventually contributed to a major riot that took dozens of lives. In recent decades, police corruption and abuse scandals have made the misuse of police power a major issue on the public agenda (Skolnick and Fyfe, 1993). Although such scandals have occurred throughout U.S. history, only in the past quarter-century has the public been keenly aware of the problems of police misconduct, especially the illegal use of violence by law enforcement officers and the criminal activities associated with police corruption. Although most officers do not engage in misconduct, these problems deserve study because they raise questions about how much the public can control and trust the police.

USE OF FORCE

Although most people cooperate with the police, officers must at times use force to make arrests, control disturbances, and deal with the drunken or mentally ill (Thompson, 2001). As noted by Jerome Skolnick and James Fyfe (1993:37),

> As long as some members of society do not comply with the law and [some] resist the police, force will remain an inevitable part of policing. Cops, especially, understand that. Indeed, anybody who fails to understand the centrality of force in police work has no business in a police uniform.

Thus, police may use *legitimate* force to do their job. It is when they use *excessive* force that they violate the law. But what is excessive force? Both officers and experts debate this question.

In cities where racial tensions are high, conflicts between police and residents often result when officers are accused of acting in unprofessional ways (Kane, 2002). Citizens use the term *police brutality* to describe a wide range of practices, from the use of profane or abusive language to physical force and violence. As shown in

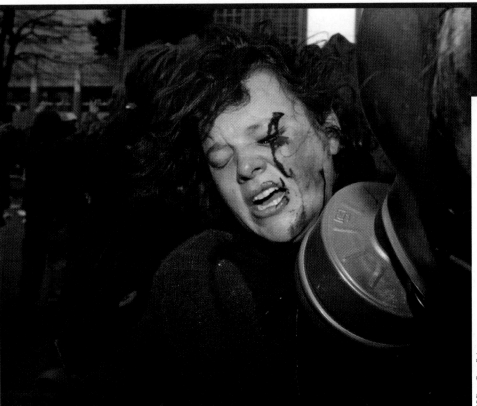

Protesters of the World Trade Organization meeting in Seattle, Washington, were sprayed with tear gas and pepper spray as well as rubber bullets by Seattle law enforcement. What factors should guide officers' use of force?

AP Photo/Peter Dejong

Go to
http://www.thomsonedu.com/
criminaljustice/cole to compare your
opinion on this issue with the opinions
of other criminal justice students.

Source: Bureau of Justice Statistics, *Source-book of Criminal Justice Statistics,* 2002 (Washington, DC: U.S. Government Printing Office, 2003), Table 2.27

"What Americans Think," most people approve a police officer striking a citizen under certain circumstances.

Stories of police brutality are not new. However, unlike the untrained officers of the early 1900s, today's officers are supposed to be professionals who know the rules and understand the need for proper conduct. Thus, reports of unjustified police shootings and beatings are particularly disturbing (Ogletree et al., 1995). Moreover, the public cannot know how often police engage in abusive behavior, even when it comes to light, because most violence remains hidden from public view (Weitzer, 2002). If a person watching from a nearby window had not videotaped the beating of Rodney King, the officers could have claimed that they had not used excessive force, and King would have had no way to prove that they had. How can we prevent such incidents, especially when they occur without witnesses?

The concept "use of force" takes many forms in practice. We can arrange the various types of force on a continuum ranging from most severe (civilians shot and killed) to least severe ("come-alongs," or being grasped by an officer). Table 6.1 lists many of these forms of force according to their frequency of use. How often must force be used? Most research has shown that in police contacts with suspects, force is used infrequently and the type of force used is usually at the low end of the continuum—toward the less severe. Research in Phoenix found that the single largest predictor of police use of force was use of force by the suspect, to which the police then responded (Garner et al., 1995). For example, resistance by a suspect can contribute to the officers' decision to use force (Garner, Maxwell, and Heraux, 2002). Research in six urban jurisdictions in which 7,512 arrests were examined showed that in 97.9 percent of contacts, the police used no weapon such as a baton, flashlight, handgun, chemical agent, or canine (Garner and Maxwell, 1999:31). Again, it is *excessive* use of force, in violation of departmental policies and state laws, that constitutes abuse of police power.

A report by the National Institute of Justice summarizes current knowledge about use of force (K. Adams, 1999):

1. Police use force infrequently.

2. Police use of force typically occurs in the lower end of the force spectrum, involving grabbing, pushing, or shoving.

3. Use of force typically occurs when police are trying to make an arrest and the suspect is resisting.

Although more studies are needed, other research indicates that use of force is not linked to an officer's personal characteristics such as age, gender, and ethnicity. However, a small percentage of officers may be disproportionately involved in use-of-force situations. In addition, use of force occurs more frequently when police are dealing with people affected by drugs, alcohol, or mental illness (K. Adams, 1999). At this point, there is a great need for additional research to tell us how frequently wrongful use of force by police occurs and whether specific departmental policies concerning hiring, training, and supervision affect officers' decisions to use force (K. Adams, 1999).

By law, the police have the authority to use force if necessary to make an arrest, keep the peace, or maintain public order. But the questions of just how much force is necessary and under what conditions it may be used are complex and and open to debate. In particular, the use of deadly force in apprehending suspects has become a deeply emotional issue with a direct connection to race relations. Research has shown that the greatest use of deadly force by the police occurs in communities with high levels of economic inequality and large minority populations (Holmes, 2000; Sorensen, Marquart, and Brock, 1993).

When police kill a suspect or bystander while trying to make an arrest, their actions may produce public outrage and hostility. Fears about the possibility of similar public disorders arose in 2005 when a police officer fired ten shots that killed a 13-year-old boy who was driving a stolen car. The officer fired in the aftermath of a chase when the boy skidded across a sidewalk and then struck a police car while backing up (Chavez, 2005). The incident led Los Angeles police officials to revise their policies about firing at moving vehicles.

In a similar incident, New Yorkers were outraged by the killing of Amadou Diallo, an unarmed West African immigrant, who died in a fusillade of 41 bullets fired by four members of New York City's Street Crime Unit. Unarmed and standing alone, Diallo was killed in the vestibule of his apartment building. The officers were looking for a rapist-murderer when they came upon Diallo. As they approached him, they said, they thought he was reaching for a gun. The killing resulted in massive protests and the indictment of the officers on second-degree murder charges. During their trial the officers said that they "reasonably believed" that Diallo was about to use deadly force against them (*New York Times*, February 26, 2000, p. A13). The Diallo killing also raised questions about New York's zero-tolerance policies and the aggressive tactics of the Street Crime Unit.

There are no accurate data on the number of people shot by the police. Researchers estimate that the police shoot about 3,600 people each year, with fatal results in as many as 1,000 of these incidents (Cullen et al., 1996:449). Although these numbers are alarming, it is important to remember that force (hit, held, choked, threatened) is used against 500,000 people each year (BJS, 1997:12). The number of police killings should not obscure the fact that most of those killed are young African American men. However, the ratio of blacks to whites killed has declined, in part because of new police policies (Sherman and Cohn, 1986; S. Walker, Spohn, and DeLeone, 2003:97).

Until the 1980s the police had broad authority to use deadly force in pursuing suspected felons. Police in about half the states were guided by the common-law principle that allowed the use of whatever force was necessary to arrest a fleeing felon. In 1985 the Supreme Court set a new standard in *Tennessee v. Garner* (1985), ruling that the police may not use deadly force in apprehending fleeing felons "unless it is necessary to prevent the escape and the officer has probable cause to believe that the suspect poses a significant threat of death or serious physical injury to the officer or others."

The standard set by *Tennessee v. Garner* presents problems because it can be hard to judge how dangerous a suspect may be. Because officers must make quick decisions in stressful situations, creating rules that will guide them in every case is impossible. The Court tried to clarify its ruling, in the case of *Graham v. Connor* (1989). Here the justices established the standard of "objective reasonableness," saying that the officer's use of deadly force should be judged in terms of the "reasonableness at the moment." This means that the use of the deadly force should be judged from the point of view of the officer on the scene. The Court's decision says that it must be recognized that "officers are often forced to make split-second judgments—in circumstances that are tense, uncertain, and rapidly evolving—about the amount of force that is necessary in a particular situation."

The risk of lawsuits by victims of improper police shootings looms over police departments and creates a further incentive for administrators to set and enforce standards for the use of force. However, as long as officers carry weapons, some improper shootings will occur. Training, internal review of incidents, and the disciplining or firing of quick-trigger officers may help reduce the use of unnecessary force (Blumberg, 1989:442; Fyfe, 1993:128).

TABLE 6.1   Reported Uses of Force by Big-City Police

Police have the legal right to use force to make an arrest, keep the peace, and maintain order. Of the many types of force available to police, the less severe types are used most often.

Type of Force	Rate per Thousand Sworn Officers
Handcuff/leg restraint	490.4
Bodily force (arm, foot, or leg)	272.2
Come-alongs	226.8
Unholstering weapon	129.9
Swarm	126.7
Twist locks/wrist locks	80.9
Firm grip	57.7
Chemical agents (mace or Cap-Stun)	36.2
Batons	36.0
Flashlights	21.7
Dog attacks or bites	6.5
Electrical devices (Taser)	5.4
Civilians shot at but not hit	3.0
Other impact devices	2.4
Neck restraints/unconsciousness-rendering holds	1.4
Vehicle rammings	1.0
Civilians shot and killed	0.9
Civilians shot and wounded but not killed	0.2

Source: Drawn from Bureau of Justice Statistics, *National Data Collection on Police Use of Force* (Washington, DC: U.S. Government Printing Office, 1996), 43.

Tennessee v. Garner (1985)
Deadly force may not be used against an unarmed and fleeing suspect unless necessary to prevent the escape and unless the officer has probable cause to believe that the suspect poses a significant threat of death or serious injury to the officers or others.

As a result of lawsuits by people injured at the hands of the police, departments have sought new means of applying force in ways that will not produce injuries. Some of the new methods center on specific holds and pressure points that officers can use to incapacitate people temporarily without causing permanent harm; officers can learn these techniques through training. In addition, police departments seek new weapons that use less-than-lethal force. Later in this chapter, when we discuss the impact of technology on police, we shall examine new weapons that use electric shocks, projectiles, and chemical sprays. Advocates claim that the use of these weapons has saved the lives of citizens and officers by permitting officers to restore order without resorting to the use of guns. Critics have raised concerns about deaths and injuries produced by less-than-lethal weapons. They also point to the risk that officers will resort too quickly to such weapons when situations could be solved through patience and persuasion (Adang and Mensink, 2004).

Although progress has been made in reducing improper and excessive use of force by police, corruption remains a major problem. We turn to this issue next.

CORRUPTION

Police corruption has a long history in America. Early in the twentieth century, city officials organized liquor and gambling businesses for their personal gain. In many cities, ties between politicians and police officials assured that favored clients would be protected and competitors harassed. Much of the Progressive movement to reform the police aimed at combating such corrupt arrangements.

Officers are often placed in situations where they can be tempted to violate the law.

Joe Rodriguez/Black Star

Sometimes corruption is defined so broadly that it ranges from accepting a free cup of coffee to robbing businesses or beating suspects. Obviously, corruption is not easily defined, and people disagree about what it includes. (See "A Question of Ethics" at the end of this chapter for more on this issue.) As a useful starting point, we can focus on the distinction between corrupt officers who are "grass eaters" and those who are "meat eaters."

"Grass eaters" are officers who accept payoffs that the routines of police work bring their way. "Meat eaters" are officers who actively use their power for personal gain. Although meat eaters are few, their actions make headlines when discovered. By contrast, because grass eaters are numerous, they make corruption seem acceptable and promote a code of secrecy that brands any officer who exposes corruption as a traitor. Grass eaters are the heart of the problem and are often harder to detect than meat eaters.

In the past, researchers have cited low salaries, politics, and poor hiring practices as factors contributing to corruption. However, these arguments fall short of explaining today's corruption. Although some claim that a few "rotten apples" should not taint an entire police force, corruption in some departments has been so rampant that the rotten-apple theory does not fully explain the situation. Some explanations focus on the structure and organization of police work. Much police work involves the enforcement of laws in situations where there is no complainant or it is unclear whether a law has been broken. Moreover, most police work is carried out at the officer's own discretion, without direct supervision. Thus, police officers may have many opportunities to gain benefits by using their discretion to protect people who engage in illegal conduct.

Examples of meat eaters in Cleveland, Ohio, came to light in January 1998 as a result of an FBI sting operation. Forty-one officers were charged with protecting cocaine trafficking. The Cleveland case was one of a series of police-corruption investigations that have struck cities across the country in recent years. From 1994 to 1997, 508 officers in 47 cities were convicted in federal corruption cases (*New York Times*, January 1, 1998, p. A16).

If police administrators judge success merely by the maintenance of order on the streets and a steady flow of arrests and traffic citations, they may not have any idea what their officers actually do while on patrol. Officers therefore may learn that they can engage in improper conduct without worrying about investigations by supervisors as long as there is order on the streets and they keep their activities out of the public spotlight.

Enforcement of vice laws, especially drug laws, creates major problems for police agencies. In many cities the rewards for vice offenders are so high that they can easily afford to make large payments to unethical officers to protect themselves against prosecution. That police operations against victimless crimes are proactive makes the problem worse. Unless drugs are being sold openly, upsetting the residents of a neighborhood, no victims will complain if officers ignore or even profit from the activities of drug dealers.

Over time, illegal activity may become accepted as normal. Ellwyn Stoddard, who studied "blue-coat crime," has said that it can become part of an "identifiable informal 'code'" (Stoddard, 1968:205). He suggests that officers are socialized to the code early in their careers. Those who "snitch" on other officers may be ostracized. Recent research shows that officers risk retaliation from peers if they break the code (Cancino and Enriquez, 2004). When corruption comes to official attention, officers protect the code by distancing themselves from the known offender rather than stopping their own improper conduct (Stoddard, 1968).

Police corruption has three major effects on law enforcement: (1) suspects are left free to engage in further crime, (2) morale is damaged and supervision becomes lax, and (3) the image of the police suffers. The image of the police agency is crucial in light of the need for citizen cooperation. When people see the police as not much different from the "crooks," effective crime control falls even further out of reach.

What is startling is that many people do not equate police corruption with other forms of crime. Some believe that police corruption is tolerable as long as the streets remain safe. This attitude ignores the fact that corrupt officers serve only themselves, not the public.

ThomsonNOW
Improve your grade on the exam with Personalized Study! For reinforcement resources and a mastery check of Political Abuse of Power, go to www.thomsonedu.com/thomsonnow

---

CHECKPOINT

Answers

1. What kinds of practices could be viewed as police abuse? ⟶ 1. Profanity, abusive language, physical force, violence.

2. How did the Supreme Court rule in *Tennessee v. Garner?* ⟶ 2. Deadly force may not be used in apprehending a fleeing felon unless it is necessary to prevent the escape and unless the officer has probable cause to believe that the suspect poses a significant threat of death or serious physical injury to the officer or to others.

3. What is the difference between grass eaters and meat eaters? ⟶ 3. Grass eaters are officers who accept payoffs that police work brings their way. Meat eaters are officers who aggressively misuse their power for personal gain.

Civic Accountability

Relations between citizens and the police depend greatly on citizen confidence that officers will behave in accordance with the law and with departmental guidelines. Rapport with the community is enhanced when citizens feel sure that the police will protect their persons and property and the rights guaranteed by the Constitution. Making the police responsive to citizen complaints without burdening them with a flood of such complaints is difficult. The main challenge in making the police more accountable is to use citizen input to force police to follow the law and departmental guidelines without placing too many limits on their ability to carry out their primary functions. At present, four less-than-perfect techniques are used in efforts to control the police: (1) internal affairs units, (2) civilian review boards, (3) standards and accreditation, and (4) civil liability lawsuits. We now look at each of these in turn.

INTERNAL AFFAIRS UNITS

Controlling the police is mainly an internal matter that administrators must treat as a top priority. The community must be confident that the department has procedures to ensure that officers will protect the rights of citizens. Yet department complaint procedures often seem designed to discourage citizen input. People with complaints cannot always be certain that the police department will take any meaningful action.

internal affairs unit A branch of a police department that receives and investigates complaints alleging violation of rules and policies on the part of officers.

Depending on the size of the department, a single officer or an entire section can serve as an **internal affairs unit** that receives and investigates complaints against officers. An officer charged with misconduct can face criminal prosecution or disciplinary action leading to resignation, dismissal, or suspension. Officers assigned to the internal affairs unit have duties similar to those of the inspector general's staff in the military. They must investigate complaints against other officers. Hollywood films and television series depict dramatic investigations of drug dealing and murder, but investigations of sexual harassment, alcohol or drug problems, misuse of force, and violations of departmental policies are more common.

The internal affairs unit must receive enough resources to carry out its mission, as well as direct access to the chief. Internal investigators who assume that a citizen complaint is an attack on the police as a whole will shield officers against such complaints. When this happens, administrators do not get the information they need to correct a problem. The public, in turn, may come to believe that the department condones the practices they complain of and that filing a complaint is pointless. Moreover, even when the top administrator seeks to attack misconduct, he or she may find persuading police to testify against other officers difficult.

Internal affairs investigators find the work stressful, because their status prevents them from maintaining close relationships with other officers. A wall of silence rises around them. Such problems can be especially severe in smaller departments where all the officers know each other well and regularly socialize together.

CIVILIAN REVIEW BOARDS

If a police department cannot show that it effectively combats corruption among officers, the public will likely demand that the department be investigated by a *civilian review board*. Such a board allows complaints to be channeled through a committee of people who are not sworn police officers. The organization and powers of civilian review boards vary, but all oversee and review how police departments handle citizen complaints. The boards may also recommend remedial action. They do not have the power to investigate or discipline individual officers, however (S. Walker and Wright, 1995).

During the 1980s, as minorities gained more political power in large cities, a revival of civilian review boards took place. A survey of the 50 largest cities found that 36 had civilian review boards, as did 13 of the 50 next-largest cities (S. Walker and Wright, 1995).

The main argument made by the police against civilian review boards is that people outside law enforcement do not understand the problems of policing. The police contend that civilian oversight lowers morale and hinders performance and that officers will be less effective if they must worry about possible disciplinary actions. In reality, however, the boards have not been harsh.

Review of police actions occurs some time after the incident has taken place and usually comes down to the officer's word against that of the complainant. Given the low visibility of the incidents that lead to complaints, a great many complaints are not substantiated (Skolnick and Fyfe, 1993:229). The effectiveness of civilian review boards has not been tested, but their presence may improve police–citizen relations.

STANDARDS AND ACCREDITATION

One way to increase police accountability is to require that police actions meet nationally recognized standards. The movement to accredit departments that meet these standards has gained momentum during the past decade. It has the support of the Commission on Accreditation for Law Enforcement Agencies (CALEA), a private nonprofit corporation formed by four professional associations: the International Association of Chiefs of Police (IACP), the National Organization of Black Law Enforcement Executives (NOBLE), the National Sheriffs Association (NSA), and the Police Executive Research Forum (PERF).

First published in 1983, the CALEA *Standards* have been periodically updated. The fourth edition, published in 1999, has 439 specific standards. Each standard is a statement, with a brief explanation, that sets forth clear requirements. For example, under "Limits of Authority," Standard 1.2.2 requires that "a written directive [govern] the use of discretion by sworn officers." The explanation states, "In many agencies, the exercise of discretion is defined by a combination of written enforcement policies, training and supervision. The written directive should define the limits of individual discretion and provide guidelines for exercising discretion within those limits" (CALEA, 1989:1). Because police departments have said almost nothing about their use of discretion, this statement represents a major shift. However, the standard still is not specific enough. For example, it does not cover stop-and-frisk actions, the handling of drunks, and the use of informants.

Police accreditation is voluntary. Departments contact CALEA, which helps them in their efforts to meet the standards. This process involves self-evaluation by departmental executives, the development of policies that meet the standards, and the training of officers. The CALEA representative acts like a military inspector general, visiting the department, examining its policies, and seeing if the standards are met in its daily operations. Departments that meet the standards receive certification. Administrators can use the standards as a management tool, training officers to know the standards and be accountable for their actions. By 1998 over 460 agencies had been accredited (S. Walker, 1999:285).

Obviously, the standards do not guarantee that police officers in an accredited department will not engage in misconduct. However, they serve as a major step toward providing clear guidelines to officers about proper behavior. Accreditation can also show the public a department's commitment to making sure officers carry out their duties in an ethical, professional manner.

CIVIL LIABILITY SUITS

Civil lawsuits against departments for police misconduct can increase civic accountability. In 1961 the U.S. Supreme Court ruled that Section 1983 of the Civil Rights Act of 1871 allows citizens to sue public officials for violations of their civil rights. The high court extended this opportunity in 1978 when it ruled that individual officials and local agencies may be sued when a person's civil rights are violated by an agency's "customs and usages." If an individual can show that harm was caused by employees whose wrongful acts were the result of these "customs, practices, and policies, including poor training and supervision," then he or she can sue (*Monell v. Department of Social Services of the City of New York*, 1978).

Lawsuits charging brutality, false arrest, and negligence are being brought in both state and federal courts. In several states people have received damage awards in the millions of dollars, and police departments have settled some suits out of court. For example, Omaha, Nebraska, paid $8 million between 1993 and 2005 to innocent victims of police chases (N. Hicks, 2005). New York City paid more than $140 million in claims for police actions between 1994 and 1999 (Flynn, 1999).

Civil liability rulings by the courts tend to be simple and severe: Officials and municipalities are ordered to pay a sum of money, and the courts can enforce that judgment. The potential for costly judgments gives police departments an incentive to improve the training and supervision of officers (Vaughn, 2001). One study asked a sample of police executives to rank the policy issues most likely to be affected by civil liability decisions. The top-ranked issues were use of force, pursuit driving, and improper arrests (C. E. Smith and Hurst, 1996). Most departments have liability insurance, and many officers have their own insurance policies.

Answers

4. What are the four methods used to increase the civic accountability of ➡ the police?

4. Internal affairs units, civilian review boards, standards and accreditation, civil liability suits.

5. What is an internal affairs unit? ───────────────────────➡

5. A unit within the police department designated to receive and investigate complaints alleging violation of rules and policies on the part of officers.

6. Why are civilian review boards relatively uncommon? ─────────➡

6. Opposition by the police.

Policing and New Technology

Policing has long made use of technological developments. For decades, police have increased their mobility (faster vehicles), communications capacity (radios and computers in patrol cars), and investigative effectiveness (fingerprints, blood samples, and polygraphs) through the use of technology. In recent decades, rapid technological changes have produced both new forms of crime and new methods for investigation.

Several issues arise as police adopt new technologies. First, law enforcement officials often struggle to keep pace with the technological advances employed by criminals, especially with respect to computer crimes. As public agencies, police departments' budgets depend in part on elected officials' decisions about policy priorities. It can be difficult for law enforcement officials, especially those in small agencies, to obtain cutting-edge equipment and to hire computer experts and other personnel with needed scientific expertise. For example, limited resources have hampered the use of DNA testing by some agencies.

Second, questions persist about the accuracy and effectiveness of investigative technologies. For example, despite its long and confident acceptance in court by police and prosecutors, the accuracy of fingerprint evidence has been questioned. In 2002 a federal judge ruled that expert witnesses could compare crime scene fingerprints with those of a defendant, but they could not testify that the prints definitely matched. The judge pointed out that, unlike DNA evidence, fingerprint evidence processes have not been scientifically verified, the error rate for such identifications has never been measured, and there are no scientific standards for determining when fingerprint samples "match" (Loviglio, 2002). Prosecutors later persuaded the judge to reverse his original decision and admit the expert testimony about a fingerprint match, but the judge's first decision raises the possibility that other judges will scrutinize fingerprint evidence more closely. Law enforcement officials must be concerned about the accuracy of scientific methods as well as the expertise, ethics, and care exercised by personnel.

Third, some observers worry that new technologies will create new collisions with citizens' constitutional rights (C. E. Smith and McCall, 2002). As police gain greater opportunities for sophisticated electronic surveillance, for example, new questions arise about what constitutes a "search" that violates the reasonable expectations of privacy of citizens. The development of technology for the interception of email messages by law enforcement agencies provides an illustration of new situations that were not foreseeable in prior decades.

CYBER CRIME

Cyber crime poses an especially difficult challenge for law enforcement. According to the FBI, individual complaints of losses from Internet fraud, such as phony email solicitations and fake websites, totaled $183 million during 2005 (National White Collar Crime Center and the FBI, 2006). Total losses to businesses and other organizations in the United States, much of which is caused by damage from worms and computer viruses as well as financial fraud, came to $67 billion in total annual costs and losses, according to an FBI survey in 2005 (FBI, 2006b). The enormous losses

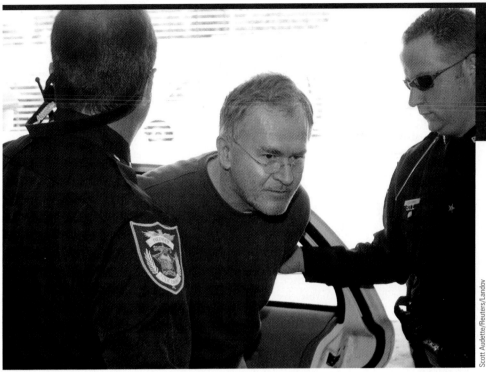

Brian Doyle, former press secretary for the U.S. Department of Homeland Security, was arrested on charges of sending pornographic messages on the Internet to someone he thought was a 14-year-old girl. The girl, in reality, was a sheriff's deputy. Use of the Internet to seduce children for sexual purposes has become an increasing problem.

Scott Audette/Reuters/Landov

from computer crime keep growing and thereby pressure law enforcement agencies to increase their efforts to counteract these crimes.

Cyber crime is an especially difficult problem because so many hackers and cyber thieves operate overseas, outside of the immediate authority of American law enforcement officials. Although much of the cyber crime that victimizes Americans originates in the United States, millions of dollars are lost each year because of the actions of criminals in Eastern Europe, China, and Africa. News reports regularly detail the millions of dollars stolen from Americans through credit card fraud, email scams, and computer withdrawals from bank accounts by thieves in such places as Russia, the Ukraine, and Nigeria (Lawal, 2006; "Meet the Hackers," 2006). Federal agencies that focus on cyber crime, especially the FBI and the Secret Service, work toward further coordination and cooperation with officials in other countries.

Cutting-edge computer equipment and expertise are essential to law enforcement's efforts to combat cyber crime (Hinduja, 2004). Computer investigations lie at the heart of police work concerning identity thieves and offenders who steal credit card numbers and engage in fraudulent financial transactions online (Collins, 2005). Computer technology is also essential to police officers who use decoy operations in order to identify sexual predators who target children through online communications. The FBI's Innocent Images National Initiative, founded in 1996, works with local law enforcement officials, often by having officers pose as young people in online conversations. From 1996 to 2005, these investigations resulted in the prosecution of 4,784 individuals for sexual abuse and child pornography (L. Miller, 2006).

State and local law enforcement officials often lack the equipment, training, and staff to pursue cyber crime vigorously. Law enforcement officials need the equipment and expertise to identify hackers who disrupt corporate and government computer systems. Hackers can steal personal information and trade secrets as well as cause expensive damage to business and government operations. As law enforcement officials and corporate security managers increase their capacity to block or identify hackers, the hackers develop new means to undertake criminal enterprises using computers. For example, in website extortion schemes, hackers threaten to shut down business websites unless they are paid significant sums of money. In 2006 two teenagers in

New York were arrested by undercover officers from the Secret Service for attempting to extort $150,000 from MySpace, the community website popular with young people (Sandoval, 2006).

Future progress against cyber crime will require the commitment of resources and the cooperation of foreign governments. Since the terrorist attacks of 9/11, the federal government has increased its attention on the use of computers for communication and money transfers by groups and individuals who threaten homeland security. The expanded attention to computer networks for antiterrorism purposes will likely also help officials increase expertise and upgrade equipment in ways that will lead to the apprehension of other criminals involved in malicious hacking, financial crimes, and child pornography.

INVESTIGATIVE TOOLS

Computers are also essential for crime analysis and "crime mapping," methods used with increasing frequency by local police departments. Through the use of Geographic Information System (GIS) technology and software, police departments can analyze hot spots, crime trends, and other crime patterns with a level of sophistication and precision never before available. By analyzing the locations and frequency of specific crimes, such as burglary, or the nature of calls for service in various neighborhoods, police can deploy their personnel more effectively and better plan targeted crime prevention programs (Stroshine, 2005).

In addition to the DNA database discussed in Chapter 5, the FBI has developed a significant database of fingerprints. Police departments throughout the country can submit fingerprints from a crime scene in hope of finding the criminal's identity from among the more than 47 million sets of fingerprints stored in the FBI computers. Local and federal law enforcement officials routinely submit the fingerprints of everyone arrested for a serious charge, so that the prints can be added to the database. If a suspect is found not guilty, the prints are supposed to be removed from the system. Fingerprints from government employees and military personnel exist in separate databases, which may also be used for background checks on people who work in regulated industries such as casinos and banks (Engber, 2005).

National databases of fingerprint, the DNA of every known felon, plus the ballistics signature of every gun ever used in a crime, are now being developed. Here, the FBI's Lead Ballistics Examiner, Walter Dandridge, studies the grooves of a .223 slug like the one used by the "D.C. Snipers."

Brooks Kraft/Corbis

A few years ago, matching fingerprints was a time-consuming process because fingerprints had to be sent to the FBI on cards. Since 1999, however, the Integrated Automated Fingerprint Identification System (IAFIS) has enabled police to send fingerprints electronically and then have those prints matched against the millions of prints in the database. The FBI can also provide electronic images of individuals' fingerprints to local enforcement agencies on request. The FBI also provides training for state and local police on taking fingerprints and transmitting those prints to the IAFIS for evaluation.

As police officers sought the snipers who terrorized Washington, D.C., in October 2002, new debates emerged about whether the government should establish a national database of ballistic evidence. Advocates argued that every gun sold should undergo a firing test so that its ballistic "fingerprint" could be stored in the database, just in case the weapon was later used in a crime. Opponents claimed that this was an undesirable step toward national gun registration and that such a database would be useless because the ballistic characteristics of a gun's fired bullets change as the gun is used over time (Chaddock, 2002). The usefulness of these databases depends on the accuracy of technology to match evidence with stored information and the accessibility of database information to police departments and individual officers. In addition, as indicated by the debate about ballistic evidence, public policy debates about what information can be gathered and how it will be used will continue to affect the nature and use of evidence databases.

As we have seen, law enforcement agencies may lack the resources to make the best use of advances in technology, including new databases. The problem of too few DNA laboratories and inadequate staff and equipment plagues many states and the federal government. It took police only five days to learn that a man's DNA sample in Vermont identified him as a murder suspect. Unfortunately, they conducted this test a full five years after the man had provided the DNA sample; it had taken this long for Vermont crime lab officials to put the sample in the state's database (Ring, 2005). The long delay prevented quick identification and arrest. A report from the Bureau of Justice Statistics estimated that reducing backlogs in DNA labs throughout the nation would require 1,900 additional laboratory staff members at a cost of more than $70 million (Peterson and Hickman, 2005).

Police have begun using surveillance cameras in many ways. American cities increasingly use surveillance cameras at intersections to monitor and ticket people who run red lights or exceed speed limits. In Scotland, England, and Australia, law enforcement officials have adopted the use of surveillance cameras that permit police to monitor activities that occur in downtown commercial areas or other selected locations. Officials in a control room can watch everyone who passes within the cameras' fields. Advances in camera technology can enable these officials to see clearly the license plate numbers of cars and other specific information. American cities, such as Chicago, New York, and Washington, have made moves toward experimenting with this approach to combating crime in targeted areas (Howlett, 2004).

Critics complain that constant surveillance by government intrudes on the privacy of innocent, unsuspecting citizens and that there is insufficient evidence that this surveillance leads to reduced crime rates (Taifa, 2002). Judges and lawyers, including civil liberties advocates, see no problem, because people do not have a reasonable expectation of privacy when they are in public places (Howlett, 2004). Public concerns loom larger, however, when government surveillance occurs in private settings, such as monitoring Americans' telephone calls, Internet usage, and conversations between lawyers and clients—forms of surveillance used by the federal government since 9/11 (Bernstein, 2006).

In the midst of these concerns, American law enforcement officials continue to experiment with surveillance and detection technologies. The National Institute of Justice provides funds to help scientists develop devices that will assist the police. For example, scanners are being developed that will permit officers to detect whether individuals are carrying weapons, bombs, or drugs. Some of these devices detect foreign masses hidden on the human body, whereas others detect trace particles and vapors that differ from those associated with human bodies and clothing (Business Wire, 2001; PR Newswire, 2001). The first versions of such scanners are undergoing testing as security measures at airports, prisons, schools, and stadiums. However, officers on the streets could eventually use smaller, more mobile versions, especially if they could point a handheld device at an individual passerby to detect whether the person is carrying weapons or contraband.

Casinos in Atlantic City also use facial-recognition technology with surveillance cameras to identify people whom they know to be skilled at cheating. Conceivably, the system could also be used to identify suspected terrorists attempting to enter the country at airports (Meyer and Gorman, 2001). This technology poses problems, however, and some cities have abandoned their initial experiments. It cannot identify faces and match them with database pictures quickly enough to prevent suspects from disappearing into a crowd and thus requiring officers to search for them. In addition, questions persist about the accuracy of the facial-recognition technology. According to one researcher who has tested some systems, "One out of every 50 people looks like Carlos the Jackal, [the infamous terrorist], and the real Carlos the Jackal has only a 50 percent chance of looking like himself" (Meyer and Gorman, 2001:1). It remains to be seen whether facial recognition technology will develop into an effective tool for police.

Scientists are working to develop technology to detect deceptions that suspects may use when questioned by police. Polygraph tests (lie detectors) are considered insufficiently reliable, because some liars may be very calm when they lie, and thereby avoid any increase in heart rate or perspiration. By contrast, some truthful people will be very nervous when being asked questions. Thus, truthful people may look like liars on a polygraph test if their palms sweat and their heart rates increase as they answer. One approach under investigation is the use of a thermal imaging camera that can detect faint blushing in the faces of people who answer questions untruthfully. Critics warn, however, that this technology may simply reproduce the problems with polygraphs by looking only at physical responses that vary by individual (R. Callahan, 2002).

less-lethal weapons Weapons such as pepper spray and air-fired bean-bags or nets that are used in an effort to incapacitate a suspect without inflicting serious injuries.

WEAPONS TECHNOLOGY

As we shall see, police officers have been sued in many cases when they injured or killed people without proper justification. Some of these lawsuits have resulted in cities and counties paying millions of dollars to people who were injured when police used guns or nightsticks improperly or in an inappropriate situation. To avoid future lawsuits, departments have given greater attention to the training of officers. They have also sought **less-lethal weapons** that could be used to incapacitate or control people with reduced risk of causing serious injuries or deaths. Traditional less-lethal weapons, such as nightsticks and pepper spray, can be used only when officers are in close contact with suspects, and they are not suitable for all situations that officers face. As discussed in "Technology Issues in Criminal Justice," police rely on new projectile weapons to subdue suspects and rioters.

For suspects who are close at hand, many police departments use the Taser, a weapon with prongs that sends an incapacitating electric jolt of 50,000 volts into people on contact (Ith, 2001). More than 5,000 law enforcement agencies in the United States use these devices. However, the human rights organization Amnesty International has documented more than 70 cases since 2001 in which people died after police used a Taser on them, and recent research raises questions about the device's effect on human hearts (Berenson, 2006). The manufacturer of Tasers as well as some researchers dispute whether the device actually caused the deaths.

Kalispell, Montana, Police Officer Mike Whitcher reacts as he receives a jolt from a Taser gun. The Taser gun fires two filaments that send an incapacitating electric jolt into the body on contact. Whitcher had to endure the jolt for a second or two in order to become certified in the use of the weapon.

AP Photo/Daily Inter Lake, Karen Nichols

Technology Issues in Criminal Justice

Less-Lethal Weapons

Police officers in the United States carry firearms. With firearms, officers can easily kill someone, including bystanders, when they pull the trigger. Many police shootings have led to lawsuits against the police that have cost taxpayers millions of dollars in court judgments favoring citizens who have been seriously injured or killed.

To avoid such incidents, the National Institute of Justice has funded projects developing less-lethal weapons. For example, projectile weapons shoot objects at people whom the police wish to subdue. Some less-lethal projectiles, such as rubber bullets, can travel a long distance. Others are employed only when suspects are within a few yards of the officers. Police have used rubber bullets for many years. Although they are generally nonlethal, they can cause serious injuries and death if they hit someone in the eye or elsewhere in the head. Many departments have turned to the use of beanbags, small canvas bags containing tiny lead beads and fired from a shotgun (Spencer, 2000). They are intended to stun people on impact without causing lasting injury. Several police departments in the Los Angeles area, however, have abandoned the use of beanbags because of concerns about injuries and a few deaths caused by these projectiles as well as dissatisfaction with their accuracy when fired at a target (Leonard, 2002).

Other departments have begun to use airguns that shoot PepperBalls, small plastic pellets filled with a peppery powder that causes coughing and sneezing upon release after the suspect is stunned by the impact of the pellet. This weapon drew increased scrutiny when an Emerson College student died after she was hit in the eye by a projectile that disperses pepper spray as police officers attempted to disperse a crowd of revelers who were celebrating a Boston Red Sox victory (CNN, 2004). Officers can also fill the pellets with green dye in order to mark and later arrest individuals in an out-of-control crowd (Randolph, 2001). Other weapons under development either shoot nets that wrap around individual suspects or spray a fountain of foam that envelops the suspect in layers of paralyzing ooze. Law enforcement agencies may also eventually have versions of new weapons being developed for the military, such as devices that send out incapacitating blasts of heat or blinding flash explosions (Hambling, 2005).

RESEARCHING THE INTERNET

To read about PepperBall projectiles and weapons, see the corresponding site listed on the Cole/Smith Criminal Justice in America Companion Website: http://www.thomsonedu.com/criminaljustice/cole.

FOR CRITICAL ANALYSIS

Will these new weapons create new problems for police? Will officers quickly employ easy-to-fire, less-lethal weapons, which can cause injury and, in rare cases, death, rather than first attempting verbal persuasion when faced with an angry, emotional, or mentally ill person? Will officers be injured or killed while employing a less-lethal weapon against a suspect who, unbeknownst to them, is armed with a gun?

CHECKPOINT

7. What challenges do law enforcement officials face in dealing with cyber crime?

8. What kinds of technologies help police with their investigative functions?

9. What kinds of new weaponry have police employed?

Answers

7. Keeping pace with computer technology and criminals' new strategies for committing crimes, the overseas locations of many cyber criminals.

8. Databases, Geographic Information Systems, DNA testing, cameras and other surveillance devices.

9. Less-lethal weapons, including beanbag projectiles, Tasers, and PepperBall projectiles.

Homeland Security

In prior chapters, we have seen how the recent emphasis on homeland security has changed policing. The federal government reorganized various agencies, including law enforcement agencies, in creating the Department of Homeland Security (DHS). Shifts in the FBI's priorities and in the availability of federal funds created new burdens, opportunities, and objectives for local law enforcement agencies. Even traditional programs, such as Neighborhood Watch, now include discussions of making contributions to homeland security in addition to crime prevention. Although the emphasis on homeland security accelerated and generated a sense of urgency after the hijackers' attacks on September 11, many police departments had gained awareness about their role in homeland security prior to that date. On February 26, 1993, radical Muslims set off a car bomb in the parking garage under the World Trade Center in New York City. Five people were killed and dozens more were injured. In Oklahoma City, Timothy McVeigh, an antigovernment radical, detonated a truck bomb in front of the Federal Building on April 19, 1995. The bomb killed 168 people and injured hundreds more. In both of these examples, local police officers, as well as firefighters, were first responders who rescued survivors, rendered first aid, and began to collect

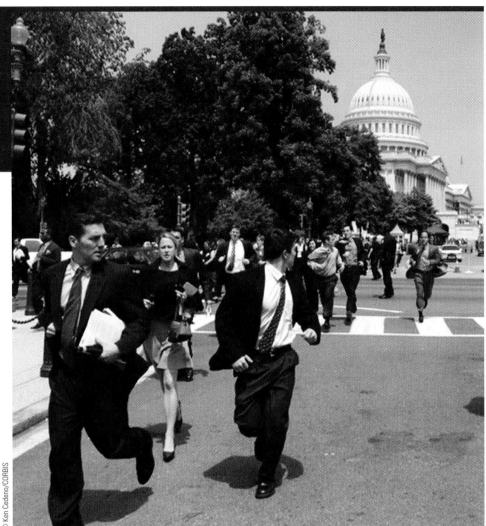

The White House and U.S. Capitol were evacuated, and U.S. Air Force planes scrambled in May, 2005, when authorities became alarmed about the approach of an unidentified aircraft. The Cessna airplane had inadvertently violated the restricted airspace surrounding Washington, D.C. Incidents such as this are treated with much more urgency since the September 11 terrorist attacks.

criminal evidence. The events of September 11 taught Americans that terrorist attacks could not be treated as isolated incidents and rare events. Instead, government officials and citizens alike needed to recognize that specific groups around the world were making plans to inflict large-scale damage on the United States and harm Americans within their own country. This lesson altered the priorities of government agencies and pushed law enforcement agencies at the federal, state, and local levels to make plans for the possibility of future significant threats to homeland security.

PREPARING FOR THREATS

As discussed in prior chapters, the FBI and DHS make concerted efforts to identify and combat risks in order to reduce the threat of additional attacks. The FBI switched a significant portion of its personnel away from traditional crime-control activities in order to gather intelligence on people within the United States who may pose a threat to the nation. The FBI also received budget allocations to enable it to expand the number of special agents and intelligence analysts working on counterterrorism issues. The creation of Joint Terrorism Task Forces reflected the agency's desire to coordinate efforts with state and local officials. Federal officials also sought greater cooperation and coordination with their counterparts in many countries around the world.

At the same time, the creation of DHS reflected a desire to have better coordination among agencies scattered through the federal government. The DHS also instituted new security procedures at airports and borders as a means of seeking to identify individuals and contraband that pose threats. Many critics believe that the federal government has not done enough to protect ports and critical infrastructure, including nuclear power plants, the information system, subway systems, and other entities that are essential for the functioning of American society. Attacks with devastating consequences could range from computer hackers disabling key military information systems or computerized controls at energy companies to a suicide airline hijacker hitting a nuclear power or chemical plant. If an attack should target and disable any of these entities, it would fall to local police to maintain order and rescue people.

Police agencies have traditionally gathered **law enforcement intelligence**, namely, information about criminal activities and organizations, especially in their efforts to monitor motorcycle gangs, hate groups, drug traffickers, and organized crime. The new emphasis on homeland security broadens the scope of information that agencies need to gather. According to Jonathan White (2004), police must be trained to look for and gather information about such things as

■ Emergence of radical groups, including religious groups

■ Suspicious subjects observing infrastructure facilities

■ Growth of phony charities that may steer money to terrorists

■ Groups with links to foreign countries

■ Unexpected terrorist information found during criminal searches

■ Discovery of bomb-making operations

Local police agencies need training about what to look for and whom to contact if any suspicious activities or materials are discovered. One of the disconcerting aspects of the September 11 tragedy was that specific agencies and officers possessed suspicions about unusual students at flight schools and individuals who had entered the country. If the agencies had shared information more effectively, some people believe that at least some of the September 11 hijackers would have been apprehended and questioned. In light of this lesson, law enforcement agencies at all levels are working harder to coordinate their efforts and share information. Local police officials still complain, however, that the FBI and other federal agencies do not share enough information with them about potential threats within their communities.

Some initiatives to gather and share information have not succeeded. For example, the federal government funded the Multistate Anti-Terrorism Information Exchange, known as MATRIX, that was to collect driver's license, criminal history, and other information from participating states so that they could share access to this information. Initially, 13 states representing nearly half the country's population indicated a willingness to participate. However, all but four of these states eventually dropped out of the project amid criticism about the threat to privacy rights as governments created larger and larger databases containing information about people who have done nothing to raise suspicions about their activities. California and Texas, for example, dropped out because of concerns that the MATRIX database, including its sensitive files, was housed in computers at a private company (Krane, 2003). Michigan dropped out amid lawsuits alleging that its participation violated a state statute forbidding the state police from participating in interstate intelligence gathering without legislative approval or outside oversight ("Michigan State Police Drop Out," 2005). Lingering public suspicion and specific laws concerning intelligence operations stem from revelations about government agents spying on American citizens for merely expressing their views about civil rights and the Vietnam War during the 1960s and 1970s. These issues have arisen again with revelations in 2005 that the National Security Agency was secretly monitoring telephone calls and Internet usage by Americans throughout the country, not just individuals under suspicion of involvement with terrorist groups (Shane and Lichtblau, 2006). As law enforcement agencies in the United States continue to develop methods to combat terrorism and protect homeland security, experts and ordinary citizens alike will reexamine the balance between providing the government with appropriate tools and safeguarding the rights of Americans against excessive government intrusions.

law enforcement intelligence
Information collected and analyzed by law enforcement officials concerning criminal activities and organizations, such as terror groups, gangs, drug traffickers, and organized crime.

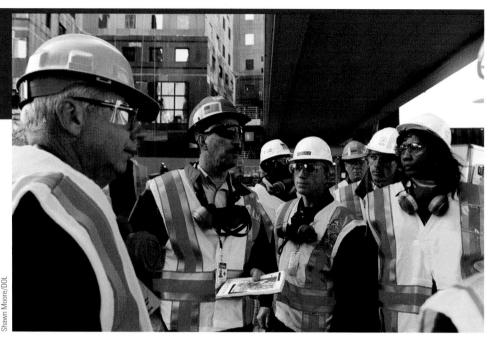

Successful implementation of the Incident Command System requires the police and other first responders such as firefighters and public health officials to develop local and regional plans to deal with terrorism and natural disasters.

Shawn Moore/DOL

The emphasis on both information analysis and coordination among agencies at all levels of U.S. government, as well as with foreign governments, also impacts law enforcement operations concerning other major problems, such as drug trafficking, money laundering, gun smuggling, and border security. Many of these problems relate directly to threats from terrorism as organizations hostile to the United States seek to finance themselves and gain entry into the country. In addition, heightened security and increased vigilance create opportunities to detect and apprehend people involved in these criminal activities but who have no connection to terrorism. For example, homeland security efforts overlap initiatives to combat transnational street gangs, such as the MS-13 gang from Central America that has spread from Los Angeles to such places as Washington, D.C., and Charlotte, North Carolina, and brought with it various criminal activities, including a series of gang-related homicides (Axtman, 2005b).

Within local police departments, the emphasis on homeland security has led to changes in training, equipment, and operations to prepare first responders to deal with the possibility of weapons of mass destruction and terrorist attacks. Local police must also develop regional coordination with neighboring communities and state governments, because large-scale emergencies require the resources and assistance of multiple agencies. Communities need plans for evacuating buildings and neighborhoods. Police officials must work more closely with firefighters, public health officials, and emergency medical services to prepare for anything from a bomb to a bioterror attack using anthrax, smallpox, or the like (Hinton, 2002). Some of these threats require the acquisition of new equipment, such as personal protection suits for suspected biological or chemical hazards or communications equipment that can be used to contact multiple agencies. Many police departments are giving renewed attention to training specialized teams, such as bomb squads and SWAT teams that will intervene in emergency situations. In addition, they must give all officers additional training on hazard materials, coordination with outside agencies, and evacuation procedures for malls, central business districts, and hospitals.

The federal government has shifted its funding priorities away from community-oriented policing in order to provide grants for state and local agencies to obtain equipment and training for emergency response and homeland security purposes. One criticism of the funding process is that funds were distributed without careful consideration for which locations had the greatest homeland security needs. For example, although many experts regard New York City as one of the top terrorism targets, as evidenced by two major attacks on the World Trade Center and several foiled plots, New York City's Fire Department had only one fully deployable hazardous materials unit for a city of 8 million people. Meanwhile, Grand Forks, North Dakota, reportedly received funds for more biochemical protective suits than they actually have officers to wear them. Wyoming was a top recipient of homeland security money, receiving funds equal to $38.31 per person in the state, whereas New York received the equivalent of $5.47 per person and was 49th in per capita funding (Kates, 2003).

Similarly, although the 9/11 target cities of New York and Washington, D.C., received significant federal funding in 2005, both cities saw significant cuts in their allocations for 2006. Because smaller cities throughout the country received significant increases for 2006, the funding decisions produced questions and complaints from elected officials (Lipton, 2006). The skewed distribution of homeland security funds led critics to conclude that there was too much emphasis on politics and insufficient attention to actual threat assessment and demonstrated needs. Many observers hoped that more effective planning would occur as DHS became better organized and more cohesive.

Just as the development of better communication and coordination among agencies can help to combat drug trafficking, gun smuggling, and other crimes unrelated to terrorism, so, too, can new training and equipment serve dual purposes. For example, new equipment for detecting and defusing bombs obtained under homeland security grants can be used for pipe bombs and other explosive devices created by people unconnected to terrorism. Similarly, training in the detection and dismantling of chemical weapons helps in police efforts to find and destroy meth labs and thereby address one of the nation's growing problems with illegal drugs.

A key element of homeland security planning is the development of the Incident Command System (ICS). The principles of the ICS were first developed to help multiple agencies coordinate their efforts in addressing large wildfires in western states. The ICS involves planning to determine what individual will take charge of managing resources and operations in response to a critical incident. It also involves the development of an incident action plan that coordinates the resources, activities, and responsibilities of various agencies and individuals who will be involved in responding to an emergency. By using the ICS, agencies are not taken by surprise when emergencies arise and they can spring into action with well-coordinated efforts to maintain order, address primary threats such as fires or bombings, evacuate endangered people, and provide medical aid. The awareness of homeland security needs after September 11 has encouraged police departments to work closely with state officials, firefighters, public health officials, hospitals, and others to develop local and regional ICS plans.

NEW LAWS AND CONTROVERSIES

The hijackers' devastating attacks on September 11 spurred a variety of government actions intended to protect homeland security and combat terrorism. The Bush administration asserted new presidential powers to arrest and detain indefinitely without trial Americans whom it accused of terrorist activities. In 2004, however, the U.S. Supreme Court ruled that the President does not possess unlimited authority and that American detainees are entitled to challenge their confinement through court procedures (*Hamdi v. Rumsfeld*, 2004). The Supreme Court's decision illustrated one aspect of the challenge facing the United States in providing the government with sufficient power to fight terrorism while also protecting individuals' constitutional rights.

Other controversies arose concerning new state and federal statutes created after September 11. Both Congress and state legislatures enacted new laws aimed at addressing various aspects of homeland security. More than 30 states added new terrorism-related laws. These laws ranged in scope, from narrowly addressing specific problems to creating broad new powers for law enforcement officials and defining new crimes. At the narrow end of the spectrum, for example, after it was discovered that several of the September 11 hijackers had Virginia drivers' licenses, Virginia passed a new law to make it more difficult for foreign nationals to obtain a driver's license without possession of specific legal documents.

An example of a broader law is Arizona's statute concerning money laundering, weapons of mass destruction, terrorism and terrorism hoaxes, and eavesdropping on communications, and including a prohibition on bail for persons accused of violent acts of terrorism. Some of the purposes and uses of these laws raise questions about whether government powers will grow beyond appropriate boundaries in a democracy that is supposed to place a high value on the protection of individuals' rights.

Because new laws provide tools for use by justice system officials, controversies can arise when those officials are accused of stretching their authority beyond the intentions of the relevant statutes. For example, prosecutors in several cases have used new terrorism laws as a means to prosecute people for criminal acts that are not commonly understood to be related to terrorism. In New York, for example, one of the first prosecutions under the state's antiterrorism laws enacted after September 11 arose when the Bronx district attorney charged street gang members of various crimes. There was no allegation that the gang members had connections to any foreign terrorist networks. Instead, the prosecutor used the state antiterrorism law to charge gang members with shootings "committed with the intent to intimidate or coerce a civilian population" (Garcia, 2005). Virginia used nearly identical language under its post–September 11 statute as one basis for applying the death penalty to John Muhammad, one of the infamous D.C. snipers who frightened the nation's capital in October 2002, even though there was no proof that he pulled the trigger in any of the shootings (Hegsted, 2005). In other examples, a North Carolina prosecutor used a terrorism statute to charge the operator of a small meth lab for "manufacturing a nuclear or chemical weapon," and a Michigan prosecutor used the state's antiterrorism law to charge a high school student for writing up a "hit list" of students and school officials ("Charging Common Criminals," 2003; "Concern Mounts over Anti-Terrorism Law," 2005). The latter two cases generated criticism in newspaper editorials and raised concerns that government officials would exploit terrorism laws for improper purposes. The language of many terrorism laws is sufficiently vague to give prosecutors greater flexibility in seeking convictions. The severe penalties for terrorism-related acts can also give prosecutors more leverage to pressure defendants to plead guilty to lesser charges.

The most controversial legislation came from Congress in the form of the "Uniting and Strengthening America by Providing Appropriate Tools Required to Intercept and Obstruct Terrorism Act." It is best known by its shorthand name, the **USA Patriot Act.** The Patriot Act moved quickly through Congress after the September 11 attacks and covered a wide range of topics, including the expansion of government authority for searches and surveillance and the expansion of definitions and penalties for crimes defined as related to terrorism. Critics raised concerns about many provisions because of fears that the government's new powers would infringe individuals' rights (Dority, 2005). The Patriot Act made it easier for law enforcement officials to monitor email communications and obtain "sneak-and-peek" warrants in which they secretly conduct searches without informing a home or business owner until much later that the premises have been searched (Sullivan, 2003). The Patriot Act also authorizes warrantless searches of third-party records, such as those at libraries, financial institutions, phone companies, and medical facilities. This provision sparked an outcry from librarians and booksellers who argued that monitoring the reading habits of citizens without sufficient evidence to obtain a warrant violates privacy and free expression rights. This provision, in particular, was cited by many of the 150 communities across the country that passed resolutions protesting the excessive authority granted to government by the Patriot Act (Jane Gordon, 2005, "In Patriots' Cradle, the Patriot Act Faces Scrutiny," *New York Times*, April 24, http://www.nytimes.com).

USA Patriot Act A federal statute passed in the aftermath of the terrorist attacks of September 11 that broadens government authority to conduct searches and wiretaps and that expands the definitions of crimes involving terrorism.

CLOSE UP

Swift Action Based on Limited Evidence

Powerful bombs rocked the train station in Madrid, Spain, on March 11, 2004, killing 191 people and injuring 2,000 others. The bombing was suspected to be the work of Muslim radicals who were targeting a country allied with the United States in the invasion of Iraq. FBI experts examined evidence in the bombing, including a partial fingerprint found on a bag of detonators. The FBI officials used their department's automated searching system for the fingerprint database and determined that the print matched Brandon Mayfield's. The fingerprints of Mayfield, a lawyer from Portland, Oregon, who had converted to Islam 20 years earlier, were in the FBI database because he had once been a U.S. Army officer, and military fingerprints are included in the FBI computer. Although Spanish authorities cast doubt on the FBI's conclusions, Mayfield was arrested as a material witness and held in jail. The FBI searched his home, examined his telephone records, and analyzed his relationships with other Muslims whom they believed to have ties to terrorist organizations. After he spent two weeks in jail, Mayfield was released because Spanish authorities matched the fingerprint to a man from Algeria. The FBI subsequently apologized to Mayfield for its errors.

RESEARCHING THE INTERNET

Read the article "Fingerprints: Not a Gold Standard" in *Issues in Science and Technology Online.* You can find it at the corresponding website listed on the Cole/Smith Criminal Justice in America Companion Website: http://www.thomsonedu.com/criminaljustice/cole.

FOR CRITICAL ANALYSIS

Should the government rely on a single, partial fingerprint for placing someone in jail? Would the FBI have acted so swiftly against Mayfield if he had belonged to a different religion? How much evidence should the government possess before taking someone into custody?

Sources: MSNBC.com, "U.S. Lawyer Freed in Madrid Bombing Case," May 20, 2004, http://www.MSNBC.com; "Editorial: The F.B.I. Messes Up," *New York Times,* May 26, 2004, p. A22.

Some of the concerns about the Patriot Act arose because it sailed through Congress in the aftermath of September 11 with very little close examination or debate. Because the law is several hundred pages long, members of Congress likely had not studied the entire law before voting on it. Some of the provisions in the Patriot Act, such as those concerning expanded powers for searches and wiretaps, were sought by some federal law enforcement officials prior to September 11. Critics claim that the terrorist attacks provided the momentum for powers that these officials sought to use for crime control purposes unrelated to homeland security. Moreover, there are concerns that there is insufficient judicial or legislative supervision over the investigatory activities of law enforcement officials.

In light of the power granted to law enforcement officials, are there risks that they will act too swiftly in investigating and even arresting people without an adequate basis for suspicion? Read the Close Up box on the arrest of an Oregon lawyer and see whether you think these risks are real.

The Patriot Act received criticism from both liberals and conservatives. Like liberals, some conservative politicians expressed concern that law enforcement officials could too easily search people's homes, obtain their personal records, and intercept their communications without a firm basis for suspicion of wrongdoing. In addition, the Patriot Act defined *domestic terrorism* as criminal acts dangerous to human life that appear intended to intimidate civilians or influence public policy by intimidation. Conservatives feared the law could be used against antiabortion protesters who block entrances at abortion clinics, and liberals feared that it could be used against environmental activists who take direct actions to prevent the destruction of forests and wildlife. Other critics of the Patriot Act pointed to provisions making it a crime to provide material support for terrorism; specifically, they raised concerns that people who donate money to the antiabortion movement or environmental causes could unwittingly find themselves prosecuted for serious terrorism offenses (Lithwick and Turner, 2003).

The debates about new laws enacted as part of homeland security and counterterrorism efforts illustrate the struggle to maintain American values of personal liberty, privacy, and individual rights while simultaneously ensuring that law enforcement personnel have sufficient power to protect the nation from catastrophic harm. There are no easy answers for the questions raised about whether the government has too much power and whether Americans' rights have been violated.

Now that we have considered the government's role in homeland security, we turn our attention to the private sector. Corporations and other entities must safeguard their assets, personnel, and facilities. They, too, have heightened concerns about homeland security issues. For example, many facilities such as nuclear power plants, chemical factories, and energy companies operate as part of the nation's critical infrastructure. Because terrorists may target such facilities, private-sector officials must address homeland security issues just as they have long needed to address other security issues such as employee theft, fires, and trade secrets.

CHECKPOINT

Answers

10. What have law enforcement officials done to enhance homeland security? ➡ 10. Planning and coordinating with other agencies, new equipment and training, Incident Command System.

11. What criticisms have been directed at the USA Patriot Act? ➡ 11. Permits too much government authority for searches and wiretaps, defines domestic terrorism in ways that might include protest groups.

Security Management and Private Policing

Only a few years ago, the term *private security* called to mind the image of security guards, people with marginal qualifications for other occupations who ended up accepting minimal wages to stand guard outside factories and businesses. This image reflected a long history of private employment of individuals who served limited police patrol functions. Private policing existed in Europe and the United States before the formation of public police forces. Examples include Fielding's Bow Street Runners in England and the bounty hunters of the American West. In the late nineteenth century, the Pinkerton National Detective Agency provided industrial spies and strikebreakers to thwart labor union activities, and Wells, Fargo and Company was formed to provide security for banks and other businesses.

In recent years, by contrast, private-sector activities related to policing functions have become more complex and important. Today, if one speaks of people employed in "private security," it would be more accurate to envision a variety of occupations ranging from traditional security guards to computer security experts to high-ranking corporate vice presidents responsible for planning and overseeing safety and security at a company's industrial plants and office complexes around the world. The training, preparation, and performance of private-sector security personnel have taken on additional importance, because governments increasingly hire private firms to perform security duties. In Iraq, private security firms provide personal protection to U.S. officials and guard specific facilities. The government even chose private firms to guard the headquarters of the Department of Homeland Security. This decision raised controversy when low-paid private guards complained to the news media that they had no training for dealing with chemical weapons and other potential terrorism threats (Margasak, 2006).

Retail and industrial firms spend nearly as much for private protection as all localities spend for police protection. Many government entities hire private companies to provide security at specific office buildings or other facilities. In addition, private groups, such as residents of wealthy suburbs, sometimes hire private police to patrol their neighborhoods. Precise figures are difficult to obtain, but a few years ago an estimated 60,000 private agencies employed more than 1.9 million people in security operations (Carlson, 1995:67). Each year businesses, organizations, and individuals together spend about $100 billion on private security. There are now three times as many officers hired by private security companies as there are public police (see Figure 6.1).

Private security presents expanding career opportunities for students who have studied criminal justice. Many jobs require investigative skills to discover employee

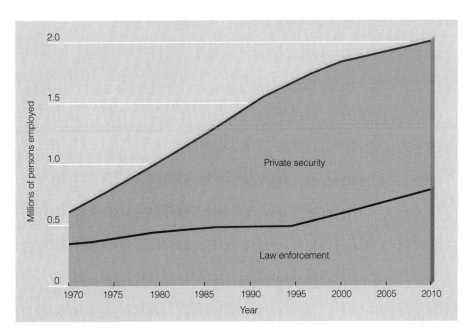

FIGURE 6.1
Employment in private and public protection, 1970–2010 (projected)
The number of people employed by private security firms has surpassed the number employed by the public police and is growing. Such a large private force presents questions for the criminal justice system.

Source: Adapted from William Cunningham, John Strauchs, and Clifford Van Meter, *Private Security: Patterns and Trends* (Washington, DC: National Institute of Justice, U.S. Government Printing Office, 1991), 3. Trend line projection to 2010 by authors.

theft, fraud, and other misconduct within businesses. Other positions require special skills in computer science or accounting in order to stop sophisticated criminal enterprises that may originate inside or outside a corporation. Still other management positions focus on occupational health and safety, fire prevention, emergency planning, and other aspects of asset protection. See "Careers in Criminal Justice" to consider career options available in the private sector.

Private agencies have gained success for several reasons. First, private companies recognize the need to be conscientious about protecting their assets, including buildings, financial resources, and personnel. They must be prepared for fires and other emergencies as well as for criminal activity. Next, many threats have spurred an expansion in security management and private policing; these include (1) an increase in crimes in the workplace; (2) an increase in fear of crime; (3) the fiscal crises of the states, which cause them to limit public police protection; and (4) increased public and business awareness of and use of cost-effective private security services (Cunningham, Strauchs, and Van Meter, 1990:236).

FUNCTIONS OF SECURITY MANAGEMENT AND PRIVATE POLICING

Top-level security managers have a range of responsibilities that require them to fulfill multiple roles that separate individuals would handle in the public sector. For their corporations, they simultaneously function as police chiefs, fire chiefs, emergency management administrators, and computer security experts. They hire, train, and supervise expert personnel to protect corporate computer systems that may contain credit card numbers, trade secrets, confidential corporate financial information, and other data sought by hackers intent on causing destruction or stealing money. Frequently they combat cyber criminals who are attacking their computer resources from overseas and are therefore beyond the reach of American law enforcement officials. They also create fire and other disaster response plans for buildings. Such plans include provisions for evacuating large buildings and coordinating their efforts with local police and fire departments in a variety of locales. In addition, they develop security systems to prevent employee theft that may involve sophisticated schemes to use company computer systems to transfer financial assets in improper ways. Because so many American companies own manufacturing plants and office buildings overseas, security companies must often implement their services in diverse countries around the globe.

CAREERS IN CRIMINAL JUSTICE

Corporate Investigator

NATURE OF THE WORK

Corporate investigators may conduct both internal and external investigations in order to protect company assets and identify individuals engaged in misconduct. Internal investigations can focus on employee theft, drug use in the workplace, abuse of expense accounts, and other misconduct by employees that affects the company. External investigations concern outsiders who direct criminal schemes at the company, such as fraudulent billing, theft of company property, and cyber crime. Corporate investigators may also be responsible for background checks on applicants for positions in the company.

Investigations may involve surveillance of individuals at work and elsewhere, interviews of suspects and witnesses, examination of documents and records, and computer analysis of financial information and other corporate data. Investigators may work irregular hours and travel frequently.

REQUIRED QUALIFICATIONS

Companies usually seek college-educated applicants for corporate investigator positions, although they may also hire individuals with investigative experience from military service or work in law enforcement. Education in criminal justice, computer science, and accounting is likely to be valued for such positions. Companies typically require a drug test, a medical examination, and a background check.

EARNINGS AND JOB OUTLOOK

Salaries vary widely, depending on the size and location of the corporation and the educational qualifications for entry-level positions. Those employers who require a four-year degree are likely to pay higher initial salaries than those that do not. The U.S. Department of Labor says that private detectives and investigators nationwide earned an average of $32,110 in 2004. Because corporate investigators have higher educational requirements and work for large businesses, their salaries are likely to be higher than this national average, which also includes private detectives who work through small agencies.

In general, employment for investigators in the private sector is expected to grow faster than the average for occupations elsewhere in the job market. Companies have become increasingly aware of the need to conduct background checks and other investigations of their employees and applicants. They also recognize that they must counteract increasingly sophisticated schemes of financial fraud and cyber crime that target businesses.

MORE INFORMATION

Information from the U.S. Department of Labor on private detectives and investigators can be found at the corresponding website listed on the Cole/Smith Criminal Justice in America Companion Website: http://www.thomsonedu.com/criminaljustice/cole. You can find additional information from the human resources offices of major corporations.

Private-sector corporations own and control security for vital facilities in the United States, including nuclear power plants, oil refineries, and military manufacturing facilities (Nalla, 2002). Because fires, tornadoes, or earthquakes at such sites could release toxic materials into the air and water, public safety depends on emergency planning. Moreover, because these sites are now recognized as potential targets of terrorist attacks, society depends more than ever on the role and effectiveness of security managers. They must work closely with law enforcement executives and other government officials to institute procedures that reduce known risks as well as participate in emergency preparedness planning.

Security managers are responsible for risk management in their facilities. They need a clear understanding of the assets to be protected in their corporations, hospitals, and other institutional settings. They must also identify the potential vulnerabilities that they face. Effective risk management depends on preparation and planning that identifies specific threats and considers how those threats can be minimized or avoided. Some security managers conduct their own risk assessments by inspecting facilities and developing a checklist of assets to be protected, vulnerabilities, and resources for surveillance, asset protection, and emergency response. Other security managers hire outside consultants to undertake such security studies, especially because many professionals believe that an "outsider" may be better positioned to take note of vulnerabilities that people who work in a facility every day minimize, take for granted, or ignore (Garvey, 2002).

At lower levels, specific occupations in private security are more directly comparable to those of police officers. Many security personnel are the equivalent of private-sector detectives. They must investigate "attacks" on company computer systems or activities that threaten company assets. Thus, for example, credit card companies have large security departments that use computers to monitor any unusual activity on individual customers' credit cards that may signal that the card is being used by a thief. Private-sector detectives must also investigate employee theft. Because this criminal activity extends beyond simple crimes such as stealing from a store's cash register, investigations might examine whether people are making false reports on expense accounts, using company computers to run private businesses, or misspending company money.

Other activities correspond more directly to those of police patrol officers, especially in the case of security officers who must guard specific buildings, apartments, or stores. The activities of these private security personnel vary greatly: Some act merely as guards and call the police at the first sign of trouble, whereas others have the power to carry out patrol and investigative duties similar to those of police officers, and still others rely on their presence and ability to make a "citizen's arrest" to deter lawbreakers. In most cases, citizens are authorized by law to make an arrest only when a felony has been committed in their presence. Thus, private security companies risk being held liable for false arrest and violation of civil rights.

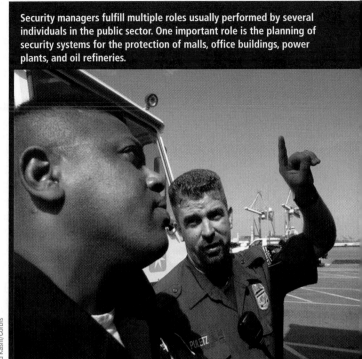

Security managers fulfill multiple roles usually performed by several individuals in the public sector. One important role is the planning of security systems for the protection of malls, office buildings, power plants, and oil refineries.

Ed Kashi/Corbis

Some states have passed laws that give civil immunity to store personnel who reasonably but mistakenly detain people suspected of shoplifting. More ambiguous is the search of the person or property of a suspect by a private guard. The suspect may resist the search and file a civil suit against the guard. If such a search yields evidence of a crime, the evidence might not be admitted in court. As yet, however, the Supreme Court has not applied the *Miranda* ruling to private police. In any case, federal law bars private individuals from engaging in wiretapping, and information so gathered cannot be entered as evidence at trial.

PRIVATE EMPLOYMENT OF PUBLIC POLICE

The officials responsible for asset protection, safety, and security at the top levels of major corporations are often retired police administrators or former military personnel. For example, New York Police Commissioner Raymond Kelly served as Senior Managing Director of Global Corporate Security for a Wall Street financial firm after he left his position as Director of the U.S. Customs Service and before he was appointed to serve as police commissioner. The reliance on people with public-sector experience for important positions in private security management reflects the fact that asset protection and security management have only recently become emphasized as topics in college and university programs. Thus, relatively few professionals have yet gained specific educational credentials in this important area. As a result, the placement of retired law enforcement officials in high-level positions has often created opportunities for strategic communication and coordination between top-level security managers and public-sector police administrators. Both entities have reason to seek cooperation throughout the hierarchy of their respective organizations. Unfortunately, however, they cannot always ensure that individual police officers and lower-level security personnel will sufficiently communicate and coordinate with each other when incidents arise.

At operations levels of security management, private security and local police often make frequent contact. Private firms are usually eager to hire public police officers on a part-time basis. About 20 percent of departments forbid their officers from "moonlighting" for private employers. By contrast, some departments simultaneously facilitate and control the hiring of their officers by creating specific rules and procedures for off-duty employment. For example, the New York City Police Department coordinates a program called the Paid Detail Unit. Event planners, corporations, and organizations can hire uniformed, off-duty officers for $30 per hour. The police department must approve all events at which the officers will work, and the department imposes an additional 10 percent administrative fee for the hiring of its officers. Thus, the department can safeguard against officers' working for organizations and events that will cause legal, public relations, or other problems for the police department. The department can also monitor and control how many hours its officers work so that private, part-time employment does not lead them to be exhausted and ineffective during their regular shifts.

These officers retain their full powers and status as police personnel even when they work for a private firm while off duty. New York and other cities have specific regulations requiring an on-duty officer to be called when a situation arises in which an arrest will be made. While the use of off-duty officers expands the number and visibility of law enforcement officers, it also raises questions, two of which are discussed here.

Conflict of Interest   Police officers must avoid any appearance of conflict of interest when they accept private employment. They are barred from jobs that conflict with their public duties. For example, they may not work as process servers, bill collectors, repossessors, or preemployment investigators for private firms. They also may not work as investigators for criminal defense attorneys or as bail bondsmen. They may not work in places that profit from gambling, and many departments do not allow officers to work in bars or other places where regulated goods, such as alcohol, are sold. No department can know the full range of situations in which private employment of an officer might harm the image of the police or create a conflict with police responsibilities. Thus, departments need to keep tabs on new situations that might require them to refine their regulations for private employment of off-duty officers.

Management Prerogatives   Another issue concerns the impact of private employment on the capabilities of the local police department. Private employment cannot be allowed to tire officers and impair their ability to protect the public when they are on duty. Late night duties as a private security officer, for example, can reduce an officer's ability to police effectively the next morning.

Departments require that officers request permission for outside work. Such permission can be denied for several reasons. Work that lowers the dignity of the police, is too risky or dangerous, is not in the "home" jurisdiction, requires more than eight hours of off-duty service, or interferes with departmental schedules is usually denied.

Several models have been designed to manage off-duty employment of officers. The *department contract model* permits close control of off-duty work, because firms must apply to the department to have officers assigned to them. Officers chosen for off-duty work are paid by the police department, which is reimbursed by the private firm, along with an overhead fee. Departments usually screen employers to make sure that the proposed use of officers will not conflict with the department's needs. When the private demand for police services exceeds the supply—and that is often the case—the department contract model provides a way of assigning staff to ensure that public needs are met. Recall the discussion of New York City's Paid Detail Unit, which uses this model.

The *officer contract model* allows each officer to find off-duty employment and to enter into a direct relationship with the private firm. Officers must apply to the department for permission, which is granted if the employment standards listed earlier are met. Problems can arise when an officer acts as an employment "agent" for other officers. This can lead to charges of favoritism and nepotism, with serious effects on discipline and morale.

In the *union brokerage model,* the police union or association finds off-duty employment for its members. The union sets the standards for the work and bargains with the department over the pay, status, and conditions of the off-duty employment.

THE PUBLIC–PRIVATE INTERFACE

The relationship between public and private law enforcement is a concern for police officials. Because private agents work for the people who employ them, their goals might not always serve the public interest. Questions have arisen about the power of private security agents to make arrests, conduct searches, and take part in undercover investigations. A key issue is the boundary between the work of the police and that of private agencies. Lack of coordination and communication between public and private agencies has led to botched investigations, destruction of evidence, and overzealousness.

Growing awareness of this problem has led to efforts to have private security agents work more closely with the police. Current efforts to enhance coordination involve emergency planning, building security, and the prevention of crime by individuals who are not employed by the private company in question. In other areas, private security managers still tend to act on their own without consulting the police.

One such area is criminal activity within a company. Many security managers in private firms tend to treat crimes by employees as internal matters that do not concern the police. They report UCR index crimes to the police, but they tend not to report employee theft, insurance fraud, industrial espionage, commercial bribery, and computer crime. In such cases private firms focus mainly on preventing losses and protecting assets. Although some such incidents are reported, most are resolved through internal procedures ("private justice"). When such crimes are discovered, the offender may be "convicted" and punished within the firm by forced restitution, loss of the job, and the spreading of information about the incident throughout the industry. Private firms often bypass the criminal justice system so they do not have to deal with prosecution policies, administrative delays, rules that would open the firms' internal affairs to public scrutiny, and bad publicity. Thus, the question arises: To what extent does a parallel system of private justice exist with regard to some offenders and some crimes (Davis, Lundman, and Martinez, 1991)?

RECRUITMENT AND TRAINING

Higher-level security managers are increasingly drawn from college graduates with degrees in criminal justice who have taken additional coursework in such subjects as business management and computer science. These graduates are attracted to the growing private-sector employment market for security-related occupations because the jobs often involve varied, complex tasks in a white-collar work environment. In addition, they often gain corporate benefits such as quick promotion, stock options, and other perks unavailable in public-sector policing.

By contrast, the recruitment and training of lower-level private security personnel present a major concern to law enforcement officials and civil libertarians. These personnel carry the important responsibility of guarding factories, stores, apartments, and other buildings. Often on the scene when criminal activity occurs, they are the private security personnel most likely to interact with the public in emergency situations. Moreover, any failure to perform their duties could lead to a significant and damaging event, such as a robbery or a fire. In spite of these responsibilities, which parallel those of police patrol officers, studies have shown that such personnel often have little education and training. Because the pay is low, the work often attracts people who cannot find other jobs or who seek temporary work. This portrait has been challenged by William Walsh (1989), who argues that differences between private and public

Private security is assuming an increasingly large role in American society. The presence of security guards in shopping malls is designed to deter wrongdoers and provide a level of calmness. In over half the states, the training and qualifications of lower-level private security personnel are not regulated. This raises concerns about the security personnel's ability to respond appropriately to emergencies.

© Syracuse Newspapers/Li-Hua Lan/The Image Works

police are not that striking. However, private security firms in San Francisco reported annual staff turnover rates as high as 300 percent because their low pay and benefits led employees continually to seek higher-paying jobs, especially when better-paid public-sector security work opened up, such as jobs as airport screeners (Lynem, 2002). City police departments and other public law enforcement agencies do not experience these kinds of staffing problems, because they have better pay and benefits. Consider the scenario posed in "Real-World Activity" at the end of the chapter to think about how you would address this issue.

The growth of private policing has brought calls for the screening and licensing of its personnel. Fewer than half the states require background checks or examine private security applicants' criminal records from states other than the one in which they currently reside. Twenty-two states have no certification or licensing requirements, and only 17 states have regulatory boards to oversee the private security industry. More than half the states have no training requirements whatsoever for people who will assume important responsibilities in guarding buildings and other private security tasks (PR Newswire, 2002). Several national organizations, such as the National Council on Crime and Delinquency, have offered model licensing statutes that specify periods of training and orientation, uniforms that permit citizens to distinguish between public and private police, and a ban on employment of people with criminal records.

ThomsonNOW
Improve your grade on the exam with Personalized Study! For reinforcement resources and a mastery check of Security Management and Private Policing, go to www.thomsonedu.com/thomsonnow

CHECKPOINT

Answers

12. What has caused the growth of security management and private policing? ➔ **12.** Companies' recognition of the need to protect assets and plan for emergencies; problems with employee theft, computer crime, and other issues that require active prevention and investigation.

13. What are the three models for private employment of police officers? ➔ **13.** Department contract model, officer contract model, union brokerage model.

A QUESTION OF ETHICS: WRITING ASSIGNMENT

Bianco's Restaurant is a popular, noisy place in a tough section of town. Open from 6:30 A.M. until midnight, it is usually crowded with regulars who like the low prices and ample portions, teenagers planning their next exploit, and people grabbing a quick bite to eat.

Officer Buchanan has just finished his late-night "lunch" before going back on duty. As he walks toward the cash register, Cheryl Bianco, the manager, takes the bill from his hand and says, "This one's on me, John. It's nice to have you with us."

Officer Buchanan protests, "Thanks, but I'd better pay for my own meal."

"Why do you say that? The other cops don't object to getting a free meal now and then."

"Well, they may feel that way, but I don't want anyone to get the idea that I'm giving you special treatment," Buchanan replies.

"Come off it. Who's going to think that? I don't expect special treatment; we just want you to know we appreciate your work."

WRITING ASSIGNMENT

What issues are involved here? If Buchanan refuses to accept Bianco's generosity, what is he saying about his role as a police officer? If he accepts the offer, what does that say? Might people who overhear the conversation draw other meanings from it? Is turning down a free $6.50 meal that important? Write a memo as if you were an officer to whom Buchanan came for advice. What advice would you give?

REAL-WORLD ACTIVITY: AN APPLICATION

You are a member of Congress examining the performance of private security firms. You are concerned that private security personnel have important responsibilities for guarding potential terrorism targets, such as nuclear power plants, chemical factories, and federal government buildings. You want to draft a law that requires private security personnel to meet specific job qualifications and training requirements.

RESEARCHING THE INTERNET

Go to InfoTrac College edition and enter the keyword *private security*. Read an article entitled "ASIS President Corrects Press Conceptions on Private Security," *Security Management*, June 2005.

APPLICATION

What requirements will you include in your law? As you list the requirements, consider whether they should include educational requirements, physical tests, or considerations of individuals' backgrounds.

SUMMARY

- Police corruption and misuse of force erode community support.

- Internal affairs units, civilian review boards, standards and accreditation, and civil liability suits increase police accountability to citizens.

- The development of new technologies has assisted police investigations through the use of computers, databases, surveillance devices, DNA testing, and methods to detect deception.

- Questions arise concerning the ability of law enforcement to keep up with new developments in cyber crime, the risks that new technologies will be ineffective, and the potential clash between law enforcement technology and constitutional rights.

- Police departments are seeking to identify less-lethal weapons that can incapacitate suspects and control unruly crowds without causing serious injuries and deaths.

- Homeland security is an important priority for law enforcement agencies at all levels of government after September 11, 2001.

- Agencies need planning and coordination in order to gather intelligence and prepare for possible threats and public emergencies.

- The expansion of security management and private policing reflects greater recognition of the need to protect private assets and to plan for emergencies.

- Security management produces new issues and problems including concerns about the recruitment, training, and activities of lower-level private security personnel.

QUESTIONS FOR REVIEW

1. What are the major forms of police abuse of power?

2. What has the Supreme Court ruled regarding police use of deadly force?

3. What are the pros and cons of the major approaches to making the police accountable to citizens?

4. What controversies exist concerning new technologies employed by the police?

5. What have law enforcement agencies done to enhance homeland security?

6. What are the problems associated with private policing?

KEY TERMS AND CASES

internal affairs unit (p. 154)
law enforcement intelligence (p. 163)
less-lethal weapons (p. 160)
USA Patriot Act (p. 166)
Tennessee v. Garner (1985) (p. 151)

GOING ONLINE

ThomsonNOW

Maximize your study time by using ThomsonNOW's diagnostic study plan to help you review this chapter. The Study Plan will

- Help you identify areas on which you should concentrate

- Provide interactive exercises to help you master the chapter concepts

- Provide a posttest to confirm you are ready to move on to the next chapter

7

Police and Constitutional Law

A Baltimore County police officer stopped a car for speeding. Within the car sat three men: Donte Partlow, the driver; Joseph Pringle, the front-seat passenger; and Otis Smith, the rear passenger. When Partlow opened the glove compartment to retrieve the vehicle registration, the officer noticed a large amount of money there. The officer asked Partlow if he could search the vehicle. After Partlow consented, the officer found five baggies of cocaine jammed between the rear-seat armrest and the rear seat. None of the men would admit to owning the cocaine or provide any information about its ownership. The officer warned them that they all would be arrested if someone did not admit to owning the cocaine. No one spoke, so he arrested all three men.

Was it fair to arrest everyone? What if one passenger had been offered a ride by his friend's cousin, someone he had just met, and had no knowledge of anyone else's involvement with drugs? Have you ever ridden in a car with someone who is merely a casual acquaintance? Do you

have any legal rights that could protect you from being arrested under such circumstances?

As you recall from Chapter 3, the Fourth Amendment provides protection against "unreasonable searches and seizures." In the cocaine case, the Fourth Amendment is relevant because all three men in the car were "seized" and therefore a court could examine whether their seizure was "unreasonable." Fundamentally, the case is about whether police officers possess the authority to arrest everyone in a vehicle if they find guns or weapons in one part of it. In other words, does the discovery of illegal items in a car make it "reasonable" to arrest everyone in the vehicle?

After the arrests, Pringle, the front-seat passenger, made incriminating statements that led prosecutors to convict him for possession of cocaine, and he was sentenced to a ten-year prison term. Pringle appealed his conviction by claiming that his Fourth Amendment rights were violated when the officer arrested him for the presence of drugs that were located next to Smith in the rear seat and that would traditionally have been considered the responsibility of Partlow, the driver, who is presumed to be in control of the vehicle and its contents. The Maryland Court of Appeals agreed with Pringle. The state court ruled that the officer did not have a sufficient basis for believing that Pringle knew about or had control over the cocaine in the rear seat. Therefore the arrest of Pringle, as well as his subsequent questioning by the police, occurred as the result of an "unreasonable seizure" in violation of the Fourth Amendment. Because Maryland prosecutors disagreed with their state court of appeals, they asked the U.S. Supreme Court to review the case.

As you think about the Pringle case, remember that the words of the Fourth Amendment do not provide an answer to the question of whether the arrest was "unreasonable." Indeed, the eighteenth-century men who wrote the phrase *unreasonable searches and seizures* could not anticipate that drugs would become a significant social problem or that motor vehicles could be used to transport and hide drugs. Thus, today's judges must decide for themselves how each situation falls within the intended purposes of the Fourth Amendment.

In December 2003 the U.S. Supreme Court provided its answer to the question raised in the case of *Maryland v. Pringle*. The justices of the Court unanimously overturned the decision of the Maryland Court of Appeals. The justices ruled that the discovery of illegal items in a vehicle can justify the arrest of everyone riding in the vehicle. Are you surprised by the U.S. Supreme Court's decision? Do you agree with it? Do you think this decision could ever apply to you? As we examine other Supreme Court decisions, think about the challenge presented by the need to apply brief phrases from the Bill of Rights to actual situations that will determine whether people can be searched and questioned and, more importantly, whether certain individuals will spend many years in prison.

In this chapter we examine individual rights and how those legal protections define the limits of police officers' powers of investigation and arrest. In particular, we look closely at two rights that were introduced in Chapter 3: the Fourth Amendment protection against unreasonable searches and seizures and the Fifth Amendment privilege against compelled self-incrimination.

QUESTIONS FOR INQUIRY

- What authority do police officers possess to stop and search people and their vehicles?
- When and how do police officers seek warrants in order to conduct searches and make arrests?
- Can police officers look in people's windows or their backyards to see if evidence of a crime is there?
- In which situations can police officers conduct searches without obtaining a warrant?
- What is the purpose of the privilege against compelled self-incrimination?
- What is the exclusionary rule?
- In what situations does the exclusionary rule apply?

Legal Limitations on Police Investigations

The provisions of Bill of Rights embody important, historic American values regarding individual rights in society. They reflect the belief that we do not want to give government officials absolute power to pursue investigations and prosecutions, because that approach to crime control would impose excessive costs on the values of individual liberty, privacy, and due process. If police could do whatever they wanted to do, then people would lack protections against arbitrary searches and arrests. On the other hand, crime control is an important policy goal. We do not want individuals' expectations about legal protections to block the ability of law enforcement officers to protect citizens from crime and punish wrongdoers. Judges must therefore seek to interpret the Constitution in ways that properly balance crime control and the protection of individual rights.

How does an officer know when his or her actions might violate laws protecting an individual's rights? Individual police officers do not have time to follow the details of the latest court decisions. That responsibility rests with those who train and supervise law enforcement officers. Officers depend on the information and training provided at the police academy and subsequent updates from city and state attorneys who monitor court decisions. Thus, police officers' compliance with the law depends on their own knowledge and decisions as well as that of their supervisors.

SEARCH AND SEIZURE CONCEPTS

The Fourth Amendment prohibits police officers from undertaking "unreasonable searches and seizures." The Supreme Court defines **searches** as actions by law enforcement officials that intrude on people's **reasonable expectations of privacy.** For example, someone who places a personal diary in a locked drawer within a bedroom of her home has demonstrated a reasonable expectation. Police officers cannot simply decide to enter her home in order to open the locked drawer and read the diary. Many situations raise questions about people's reasonable expectations. Should people reasonably expect a police officer to reach into their pockets in order to see if they have guns? Should people reasonably expect an officer not to walk up to their houses and peer into the windows? Although judges do not always answer these questions in clear, consistent ways, people's reasonable expectations about their privacy play a key role in judges' determinations about legal guidelines for police investigations. Read "Technology Issues in Criminal Justice" to consider what reasonable expectation of privacy should exist with respect to people's computers and electronic communications.

In defining **seizures,** the Supreme Court focuses on the nature and extent of officers' interference with people's liberty and freedom of movement. If an officer who is

search Government officials' examination of and hunt for evidence in or on a person or place in a manner that intrudes on reasonable expectations of privacy.

reasonable expectation of privacy The objective standard developed by courts for determining whether a government intrusion into an individual's person or property constitutes a search because it interferes with the individual's interests that are normally protected from government examination.

seizure Situations in which police officers use their authority to deprive people of their liberty or property and which must not be "unreasonable" according to the Fourth Amendment.

TECHNOLOGY ISSUES IN CRIMINAL JUSTICE

Monitoring Computer Keystrokes

A cting under a search warrant, the FBI installed a keystroke-logging device on the computer of a suspected organized crime figure named Nicodemo Scarfo, Jr. The device detects the exact keystrokes typed, and the agents hoped to use it to discover the suspect's passwords. If police can monitor the exact keystrokes on a computer, they can learn the content of documents, outgoing Internet messages, and passwords to enable them to overcome encryption software. With such monitoring devices in place, little remains private on an individual's computer.

The use of such technology is likely to expand as part of the government's efforts to identify suspected terrorists. The USA Patriot Act enhances federal law enforcement officials' authority to monitor electronic communications, including the use of "roving" surveillance aimed at particular individuals without identifying or limiting specific facilities and devices to be monitored. Because there are proposals for additional government surveillance powers to combat terrorism, privacy advocates fear that computers and electronic communications will have few Fourth Amendment protections. By contrast, advocates for the expanded use of new surveillance technologies believe that the government's need to stop crime and terrorism

outweighs individuals' privacy interests with respect to computer documents and communications. See "What Americans Think" for recent survey data concerning one aspect of this issue.

 RESEARCHING THE INTERNET

Read online about surveillance software available to police departments; see the corresponding site listed on the Cole/Smith Criminal Justice in America Companion Website: http://www.thomsonedu.com/criminaljustice/cole.

FOR CRITICAL ANALYSIS

Would you feel that your rights were violated if the government secretly monitored the keystrokes on your computer, or do you believe that the government needs broad authority to undertake such surveillance freely as part of the battle against potential terrorists and criminals?

Sources: George A. Chidi, Jr., "FBI's Use of Keystroke Capture Tool Was Permitted for Investigation, Court Says," *PC World,* January 4, 2002, http://www.pcworld.com/news/article/O,aid,78284,000.asp; Harry F. Tepker, "The USA Patriot Act," *Extensions,* Fall 2002, p. 11.

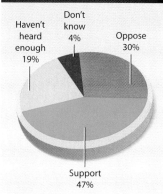
stop Government officials' interference with an individual's freedom of movement for a duration that typically lasts less than one hour and only rarely extends for as long as several hours.

reasonable suspicion A police officer's belief based on articulable facts that would be recognized by others in a similar situation as indicating that criminal activity is afoot and necessitates further investigation that will intrude on an individual's reasonable expectation of privacy.

probable cause An amount of reliable information indicating that it is more likely than not that evidence will be found in a specific location or that a specific person is guilty of a crime.

leaning against the wall of a building says to a passing pedestrian, "Where are you going?" and the person replies, "To the sandwich shop down the street" as she continues to walk without interference by the officer, there is virtually no intrusion on her liberty and freedom of movement. Thus, officers are free to speak to people on the street. If people voluntarily stop in order to speak with the officer, they have not been "seized," because they are free to move along their way whenever they choose. However, if people are not free to leave when officers assert their authority to halt someone's movement, then a seizure has occurred and the Fourth Amendment requires that the seizure be reasonable.

One form of seizure is an arrest. This involves taking a suspect into custody. Property can also be subject to seizure, especially if it is evidence in a criminal case.

A **stop** is a brief interference with a person's freedom of movement for a duration that can be measured in minutes. An interference with freedom of movement that lasts several hours risks being viewed as exceeding the proper duration of a stop and would require greater justification. When police require a driver to pull over in order to receive a traffic citation, that is a stop. In order to be permissible under the Fourth Amendment, stops must be justified by **reasonable suspicion**—a situation in which specific articulable facts lead officers to conclude that the person may be engaging in criminal activity. Officers cannot legally make stops based on hunches; they must be able to describe specific aspects of the person's appearance, behavior, and circumstances that led them to conclude that the person should be stopped in order to investigate the occurrence of a crime. As we shall see, however, the courts permit police officers to make many kinds of stops without reasonable suspicion. Such stops can occur, for example, at border crossing points where preventing illegal activities, such as smuggling and drug trafficking, is especially important. Thus, everyone can be stopped in certain situations even if there is no specific basis to suspect them of wrongdoing.

THE CONCEPT OF ARREST

An arrest is a significant deprivation of liberty, because a person is taken into police custody, transported to the police station or jail, and processed into the criminal justice system. A seizure need not be lengthy to be an arrest. Indeed, some stops may be longer than arrests if, for example, a person taken to the police station is released on bail within an hour while a person stopped along a roadside must wait a longer period for the officer to write out several traffic citations. Typically, however, stops take much less time than do arrests.

Because arrests involve a more significant intrusion on liberty, they require a higher level of justification. Unlike stops, which require only reasonable suspicion, all arrests must be supported by probable cause. With **probable cause,** sufficient evidence exists to support the reasonable conclusion that a person has committed a crime. To obtain an arrest warrant, the police must provide a judicial officer with sufficient evidence to support a finding of probable cause. Alternatively, police officers' on-the-street determinations of probable cause can produce discretionary warrantless arrests. A judge subsequently examines such arrests for probable cause, in a hearing that must occur shortly after the arrest, typically within 48 hours. If the judge determines that the police officer was wrong in concluding that probable cause existed to justify the arrest, the suspect is released from custody.

WARRANTS AND PROBABLE CAUSE

Imagine that you are a judge. Two police officers come to your chambers to ask you to authorize a search warrant. They swear that they observed frequent foot traffic of suspicious people going in and out of a house. Moreover, they swear that a reliable informant told them that he was inside the house two days earlier and saw crack cocaine being sold. Does this information rise to the level of probable cause, justifying issuance of a search warrant? Can you grant a warrant based purely on the word of police officers, or do you need more concrete evidence?

Arrest is the physical taking of a person into custody. What legal requirements must be met to make this a valid arrest? What limits are placed on the officers?

These questions are important not only for judges but for prosecutors as well. Police and prosecutors must work closely together. If the police have made errors in seeking warrants or conducting searches, evidence could be excluded from use at trial and, as a result, prosecutors could lose their cases through no fault of their own.

The Fourth Amendment requires that "no Warrants shall issue, but upon probable cause, supported by Oath or affirmation, and particularly describing the place to be searched, and the persons or things to be seized." These particular elements of the Amendment must be fulfilled in order to issue a warrant. If they are not, then a defendant may later challenge the validity of the warrant. The important elements are, first, the existence of probable cause. Second, evidence must be presented to the judicial officer and be supported by "oath or affirmation," which typically means that police officers must say "yes" when the judicial officer asks them if they swear or affirm that all information presented is true to the best of their knowledge. This requirement may be fulfilled by presenting an **affidavit** from the police officers, which is a written statement confirmed by oath or affirmation. Third, the warrant must describe the specific place to be searched. A "general warrant" that can be used to search many locations cannot be issued. Fourth, the warrant must describe the person or items to be seized. Thus, if the warrant authorizes a search for a person suspected of robbery, the officers should not open small dresser drawers or other places a person could not be hiding.

The U.S. Supreme Court has attempted to guide judicial officers in identifying the existence of probable cause. Mere suspicion cannot constitute probable cause, yet the level of evidence to establish probable cause need not fulfill the high level of proof needed to justify a criminal conviction. In essence, probable cause is a level of evidence sufficient to provide a reasonable conclusion that the proposed objects of a search will be found in a location that law enforcement officers request to search. For an arrest warrant, the essential issue is whether sufficient evidence is presented to lead to the reasonable conclusion that a specific person should be prosecuted for a criminal offense. There is no hard-and-fast definition of *probable cause* that can be applied to every situation. It is a flexible concept that various judicial officers apply differently. In *Illinois v. Gates* (1983), the Supreme Court announced a flexible **totality of circumstances** test for determining the existence of probable cause. Judges are permitted to make a generalized determination about whether the evidence is both sufficient and reliable enough to justify a warrant.

affidavit Written statement of fact, supported by oath or affirmation, submitted to judicial officers to fulfill the requirements of probable cause for obtaining a warrant.

totality of circumstances Flexible test established by the Supreme Court for identifying whether probable cause exists to justify a judge's issuance of a warrant.

1. What is a search?

2. What is the difference between an arrest and a stop?

3. What do police officers need to demonstrate in order to obtain a warrant?

Answers

1. A government intrusion into an individual's reasonable expectation of privacy.

2. An arrest requires probable cause and involves taking someone into custody for prosecution, whereas a stop is a brief deprivation of freedom of movement based on reasonable suspicion.

3. The existence of probable cause by the totality of circumstances in the case.

Plain View Doctrine

plain view doctrine Officers may examine and use as evidence, without a warrant, contraband or evidence that is in open view at a location where they are legally permitted to be.

Although the warrant requirement is a central feature of the Fourth Amendment, the Supreme Court has identified situations in which warrants are not required. What if a police officer is walking down the street and sees a marijuana plant growing in the front window of a home? Has the officer conducted a search by looking into the window? If so, is the search illegal because it took place by chance but was not supported by reasonable suspicion or probable cause? In *Coolidge v. New Hampshire* (1971) the Court discussed the **plain view doctrine,** which permits officers to notice and use as evidence items that are visible to them when they are in a location where they are permitted to be. Officers may not break into a home and then claim that the drugs found inside were in plain view on a table. However, if a homeowner invited officers into his home in order to file a report about a burglary, the officers do not need to obtain a warrant in order to seize drugs that they see lying on the kitchen table. Because the drugs were in plain view and the officers had a legal basis for their presence in the house, the owner lost any reasonable expectation of privacy that would otherwise require officers to demonstrate probable cause for a search.

OPEN FIELDS DOCTRINE

open fields doctrine Supreme Court doctrine under which property owners have no reasonable expectation of privacy in open fields on and around their property.

Related to the plain view doctrine is the **open fields doctrine.** Under this doctrine, first announced by the Supreme Court in *Hester v. United States* (1924), property owners have no reasonable expectation of privacy in open fields on and around their property. Thus, if criminal evidence is visible, then probable cause has been established for its seizure without a warrant. The Court has approved cases in which police officers, acting without a warrant, walked past "no trespassing" signs and found marijuana plants in fields on private property (*Oliver v. United States*, 1984). The Court limited this doctrine by refusing to apply it to the *curtilage*, or the yard area immediately surrounding the home. Although protected against physical intrusion by officers, that area remains subject to the plain view doctrine if evidence of criminal activity is clearly visible from the vantage point of a location where officers can lawfully stand. For example, the plain view doctrine includes any areas visible from the air when police officers hover above property in a helicopter.

PLAIN FEEL AND OTHER SENSES

If law enforcement officers are permitted to conduct a warrantless search under the plain view doctrine, what about detection of criminal evidence using other senses such as smell and feel? If officers smell the distinctive odor of an illegal substance, such as marijuana, they are justified in investigating further.

Does an officer's sense of "feel" apply to searches of property? The Supreme Court has

Under the plain view doctrine, are the police allowed to seize the marijuana plant taken from the yard of this home without a search warrant?

A. Ramey/PhotoEdit

TABLE 7.1   Searches by Sight and Feel

The Fourth Amendment's protection for reasonable expectations of privacy does not cover criminal evidence that can be seen or felt by officers in specific situations.

Case	Decision
Plain View *Coolidge v. New Hampshire* (1971)	Officers are permitted to notice and use as evidence items in plain view when the officers are where they are legally permitted to be.
Open Fields *Oliver v. U.S.* (1984)	Officers are permitted to intrude on private lands that are open areas, such as fields and pastures, but they may not search the yard area immediately surrounding a house (*curtilage*) without a warrant or a specific justification for a warrantless search.
Plain Feel *Minnesota v. Dickerson* (1993)	While conducting a pat-down search of a suspect's outer clothing, police may seize items in pockets or clothing as evidence if they are immediately identifiable by touch as weapons or contraband.

ruled that if the officer feels something that is immediately recognizable as a weapon, crack pipe, or other contraband, the item may be seized (*Minnesota v. Dickerson*, 1993). However, police officers cannot aggressively feel and manipulate people's property, such as a duffel bag, in an attempt to detect criminal evidence, unless the luggage examination is part of a standard search in boarding a commercial airliner or crossing an international border into the United States (*Bond v. United States*, 2000). Table 7.1 reviews selected cases concerning the Fourth Amendment's protection for reasonable expectations of privacy involving searches by sight and feel.

CHECKPOINT

4. What is the plain view doctrine?

5. May officers use senses other than sight to find evidence of crime without a warrant?

Answers

4. Officers can examine and use as evidence contraband and criminal evidence that is in open sight at a place where the officers are legally permitted to be.

5. Officers may use their sense of smell, especially for distinctive odors like marijuana, but the Supreme Court has limited police authority to feel and manipulate luggage and other objects.

Warrantless Searches

In day-to-day police work, the majority of searches take place without a warrant. It is in this area that the courts have been most active in defining the term *unreasonable*. Six kinds of searches may be legally conducted without a warrant and still uphold the Fourth Amendment: (1) special needs beyond the normal purposes of law enforcement, (2) stop and frisk on the streets, (3) search incident to a lawful arrest, (4) exigent circumstances, (5) consent, and (6) automobile searches.

SPECIAL NEEDS BEYOND THE NORMAL PURPOSES OF LAW ENFORCEMENT

In certain specific contexts, law enforcement officials have a justified need to conduct warrantless searches of every individual passing through. The use of metal detectors to examine airline passengers, for example, occurs in a specific context in which the need to prevent hijacking justifies a limited search of every passenger. Here the Supreme Court does not require officers to have any suspicions, reasonable or otherwise, about the illegal activities of any individual.

Similarly, warrantless searches take place at the entry points into the United States—border crossings, ports, and airports. The government's interests in guarding against the entry of people and items (weapons, drugs, toxic chemicals, and so forth)

[handwritten margin notes: 1. AIRPORT + BORDER   2. ENTERING CERTAIN BUILDINGS]

The Supreme Court has upheld systematic highway stops without a warrant to look for drunken drivers. Each vehicle must be stopped and the driver briefly questioned.

Photo by Joe Raedle/Getty Images

that are harmful to national interests outweigh the individuals' expectations of privacy. Typically, these border stops involve only a few moments as customs officers check any required documents such as passports and visas, ask where the person traveled, and ask what the person is bringing into the United States. The customs officers may have a trained dog sniff around people and their luggage, checking for drugs or large amounts of cash. At the Mexican and Canadian borders and at international airports, people may be chosen at random to have their cars and luggage searched. They may also be chosen for such searches because their behavior or their answers to questions arouse the suspicions of customs officers.

Border Patrol agents have especially important jobs because they guard against common crimes, such as smuggling, as well as focus on national security issues, such as terrorists attempting to sneak into the country. Their jobs are especially challenging because they must know about laws related to searches and seizures, common to all American law enforcement officials, in addition to laws about immigration. They must also be fluent in Spanish. Despite these extra challenges, opportunities in these positions are expanding because of the nation's increased attention to issues of immigration and border security (Archibold, 2006). Read "Careers in Criminal Justice" to learn about career opportunities as a federal Border Patrol agent.

The Supreme Court has expanded the checkpoint concept by approving systematic stops to look for drunken drivers along highways within the nation's interior. Michigan's state police implemented a sobriety checkpoint program in order to combat drunken driving. They set up a checkpoint at which they stopped every vehicle and briefly questioned each driver (*Michigan Department of State Police v. Sitz*, 1990). A drunken driver caught at the checkpoint claimed that he was stopped improperly. However, the Court said that police can systematically stop drivers in order to seek information. The Court more recently approved checkpoints to ask drivers whether they had witnessed an accident (*Illinois v. Lidster*, 2004).

Although the U.S. Supreme Court has approved certain kinds of vehicle checkpoints as contexts for permissible warrantless stops and searches, this does not mean that these checkpoints are permissible everywhere in the United States. As you read the Close Up box on page 186 about legal developments in Michigan, think about how the definitions of rights and police authority can differ from state to state.

The U.S. Supreme Court has not given blanket approval for every kind of checkpoint or traffic stop that police might wish to use. The Court forbids random stops of vehicles by officers on patrol (*Delaware v. Prouse*, 1979). Officers must have a basis for a vehicle stop, such as an observed violation of traffic laws. The Court also ruled that a city cannot set up a checkpoint in order to check drivers and passengers for possible involvement in drugs. Even though police officers in the given case stopped vehicles only briefly in order to ask a few questions and circle the car with a drug-sniffing dog, the Court declared a general search for criminal evidence does not justify the use of a checkpoint. Again, such stops must be narrowly focused on a specific objective, such as checking for drunken drivers (*City of Indianapolis v. Edmond*, 2000).

STOP AND FRISK ON THE STREETS

Police officers possess the authority to make stops and limited searches of individuals on the streets when specific circumstances justify such actions. In the landmark

CAREERS IN CRIMINAL JUSTICE

Border Patrol Agent

NATURE OF THE WORK

U.S. Border Patrol agents are armed, uniformed law enforcement officers with a very specific mission. They are responsible for the detection, prevention, and apprehension of smugglers and of people entering the country illegally. They work primarily along the Mexican border in Texas, New Mexico, Arizona, and California. They patrol the border as well as undertake surveillance, often with infrared night scopes, low-light television systems, and other high-tech tools. To follow and apprehend illegal entrants who move north into the country through undeveloped areas of the desert Southwest, they adeptly interpret and follow tracks and other physical evidence. They also inspect farms and ranches for the presence of undocumented aliens. Finally, they set up checkpoints on incoming highways to determine if vehicles are carrying smuggled goods or illegal entrants into the country.

REQUIRED QUALIFICATIONS

Entry-level Border Patrol agents must have a four-year college degree in any major or work experience involving interviewing, private security, or leadership that would be equivalent to a college degree. Applicants with a college degree and one year of experience in law enforcement can begin their careers at a higher salary level.

Applicants must be U.S. citizens who have resided in the United States (except for vacation travel, military service, or federal contract work) for the three years preceding application. They must be under the age of 40, take a written exam, and pass a background check, including a criminal record check. They must also pass a medical exam, including specific standards for hearing and vision, and a drug test. At the Border Patrol Academy in Artesia, New Mexico, they must pass a timed physical fitness test that includes push-ups, sit-ups, a 1.5 mile run, a 220-yard dash, and an obstacle course. Applicants are also expected to become fluent in Spanish as well as English. The Border Patrol provides Spanish-language instruction.

EARNINGS AND JOB OUTLOOK

Applicants with a four-year college degree or appropriate work experience have a starting salary of $34,966 per year. College graduates with law enforcement experience may start at $39,797. Border Patrol agents can earn substantial additional compensation through overtime work. The agency also offers annual salary increases and opportunities for promotion. Further, agents can retire after 25 years of service at any age, or after 20 years if they have reached the age of 50. The mandatory retirement age is 57.

Opportunities for careers as Border Patrol agents have grown more dramatically than those for other careers in law enforcement. Between 1991 and 2006, the number of Border Patrol agents increased from 4,000 to 11,000. President Bush has proposed hiring 6,000 additional agents by 2008. If this expansion takes place, the Border Patrol will overtake the FBI as the largest federal law enforcement agency (Archibold, 2006).

MORE INFORMATION

More information is available at the U.S. Customs and Border Protection website listed on the Cole/Smith Criminal Justice in America Companion Website: http://www.thomsonedu.com/criminaljustice/cole.

---

case of *Terry v. Ohio* (1968) the Court upheld the stop-and-frisk procedure when a police officer had reason to believe that the person might be dangerous. In the *Terry* case, a plainclothes detective in downtown Cleveland observed men walking back and forth to look in the window of a store and then conferring with each other. He suspected that they might be preparing to rob the store. He approached the men, identified himself as a police officer, patted down their clothing, and found unlicensed handguns on two individuals. Those individuals challenged the legality of the search. NOT SATISFIED W/ THEIR RESPONSE

Although the justices supported the detective's authority to conduct the pat-down search based on his observations of the men's suspicious behavior, they struck a careful balance between police authority and individuals' rights by specifying the circumstances in which such a pat-down search—more commonly known as a **stop-and-frisk search**—can occur. The Court requires that several specific facts exist in each situation

Terry v. Ohio (1968) Supreme Court decision endorsing police officers' authority to stop and frisk suspects on the streets when there is reasonable suspicion that they are armed and involved in criminal activity.

stop-and-frisk search Limited search approved by the Supreme Court in *Terry v. Ohio* that permits police officers to pat down the clothing of people on the streets if there is reasonable suspicion of dangerous criminal activity.

CLOSE UP

State Supreme Courts and Constitutional Rights

Ironically, although the Michigan case established the legality of sobriety checkpoints for the entire nation, the Michigan Supreme Court later barred the use of such checkpoints within the state of Michigan. The Michigan Supreme Court examined the protection against unreasonable searches and seizures contained in Article I, Section 11, of the Michigan Constitution and found that such checkpoints violate its interpretation of the state constitution. Michigan's high court used a balancing test, but simply struck a different balance than that applied by the U.S. Supreme Court majority. The Michigan court concluded that the government's interest in reducing drunken driving did not outweigh the liberty and privacy interests of individual drivers.

The *Sitz* case serves as a reminder that states can make authoritative decisions about many of their own affairs in the U.S. government system. The U.S. Supreme Court is the final authority over decisions concerning the interpretation of the U.S. Constitution, but state supreme courts control the interpretation of their own constitutions. State supreme courts can interpret their own constitutions to provide stronger rights, but not weaker ones, than those recognized by the U.S. Supreme Court. This is what happened in the Michigan sobriety checkpoint case. It happens in other cases, too, and thus constitutional rights vary to some degree from state to state.

RESEARCHING THE INTERNET

The California Supreme Court is often regarded as a leader in establishing its own interpretations of rights under a state constitution. You can read its opinions at the corresponding website listed on the Cole/Smith Criminal Justice in America Companion Website: http://www.thomsonedu.com/criminaljustice/cole.

FOR CRITICAL ANALYSIS

Should rights vary from state to state even though all of the U.S. states are part of one country? If people in Michigan are protected against surprise sobriety checkpoints as an invasion of their right against unreasonable seizures, is it fair that other Americans do not enjoy the same constitutional protection?

---

in which a permissible stop and frisk can legally occur. In the *Terry* decision the justices say,

> We merely hold today that
>
> [1] where a police officer observes unusual conduct
>
> [2] which leads him reasonably to conclude in light of his experience
>
> [3] that criminal activity may be afoot and
>
> [4] that the persons with whom he is dealing may be armed and presently dangerous,
>
> [5] where in the course of investigating this behavior
>
> [6] he identifies himself as a policeman and makes reasonable inquiries,
>
> [7] and where nothing in the initial stages of the encounter serves to dispel his reasonable fear for his own or others' safety,
>
> [8] he is entitled for the protection of himself and others in the area to conduct a carefully limited search of the outer clothing of such persons in an attempt to discover weapons which might be used to assault him.

The stopping and frisking of an individual must be carried out according to the law. What does the law require in this situation?

AP Photo/Gregory Bull

These specified factors imposed an obligation on police officers to make observations, draw reasonable conclusions, identify themselves, and make inquiries before conducting the stop-and-frisk search. In addition, the reasonableness of the search was justified by a reasonable conclusion that a person was armed, thereby requiring the officer to act in order to protect him- or herself and the public. See "Real-World Activity" at the end of this chapter for more on stop and frisk.

Court decisions have given officers significant discretion to decide when these factors may exist. For example, if officers see someone running at the sight of police in a high-crime neighborhood, their observation can provide the basis for sufficient suspicion to justify a stop and frisk (*Illinois v. Wardlow*, 2000). Thus, officers need not actually see evidence of a weapon or interact with the suspect prior to making the stop.

The Supreme Court also expanded police authority by permitting officers to rely on reports from reliable witnesses as the basis for conducting the stop and frisk (*Adams v. Williams*, 1972). However, an unverified anonymous tip does not serve as an adequate reason for a stop-and-frisk search (*Florida v. J. L.*, 2000).

SEARCH INCIDENT TO A LAWFUL ARREST

The authority to undertake a warrantless search incident to a lawful arrest is not limited by the crime for which the arrestee has been taken into custody. Even someone arrested for a traffic offense can be searched. Although there is no reason to suspect the person has a weapon nor to believe that evidence related to the offense will be found in the person's pockets (*United States v. Robinson*, 1973), the arrestee is subject to the same arrest scene search as someone taken into custody for murder.

The justification for searches of arrestees emerged in the Supreme Court's decision in *Chimel v. California* (1969). The officers must make sure that the arrestee does not have a weapon that could endanger the officers or others in the vicinity. The officers must also look for evidence that might be destroyed or damaged by the arrestee before or during the process of transporting the arrestee to jail. Officers can search the arrestee and the immediate area around the arrestee. Officers can also make a protective sweep through other rooms where the suspect may recently have been. However, the arrest would not justify opening drawers and conducting a thorough search of an entire house. If, after the arrest, officers have probable cause to conduct a more thorough search, they must obtain a warrant that specifies the items that they seek and the places where they will search.

Although a lawful arrest justifies a limited search and protective sweep, the Court has been unwilling to permit thorough warrantless searches at crime scenes, even when a murder victim is discovered. Officers should obtain a warrant to open luggage, packages, and filing cabinets at the murder scene (*Flippo v. West Virginia*, 1999).

> **Chimel v. California (1969)**
> Supreme Court decision that endorsed warrantless searches for weapons and evidence in the immediate vicinity of people who are lawfully arrested.

EXIGENT CIRCUMSTANCES

Officers can make an arrest without a warrant when there are **exigent circumstances.** This means that officers are in the middle of an urgent situation in which they must act swiftly and do not have time to go to court to seek a warrant. With respect to arrests, for example, when officers are in hot pursuit of a fleeing suspected felon, they need not stop to seek a warrant and thereby risk permitting the suspect to get away (*Warden v. Hayden*, 1967). Similarly, exigent circumstances can justify the warrantless entry into a home or other building and an accompanying search that flows from the officers' response to the urgent situation. When the ex-wife of football Hall-of-Famer O. J. Simpson was stabbed to death in front of her home, police officers went to Simpson's home and climbed the wall to gain entry to his backyard. They claimed that they found a bloody glove in the backyard, and that glove was admitted into evidence against Simpson because a judge was persuaded that the officers made the warrantless entry and search based on the urgency of their need to make sure that no one at the Simpson house was injured or in danger. This point was reaffirmed in 2006 when the Supreme Court approved police officers' warrantless entry into a home when, on being called to the scene of a loud party, they observed through the home's window a violent altercation between a teenager and an adult (*Brigham City, Utah v. Stuart*). The unanimous decision by Chief Justice John Roberts said, "[L]aw enforcement officers may enter a home without a warrant to render emergency assistance to an injured occupant or to protect an occupant from imminent injury." After the officers make the warrantless entry, the plain view doctrine permits them to examine and seize any criminal evidence that they can see in the course of actions taken to address the exigent circumstances.

In *Cupp v. Murphy* (1973) a man voluntarily complied with police officers' request that he come to the police station to answer questions concerning his wife's murder. The couple resided in separate homes at the time. At the station, officers noticed a substance on the man's fingernails that they thought might be dried blood.

> **exigent circumstances** When there is an immediate threat to public safety or the risk that evidence will be destroyed, officers may search, arrest, or question suspects without obtaining a warrant or following other usual rules of criminal procedure.

OJ SIMPSON

Over his objections, they took a sample of scrapings under his fingernails and ultimately used that tissue as evidence against him when he was convicted of murdering his wife. The Supreme Court said the search was properly undertaken under exigent circumstances. If officers had taken the time to seek a warrant, the suspect could have washed his hands and the evidence would have been lost.

Police officers can use the exigent circumstances justification for warrantless searches for the purpose of seeking evidence. To justify such searches, they do not need to show that there was a potential threat to public safety. As a practical matter, police officers make quick judgments about undertaking certain searches. If incriminating evidence is discovered, courts may be asked after the fact to determine whether the urgency of the situation justified a warrantless search and whether the nature and purpose of the search were reasonable. Judges are usually reluctant to second-guess a police officer's on-the-spot decision that the urgency of a situation required an immediate warrantless search.

CONSENT

If people consent to a search, officers do not need probable cause or even any level of suspicion to justify the search. Consent effectively absolves law enforcement officers of any risk that evidence will be excluded from use at trial or that they will be found liable in a civil lawsuit alleging a violation of Fourth Amendment rights.

Consent searches provide a valuable investigatory tool for officers who wish to conduct warrantless searches. Officers in many police departments are trained to ask people if they will consent to a search. Thus, some officers ask every motorist during a traffic stop, "Can I search your car?" Or, if called to the scene of a domestic dispute or a citizen complaint about noise, the officers may say, "Do you mind if I look around the downstairs area of your house?" Criminal evidence is often uncovered in such consent searches—a fact that may indicate that many citizens do not know that they have the option to say "no" when officers ask for permission to search. Moreover, some citizens may fear that they will look more suspicious to the officers if they say "no," so they agree to searches in order to act as if they have nothing to hide. In addition, in *United States v. Drayton* (2002) the Supreme Court said that police officers do not have to inform people of their right to say "no" when asked if they wish to consent to a search.

In deciding if a permissible consent search has occurred, one must address two key issues. First, the consent must voluntary. Police officers may not use coercion or threats to obtain consent. Even subtler tricks, such as dishonestly telling someone that there is a search warrant and thereby implying that the person has no choice but to consent, will result in the search being declared improper (*Bumper v. North Carolina*, 1968). Second, the consent must be given by someone who possesses authority to give consent and thereby waive the right. Someone cannot, for example, consent to have his or her neighbor's house searched. Normally, the resident in a dwelling can consent to a search of that dwelling. In 2006, however, the Supreme Court declared that the police may not search when one resident of a dwelling objects, even if another resident consents to the search of the house (*Georgia v. Randolph*).

AUTOMOBILE SEARCHES

The U.S. Supreme Court first addressed automobile searches in *Carroll v. United States* (1925) a case in which federal agents searched a car for illegal alcohol. The *Carroll* case, in which the warrantless search was approved, provided an underlying justification for permitting such searches of automobiles. In essence, because cars are mobile, they differ greatly from houses and other buildings. Automobiles can be driven away and disappear in the time that it would take officers to ask a judicial officer for a search warrant.

Police officers have significant authority to search automobiles and to issue commands to people riding in vehicles. For example, during a traffic stop, officers can order passengers as well as the driver to exit the vehicle, even if there is no basis for suspicion that the passengers engaged in any wrongdoing (*Maryland v. Wilson*, 1997).

United States v. Drayton
(2002) Legal decision declaring that police officers are not required to inform people of their right to decline to be searched when police ask for consent to search.

Warrantless searches of automobiles may be conducted when there is probable cause. California Highway Patrol Sgt. Hal Rosendahl dismantles the dashboard of a car allegedly used to smuggle drugs. What is necessary to establish probable cause to conduct this search?

Two key questions arise in automobile searches: (1) When can officers stop a car? and (2) How extensively can they search the vehicle? Many automobile searches arise as a result of traffic stops. A stop can occur when an officer observes a traffic violation, including defective safety equipment, or when there is a basis for reasonable suspicion concerning the involvement of the car, its driver, or its passengers in a crime. Police officers are free to make a visible inspection of a car's interior as they question a driver and ask for identification when preparing a citation for a traffic violation. All sworn officers can make traffic stops, even if they are in unmarked vehicles and serving in special vice or detective bureaus that do not normally handle traffic offenses (*Whren v. United States*, 1996). A traffic violation by itself, however, does not provide an officer with the authority to search an entire vehicle (*Knowles v. Iowa*, 1998). Only specific factors creating reasonable suspicion or probable cause will justify officers' doing anything more than looking inside the vehicle.

For example, the lawful arrest of a driver for violating the law justifies a search of the entire passenger compartment of the automobile for evidence or weapons (*New York v. Belton*, 1981). Moreover, the arrest of a driver justifies the search of a passenger's property (*Wyoming v. Houghton*, 1999). In addition, the Court has expanded officers' authority to search automobiles even when no formal arrest has yet occurred. In *Michigan v. Long* (1983) the Court approved a search of the car's interior around the driver's seat after officers found the car in a ditch and the apparently intoxicated driver standing outside the car. The Supreme Court justified the search as an expansion of the *Terry* doctrine. In effect, the officers were permitted to "frisk" the car in order to protect themselves and others by making sure no weapon was available to the not-yet-arrested driver. Such a search requires that the officers have reasonable suspicion that the person stopped may be armed and may pose a threat to the officers.

Until the Court's decision in *California v. Acevedo* (1991), even when officers had probable cause to search a car's trunk, they were expected to obtain a warrant for any containers found within the trunk. In the *Acevedo* ruling the Court said that officers could search anywhere in the car for which they have probable cause to search. Further, the officers themselves, rather than a judge, determine whether probable cause exists before conducting the warrantless search of the vehicle. If, however, a judge later disagrees with the officer's conclusion about the existence of probable cause, any evidence found in the search of the automobile might be excluded from use at trial.

Even if officers lack probable cause to believe that the vehicle has been stolen, an officer may enter the vehicle to see the vehicle identification number by the windshield when a car has been validly stopped pursuant to a traffic violation or other permissible justification (*New York v. Class*, 1986). In addition, the Court permits thorough searches of vehicles, without regard to probable cause, when police officers inventory the contents of impounded vehicles (*South Dakota v. Opperman*, 1976). This means that containers found within the course of the inventory search may also be opened and searched when the examination of such containers is consistent with a police department's inventory policies.

Table 7.2 reviews selected Supreme Court cases concerning those circumstances in which the police do not need a warrant to conduct a search or to seize evidence.

TABLE 7.2   Warrantless Searches

The Supreme Court has ruled that there are circumstances when a warrant is not required.

Case	Decision
Special Needs	
Michigan Department of State Police v. Sitz (1990)	Stopping motorists systematically at roadblocks designed for specific purposes, such as detecting drunken drivers, is permissible.
City of Indianapolis v. Edmond (2000)	Police traffic checkpoints cannot be justified as a generalized search for criminal evidence; they must be narrowly focused on a specific objective.
Stop and Frisk	
Terry v. Ohio (1968)	Officers may stop and frisk suspects on the street when there is reasonable suspicion that they are armed and involved in criminal activity.
Adams v. Williams (1972)	Officers may rely on reports from reliable witnesses as the basis for conducting a stop and frisk.
Illinois v. Wardlow (2000)	When a person runs at the sight of police in a high-crime area, officers are justified in using that person's flight as a basis for forming reasonable suspicion to justify a stop and frisk.
Incident to an Arrest	
Chimel v. California (1969)	To preserve evidence and protect the safety of the officer and the public after a lawful arrest, the arrestee and the immediate area around the arrestee may be searched for weapons and criminal evidence.
United States v. Robinson (1973)	A warrantless search incident to an arrest is not limited by the seriousness of the crime for which the arrestee has been taken into custody.
Exigent Circumstances	
Warden v. Hayden (1967)	When officers are in hot pursuit of a fleeing suspect, they need not stop to seek a warrant and thereby risk permitting the suspect to get away.
Cupp v. Murphy (1973)	Officers may seize evidence to protect it if taking time to seek a warrant creates a risk of its destruction.
Consent	
Bumper v. North Carolina (1968)	Officers may not tell falsehoods as a means of getting a suspect to consent to a search.
United States v. Drayton (2002)	An officer does not have to inform people of their right to refuse when he or she asks if they wish to consent to a search.
Automobiles	
Carroll v. United States (1925)	Because by their nature automobiles can be easily moved, warrantless searches are permissible when reasonable suspicion of illegal activity exists.
New York v. Class (1986)	An officer may enter a vehicle to see the vehicle identification number when a car has been validly stopped pursuant to a traffic violation or other permissible justification.
California v. Acevedo (1991)	Officers may search throughout a vehicle when they believe they have probable cause to do so.
Maryland v. Wilson (1997)	During traffic stops, officers may order passengers as well as the driver to exit the vehicle, even if there is no basis for suspicion that the passengers engaged in any wrongdoing.
Knowles v. Iowa (1998)	A traffic violation by itself does not provide an officer with the authority to search an entire vehicle. There must be reasonable suspicion or probable cause before officers can extend their search beyond merely looking inside the vehicle's passenger compartment.

Answers

6. In what situations do law enforcement's special needs justify stopping an automobile without reasonable suspicion? ➞ **6.** Warrantless stops of automobiles are permitted at international borders and sobriety checkpoints (unless barred within a specific state by its own supreme court) or when there is reasonable suspicion of a traffic violation or other wrongdoing.

7. What is an exigent circumstance? ➞ **7.** An urgent situation in which evidence might be destroyed, a suspect might escape, or the public would be endangered by taking the time to seek a warrant for a search or an arrest.

8. What two elements must be present for a valid consent to permit a warrantless search? ➞ **8.** Voluntariness and a person with proper authority to consent.

Questioning Suspects

The Fifth Amendment contains various rights, including the one most relevant to police officers' actions in questioning suspects. The relevant words of the Amendment are "No person shall . . . be compelled in any criminal case to be a witness against himself." The privilege against compelled self-incrimination should not be viewed as simply a legal protection that seeks to assist individuals who may be guilty of crimes. By protecting individuals in this way, the Fifth Amendment discourages police officers from using violent or otherwise coercive means to push suspects to confess.

In addition to discouraging the physical abuse of suspects, the privilege against compelled self-incrimination can also diminish the risk of erroneous convictions. When police officers use coercive pressure to seek confessions, they create a significant risk that innocent people will confess to crimes they did not commit. The worst-case scenario took place in the film *In the Name of the Father,* based on a true story in England in which police officers gain a confession from a bombing suspect, whom they know to be innocent, by placing a gun in the suspect's mouth and threatening to pull the trigger.

MIRANDA RULES

The 1966 decision by the Supreme Court in **Miranda v. Arizona** said that as soon as the investigation of a crime begins to focus on a particular suspect and he or she is taken into custody, the so-called *Miranda* warnings must be read aloud before questioning can begin. Suspects must be told four things:

1. They have the right to remain silent.

2. If they decide to make a statement, it can and will be used against them in court.

3. They have the right to have an attorney present during interrogation or to have an opportunity to consult with an attorney.

4. If they cannot afford an attorney, the state will provide one.

Prior to the *Miranda* decision, police officers in some places solved crimes by picking up a poor person or African American and torturing him or her until a confession was produced. In *Brown v. Mississippi* (1936) the Supreme Court ruled that statements produced after police beat suspects were inadmissible, but it did not insist that counsel be available at the early stages of the criminal process.

Two rulings in 1964 laid the foundation for the *Miranda* decision. In *Escobedo v. Illinois* the Court made the link between the Fifth Amendment right against self-incrimination and the Sixth Amendment right to counsel. Danny Escobedo was questioned at the police station for 14 hours without counsel even

Miranda v. Arizona (1966)
U.S. Supreme Court decision declaring that suspects in custody must be informed of their rights to remain silent and be represented during questioning.

The Fifth Amendment protects suspects against compelled self-incrimination. What are the rights of suspects before and during police interrogation?

© Mark Richards/PhotoEdit

though he asked to see his attorney. He finally made incriminating statements that the police said were voluntary. The Court's ruling specified that defendants have a right to counsel

> when the investigation is no longer a general inquiry into an unsolved crime, but has begun to focus on a particular suspect, the suspect has been taken into police custody, [and] the police carry out a process of interrogations that lends itself to eliciting incriminating statements.

The Court effectively expanded the right to counsel to apply at an early point in the criminal justice process as a means to guard against law enforcement officers' actions that might violate the Fifth Amendment privilege against compelled self-incrimination. In *Massiah v. United States* (1964) the Supreme Court declared that the questioning of the defendant by a police agent outside of the presence of defense counsel violated the defendant's rights.

The *Miranda* warnings only apply to what are called custodial interrogations. If police officers walk up to someone on the streets and begin asking questions, there is no need to inform the person of his rights. The justices say that people know they can walk away when an officer asks them questions in a public place. When police have taken someone into custody, however, the Supreme Court sees an inherently coercive situation. The loss of liberty and isolation experienced by detained suspects can make them vulnerable to abusive interrogation techniques, especially when interrogations take place out of view of anyone other than police officers. When a suspect is alone in a room with the police, will anyone believe the suspect if he or she claims to have been beaten? If the police say that the suspect confessed, will anyone believe the suspect if he or she denies this? The *Miranda* warnings and presence of counsel during questioning are supposed to prevent such abuses.

One circumstance in which the Court has permitted police officers to forgo *Miranda* warnings is when there would be a threat to public safety by taking the time to provide the warnings. This exception is similar to the exigent circumstance justification for warrantless searches. The underlying premise is that some urgent, socially significant situation outweighs the necessity of respecting individuals' rights. In the case that created this "public safety" exception, police officers chased an armed man into a supermarket after a reported assault. When they found him with an empty shoulder holster, they asked, "Where's the gun?" after he was handcuffed but before he had been informed of his *Miranda* rights (*New York v. Quarles*, 1984). His statement in response to the question could be used against him in court because the public's safety might have been threatened if the police had taken the time to read him his rights before asking any questions.

Although some legal commentators and police officials have criticized the *Miranda* warnings, the Supreme Court strongly repeated its endorsement of the *Miranda* requirement in 2000 (*Dickerson v. United States*). In declaring that *Miranda* warnings are required by the Constitution, Chief Justice William Rehnquist's majority opinion stated that "*Miranda* has become embedded in routine police practice to the point where the warnings have become part of our national culture."

"public safety" exception
Exception to *Miranda* requirements that permits police to immediately question a suspect in custody without providing any warnings, when public safety would be jeopardized by taking the time to supply the warnings.

THE CONSEQUENCES OF *MIRANDA*

Miranda rights must be provided before questions are asked during custodial interrogations. However, police officers have adapted their techniques in various ways in order to question suspects without any impediment from the warnings. For example, officers may ask questions while standing on the suspect's doorstep before making an arrest. Even after arrest, the courts do not require that police inform suspects of their rights immediately. Thus, after taking a suspect into custody, some officers may delay providing *Miranda* warnings in case the suspect talks on his or her own. The suspect may be kept in the backseat of a car as officers drive around town, or the suspect may be left alone in a room at the police station. Some suspects will take the initiative to talk to officers because of feelings of guilt. Other suspects may start conversations with officers because they are so eager to convince the officers that they have an alibi or that they want to cooperate. This may lead the suspect to provide contradictory statements that will help build the case.

Officers are also trained in interrogation techniques that are intended to encourage suspects to talk despite *Miranda* warnings. The words of the warnings are so familiar from television police shows that many suspects never stop to think about the message being conveyed. In addition, officers may pretend to sympathize with the suspect (Leo, 1996). They may say, for example, "We understand how bad stuff can happen that you never want to have happen. We know that you had a good reason to get mad and go after that guy with your knife. We probably would have done the same thing if we were in your situation. We know that you never really planned to stab him." Such statements are not honest. But police officers are allowed to use deception to induce suspects to talk. It is not uncommon for officers to say, untruthfully, "We have five witnesses that saw you do it. If you tell us everything right now, we may be able to get you a good deal. If you don't help us, we don't know what we can do for you." Do such statements constitute coercion that would be regarded as improper pressure in violation of *Miranda*? Probably not—as long as the officers do not threaten suspects in ways that make them fear for their physical safety or the safety of their loved ones. See "A Question of Ethics" at the end of the chapter for more on this.

In 2004 the Supreme Court warned police officers not to use a particular technique that had begun to emerge as a routine strategy in some departments. Officers would question suspects without providing *Miranda* warnings. After gaining incriminating statements, the officers would give *Miranda* warnings and ask the suspects to repeat what they had just said. Not realizing that their first statements were inadmissible because of a *Miranda* violation, the suspects would repeat the incriminating statements, reasonably assuming that the police had already heard the statement so that there would be nothing to gain by refusing to speak the second time. In *Missouri v. Seibert* (2004) Justice Souter's majority opinion concluded,

> Upon hearing warnings only in the aftermath of interrogation and just after making a confession, a suspect would hardly think he had a genuine right to remain silent, let alone persist in so believing once the police began to lead him over the same ground again. . . . Thus, when *Miranda* warnings are inserted in the midst of coordinated and continuing interrogation, they are likely to mislead and "depriv[e] a defendant of knowledge essential to his ability to understand the nature of his rights and the consequences of abandoning them."

Many suspects talk to the police despite being informed of their right to remain silent and their right to have an attorney present during questioning. Some suspects do not fully understand their rights. They may believe that they will look guilty by remaining silent or asking for an attorney. They therefore feel that they must talk to officers in order to have any hope of claiming innocence. More importantly, many suspects believe (often accurately) that they will gain a more favorable charge or plea bargain if they cooperate with officers as fully and as early as possible.

Following the September 11 terrorist attacks, the U.S. government jailed U.S. citizens even though it had not charged them with any crimes, had not given them access to court proceedings, and had not permitted them to meet with an attorney, all because they were suspected of being "enemy combatants." As shown in "What Americans Think," many people believe that individual rights should be curtailed in the fight against terrorism.

WHAT AMERICANS THINK

Question: The federal government has taken aggressive actions, without the approval of legislators or judges, to monitor, detain, and question terrorism suspects—actions that would violate the usual rights of criminal suspects. "Do Americans believe such actions are necessary to stop terrorism? Alternatively, is the government trampling on rights guaranteed by the Constitution?"

In order to curb terrorism, it will be necessary to give up some of our liberties.

Agree — 45.3%

Government should be able to arrest and detain a noncitizen indefinitely if the person is suspected of belonging to a terrorist organization.

Agree — 47%

Government should be able to search property without a warrant solely on the suspicion that a crime or terrorist act is being planned there.

Agree — 23%

Go to http://www.thomsonedu.com/criminaljustice/cole to compare your opinion on this issue with the opinions of other criminal justice students.

Source: "Americans Unwilling to Give up Liberties," *Inside IPPSR* [Institute for Public Policy and Social Research, Michigan State University], September 2002, p. 3, http://www.ippsr.msu.edu/AboutIPPSR/CivilLiberties.htm.

ThomsonNOW

Improve your grade on the exam with Personalized Study! For reinforcement resources and a mastery check of Questioning Suspects, go to www.thomsonedu.com/thomsonnow

CHECKPOINT

Answers

9. What are *Miranda* rights? → **9.** Officers must inform suspects before custodial interrogation of the right to remain silent, the prosecution's authority to use any of the suspect's statements, the right to the presence of an attorney during questioning, and the right to have an attorney appointed if the suspect is too poor to hire one.

10. What is the "public safety" exception? → **10.** Officers can ask questions of suspects in custody without first providing *Miranda* warnings, if the public safety would be threatened by taking the time to supply the warnings.

11. How have police officers adapted their practices in light of *Miranda*? → **11.** Officers ask questions before suspects are in custody, use techniques to pretend to befriend or empathize with suspects being questioned, and misinform suspects about the existence of evidence demonstrating their guilt.

The Exclusionary Rule

What happens when police commit rights violations? One primary remedy is the exclusion of evidence from court. In 1914 the U.S. Supreme Court declared in *Weeks v. United States* that federal courts must exclude any evidence that was obtained through an improper search by federal law enforcement agents. In *Weeks*, U.S. marshals searched a home without a warrant and found incriminating evidence. According to the Court,

> If letters and private documents can thus be seized and held and used in evidence against a citizen accused of an offense, the protection of the 4th Amendment, declaring his right to be secure against such searches and seizures, is of no value, and, so far as those thus placed are concerned, might as well be stricken from the Constitution.

Thus, the Court required that the improperly obtained evidence be excluded from use in court, even if it meant that a guilty person may go free because the prosecution no longer has enough evidence to gain a conviction. As a result of this **exclusionary rule** created by the Court, it was assumed that law enforcement officers would obey the Fourth Amendment in order to avoid the loss of incriminating evidence. The exclusionary rule was later also applied to Fifth Amendment violations caused by improper questioning, such as a failure to inform arrested individuals of their *Miranda* rights.

The exclusionary rule does not necessarily require that cases against defendants be dismissed when constitutional rights have been violated. The prosecution can continue, but it may not use improperly obtained evidence. In some cases, other valid evidence of guilt may exist in the form of witness testimony or confessions. Without such alternative evidence, however, the exclusionary rule can lead to charges being dropped.

exclusionary rule The principle that illegally obtained evidence must be excluded from trial.

THE APPLICATION OF THE EXCLUSIONARY RULE TO THE STATES

In *Wolf v. Colorado* (1949) the Supreme Court incorporated the Fourth Amendment. However, the justices declined to apply the exclusionary rule to the states, because they believed states could develop their own remedies to handle improper searches by police. The situation changed during the Supreme Court tenure of Chief Justice Earl Warren (1953–1969), when the Court incorporated most of the criminal justice–related rights in a way that required state law enforcement officials to adhere to the same rules federal law enforcement officials had to follow. Not until *Mapp v. Ohio* (1961) did the Court apply the exclusionary rule to the states.

Why did the Supreme Court see the exclusionary rule as necessary? Several reasons emerge in *Weeks v. United States* (1914) and *Mapp*. First, *Weeks* declared that the exclusionary rule is essential to make the Fourth Amendment meaningful. In essence, the justices believed that constitutional rights are nullified if government officials are permitted to benefit by violating those rights. Second, the *Mapp* decision indicates that the exclusionary rule is required by the Constitution. Third, the majority opinion in *Mapp* concluded that alternatives to the exclusionary rule do not work. The opinion noted that many states had found that nothing short of exclusion of evidence would work to correct constitutional rights violations and limit the number of violations that occur. Fourth, the *Mapp* opinion argued that the use of improperly obtained evidence by officials who are responsible for upholding the law only serves to diminish respect for the law. Fifth, the *Mapp* decision indicates that the absence of an exclusionary rule diminishes the protection of all rights because it would permit all constitutional rights "to be revocable at the whim of any police officer who, in the name of law enforcement itself, chooses to suspend . . . [the] enjoyment [of rights]." Sixth, the exclusionary rule is justified in *Mapp* as an effective means of deterring police and prosecutors from violating constitutional rights.

The existence of the exclusionary rule demonstrates the Supreme Court's conclusion that it is sometimes necessary to risk setting a guilty criminal free in order to

WHAT AMERICANS THINK

Question: "Should putting guilty people in jail be the most important goal of the criminal justice system?"

It's just as important to protect the rights of the accused as it is to put the guilty people in jail.

50%

Putting guilty people in jail should be the most important goal of the criminal justice system.

29%

Even if it means that some guilty people go free, it's important to protect the rights of the accused.

18%

None of the above choices.

2%

Don't know.

2%

Go to http://www.thomsonedu.com/criminaljustice/cole to compare your opinion on this issue with the opinions of other criminal justice students.

Source: Survey based on telephone interviews of a national adult sample conducted July 10–24, 2002, by the Public Agenda Foundation. Data provided by the Roper Center for Public Opinion Research, University of Connecticut.

make sure that constitutional rights are protected. Look at "What Americans Think" to see what whether other people agree with this emphasis on constitutional rights.

EXCEPTIONS TO THE EXCLUSIONARY RULE

The exclusionary rule has many critics who have claimed that the Court's decision hampers police investigations and allows guilty criminals to go free. However, research has not clearly supported claims about the negative consequences of the exclusionary rule. Studies of the impact of the exclusionary rule have produced two consistent findings. First, only a small minority of defendants file a "motion to suppress," which is used to ask a judge to exclude evidence that has allegedly been obtained in violation of the defendant's rights. Second, only a very small fraction of motions to suppress evidence are granted (Davies 1983; Uchida and Bynum, 1991; S. Walker, 2001:90–91). Despite continuing debates about the rule's impact and effectiveness, the Supreme Court began creating exceptions to the exclusionary rule after Warren Burger became chief justice in 1969.

"Good Faith" Exception   The Supreme Court created a **"good faith" exception** to the exclusionary rule when officers use search warrants (*United States v. Leon,* 1984). "Good faith" means that the officers acted with the honest belief that they were following the proper rules, but the judge issued the warrant improperly. In addition, the reliance and honest belief must be reasonable. If officers knew that a judge issued a warrant based on no evidence whatsoever, the officers could not claim that they reasonably and honestly relied on the warrant. But when officers present evidence of probable cause to the judge and the judge issues a warrant based on information that actually falls below the standard of probable cause, the officers may use evidence found in the resulting search, because it was the judge who made the error, not the police. However, evidence can still be excluded if officers undertake a warrantless search based on their own discretionary decision, even if they honestly (but wrongly) believe that such a search is permitted in such circumstances.

"good faith" exception
Exception to the exclusionary rule that permits the use of improperly obtained evidence when police officers acted in honest reliance on a defective statute, a warrant improperly issued by a magistrate, or a consent to search by someone who lacked authority to give such permission.

Inevitable Discovery Rule   Another important exception to the exclusionary rule is the **inevitable discovery rule.** This rule arose from a case involving the tragic abduction and murder of a young girl. The police sought an escapee from a psychiatric hospital who was seen carrying a large bundle. The man being sought contacted an attorney

inevitable discovery rule
Supreme Court ruling that improperly obtained evidence can be used when it would later have been inevitably discovered by the police.

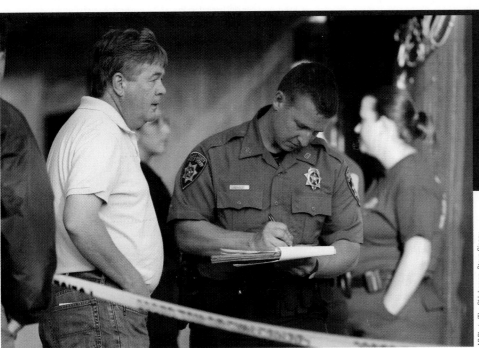

District Attorney Tim Kuykendall, left, and police officers wait for a search warrant before entering an apartment where Jamie Rose Bolin, who had been missing for two days, lived in Purcell, Oklahoma. Authorities found a body believed to be Bolin's in the apartment of Kevin Ray Underwood. Police arrested Underwood on a first-degree murder charge. Which exceptions to the exclusionary rule might apply in this case?

AP Photo/The Oklahoman, Steve Sisney

and arranged to surrender to police in a town 160 miles away from the scene of the abduction. The Supreme Court subsequently found that the police improperly questioned the suspect outside of the presence of his attorney while driving him back to the city where the abduction occurred (*Brewer v. Williams*, 1977). The Court declared that the girl's body and the suspect's statements had to be excluded from evidence because they were obtained in violation of his rights. Thus, his murder conviction was overturned and he was given a new trial. At the second trial, he was convicted again. However, at the second trial, the prosecution used the body in evidence against him based on the claim that search parties would have found the body eventually even without his confession. There was a search team within two and one-half miles of the body at the time that it was found. In *Nix v. Williams* (1984) the Supreme Court agreed that the improperly obtained evidence can be used when it would later have been inevitably discovered anyway without improper actions by the police. Table 7.3 summarizes selected Supreme Court decisions regarding the exclusionary rule as it applies to the Fourth and Fifth Amendments.

When the Court issued its decisions in *Weeks* and *Mapp*, it appeared that the exclusion of evidence would be guided by a trial judge's answer to the question, "Did police violate the suspect's rights?" By contrast, through the development of exceptions to the rule, the Court shifted its focus to the question, "Did the police make an error that was so serious that the exclusion of evidence is required?" For example, the "good faith" exception established in *United States v. Leon* (1984) emphasizes the fact that officers did what they thought they were supposed to do. The decision did not rest on the fact that the suspect's Fourth Amendment rights were violated by a search conducted with an improper warrant. Thus, the Supreme Court's creation of exceptions to the exclusionary rule has given police officers the flexibility to make specific kinds of errors without jeopardizing the admissibility of evidence that may help establish a defendant's guilt.

Nix v. Williams (1984) Legal decision in which the Supreme Court created the inevitable discovery exception to the exclusionary rule.

ThomsonNOW™
Improve your grade on the exam with Personalized Study! For reinforcement resources and a mastery check of The Exclusionary Rule, go to www.thomsonedu.com/thomsonnow

CHECKPOINT

12. Why was the exclusionary rule created and eventually applied to the states?

13. What are the criticisms of the exclusionary rule?

14. What are the main exceptions to the exclusionary rule?

Answers

12. The exclusionary rule was created to deter officers from violating people's rights, and the Supreme Court considers it an essential component of the Fourth and Fifth Amendments.

13. The rule is criticized for hampering police investigations and permitting some guilty people to go free.

14. A "good faith" exception in warrant situations; cases in which evidence would have been discovered by the police inevitably anyway (inevitable discovery rule).

TABLE 7.3 Exclusionary Rule	
The Supreme Court has created the exclusionary rule as a means of insuring that Fourth and Fifth Amendment rights are protected. It has also provided exceptions to this rule.	
Case	**Decision**
Exclusionary Rule	
Mapp v. Ohio (1961)	Because the Fourth Amendment protects people from unreasonable searches and seizures by all law enforcement officials, evidence found through improper searches or seizures must be excluded from use at state and federal trials.
"Good Faith" Exception	
United States v. Leon (1984)	When officers act in good faith reliance on a warrant, the evidence will not be excluded even if the warrant was issued improperly.
"Inevitable Discovery" Exception	
Nix v. Williams (1984)	Improperly obtained evidence can be used when it would later have inevitably been discovered without improper actions by the police.

A QUESTION OF ETHICS: WRITING ASSIGNMENT

The desk sergeant approached Detectives Alicia Baird and Eric Houston at 10:00 P.M. "An attorney just called and said that he is representing Linda Franklin. He said that he would come in if you were going to question her, but I told him that you had just finished booking her. Since it's so late, I knew you'd be leaving for home so I told him that no questioning would start until tomorrow."

"OK," said Detective Baird as the desk sergeant turned and walked down the hall. She turned to Detective Houston. "That's too bad, because I really thought she might start talking about the murder if we asked her some questions right away."

"I agree," said Houston. "So I don't think we can afford to let this opportunity pass by. C'mon."

With a puzzled look on her face, Baird followed him into the interrogation room where Franklin sat at a table looking tired and frightened.

As Baird stood by the door, Houston read the suspect her *Miranda* rights again—she had already been informed of her rights during the booking process. "Do you understand these rights?" Houston asked.

Franklin nodded her head. "I know. I know." She hesitated before saying, "I guess I don't have any attorney, do I?"

"I don't see one here, do you?" replied Houston. "But you can talk to us if you want to. Just sign this form indicating that you were informed of your rights and that you understand them."

Franklin signed the form and Houston began to ask her questions about the events of the evening that led to the discovery of a murder victim at her apartment.

Baird could not stop thinking about the conversation with the desk sergeant and the fact that the attorney had been told that no questioning would begin until the next day. If the questioning continued, that would mean that the police had deceived the defense attorney and, in effect, been untruthful in stating when questioning would take place.

WRITING ASSIGNMENT

What should Detective Baird do? Should she stop Houston from questioning Franklin? Should she call the attorney to tell him that the questioning of his client has begun? Is she obligated to take any action at all? Write a memo to Detective Baird explaining the legal and ethical implications of the situation. Also give her advice about what she might do. After you write the memo, go to the Findlaw website and search for the case *Moran v. Burbine* (1986). The website is listed on the Cole/Smith Criminal Justice in America Companion Website: http://www.thomsonedu.com/criminaljustice/cole. How does your advice compare with the decision of the U.S. Supreme Court?

REAL-WORLD ACTIVITY: AN APPLICATION

You are a police officer on foot patrol. You notice a teenager wearing a bulky New York Yankees jacket on a hot summer day. He stands and peers for a while into the window of a pawn shop. Then he walks around the corner and makes a call on a cell phone. After the call, he returns to the front window of the pawn shop.

He walks around the corner and makes another call on the cell phone. Subsequently, he looks in the pawn shop window again. You think his actions are suspicious.

RESEARCHING THE INTERNET

Go to InfoTrac College Edition and search for *Terry v. Ohio*. Read "*Terry v. Ohio* in Hindsight: The Perils of Predicting the Past," by Susan Bandes, *Constitutional Commentary*, 1999.

APPLICATION

Do you have grounds to conduct a stop-and-frisk search based on the doctrine of *Terry v. Ohio?* What, if anything, would you do? Why?

SUMMARY

- The Supreme Court has defined rules for the circumstances and justifications for stops, searches, and arrests in light of the Fourth Amendment's prohibition on unreasonable searches and seizures.

- Most stops must be supported by reasonable suspicion; an arrest or a search warrant must be supported by enough information to constitute probable cause.

- The plain view doctrine permits officers to visually examine and use as evidence, without a warrant, any contraband or criminal evidence that is in open sight when the officers are in a place where they are legally permitted to be.

- Searches are considered "reasonable" and may be conducted without warrants in specific circumstances, such as border checkpoints and airport security, that present special needs beyond the normal purposes of law enforcement.

- Limited searches may be conducted without warrants when officers have reasonable suspicions to justify a stop and frisk for weapons on the streets, when officers make a lawful arrest, when exigent circumstances exist, when people voluntarily consent to searches of their persons or property, or in certain situations involving automobiles.

- The Fifth Amendment privilege against compelled self-incrimination helps protect citizens against violence and coercion by police as well as helping maintain the legitimacy and integrity of the legal system.

- The Supreme Court's decision in *Miranda v. Arizona* required officers to inform suspects of specific rights before custodial questioning, although officers have adapted their practices to accommodate this rule and several exceptions have been created.
- By barring the use of illegally obtained evidence in court, the exclusionary rule is designed to deter police from violating citizens' rights during criminal investigations.
- The Supreme Court has created several exceptions to the exclusionary rule, including the inevitable discovery rule and the "good faith" exception in defective warrant situations.

QUESTIONS FOR REVIEW

1. What are the requirements for police officers with respect to stops, searches, arrests, and warrants?

2. What are the plain view doctrine and the open fields doctrine?

3. Under what circumstances are warrantless searches permissible?

4. How have police officers adapted to the requirements of *Miranda v. Arizona?*

5. What are the main exceptions to the exclusionary rule?

KEY TERMS AND CASES

affidavit (p. 181)
exclusionary rule (p. 194)
exigent circumstances (p. 187)
"good faith" exception (p. 195)
inevitable discovery rule (p. 195)
open fields doctrine (p. 182)
plain view doctrine (p. 182)

probable cause (p. 180)
"public safety" exception (p. 192)
reasonable expectation of privacy (p. 179)
reasonable suspicion (p. 180)
search (p. 179)
seizure (p. 179)
stop (p. 180)

stop-and-frisk search (p. 185)
totality of circumstances (p. 181)
Chimel v. California (1969) (p. 187)
Miranda v. Arizona (1966) (p. 191)
Nix v. Williams (1984) (p. 196)
Terry v. Ohio (1968) (p. 185)
United States v. Drayton (2002) (p. 188)

GOING ONLINE

ThomsonNOW

Maximize your study time by using ThomsonNOW's diagnostic study plan to help you review this chapter. The Study Plan will

- Help you identify areas on which you should concentrate
- Provide interactive exercises to help you master the chapter concepts
- Provide a posttest to confirm you are ready to move on to the next chapter

Written by Chuck Terry

INSIDE THE CRIMINAL JUSTICE SYSTEM AND BEYOND: ONE MAN'S JOURNEY

Stepping into a New World: Arrested, Booked, Charged, Jailed, and Investigated

By the mid-1970s I had spent time in jail and was on probation for burglary. My probation officer, thinking I could never stay "clean" (not use heroin), thought I belonged in San Quentin and told me he'd do everything within his power to send me there. He tested my urine for drugs and checked my arms for needle marks with a magnifying glass two or three times a week until I couldn't take it anymore. Eventually I quit reporting and went "on the run." The fact that I had skipped probation and there was now an arrest warrant with my name on it left me feeling like a desperado. Now it was time to get really hooked.

I began selling dope to support my habit. I was living in a Manhattan Beach motel and selling about a thousand dollars' worth of heroin a week. For me this was "doing good," because I wasn't stealing. Not only that, my customers seemed to appreciate my services.

Arrest

One Thursday afternoon, while calling my connection from a phone booth in front of my motel, I noticed several men in suits knocking on the door of my room. I instantly knew they were cops and that I needed to get away from there fast. Trying to be discreet, I opened the booth door and quietly started walking away. Before I took two steps a woman came running out of the nearby motel office, pointing at me and yelling, "There he is! There he is!" Because of the many people she had observed coming and going from my room, she suspected me of dealing and called the Manhattan Beach City Police Department.

I started running but didn't get far. Besides the cops upstairs, other officers were surrounding the motel. Though I hadn't noticed, two of them were within ten feet of where I stood. As soon as I realized that I had been spotted by the police, I bolted from that phone booth as if my life depended on it. Ignoring their commands to "halt," I ran as fast as I could. Before I had gone a hundred yards, they tackled me to the ground and cuffed me. At that moment I felt a sense of fear, helplessness, and anger that is difficult to describe. I was under arrest—again. While one cop held me from behind, the other went into my pockets and pulled out eleven balloons filled with heroin. The plainclothes cops found more heroin, other drugs, and several hundred dollars in my room. Next thing I knew somebody was reading me my *Miranda* rights ("You have the right to remain silent. . . .") and I found myself sitting in the back seat of a cop car, alone, angry, scared, and cuffed, the crackling sounds and voices from the police radio relentlessly assaulting my ears. Welcome to my nightmare—live from Los Angeles County.

During the ride to the Manhattan Beach City Jail, the police lockup, I felt helpless and desperate, like a captured animal. The cops in the front seat seemed excited as they talked about what had just gone down—the chase, the bust. As I listened to their conversation I got a sense of what I must mean to them—a good catch, evidence of a job well done, but little else. They talked about me as if I were invisible. That my whole world had just caved in was apparently insignificant to them. Underneath all these feelings was the unquestionable certainty that I would soon become sick from heroin withdrawal.

Booking

We quickly arrived at the local police lockup—a small facility that functioned as a way station, a place where recently captured "suspects" are held until they can bail out or be transported to the county jail. Once inside I was promptly booked, a process that included being notified of my charges (given paperwork clarifying the specific crimes I was being accused of—possession of heroin with the intent to sell was the most serious) and the amount of my bail (which was high), photographed, fingerprinted, and strip-searched. Because I could not make bail, I was held for a court appearance and confined to a small cell block (the tank), where I was given a blanket, toilet paper, and food twice a day. Because Friday was a holiday I would not be sent to the county jail until Monday. It was here that I began kicking a heroin habit that was so bad I did not sleep for the following three weeks.

For the next four days this cell block was my home. I had never been so physically addicted or experienced such severe withdrawal. I was weak, couldn't eat, ached all over, and had the sweats, chills, and diarrhea.

While I was in the lockup, a few other men came and went. Most had been arrested for crimes that were not as serious as mine—not paying traffic tickets and the like. But they say misery loves company, and having other people around did help. In such facilities there is usually a high level of camaraderie among inmates. Having been stripped of everything we take for granted "on the streets," like personal autonomy, heterosexual relations, jobs, safety, and loved ones, we are left with just about all there is to associate with and find meaning from on the inside—each other.

On the third day I was called out of the tank and placed inside a room with two men who looked like addicts. One was Chicano and the other white. They had tattoos, tracks on their arms (scars from needle marks), and talked like convicts. By this time I was extremely weak—neither my vision nor my perception was very sharp. To my surprise these guys turned out to be narcotics officers who worked for the local police department. I felt like I was in the Twilight Zone. They wanted me to tell on my connection. "We know you were scoring ounces. We figure if you tell us who your man is, we can get to the guy who has the pounds." My head began to spin.

Even though it happens a lot, being a police informant is taboo among prisoners. Informants often spend years in protective custody (special sections of jails or prisons separated from the main population) or are killed for providing information that leads to further arrests. Nevertheless, police relentlessly seek new informants. Payment for cooperation varies. A good example of this is the witness protection programs that keep all sorts of people, including murderers, out of prison in exchange for the information they provide.

I was still consumed by my need for heroin as I sat facing these guys. Sick as I was, I would do just about anything for a shot. Except tell. They said if I cooperated they would give me enough dope to "get well." I told them I could never give up my connection because he was my friend. How could I live with myself if I did that? They told me they'd set it up so nobody would have to know (apparently they didn't understand why I couldn't do it). Their plan was for me to have my connection meet me on a street corner and sell me some dope while they watched from a hidden location. Once the buy was made they would rush in, arrest us, take us both to jail, and then let me go. All my charges would be dropped and they would cut me loose. Luckily, their offer did not tempt me. I knew what time it was. I went to bed in the tank that night sick as a dog, but I still had my dignity. The following Monday I was transported in chains to the county jail.

8

Courts and Adjudication

In February 2001, as Grammy-winning recording artist Lil' Kim departed from an interview at a New York City radio station, her entourage encountered the companions of rap group Capone-N-Noreaga entering the building. A shoot-out ensued in broad daylight. Nearly two dozen shots were fired, and a friend of rapper Noreaga went to the hospital with a bullet wound in his back. The gunplay reportedly stemmed from a simmering dispute between Lil' Kim and Foxy Brown, a rapper who performed on Capone-N-Noreaga songs. The two women had exchanged verbal insults as parts of songs released on their respective CDs ("What Was She Thinking?" 2005).

Lil' Kim, whose real name is Kimberly Jones, reportedly failed to cooperate with police during the initial investigation of the shooting. Federal prosecutors took over the case because two prime suspects—Lil' Kim's manager, Damion Butler, and Suif Jackson, who reportedly accompanied Lil' Kim to the radio station—had prior criminal records and allegedly violated federal law by obtaining firearms and

illegally transporting them across state lines from New Jersey to New York ("What Was She Thinking?" 2005). As the investigation continued, prosecutors decided to use one of their primary tools for seeking witness testimony: the grand jury. A *grand jury* is comprised of a body of citizens summoned to hear evidence about whether a specific individual should be charged with a crime. They called Lil' Kim before a grand jury and asked her to answer questions while under oath. Because defense attorneys are not allowed to be present in the grand jury room, many observers regard grand juries as significantly influenced by the prosecutors, who have complete control over the witnesses and evidence presented in the secret proceedings. The authority of prosecutors to use grand juries as well as their own discretion to decide whether charges should be pursued contributes to the perception that prosecutors are the most powerful actors in the criminal justice process.

During her grand jury testimony, Lil' Kim denied that she had seen Butler at the radio station, and when shown

Jackson's photo, she claimed that she did not know him. Eventually, Butler and Jackson pleaded guilty to federal charges and received prison sentences of 10 and 12 years, respectively. Based on her grand jury testimony, Lil' Kim was charged with *perjury:* lying under oath in a court proceeding. For many months, Lil' Kim continued to proclaim her innocence. Her lawyer, Mel Sachs, told the reporters that parts of her grand jury testimony had been taken out of context.

During Lil' Kim's trial in 2005, Sachs had to make an important strategic decision: Would he let his client testify and face questioning by the prosecution? The Fifth Amendment protection against compelled self-incrimination protects defendants from feeling forced to testify about their own actions. However, defendants can choose to testify if they are willing to take the risk that questions asked by the prosecutor might make them appear to be untruthful in front of the jury. Ultimately, Lil' Kim took the stand and swore an oath to tell the truth. She continued to assert her innocence, but she claimed that she had a faulty memory that had affected her grand jury testimony. When it came time for the prosecutor, Assistant U.S. Attorney Cathy Seibel, to ask questions, she confronted the rapper with security photos showing Butler holding the door for her as she entered the radio station on the day of the shoot-out. Lil' Kim blamed her memory and the shock from bullets flying around her for her failure to remember Butler's presence that day. She also admitted that she knew Jackson, although she claimed that she was too traumatized by the shoot-out to remember that Jackson was present on that day (Hurtado, 2005). In addition, Jackson was brought to the courtroom from prison in order to testify against her. The prosecution's evidence persuaded the jury that Lil' Kim had lied to the grand jury. She was convicted of three counts of perjury and one count of conspiracy, resulting in a one-year prison sentence and a $50,000 fine (CNN, 2005d).

Lil' Kim's case demonstrates the power and importance of prosecutors and defense attorneys. Prosecutors determine who will be charged with a crime and which charges they will face. Prosecutors also organize and present evidence to prove guilt when defendants decline to plead guilty and instead seek a trial. Defense attorneys must advise their clients and make strategic decisions about whether to plead guilty and what tactics to use during trial. Because of her prominence and wealth, the celebrity rapper could afford to hire a well-known defense attorney and fight her case through the entire trial process. Many defendants cannot afford to hire their own attorneys. Among those with sufficient funds to hire an attorney, a large percentage will still plead guilty for reduced charges rather than risk facing a guilty verdict at trial.

The American system places great power and responsibility in the hands of attorneys for each side in a criminal case. The prosecutor and defense attorney are the most influential figures in determining the outcomes of criminal cases. Their discretionary decisions and negotiations determine people's fates. As we shall see in this chapter, the justice system's ability to handle cases and produce fair results depends on the dedication, skill, and enthusiasm of these lawyers. In addition, the lawyers who become judges assume important duties for overseeing court proceedings that decide whether accused defendants will be found guilty and punished. Later in the chapter, when you read "Careers in Criminal Justice" about employment as a lawyer, imagine how you could use a career as a lawyer to become a prosecutor, a defense attorney, or a judge.

QUESTIONS FOR INQUIRY

- What are the functions and structure of the American court system?
- What qualities should a judge have, and how are judges chosen?
- What roles does the prosecuting attorney play?
- What is the process by which criminal charges are filed, and what role does the prosecutor's discretion play in that process?
- With whom does the prosecutor interact in decision making?
- What is the day-to-day reality of criminal defense work in the United States?
- How is counsel provided for defendants who cannot afford a private attorney?
- What is the local legal culture?
- What is the courtroom workgroup?

The Functions and Structure of American Courts

The United States has a dual court system. Separate federal and state court systems handle matters throughout the nation. Other countries have a single national court system, but American rules and traditions permit states to create their own court systems to handle most legal matters, including most crimes.

In the United States, both state and federal courts use the **adversary process** to protect the rights of defendants and examine evidence to determine whether a defendant is guilty. In the adversary process, a professional attorney, trained in the rules of evidence and the strategies of advocacy, represents each side—the prosecution (government) and defense (defendant). These attorneys challenge each other's evidence and arguments while trying to persuade the judge or jury about the defendant's guilt or lack thereof. Even when the attorneys negotiate a guilty plea without going to trial, they are supposed to adopt an adversarial stance that represents the interests of their side. Although they may hold friendly and cooperative discussions, the content of these discussions often reflects probing, bluffing, compromising, and disagreeing. In the adversarial context of American courts, judges often act like referees at a sporting event. They oversee the interactions and enforce the rules without imposing their will on the presentation of evidence by attorneys. The adversary process came from England and can be found in the United States and other former British colonies. By contrast, other countries typically use an **inquisitorial process,** in which the judge takes an active role in questioning witnesses and asserts herself into the investigation of the case and the examination of evidence.

The federal courts oversee a limited range of criminal cases. For example, they deal with people accused of violating the criminal laws of the national government. Federal crimes include counterfeiting, kidnapping, smuggling, and drug trafficking, among others. But such cases account for only a small portion of the criminal cases that pass through U.S. courts each year. For every felony conviction in federal courts, more than 20 felony convictions take place in state courts, because most crimes are defined by state laws (BJS, 2002d). This disparity may grow wider as federal law enforcement agencies increasingly emphasize antiterrorism activities rather than traditional crime-control investigations. The gap is even greater for misdemeanors, because state courts bear the primary responsibility for processing the lesser offenses, such as disorderly conduct, that arise on a daily basis.

State supreme courts monitor the decisions of lower courts within their own states by interpreting state constitutions and statutes. The U.S. Supreme Court oversees both court systems by interpreting the U.S. Constitution, which protects the rights of defendants in federal and state criminal cases.

A third court system operates in several states; this adds to the issues of complexity and coordination that the country's decentralized courts face. Native Americans have tribal courts, whose authority is endorsed by congressional statutes and Supreme Court decisions, with **jurisdiction** over their own people on tribal land. The existence of tribal courts permits Native American judges to apply their people's cultural values in resolving civil lawsuits and processing certain criminal offenses (Vicenti, 1995).

THE FUNCTIONS OF COURTS

Courts serve many important functions for society. We often picture courts as the settings for criminal trials, much like those portrayed on television shows such as *Law and Order.* When courts focus on criminal matters, through bail hearings, preliminary hearings, plea bargaining, and trials, they are serving a *norm enforcement* function for society. A *norm* is a value, standard, or expectation concerning people's behavior. In other words, courts play a central role in enforcing society's rules and standards for behavior—a function that contributes to peace and stability in society. In addition, courts handle a wide variety matters beyond criminal justice and, in so doing, benefit society in ways that extend beyond merely determining the guilt of and punishments for criminal defendants.

adversary process Court process employed in the United States and other former British colonies in which lawyers for each side represent their clients' best interests in presenting evidence and formulating arguments as a means to discover the truth and protect the rights of defendants.

inquisitorial process Court process employed in most countries of the world in which the judge takes an active role in investigating the case and examining evidence by, for example, questioning witnesses.

jurisdiction The geographic territory or legal boundaries within which control may be exercised; the range of a court's authority.

Courts also handle *dispute processing* for society. When people disagree about contracts, money, property, and personal injuries in ways that they cannot resolve on their own, they file lawsuits in order to seek government intervention on their behalf. Presumably the availability of courts for dispute processing helps avoid the possibility that people will resort to violence when they become angry about disagreements with business partners, neighbors, and others. In criminal justice, the dispute-processing function plays a significant role when people file lawsuits against police officers or correctional officials for violating constitutional rights. As a result of such lawsuits, judges may order prisons to change their procedures or order police officers or their departments to pay thousands of dollars to compensate a citizen for an erroneous arrest, excessive use of force, or improper search of a home.

Courts also engage in *policy making*, especially the highest courts, such as state supreme courts and the U.S. Supreme Court. When judges interpret the U.S. Constitution or other forms of law and thereby define the rights of individuals, they are simultaneously telling police officers, correctional officers, and other officials what they can and cannot do. Such judicial decisions determine how searches will be conducted, how suspects will be questioned, and how prisons will be managed. This function makes courts in the United States especially important and powerful, because judges in other countries usually do not have the authority to tell officials throughout all levels of government how to carry out their jobs.

THE STRUCTURE OF COURTS

trial courts of limited jurisdiction Criminal courts with trial jurisdiction over misdemeanor cases and preliminary matters in felony cases. Sometimes these courts hold felony trials that may result in penalties below a specific limit.

trial courts of general jurisdiction Criminal courts with jurisdiction over all offenses, including felonies. In some states these courts also hear appeals.

appellate courts Courts that do not try criminal cases but hear appeals of decisions of lower courts.

Both the federal and state court systems have trial and appellate courts. There are three levels of courts: appellate courts, trial courts of general jurisdiction, and trial courts of limited jurisdiction.

Cases begin in a trial court, which handles determinations of guilt and sentencing. **Trial courts of limited jurisdiction** handle only misdemeanors, lawsuits for small amounts of money, or specific kinds of cases. The full range of felony cases and all other civil lawsuits are heard in **trial courts of general jurisdiction.** Trial courts are the arenas in which evidence is presented, witnesses give testimony and are questioned by attorneys, and lawyers make arguments about the guilt (or lack thereof) of criminal defendants. These are the courts in which jury trials take place and judges impose prison sentences. The federal system has no limited jurisdiction trial courts. All federal cases begin in the general jurisdiction trial courts, the U.S. district courts.

Cases move to intermediate **appellate courts** if defendants claim that errors by police or the trial court contributed to their convictions. Further appeals may be

The Supreme Court of the United States has the final word on questions concerning interpretations of the Constitution.

Photo of the Supreme Court Justices 2006: a work of the United States Federal Government filed with a state supreme court or the U.S. Supreme Court, depending on which court system the case is in and what kind of legal argument is being made. Unlike trial courts, appellate courts do not have juries, nor do lawyers present evidence. Instead, lawyers for each side make arguments about specific alleged errors of law or procedure that the trial judge failed to correct during the proceeding that determined the defendant's guilt. Thus, the written and oral arguments presented in an entire appellate case may focus on a single question, such as "Should the trial judge have excluded the defendant's confession because the police did not adequately inform her about *Miranda* rights?" Appellate judges often decide cases by issuing elaborate written opinions to explain why they answered the question at issue in a certain way.

All states have courts of last resort (usually called state supreme courts), and all but a few have an intermediate-level appellate court (usually called courts of appeals). In the federal system, the U.S. Supreme Court is the court of last resort, and the U.S. circuit courts of appeals are the intermediate appellate courts.

Although this basic, three-tiered structure is found throughout the United States, the number of courts, their names, and their specific functions vary widely. For example, the federal system has no trial courts of limited jurisdiction. In state systems, 13,000 trial courts of limited jurisdiction typically handle traffic cases, small claims, misdemeanors, and other less serious matters. These courts handle 90 percent of all criminal matters. Some limited jurisdiction courts bear responsibility for a specific category of cases, sometimes including serious offenses. Drug courts, for example, attempt to combine rehabilitation, close supervision, and the threat of punishment in order to push drug offenders to shake free from substance abuse problems (Kassebaum and Okamoto, 2001). Mental health courts, which are expanding across the country, seek to handle cases of nonviolent offenders with mental disorders and to develop appropriate treatment, supervision, and assistance instead of incarceration (Watson et al., 2001).

The federal system begins with the U.S. district courts, its trial courts of general jurisdiction. In the states, these courts have a variety of names (circuit, district, superior, and others) and are reserved for felony cases or substantial lawsuits. These are the courts in which trials take place, judges rule on evidence, and juries issue verdicts. Figure 8.1 shows the basic structure of the dual court system.

American trial courts are highly decentralized. Local political influences and community values affect the courts: Local officials determine their budgets, residents make up the staff, and operations are managed so as to fit community needs. Only a few small states have a court system organized on a statewide basis, with a central administration and state funding. In most of the country, the criminal courts operate under the state penal code but are staffed, managed, and financed by county or city governments. The federal courts, by contrast, have central administration and funding, although judges in each district help shape their own courts' practices and procedures.

Lower courts, especially at the state level, do not always display the dignity and formal procedures of general jurisdiction trial courts and appellate courts. Instead, they may function informally. Decisions and processes in one judge's courtroom may differ from those in another courtroom. In most urban areas, local courts

FIGURE 8.1

The dual court system of the United States and routes of appeal

Whether a case enters through the federal or state court system depends on which law has been broken. The right of appeal to a higher court exists in either system.

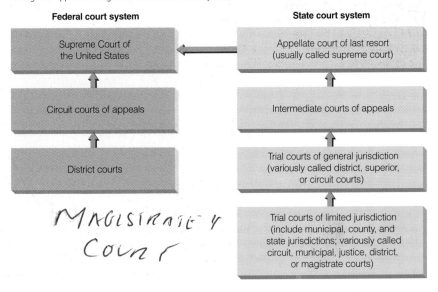

Federal court system	State court system
Supreme Court of the United States	Appellate court of last resort (usually called supreme court)
Circuit courts of appeals	Intermediate courts of appeals
District courts	Trial courts of general jurisdiction (variously called district, superior, or circuit courts)
	Trial courts of limited jurisdiction (include municipal, county, and state jurisdictions; variously called circuit, municipal, justice, district, or magistrate courts)

MAGISTRATE Y
COURT

TECHNOLOGY ISSUES IN CRIMINAL JUSTICE

The Electronic Courtroom

Increasing numbers of courtrooms in the United States rely on technology for conferences, hearings, and trials. Lawyers make PowerPoint presentations with video clips of witnesses. Judges and attorneys can have Internet access to check relevant judicial decisions and statutes during the hearings and conferences. The jury box may have multiple flat-screen monitors to give jurors a close up view of information from attorneys' laptop computers or of objects placed in evidence. The screens can also enable them to read documents and jury instructions. Hearings can be held with participants in distant locations who communicate with each other through video-conferencing technologies. Computer simulations can re-create the events leading up to a crime while enabling the jury to see the rooms or other locations that are relevant to the crime. Technology can improve communication and comprehension while it makes judicial proceedings more efficient. However, there may be unknown risks, such as issues related to computer simulations that could distort jurors' perceptions of events.

RESEARCHING THE INTERNET

Examine the details of the Courtroom 21 Project, an experimental courtroom at the law school of the College of William and Mary in Virginia. The project is designed to test new aspects of technology and demonstrate new innovations for the benefit of judicial proceedings. You can learn about this project at the corresponding website listed on the Cole/Smith Criminal Justice in America Companion Website: http://www.thomsonedu.com/criminaljustice/cole.

FOR CRITICAL ANALYSIS

Do citizens who live in jurisdictions with less tax money available for courts receive second-class justice when courts in other communities are benefiting from technologies unavailable to them?

Sources: Drawn from Sherri Day, "Electronic Order in the Court," *New York Times*, May 29, 2003, http://www.nytimes.com; John McCormick, "Scene of the Crime," *Newsweek*, February 28, 2000, p. 60.

process seemingly endless numbers of people through the crime control model (see Chapter 1), and each defendant's "day in court" usually lasts only a few minutes. People expect their local courts to adhere to the standards that reflect American values of justice. Many are critical when the courts do not meet these ideals. See "Technology Issues in Criminal Justice" for a look at how the latest devices affect courtroom justice.

CHECKPOINT

1. What is the dual court system?

2. What different categories of courts exist within each court system?

3. What does it mean for courts to be decentralized?

Answers

1. Separate federal and state court systems handling cases in the United States.

2. The federal system is made up of the Supreme Court of the United States, circuit courts of appeals, and district courts. State court systems are made up of an appellate court of last resort, intermediate appellate courts (in most states), trial courts of general jurisdiction, and trial courts of limited jurisdiction.

3. Operated, controlled, and funded by local communities, not a statewide administration. Most state and county courts are decentralized.

To Be a Judge

People tend to see judges as the most powerful actors in the criminal justice process. Their rulings and sentencing decisions influence the actions of police, defense attorneys, and prosecutors. If judges treat certain crimes lightly, for example, police and prosecutors may be less inclined to arrest and prosecute people who commit those offenses. Although judges are thought of primarily in connection with trials, some of their work—signing warrants, setting bail, arraigning defendants, accepting guilty pleas, scheduling cases—takes place outside the formal trial process.

More than any other person in the system, the judge is expected to embody justice, ensuring that the right to due process is upheld and that the defendant receives fair treatment. The prosecutor and the defense attorney each represent a "side" in a criminal case. By contrast, the judge's black robe and gavel symbolize impartiality. Both within and outside the courthouse the judge is supposed to act according to a well-defined role. Judges are expected to make careful, consistent decisions that uphold the ideal of equal justice for all citizens.

WHO BECOMES A JUDGE?

In American society the position of judge, even at the lowest level of the judicial hierarchy, brings high status. Public service, political power, and prestige in the community may matter more than a high-paying job to those who aspire to the judiciary. Many judges take a significant cut in pay to assume a position on the bench. Unlike private practice attorneys, who often work over 40 hours per week preparing cases and counseling clients, judges can typically control their own working hours and schedules better. Although judges carry heavy caseloads, they frequently decide for themselves when to go home at the end of the workday. The ability to control one's own work schedule is therefore an additional attraction for lawyers interested in becoming judges.

Historically, the vast majority of judges have been white men with strong political connections. Women and members of minority groups had few opportunities to enter the legal profession prior to the 1960s and thus were seldom considered for judgeships. By the late twentieth century, political factors in many cities dictated that judges be drawn from specific racial, religious, and ethnic groups. One study found, however, that only 3.6 percent of state court judges were African American, most of them serving in the lower criminal courts (Graham, 1995:219). Comparing the racial and ethnic makeup of the judiciary with the race and ethnicity of many of the defendants in urban courts raises important questions. If middle-aged white men hold nearly all the power to make judgments about people from other segments of society, will people believe that decisions about guilt and punishment are being made in an unfair manner? Will people think that punishment is being imposed on behalf of a privileged segment of society rather than on behalf of the entire, diverse U.S. society?

Further, within these questions lurk concerns regarding the essential American values of equality, fairness, and equal opportunity. Indeed, the equal protection clause of the Fourteenth Amendment of the Constitution demonstrates a formal commitment to use law to combat discrimination. However, the political connections necessary to gain judgeships continue to disadvantage women and members of racial minority groups in many communities. Because judges symbolize the law as well as make important decisions about law, the lack of diversity in the judiciary provides a visible contrast with American values related to equal opportunity.

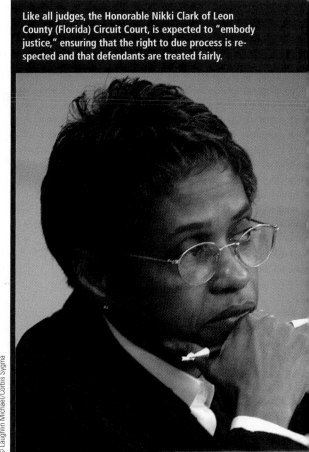

Like all judges, the Honorable Nikki Clark of Leon County (Florida) Circuit Court, is expected to "embody justice," ensuring that the right to due process is respected and that defendants are treated fairly.

© Laughlin Michael/Corbis Sygma

FUNCTIONS OF THE JUDGE

Although people usually think that a judge's job is to preside at trials, in reality the work of most judges extends to all aspects of the judicial process. Defendants see a judge whenever decisions about their future are being made: when bail is set, pretrial motions are made, guilty pleas are accepted, a trial is conducted, a sentence is pronounced, and appeals are filed (see Figure 8.2). However, judges' duties are not limited to making such decisions about criminal defendants within the courtroom; judges also perform administrative tasks outside of it. Judges have three major roles: adjudicator, negotiator, and administrator.

Adjudicator   Judges must assume a neutral stance in overseeing the contest between the prosecution and the defense. They must apply the law in ways that uphold the rights of the accused in decisions about detention, plea, trial, and sentence. Judges receive a certain amount of discretion in performing these tasks—for example, in setting bail—but they must do so according to the law. They must avoid any conduct that could appear biased (Goldschmidt and Shaman, 1996).

Negotiator   Many decisions that determine the fates of defendants take place outside of public view, in the judge's private chambers. These decisions come about through negotiations between prosecutors and defense attorneys about plea bargains,

FIGURE 8.2
Actions of a trial court judge in processing a felony case
Throughout the process, the judge ensures that legal standards are upheld; he or she maintains courtroom decorum, protects the rights of the accused, meets the requirement of a speedy trial, and ensures that case records are maintained properly.

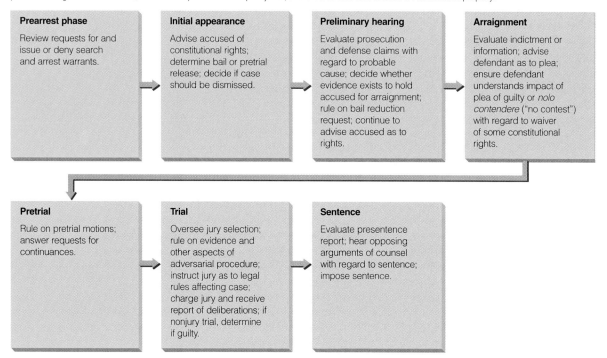

Prearrest phase

Review requests for and issue or deny search and arrest warrants.

Initial appearance

Advise accused of constitutional rights; determine bail or pretrial release; decide if case should be dismissed.

Preliminary hearing

Evaluate prosecution and defense claims with regard to probable cause; decide whether evidence exists to hold accused for arraignment; rule on bail reduction request; continue to advise accused as to rights.

Arraignment

Evaluate indictment or information; advise defendant as to plea; ensure defendant understands impact of plea of guilty or *nolo contendere* ("no contest") with regard to waiver of some constitutional rights.

Pretrial

Rule on pretrial motions; answer requests for continuances.

Trial

Oversee jury selection; rule on evidence and other aspects of adversarial procedure; instruct jury as to legal rules affecting case; charge jury and receive report of deliberations; if nonjury trial, determine if guilty.

Sentence

Evaluate presentence report; hear opposing arguments of counsel with regard to sentence; impose sentence.

sentencing, and bail conditions. Judges spend much of their time in their chambers talking with prosecutors and defense attorneys. They often encourage the parties to work out a guilty plea or agree to proceed in a certain way. The judge may act as a referee, keeping both sides on track in accordance with the law. Sometimes the judge takes a more active part in the negotiations, suggesting terms for an agreement or even pressuring one side to accept an agreement.

Administrator   A seldom-recognized function of most judges is managing the courthouse. In urban areas a professional court administrator may direct the people who keep records, schedule cases, and do the many other jobs that keep a system functioning. But even in cities, judges are in charge of their own courtroom and staff. In rural areas, which do not usually employ professional court administrators, the judges' administrative tasks may expand to include managing labor relations, budgeting, and maintenance of the courthouse building. As administrator, the judge must deal with political actors such as county commissioners, legislators, and members of the state executive bureaucracy. Chief judges in large courts may also use their administrative powers to push other judges to cooperate in advancing the court's goals of processing cases in a timely manner (Jacob, 1973). For judges whose training as lawyers focused on learning law and courtroom advocacy skills, managing a complex organization with a sizable budget and many employees can pose a major challenge (C. E. Smith and Feldman, 2001; Wasby, 2003).

HOW TO BECOME A JUDGE

The quality of justice depends to a great extent on the quality of those who make decisions about guilt and punishment. Because judges have the power to deprive a citizen of his or her liberty through a prison sentence, judges should be thoughtful, fair, and impartial. When a judge is rude or hasty or allows the courtroom to become noisy and crowded, the public may lose confidence in the fairness and effectiveness of the criminal justice process (see the Close Up box).

CLOSE UP

Improper Judicial Behavior

During an arraignment in New York for a defendant charged with assaulting his wife, the judge reportedly said, "What's wrong with that? You've got to keep them in line once in a while." When authorities acted to remove the judge from office, the judge's lawyer said that the judge makes lighthearted comments from the bench but does not misuse his position. In California a judge reportedly indicated to a good-looking defendant that other inmates at the prison would find him attractive. The judge also allegedly called a prosecutor in a drunken-driving case a "hypocrite" who was in all probability guilty of the same offense as the defendant. When a complaint was filed with the state's Commission on Judicial Performance, the judge's attorney claimed that the comments were taken out of context. In another New York case, a judge charged off the bench, grabbing and screaming at a lawyer during a courtroom proceeding.

 RESEARCHING THE INTERNET

To read about ethics rules for judges, see the Code of Judicial Conduct for judges in Illinois at the corresponding website listed on the Cole/Smith Criminal Justice in America Companion Website: http://www.thomsonedu.com/criminaljustice/cole.

FOR CRITICAL ANALYSIS

Do the statements reportedly made by these judges harm the image of the courts? If so, how? If these statements are improper, what should happen to judges who say such things? If the judges apologize, should they receive another opportunity to behave properly? Is there any way to make sure that judges act at all times in accordance with the proper image of their office?

Sources: Drawn from "Court Upholds Removal of Rockland Judge," *New York Times,* March 31, 1999 (Metro News); Richard Marosi, "Hard-line Judge Is Being Judged Herself," *Los Angeles Times,* May 7, 1999, p. B1; Robert H. Tembeckjian, "How Judges Hide from Justice," *New York Times,* May 22, 2005, http://www.nytimes.com.

TABLE 8.1   Methods Used by States to Select Judges

States use different methods to select judges. Note that many judges are initially appointed to fill a vacancy, giving them an advantage if they must run for election at a later date.

Partisan Election	Nonpartisan Election	Gubernatorial Appointment	Legislative Selection	Merit Selection
Alabama	Arizona (some trial courts)	Connecticut	Rhode Island (appellate)	Alaska
Arkansas	California (trial)	Delaware	South Carolina	Arizona (appellate)
Illinois	Florida (trial)	Maine	Virginia	California (appellate)
Indiana (trial)	Georgia	Massachusetts		Colorado
Mississippi	Idaho	New Hampshire		Florida (appellate)
New Mexico (retention)	Kentucky	New Jersey		Hawaii
New York (trial)	Louisiana	New York (appellate)		Indiana (appellate)
North Carolina	Michigan	Rhode Island (trial)		Iowa
Pennsylvania (initial)	Minnesota			Kansas
Tennessee (supreme and trial)	Montana			Maryland
Texas	Nevada			Missouri
West Virginia	North Dakota			Nebraska
	Ohio			New Mexico (initial)
	Oklahoma (trial)			Oklahoma (appellate)
	Oregon			South Dakota (appellate)
	Pennsylvania (retention)			Tennessee (intermediate appellate)
	South Dakota (trial)			Utah
	Washington			Vermont
	Wisconsin			Wyoming

Source: *The Book of the States, 1998–1999 Edition* (Lexington, KY: Council of State Governments, 1998), 135–37.

Six methods are used to select state trial court judges: gubernatorial appointment, legislative selection, merit selection, **nonpartisan election, partisan election,** and a mixture of methods. Table 8.1 shows the method used in each of the states. All the methods bring up persistent concerns about the desired qualities of judges.

Selection by public voting occurs in more than half the states and has long been part of this nation's tradition. This method of judicial selection embodies the

nonpartisan election An election in which candidates' party affiliations are not listed on the ballot.

partisan election An election in which candidates openly endorsed by political parties are presented to voters for selection.

WHAT AMERICANS THINK

Question 1: "Do you agree or disagree with the statement 'Judges' decisions are influenced by political considerations'?"

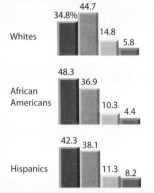

Whites
34.8% 44.7
       14.8
            5.8

African Americans
48.3 36.9
      10.3 4.4

Hispanics
42.3 38.1
      11.3 8.2

Question 2: "Do you agree or disagree with the statement 'Elected judges are influenced by having to raise campaign funds'?"

Whites
31% 46.5
     15.8 6.7

African Americans
44.3 35.1
      13.9 6.7

Hispanics
42.1 38.2
      12.9 6.7

■ Strongly agree   ■ Somewhat agree
■ Somewhat disagree ■ Strongly disagree

Go to http://www.thomsonedu.com/criminaljustice/cole to compare your opinion on this issue with the opinions of other criminal justice students.

Source: National Center for State Courts, *How the Public Views the State Courts: A 1999 National Survey*, report presented at the National Conference on Public Trust and Confidence in the Justice System, Washington, DC, May 14, 1999.

merit selection A reform plan by which judges are nominated by a commission and appointed by the governor for a given period. When the term expires, the voters approve or disapprove the judge for a succeeding term. If the judge is disapproved, the committee nominates a successor for the governor's appointment.

underlying American value of democracy because it permits the citizens to control the choice of individuals who will receive the power to make decisions in civil and criminal cases. The fulfillment of this American value also helps ensure that judges remain connected to the community and demonstrate sensitivity to the community's priorities and concerns. The American value of democracy may, however, have detrimental consequences if it pressures judges to follow a community's prejudices rather than make independent decisions using their best judgment in each case.

When lawyers are first elected to serve as judges, they obviously have no prior experience in deciding cases and supervising courthouse operations. As a result, judges must learn on the job. This clashes with the belief that judges are trained to "find the law" and apply neutral judgments (M. G. Hall, 1995). In Europe, by contrast, prospective judges are given special training in law school to become professional judges. These trained judges must serve as assistant judges and lower court judges before they can become judges in general trial and appellate courts (Provine, 1996).

Election campaigns for lower-court judgeships tend to be low-key contests marked by little controversy. Usually, only a small portion of the voters participate, judgeships are not prominent on the ballot, and candidates do not discuss controversial issues because of ethical considerations. Most candidates run on the same two claims that reveal relatively little to the voters about how they will make specific decisions as judges: "I have the best prior experience" and "I'll be tough on crime." Recent research reveals, however, that even lower-level judicial races are becoming more competitive as candidates raise money and seek connections with interest groups (Abbe and Herrnson, 2002). Political parties typically want local judgeships to be elected posts, because they can use courthouse staff positions to reward party loyalists. When a party member wins a judgeship, courthouse jobs may become available for campaign workers, because the judge often chooses clerks, bailiffs, and secretaries.

In contrast, elections for seats on state supreme courts frequently receive statewide media attention. Because of the importance of state supreme courts as policy-making institutions, political parties and interest groups may devote substantial energy to organizing and funding the election campaigns of their preferred candidates. When organized interests contribute tens of thousands of dollars to judicial campaigns, questions sometimes arise about whether the successful candidates who received those contributions will favor the interests of their donors when they begin to decide court cases (Champagne and Cheek, 1996; T. V. Reid, 1996).

Some states have tried to reduce the influence of political parties in the selection of judges while still allowing voters to select judges. These states hold nonpartisan elections in which only the names of candidates, not their party affiliations, appear on the ballot. However, political parties are often strongly involved in such elections. In Ohio, for example, the Republican and Democratic political parties hold their own primary elections to choose the judicial candidates whose names will go on the nonpartisan ballot for the general election (Felice and Kilwein, 1992). In other states, party organizations raise and spend money on behalf of candidates in nonpartisan elections.

Public opinion data show that Americans express concern about the influence of politics on judges, especially with respect to elected judges (see "What Americans Think"). If so many Americans are concerned about judges' involvement in political campaigns, why do so many states still rely on elections to select judges? See "Real-World Activity" at the end of this chapter to consider an application of this issue.

Merit selection, which combines appointment and election, was first used in Missouri in 1940 and has since spread to other states. When a judgeship becomes vacant, a nominating commission made up of citizens and attorneys evaluates potential appointees and sends the governor the names of three candidates, from which the replacement is chosen. After one year, a referendum is held to decide whether the judge will stay on the bench. The ballot asks, "Shall Judge X remain in office?" The judge who wins a majority vote serves out the term and can then be listed on the ballot at the next election.

Merit selection is designed to remove politics from the selection of judges and supposedly allows the voters to unseat judges. However, interest groups sometimes mount publicity campaigns during retention elections in order to turn out judges with whom they disagree on a single issue or to open an important court seat so that a like-minded governor can appoint a sympathetic replacement. It may be difficult for judges to counteract a barrage of one-sided inflammatory television commercials focusing on a single issue such as capital punishment (T. V. Reid, 2000). If merit-selected judges feel intimidated by interest groups that might threaten their jobs at the next retention election, the independence of the judiciary will diminish.

CHECKPOINT

Answers

4. What are judges' main functions? ———————→ 4. Adjudicator, negotiator, administrator.

5. Why do political parties often prefer that judges be elected? ———→ 5. To ensure that courthouse positions are allocated to party workers.

6. What are the steps in the merit selection process? ————→ 6. When a vacancy occurs, a nominating commission is appointed that sends the governor the names of approved candidates. The governor must fill the vacancy from the list. After a year's term, a referendum is held to ask the voters whether the judge should be retained.

The Prosecutorial System

Prosecuting attorneys make discretionary decisions about whether to pursue criminal charges, which charges to make, and what sentence to recommend. They represent the government in pursuing criminal charges against the accused. Except in a few states, no higher authority second-guesses or changes these decisions. Thus, prosecutors are more independent than most other public officials. As with other aspects of American government, prosecution is mainly a task of state and local governments. Because most crimes violate state laws, county prosecutors bring charges against suspects in court.

Federal cases are prosecuted by **United States attorneys.** One U.S. attorney and a staff of assistant U.S. attorneys prosecute cases in each of the 94 U.S. district courts (Lochner, 2002). Each state has an elected **state attorney general,** who usually has the power to bring prosecutions in certain cases. A state attorney general may, for example, handle a statewide consumer fraud case if a chain of auto repair shops is suspected of overcharging customers. In Alaska, Delaware, and Rhode Island, the state attorney general also directs all local prosecutions. However, the vast majority of state criminal cases are handled in the 2,341 county-level offices of the prosecuting attorney—known in various states as the district attorney, state's attorney, commonwealth attorney, or county attorney—who pursues cases that violate state law. The number of prosecutors who work in these offices increased by more than 35 percent between 1990 and 2001 (DeFrances, 2002). Prosecutors have the power to make independent decisions about which cases to pursue and what charges to file. They can also drop charges and negotiate arrangements for guilty pleas.

In rural areas the prosecutor's office may consist of merely the prosecuting attorney and a part-time assistant. By contrast, some urban jurisdictions such as Los Angeles have 500 assistant prosecutors and numerous legal assistants and investigators, and the office is organized according to various types of crimes. Many assistant prosecutors seek to use the trial experience gained in the prosecutor's office as a means of moving on to a more highly paid position in a private law firm.

prosecuting attorney A legal representative of the state with sole responsibility for bringing criminal charges. In some states this person is referred to as the district attorney, state's attorney, or county attorney.

United States attorneys Officials responsible for the prosecution of crimes that violate the laws of the United States. Appointed by the president and assigned to a U.S. district court jurisdiction.

state attorney general Chief legal officer of a state, responsible for both civil and criminal matters.

POLITICS AND PROSECUTION

In all states except Connecticut and New Jersey, prosecutors are elected, usually for a four-year term; local politics thus heavily influence the office. By seeking to please voters, many prosecutors have tried to use their local office as a springboard to a higher office—such as state legislator, governor, or member of Congress. Further, although the power of prosecutors flows directly from their legal duties, prosecutors can often mesh their own ambitions with the needs of a political party. The appointment of assistant prosecutors offers a chance to recruit bright young lawyers for the party.

Prosecutors may choose certain cases for prosecution in order to gain the favor of voters, or investigate charges against political opponents and public officials to get the public's attention. Political factors may also cause prosecutors to apply their powers unevenly within a community. Prosecutors' discretionary power can create the impression that some groups or individuals receive harsh treatment while others receive protection.

Discretion in decision making also creates the risk of discrimination. For example, some scholars see prosecutors' decisions as reflecting biases based on race, social class, and gender (Frohmann, 1997), but other researchers believe that studies have not yet documented the full extent of discrimination by prosecutors (S. Walker, Spohn, and DeLeone, 2003). Several studies raise questions about discrimination in specific situations, such as prosecutors' decisions to seek the death penalty (Sorensen and Wallace, 1999). For the criminal justice system to fulfill American values concerning equality and fairness, prosecutors must use their decision-making authority carefully to avoid inequality and injustice.

THE PROSECUTOR'S INFLUENCE

Prosecutors have great influence because they are concerned with all aspects of the criminal justice process. By contrast, other decision makers are involved in only part of the process. From arrest to final disposition of a case, prosecutors can make decisions that largely determine the defendant's fate. The prosecutor chooses the cases to be prosecuted, selects the charges to be brought, recommends the bail amount, approves agreements with the defendant, and urges the judge to impose a particular sentence (Kingsnorth, MacIntosh, and Sutherland, 2002).

Throughout the justice process, prosecutors' links with the other actors in the system—police, defense attorneys, judges—shape the prosecutors' decisions. Prosecutors may, for example, recommend bail amounts and sentences that match the preferences of particular judges. They may make "tough" recommendations in front of "tough" judges but tone down their arguments before judges who favor leniency or rehabilitation. Similarly, the other actors in the system may adjust their decisions and actions to match the preferences of the prosecutor. For example, police officers' investigation and arrest practices tend to reflect the prosecutor's priorities. Thus, prosecutors influence the decisions of others while also shaping their own actions in ways that reinforce their relationships with police, defense attorneys, and judges.

Prosecutors gain additional power from the fact that their decisions and actions take place away from public view. For example, a prosecutor and a defense attorney

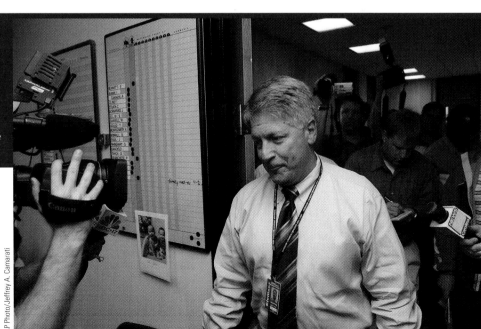

District Attorney Mike Nifong returns to his office while being questioned by the media at the Durham County (North Carolina) Judicial Building, April 2006. Nifong was the lead prosecutor in the rape allegations against members of the Duke University lacrosse team. Prosecutors have great influence over the decisions of others—police, defense attorneys, and judges.

AP Photo/Jeffrey A. Camarati

may strike a bargain whereby the prosecutor reduces a charge in exchange for a guilty plea or drops a charge if the defendant agrees to seek psychiatric help. In such instances they reach a decision on a case in a way that is nearly invisible to the public.

THE PROSECUTOR'S ROLES

As "lawyers for the state," prosecutors face conflicting pressures to press charges vigorously against lawbreakers while also upholding justice and the rights of the accused. These pressures are often called "the prosecutor's dilemma." In the adversary system, prosecutors must do everything they can to win a conviction, yet as members of the legal profession they must see that justice is done even if it means that the accused is not convicted. Even so, they always face the risk of "prosecutor's bias," sometimes called a "prosecution complex." Although they are supposed to represent all the people, including the accused, prosecutors may view themselves as instruments of law enforcement. Thus, as advocates on behalf of the state, their strong desire to close each case with a conviction may keep them from recognizing unfair procedures or evidence of innocence.

Although all prosecutors must uphold the law and pursue charges against lawbreakers, they may perform these tasks in different ways. Their personal values and professional goals, along with the political climate of their city or county, may cause them to define the prosecutor's role differently than do prosecutors in other places. For example, a prosecutor who believes that young offenders can be rehabilitated may define the role differently than one who believes that young offenders should receive the same punishments as adults. One might send juveniles to counseling programs, whereas the other would seek to process them though the adult system of courts and corrections. A prosecutor with no assistants and few resources for conducting full-blown jury trials may be forced to embrace effective plea bargaining, whereas a prosecutor in a wealthier county may have more options when deciding whether to take cases to trial.

When prosecutors are asked about their roles, the following four emerge:

1. *Trial counsel for the police.* Prosecutors who see their main function in this light believe that they should reflect the views of law enforcement in the courtroom and take a crime-fighter stance in public.

2. *House counsel for the police.* These prosecutors believe that their main function is to give legal advice so that arrests will stand up in court.

3. *Representative of the court.* Such prosecutors believe that their main function is to enforce the rules of due process to ensure that the police act according to the law and uphold the rights of defendants.

4. *Elected official.* These prosecutors may be most responsive to public opinion. The political impact of their decisions is one of their major concerns.

Each of these roles involves a different view of the prosecutor's "clients" as well as his or her own responsibilities. In the first two roles, prosecutors appear to believe that the police are the clients of their legal practice. Take a moment to think about who might be the clients of prosecutors who view themselves as representatives of the court or as elected officials.

DISCRETION OF THE PROSECUTOR

Because they have such broad discretion, prosecutors can shape their decisions to fit different interests. They might base their decisions on a desire to impress voters through tough "throw-the-book-at-them" charges in a highly publicized case (Maschke, 1995). Their decisions might stem from their personal values, such as an emphasis on leniency and rehabilitation for young offenders. They may also shape their decisions to please local judges by, for example, accepting plea agreements that will keep the judges from being burdened by too many time-consuming trials. Prosecutors who have doubts about whether the available evidence actually proves the defendant's guilt may just shrug their shoulders and say, "I'll just let the jury decide" rather than face public criticism for dropping charges. Any or all of these motives may shape prosecutors' decisions because there is generally no higher authority to tell prosecutors how they must do their jobs. From the time the police turn a case over to the prosecutor, the prosecutor has almost complete control over decisions about charges and plea agreements.

Research has also shown that the staffing levels of individual prosecutor's offices may affect decisions to pursue felony charges (P. Walker, 1998). If offices lack sufficient resources to pursue all possible cases, prosecutors may establish priorities and then reduce or dismiss charges in cases deemed less important.

If you were a prosecutor, what would you consider to be the most important factors in deciding whether to pursue a case? Would you have any concerns about the possibility of prosecuting an innocent person? If a prosecutor pursues a case against someone who the prosecutor does not really believe is guilty of a crime, does this pose an ethical problem? As you read "A Question of Ethics" at the end of the chapter, consider what you would do if you were the prosecutor assigned to the case.

After deciding that a case should be prosecuted, the prosecutor has great freedom in deciding what charges to file. Criminal incidents may involve several laws, so the prosecutor can often bring a single charge or more than one. Suppose that Smith, who is armed, breaks into a grocery store, assaults the proprietor, and robs the cash drawer. What charges can the prosecutor file? By virtue of having committed the robbery, the accused can be charged with at least four crimes: breaking and entering, assault, armed robbery, and carrying a dangerous weapon. Other charges or **counts** may be added, depending on the nature of the incident. A forger, for instance, may be charged with one count for each act of forgery committed. By filing as many charges as possible, the prosecutor strengthens his or her position in plea negotiations. In effect, the prosecutor can use discretion in deciding the number of charges and thus increase the prosecution's supply of "bargaining chips."

The discretionary power to set charges does not give the prosecutor complete control over plea bargaining, however. Defense attorneys strengthen their position in the **discovery** process, in which information from the prosecutor's case file must be made available to the defense. For example, the defense has the right to see any statements made by the accused during interrogation by the police, as well as the results of any physical or psychological tests. This information tells the defense attorney about the strengths and weaknesses of the prosecution's case. The defense attorney may use it to decide whether a case is hopeless or whether engaging in tough negotiations is worthwhile.

The prosecutor's discretion does not end with the decision to file a certain charge. After the charge has been made, the prosecutor may reduce it in exchange for a guilty plea or enter a notation of *nolle prosequi* (*nol. pros.*). The latter is a freely made decision to drop the charge, either as a whole or as to one or more counts. When a prosecutor decides to drop charges, no higher authorities can force him or her to reinstate them. When guilty pleas are entered, the prosecutor uses discretion in recommending a sentence.

KEY RELATIONSHIPS OF THE PROSECUTOR

Prosecutors do not base their decisions solely on formal policies and role conceptions (Fridell, 1990). Relationships with other actors in the justice system also influence their choices. Despite their independent authority, prosecutors must consider how police, judges, and others will react. They depend on these other officials in order to prosecute cases successfully. In turn, the success of police, judges, and correctional officials depends on prosecutors' effectiveness in identifying and convicting lawbreakers. Thus, these officials build exchange relationships in which they cooperate with each other.

Police   Prosecutors depend on the police to provide both the suspects and the evidence needed to convict lawbreakers. Because they cannot investigate crimes on their own, prosecutors cannot control the types of cases brought to them. Thus, the police control the initiation of the criminal justice process by investigating crimes and arresting suspects. These actions may be influenced by various factors, such as pressure on police to establish an impressive crime-clearance record. As a result,

count Each separate offense of which a person is accused in an indictment or an information.

discovery A prosecutor's pretrial disclosure to the defense of facts and evidence to be introduced at trial.

nolle prosequi An entry, made by a prosecutor on the record of a case and announced in court, indicating that the charges specified will not be prosecuted. In effect, the charges are thereby dismissed.

police actions may create problems for prosecutors if, for example, the police make many arrests without gathering enough evidence to ensure conviction.

Victims and Witnesses   Prosecutors depend on the cooperation of victims and witnesses. Although prosecutors can pursue a case whether or not a victim wishes to press charges, many prosecutors will not do so when the key testimony and other necessary evidence must come from a victim who is unwilling to cooperate (Dawson and Dinovitzer, 2001). Prosecutors need the cooperation of people who have witnessed crimes.

The decision to prosecute is often based on an assessment of the victim's role in his or her own victimization and the victim's credibility as a witness. If a victim has a criminal record, the prosecutor may choose not to pursue the case, in the belief that a jury would not consider the victim a credible witness—despite the fact that the jury will never learn that the victim has a criminal record. If a victim is poorly dressed, uneducated, or somewhat inarticulate, the prosecutor may be inclined to dismiss charges out of fear that a jury would find the victim unpersuasive (Stanko, 1988). Research indicates that victim characteristics, such as moral character, behavior at time of incident, and age, influence decisions to prosecute sexual assault cases more than does the actual strength of the evidence against the suspect (Spears and Spohn, 1997). Studies have shown that prosecutions succeed most when aimed at defendants accused of committing crimes against strangers (Boland et al., 1983). When the victim is an acquaintance, a friend, or even a relative of the defendant, he or she may refuse to act as a witness, and prosecutors and juries may view the offense as less serious.

Judges and Courts   The sentencing history of each judge gives prosecutors an idea of how a case may be treated in the courtroom. Prosecutors may decide to drop a case if they believe that the judge assigned to it will not impose a serious punishment. Because prosecutors' offices have limited resources, they cannot afford to waste time pursuing charges in front of a specific judge if that judge shows a pattern of dismissing those types of charges.

The Community   Public opinion and the media can play a crucial role in creating an environment that either supports or scrutinizes the prosecutor. Like police chiefs and school superintendents, county prosecutors will not remain in office long if they fall out of step with community values. They will likely lose at the next election to an opponent who has a better sense of the community's priorities.

Many cities are experimenting with innovations designed to enhance communication and understanding between prosecutors and the community. One innovation called *community prosecution* gives specific assistant prosecutors continuing responsibilities for particular neighborhoods. These prosecutors can become known to people in the neighborhood, they can attend community meetings and social functions, and they can learn about residents' specific concerns. At the same time, they are building relationships that will help them gather information and identify witnesses when crimes occur (Boland, 2001).

Prosecutors' relationships and interactions with police, victims, defense attorneys, judges, and the community form the core of the exchange relations that shape decision making in criminal cases. Other relationships, such as those with news media, federal and state officials, legislators, and political party officials, also influence prosecutors' decisions. This long list of actors illustrates that prosecutors do not base their decisions solely on whether a law was broken. The occurrence of a crime is only the first step in a decision-making process that may vary from one case to the next. Sometimes charges are dropped or reduced. Sometimes plea bargains are negotiated quickly. Sometimes cases move through the system to a complete jury trial. In every instance, relationships and interactions with a variety of actors both within and outside the justice system shape prosecutors' discretionary decisions.

DECISION-MAKING POLICIES

Despite the many factors that potentially affect prosecutors' decisions, we can draw some general conclusions about how prosecutors approach their office. Prosecutors develop their own policies on how cases will be handled. These policies shape the decisions made by the assistant prosecutors and thus greatly affect the administration of justice. Within the same state, prosecutors may pursue different goals in forming policies on which cases to pursue, which ones to drop, and which ones to plea bargain. For example, prosecutors who wish to maintain a high conviction rate will drop cases with weak evidence. Others, concerned about using limited resources effectively, will focus most of their time and energy on the most serious cases.

Some prosecutors' offices make extensive use of screening and tend not to press charges. Guilty pleas are the main method of processing cases in some offices, whereas pleas of not guilty strain the courts' trial resources in others. Some offices process cases soon after the police bring them to the prosecutor's attention, sometimes diverting or referring them to other agencies; others have disposition occurring as late as the first day of trial. The period from the receipt of the police report to the start of the trial is thus a time of review in which the prosecutor uses discretion to decide what actions should be taken.

The **accusatory process** is the series of activities that take place from the moment a suspect is arrested and booked by the police to the moment the formal charge—in the form of an indictment or information—is filed with the court. In an indictment, evidence is presented to a grand jury made up of citizens who determine whether to issue a formal charge. Grand juries are used in the federal system and in states where legislatures have mandated their use for serious crime. In jurisdictions that do not use grand juries, the prosecutor has full control of the charging decision when the filing of an information initiates prosecution. In other words, when an information is used to present formal charges, no body of citizens can protect a suspect from wrongful prosecution until the case goes to trial and a trial jury hears the case. However, earlier in the process judges may decide at preliminary hearings that there is insufficient evidence to support the pursuit of the charges; in such circumstances, a judge can order that the charges be dismissed.

Clearly the prosecutor's established policies and decisions play a key role in determining whether charges will be filed against a defendant. Keep in mind, though, that the prosecutor's decision-making power is not limited to decisions about charges. As shown in Figure 8.3, the prosecutor makes important decisions at each stage, both before and after a defendant's guilt is determined. Because the prosecutor's involvement

accusatory process The series of events from the arrest of a suspect to the filing of a formal charge (through an indictment or information) with the court.

ThomsonNOW

Improve your grade on the exam with Personalized Study! For reinforcement resources and a mastery check of The Prosecutorial System, go to www.thomsonedu.com/thomsonnow.

FIGURE 8.3

Typical actions of a prosecuting attorney in processing a felony case

The prosecutor has certain responsibilities at various points in the process. At each point the prosecutor is an advocate for the state's case against the accused.

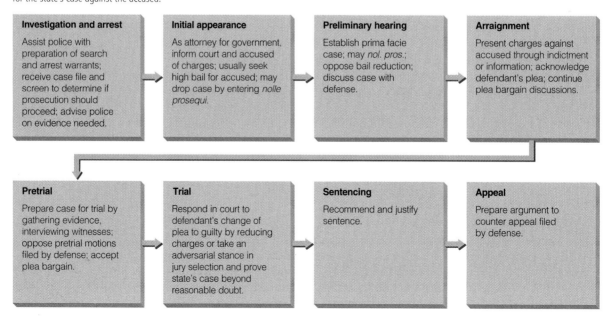

Investigation and arrest	Initial appearance	Preliminary hearing	Arraignment
Assist police with preparation of search and arrest warrants; receive case file and screen to determine if prosecution should proceed; advise police on evidence needed.	As attorney for government, inform court and accused of charges; usually seek high bail for accused; may drop case by entering *nolle prosequi*.	Establish prima facie case; may *nol. pros.*; oppose bail reduction; discuss case with defense.	Present charges against accused through indictment or information; acknowledge defendant's plea; continue plea bargain discussions.

Pretrial	Trial	Sentencing	Appeal
Prepare case for trial by gathering evidence, interviewing witnesses; oppose pretrial motions filed by defense; accept plea bargain.	Respond in court to defendant's change of plea to guilty by reducing charges or take an adversarial stance in jury selection and prove state's case beyond reasonable doubt.	Recommend and justify sentence.	Prepare argument to counter appeal filed by defense.

and influence span the justice process, from seeking search warrants during early investigations to arguing against postconviction appeals, the prosecutor is a highly influential actor in criminal cases. No other participant in the system is involved in so many different stages of the criminal process.

CHECKPOINT

Answers

7. What are the roles of the prosecutor? ⟶ 7. Trial counsel for the police, house counsel for the police, representative of the court, elected official.

8. How does the prosecutor use discretion to decide how to treat each defendant? ⟶ 8. The prosecutor can determine the type and number of charges, reduce the charges in exchange for a guilty plea, or enter a *nolle prosequi* (thereby dropping some or all of the charges).

9. What are the prosecutor's key exchange relationships? ⟶ 9. Police, victims and witnesses, defense attorneys, judges, the community.

The Defense Attorney: Image and Reality

In an adversary process, the **defense attorney** is the lawyer who represents accused and convicted persons in their dealings with the criminal justice system. Most Americans have seen defense attorneys in action on television dramas such as *Boston Legal* and *Law and Order*. In these dramas defense attorneys vigorously battle the prosecution, and the jury often finds their clients innocent. These images gain strength from news stories about defense attorneys such as Johnnie Cochran and Robert Shapiro, whose efforts helped acquit O. J. Simpson of murder charges in 1995. Although these images are drawn from reality, they do not give a true picture of the typical defense attorney, focusing as they do on the few highly publicized cases that result in jury trials. By contrast, most cases find resolution through plea bargaining, discretionary dismissals, and similar decisions by actors in the justice system. In these cases the defense attorney may seem less like the prosecutor's adversary and more like a partner in the effort to dispose of cases as quickly and efficiently as possible through negotiation.

All the key courtroom actors discussed in this chapter—judges, prosecutors, and defense attorneys—are lawyers who met the same educational requirements. After becoming lawyers, however, they made different decisions about what career to pursue. As you read "Careers in Criminal Justice," imagine which legal career would appeal most to you. Some people cannot understand why anyone would want to be a defense attorney and work on behalf of criminals. But remember that defense attorneys work for people who are *accused* of crimes. Under the American system of criminal justice, defendants are supposedly presumed to be innocent. Indeed, many of them will have charges reduced or dismissed. Others will be not guilty. Thus, characterizing defense attorneys as representing only criminals is simply not accurate. Moreover, many lawyers who choose to work as defense attorneys see themselves as defending the Bill of Rights by ensuring that prosecutors actually respect the Constitution and provide proof beyond a reasonable doubt before defendants are convicted and punished.

THE ROLE OF THE DEFENSE ATTORNEY

To be effective, defense attorneys must have knowledge of law and procedure, skill in investigation, experience in advocacy, and, in many cases, relationships with prosecutors and judges that will help a defendant obtain the best possible outcome. In the American legal system the defense attorney performs the key function of making sure that the prosecution proves its case in court or has substantial evidence of guilt before a guilty plea leads to conviction and punishment.

As shown in Figure 8.4, the defense attorney advises the defendant and protects his or her constitutional rights at each stage of the criminal justice process. The defense attorney advises the defendant during questioning by the police, represents him or her at each arraignment and hearing, and serves as advocate for the defendant during the appeal process. Without knowing the technical details of law

defense attorney The lawyer who represents accused offenders and convicted offenders in their dealings with criminal justice.

Billy Martin, attorney for former New Jersey Nets basketball star Jayson Williams, gives closing arguments during William's manslaughter trial in a New Jersey courtroom. An effective defense requires respect, openness, and trust between attorney and client.

AP Photo/Ed Pagliarini, Pool

CAREERS IN CRIMINAL JUSTICE

Lawyer

NATURE OF THE WORK

Lawyers who work as judges, prosecutors, and defense attorneys all spend a significant amount of time in offices doing legal research, preparing legal documents, and reviewing legal papers drawn up by others. In the courtroom, they listen to the arguments of lawyers and, if representing clients, prepare and present their own arguments. Judges must listen carefully in order to make rulings on disputes between lawyers about evidence and procedure. Judges may also be responsible for determining guilt in cases tried without a jury. All three actors may participate in developing and approving negotiated guilty pleas in the plea-bargaining process.

Unlike judges, who work exclusively in offices and courtrooms within a courthouse, lawyers must also interact with members of the public by interviewing witnesses, victims, and police officers. Defense attorneys in particular may find themselves conducting interviews in unpleasant settings such as jail cells or street corners as they try to find information to help their clients.

REQUIRED QUALIFICATIONS

To become a lawyer in the United States, people must earn a four-year college degree in any subject before going to law school for three years of postgraduate study. Gaining admission to law school is a competitive process, so people interested in legal careers must work hard during college, earn good grades, and gain good scores on the Law School Admissions Test (LSAT). After graduating from law school, prospective lawyers must pass a state's bar exam in order to receive a license to practice law or serve as a judge in that state. Each state has its own bar exam which typically lasts two days. A separate ethics exam may also be required. In most states, one day is devoted to a six-hour multiple-choice test on six subjects that are common to all states (contract, criminal, tort, evidence, property, and constitutional law). The other day involves six hours of essays on 12 or more subjects focused on state law, including business associations, taxation, and family law.

After passing a state's bar exam and being granted a law license, new lawyers can seek jobs as assistant prosecutors or public defenders. Lawyers typically only become judges after practicing law for several years in order to build a reputation that will permit them to win elections or be appointed to the bench.

EARNINGS AND JOB OUTLOOK

The U.S. Department of Labor projects that jobs as lawyers and judges will increase as fast as other occupations in the United States. More jobs will be created as the country's population increases and needs more courts and judges.

Salaries vary. Annual salaries for new public defenders range from $30,000 to $45,000, depending on the city or state in which the public defender is employed. Private practice attorneys who handle criminal cases must build their careers—and incomes—through successful work in low-paid appointed cases that help develop the lawyer's reputation in order to attract paying clients. Starting salaries for prosecutors are similar to those of starting salaries for defense attorneys, except that federal prosecutors have starting salaries of $40,000 to $65,000, depending on whether they had experience in private practice before becoming prosecutors.

Salaries for state judges in general jurisdiction trial courts averaged $113,504 in 2004, although the exact salary varied by state. U.S. district court judges earn $162,000 per year.

MORE INFORMATION

The U.S. Department of Labor provides online information about lawyers' and judges' careers. See the corresponding sites listed on the Cole/Smith Criminal Justice in America Companion Website: http://www.thomsonedu.com/criminaljustice/cole.

Sources: Carol J. DeFrances, "Prosecutors in State Courts, 2001," Bureau of Justice Statistics *Bulletin* (May 2002); Carol J. DeFrances, "State-Funded Indigent Defense Services, 1999," Bureau of Justice Statistics *Special Report* (September 2001).

and court procedures, defendants have little ability to represent themselves in court effectively. The defense attorney therefore ensures that prosecutors and judges understand and respect the defendant's rights.

While filling their roles in the criminal justice system, defense attorneys also psychologically support defendants and their families. Relatives are often bewildered, frightened, and confused. The defense attorney is the only legal actor available to answer the question, "What will happen next?" In short, the attorney's relationship

FIGURE 8.4

Typical actions of a defense attorney processing a felony case

Defense attorneys are advocates for the accused. They have an obligation to challenge points made by the prosecution and advise clients about constitutional rights.

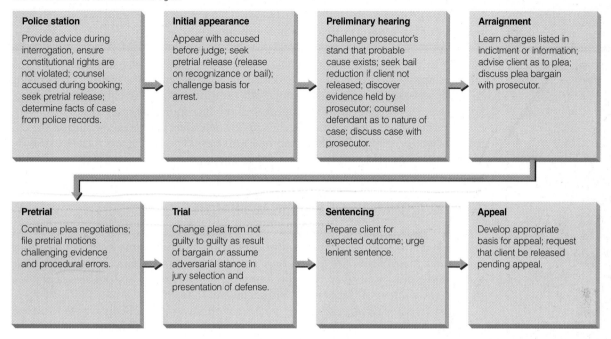

Police station

Provide advice during interrogation, ensure constitutional rights are not violated; counsel accused during booking; seek pretrial release; determine facts of case from police records.

Initial appearance

Appear with accused before judge; seek pretrial release (release on recognizance or bail); challenge basis for arrest.

Preliminary hearing

Challenge prosecutor's stand that probable cause exists; seek bail reduction if client not released; discover evidence held by prosecutor; counsel defendant as to nature of case; discuss case with prosecutor.

Arraignment

Learn charges listed in indictment or information; advise client as to plea; discuss plea bargain with prosecutor.

Pretrial

Continue plea negotiations; file pretrial motions challenging evidence and procedural errors.

Trial

Change plea from not guilty to guilty as result of bargain *or* assume adversarial stance in jury selection and presentation of defense.

Sentencing

Prepare client for expected outcome; urge lenient sentence.

Appeal

Develop appropriate basis for appeal; request that client be released pending appeal.

with the client matters a great deal. An effective defense requires respect, openness, and trust between attorney and client. If the defendant refuses to follow the attorney's advice, the lawyer may feel obliged to withdraw from the case in order to protect his or her own professional reputation.

REALITIES OF THE DEFENSE ATTORNEY'S JOB

How well do defense attorneys represent their clients? Attorneys who are inexperienced, uncaring, or overburdened have trouble representing their clients effectively. The attorney may quickly agree to a plea bargain and then work to persuade the defendant to accept the agreement. The attorney's self-interest in disposing of cases quickly, receiving payment, and moving on to other cases may cause the attorney to, in effect, work with the prosecutor to pressure the defendant to plead guilty. Skilled defense attorneys also consider plea bargaining in the earliest stages of a case; however, unlike their unskilled counterparts, these lawyers would be guided by their role as advocate for the defendant, not by outside pressures. In many cases, a negotiated plea with a predictable sentence serves the defendant better than does a trial spent fending off more serious charges. An effective defense attorney does not try to take every case all the way to trial.

The defense attorney's job is all the more difficult because neither the public nor defendants fully understand the attorney's duties and goals. The public often views defense attorneys as protectors of criminals. In fact, the attorney's basic duty is not to save criminals from punishment but to protect constitutional rights, keep the prosecution honest in preparing and presenting cases, and prevent innocent people from being convicted. Look at the question presented in "What Americans Think" on the next page. Do you think that the public overestimates the necessity of representation by an attorney?

Three groups of private practice lawyers can be called specialists in criminal defense because they handle criminal cases on a regular basis. The first group is composed of nationally known attorneys who charge large fees in highly publicized cases. The second group, found in each large city, is the lawyers of choice for defendants who can afford to pay high fees. These attorneys make handsome incomes by representing white-collar criminals, drug dealers, and affluent people charged with crimes. The third and largest group of attorneys in full-time criminal practice is courthouse

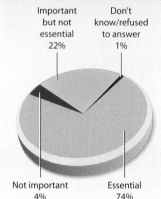

Question: "Is the right to have the government provide a defense attorney for someone who cannot afford one essential, important but not essential, or not important?"

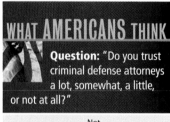

Important but not essential 22%

Don't know/refused to answer 1%

Not important 4%

Essential 74%

Go to http://www.thomsonedu.com/criminaljustice/cole to compare your opinion on this issue with the opinions of other criminal justice students.

Source: Telephone interviews of a national adult sample by the Center for Survey Research and Analysis, University of Connecticut, February 17–March 7, 2000. Data provided by the Roper Center for Public Opinion Research, University of Connecticut.

Question: "Do you trust criminal defense attorneys a lot, somewhat, a little, or not at all?"

Don't know/refused to answer 3%

Not at all 19%

A lot 6%

A little 34%

Somewhat 38%

Go to http://www.thomsonedu.com/criminaljustice/cole to compare your opinion on this issue with the opinions of other criminal justice students.

Source: Based on a national telephone survey of an adult sample conducted by the Center for Survey Research and Analysis, University of Connecticut, February 17–March 7, 2000. Data provided by the Roper Center for Public Opinion Research, University of Connecticut.

regulars who accept many cases for small fees and who participate daily in the criminal justice system as either retained or assigned counsel. These attorneys handle a large volume of cases quickly. They negotiate guilty pleas and try to convince their clients that these agreements are beneficial. They depend on the cooperation of prosecutors, judges, and other courtroom actors, with whom they form exchange relationships in order to reach plea bargains quickly.

In addition to these defense specialists, many private attorneys sometimes take criminal cases. These attorneys often have little trial experience and lack well-developed relationships with other actors in the criminal justice system. In fact, their clients might be better served by a courthouse regular who has little interest in each case but whose relationships with prosecutors and judges will produce more favorable plea bargains.

Government-salaried attorneys called *public defenders* handle criminal cases for defendants who are too poor to hire their own attorneys. These attorneys focus exclusively on criminal cases and usually develop significant expertise. They cannot always devote as much time as they want to each case, because they often have heavy caseloads.

THE ENVIRONMENT OF CRIMINAL PRACTICE

Defense attorneys have a difficult job. Much of their work involves preparing clients and their relatives for the likelihood of conviction and punishment. Even when they know that their clients are guilty, they may become emotionally involved because they are the only judicial actors who know the defendants as human beings and see them in the context of their family and social environment.

Most defense lawyers constantly interact with lower-class clients whose lives and problems are depressing. They might also visit the local jail at all hours of the day and night. Thus, their work setting is far removed from the fancy offices and expensive restaurants of the world of corporate attorneys. As described by one defense attorney, "The days are long and stressful. I spend a good deal of time in jail, which reeks of stale food and body odor. My clients often think that because I'm court-appointed, I must be incompetent" (Lave, 1998:14).

Defense lawyers must also struggle with the fact that criminal practice does not pay well. Public defenders garner fairly low salaries, and attorneys appointed to represent poor defendants receive small sums. If private attorneys do not demand payment from their clients at the start of the case, they may find that they must persuade the defendants' relatives to pay—because many convicted offenders have no incentive to pay for legal services while sitting in a prison cell. To perform their jobs well and gain satisfaction from their careers, defense attorneys must focus on goals other than money, such as their key role in protecting people's constitutional rights. However, that they are usually on the losing side can make it hard for them to feel like professionals—with high self-esteem and satisfying work. In addition, because they work on behalf of criminal defendants, they also face suspicion from the public (see "What Americans Think"). If you were a defense attorney, would it bother you if most members of the public did not trust you?

COUNSEL FOR INDIGENTS

Since the 1960s, the Supreme Court has interpreted the "right to counsel" in the Sixth Amendment to the Constitution as requiring that the government provide attorneys for indigent defendants who face the possibility of going to prison or jail. *Indigent defendants* are those who are too poor to afford their own lawyers. The Court has also required that attorneys be provided early in the criminal justice process, to protect suspects' rights during questioning and pretrial proceedings. See Table 8.2 for a summary of key rulings on the right to counsel.

Research on felony defendants indicates that 78 percent of those prosecuted in the 75 largest counties and 66 percent of those prosecuted in federal courts received publicly provided legal counsel (Harlow, 2000). The portion of defendants who are provided with counsel because they are indigent has increased greatly in the past three decades.

The quality of counsel given to indigent defendants has spurred debate. Ideally, experienced lawyers would be appointed soon after arrest to represent the defendant

TABLE 8.2   The Right to Counsel: Major Supreme Court Rulings

Case	Year	Ruling
Powell v. Alabama ✓	1932	Indigents facing the death penalty who are not capable of representing themselves must be given attorneys.
Johnson v. Zerbst ✓	1938	Indigent defendants must be provided with attorneys when facing serious charges in federal court.
Gideon v. Wainwright ✓	1963	Indigent defendants must be provided with attorneys when facing serious charges in state court.
Douglas v. California	1963	Indigent defendants must be provided with attorneys for their first appeal.
Miranda v. Arizona	1966	Criminal suspects must be informed about their right to counsel before being questioned in custody.
United States v. Wade	1967	Defendants are entitled to counsel at "critical stages" in the process, including postindictment lineups.
Argersinger v. Hamlin ✓	1972	Indigent defendants must be provided with attorneys when facing misdemeanor and petty charges that may result in incarceration.
Ross v. Moffitt	1974	Indigent defendants are not entitled to attorneys for discretionary appeals after their first appeal is unsuccessful.
Strickland v. Washington ✓	1984	To show ineffective assistance of counsel violated the right to counsel, defendants must prove that the attorney committed specific errors that affected the outcome of the case.
Murray v. Giarratano	1989	Death row inmates do not have a right to counsel for habeas corpus proceedings asserting rights violations in their cases.

in each stage of the criminal justice process. Ideal conditions do not always exist, however. As we have seen, inexperienced and uncaring attorneys may be appointed. Some attorneys have little time to prepare the case. Even conscientious attorneys may be unable to provide top-quality counsel if they have heavy caseloads or do not receive enough money to enable them to spend the time required to handle the case well. If they lack the time and desire to interview the client and prepare the case, the appointed counsel may simply persuade defendants to plead guilty right there in the courtroom during their first and only brief conversation. Of course, not all publicly financed lawyers who represent poor defendants ignore their clients' best interests. Even so, the quality of counsel received by the poor may vary from courthouse to courthouse, depending on the quality of the attorneys, conditions of defense practice, and administrative pressure to reduce the caseload.

Ways of Providing Indigents with Counsel   There are three main ways of providing counsel to indigent defendants: (1) the **assigned counsel** system, in which a court appoints a private attorney to represent the accused; (2) the **contract counsel** system, in which an attorney, a nonprofit organization, or a private law firm contracts with a local government to provide legal services to indigent defendants for a specified dollar amount; and (3) **public defender** programs, which are public or private nonprofit organizations with full-time or part-time salaried staff. Figure 8.5 shows the system in use in the majority of counties in each of the 50 states. Note, however, that 23 percent of counties use both public defenders and assigned counsel to provide representation (S. K. Smith and DeFrances, 1996).

The methods for providing defense attorneys and the quality of defense services may depend on the money available to pay attorneys. Twenty-seven states pay for indigent criminal defense, but in the remaining states each county must fund its own defense service. As a result, resources—and the quality of indigent defense—may vary from county to county within a single state. In 2003 Quitman County, Mississippi, sued the state government because it could not provide sufficient county funds to pay for defense attorneys by itself (Liptak, 2003).

Assigned Counsel   In the assigned counsel system, the court appoints a lawyer in private practice to represent an indigent defendant. This system is widely used in small cities and in rural areas, but even some city public defender systems assign counsel in some cases, such as a case with multiple defendants, where a conflict of interest might result if a public lawyer represented all of them.

assigned counsel An attorney in private practice assigned by a court to represent an indigent. The attorney's fee is paid by the government with jurisdiction over the case.

contract counsel An attorney in private practice who contracts with the government to represent all indigent defendants in a county during a set period of time and for a specified dollar amount.

public defender An attorney employed on a full-time, salaried basis by a public or private nonprofit organization to represent indigents.

Sean Sullivan, a lawyer who represents indigent clients, carries a heavy caseload under trying conditions. The quality of counsel received by the poor may vary from courthouse to courthouse, depending on the quality of the attorneys, conditions of defense practice, and administrative pressures to reduce caseloads.

Ruth Fremson/The New York Times/Redux

FIGURE 8.5
Indigent defense system used by the majority of counties in each state
Note that some states use a mixture of methods to provide counsel for indigents; this figure shows only the predominant method per state.

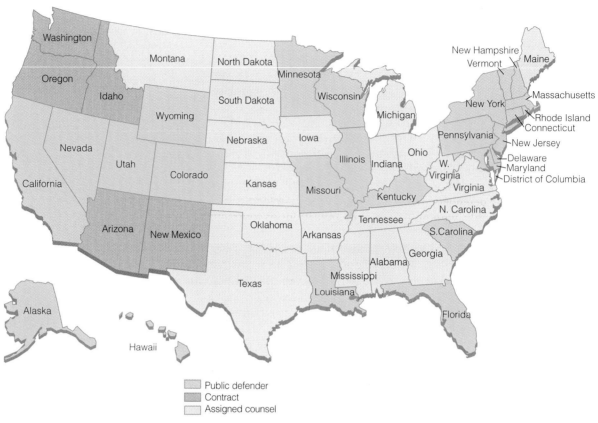

Public defender
Contract
Assigned counsel

Source: Bureau of Justice Statistics, *Bulletin,* September 1988.

Assigned counsel systems are organized on either an ad hoc or a coordinated basis. In ad hoc assignment systems, private attorneys tell the judge that they are willing to take the cases of indigent defendants. When an indigent requires counsel, the judge either assigns lawyers in rotation from a prepared list or chooses one of the attorneys who are known and present in the courtroom. In coordinated assignment systems, a court administrator oversees the appointment of counsel.

Use of the ad hoc system raises questions about the loyalties of the assigned counsel. Are they trying to vigorously defend their clients or are they trying to please the judges to ensure future appointments? For example, Texas has been criticized for giving judges free rein to assign lawyers to cases without any supervising authority to ensure that the attorneys actually do a good job (Novak, 1999). Additional concerns in Texas and other states where judges run for election center on lawyers' donating to judges' political campaigns. Judges could return the favor by supplying their contributors with criminal defense assignments.

The fees paid to assigned defenders are often low compared with what a lawyer might otherwise charge (see Table 8.3, which shows the fees paid in New Hampshire). In 1999 the average hourly overhead cost for attorneys—the amount they must make just to pay their secretaries, office rent, and telephone bills—was $58 (National Legal Aid and Defender Association, 1999). Low fees discourage skilled attorneys from taking criminal cases. Low fees may also induce a defender to persuade the client to plead guilty to a lesser charge. Note in Table 8.3 that the maximum hourly rate paid to appointed counsel in New Hampshire is $60. This falls well below the rate of $171 average per hour fee that Wisconsin lawyers charge their paying clients ("2005 Economics of Law Practice Survey," 2005).

Contract System A few counties, mainly in Western states that do not have large populations, use the contract system. The government contracts with an attorney, a nonprofit association, or a private law firm to handle all indigent cases (Worden, 1994). Some jurisdictions use public defenders for most cases but contract for services in multiple-defendant cases that might present conflicts of interest, in extraordinarily complex cases, or in cases that require more time than the government's salaried lawyers can provide.

This system has its problems. According to Robert Spangenberg and Marea Beeman (1995:49), "There are serious potential dangers with the contract model, such as expecting contract defenders to handle an unlimited caseload or awarding contracts on a low-bid basis only, with no regard to qualifications of contracting attorneys."

TABLE 8.3 Fees Paid to Assigned Counsel in New Hampshire	
New Hampshire's statewide maximum fee schedule for appointed counsel is contained in the *Rules of the Supreme Court of the State of New Hampshire*.	
Maximum hourly rate	$60
Maximum fee per day	$400
Maximum fee for a misdemeanor case	$1,000
Maximum fee for a felony case	$3,000
Maximum fee for a homicide case	$15,000
Maximum fee for a state supreme court appeal	$1,500

Source: Rule 47: "Counsel Fees and Expenses—Indigent Criminal Cases," in *Rules of the Supreme Court of the State of New Hampshire* (2006), http://www.nh.gov/judiciary/rules/scr/scr-47.htm.

Public Defenders The position of public defender developed as a response to the legal needs of indigent defendants. The most recent national survey of the 100 most populous counties found that public defender systems handled 82 percent of the 4.2 million indigent criminal cases, whereas appointed counsel handled 15 percent and contract counsel represented only 3 percent of defendants (DeFrances and Litras, 2000). The public defender system, which is growing fast, is used in 43 of the 50 most populous counties and in most large cities. There are about 20 statewide, state-funded systems; in other states, the counties organize and pay for indigent defense, and some counties in 28 states choose to use full-time public defenders. Only two states, North Dakota and Maine, do not have public defenders either statewide or in any individual counties.

Experts and others often view the public defender system as better than the assigned counsel system, because public defenders are specialists in criminal law. Because they are full-time government employees, public defenders, unlike appointed counsel and contract attorneys, do not sacrifice their clients' cases to protect their own financial interests. Public defenders do face certain special problems, however.

They may have trouble gaining the trust and cooperation of their clients. Criminal defendants may assume that attorneys on the state payroll, even with the title public defender, have no reason to protect the defendants' rights and interests. Lack of cooperation from the defendant may make it harder for the attorney to prepare the best possible arguments for use during hearings, plea bargaining, and trials.

Public defenders may also face heavy caseloads. In New York City's public defender program, for example, Legal Aid lawyers may handle as many as 100 felony cases at any time. A public defender in Atlanta may be assigned as many as 45 new cases at a single arraignment (Bright, 1994). Although the National Legal Aid and Defender Association recommends that defense attorneys handle no more than 400 cases per year, public defenders in Connecticut averaged 618 cases in 1999 (Casey, 1999). Such heavy caseloads do not allow time for attorneys to become familiar with each case. Public defender programs are most effective when they have enough money to keep caseloads manageable. However, these programs do not control their own budgets, and state and local governments usually do not see them as high priorities. Thus, they find it hard to gain the funds they need to give adequate attention to each defendant's case.

If public defenders work effectively on behalf of criminal defendants, they may become the focus of political efforts to reduce their resources or involvement in cases. In 2003 Governor Jeb Bush of Florida proposed cutting state funding for the public defenders who handle death penalty cases. Although he argued that it would be less expensive to hire private attorneys as assigned counsel for capital cases, critics worried that such a move would reduce the quality of representation and increase the risk of errors in such cases (Richey, 2003).

Attorney Effectiveness and Competence   Do defendants who can afford their own counsel get better legal services than those who cannot? Many convicted offenders say, "You get what you pay for," meaning that they would have received better counsel if they had been able to pay for their own attorneys. At one time, researchers thought public defenders entered more guilty pleas than did lawyers who had been either privately retained or assigned to cases. However, studies show little variation in case outcomes by various types of defense (Hanson and Chapper, 1991).

The right to counsel is of little value when the counsel is not competent and effective. Even in death penalty cases, attorneys have shown up for court so drunk that they could not stand up straight (Bright, 1994). In other cases, attorneys with almost no knowledge of criminal law have made blunders that have needlessly sent their clients to death row (C. E. Smith, 1997). For example, lawyers have fallen asleep during their clients' death penalty trials, yet one Texas judge found no problem with such behavior. He wrote that everyone has a constitutional right to have a lawyer, but "the Constitution does not say that the lawyer has to be awake" (Shapiro, 1997:27). An appellate court later disagreed with this conclusion.

The U.S. Supreme Court has examined the question of what requirements must be met if defendants are to receive effective counsel. To prevail in claims that their counsel has been ineffective, defendants must identify specific errors, made by their attorneys, that affected the result of the case and made the case unfair. By focusing on whether errors by an attorney were bad enough to make the trial result unreliable, thereby denying a fair trial, the Court has made it hard for defendants to prove that they were denied effective counsel, even when defense attorneys perform very poorly. As a result, innocent people who were poorly represented have been convicted, even of the most serious crimes (Radelet, Bedeau, and Putnam, 1992).

CHECKPOINT

10. What special pressures do defense attorneys face? ⟶

11. What are the three main methods of providing attorneys for indigent defendants? ⟶

Answers

10. Securing cases, collecting fees, persuading clients to accept pleas, accepting the fact that they will lose most cases.

11. Assigned counsel, contract counsel, public defender.

The Courtroom: How It Functions

Criminal cases throughout the nation follow similar rules and procedures. However, courts differ in the precise ways they apply them. Social scientists are aware that the culture of a community greatly influences how its members behave. *Culture* implies shared beliefs about proper behavior. These beliefs can span entire nations or exist in smaller communities, including organizations such as corporations, churches, or neighborhoods. In any community, large or small, the culture can strongly affect people's decisions and behaviors.

Researchers have identified a **local legal culture** of values and norms shared by members of a particular court community (judges, attorneys, clerks, bailiffs, and others) about how cases should be handled and the way court officials should behave (Church, 1985). The local legal culture influences court operations in three ways:

1. Norms (shared values and expectations) help participants distinguish between "our" court and other courts. Often a judge or prosecutor will proudly describe how "we" do the job differently and better than officials in a nearby county or city.

2. Norms tell members of a court community how they should treat one another. For example, mounting a strong adversarial defense may be viewed as not in keeping with the norms of one court, but it may be expected in another.

3. Norms describe how cases should be processed. The best example of such a norm is the **going rate**, the local view of the proper sentence, which considers the offense, the defendant's prior record, and other factors. The local legal

local legal culture   Norms shared by members of a court community as to how cases should be handled and how a participant should behave in the judicial process.

going rate   Local court officials' shared view of the appropriate sentence, given the offense, the defendant's prior record, and other case characteristics.

culture also includes attitudes on such issues as whether a judge should take part in plea negotiations, when **continuances**—lawyers' requests for delays in court proceedings—should be granted, and which defendants qualify for a public defender.

Differences among local legal cultures help explain why court decisions may differ, even though the formal rules of criminal procedure are basically the same. For example, although judges play a key role in sentencing, sentences also stem from shared understandings—the going rate—among the prosecutor, defense attorney, and judge. In one court, shared understandings may mean that a court imposes probation on a first-time thief; in other courts, different shared values may send first offenders to jail or prison for the same offense.

Decision making in criminal cases is influenced by the fact that participants are organized in **workgroups.** The judge, prosecutor, and defense attorney, along with the support staff (clerk, reporter, and bailiff), interact in the workplace on a continuing basis, share goals, develop norms regarding how activities should be carried out, and eventually establish a network of roles that differentiates the group from others and that facilitates cooperation. These relationships are necessary if the group is to carry out its task of disposing of cases. The workgroup concept is especially important in analyzing urban courts, which have many courtrooms; large numbers of lawyers, judges, and other court personnel; and a heavy caseload.

Given the factors that define the workgroup, workgroups in various courthouses differ, depending on the strength of these factors in each setting. For example, a rotation system that moves judges among courtrooms in a large courthouse may limit the development of workgroup norms and roles. Although the same prosecutors and defense attorneys may be present every day, the arrival of a new judge every week or month will require them to learn and adapt to new ideas about how cases should be negotiated or tried. When shared norms cannot develop, cases will tend to proceed in a more formal manner. The actors in such a courtroom have fewer chances to follow agreed-on routines than would a workgroup with a well-developed pattern of interactions.

By contrast, when there are shared expectations and consistent relationships, the business of the courtroom proceeds in a regular but informal manner, with many shared understandings among members easing much of the work (Worden, 1995). Through cooperation, each member can achieve his or her goals as well as those of the group. The prosecutor wants to gain quick convictions, the defense attorney wants fair and prompt resolution of the defendant's case, and the judge wants cooperative agreements on guilt and sentencing. All of these actors want efficient processing of the steady flow of cases that burden their working lives.

Judges are the leaders of the courtroom team. They ensure that procedures are followed correctly. Even if prosecutors and defense attorneys appear to make the key decisions, the judge must approve them. Judges coordinate the processing of cases. Further, each judge can perform this role somewhat differently. Judges who run a loose administrative ship see themselves as somewhat above the battle. They give other members of the team a great deal of freedom in carrying out their duties and will usually approve group decisions, especially when the members of the group have shared beliefs about the court's goals and the community's values. Judges who exert tighter control over the process play a more active role. They anticipate problems, provide cues for

Mesa County District Judge David Bottger listens at a bench conference with prosecutors and defense attorneys during Michael Blagg's murder trial in Grand Junction, Colorado. Even in the most adversarial cases, courtroom participants form a workgroup that requires constant interaction, cooperation, and negotiation.

AP Photo/Pool, George Kochaniec Jr.

continuance An adjournment of a scheduled case until a later date.

workgroup A collection of individuals who interact in the workplace on a continuing basis, share goals, develop norms regarding how activities should be carried out, and eventually establish a network of roles that differentiates the group from others and that facilitates cooperation.

other actors, and threaten, cajole, and move the group toward the efficient achievement of its goals. Such judges command respect and participate fully in the ongoing courtroom drama. Judges' actions can, for example, pressure defense attorneys to encourage their clients to plead guilty instead of insisting on a trial (D. Lynch, 1999).

CHECKPOINT

12. How does the local legal culture affect criminal cases? ➞

13. What is the courtroom workgroup? ➞

Answers

12. The local legal culture consists of norms that distinguish a given court from other jurisdictions, that stipulate how members should treat one another, and that describe how cases should be processed.

13. The courtroom workgroup is made up of the judge, prosecutor, defense counsel, and support staff assigned regularly to a specific courtroom. Through the interaction of these members, goals and norms are shared and a set of roles becomes stabilized.

A QUESTION OF ETHICS: WRITING ASSIGNMENT

Assistant County Prosecutor Adam Dow entered the office of his boss, County Prosecutor Susan Graham. "You wanted to see me?" he asked as he closed the door.

"Yes, I do," Graham replied with a flash of anger. "I don't agree with your recommendation to dismiss charges in the Richardson case."

"But the victim was so uncertain in making the identification at the lineup, and the security video from the ATM machine is so grainy that you can't really tell if Richardson committed the robbery."

"Look. We've had six people robbed while withdrawing money at ATM machines in the past month. The community is upset. The banks are upset. The newspapers keep playing up these unsolved crimes. I want to put an end to this public hysteria. Richardson has a prior record for a robbery and the victim picked him out of the lineup eventually." Graham stared at him coldly. "I'm not going to dismiss the charges."

Dow shifted his feet and stared at the floor. "I'm not comfortable with this case. Richardson may be innocent. The evidence just isn't very strong."

"Don't worry about the strength of the evidence. That's not your problem," said Graham. "We have enough evidence to take the case to trial. The judge said so at the preliminary hearing. So we'll just let the jury decide. Whatever happens, the community will know that we took action against this crime problem."

"But what if he's innocent? The jury could make a mistake in thinking that he's the robber in the grainy videotape. I wouldn't want that on my conscience."

WRITING ASSIGNMENT

Should Assistant Prosecutor Dow act as if he is the judge and jury by deciding on the certainty of the defendant's guilt before agreeing to take a case forward? Should Prosecutor Graham take the community's feelings into consideration in deciding whether to pursue charges against Richardson? Is there an actual risk that an innocent person could be convicted in a jury trial under such circumstances if the prosecutor is reluctant to dismiss questionable charges? Write a memo as if you were a senior assistant prosecutor who has been asked to give advice about what to do in this case.

REAL-WORLD ACTIVITY: AN APPLICATION

You have been appointed to a commission to evaluate the selection of judges in a state that uses partisan elections. Newspaper editorials have been complaining that campaign fund-raising by judicial candidates makes it appear as if the judges owe favors to specific lawyers, interest groups, and wealthy individuals who support them with campaign contributions during elections.

RESEARCHING THE INTERNET

Go to **InfoTrac** College Edition. Enter the keyword *merit selection judges* and read the article entitled "Alaska's Merit Selection for Judges," by Susie Dosik, *Alaska Law Review,* December 2004.

APPLICATION

Write an advisory report that addresses several important questions. What is the best method for selecting judges? Would you recommend that the state change its method of judicial selection? Could your recommended change produce any undesirable consequences?

SUMMARY

- The United States has a dual court system consisting of state and federal courts that are organized into separate hierarchies.

- Trial courts and appellate courts have different jurisdictions and functions.

- The judge is a key figure in the criminal justice process who assumes the roles of adjudicator, negotiator, and administrator.

- State judges are selected through various methods, including partisan elections, nonpartisan elections, gubernatorial appointment, legislative selection, and merit selection.

- American prosecutors, both state and federal, have significant discretion to determine how to handle criminal cases.

- There is no higher authority over most prosecutors that can overrule a decision to pursue multiple counts against a defendant or to decline to prosecute (*nolle prosequi*).

- The prosecutor can play various roles, including trial counsel for the police, house counsel for the police, representative of the court, and elected official.

- Prosecutors' decisions and actions are affected by their exchange relationships with many other important actors and groups, including police, judges, defense attorneys, victims and witnesses, and the public.

- Often the image of defense attorneys as courtroom advocates differs vastly from the reality of pressured, busy negotiators constantly involved in bargaining with the prosecutor over guilty plea agreements.

- Relatively few private defense attorneys make significant incomes from criminal work, but larger numbers of private attorneys accept court appointments to handle indigent defendants' cases quickly for relatively low fees.

- Three primary methods for providing attorneys to represent indigent defendants are appointed counsel, contract counsel, and public defenders.

- Defense attorneys must often wrestle with difficult working conditions and uncooperative clients as they seek to provide representation, usually in plea negotiations.

- Although the quality of representation provided to criminal defendants is of significant concern, U.S. Supreme Court rulings have made it difficult for convicted offenders to prove that their attorneys did not provide a competent defense.

- The outcomes in criminal cases depend significantly on a court's local legal culture, which defines the going rates of punishment for various offenses.

- Courtroom workgroups made up of judges, prosecutors, defense attorneys, and staff who work together can smoothly and efficiently handle cases through cooperative plea-bargaining processes.

QUESTIONS FOR REVIEW

1. The judge plays several roles. What are they? Do they conflict with one another?

2. What is the best method for selecting judges? Why? What are the flaws or risks of alternative selection methods?

3. What are the formal powers of the prosecuting attorney?

4. How do politics affect prosecutors?

5. What considerations influence the prosecutor's decision about whether to bring charges and what to charge?

6. Why is the prosecuting attorney often cited as the most powerful office in the criminal justice system?

7. What are some of the problems faced by attorneys who engage in private defense practice?

8. What are the methods by which defense services are provided to indigents?

9. Why might it be argued that publicly financed counsel serves defendants better than does privately retained counsel?

10. What is the courtroom workgroup and what does it do?

KEY TERMS

accusatory process (p. 216)
adversary process (p. 203)
appellate courts (p. 204)
assigned counsel (p. 221)
continuance (p. 225)
contract counsel (p. 221)
count (p. 214)
defense attorney (p. 217)
discovery (p. 214)

going rate (p. 224)
inquisitorial process (p. 203)
jurisdiction (p. 203)
local legal culture (p. 224)
merit selection (p. 210)
nolle prosequi (p. 214)
nonpartisan election (p. 209)
partisan election (p. 209)
prosecuting attorney (p. 211)

public defender (p. 221)
state attorney general (p. 211)
trial courts of general jurisdiction (p. 204)
trial courts of limited jurisdiction (p. 204)
United States attorneys (p. 211)
workgroup (p. 225)

GOING ONLINE

ThomsonNOW™

Maximize your study time by using ThomsonNOW's diagnostic study plan to help you review this chapter. The Study Plan will

- help you identify areas on which you should concentrate

- provide interactive exercises to help you master the chapter concepts

- provide a posttest to confirm you are ready to move on to the next chapter

9

Pretrial Procedures, Plea Bargaining, and the Criminal Trial

J ayson Williams, the former NBA basketball player, waited anxiously in the Somerset County, New Jersey, courtroom. After 23 hours of deliberations over four days, a jury of eight women and four men filed into the courtroom to deliver the verdict from the trial that had lasted ten weeks. On the charge of aggravated manslaughter, Williams could receive 30 years in prison; he also faced seven lesser charges related to the shooting death of Costas Christofi, a limousine driver who died in the bedroom of Williams's 40-room mansion. The jury's verdict on April 30, 2004, would represent the conclusion of a trial process that had begun with the police investigation at the scene of Christofi's death in the early morning hours of February 14, 2002 (Reilly, 2004a).

Williams had hired Christofi to drive his friends, including several former NBA players, to the mansion after a night of eating and drinking. Christofi followed along as Williams gave a tour of the mansion. In the bedroom Williams, who owned several guns, grabbed a shotgun.

After he cracked the gun open and then snapped it closed, the weapon discharged. Christofi was struck in the chest and died a few minutes later. The prosecution alleged that Williams, who reportedly cursed at Christofi prior to the shooting, pointed the gun at the driver and pulled the trigger. Alternatively, they alleged that Williams demonstrated criminal recklessness in the manner in which he handled and pointed the gun. The prosecution relied on testimony from several of Williams's friends who were present in the bedroom. The prosecution's witnesses included two friends who agreed to cooperate in exchange for reduced charges and sentences when they admitted that they had helped Williams wipe his fingerprints from the weapon and place the gun in Christofi's hands to make it look like a suicide. In response, the defense claimed that the shooting was an accident and that a mechanical malfunction caused the shotgun to fire (Ryan, 2004).

When the verdict was read, Williams's face showed his sense of relief as he leaned over to kiss his wife, who was sitting in the first row behind the defense table. The jury had found Williams not guilty of the serious charges of aggravated manslaughter and aggravated assault. However, they did find him guilty of tampering with witnesses and evidence, charges for which most observers expected him to receive a sentence of probation and fines. In the aftermath of the verdict, it became clear that Williams's relief had to be tempered with a sense of uncertainty about the future. Because the jury had deadlocked 8–4 in favor of acquittal on the reckless manslaughter count, a charge that could lead to a ten-year prison sentence, the prosecution announced that it would put Williams on trial again for that single charge (Reilly, 2004b). Williams filed an appeal claiming that his Fifth Amendment right against double jeopardy would be violated if he faced another trial. However, the state court of appeals rejected his claim in 2006, thereby permitting the prosecution to move ahead in planning the new trial (Gold, 2006).

The American system regards the trial as the best method for determining a defendant's guilt. Williams was fortunate that his wealth enabled him to use all available resources to challenge the prosecutor's theory and present his own evidence. His defense team included a nationally known attorney from Washington, D.C.; a retired local judge; a jury consultant to provide advice on what kinds of people to seek in jury selection; and a media consultant to shape the information provided to the news media and the public ("The Trial," 2004). Thus, as one of those celebrated cases that go to trial and command great public attention, his case occupies the top layer of the criminal justice wedding cake (see Chapter 1).

Because of the high stakes and uncertainty that surround criminal trials, most defendants plead guilty as they get closer to the prospect of being judged by a random group of citizens drawn from the community. A guilty plea creates greater certainty about what the punishment will be. Prosecutors create incentives for guilty pleas by offering reductions in charges and sentences in exchange for admissions of guilt. As in the case of the friends who testified against Williams, the prosecutor may also demand cooperation in exchange for an offer of reduced charges.

In this chapter, we examine the steps in the criminal justice process from arrest to dismissal or conviction. We give particular attention to bail, plea bargaining, and trials—the processes and decisions that most influence whether people will lose their liberty or otherwise receive punishment. As we shall see, interactions and decisions involving judges, prosecutors, and defense attorneys guide the outcomes from these important processes.

QUESTIONS FOR INQUIRY

- How does the bail system work, and how is bail set?
- What conditions do people face during pretrial detention?
- How and why does plea bargaining occur?
- What are the stages of the criminal trial?
- How are juries chosen?
- What is the basis for an appeal of a conviction?

From Arrest to Trial or Plea

At each stage of the pretrial process, key decisions are made that move some defendants to the next stage of the process and filter others out of the system. An innocent person could be arrested on the basis of mistaken identification or misinterpreted evidence (Huff, 2002; Kridler, 1999). However, pretrial processes ideally force prosecutors and judges to review the available evidence and dismiss unnecessary charges against people who should not face trial and punishment. These processes stem from the American value of due process. Americans believe that people should be entitled to a series of hearings and other procedural steps in which their guilt is proven, before they should be subjected to punishments such as the loss of liberty through incarceration.

After arrest, the accused is booked at the police station. This process includes taking photographs and fingerprints, which form the basis of the case record. Within 48 hours of a warrantless arrest, the defendant is usually taken to court for the initial appearance to hear which charges are being pursued, to be advised of his or her rights, and to receive the opportunity to post bail. At the initial appearance, the judge also must confirm that evidence exists to establish probable cause that the accused committed a crime and thereby is eligible to be prosecuted. If the police used an arrest warrant to take the suspect into custody, evidence has already been presented to a judge who believed that it was strong enough to support a finding of probable cause to proceed against the defendant.

Often, the first formal meeting between the prosecutor and the defendant's attorney is the **arraignment**: the formal court appearance in which the charges against the defendant are read and the defendant, advised by his or her lawyer, enters a plea of either guilty or not guilty. Most defendants will initially plead not guilty, even if they are likely to plead guilty at a later point. This is because, thus far, the prosecutor and defense attorney usually have had little chance to discuss a potential plea bargain. The more serious the charges, the more likely the prosecutor and defense attorney will need time to assess the strength of the other side's case. Only then can plea bargaining begin.

At the time of arraignment, prosecutors begin to evaluate the evidence. This screening process greatly affects the lives of accused persons, whose fate rests largely on the prosecutor's discretion. If the prosecutor believes the case against the defendant is weak, the charges may be dropped. Prosecutors do not wish to waste their limited time and resources on cases that will not stand up in court. A prosecutor may also drop charges if the alleged crime is minor, if the defendant is a first offender, or if the prosecutor believes that the few days spent in jail before arraignment have provided enough punishment for the alleged offense. Jail overcrowding or the need to work on more serious cases may also influence the decision to drop charges. In making these decisions, prosecutors at times may discriminate against the accused because of race, wealth, or some other factor, or they may discriminate against certain victims, such as women who have been sexually assaulted by an intimate partner or other acquaintance (Spohn and Holleran, 2001).

Defense attorneys use pretrial proceedings to challenge the prosecution's evidence. They make **motions** to the court requesting that an order be issued to bring about a specific action. For example, the defense may seek an order for the prosecution to share certain evidence, or for the exclusion of evidence based on the claim that it was obtained through improper questioning of the suspect or an improper search.

As Figure 9.1 shows, prosecutors use their decision-making power to filter many cases out of the system. The 100 cases illustrated are typical felony cases. The percentage of cases varies from city to city, depending on such factors as the effectiveness of police investigations and prosecutors' policies about which cases to pursue. In the figure, nearly half of those arrested did not ultimately face felony prosecutions. A small number of defendants were steered toward diversion programs. A larger number had

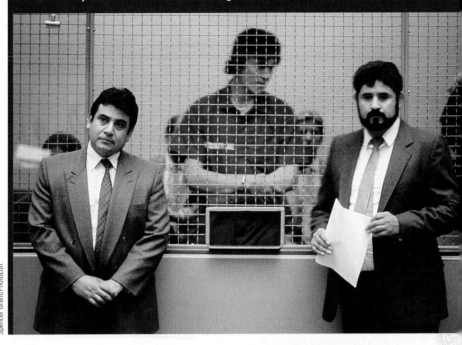

"Night Stalker" Richard Ramirez, flanked by his attorneys, is arraigned on rape and murder charges in Santa Ana, California. When defendants are thought to pose a threat, they may have their "day in court" from within a wired cage.

Spencer Grant/PhotoEdit

arraignment The court appearance of an accused person in which the charges are read and the accused, advised by a lawyer, pleads guilty or not guilty.

motion An application to a court requesting that an order be issued to bring about a specific action.

FIGURE 9.1

Typical outcomes of 100 urban felony cases

Prosecutors and judges make crucial decisions during the period before trial or plea. Once cases are bound over for disposition, guilty pleas are many, trials are few, and acquittals are rare.

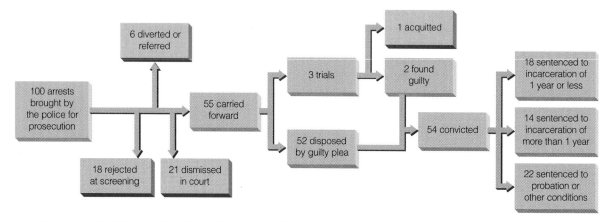

Source: Barbara Boland, Paul Mahanna, and Ronald Stones, *The Prosecution of Felony Arrests, 1988* (Washington, DC: Bureau of Justice Statistics, U.S. Government Printing Office, 1992), 2.

their cases dismissed for various reasons, including lack of evidence, the minor nature of the charges, or first-time offender status. Some of the 22 sentenced to probation or other conditions may actually be imprisoned if the offenders commit a crime after release into the community. In these cases, the prosecutor simply chooses to pursue revocation of probation or parole, typically an easier and quicker process than proving guilt for a new crime (Kingsnorth, MacIntosh, and Sutherland, 2002).

During the pretrial process, defendants are exposed to the informal, "assembly-line" atmosphere of the lower criminal courts. Often, decisions are quickly made about bail, arraignment, pleas, and the disposition of cases. Moving cases as quickly as possible seems to be the major goal of many judges and attorneys during the pretrial process. Courts throughout the nation face pressure to limit the number of cases going to trial. This pressure may affect the decisions of both judges and prosecutors, as well as the defense attorneys who seek to maintain good relationships with them. American courts often have too little money, too few staff members, and not enough time to give detailed attention to each case, let alone a full trial.

CHECKPOINT

1. What are the purposes of the initial appearance, arraignment, and motions?

2. Why and how are cases filtered out of the system?

Answers

1. The initial appearance determines if there is probable cause to support the arrest. Arraignments involve the formal reading of charges and the entry of a plea. Motions seek information and the vindication of defendants' rights.

2. Cases are filtered out through the discretionary decisions of prosecutors and judges when they believe that there is inadequate evidence to proceed, or when prosecutors believe that their scarce resources are best directed at other cases.

Bail: Pretrial Release

It is often stated that defendants are presumed innocent until proved guilty or until they enter a guilty plea. However, people who are arrested are taken to jail. They are deprived of their freedom and, in many cases, subjected to miserable living conditions while they await the processing of their cases. The idea that people who are presumed innocent can lose their freedom—sometimes for many months—as their cases work their way toward trial, clashes with the American values of freedom and liberty. It is not clear how committed Americans are to preserving the ideal of freedom for people who have not yet been convicted of crimes. As indicated by one public opinion study (see "What Americans Think"), members of the public may be less concerned than lawyers about the ideal of freedom when it applies to suspected criminals. Such concerns may have further diminished in the aftermath of September 11, as the federal government began to hold terrorism suspects whom they labeled "enemy combatants" without providing any bail hearing, evidence of guilt, or access to defense attorneys. The outcry about such deprivations of liberty has come from specific civil rights groups and attorneys rather than from the general public.

A conflict is bound to occur between the American value of individual liberty and the need to keep some criminal suspects in jail in order to protect society from violent people or from those who may try to escape prosecution. However, not every person charged with a criminal offense need be detained. Thus, bail and other release methods are used on the condition that the defendants will appear in court as required.

Bail is a sum of money or property, specified by the judge, that defendants present to the court as a condition of pretrial release. They forfeit the bail if they do not appear in court as scheduled. Although people are generally entitled to a bail hearing as part of their right to due process, there is no constitutional right to release on bail, nor even a right to have the court set an amount as the condition of release. The Eighth Amendment to the U.S. Constitution forbids excessive bail, and state bail laws are usually designed to prevent discrimination in setting bail. They do not guarantee, however, that all defendants will have a realistic chance of being released before trial.

Because the accused is presumed to be innocent, bail should not be used as punishment. The amount of bail should therefore be high enough to ensure that the defendant appears in court for trial—but no higher. As we have seen, however, this is not the only purpose of bail. The community must be protected from the crimes that some defendants would likely commit while out on bail. Congress and some of the states have passed laws that permit preventive detention of defendants when the judge concludes that they pose a threat to the community while awaiting trial.

THE REALITY OF THE BAIL SYSTEM

The reality of the bail system is far from the ideal. The question of bail may arise at the police station, at the initial court appearance in a misdemeanor case, or at the arraignment in most felony cases. For minor offenses, police officers may have a standard list of bail amounts. For serious offenses, a judge will set bail in court. In both cases, those setting bail may have discretion to set differing bail amounts for various suspects, depending on the circumstances of each case. As you read "Real-World Activity" at the end of the chapter, consider whether it is fair and appropriate to set bail at significantly different amounts for people involved in the same alleged crime.

In almost all courts, the amount of bail is based mainly on the judge's view of the seriousness of the crime and of the defendant's record. In part, this emphasis results from a lack of information about the accused. Because bail is typically determined 24 to 48 hours after an arrest, there is little time to conduct a more thorough assessment. As a result, judges in many communities have developed standard rates: so many dollars for such-and-such an offense. In some cases, a judge may set a high bail if the police or prosecutor want a certain person to be kept off the streets.

Critics of the bail system argue that it discriminates against poor people. Imagine that you have been arrested and have no money. Should you be denied a chance for freedom before trial just because you are poor? What if you have a little money, but if you use it to post bail you will not have any left to hire your own attorney? Professional criminals and the affluent have no trouble making bail; many drug dealers, for instance, can readily make bail and go on dealing while awaiting trial. In contrast, a poor person arrested for a minor violation may spend the pretrial period in jail. Should dangerous, wealthy offenders be allowed out on bail while nonviolent, poor suspects are locked up?

According to a study of felony defendants in the nation's most populous counties, 62 percent were released before disposition of their cases, 32 percent were unable to make bail, and 6 percent were detained without bail (T. H. Cohen and Reaves, 2006).

bail An amount of money, specified by a judge, to be paid as a condition of pretrial release to ensure that the accused will appear in court as required.

WHAT AMERICANS THINK

Question: "Do you favor allowing the government to hold suspected criminals for more than 48 hours without being charged for a specific crime?"

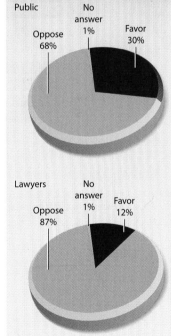

Public

Oppose 68%
No answer 1%
Favor 30%

Lawyers

Oppose 87%
No answer 1%
Favor 12%

Go to http://www.thomsonedu.com/criminaljustice/cole to compare your opinion on this issue with the opinions of other criminal justice students.

Source: Schmuel Lock, *Crime, Public Opinion, and Civil Liberties* (Westport, CT: Praeger, 1999), 193, 217. Reproduced with permission of Greenwood Publishing Group, Inc., Westport, CT.

FIGURE 9.2

Bail amounts for felony defendants by type of offense
The amount of bail varies according to the offense.

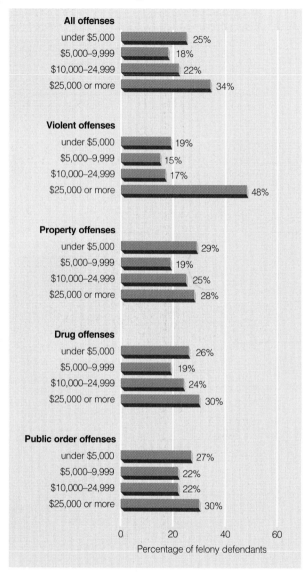

Source: Thomas H. Cohen and Brian A. Reaves, *Felony Defendants in Large Urban Counties, 2002* (Washington, DC: U.S. Government Printing Office, 2006), 18.

Among those who gained release, 25 percent had bail set at less than $5,000. Figure 9.2 shows the amounts of bail set for various types of felony offenses. Those who cannot make bail must remain in jail awaiting trial, unless they can obtain enough money to pay a bail bondsman's fee. Given the length of time between arraignment and trial in most courts and the hardships of pretrial detention, bondsmen are important to defendants in many cities.

BAIL BONDSMEN

The bail bondsman is a key figure in the bail process. Bail bondsmen (or women) are private businesspeople who are paid fees by defendants who lack the money to make bail. They are licensed by the state and can choose their own clients. In exchange for a fee, which may be 5 to 10 percent of the bail amount, the bondsman will put up the money (or property) to gain the defendant's release. Bondsmen are not obliged to provide bail money for every defendant who seeks to use their services. Instead, they decide which defendants are likely to return for court appearances. If the defendant skips town, the bondsman's money is forfeited and the bondman has a strong incentive to try to locate the missing defendant. Sometimes bondsmen and their employees have used violence or otherwise gone outside the boundaries of the law in their efforts to capture missing defendants.

Bondsmen may build relationships with police officers and jailers to obtain referrals. Many defendants may not know whom to call for help in making bail, and officers can steer them to a particular bondsman. This can lead to corruption if a bondsman pays a jailer or police officer to make such referrals. Moreover, these relationships may lead to improper cooperation, such as a bondsman refusing to help a particular defendant if the police would like to see that defendant remain in jail.

Despite the problems posed by the bondsmen's role, and although bondsmen act in their own interest, they contribute to the smooth processing of cases (Dill, 1975). A major reason that defendants fail to appear for scheduled court appearances is forgetfulness and confusion about when and where they must appear. Courthouses in large cities are huge bureaucracies that do not always clearly communicate to a defendant a change in the time and location of a hearing. Bondsmen can help by reminding defendants about court dates, calling defendants' relatives to make sure that the defendant will arrive on time, and warning defendants about the penalties for failing to appear.

Although the justice system benefits from the activities of bondsmen, court and law enforcement officials could handle the same functions as well or better if they had the resources, time, and interest to make sure that released defendants return to court. If all courts had pretrial services offices such as those in the federal courts, defendants could be monitored and reminded to return to court but avoid the risks of discrimination and corruption associated with the use of bail bondsmen (Carr, 1993; Marsh, 1994; Peoples, 1995).

Further, the problems caused by bondsmen and bounty hunters in using their own means to find and capture fugitives could be avoided if pretrial services offices reduced the role of bail bondsmen. The hunt for fugitives, such as defendants who skip bail, could remain the exclusive responsibility of trained law enforcement personnel. In the federal system, U.S. marshals are the main law enforcement officials in the court system, responsible for court security, prisoner transport, and tracking down fugitives. Read "Careers in Criminal Justice" to learn about the job of a U.S. marshal.

SETTING BAIL

When the police set bail at the station house for minor offenses, they usually apply a standard amount for a particular charge. By contrast, when a judge sets bail, the amount of bail and conditions of release result from interactions among the judge, prosecutor, and defense attorney. These actors discuss the defendant's personal qualities and prior record. The prosecutor may stress the seriousness of the crime, the defendant's record, and negative personal characteristics. The defense attorney, if one has been hired or appointed at this point in the process, may stress the defendant's good job, family responsibilities, and place in the community. Like other aspects of bail, these factors may favor affluent defendants over the poor, the unemployed, and people with unstable families. Yet many of these factors provide no clear information about how dangerous a defendant is or whether he or she will appear in court.

Research studies highlight the disadvantages of the poor in the bail process. A study of Hispanic arrestees in the Southwest found that those who could afford to hire their own attorneys were seven times more likely to gain pretrial release than were those represented at public expense (Holmes et al., 1996). This result may reflect the fact that affluent defendants are better able to come up with bail money, as well as the possibility that private attorneys fight harder for their clients in the early stages of the criminal process.

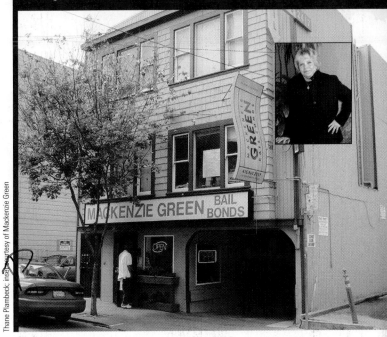

Mackenzie Green is a well-known California bondsman and bounty hunter. Each year 20 percent of felony defendants out on bail skip trial, but 97 percent are brought back to court, 82 percent by bondsmen and their agents.

Thane Plambeck; inset courtesy of Mackenzie Green

The amount of bail may also reflect the defendant's social class or even racial or ethnic discrimination by criminal justice officials. A study by the State Bail Commission of cases in Connecticut showed that at each step in the process African American and Hispanic men with clean records received bail amounts double those given whites. One reason for the difference might be that poor defendants often do not have jobs and a permanent residence, factors that strongly influence setting bail. The study also recognized that the higher bail might result from the fact that African Americans and Hispanics were more likely than whites to be charged with a felony. However, the largest disparities in bail appeared in felony drug cases. In these cases the average bail for African Americans and Hispanics was four times higher than for whites at the same courthouse (Houston and Ewing, 1991).

REFORMING THE BAIL SYSTEM

Studies of pretrial detention in such cities as Philadelphia and New York have raised questions about the need to hold defendants in jail. Criticisms of the bail system focus on judges' discretion in setting bail amounts, the fact that the poor are deprived of their freedom while the affluent can afford bail, the negative aspects of bail bondsmen, and jail conditions for those detained while awaiting trial.

In response to such criticisms, efforts to reform the bail system have arisen. Such efforts often focus on reducing the number of defendants held in jail. As such, the percentage of defendants released on bail has increased in recent decades, in part because of the use of certain pretrial release methods, which we now discuss.

Citation   A **citation**, or summons, to appear in court—a "ticket"—is often issued to a person accused of committing a traffic offense or some other minor violation. By issuing the citation, the officer avoids taking the accused person to the station house for booking and to court for arraignment and setting of bail. Citations are now being used for more serious offenses, in part because the police want to reduce the amount

citation A written order or summons, issued by a law enforcement officer, directing an alleged offender to appear in court at a specific time to answer a criminal charge.

CAREERS IN CRIMINAL JUSTICE

U.S. Marshal

NATURE OF THE WORK

U.S. marshals are the federal court system's law enforcement division. Marshals provide security at courthouses, including checking people who enter the building and maintaining order in courtrooms. They also transport prisoners from jail to court and from court to prison. In this role, they must conduct body searches and watch closely for escape attempts. Marshals also provide security for witnesses who need protection and supervise juries that are kept overnight in hotels during a trial (sequestered juries, discussed later). In addition, marshals conduct detective work in tracking and capturing fugitives who have skipped bail. Locating and capturing fugitives can place marshals in dangerous situations, from high-speed pursuits to encountering desperate, armed offenders. Marshals are highly trained, armed, law enforcement officers dedicated to supporting the mission of the courts.

REQUIRED QUALIFICATIONS

To apply for a position with the U.S. Marshals Service, applicants must be U.S. citizens between the ages of 21 and 36. They must possess a four-year college degree or an equivalent combination of education and experience. They must be in excellent physical condition, pass medical exams including screenings for vision and hearing, and have a good driving record.

To be placed on the eligibility list, applicants must pass an initial written exam. Selection for initial interviews is based on the scores from this test. Those who pass the initial interviews must undergo a medical exam, physical fitness test, and background check. Afterward, applicants attend a ten-week training course at the U.S. Marshals training center in Glynco, Georgia. The training programs include instruction in law, firearms, court security, protective service, surveillance, prisoner restraint, and other essential skills and knowledge.

EARNINGS AND JOB OUTLOOK

New deputy U.S. marshals are hired at the GS-5 level ($35,000), but those with law enforcement experience may start at the GS-7 level ($39,000). Unlike some criminal justice–related occupations that are expanding rapidly in the aftermath of 9/11 (such as Border Patrol and Transportation Security), openings for U.S. marshal are likely to depend on the retirement of current marshals or on authorizations by Congress to build new courthouses or increase security at existing ones. People interested in a career as a U.S. marshal should seek information about the qualifying exam in order to be placed on the eligibility list so that they are available for consideration as openings develop.

MORE INFORMATION

For more information about a career as a U.S. marshal, see the website of the U.S. Marshals Service, listed on the Cole/Smith Criminal Justice in America Companion Website: http://www.thomsonedu.com/criminaljustice/cole.

---

of time they spend booking minor offenders and waiting in arraignment court for their cases to come up.

Release on Recognizance   Pioneered in the 1960s by the Vera Institute of Justice in New York City, the **release on recognizance (ROR)** approach is based on the assumption that judges will grant releases if the defendant is reliable and has roots in the community. Soon after the arrest, court personnel talk to defendants about their job, family, prior record, and associations. They then decide whether to recommend release. In the first three years of the New York project, more than ten thousand defendants were interviewed and about 3,500 were released. Only 1.5 percent failed to appear in court at the scheduled time, a rate almost three times better than the rate for those released on bail (Goldfarb, 1965). Programs in other cities have had similar results, although Sheila Royo Maxwell's research raises questions about whether women and property crime defendants on ROR are less likely than other defendants to appear in court (Maxwell, 1999).

release on recognizance (ROR)
Pretrial release granted, on the defendant's promise to appear in court, because the judge believes that the defendant's ties to the community guarantee that he or she will appear.

Ten Percent Cash Bail   Although ROR is a useful alternative to money bail, judges are unwilling to release some defendants on their own recognizance. Some states (Illinois, Kentucky, Nebraska, Oregon, and Pennsylvania) have **percentage bail** programs in which the defendants deposit with the court an amount of cash equal to 10 percent of their bail. When they appear in court as required, this amount is returned minus a 1 percent fee for administrative costs. Begun in Illinois in 1964, this plan is designed to release as many defendants as possible without using bail bondsmen.

Bail Guidelines   To deal with the problem of unequal treatment, reformers have written guidelines for setting bail. The guidelines specify the standards judges should use in setting bail and also list appropriate amounts. Judges are expected to follow the guidelines but may deviate from them in special situations. The guidelines take into account the seriousness of the offense and the defendant's prior record in order to protect the community and ensure that released suspects will likely return for court appearances.

Preventive Detention   Reforms have been suggested not only by those concerned with unfairness in the bail system but also by those concerned with stopping crime. Critics of the bail system point to a link between release on bail and the commission of crimes, arguing that the accused can commit other crimes while awaiting trial. A study of the nation's most populous counties found that 18 percent of felony defendants released on bail were rearrested for another crime (Cohen and Reaves, 2006). To address this problem, legislatures have passed laws permitting detention of defendants without bail.

For federal criminal cases, Congress enacted the Bail Reform Act of 1984, which authorizes **preventive detention.** Under the act, if prosecutors recommend that defendants be kept in jail, a federal judge holds a hearing to determine (1) if there is a serious risk that the person will flee; (2) if the person will obstruct justice or threaten, injure, or intimidate a prospective witness or juror; or (3) if the offense is one of violence or one punishable by life imprisonment or death. On finding that one or more of these factors make setting bail impossible without endangering the community, the judge can order the defendant held in jail until the case is completed (C. E. Smith, 1990).

Critics of preventive detention argue that it violates the Constitution's due process clause because the accused is held in custody until a verdict is rendered. However, the Supreme Court has ruled that it is constitutional. The preventive detention provisions of the Bail Reform Act of 1984 were upheld in *United States v. Salerno and Cafero* (1987). The justices said that preventive detention was a legitimate use of government power because it was not designed to punish the accused. Instead, it deals with the problem of people who commit crimes while on bail. By upholding the federal law, the Court also upheld state laws dealing with preventive detention (M. Miller and Guggenheim, 1990).

Supporters of preventive detention claim that it ensures that drug dealers, who often treat bail as a business expense, cannot flee before trial. Research has shown that the nature and seriousness of the charge, a history of prior arrests, and drug use all have a strong bearing on the likelihood that a defendant will commit a crime while on bail.

percentage bail Defendants may deposit a percentage (usually 10 percent) of the full bail with the court. The full amount of the bail is required if the defendant fails to appear. The percentage of bail is returned after disposition of the case, although the court often retains 1 percent for administrative costs.

preventive detention Holding a defendant for trial, based on a judge's finding that if the defendant were released on bail, he or she would endanger the safety of any other person and the community or would flee.

United States v. Salerno and Cafero (1987) Preventive detention provisions of the Bail Reform Act of 1984 are upheld as a legitimate use of government power designed to prevent people from committing crimes while on bail.

ThomsonNOW™
Improve your grade on the exam with Personalized Study! For reinforcement resources and a mastery check of Bail: Pretrial Release, go to www.thomsonedu.com/thomsonnow.

CHECKPOINT

3. What factors affect whether bail is set and how much money or property a defendant must provide to gain pretrial release?

4. What methods are used to facilitate pretrial release for certain defendants?

Answers

3. Bail decisions are based primarily on the judge's evaluation of the seriousness of the offense and the defendant's prior record. The decisions are influenced by the prosecutor's recommendations and the defense attorney's counterarguments about the defendant's personal qualities and ties to the community.

4. Police citations, release on own recognizance (ROR), and 10 percent cash bail.

Pretrial Detention

People who are not released before trial must remain in jail. Often called the ultimate ghetto, American jails hold almost 750,000 people on any one day. Most are poor, half are in pretrial detention, and the rest are serving sentences (normally of less than one year) or are waiting to be moved to state prison or to another jurisdiction (Clear, Cole, and Reisig, 2006).

Urban jails also contain troubled people, many with mental health and drug abuse problems, whom police have swept off the streets. Michael Welch calls this process, in which the police remove socially offensive people from certain areas, "social sanitation" (1994:262). Conditions in jails are often much harsher than those in prisons. People awaiting trial are often held in barracks-like cells with sentenced offenders. Thus, a "presumed innocent" pretrial detainee might spend weeks in the same confined space with troubled people or sentenced felons (Beck, Karberg, and Harrison, 2002).

The period just after arrest is the most frightening and difficult time for suspects. Imagine freely walking the streets one minute and being locked in a small space with a large number of troubled and potentially dangerous cell mates the next. Suddenly you have no privacy and must share an open toilet with hostile strangers. You have been fingerprinted, photographed, and questioned—treated like the "criminal" that the police and the criminal justice system consider you to be. You are alone with people whose behavior you cannot predict. You are left to worry about what might happen. If you are female, you may be placed in a cell by yourself (Steury and Frank, 1990). Given the stressful nature of arrest and jailing, it is little wonder that most jail suicides and psychotic episodes occur during the first hours of detention.

Often, jails holding pretrial detainees are crowded and have no programs. Awaiting disposition of a case is the most frightening and difficult time for most suspects. The suicide rate in jails is much higher than that in prisons.

AP Photo/Matt York

Other factors can make the shock of arrest and detention even worse. Many people are arrested for offenses they committed while under the influence of drugs or alcohol. They may be less able than others to cope with their new situation. Young arrestees who face the risk of being victimized by older, stronger cell mates may sink into depression. Detainees also worry about losing their jobs while in jail, because they do not know if or when they will be released.

As you read the Comparative Perspective concerning pretrial detention in Russia, ask yourself whether individual U.S. jails could ever have comparable conditions, especially if the county administering the jail has budget problems that hinder upgrading facilities and training personnel. What factors help keep detainees in American jails from experiencing the hardships endured by those in Russian jails?

Although most Americans arrested for felonies have their cases adjudicated within three months, 31 percent wait for more than six months and 13 percent for more than a year (Cohen and Reaves, 2006). Imagine the hardships for the 38 percent of arrestees who cannot gain pretrial release if they are among those who must wait six months or a year before the courts complete the processing of their cases. The psychological and economic hardships faced by pretrial detainees and their families can be major and prolonged.

Pretrial detention not only imposes stresses and hardships that may reach a crisis level; it can also affect the outcomes of cases. People in jail can give little help to their attorneys. They cannot help find witnesses and perform other useful tasks on their own behalf. In addition, they may feel pressured to plead guilty in order to end their indefinite stay in jail. Even if they believe that they should not be convicted of the crime charged, they may prefer to start serving

COMPARATIVE PERSPECTIVE

Pretrial Detention in Russia

Prisoners almost always swear they are not guilty. In Russian pretrial detention centers, many inmates insist that they no longer care about proving their innocence. Pretrial detainees spend long periods in unhealthy conditions while investigations of their alleged offense are conducted.

"At first, all I wanted was a fair trial," Pyotr Kuznetsov, 51, said in a dank and stinking cell of Matrosskaya Tishina, one of Moscow's largest and most infamous detention centers.

He said he had been arrested and brutally beaten for stealing less than $5 and had already spent 10 months behind bars awaiting trial. His lice-ridden eighteenth-century cell, built for 30, currently warehouses more than 100 men. The inmates share beds, sleeping in three shifts.

"All I want now is to get out of here, even to a labor camp," Mr. Kuznetsov said. "I've been in prison before, and it is not as bad as this."

Perhaps the most terrifying aspect of the Russian penal system is pretrial detention. Close to 300,000 people awaiting trial are now in jail. There, a death sentence stalks people who have not yet been convicted of a crime.

Unprotected from the TB (tuberculosis) epidemic (as many as 50 percent of Russian prisoners are believed to be infected) and other infectious diseases, many detainees end up spending two, three, and even four years awaiting their day in court in cells as packed as a rush-hour subway car.

The Russian legal system is so tortuous that people can find themselves detained for months or years even on minor charges. Prosecutors are legally required to complete a criminal investigation within

two years, but there is no time limit for judges, who can keep a suspect waiting for trial indefinitely. The average stay in detention is 10 months.

In Soviet times, bail was dismissed as a capitalist folly. Today, bail is legal, but it remains a novelty, granted to less than 2 percent of the country's accused—usually to mobsters who have ready cash and connections to a compliant judge.

"Under our system, it is much harder to acquit than find a person guilty," Sergei Pasin, a judge in a Moscow appeals court explained. "Less than 1 percent of all cases end in an acquittal, and that is because before a judge can acquit, he must do a huge amount of work that is not done by the police: requesting information, soliciting expert testimony, etc."

"The fact that time served before trial is subtracted from convicted prisoners' sentences can hardly be viewed as justice," Judge Pasin said. "The pre-detention centers are a far worse punishment than prison," he said. Prisons and labor camps in Russia are grim, but they are not nearly as overcrowded.

In a report on torture in Russia, Amnesty International said that "torture and ill-treatment occur at all stages of detention and imprisonment," but noted that it was most often reported in pretrial detention.

"Its main purpose appears to be to intimidate detainees and obtain confessions," the report said. Confessions, more than evidence, are a major part of criminal investigations in Russia.

How does the American criminal justice system differ from Russia's? How do those differences affect the conditions of pretrial detention?

Source: Alessandra Stanley, "Russians Lament the Crime of Punishment," *New York Times*, January 1, 1998, p. A1. Copyright © 1998 by the New York Times Co. Reprinted by permission.

---

a prison or jail sentence with a definite end point. Some may even gain quicker release on probation or in a community corrections program by pleading guilty, whereas they might stay in jail for a longer period by insisting on their innocence and awaiting a trial.

CHECKPOINT

5. What categories of people are found in jails?

6. What are the sources of stress for people in jail awaiting trial?

Answers

5. Pretrial detainees for whom bail was not set or those who are too poor to pay the bail amount required, people serving short sentences for misdemeanors, people convicted of felonies awaiting transfer to prison, and people with psychological or substance abuse problems who have been swept off the streets.

6. Living with difficult and potentially dangerous cell mates; uncertainty about what will happen to their case, their families, their jobs, and their ability to contribute to preparing a defense.

Plea Bargaining

For the vast majority of cases, plea bargaining—also known as negotiating a settlement, copping a plea, or copping out—is the most important step in the criminal justice process. Very few cases go to trial; instead, a negotiated guilty plea arrived at through the interactions of prosecutors, defense lawyers, and judges determines what will happen to most defendants. The courtroom workgroup, as discussed in Chapter 8,

Jack Abramoff leaves federal court in Washington on January 3, 2006. The once-powerful lobbyist pleaded guilty to federal charges of conspiracy, tax evasion, and mail fraud, agreeing to cooperate with prosecutors investigating influence peddling that has threatened powerful members of the U.S. Congress.

AP Photo/Gerald Herbert

Santobello v. New York (1971)
When a guilty plea rests on a promise of a prosecutor, the promise must be fulfilled.

uses plea bargaining to determine the outcomes of cases quickly and efficiently in those courthouses where the same actors work together repeatedly in processing cases.

Quick resolution of cases through negotiated guilty pleas became common and was upheld by the Supreme Court in the 1971 case of *Santobello v. New York*. In the decision Chief Justice Warren Burger described plea bargaining in favorable terms in ruling that prosecutors were obliged to fulfill promises made during plea negotiations. According to Burger, "'Plea bargaining' is an essential component of the administration of justice. Properly administered, it is to be encouraged" because it saves time and criminal justice resources while also protecting the community.

In 1976 Justice Potter Stewart revealed the heart and soul of plea bargaining when he wrote in *Blackledge v. Allison* that plea bargaining "can benefit all concerned" in a criminal case. There are advantages for defendants, prosecutors, defense attorneys, and judges. Defendants can have their cases completed more quickly and know what the punishment will be, instead of facing the uncertainty of a judge's sentencing decision. Moreover, the defendant is likely to receive less than the maximum punishment that might have been imposed after a trial. Prosecutors are not being "soft on crime" when they plea bargain. Instead, they gain an easy conviction, even in cases in which enough evidence may not have been gathered to convince a jury to convict the defendant. They also save time and resources by disposing of cases without having to prepare for a trial. Private defense attorneys also save the time needed to prepare for a trial. They earn their fee quickly and can move on to the next case. Similarly, plea bargaining helps public defenders cope with large caseloads. Judges, too, avoid time-consuming trials and the prospect of having to decide what sentence to impose on the defendant. Instead, they often adopt the sentence recommended by the prosecutor in consultation with the defense attorney, provided that it is within the range of sentences that they deem appropriate for a given crime and offender.

Because plea bargaining benefits all involved, it is little wonder that it still exists, even when prosecutors, legislators, or judges claim that they wish to abolish it. In California, for example, voters decided to ban plea bargaining for serious felony cases. Research showed, however, that when plea bargaining was barred in the felony trial courts, it did not disappear. It simply occurred earlier in the justice process, at the suspect's first appearance in the lower-level municipal court (McCoy, 1993). Efforts to abolish plea bargaining may also result in bargaining over the charges instead of over the sentence that will be recommended in exchange for a guilty plea. And if a

CLOSE UP

Banning Plea Bargaining in Tennessee

In January 1997, William Gibbons, the district attorney for Shelby County, Tennessee, which includes the City of Memphis, introduced a policy of refusing to reduce charges of first- and second-degree murder and charges of robbery or rape that involved the use of a deadly weapon. Under the policy, anyone indicted for these crimes must either plead guilty to the charge specified or go to trial. The operation of the policy raises interesting questions about the impact of bans on plea bargaining.

The District Attorney's Office hoped that the "no deal" policy and the resulting tough sentences would deter other potential offenders from committing violent crimes. Thus, the ban on plea bargaining was accompanied by a public relations campaign to spread the word about the new policy. "No Deal" signs, decals, and bumper stickers were distributed to businesses and neighborhood watch groups.

The District Attorney's Office claims that the ban "had a positive impact in reducing violent felonies." But can one truly know whether crime reductions are due to the plea-bargaining policy rather than a general social trend?

The District Attorney's Office says that the effectiveness of the new policy is due to cooperation between the prosecutor and local law enforcement agencies. Under the new policy, representatives of the District Attorney's Office meet with representatives of the Memphis Police Department and the Shelby County Sheriff's Office to screen cases involving the violent crimes covered by the policy. This early review helps insure that the DA's Office has a good case with strong evidence before someone is charged and a proposed indictment is presented to the grand jury.

By filtering out cases for which the most serious charges are not provable, does this review and screening process perhaps fulfill the function served by plea bargaining in other cities? Elsewhere, the plea negotiation process involves discussions between defense attorneys and prosecutors about the provable facts of a case so that both sides can reach agreement about the going rate of punishment for that particular offender and crime. In effect, then, might the Memphis screening process really just produce the same results in "no deal" cases that would have been produced anyway through plea negotiations in other cities?

In reality, the Memphis ban on plea bargaining is not absolute, even for the specified crimes to which it applies. There can be "exceptions based on legal, factual, or ethical grounds [that] must be approved by a supervisor [in the District Attorney's Office] and documented in writing." Does the possibility of exceptions create incentives for defense attorneys to seek special deals for their clients? Does it create opportunities for prosecutors to use discretion to reduce charges against particular defendants or the clients of particular attorneys?

Consider the following results from the "no deal" policy in 2003. Out of 560 "no deals" cases, 323 defendants entered guilty pleas to the charges and an additional 114 defendants were convicted at trial. Small numbers of defendants were acquitted at trial and dozens had their charges dismissed. The most interesting number represents the 90 defendants who pleaded guilty to lesser charges under the "no deal" system. According to the prosecutor's office, the charge reductions were usually the result of the inability of the police to locate crucial witnesses needed for gaining a conviction at trial. In light of those numbers, does the "no deal" policy really live up to its name? Would the public be surprised to learn that a "no deal" policy permits so many plea bargains resulting in reduced charges? Alternatively, in light of how the criminal justice system operates and its dependence on witnesses and discretionary decisions, would it be unrealistic to have a policy in which there were actually never any charge reductions?

RESEARCHING THE INTERNET

To see a report evaluating Alaska's early effort to abolish plea bargaining, read the report of the Alaska Judicial Council at the corresponding website listed on the Cole/Smith Criminal Justice in America Companion Website: http://www .thomsonedu.com/criminaljustice/cole.

FOR CRITICAL ANALYSIS

Are the "no deal" policy and the accompanying advertising campaign primarily a public relations effort to gain support and credit for the District Attorney's Office? Is it possible that the district attorney honestly believes that the "no deal" policy has positive benefits even if it may have produced little change? What do you think?

Sources: Thomas D. Henderson, "No Deals Policy," Office of the District Attorney General, 30th Judicial District of Tennessee, 1999, http://www.scdag.com/nodeals/htm#top; Michael J. Sniffen, "Crime Down for 7th Straight Year," Associated Press, October 17, 1999; *2003 Annual Report of District Attorney General's Office, Shelby County, Tennessee,* 2004, http://www.scdag.com/ar2003.pdf.

---

prosecutor forbids his or her staff to plea bargain, judges may become more involved in negotiating and facilitating guilty pleas that result in predictable punishments for offenders. Consider the ban on plea bargaining for several serious violent crimes in Memphis, Tennessee, described in the Close Up box.

EXCHANGE RELATIONSHIPS IN PLEA BARGAINING

As we have seen, plea bargaining is a set of exchange relationships in which the prosecutor, the defense attorney, the defendant, and sometimes the judge participate. All have specific goals, all try to use the situation to their own advantage, and all are likely to see the exchange as a success.

Plea bargaining does not always occur in a single meeting between the prosecutor and defense attorney. One study showed that plea bargaining is a process in which prosecutors and defense attorneys interact again and again as they move further along in the judicial process. As time passes, the discovery of more evidence or new information about the defendant's background may strengthen the prosecutor's hand (Emmelman, 1996). Often the prosecution rather than the defense is in the best position to obtain new evidence (Cooney, 1994). However, the defense attorney's position may gain strength if the prosecutor does not wish to spend time preparing for a trial.

TACTICS OF PROSECUTOR AND DEFENSE

Plea bargaining between defense counsel and prosecutor is a serious game in which friendliness and joking can mask efforts to advance each side's cause. Each side tries to impress the other with its confidence in its own case while pointing out weaknesses in the other side's case. An unspoken rule of openness and candor usually keeps the relationship on good terms. Little effort is made to conceal information that could later be useful to the other side in the courtroom. Studies show that the outcomes of plea bargaining may depend on the relationships between prosecutors and individual attorneys, as well as the defense counsel's willingness to fight for the client (Champion, 1989).

A tactic that many prosecutors bring to plea-bargaining sessions is the multiple-offense indictment. Multiple-offense charges are especially important to prosecuting attorneys in difficult cases—in which, for instance, the victim is reluctant to provide information, the value of the stolen item is unclear, and the evidence may not be reliable. The police often file charges of selling a drug when they know they can probably convict only for possession. Because the accused persons know that the penalty for selling is much greater, they are tempted to plead guilty to the lesser charge rather than risk a severer punishment, even if the probability of conviction on the more serious charge is uncertain.

Defense attorneys may threaten to ask for a jury trial if concessions are not made. To strengthen their hand further, they may also file pretrial motions that require a formal response by the prosecutor. Another tactic is to seek to reschedule pretrial activities in the hope that, with delay, witnesses will become unavailable, media attention will die down, and memories of the crime will grow weaker by the time of the trial. Rather than resort to such legal tactics, however, some attorneys prefer to bargain on the basis of friendship.

PLEAS WITHOUT BARGAINING

Studies have shown that in many courts give-and-take plea bargaining does not occur for certain types of cases, yet they have as many guilty pleas as do other courts (Eisenstein, Flemming, and Nardulli, 1988). The term *bargaining* may be misleading in that it implies haggling. Many scholars argue that guilty pleas emerge after the prosecutor, the defense attorney, and sometimes the judge have reached an agreement to "settle the facts" (Utz, 1978). In this view the parties first study the facts of a case. What were the circumstances of the event? Was it really an assault or was it more of a shoving match? Did the victim antagonize the accused? Each side may hope to persuade the other that its view of the defendant's actions is backed up by provable facts. The prosecution wants the defense to believe that strong evidence proves its version of the event. The defense attorney wants to convince the prosecution that the evidence is not solid and that there is a risk of acquittal if the case is heard by a jury.

In some cases, the evidence is strong and the defense attorney has little hope of persuading the prosecutor otherwise. Through their discussions, the prosecutor and defense attorney seek to reach a shared view of the provable facts in the case. Once they agree on the facts, they will both know the appropriate charge, and they can agree on the sentence according to the locally defined going rate. At that point a guilty plea can be entered without any formal bargaining, because both sides agree on what the case is worth in terms of the seriousness of the charge and the usual punishment. This process may be thought of as *implicit plea bargaining* because shared understandings create the expectation that a guilty plea will lead to a less-than-maximum sentence, even without any exchange or bargaining.

As we saw in Chapter 8, the going rates for sentences for particular crimes and offenders depend on local values and sentencing patterns. Often both the prosecutor and the defense attorney belong to a particular local legal culture and thus share an understanding about how cases should be handled. On the basis of their experiences in interacting with other attorneys and judges, they become keenly aware of local practices in the treatment of cases and offenders (Worden, 1995). Thus, they may both know right away what the sentence will be for a first-time burglar or second-time robber. The sentence may differ in another courthouse because the local legal culture and going rates vary.

LEGAL ISSUES IN PLEA BARGAINING

In *Boykin v. Alabama* (1969), the U.S. Supreme Court ruled that defendants must state that the plea was made voluntarily before a judge may accept the plea. Judges have created standard forms with questions for the defendant to affirm in open court before the plea is accepted. Trial judges also must learn whether the defendant understands the consequences of pleading guilty and ensure that the plea is not obtained through pressure.

Can a trial court accept a guilty plea if the defendant claims to be innocent? In *North Carolina v. Alford* (1970), the Court allowed a defendant to enter a guilty plea for the purpose of gaining a lesser sentence, even though he maintained that he was innocent. However, the Supreme Court also stated that trial judges should not accept such a plea unless a factual basis exists for believing that the defendant is in fact guilty.

Another issue is whether the plea agreement will be fulfilled. If the prosecutor has promised to recommend a lenient sentence, the promise must be kept (*Santobello v. New York*, 1971). As ruled in *Ricketts v. Adamson* (1987), defendants must also keep their side of the bargain, such as testifying against a codefendant. However, in *Bordenkircher v. Hayes* (1978), the justices ruled that prosecutors may threaten to seek more serious charges, as long as such charges are supported by evidence, if defendants refuse to plead guilty.

CRITICISMS OF PLEA BARGAINING

Although widely used, plea bargaining receives many criticisms, of two main types. The first argues that plea bargaining is unfair because defendants give up some of their constitutional rights, especially the right to trial by jury. The second stresses sentencing policy and points out that plea bargaining reduces society's interest in appropriate punishments for crimes. In urban areas with high caseloads, harried judges and prosecutors are said to make concessions based on administrative needs, resulting in lighter sentences than those required by the penal code.

Plea bargaining also comes under fire because it is hidden from judicial scrutiny. Because the agreement is most often made at an early stage, the judge has little information about the crime or the defendant and thus cannot adequately evaluate the case. The result of "bargain justice" is that the judge, the public, and sometimes even the defendant cannot know for sure who got what from whom in exchange for what.

Other critics believe that overuse of plea bargaining breeds disrespect and even contempt for the law. They say criminals look at the judicial process as a game or a sham, much like other "deals" made in life.

Critics also contend that it is unjust to penalize people who assert their right to a trial, by giving them stiffer sentences than they would have received if they had pleaded guilty. The evidence here is unclear, although it is widely believed that an extra penalty is imposed on defendants who take up the court's time by asserting their right to a trial (Spohn, 1992). Critics note that federal sentencing guidelines also encourage avoidance of trial because they include a two-point deduction from an offender's base score for a guilty plea—thus lowering the sentence—for "acceptance of responsibility" (McCoy, 1995).

Finally, another concern about plea bargaining is that innocent people will plead guilty to acts that they did not commit. Although it is hard to know how often this happens, some defendants have entered guilty pleas when they have not committed the offense. It may be hard for middle-class people to understand how anyone could possibly plead guilty when innocent. However, people with little education and low social status may lack the confidence to say "no" to an attorney who pressures them to plead guilty.

Boykin v. Alabama (1969)
Defendants must state that they are voluntarily making a plea of guilty before a judge may accept the plea.

North Carolina v. Alford (1970) A plea of guilty by a defendant who maintains his or her innocence may be accepted for the purpose of a lesser sentence.

Ricketts v. Adamson (1987)
Defendants must uphold the plea agreement or suffer the consequences.

Bordenkircher v. Hayes (1978)
A defendant's rights were not violated by a prosecutor who warned that refusing to enter a guilty plea would result in a harsher sentence.

People may also lack confidence in court processes. What if you feared that a jury might convict you and send you to prison for 20 years based on circumstantial evidence (such as being in the vicinity of the crime and wearing the same color shirt as the robber that day). Might you plead guilty and take a five-year sentence, even if you knew that you were innocent? How much confidence do you have that juries and judges will always reach the correct result? Poor people may feel helpless in the stressful climate of the courthouse and jail. If they lack faith in the system's ability to protect their rights and find them not guilty, they may accept a lighter punishment rather than risk being convicted for a serious offense.

Examine the scene in "A Question of Ethics" at the end of the chapter. Are all of the courtroom actors behaving in an honest, ethical manner? Does this scene raise questions about how plea bargains operate?

ThomsonNOW
Improve your grade on the exam with Personalized Study! For reinforcement resources and a mastery check of Plea Bargaining, go to www.thomsonedu.com/thomsonnow.

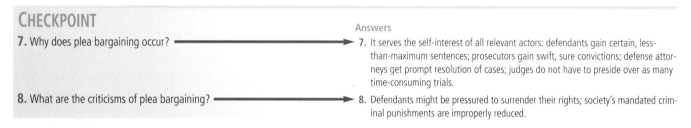

CHECKPOINT

7. Why does plea bargaining occur? ➤

8. What are the criticisms of plea bargaining? ➤

Answers

7. It serves the self-interest of all relevant actors: defendants gain certain, less-than-maximum sentences; prosecutors gain swift, sure convictions; defense attorneys get prompt resolution of cases; judges do not have to preside over as many time-consuming trials.

8. Defendants might be pressured to surrender their rights; society's mandated criminal punishments are improperly reduced.

Trial: The Exceptional Case

If cases are not dismissed or terminated through plea bargaining, they move forward for trial. The seriousness of the charge is probably the most important factor influencing the decision to go to trial. Murder, felonious assault, or rape—all charges that bring long prison terms—may require judge and jury, unless the defendant fears a certain conviction and therefore seeks a negotiated plea deal. In a study of the nation's 75 largest counties, trials occurred in 5 percent of cases or less. Sixty-one percent of these trials were **bench trials,** presided over by a judge without a jury. Only 39 percent were **jury** trials (Cohen and Reaves, 2006). When the penalty is harsh, many defendants seem willing to risk the possibility of conviction at trial. Table 9.1

bench trials Trials conducted by a judge who acts as fact finder and determines issues of law. No jury participates.

jury A panel of citizens selected according to law and sworn to determine matters of fact in a criminal case and to deliver a verdict of guilty or not guilty.

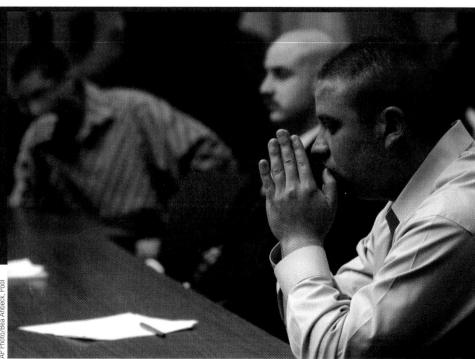

Although only 9 percent of felony cases go to trial, they often attract great attention, as did the case of Jason Cazares (right), Jose Merel (left), and Michael Magidson (center). The three were charged with killing Gwen Araujo, a transgender teen. On September 12, 2005, the jury found Merel and Madison guilty of second-degree murder but were unable to reach a decision on Cazares. Like other trials where the stakes are high, skilled attorneys for the prosecution and defense battled over the law and the evidence. On January 27, 2006, Merel and Magidson received sentences of 15 years to life. Cazares pleaded no contest to manslaughter and received a 6-year sentence.

AP Photo/Bea Ahbeck, Pool

TABLE 9.1	Percentage of Felony Convictions by Trial and Guilty Pleas, by Offense		

Defendants facing severe punishments for the most serious offenses are mostly likely to go to trial rather than plead guilty.

Offense	Bench Trial	Jury Trial	Guilty Plea
All offenses	3%	2%	95%
Murder/nonnegligent manslaughter	5	27	68
Rape	4	12	84
Robbery	3	6	91
Aggravated assault	4	4	92
Weapons offenses	4	3	93
Drug trafficking	3	2	95
Burglary	2	2	96
Motor vehicle theft	1	2	97
Fraud/forgery	2	1	97

Source: *Sourcebook of Criminal Justice Statistics, 2002* (Washington, DC: U.S. Government Printing Office, 2003), Table 5.46.2002.

shows the differences in the percentages of defendants going to trial for offenses of varying severity. Notice that crimes with greater punishments—murder, manslaughter, and rape—produce a higher percentage of trials than do other crimes.

The rates of trials also vary from city to city depending, in part, on the local legal culture. Think about how prosecutors' policies or sentencing practices in different cities may increase or decrease the incentives for a defendant to plead guilty. In addition, defense attorneys and prosecutors in different courthouses may have their own understandings about which cases should produce a plea bargain because of agreements (or disagreements) about the provable facts and the going rate of sentences for an offense.

Trials determine the fates of very few defendants. Although the right to trial by jury is ingrained in American ideology—it is mentioned in the Declaration of Independence, three amendments to the Constitution, and myriad opinions of the Supreme Court—year in and year out fewer than 10 percent of felony cases go to trial. Defendants may choose a bench trial if they believe a judge will be more capable of making an objective decision, especially if the charges or evidence will likely arouse emotional reactions in jurors.

Trials take considerable time and resources. Attorneys frequently spend weeks or months preparing—gathering evidence, responding to their opponents' motions, planning trial strategy, and setting aside from one day to several weeks to present the case in court. From the perspective of judges, prosecutors, and defense attorneys, plea bargaining presents an attractive alternative for purposes of completing cases quickly.

JURY TRIAL

Trials are based on the idea that the prosecution and defense will compete as adversaries before a judge and jury so that the truth will emerge. As such, the rules of criminal law, procedure, and evidence govern the conduct of the trial. Above the battle, the judge sees to it that the rules are followed and that the jury impartially evaluates the evidence and reflects the community's interests. In a jury trial, the jury alone evaluates the facts in a case. The adversarial process and inclusion of jurors in decision making often make trial outcomes difficult to predict. The verdict hinges not only on the nature of the evidence but also on the effectiveness of the prosecution and defense and on the jurors' attitudes. Does this adversarial and citizen-involved process provide the best mechanism for finding the truth and doing justice in our most serious criminal cases?

However one assesses their effectiveness, juries perform six vital functions in the criminal justice system:

1. Prevent government oppression by safeguarding citizens against arbitrary law enforcement

2. Determine whether the accused is guilty on the basis of the evidence presented

3. Represent diverse community interests so that no one set of values or biases dominates decision making

4. Serve as a buffer between the accused and the accuser

5. Promote knowledge about the criminal justice system by learning about it through the jury duty process

6. Symbolize the rule of law and the community foundation that supports the criminal justice system

As a symbol of law, juries demonstrate to the public, as well as to defendants, that decisions about depriving individuals of their liberty will be made carefully by a group of citizens who represent the community's values. In addition, juries provide the primary element of direct democracy in the judicial branch of government.

Through participation on juries, citizens use their votes to determine the outcomes of cases (C. E. Smith, 1994). This branch of government, which is dominated by judges and lawyers, offers few other opportunities for citizens to shape judicial decisions directly.

In the United States, a jury in a criminal trial traditionally comprises 12 citizens, but some states now allow as few as 6 citizens to make up a jury. This reform was recommended to modernize court procedures and reduce expenses. It costs less for the court to contact, process, and pay a smaller number of jurors. The use of small juries was upheld by the Supreme Court in ***Williams v. Florida*** (1970). Six states use juries with fewer than 12 members in noncapital felony cases, and a larger number of states use small juries for misdemeanors. In *Burch v. Louisiana* (1979), the Supreme Court ruled that 6-member juries must vote unanimously to convict a defendant, but unanimity is not required for larger juries. Some states permit juries to convict defendants by votes of 10 to 2 or 9 to 3. The change to 6-person juries has its critics, who charge that the smaller group is less representative of the conflicting views in the community and too quick to bring in a verdict (Amar, 1997).

***Williams v. Florida* (1970)** Juries of fewer than 12 members are constitutional.

FIGURE 9.3
Jury selection process for a 12-member jury

Potential jurors are drawn at random from a source list. From this pool, a panel is selected and presented for duty. The voir dire examination may remove some, whereas others will be seated. The 14 jurors selected include two alternates.

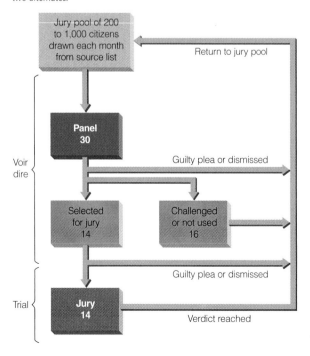

THE TRIAL PROCESS

The trial process generally follows eight steps: (1) selection of the jury, (2) opening statements by prosecution and defense, (3) presentation of the prosecution's evidence and witnesses, (4) presentation of the defense's evidence and witnesses, (5) presentation of rebuttal witnesses, (6) closing arguments by each side, (7) instruction of the jury by the judge, and (8) decision by the jury. The details of each step may vary according to each state's rules. Although the proportion of trials may be small, understanding each step in the process and considering the broader impact of this institution are both important.

Jury Selection   The selection of the jury, outlined in Figure 9.3, is a crucial first step in the trial process. Because people always apply their experiences, values, and biases in their decision making, prosecutors and defense attorneys actively seek to identify potential jurors who may be automatically sympathetic or hostile to their side. When they believe they have identified such potential jurors, they try to find ways to exclude those who may sympathize with the other side, while striving to keep those who may favor their side. Lawyers do not necessarily achieve these goals, because the selection of jurors involves the decisions and interactions of prosecutors, defense attorneys, and judges, each of whom has different objectives in the selection process.

Jurors are selected from among the citizens whose names have been placed in the jury pool. The composition of the jury pool tremendously affects the ultimate composition of the trial jury. In most states the jury pool is drawn from lists of registered voters, but research has shown that nonwhites, the poor, and young people register to vote at much lower rates than does the rest of the population. As a result, members of these groups are underrepresented on juries (Fukurai, 1996).

In many cases, the presence or absence of these groups may make no difference in the ultimate verdict. In some situations, however, members of these groups may interpret evidence differently than do their older, white, middle-class counterparts who dominate the composition of juries (Ugwuegbu, 1999). For example, the poor, nonwhites, and young people may be more likely to have had unpleasant experiences with police officers and therefore be less willing to believe automatically that police officers always tell the truth. Today courts may supplement the lists of registered voters with other lists, such as those for driver's licenses, hunting licenses, and utility bills, in order to diversify the jury pool (Newman, 1996). Several states are also considering increases in jurors' daily pay, such as a Texas's move from $6 per day to $40 per day in trials lasting more than one day. It is hoped that such efforts will make jury service more attractive for poor people who might otherwise avoid participating because they cannot afford to lose pay by missing work (Axtman, 2005a).

Only about 15 percent of adult Americans have ever been called for jury duty. Retired people and homemakers with grown children tend to be overrepresented on juries because they are less inconvenienced by serving and are often less likely to ask to be excused because of job responsibilities or child care problems. To make jury duty less onerous, many states have moved to a system called "one-day-one-trial," in which jurors serve for either one day or for the duration of one trial.

The courtroom process of **voir dire** (which means "to speak the truth") is used to question prospective jurors in order to screen out those who might be biased or otherwise incapable of making a fair decision. Attorneys for each side, as well as the judge, may question jurors about their background, knowledge of the case, and acquaintance with any participants in the case. Jurors will also be asked whether they or their immediate family members have been crime victims or otherwise involved in a criminal case in a manner that may prevent them from making open-minded decisions about the evidence and the defendant. If a juror's responses indicate that he or she will not be able to make fair decisions, the juror may be **challenged for cause.** The judge must rule on the challenge, but if the judge agrees with the attorney, then the juror is excused from that specific case. There is usually no limit on the number of jurors that the attorneys may challenge for cause. It is not easy, however, for attorneys to identify all of a juror's biases through brief questioning (Dillehay and Sandys, 1996).

Although challenges for cause ultimately fall under the judge's control, the prosecution and defense can exert their own control over the jury's composition through the use of **peremptory challenges.** With these, the prosecution and defense can exclude prospective jurors without giving specific reasons. Attorneys use peremptory challenges to exclude jurors who they think will be unsympathetic to their arguments (Hoffman, 1999). Attorneys usually use hunches about which jurors to challenge; little evidence suggests that they can accurately identify which jurors will sympathize with their side or not (M. S. White, 1995). Normally, the defense is allowed eight to ten peremptory challenges, and the prosecution six to eight.

The use of peremptory challenges has raised concerns that attorneys can use them to exclude, for example, African American jurors when an African American is on trial (Kennedy, 1997). In a series of decisions in the late 1980s and early 1990s (such as *Batson v. Kentucky*, 1986), the Supreme Court prohibited using peremptory challenges to systematically exclude potential jurors because of their race or gender. In practice, however, the enforcement of this prohibition is up to the trial judge (C. E. Smith and Ochoa, 1996). If a trial judge is willing to accept flimsy excuses for race-based and gender-based exclusions, then the attorneys can ignore the ban on discrimination (Bray, 1992).

Some lawyers say that trials are won or lost in jury selection. If a lawyer succeeds in seating a favorable jury, he or she may have a receptive audience that will readily support the lawyer's arguments and evidence.

voir dire A questioning of prospective jurors to screen out people the attorneys think might be biased or otherwise incapable of delivering a fair verdict.

challenge for cause Removal of a prospective juror by showing that he or she has some bias or some other legal disability. The number of such challenges available to attorneys is unlimited.

peremptory challenge Removal of a prospective juror without giving any reason. Attorneys are allowed a limited number of such challenges.

Opening Statements   After the jury has been selected, the trial begins. The clerk reads the complaint (indictment or information) detailing the charges, and the prosecutor and the defense attorney may, if they desire, make opening statements to the jury to summarize the position that each side intends to take. The statements are not evidence. The jury is not supposed to regard the attorneys' statements as proving or disproving anything about the case.

Presentation of the Prosecution's Evidence   One of the basic protections of the American criminal justice system is the assumption that the defendant is innocent until proved guilty. The prosecution carries the burden of proving beyond a reasonable doubt, within the demands of the court procedures and rules of evidence, that the individual named in the indictment committed the crime. This does not mean that absolute certainty is required, only that the evidence sufficiently excludes all reasonable doubt.

In presenting evidence to the jury, the prosecution must establish a case showing that the defendant is guilty. Evidence is classified as real evidence, demonstrative evidence, testimony, direct evidence, and circumstantial evidence. **Real evidence** might include such objects as a weapon, business records, fingerprints, or stolen property. These are real objects involved in the crime. **Demonstrative evidence** is presented for jurors to see and understand without testimony. Real evidence is one form of demonstrative evidence; other forms include maps, X-rays, photographs, models, and diagrams. Most evidence in a criminal trial, however, consists of the **testimony** of witnesses. Witnesses at a trial must be legally competent. Thus, the judge may be required to determine whether the witness whose testimony is challenged has the intelligence to tell the truth and the ability to recall what was seen. Witnesses with inadequate intelligence or mental problems might not be regarded as qualified to present testimony. **Direct evidence** refers to eyewitness accounts such as "I saw John Smith fire the gun." **Circumstantial evidence** requires that the jury infer a fact from what the witness observed: "I saw John Smith walk behind his house with a gun. A few minutes later I heard a gun go off, and then Mr. Smith walked toward me holding a gun." The witness's observation that Smith had a gun and that the witness then heard a gun go off does not provide direct evidence that Smith fired his gun; however, the jury may link the described facts and infer that Smith fired his gun. (See "Technology Issues in Criminal Justice" for a look at one role of technology in presenting evidence.) After a witness has given testimony, counsel for the other side may cross-examine him or her.

The attorney for each side challenges the other side's presentation of evidence. If evidence violates the rules, reflects untrustworthy hearsay, is a statement of opinion, or is not relevant to the issues in the case, an attorney will object to the presentation of it. In effect, the attorney is asking the judge to rule that the jury cannot consider the opponent's questionable evidence.

After the prosecution has presented all of the state's evidence against the defendant, the court is informed that the people's case rests. It is common for the defense then to ask the court to direct the jury to bring forth a verdict of not guilty. Such a motion is based on the defense argument that the state has not presented enough evidence to prove its case. If the motion is sustained by the judge (it rarely is), the trial ends; if it is overruled, the defense presents its evidence.

Presentation of the Defense's Evidence   The defense is not required to answer the case presented by the prosecution. As it is the state's responsibility to prove the case beyond a reasonable doubt, it is theoretically possible—and in fact sometimes happens—that the defense rests its case immediately. Usually, however, the accused's attorney employs one strategy or a combination of three strategies: (1) contrary evidence is introduced to rebut or cast doubt on the state's case, (2) an alibi is offered, or (3) an affirmative defense is presented. As discussed in Chapter 3, defenses include self-defense, insanity, duress, and necessity.

A key issue for the defense is whether the accused will take the stand. The Fifth Amendment protection against self-incrimination means that the defendant does not have to testify. The Supreme Court has ruled that the prosecutor may not comment on, nor can the jury draw inferences from, the defendant's decision not to appear in

---

real evidence Physical evidence—such as a weapons, records, fingerprints, and stolen property—involved in the crime.

demonstrative evidence Evidence that is not based on witness testimony but that demonstrates information relevant to the crime, such as maps, X-rays, and photographs; includes real evidence involved in the crime.

testimony Oral evidence provided by a legally competent witness.

direct evidence Eyewitness accounts.

circumstantial evidence Evidence provided by a witness from which a jury must infer a fact.

TECHNOLOGY ISSUES IN CRIMINAL JUSTICE

Computer Simulations in the Courtroom

I n jury trials, prosecutors and defense attorneys have traditionally attempted to use their words to "paint a picture" for the jurors. Each attorney wants the jurors to envision a specific chain of events. It is entirely possible that after hearing the same presentations individual jurors will leave the courtroom with very different perceptions about what happened at the crime scene and whether the defendant played a role. In recent years, attorneys have attempted to use computer technology to present clearer images of events. Just as computer programmers have developed realistic games for computers, similar realism has now been developed in computer-generated re-creations of crime scenes. If the jury needs to understand how an injury occurred, the prosecution may present a computer-generated film of a person being struck from behind or falling in a manner consistent with the victim's injuries. If a defendant has sufficient money to hire computer experts, the defendant may attempt to develop a computer presentation that re-creates events in a way that absolves the defendant of responsibility.

Observers have serious concerns about the use of such computer programs in trials. Such re-creations are available only to those who can afford them. Thus, poor defendants have little hope of using this technology to present their side of the story. In addition, computer scenes could be developed or manipulated in ways that are not consistent with the available evidence. Jurors may believe the realistic scenes that they watch on the screen despite contrary evidence that they hear from witness testimony. The image of the re-creation may stick in jurors' minds even when there is strong evidence to show that the re-creation was not accurate.

RESEARCHING THE INTERNET

Consultants offer computer simulation services to attorneys who conduct trials. For one example, see the website listed on the Cole/Smith Criminal Justice in America Companion Website: http://www.thomsonedu.com/criminaljustice/cole.

FOR CRITICAL ANALYSIS

Should computer-generated re-creations of crimes be shown during trials? How can we reduce the risks that such re-creations will distort reality or otherwise be misused?

Source: Drawn from John McCormick, "Scene of the Crime," *Newsweek,* February 28, 2000, p. 60. Copyright © 2000 Newsweek, Inc. All rights reserved. Reprinted by permission.

---

his or her own defense. The decision is not made lightly, because if the defendant does testify, the prosecution may cross-examine. Cross-examination, which is questioning by the opposing attorney, is broader than direct examination. The prosecutor may question the defendant not only about the crime but also about his or her past, including past criminal convictions. On the other hand, if the defendant does not testify, jurors may make assumptions about the defendant's guilt, even though they have been instructed not to do so.

For example, when Michael Skakel, a cousin of the Kennedy family, was convicted in 2002 of bludgeoning a girl with a golf club 27 years earlier as a teenager, he never took the witness stand in his own defense. The prosecution gained the conviction based on testimony from several witnesses who claimed that Skakel had told them years earlier about killing a girl with a golf club. Skakel's attorneys used an alibi defense by presenting testimony from witnesses who said that he had been at home watching television with friends at the time of the murder. The defense also sought to cast suspicion on another suspect. The jury, however, accepted the version of events presented by the prosecution's witnesses and, upon conviction, Skakel received a sentence of 20 years to life (Goldman, 2002).

Presentation of Rebuttal Witnesses   When the defense's case is complete, the prosecution may present witnesses whose testimony is designed to discredit or counteract testimony presented on behalf of the defendant. If the prosecution brings rebuttal witnesses, the defense has the opportunity to question them and to present new witnesses in rebuttal.

Closing Arguments by Each Side   When each side has completed its presentation of the evidence, the prosecution and defense make closing arguments to the

Defense Attorney John Thebes presents "real" evidence during the trial of Rev. Gerald Robinson, a Roman Catholic priest, in Toledo, Ohio. Robinson is on trial for the 1980 death of Sister Margaret Ann Pahl. In May 2006 Father Robinson was found guilty and sentenced to 15 years to life in prison.

AP Photo/Andy Morrison, Pool

jury. The attorneys review the evidence of the case for the jury, presenting interpretations of the evidence that favor their own side. The prosecutor may use the summation to connect the individual pieces of evidence in a way that forms a basis for concluding that the defendant is guilty. The defense may set forth the applicable law and try to show that the prosecution has not proved its case beyond a reasonable doubt. Each side may remind the jury of its duty to evaluate the evidence impartially and not to be swayed by emotion. Yet, some attorneys may hope that the jurors react emotionally, especially if they think that those emotions will benefit their side.

Judge's Instructions to the Jury   The jury decides the facts of the case, but the judge determines the law. Before the jurors depart for the jury room to decide the defendant's fate, the judge instructs them on how the law should guide their decision. The judge may discuss basic legal principles such as proof beyond a reasonable doubt, the legal requirements necessary to show that all the elements have been proved by the prosecution, or the rights of the defendant. More-specific aspects of the law bearing on the decision—such as complicated court rulings on the nature of the insanity defense or the ways certain types of evidence have been gathered—may be included in the judge's instructions. In complicated trials, the judge may spend an entire day instructing the jury.

reasonable doubt The standard used by a jury to decide if the prosecution has provided enough evidence for conviction.

The concept of **reasonable doubt** forms the heart of the jury system. As we have seen, the prosecution is not required to prove the guilt of the defendant beyond all doubt. Instead, if a juror is

> satisfied to a moral certainty that this defendant . . . is guilty of any one of the crimes charged here, you may safely say that you have been convinced beyond a reasonable doubt. If your mind is wavering, or if you are uncertain . . . you have not been convinced beyond a reasonable doubt and must render a verdict of not guilty. (Phillips, 1977:214)

Listening to the judge may become an ordeal for the jurors, who must hear and understand perhaps two or three hours of instruction on the law and the evidence (Bradley, 1992). It is assumed that somehow jurors will fully absorb these details on first hearing them, so that they will thoroughly understand how they are supposed to decide the case in the jury room (G. P. Kramer and Koenig, 1990).

Decision by the Jury   After they have heard the case and received the judge's instructions, the jurors retire to a room where they have complete privacy. They elect a foreperson to run the meeting, and deliberations begin. Until now, the jurors have been passive observers of the trial, unable to question witnesses or to discuss the case among themselves; now they can discuss the facts that have been presented. Throughout their deliberations the jurors may be *sequestered*—kept together day and night, away from the influences of newspapers and conversations with family and friends. If jurors are allowed to spend nights at home, they are ordered not to discuss the case with anyone. The jury may request that the judge reread to them portions of the instructions, ask for additional instructions, or hear portions of the transcript detailing what was said by specific witnesses.

If the jury becomes deadlocked and cannot reach a verdict, the trial ends with a hung jury and the prosecutor must decide whether to try the case all over again in front of a new jury. When a verdict is reached, the judge, prosecution, and defense reassemble in the courtroom to hear it. The prosecution or the defense may request that the jury be polled: Each member individually tells his or her vote in open court. This procedure presumably ensures that no juror has felt pressured to agree with the other jurors.

EVALUATING THE JURY SYSTEM

Early research found that, consistent with theories of group behavior, participation and influence in the jury process are related to social status. Men were found to be more active participants than women, whites more active

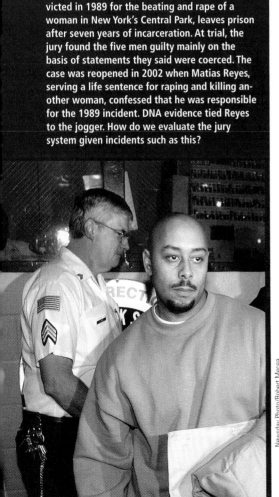

Raymond Santana, one of five teenagers convicted in 1989 for the beating and rape of a woman in New York's Central Park, leaves prison after seven years of incarceration. At trial, the jury found the five men guilty mainly on the basis of statements they said were coerced. The case was reopened in 2002 when Matias Reyes, serving a life sentence for raping and killing another woman, confessed that he was responsible for the 1989 incident. DNA evidence tied Reyes to the jogger. How do we evaluate the jury system given incidents such as this?

Newsday Photo/Robert Mecea

than minority members, and the better educated more active than those less educated. Much of the discussion in the jury room did not center on the testimony but rather on trial procedures, opinions about the witnesses, and personal reminiscences (Strodtbeck, James, and Hawkins, 1957). In 30 percent of the cases, a vote taken soon after entering the jury room was the only one necessary to reach a verdict; in the rest of the cases, the majority on the first ballot eventually prevailed in 90 percent of the cases (Broeder, 1959). Because of group pressure, only rarely did a single juror produce a hung jury. Although some individual jurors may view the case differently, they may doubt their own views or go along with the others if everyone else disagrees. More recent findings have upheld the influence of group pressure on decision making (Hastie, Penrod, and Pennington, 1983).

A recent examination of trials in the 75 largest counties found that 88 percent of bench trials ended in convictions but only 80 percent of jury trials ended so (Cohen and Reaves, 2006). These numbers alone do not reveal whether judges and juries decide cases differently. However, research on trials provides clues about differences between these two decision makers.

Juries tend to take a more liberal view of such issues as self-defense than do judges and are likely to minimize the seriousness of an offense if they dislike some characteristic of the victim (S. J. Adler, 1994:200–207). For example, if the victim of an assault is a prostitute, the jury may minimize the assault. Perceived characteristics of the defendant may also influence jurors' assessments of guilt (Abwender and Hough, 2001). Because judges have more experience with the justice process, they are more likely than juries to base their convictions on evidence that researchers characterize as moderately strong (Eisenberg et al., 2005).

ThomsonNOW
Improve your grade on the exam with Personalized Study! For reinforcement resources and a mastery check of Trial: The Exceptional Case, go to www.thomsonedu.com/thomsonnow.

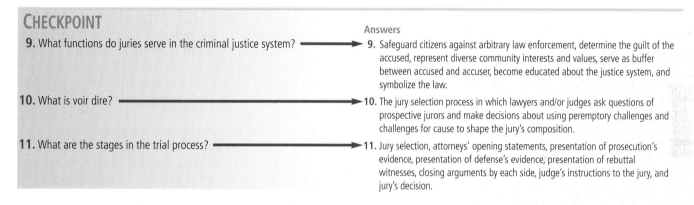

CHECKPOINT

Answers

9. What functions do juries serve in the criminal justice system? ——➤ 9. Safeguard citizens against arbitrary law enforcement, determine the guilt of the accused, represent diverse community interests and values, serve as buffer between accused and accuser, become educated about the justice system, and symbolize the law.

10. What is voir dire? ——➤ 10. The jury selection process in which lawyers and/or judges ask questions of prospective jurors and make decisions about using peremptory challenges and challenges for cause to shape the jury's composition.

11. What are the stages in the trial process? ——➤ 11. Jury selection, attorneys' opening statements, presentation of prosecution's evidence, presentation of defense's evidence, presentation of rebuttal witnesses, closing arguments by each side, judge's instructions to the jury, and jury's decision.

Appeals

Imposition of a sentence does not mean that the case is necessarily over; the defendant typically has the right to appeal the verdict to a higher court, and the right to counsel continues through the first appeal (Priehs, 1999). Some states have limited the right to appeal when defendants plead guilty. An **appeal** is based on a claim that one or more errors of law or procedure were made during the investigation, arrest, or trial process (C. E. Smith, 2000). Such claims usually assert that the trial judge made errors in courtroom rulings or in improperly admitting evidence that the police gathered in violation of some constitutional right. A defendant might base an appeal, for example, on the claim that the judge did not instruct the jury correctly or that a guilty plea was not made voluntarily.

Appeals are based on questions of procedure, not on issues of the defendant's guilt or innocence. The appellate court will not normally second-guess a jury. Instead it will check to make sure that the trial followed proper procedures. If there were significant errors in the trial, then the conviction is set aside. The defendant may be tried again if the prosecutor decides to pursue the case again. Most criminal defendants must file an appeal shortly after trial to have an appellate court review the case. By contrast, many states provide for an automatic appeal in death penalty cases.

appeal A request to a higher court that it review actions taken in a trial court.

The quality of defense representation is important because the appeal must usually meet short deadlines and carefully identify appropriate issues (Wasserman, 1990).

A case originating in a state court is first appealed through that state's judicial system. When a state case involves a federal constitutional question, however, a later appeal can go to the U.S. Supreme Court. State courts decide almost four-fifths of all appeals.

Most appeals do not succeed. In almost 80 percent of the cases examined in one study (Chapper and Hanson, 1989), the decision of the trial courts was affirmed. Most of the other decisions produced new trials or resentencing; relatively few decisions (1.9 percent) produced acquittals on appeal.

HABEAS CORPUS

habeas corpus A writ or judicial order requesting the release of a person being detained in a jail, prison, or mental hospital. If a judge finds the person is being held improperly, the writ may be granted and the person released.

After people use their avenues of appeal, they may pursue a writ of habeas corpus if they claim that their federal constitutional rights were violated during the lower-court processes. Known as "the great writ" from its traditional role in English law and its enshrinement in the U.S. Constitution, **habeas corpus** is a judicial order requesting that a judge examine whether an individual is being properly detained in a jail, prison, or mental hospital. If there is no legal basis for the person to be held, then the judge may grant the writ and order the person to be released. In the context of criminal justice, convicted offenders claim that their imprisonment is improper because one of their constitutional rights was violated during the investigation or adjudication of their case. Statutes permit offenders convicted in both state and federal courts to pursue habeas corpus actions in the federal courts. After first seeking favorable decisions by state appellate courts, convicted offenders can start their constitutional claims anew in the federal trial-level district courts and subsequently pursue their habeas cases in the federal circuit courts of appeal and the U.S. Supreme Court.

Only about 1 percent of habeas petitions are successful (Flango, 1994). One reason may be that an individual has no right to be represented by counsel when pursuing a habeas corpus petition. Few offenders have sufficient knowledge of law and legal procedures to identify and present constitutional claims effectively in the federal courts (Hanson and Daley, 1995). In the late 1980s and early 1990s, the U.S. Supreme Court issued many decisions that made filing habeas corpus petitions more difficult for convicted offenders (Alexander, 1993; C. E. Smith, 1995a). Specifically, the Court created tougher procedural rules that are more difficult for convicted offenders to follow. The rules also unintentionally created some new problems for state attorneys general and federal trial courts, because they must now examine the procedural rules affecting cases rather than simply addressing the constitutional violations that the offender claims occurred (C. E. Smith, 1995c). In 1996 the Antiterrorism and Effective Death Penalty Act placed additional restrictions on habeas corpus petitions. The statute was quickly approved by the U.S. Supreme Court. These reforms were based, in part, on a belief that prisoners' cases were clogging the federal courts (C. E. Smith, 1995b). Ironically, habeas corpus petitions in the federal courts have increased by 50 percent since the passage of the restrictive legislation (Scalia, 2002). By imposing strict filing deadlines for petitions, the legislation may have inadvertently focused more prisoners' attention on the existence of habeas corpus and thereby encouraged them to move forward with petitions in order to meet the deadlines.

EVALUATING THE APPELLATE PROCESS

The public seems to believe that many offenders are being "let off" through the appellate process. In addition, frustrated by the problems of crime, some conservatives have argued that opportunities for appeal should be limited. They claim that too many offenders delay imposition of their sentences and that others completely evade punishment by filing appeals endlessly. This practice not only increases the workload of the courts but also jeopardizes the concept of the finality of the justice process. However, given that 90 percent of accused persons plead guilty, the number of cases that might be appealed is relatively small.

The appeals process performs the important function of righting wrongs. It also helps to ensure consistency in the application of law by judges in different courts.

Beyond that, its presence constantly influences the daily operations of the criminal justice system, as prosecutors and trial judges must consider how a higher court might later evaluate their decisions and actions.

CHECKPOINT

Answers

12. How does the appellate court's job differ from that of the trial court? ➤ **12.** Unlike trial courts, which have juries, hear evidence, and decide if the defendant is guilty or not guilty, appellate courts focus only on claimed errors of law or procedure in trial court proceedings. Victory for a defendant in a trial court means an acquittal and instant freedom. Victory in an appellate court may mean only a chance at a new trial—which often leads to a new conviction.

13. What is a habeas corpus petition? ➤ **13.** The habeas corpus process may be started after all appeals have been filed and lost. Convicted offenders ask a federal court to review whether any constitutional rights were violated during the course of a case investigation and trial. If rights were violated, the person's continued detention in prison or jail may be improper.

A QUESTION OF ETHICS: WRITING ASSIGNMENT

Lisa Davidson stood silently in the courtroom of Judge Helen Iverson. Defense attorney Bill Dixon whispered in Davidson's ear as they waited for Judge Iverson to finish reading Davidson's file. "Are we ready to proceed?" asked the judge.

"Yes, your honor," came the simultaneous replies from both Dixon and the prosecutor standing nearby.

Judge Iverson stared at Davidson momentarily with a serious expression. "Ms. Davidson, you are charged with larceny. Because it is your third offense, I can send you to prison. Do you understand that?"

"Yes, your honor," replied Davidson, her voice quivering.

"Are you pleading guilty to this crime because you are guilty?" asked the judge.

"Yes, your honor."

The judge continued. "Are you pleading guilty of your own free will?"

"Yes, your honor."

"Did anyone threaten you to make you plead guilty?"

"No, your honor."

"Did anyone make any promises to you to induce you to plead guilty?"

Davidson nodded her head. "Yes. Mr. Dixon said that if I plead guilty to this charge then the prosecutor promised that my sentence would be only. . . ."

"Excuse me, Judge Iverson!" Dixon interrupted in a loud voice. "Could I please have a moment to speak with my client?" Judge Iverson nodded. Taking Davidson by the arm, Dixon moved her three feet farther away from the judge's bench. Dixon whispered into Davidson's ear as his hands punched the air with emphatic gestures. A few moments later, they returned to their positions, standing in front of the judge. "We are ready to continue, your honor," said Dixon.

Judge Iverson looked at Davidson once again. "Did anyone promise you anything to induce you to plead guilty?"

Davidson glanced sideways at Dixon before replying "No, your honor."

"You understand that you are waiving your constitutional right to a trial and you are freely waiving that right?"

"Yes, your honor."

"Then I find you guilty as charged and I will set sentencing for one month from today at 10:00 A.M."

WRITING ASSIGNMENT

Imagine that you are an ethics expert who has been asked to evaluate court processes. Write a memo addressing the following questions. Should Judge Iverson have accepted the guilty plea? What role did the defense attorney play in staging the guilty plea ceremony? Were there any ethical problems? What would you have done if you were the judge?

REAL-WORLD ACTIVITY: AN APPLICATION

In 2002 John Rigas, the 78-year-old founder of Adelphia Communication Corporation, one of the nation's largest cable television systems, was arrested along with two of his sons and two company employees for improperly taking the company's money for personal use. Rigas, who had an annual salary of $1.9 million, allegedly took an additional $1 million per month from the company for a total theft of $62 million. The total amount that all of the defendants improperly took from the company allegedly exceeded $1 billion. The company eventually collapsed, and shareholders suffered massive financial losses.

After appearing in court to hear the formal charges, the two company employees were released on their own recognizance, meaning that they merely had to promise to appear at future court hearings. By contrast, Rigas and his two sons were each required to post $10 million in property and cash in order to gain release on bail. They would forfeit these assets if they failed to appear for scheduled hearings.

RESEARCHING THE INTERNET

Go to **InfoTrac** College Edition and enter the keyword *bail hearing*. Read the article entitled "Friends in High Places No Help at Bail Hearing," *Philadelphia Daily News*, April 2006.

APPLICATION

In light of the purposes of bail—to protect the community and ensure that defendants appear in court—why was bail set so high for members of the Rigas family? Is it fair and appropriate that they faced a high bail while the other defendants were released without putting up any cash or property? Write a memo as if you were a judge explaining how you would have set bail for the defendants in this case.

Source: Drawn from M. Farrell, "No Surrender: Rigases Arrested; Adelphia Five Face Charges They 'Looted on a Massive Scale.'" Multichannel News [Reed Business Information], July 29, 2002. Available on Lexis-Nexis.

SUMMARY

- Pretrial processes determine the fates of nearly all defendants through case dismissals, decisions defining charges, and plea bargains, all of which affect more than 90 percent of cases.

- The bail process provides opportunities for many defendants to gain pretrial release, but poor defendants may be disadvantaged by their inability to come up with the money or property needed to secure release. Some preventive detention statutes permit judges to hold defendants considered dangerous or likely to flee.

- Bail bondsmen are private businesspeople who charge a fee to provide money for defendants' pretrial release. Their activities create risks of corruption and discrimination in the bail process, but bondsmen may also help the system by reminding defendants about court dates.

- Although judges bear the primary responsibility for setting bail, prosecutors are especially influential in recommending amounts and conditions for pretrial release.

- Initiatives to reform the bail process include police-issued citations, release on own recognizance (ROR), percentage bail, bail guidelines, and preventive detention. *CONDITIONS*

- Despite the presumption of innocence, pretrial detainees endure difficult conditions in jails containing mixed populations of convicted offenders, detainees, and troubled people. The shock of being jailed creates risks of suicide and depression.

- Most convictions are obtained through plea bargaining, a process that exists because it fulfills the self-interest of prosecutors, judges, defense attorneys, and defendants.

- Plea bargaining is facilitated by exchange relations between prosecutors and defense attorneys. In many courthouses, there is little actual bargaining, as outcomes are determined through the implicit bargaining process of settling the facts and assessing the going rate of punishment according to the standards of the local legal culture.

- Plea bargaining has been criticized for pressuring defendants to surrender their rights and reducing the sentences imposed on offenders.

- Through the dramatic courtroom battle of prosecutors and defense attorneys, trials are presumed to provide the best way to discover the truth about a criminal case.

- Only about 5 percent of cases go to trial, and half of those are typically bench trials in front of a judge, not jury trials.

- Typically, cases go to trial because they involve defendants who are wealthy enough to pay attorneys to fight to the very end or because they involve charges that are too serious to create incentives for plea bargaining.

- The U.S. Supreme Court has ruled that juries need not be made up of 12 members, and 12-member juries can, if permitted by state law, convict defendants by a majority vote instead of a unanimous vote.

- Juries serve vital functions for society by preventing arbitrary action by prosecutors and judges, educating citizens about the justice system, symbolizing the rule of law, and involving citizens from diverse segments of the community in judicial decision making.

- The jury selection process, especially in the formation of the jury pool and the exercise of peremptory challenges, often creates juries that do not fully represent all segments of a community.

- The trial process consists of a series of steps: jury selection, opening statements, presentation of prosecution's evidence, presentation of defense's evidence, presentation of rebuttal witnesses, closing arguments, judge's jury instructions, and jury's decision.

- Rules of evidence dictate what kinds of information may be presented in court for consideration by the jury. Types of evidence are real evidence, demonstrative evidence, testimony, direct evidence, and circumstantial evidence.

- Convicted offenders have the opportunity to appeal, although defendants who plead guilty, unlike those convicted through a trial, often have few grounds for an appeal.

- Appeals focus on claimed errors of law or procedure in the investigation by police and prosecutors or the decisions by trial judges. Relatively few offenders win their appeals, and most of those simply gain an opportunity for a new trial, not release from jail or prison.

- After convicted offenders have used all of their appeals, they may file a habeas corpus petition to seek federal judicial review of claimed constitutional rights violations in their cases. Very few of such petitions succeed.

QUESTIONS FOR REVIEW

1. What is bail and how has it been reformed to limit its traditionally harsh impact on poor defendants?

2. Why are some defendants held in pretrial detention?

3. Why does plea bargaining exist?

4. Given that there are so few jury trials, what types of cases would you expect to find adjudicated in this manner? Why?

5. What is the purpose of the appeals process?

KEY TERMS AND CASES

appeal (p. 251)

arraignment (p. 231)

bail (p. 233)

bench trials (p. 244)

challenge for cause (p. 247)

circumstantial evidence (p. 248)

citation (p. 235)

demonstrative evidence (p. 248)

direct evidence (p. 248)

habeas corpus (p. 252)

jury (p. 244)

motion (p. 231)

percentage bail (p. 237)

peremptory challenge (p. 247)

preventive detention (p. 237)

real evidence (p. 248)

reasonable doubt (p. 250)

release on recognizance (ROR) (p. 236)

testimony (p. 248)

voir dire (p. 247)

Bordenkircher v. Hayes (1978) (p. 243)

Boykin v. Alabama (1969) (p. 243)

North Carolina v. Alford (1970) (p. 243)

Ricketts v. Adamson (1987) (p. 243)

Santobello v. New York (1971) (p. 240)

United States v. Salerno and Cafero (1987) (p. 237)

Williams v. Florida (1970) (p. 246)

GOING ONLINE

ThomsonNOW™

Maximize your study time by using ThomsonNOW's diagnostic study plan to help you review this chapter. The Study Plan will

- Help you identify areas on which you should concentrate
- Provide interactive exercises to help you master the chapter concepts
- Provide a posttest to confirm you are ready to move on to the next chapter

10

Punishment and Sentencing

The Goals of Punishment

Forms of the Criminal Sanction

The Sentencing Process

AP Photo/Nick Ut

The movie actor Tom Sizemore, best known for his roles in such films as *Saving Private Ryan* and *Blackhawk Down,* was overcome with emotion as he awaited sentencing for probation violations in the courtroom of Los Angeles Superior Court Judge Antonio Barreto, Jr. On this day in March 2005, Sizemore faced the consequences of violating the conditions of probation imposed after his 2003 domestic violence conviction. While on probation, Sizemore failed seven drug tests, missed several drug tests, and admitted to using methamphetamine. During a rambling statement in the courtroom, Sizemore sobbed and begged the judge for another chance to continue on probation: "I assure your honor that I'm not acting now. I'm not acting. I'm begging. I'm beseeching you. I can't imagine my future without performing" ("Actor Tom Sizemore," 2005).

After listening to the actor and considering the evidence of probation violations, Judge Barreto sentenced Sizemore to 17 months in jail and four months in a drug treatment facility. Later that same day in another courtroom, Judge Paula Adele Mabrey sentenced Sizemore to drug treatment on a separate conviction for methamphetamine possession ("Actor Tom Sizemore," 2005).

What did these judges accomplish with the sentences they imposed on Sizemore? Will Sizemore learn a lesson from spending time in jail? Does the sentence send a message to the community that court orders concerning probation and other matters must be taken seriously and obeyed? In light of Sizemore's drug abuse problem, does a jail sentence ignore the fundamental nature of his problems? On the other hand, should society care at all about addressing his personal problems—after all, his original conviction was for a crime of violence? These are difficult questions to answer. Thus, it is not surprising that many judges say that sentencing is the most difficult part of their jobs.

Sentencing is a crucial point in the criminal justice system. After guilt is established, someone must decide what to do with the defendant. In some states, statutes determine sentences by mandating specific punishments for various crimes. In other states, judges have discretion to choose a sentence from within a range of permissible punishments. For the offender, sentencing is the beginning of corrections.

The criminal justice system aims to solve three basic questions: (1) What conduct is criminal? (2) What determines guilt? (3) What should be done with the guilty? Earlier chapters emphasized the first two questions. The legal system's answers to the first question compose the basic rules of society: Do not murder, rob, sell drugs, commit treason, and so forth. Regarding the second question, the law spells out the process for determining guilt or innocence, and the administrative and interpersonal considerations of the actors in the criminal justice system greatly influence that process. In this chapter we begin to examine the third question, which involves the problem of sanction and punishment. First we consider the four goals of punishment: retribution, deterrence, incapacitation, and rehabilitation. We then explore the forms that punishment takes to achieve its goals. These are incarceration, intermediate sanctions, probation, and death. Finally, we look at the sentencing process in the context of the courts.

QUESTIONS FOR INQUIRY

- What are the goals of punishment?
- What really happens in sentencing?
- What types of sentences can judges impose?
- Does the system treat wrongdoers equally?

retribution Punishment inflicted on a person who has infringed on the rights of others and so deserves to be penalized.

The Goals of Punishment

Criminal sanctions in the United States have four main goals: retribution (deserved punishment), deterrence, incapacitation, and rehabilitation. Ultimately, all criminal punishment aims at maintaining the social order, but the justifications for sentencing proceed from the American values of justice and fairness. There is not universal agreement, however, on how to make the severity of punishment just and fair. Further, the justice sought by crime victims often conflicts with fairness to offenders.

Punishments reflect the dominant values of a particular moment in history. By the end of the 1960s, for example, the number of Americans who were sentenced to imprisonment decreased because of a widespread commitment to rehabilitating offenders. By contrast, since the mid-1970s an emphasis on imposing strong punishments for the purposes of retribution, deterrence, and incapacitation has resulted in record numbers of offenders being sentenced to prison (see "What Americans Think"). At the beginning of the twenty-first century, voices are calling for the addition of restorative justice as a fifth goal of the criminal sanction.

RETRIBUTION—DESERVED PUNISHMENT

Retribution is punishment inflicted on a person who has infringed on the rights of others and so deserves to be penalized. The biblical expression "An eye for an eye, a tooth for a tooth" illustrates the philosophy underlying this kind of punishment. Retribution means that those who commit a particular crime should be punished alike, in proportion to the gravity of the offense or to the suffering it has caused others. Retribution is deserved punishment; offenders must "pay their debts."

Some scholars claim that the desire for retribution is a basic human emotion. They maintain that if the state does not provide retributive sanctions to reflect community revulsion at offensive acts, citizens will take the law into their own hands to punish offenders. Under this view, the failure of government to satisfy the people's desire for retribution could produce social chaos.

This argument may not be valid for all crimes, however. If a rapist is inadequately punished, then the victim's family and other members of the community may be tempted to exact their own retribution. But what about a young adult smoking marijuana? If the government failed to impose retribution for this offense, would the community care? The same apathy may hold true for offenders who commit other nonviolent crimes that modestly impact society. Even in these seemingly trivial situations, however, retribution may serve as a necessary public reminder of the general rules of law and the important values they protect.

Since the late 1970s, retribution as a justification for the criminal sanction has aroused new interest, largely because of dissatisfaction with the philosophical basis and practical results of rehabilitation. Using the concept of "just deserts or deserved punishment" to define retribution, some theorists argue that one who infringes on the rights of others deserves to be punished. This approach rests on the philosophical view that punishment is a moral response to harm inflicted on society. In effect, these theorists believe that basic morality demands that wrongdoers be punished (von Hirsch, 1976:49). According to this view, punishment should be applied only for the wrong inflicted and not primarily to achieve other goals such as deterrence, incapacitation, or rehabilitation.

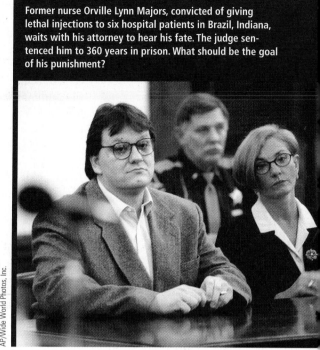

Former nurse Orville Lynn Majors, convicted of giving lethal injections to six hospital patients in Brazil, Indiana, waits with his attorney to hear his fate. The judge sentenced him to 360 years in prison. What should be the goal of his punishment?

AP/Wide World Photos, Inc.

DETERRENCE

Many people see criminal punishment as a basis for affecting the future choices and behavior of individuals. Politicians frequently talk about being "tough on crime" in order to send a message to would-be criminals. The roots of this approach, called deterrence, lie in eighteenth-century England among the followers of the social philosopher Jeremy Bentham.

Bentham was struck by what seemed to be the pointlessness of retribution. His fellow reformers adopted Bentham's theory of utilitarianism, which holds that human behavior is governed by the individual's calculation of the benefits versus the costs of his or her acts. Before stealing money or property, for example, potential offenders would consider the punishment that others have received for similar acts and would thereby be deterred.

There are two types of deterrence. **General deterrence** presumes that members of the general public, on observing the punishments of others, will conclude that the costs of crime outweigh the benefits. For general deterrence to be effective, the public must receive constant reminders of the likelihood and severity of punishment for various acts. They must believe that they will be caught, prosecuted, and given a specific punishment if they commit a particular crime. Moreover, the punishment must be severe enough to instill fear of the consequences of committing crimes. For example, public hanging was once considered to be an effective general deterrent.

By contrast, **specific deterrence** targets the decisions and behavior of offenders who have already been convicted. Under this approach, the amount and kind of punishment are calculated to discourage that criminal from repeating the offense. The punishment must be severe enough to cause the criminal to say, "The consequences of my crime were too painful. I will not commit another crime, because I do not want to risk being punished again."

The concept of deterrence presents obvious difficulties (Stafford and Warr, 1993). Deterrence assumes that all people think before they act. As such, deterrence does not account for the many people who commit crimes while under the influence of drugs or alcohol, or those whose harmful behavior stems from psychological problems or mental illness. Deterrence also does not account for people who act impulsively in stealing or damaging property. In other cases, the low probability of being caught defeats both general and special deterrence. To be generally deterrent, punishment

general deterrence Punishment of criminals that is intended to be an example to the general public and to discourage the commission of offenses.

specific deterrence Punishment inflicted on criminals to discourage them from committing future crimes.

must be perceived as relatively fast, certain, and severe. But punishment does not always occur that way.

Knowledge of the effectiveness of deterrence is limited as well (Nagin, 1998). For example, social science cannot measure the effects of general deterrence, because only those who are not deterred come to the attention of researchers. A study of the deterrent effects of punishment would have to examine the impact of different forms of the criminal sanction on various potential lawbreakers. How can we truly determine how many people—or even if any people—stopped themselves from committing a crime, because they were deterred by the prospect of prosecution and punishment? Therefore, although legislators often cite deterrence as a rationale for certain sanctions, no one really knows the extent to which sentencing policies based on deterrence achieve their objectives. Because contemporary U.S. society has shown little ability to reduce crime by imposing increasingly severe sanctions, the effectiveness of deterrence for many crimes and criminals should be questioned.

INCAPACITATION

incapacitation Depriving an offender of the ability to commit crimes against society, usually by detaining the offender in prison.

Incapacitation assumes that society can keep offenders from committing further crimes by detention in prison or by execution. Many people express such sentiments, urging officials to "lock 'em up and throw away the key!" In primitive societies, banishment from the community was the usual method of incapacitation. In early America, offenders often agreed to move away or to join the army as an alternative to some other form of punishment. In the United States today, imprisonment serves as the usual method of incapacitation. Offenders can be confined within secure institutions and effectively prevented from committing additional harm against society for the duration of their sentence. Capital punishment is the ultimate method of incapacitation. Any sentence that physically restricts an offender may incapacitate the person, even when the underlying purpose of the sentence is retribution, deterrence, or rehabilitation.

Sentences based on incapacitation are future oriented. Whereas retribution requires focusing on the harmful act of the offender, incapacitation looks at the offender's potential actions. If the offender is likely to commit future crimes, then the judge may impose a severe sentence—even for a relatively minor crime.

For example, under the incapacitation theory, a woman who kills her abusive husband as an emotional reaction to his verbal insults and physical assaults could receive a light sentence. As a one-time impulse killer who felt driven to kill by unique circumstances, she is not likely to commit additional crimes. By contrast, someone who shoplifts merchandise and has been convicted of the offense on ten previous occasions may receive a severe sentence. The criminal record and type of crime indicate that he or she will commit additional crimes if released. Thus, incapacitation focuses on characteristics of the offenders instead of aspects of their offenses.

Does it offend your sense of justice that a person could receive a severer sentence for shoplifting than for manslaughter? This question embodies one of the criticisms of incapacitation. Questions also arise about how to determine the length of sentence. Presumably, offenders will not be released until the state is reasonably sure that they will no longer commit crimes. However, can we accurately predict any person's behavior? Moreover, on what grounds can we punish people for anticipated behavior that we cannot accurately predict?

selective incapacitation Making the best use of expensive and limited prison space by targeting for incarceration those individuals whose incapacity will do the most to reduce crime in society.

In recent years greater attention has been paid to the concept of **selective incapacitation,** whereby offenders who repeat certain kinds of crimes receive long prison terms. Research has suggested that a relatively small number of offenders commit a large number of violent and property crimes (Clear, 1994:103). Burglars, for example, tend to commit many offenses before they are caught. Thus, these "career criminals" should be locked up for long periods (Auerhahn, 1999). Such policies could be costly, however. Not only would correctional facilities have to be expanded, but the number of expensive, time-consuming trials also might increase if severer sentences caused more repeat offenders to plead not guilty. Another difficulty with this policy is that we cannot accurately predict which offenders will commit more crimes upon release.

REHABILITATION

Rehabilitation refers to the goal of restoring a convicted offender to a constructive place in society through some form of training or therapy. Americans want to believe that offenders can be treated and resocialized in ways that allow them to lead a crime-free, productive life upon release. Over the last hundred years, rehabilitation advocates have argued for techniques that they claim identify and treat the causes of criminal behavior. If the offender's criminal behavior is assumed to result from some social, psychological, or biological imperfection, the treatment of the disorder becomes the primary goal of corrections.

Rehabilitation focuses on the offender. Its objective does not imply any consistent relationship between the severity of the punishment and the gravity of the crime. People who commit lesser offenses can receive long prison sentences if experts believe that the rehabilitation requires it. By contrast, a murderer might win early release by showing signs that the psychological or emotional problems that led to the killing have been corrected.

According to the concept of rehabilitation, offenders are treated, not punished, and they will return to society when they are "cured." Consequently, judges should not set fixed sentences but rather ones with maximum and minimum terms so that parole boards can release inmates when they have been rehabilitated.

From the 1940s until the 1970s, the goal of rehabilitation was so widely accepted that treatment and reform of the offender were generally regarded as the only issues worth serious attention. Crime was assumed to be caused by problems affecting individuals, and modern social sciences had the tools to address those problems. During the past 30 years, however, researchers and others have questioned the assumptions of the rehabilitation model. Studies of the results of rehabilitation programs have challenged the idea that criminal offenders can be cured (Martinson, 1974). Moreover, scholars no longer take for granted that crime is caused by identifiable, curable problems such as poverty, lack of job skills, low self-esteem, and hostility toward authority. Instead, some argue that we cannot identify the cause of criminal behavior for individual offenders.

> **rehabilitation** The goal of restoring a convicted offender to a constructive place in society through some form of vocational or educational training or therapy.

A NEW APPROACH TO PUNISHMENT: RESTORATIVE JUSTICE

In keeping with the focus on community justice for police, courts, and corrections, many people are calling for **restorative justice** to be added to the goals of the criminal sanction (Basemore and Umbreit, 1994). The restorative justice perspective views crime as more than a violation of penal law. The criminal act practically and symbolically denies community. It breaks trust among citizens and requires community members to determine how "to contradict the moral message of the crime that the offender is above the law and the victim beneath its reach" (Clear and Karp, 1999). Crime victims suffer losses involving damage to property and self. The primary aim of criminal justice should be to repair these losses. Crime also challenges the heart of community, to the extent that community life depends on a shared sense of trust, fairness, and interdependence.

Shifting the focus to restorative justice requires a three-way approach that involves the offender, the victim, and the community. This approach may include mediation in which the three actors devise ways that all agree are fair and just for the offender to repair the harm done to victim and community.

> **restorative justice** Punishment designed to repair the damage done to the victim and community by an offender's criminal act.

Restorative justice seeks to repair the damage done to the victim and community by an offender's criminal act. Here, Susanna Kay Cooper sits next to David Lee Myers as she looks at the photo of his dead wife. Cooper pled guilty to vehicular homicide in the death of Elaine Myers, received a 34-month prison sentence, and agreed to enter into talks with the victim's family.

Rose Howerter/The Oregonian

CLOSE UP

Restorative Justice in Vermont

One night in Morrisville, Vermont, Newton Wells went looking for a good time and wound up in an experiment. The 22-year-old college student was charged with assault after nearly driving into two police officers who were breaking up a party. Facing a felony conviction, Wells took a different way out. He pleaded guilty to a lower charge and volunteered to be sentenced by a county "reparative" board. Instead of a judge, a businessman, a counselor, a retired chemistry teacher, and a civil servant issued his punishment.

Restorative justice programs are designed to compensate victims, rehabilitate offenders, and involve the community in a new and direct way in the justice process. Today some Vermont offenders may be sentenced to make public apologies, make restitution, or chop wood for the elderly—to "repair" the community.

Vermont's sentencing boards, typically four to six volunteers, handle misdemeanors and low-grade felonies such as drunken driving and writing bad checks. Although such crimes normally would not merit jail time, removing the cases from the traditional criminal justice system frees up correctional department resources.

Board members meet with offenders in hour-long sessions, hear explanations and apologies, and tailor the penalties. The idea is to make the punishment related to the crime, which often occurs in novel ways:

- In Morrisville, college student Wells was ordered to work 30 hours with troubled youths and to meet with the police he menaced so that they could vent their anger about his driving.

- In Rutland, a man who drove 105 mph down a residential street was sentenced to work with brain-injured adults, some of them survivors of high-speed crashes.

- In Hyde Park, a teenager who vandalized a home got 55 hours on a work crew. His job was repairing plaster on an aging opera house.

Panel members get involved in ways they never could if they were serving as jurors. In Rutland, Jack Aicher tells shoplifters they've committed crimes against the "community." Everyone pays higher prices, he says, to cover the store's loss.

Proponents say board sanctions are typically tougher than conventional probation.

But offenders opt for the citizen panels to get their sentences concluded quickly. In Vermont, probation can last more than a year and can include special sanctions such as drug tests and rehabilitation programs. Reparative board punishments are concluded within 90 days.

The percentage of nonviolent offenders in the state's eight prisons has dropped from about 50 percent to 28 percent. The decline is ascribed, in part, to the effect of the boards. By handling low-level offenders, the community panels have freed state probation officers to deal with more serious cases. Those probation officers can then monitor criminals serving their sentences in work camps or on furlough rather than in jail, as a way of relieving overcrowding.

RESEARCHING THE INTERNET

Using **InfoTrac** College Edition, enter the keyword *restorative justice* and access the article entitled "Restorative Justice: What Is It? Can It Work? What Do Women Think?" by Stephani Coward-Yaskin, *Horizons*, Spring 2002, p. 22.

FOR CRITICAL ANALYSIS

Would the restorative justice approach work in your community? What criticisms is such a program likely to face?

Source: *USA Today*, February 12, 1997, http://www.usatoday.com. Copyright (c) 1997 USA Today. Reprinted by permission.

This new approach to criminal justice means that losses suffered by the crime victim are restored, the threat to local safety is removed, and the offender again becomes a fully participating member of the community. The Vermont Reparative Sentencing Boards, described in the Close Up box, exemplify one way of implementing restorative justice.

As yet, restorative justice represents a small minority of sanctions. To see how the four main punishment goals might be enacted in real life, consider again the sentencing of actor Tom Sizemore for probation violations. Table 10.1 shows various hypothetical sentencing statements that the judge might have given, depending on prevailing correctional goals.

As we next consider the ways that the goals are applied though the various forms of punishment, keep in mind the underlying punishment goal—or mix of goals—that justifies each form of sanction.

ThomsonNOW
Improve your grade on the exam with Personalized Study! For reinforcement resources and a mastery check of The Goals of Punishment, go to www.thomsonedu.com/thomsonnow.

CHECKPOINT

1. What are the four primary goals of the criminal sanction?

2. What are the difficulties in showing that a punishment acts as a deterrent?

Answers

1. Retribution, deterrence, incapacitation, rehabilitation.

2. It is impossible to show who has been deterred from committing crimes; punishment isn't always certain; people act impulsively rather than rationally; people commit crimes while on drugs.

TABLE 10.1   The Goals of Punishment

At sentencing, the judge usually gives reasons for the punishments imposed. Here are statements that Judge Antonio Barreto might have given Tom Sizemore, each promoting a different goal for the sanction.

Goal	Judge's Possible Statement
Retribution	I am imposing this sentence because you deserve to be punished for your deliberate violations of your conditions of probation and for the domestic violence charge that was the original basis for your sentence. Your criminal behavior is the basis of the punishment. Justice requires that I impose a sanction at a level that illustrates the importance that the community places on punishing domestic violence and ensuring that people respect the requirements of the legal system.
Deterrence	I am imposing this sentence so that your punishment will serve as an example and deter others who might contemplate committing acts of domestic violence or violating the conditions of probation. In addition, I hope that this sentence will deter you from ever again committing an illegal act.
Incapacitation	I am imposing this sentence so that you will be incapacitated and hence unable to commit acts of violence or abuse drugs during the length of this term.
Rehabilitation	The trial testimony and information contained in the presentence report makes me believe that there are aspects of your personality, especially your propensity to abuse illegal drugs, that led to your criminal acts. I am therefore imposing this sentence so that you can receive treatment that will rectify your behavior so you will not commit another crime.

Forms of the Criminal Sanction

Incarceration, intermediate sanctions, probation, and death are the basic ways that the criminal sanction, or punishment, is applied. The United States does not have a single, uniform set of sentencing laws. The criminal codes of each of the states and of the federal government specify the punishments. Each codes differs to some extent in the severity of the punishment for specific crimes and in the amount of discretion given judges to tailor the sanction to the individual offender.

As we examine the various forms of criminal sanction, bear in mind that applying these legally authorized punishments gives rise to complex problems. Judges often receive wide discretion in determining the appropriate sentence within the parameters of the penal code.

INCARCERATION

Imprisonment is the most visible penalty imposed by U.S. courts. Although less than 30 percent of people under correctional supervision are in prisons and jails, incarceration remains the standard for punishing those who commit serious crimes. Imprisonment is thought to contribute significantly to deterring potential offenders.

Of all correctional measures, incarceration represents the greatest restriction on freedom. These inmates at Alabama's Staton Prison are part of America's huge incarcerated population. Since 1980 the number of Americans held in prisons and jails has quadrupled.

AP Photo/Rob Carr

However, incarceration is expensive. It also creates the problem of reintegrating offenders into society upon release.

In penal codes, legislatures stipulate the types of sentences and the amount of prison time that can be imposed for each crime. Three basic sentencing structures are used: (1) indeterminate sentences (36 states), (2) determinate sentences (14 states), and (3) mandatory sentences (all states). Each type of sentence makes certain assumptions about the goals of the criminal sanction, and each provides judges with varying degrees of discretion.

Indeterminate Sentences

When the goal of rehabilitation dominated corrections, legislatures enacted **indeterminate sentences** (often called indefinite sentences). In keeping with the goal of treatment, indeterminate sentencing gives correctional officials and parole boards significant control over the amount of time a prisoner serves. Penal codes with indeterminate sentences stipulate a minimum and a maximum amount of time to be served in prison (for example, 1–5 years, 10–15 years, or 1 year to life). At the time of sentencing, the judge informs the offender about the range of the sentence. The offender also learns that he or she will probably be eligible for parole at some point after the minimum term has been served. The parole board determines the actual release date.

Determinate Sentences

Dissatisfaction with the rehabilitation goal and support for the concept of deserved punishment led many legislatures in the 1970s to shift to **determinate sentences.** With a determinate sentence, a convicted offender is imprisoned for a specific period (for example, 2 years, 5 years, 15 years). At the end of the term, minus credited good time (discussed shortly), the prisoner is automatically freed. The time of release depends neither on participation in treatment programs nor on a parole board's judgment concerning the offender's likelihood of returning to criminal activities.

Some determinate-sentencing states have adopted penal codes that stipulate a specific term for each crime category. Others allow the judge to choose a range of time to be served. Some states emphasize a determinate **presumptive sentence;** the legislature or often a commission specifies a term based on a time range (for example, 14–20 months) into which most cases should fall. Only in special circumstances should judges deviate from the presumptive sentence. Whichever variation is used, however, the offender theoretically knows at sentencing the amount of time to be served. One result of determinate sentencing is that, by reducing the judge's discretion, legislatures have tended to limit sentencing disparities and to ensure that terms correspond to those the elected body thinks are appropriate (Griset, 1993).

Mandatory Sentences

Politicians and the public have continued to complain that offenders are released before serving long enough terms, and legislatures have responded. All states and the federal government now have some form of **mandatory sentences** (often called mandatory minimum sentences), stipulating some minimum period of incarceration that people convicted of selected crimes must serve. The judge may not consider the circumstances of the offense or the background of the offender, and he or she may not impose nonincarcerative sentences. Mandatory prison terms are most often specified for violent crimes, drug violations, habitual offenders, or crimes in which a firearm was used (see "What Americans Think").

The "three strikes and you're out" laws adopted by 26 states and the federal government provide an example of mandatory sentencing (Schultz, 2000). These laws require that judges sentence offenders with three felony convictions (in some states two or four convictions) to long prison terms, sometimes to life without parole. In California and Georgia, the two states making the greatest use of them, these laws have inadvertently clogged the courts, lowered the rates of plea bargaining, and caused desperate offenders to violently resist arrest (Butterfield, 1996). Mandatory minimum sentences have resulted in a great increase in drug offenders, most for nonviolent offenses, serving very long terms in America's prisons. One study shows that the law has not significantly reduced rates for serious crime or petty theft (Stolzenberg and D'Alessio, 1997).

indeterminate sentence A period, set by a judge, that specifies a minimum and a maximum time to be served in prison. Sometime after the minimum, the offender may be eligible for parole. Because it is based on the idea that the time necessary for treatment cannot be set, the indeterminate sentence is closely associated with rehabilitation.

determinate sentence A sentence that fixes the term of imprisonment at a specific period.

presumptive sentence A sentence for which the legislature or a commission sets a minimum and maximum range of months or years. Judges are to fix the length of the sentence within that range, allowing for special circumstances.

mandatory sentence A sentence determined by statutes and requiring that a certain penalty be imposed and carried out for convicted offenders who meet certain criteria.

In March 2003 the U.S. Supreme Court in two 5–4 rulings upheld California's three-strikes law. The offenders in the two cases argued that their third felonies were minor and their long sentences were unconstitutional "cruel and unusual punishments." Leondro Andrade's third felony was for stealing two video tapes, for which he was sentenced to 50 years without the possibility of parole. Gary Ewing's theft of golf clubs earned him a sentence of 25 years to life. Justices in the majority said that the California law reflected a legislative judgment and that the court should not second-guess this policy choice. The four justices in the minority argued that there was a "gross" disparity between the pettiness of the crime and the severity of the sentence (*Ewing v. California*, 2003; *Lockyer, Attorney General of California v. Andrade*, 2003). Which side would you choose?

The Sentence versus Actual Time Served   Regardless of how much discretion judges have to fine-tune the sentences they give, the prison sentences that are imposed may bear little resemblance to the actual amount of time served. In reality, parole boards in indeterminate-sentencing states have broad discretion in release decisions once the offender has served a minimum portion of the sentence. In addition, offenders can have their prison sentence reduced by earning **good time** for good behavior, at the discretion of the prison administrator.

Most states have good-time policies. Days are subtracted from prisoners' minimum or maximum term for good behavior or for participating in various types of vocational, educational, or treatment programs. Correctional officials consider these policies necessary for maintaining institutional order and for reducing crowding. Good-time credit serves as an incentive for prisoners to follow institutional rules. Prosecutors and defense attorneys also take good time into consideration during plea bargaining. In other words, they think about the actual amount of time a particular offender will likely serve.

The amount of good time one can earn varies among the states, usually from 5 to 10 days a month. In some states, once 90 days of good time are earned, they are vested; that is, the credits cannot be taken away as a punishment for misbehavior. Prisoners who then violate the rules risk losing only days not vested.

Judges in the United States often prescribe long periods of incarceration for serious crimes, but good time and parole reduce the amount of time spent in prison. Figure 10.1 shows the estimated time actually served by offenders sent to state prisons versus the average (mean) sentence. Note that the national average for time served is 27 months, or 51 percent of the mean sentence of 53 months.

This type of national data often hides the impact of variations in sentencing and releasing laws in individual states. In many states, because of prison crowding and release policies, offenders serve less than 20 percent of their sentences. In other states, where three-strikes and truth-in-sentencing laws are employed, the average time served will be longer than the national average.

Truth-in-Sentencing   *Truth-in-sentencing* refers to laws that require offenders to serve a substantial proportion (usually 85 percent for violent crimes) of their prison sentence before being released on parole. Truth-in-sentencing has become such a politically attractive idea that the federal government has allocated almost $10 billion for prison construction to those states adopting truth-in-sentencing (Donziger, 1996:24). Critics maintain, however, that truth-in-sentencing will increase prison populations at a tremendous cost.

INTERMEDIATE SANCTIONS

Prison crowding and the low levels of probation supervision have spurred interest in the development of **intermediate sanctions,** punishments that are less severe and costly than prison but more restrictive than traditional probation (Morris and Tonry, 1990). Intermediate sanctions provide a variety of restrictions on freedom, such as fines, home confinement, intensive probation supervision, restitution to victims, community service, boot camp, and forfeiture of possessions or stolen property.

In advocating intermediate punishments, Norval Morris and Michael Tonry (1990:37) stipulate that these sanctions should not be used in isolation, but rather in

WHAT AMERICANS THINK

Question: "Would you favor or oppose a law requiring mandatory life imprisonment for anyone convicted of a violent felony for the third time?"

No opinion 4%

Oppose 14%

Favor 82%

Go to http://www.thomsonedu.com/criminaljustice/cole to compare your opinion on this issue with the opinions of other criminal justice students.

Source: Telephone interviews of a national adult sample by ABC News, February 27–March 3, 2002. Data provided by the Roper Center for Public Opinion Research, University of Connecticut.

good time   A reduction of an inmate's prison sentence, at the discretion of the prison administrator, for good behavior or participation in vocational, educational, or treatment programs.

intermediate sanctions   A variety of punishments that are more restrictive than traditional probation but less severe and costly than incarceration.

FIGURE 10.1
Estimated time served in state prison compared with mean length of sentence
Most offenders serve a third or less of their mean sentences. Why is there such a difference between the sentence and actual time served?

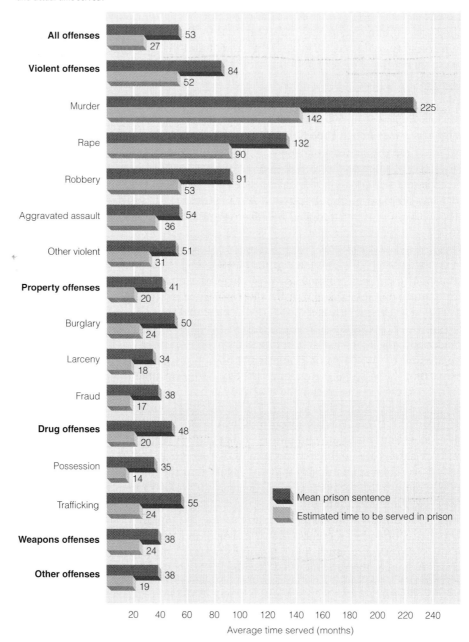

Average time served (months)

Source: Matthew R. Durose and Patrick A. Langan, "Felony Sentences in State Courts, 2002," Bureau of Justice Statistics *Bulletin*, December 2004, p. 5.

combination, to reflect the severity of the offense, the characteristics of the offender, and the needs of the community. In addition, intermediate punishments must be supported and enforced by mechanisms that take seriously any breach of the conditions of the sentence. Too often, criminal justice agencies have devoted few resources to enforcing sentences that do not involve incarceration. If the law does not fulfill its promises, offenders may feel that they have "beaten" the system, which makes the punishment meaningless. Citizens viewing the ineffectiveness of the system may develop the attitude that nothing but stiffer sentences will work.

PROBATION

The most frequently applied criminal sanction is **probation,** a sentence that an offender serves in the community under supervision. Nearly 60 percent of adults under correctional supervision are on probation. Ideally, under probation, offenders attempt to straighten out their lives. Probation is a judicial act granted by the grace of the state, not extended as a right. Conditions are imposed specifying how an offender will behave through the length of the sentence. Probationers may have to undergo regular drug tests, abide by curfews, enroll in educational programs or remain employed, stay away from certain parts of town or certain people, and meet regularly with probation officers. If probationers do not meet the required conditions, the supervising officer recommends to the court that the probation be revoked and that the remainder of the sentence be served in prison. Probation may also be revoked for commission of a new crime.

Although probationers serve their sentences in the community, the sanction is often tied to incarceration. In some jurisdictions, the court is authorized to modify an offender's prison sentence, after a portion is served, by changing it to probation. This is often referred to as **shock probation** (or split probation): an offender is released after a period of incarceration (the "shock") and resentenced to probation. An offender on probation may be required to spend intermittent periods, such as weekends or nights, in jail. Whatever its specific terms, a probationary sentence will emphasize guidance and supervision in the community.

Probation is generally advocated as a way of rehabilitating offenders whose crimes are not serious or whose past records are clean. It is viewed as less expensive than imprisonment, and more effective. For example, imprisonment may embitter youthful or first-time offenders and mix them with hardened criminals so that they learn more-sophisticated criminal techniques.

DEATH

Although other Western democracies abolished the death penalty years ago, the United States continues to use it. Capital punishment was imposed and carried out regularly prior to the late 1960s. Amid debates about the constitutionality of the death penalty and with public opinion polls showing opposition to it, the U.S. Supreme Court suspended its use from 1968 to 1976. Eventually the Court decided that capital punishment does not violate the Eighth Amendment's prohibition of cruel and unusual punishments. Executions resumed in 1977 as a majority of states began, once again, to sentence murderers to death.

The numbers of people facing the death penalty has increased dramatically, as Figure 10.2 reveals. As of April 1, 2006, 3,370 people awaited execution in death penalty states. Two-thirds of those on death row are in the South. The greatest number of death row inmates are in California, Texas, Florida, and Pennsylvania (see Figure 10.3). Although about 200 people are sent to death row each year, since 1977 the annual number of executions has never exceeded 98 (which occurred in 1999).

The Death Penalty and the Constitution   Death differs from other punishments in that it is final and irreversible. The Supreme Court has therefore examined the decision-making process in capital cases to ensure that it fulfills the Constitution's requirements regarding due process, equal protection, and cruel and unusual punishment. Because life is in the balance, capital cases must be conducted according to higher standards of fairness and more-careful procedures than are other kinds of cases. Several important Supreme Court cases illustrate this concern.

In *Furman v. Georgia* (1972), the Supreme Court ruled that the death penalty, as administered, constituted cruel and unusual punishment. The decision invalidated the death penalty laws of 39 states and the District of Columbia. A majority of justices found that the procedures used to impose death sentences were arbitrary and unfair. Over the next several years, 35 states eventually enacted new capital punishment statutes that provided for different procedures and methods of execution, such as lethal injection.

probation A sentence that the offender is allowed to serve under supervision in the community.

shock probation A sentence in which the offender is released after a short incarceration and resentenced to probation.

***Furman v. Georgia* (1972)** The death penalty, as administered, constitutes cruel and unusual punishment.

FIGURE 10.2
People under sentence of death and people executed, 1953–2006

Since 1976 about 250 new offenders, on average, have been added to death row each year, yet the number of executions has never exceeded 98. What explains this fact?

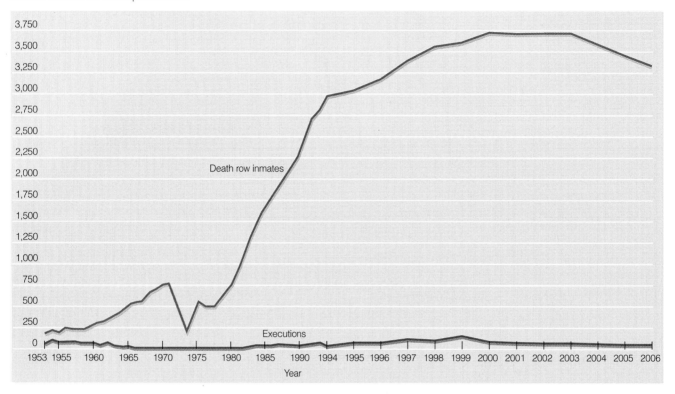

Sources: NAACP Legal Defense and Education Fund, *Death Row USA,* Spring 2006; Death Penalty Information Center, http://www.deathpenaltyinfo.org/.

Gregg v. Georgia (1976) Death penalty laws are constitutional if they require the judge and jury to consider certain mitigating and aggravating circumstances in deciding which convicted murderers should be sentenced to death. Proceedings must be also be divided into a trial phase and a punishment phase, and there must be opportunities for appeal.

The new laws were tested before the Supreme Court in *Gregg v. Georgia* (1976). The Court upheld those laws that required the sentencing judge or jury to take into account specific aggravating and mitigating factors in deciding which convicted murderers should be sentenced to death. Further, the Court decided that, rather than having a single proceeding determine the defendant's guilt and whether the death sentence would be applied, states should use "bifurcated proceedings." In this two-part process, the defendant has a trial that finds him guilty or not guilty and then a separate hearing that focuses exclusively on the issues of punishment. It seeks to ensure a thorough deliberation before someone receives the ultimate punishment.

Under the *Gregg* decision, the prosecution uses the punishment phase hearing to focus attention on the existence of aggravating factors, such as excessive cruelty or a defendant's prior record of violent crimes. The defense may focus on mitigating factors, such as the offender's youthfulness, mental condition, or lack of a criminal record. Before the judge or jury can decide to impose a death sentence, they must weigh these aggravating and mitigating factors. The Supreme Court has ruled that the defendant may not be brought into court for the sentencing hearing wearing chains and shackles. Such visible restraints may influence the jury to favor the death in that they might make the individual seem exceptionally dangerous (*Deck v. Missouri*, 2005). Because of the Court's emphasis on fair procedures and individualized decisions, state appellate courts review trial court procedures in virtually every capital case.

McCleskey v. Kemp (1987) The Supreme Court rejects a challenge of Georgia's death penalty on grounds of racial discrimination.

In *McCleskey v. Kemp* (1987), opponents of the death penalty felt that the U.S. Supreme Court severely limited their movement. In this case the Court rejected a challenge to Georgia's death penalty law, made on the grounds of racial discrimination. Warren McCleskey, an African American, was sentenced to death for killing a white police officer. Before the U.S. Supreme Court, McCleskey's attorney cited research that showed a disparity in the imposition of the death penalty in Georgia,

FIGURE 10.3
Death row census, April 1, 2006

Many of the inmates on death row are concentrated in certain states. African Americans make up about 13 percent of the U.S. population but 42 percent of the death row population. How might you explain this higher percentage of death sentences in proportion to the population?

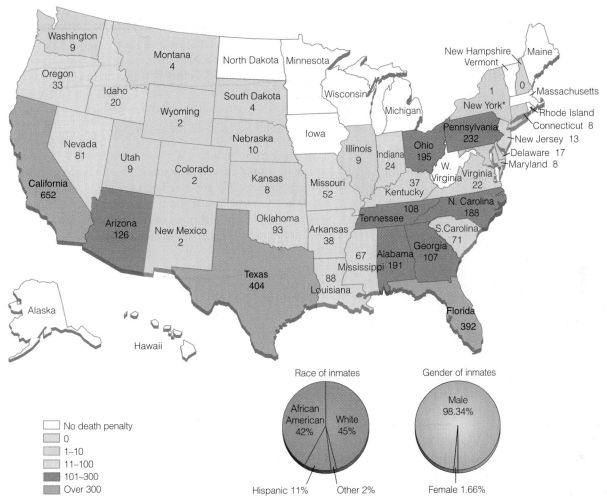

*New York's Court of Appeals declared that state's death penalty law to be unconstitutional in 2004 (*People v. LaValle*).

Source: NAACP Legal Defense and Education Fund, *Death Row USA,* Spring 2006.

based on the race of the victim and, to a lesser extent, the race of the defendant (Baldus, Woodworth, and Pulaski, 1994).

By a 5–4 vote, the justices rejected McCleskey's assertion that Georgia's capital-sentencing practices violated the equal protection clause of the Constitution by producing racial discrimination. The slim majority of justices declared that McCleskey would have to prove that the decision makers acted with a discriminatory purpose in deciding his particular case. The Court also concluded that statistical evidence showing discrimination throughout the Georgia courts did not provide adequate proof. McCleskey was executed in 1991.

In June 2002 the Supreme Court broke new ground in a way that heartened opponents of the death penalty. First, in *Atkins v. Virginia* it ruled that execution of the mentally retarded was unconstitutional. Daryl Atkins, who has an IQ of 59, was sentenced to death for killing Eric Nesbitt in a 7-Eleven store parking lot. As the majority opinion notes, the characteristics of mentally retarded offenders, people with IQs of less than 70, "undermine the strength of the procedural protections." This point is in keeping with the argument of mental health experts who say their suggestibility and

***Atkins v. Virginia* (2002)**
Execution of the mentally retarded is unconstitutional.

Scott Panetti, a death row inmate in Texas, understands that the state intends to execute him for the murder of his wife's parents. However, he says that the state, in league with Satan, wants to kill him to keep him from preaching the gospel. That delusion has been documented by doctors and acknowledged by judges and prosecutors. It poses the question: When is someone too mentally ill to be executed?

Brett Coomer/The New York Times/Redux

willingness to please leads retarded people to confess. At trial they have problems remembering details, locating witnesses, and testifying credibly in their own behalf.

Second, in *Ring v. Arizona* (2002) the Supreme Court ruled that juries, rather than judges, must make the crucial factual decisions as to whether a convicted murderer should receive the death penalty. *Ring v. Arizona* overturned the law of that state and four others—Colorado, Idaho, Montana, and Nebraska—where judges alone decided on aggravating factors that warrant capital punishment. The decision also raised questions about the procedure in four other states—Alabama, Delaware, Florida, and Indiana—where judges decide life imprisonment or death after hearing a jury's recommendation. The *Ring* opinion also says that any aggravating factors must be stated in the indictment, thus also requiring a change in federal death penalty laws.

The Supreme Court made a further reduction in the scope of capital punishment in *Roper v. Simmons* (2005). A slim majority of justices decided that offenders cannot be sentenced to death for crimes that they committed before they reached the age of 18. Prior to that decision, the United States was among only a half-dozen countries in the entire world with laws that permitted death sentences for juveniles. Because the Court was divided on the issue, some observers wonder if further changes in the Court's composition may lead to a reversal of this decision.

Roper v. Simmons (2005)
Execution of offenders for crimes committed while under the age of 18 is unconstitutional.

Continuing Legal Issues   The case law since *Furman* indicates that capital punishment is legal so long as it is imposed fairly. However, opponents continue to raise several issues in litigation. Now that the mentally retarded and juvenile offenders have been excluded from eligibility for the death penalty, some people argue that mentally ill offenders should also be excluded. Issues have arisen about the effectiveness of representation provided for capital defendants by defense attorneys. Many critics are concerned about the impact of using death-qualified juries. Other cases continue to raise issues about methods of execution and the lengthy periods that condemned offenders spend on death row because of appeals. Finally, issues have arisen concerning the requirements of international law on the administration of capital punishment in the United States.

EXECUTION OF THE MENTALLY ILL As we saw in Chapter 3, insanity is a recognized defense for commission of a crime. Moreover, the Supreme Court has said that people who become insane after entering prison cannot be executed (*Ford v. Wainwright*, 1986). But many people with mental illnesses do not meet the legal tests for insanity. They can be convicted of crimes and punished, and there is no guarantee that they will receive psychiatric treatment in prison. What happens if these people commit capital crimes? Is it appropriate to execute people whose mental illnesses may have affected their behavior? Opponents of the death penalty will undoubtedly seek to persuade the Supreme Court that mentally ill offenders should be excluded from capital punishment in the same manner in which the Court removed the mentally retarded and juveniles from eligibility for execution.

Critics have also raised questions about medical ethics in treating an offender's mental illness so that he or she can be executed. In 2003 the U.S. 8th Circuit Court of Appeals held that Arkansas could force a death row inmate to take antipsychotic drugs to make him sane enough to execute. Similarly, ethical concerns related to the physicians' oath to "do no harm" led California to postpone executions by lethal injection because doctors refused to participate. Such issues may be raised on behalf of mentally ill offenders in future court cases.

EFFECTIVE COUNSEL In *Strickland v. Washington* (1984) the Supreme Court ruled that defendants in capital cases had the right to representation that meets an "objective standard of reasonableness." As noted by Justice Sandra Day O'Connor, the appellant must show "that there is a reasonable probability that, but for the counsel's unprofessional errors, the result of the proceeding would be different."

David Washington was charged with three counts of capital murder, robbery, kidnapping, and other felonies, and an experienced criminal lawyer was appointed as counsel. Against his attorney's advice, Washington confessed to two murders, waived a jury trial, pleaded guilty to all charges, and chose to be sentenced by the trial judge. Believing the situation was hopeless, his counsel did not adequately prepare for the sentencing hearing. On being sentenced to death, Washington appealed. The Supreme Court, however, rejected Washington's claim that his attorney was ineffective because he did not call witnesses, seek a presentence investigation report, or cross-examine medical experts on the defendant's behalf. In this case, the Court set standards that Washington's case did not meet. In other words, although his lawyer did not do as good a job as he wanted, Washington nonetheless received a fair trial.

In recent years the public has learned of cases placing the defense attorney's competency in doubt, even to the point of sleeping at trial. In 1999 the *Chicago Tribune* conducted an extensive investigation of capital punishment in Illinois. Reporters found that 33 defendants sentenced to death since 1977 were represented by an attorney who had been, or was later, disbarred or suspended for conduct that was "incompetent, unethical or even criminal." These attorneys included David Landau, who was disbarred one year after representing a Will County defendant sentenced to death, and Robert McDonnell, a convicted felon and the only lawyer in Illinois to be disbarred twice. McDonnell represented four men who landed on death row (Armstrong and Mills, 1999).

In March 2000 a federal judge in Texas ordered the release of Calvin Jerold Burdine after 16 years on death row. At his 1984 trial, Burdine's counsel slept through long portions of the proceedings. As the judge said, "Sleeping counsel is equivalent to no counsel at all" (*New York Times,* March 2, 2000:A19).

These highly publicized cases may have caught the attention of the Supreme Court. In 2003, the Court issued a decision that seemed designed to remind lawyers and judges about the need for competent defense attorneys in capital cases. In *Wiggins v. Smith* (2003) the Court found that the Sixth Amendment right to counsel was violated when a defense attorney failed to present mitigating evidence concerning the severe physical and sexual abuse suffered by the defendant during childhood. Whether the justices create clearer or stricter standards for defense attorneys remains to be seen.

DEATH-QUALIFIED JURIES Should people who are opposed to the death penalty be excluded from juries in capital cases? In *Witherspoon v. Illinois* (1968), the Supreme Court held that potential jurors who have general objections to the death penalty or whose religious convictions oppose its use cannot be automatically excluded from jury service in capital cases. However, it upheld the practice of removing, during voir dire (preliminary examination), those people whose opposition is so strong as to "prevent or substantially impair the performance of their duties." Such jurors have become known as "*Witherspoon* excludables." The decision was later reaffirmed in *Lockhart v. McCree* (1986).

Because society is divided on capital punishment, opponents argue that death-qualified juries do not represent a cross section of the community. Researchers have also found that "juries are likely to be nudged toward believing the defendant is guilty and toward an imposition of the death sentence by the very process of undergoing death qualification" (Luginbuhl and Burkhead, 1994:107).

Mark Costanzo (1997:24–25) points to research that indicates that death qualification has several impacts. First, those who are selected for jury duty are more conviction prone and more receptive to aggravating factors presented during the penalty phase. A second, subtler impact is that jurors answering the questions about their willingness to vote for a death sentence often conclude that both defenders and prosecutors anticipate a conviction and a death sentence.

Witherspoon v. Illinois **(1968)**
Potential jurors who object to the death penalty cannot be automatically excluded from service; however, during voir dire those who feel so strongly about capital punishment that they could not give an impartial verdict may be excluded.

METHODS OF EXECUTION Over the years, states have sought new methods of execution that are believed to be more humane than older methods. Thus, during the twentieth century most states moved from execution by hanging and firing squad to the use of the gas chamber and the electric chair (Moran, 2002). During the 1980s and 1990s, however, these methods were challenged because they do not kill instantly and highly publicized mishaps highlighted the severe pain and suffering that can occur during the several minutes that condemned offenders can take to die. In 1994, for example, a federal district judge declared California's use of the gas chamber to be unconstitutional because "inmates suffer intense, visceral pain, primarily as a result of the lack of oxygen to the cells. . . . Cyanide-induced cellular suffocation causes anxiety, panic, terror, and pain" (*Fierro v. Gomez*). The Georgia Supreme Court declared the use of the electric chair to be unconstitutional in 2001 because "death by electrocution, with its specter of excruciating pain and its certainty of cooked brains and blistered bodies, violates the prohibition on cruel and unusual punishment" (*Dawson v. State*).

By 2004 all capital punishment states except Nebraska had authorized the use of lethal injection as the preferred method of execution. However, lethal injection faces close scrutiny and potential challenges. Botched executions have occurred in which needles have popped out of offenders' arms during executions or technicians have misapplied the drugs. Although lethal injection was intended to kill offenders by peacefully rendering them unconscious as they die, the reality can be quite different. For example, during one execution witnessed and described by a journalist, the condemned man "continued to gasp and violently gag until death came, some eleven minutes after the drugs were administered" (Radelet, 2004).

In 2004 the Supreme Court issued its first decision concerning lethal injection when it permitted a condemned man to pursue a civil rights lawsuit to challenge officials' plans to cut a 2-inch incision into his arm in order to find a usable vein for the execution. The justices remanded the case to a lower court to determine whether the cut-down procedure, to be performed without any assurance that a physician would be present, violates the Eighth Amendment (*Nelson v. Campbell*). In a case in 2006, the Supreme Court said that a death row inmate could use a civil rights lawsuit to allege that the use of lethal injections violates the Eighth Amendment prohibition on cruel and unusual punishments (*Hill v. McDonough*). Undoubtedly, we shall see additional legal challenges to lethal injection procedures and any other method of execution subsequently developed.

APPEALS Ongoing controversy surrounds the long appeals process for death penalty cases. The 65 prisoners executed in 2003 had been under sentence of death an average of 10 years and 11 months (Bonczar and Snell, 2004). During this time, sentences were reviewed by the state courts and through the writ of habeas corpus by the federal courts.

The late Chief Justice William Rehnquist, who served as chief justice from 1986 to 2005, actively sought to reduce the opportunities for capital punishment defendants to have their appeals heard by multiple courts. In 1996 President Bill Clinton signed the Anti-Terrorism and Effective Death Penalty Act that requires death row inmates to file habeas appeals within one year and requires federal judges to issue their decisions within strict time limits.

Appellate review is a time-consuming and expensive process, but it also makes an impact. From 1977 through 2003, 7,061 people entered prison under sentence of death. During those 26 years, 885 people were executed, 282 died of natural causes, and 2,542 were removed from death row as a result of appellate court decisions and reviews, commutations, or death while awaiting execution (Bonczar and Snell, 2004).

Michael Radelet and his colleagues have examined the cases of 68 death row inmates later released because of doubts about their guilt (Radelet, Lofquist, and Bedau, 1996:907). This number is equivalent to one-fifth of the inmates executed during the period 1970–1996. Correction of the miscarriage of justice for about one-third of the defendants took four or less years, but it took nine years or longer for another third of the defendants. Had the expedited appeals process and limitations on habeas corpus been in effect, would these death sentences have been overturned?

INTERNATIONAL LAW The United States is a signatory of the Vienna Convention on Consular Relations that requires notification of consular officials when a foreign national is arrested. This aspect of international law benefits Americans who are arrested abroad, by enabling the U.S. embassy to help find a lawyer and monitor the prosecution of Americans who face criminal punishment in foreign countries. However, individual prosecutors and police throughout the United States are apparently unaware of the law because several dozen foreign nationals have been convicted and sentenced to death in the United States without their consular officials being informed.

Mexico, Germany, and Paraguay filed complaints against the United States for violating the Vienna Convention in death penalty cases. In April 2004 the International Court of Justice in the Hague, Netherlands, ruled that international law had been violated and ordered the United States to review the death sentences of Mexicans held on American death rows. The International Court has no power to force the United States to take action, but President George W. Bush announced in February 2005 that the United States will comply with the Vienna Convention in the future. President Bush does not, however, have any means to insure that each county prosecutor throughout the United States follows the Vienna Convention. In light of President Bush's announcement, the Supreme Court decided not to rule in a pending case brought to it by a Mexican citizen on death row in Texas (*Medellin v. Dretke*, 2005). Instead, the majority of justices decided to wait and see how the Texas courts handle the issue.

It remains to be seen whether international law will spur additional issues and arguments concerning the death penalty. For example, in 2002 the Supreme Court declined to rule in a death row petitioner's case that asserted a violation of the cruel and unusual punishments clause because he had spent 27 years in solitary confinement on death row under exceptionally restrictive conditions (*Foster v. Florida*). The condemned man cited judicial decisions by foreign courts, such as the Privy Council of Great Britain and the European Court of Human Rights, that stated a delay of 15 years between trial and execution can render a capital punishment conviction "degrading, shocking, or cruel." Several justices of the Supreme Court have made it clear that they do not believe international law has any application to the American criminal justice system, but other justices have cited foreign cases to support specific decisions.

The Death Penalty: A Continuing Controversy On January 13, 2000, Governor George Ryan of Illinois, a longtime supporter of the death penalty, called for a moratorium on executions in his state. Ryan said that he was convinced that the death penalty in Illinois was "fraught with errors," noting that since 1976 Illinois had executed 12 people yet freed 13 from death row as innocent. Similar calls followed from Kansas Governor Bill Graves, Maryland Governor Paris Glendening, the Louisiana Bar Association, and the Philadelphia City Council. In May 2000 the New Hampshire legislature became the first in more than two decades to vote to repeal the death penalty; the governor vetoed it, however. In January 2003 Governor Ryan pardoned four death-row inmates and commuted the sentences of 167 to life imprisonment without parole.

Both Illinois and Massachusetts appointed commissions to study whether and how the courts could process death penalty cases fairly and with little risk that an innocent person would be erroneously convicted. The recommendations from commissions in both states emphasized providing high-quality representation for defendants; using scientific evidence, such as DNA testing, when appropriate; and careful appeals processes. Governor Mitt Romney of Massachusetts has sought to use his commission report as the basis for proposing the limited use of capital punishment in a state that currently does not use the death penalty.

Although public opinion polls show high support for the death penalty (see "What Americans Think"), the number of executions remains low. Recent surveys show that the public is split when asked to choose between life imprisonment (without parole) and death. Does this mean that Americans are ambivalent about carrying

WHAT AMERICANS THINK

Question: "If you could choose between the following two approaches, which do you think is the better penalty for murder—the death penalty or life imprisonment with absolutely no possibility of parole?"

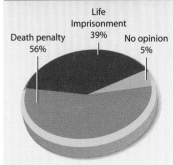

Death penalty 56%

Life Imprisonment 39%

No opinion 5%

Go to http://www.thomsonedu.com/criminaljustice/cole to compare your opinion on this issue with the opinions of other criminal justice students.

Source: Gallup Poll, May 2–5, 2005, http://www.gallup.com.

THE POLICY DEBATE

Should the Death Penalty Be Abolished?

The execution moratorium imposed by Illinois Governor George Ryan in January 2000 reinvigorated debate on the death penalty. His announcement was soon followed by a national poll that found support for the penalty to be the lowest in 19 years, the release of a national study of appeals that found two-thirds of death sentences overturned, and research questioning the quality of counsel given to many defendants. Within months, the policy debate shifted to whether it was possible to construct a system that could ensure that innocent people were not executed.

Opponents of capital punishment continue the fight to abolish it. They argue that poor people and minorities receive a disproportionate number of death sentences. They also point to the numbers of innocent people discovered on death row, to argue that the system is too fallible and flawed ever to produce error-free results.

Even the proponents of capital punishment remain dissatisfied with how it is applied. They point to the fact that although there are more than 3,300 convicted murderers on death row, the number of executions since 1976 has never exceeded 98 in a year. The appeals process is a major factor halting this pace, given that executions are delayed for years as cases are appealed through the courts.

For the Death Penalty

Supporters argue that society should apply swift, severe punishments to killers to address the continuing problems of crime and violence. Execution should occur quite soon after conviction so that the greatest deterrent value will result. They say that justice requires that a person who murders another must be executed. To do less is to denigrate the value of human life.

The arguments for the death penalty include the following:

- The death penalty deters criminals from committing violent acts.

- The death penalty achieves justice by paying killers back for their horrible crimes.

- The death penalty prevents criminals from doing further harm while on parole.

- The death penalty is less expensive than holding murderers in prison for life.

Against the Death Penalty

Opponents believe that the death penalty lingers as a barbaric practice from a less civilized age. They point out that most other developed democracies in the world have ceased to execute criminals. Opponents challenge the death penalty's claims for effectiveness in reducing crime. They also raise concerns about whether the punishment can be applied without errors and discrimination.

The arguments against the death penalty include the following:

- No hard evidence proves that the death penalty is a deterrent.

- It is wrong for a government to participate in the intentional killing of citizens.

- The death penalty is applied in a discriminatory fashion.

- Innocent people have been sentenced to death.

- Some methods of execution are inhumane, causing painful, lingering deaths.

What Should U.S. Policy Be?

With more and more people now being sentenced to death row but fewer than one hundred individuals executed each year, death penalty policy is at a significant crossroads. Will the United States increase the pace of executions, allow the number of capital offenders in prison to keep growing, or take a middle ground that satisfies neither side completely, such as life imprisonment without parole for convicted murderers?

RESEARCHING THE INTERNET

Compare the perspectives presented at the websites of Pro-Death Penalty and the Death Penalty Information Center. Both are listed on the Cole/Smith Criminal Justice in America Companion Website: http://www.thomsonedu.com/criminaljustice/cole.

FOR CRITICAL ANALYSIS

Evaluate the pros and cons of the death penalty debate. What political factors might influence your state's legislators to abolish, modify, or retain the death penalty?

---

out the punishment? What might it say about capital punishment in the next decade? Debate on this important public policy issue has gone on for more than two hundred years, yet there is still no consensus (see "The Policy Debate" for more).

The criminal sanction takes many forms, with offenders punished in various ways to serve various purposes. Table 10.2 summarizes how these sanctions operate and how they reflect the underlying philosophies of punishment.

CHECKPOINT

3. What are the three types of sentences used in the United States?

4. What are thought to be the advantages of intermediate sanctions?

5. What requirements specified in *Gregg v. Georgia* must exist before a death sentence can be imposed?

Answers

3. Determinate, indeterminate, and mandatory sentences.

4. Intermediate sanctions give judges a greater range of sentencing alternatives, reduce prison populations, cost less than prison, and increase community security.

5. Judge and jury must be able to consider mitigating and aggravating circumstances, proceedings must be divided into a trial phase and a punishment phase, and there must be opportunities for appeal.

TABLE 10.2   The Punishment of Offenders

The goals of the criminal sanction are carried out in a variety of ways, depending upon the provisions of the law, the characteristics of the offender, and the discretion of the judge. Judges may impose sentences that combine several forms to achieve punishment objectives.

Form of Sanction	Description	Purposes
Incarceration	Imprisonment	
Indeterminate sentence	Specifies a maximum and minimum length of time to be served	Incapacitation, deterrence, rehabilitation
Determinate sentence	Specifies a certain length of time to be served	Retribution, deterrence, incapacitation
Mandatory sentence	Specifies a minimum amount of time that must be served for given crimes	Incapacitation, deterrence
Good time	Subtracts days from an inmate's sentence because of good behavior or participation in prison programs	Rewards behavior, relieves prison crowding, helps maintain prison discipline
Intermediate sanctions	Punishment for those requiring sanctions more restrictive than probation but less restrictive than prison	Retribution, deterrence
Administered by the judiciary		
Fine	Money paid to state by offender	Retribution, deterrence
Restitution	Money paid to victim by offender	Retribution, deterrence
Forfeiture	Seizure by the state of property illegally obtained or acquired with resources illegally obtained	Retribution, deterrence
Administered in the community		
Community service	Requires offender to perform work for the community	Retribution, deterrence
Home confinement	Requires offender to stay in home during certain times	Retribution, deterrence, incapacitation
Intensive probation supervision	Requires strict and frequent reporting to probation officer	Retribution, deterrence, incapacitation
Administered institutionally		
Boot camp/shock incarceration	Short-term institutional sentence emphasizing physical development and discipline, followed by probation	Retribution, deterrence, rehabilitation
Probation	Allows offender to serve a sentence in the community under supervision	Retribution, incapacitation, rehabilitation
Death	Execution	Incapacitation, deterrence, retribution

The Sentencing Process

Regardless of how and where guilt has been determined—misdemeanor court or felony court, plea bargain or adversarial context, bench or jury trial—judges hold the responsibility for imposing sentences. Often difficult, sentencing usually involves more than applying clear-cut principles to individual cases. In one case, a judge may decide to sentence a forger to prison as an example to others, even though the offender poses no threat to community safety and probably does not need rehabilitative treatment. In another case, the judge may impose a light sentence on a youthful offender who has committed a serious crime but may be a candidate for rehabilitation if moved quickly back into society.

Legislatures establish the penal codes that set forth the sentences judges can impose. These laws generally give judges discretion in sentencing. Judges may combine various forms of punishment in order to tailor the sanction to the offender. The judge may specify, for example, that the prison terms for two charges are to run either concurrently (at the same time) or consecutively (one after the other), or that all or part of the period of imprisonment may be suspended. In other situations, the offender may receive a combination of a suspended prison term, a fine, and probation. Judges may suspend a sentence as long as the offender stays out of trouble, makes restitution, or seeks medical treatment. They may also delay imposing any sentence but retain the power to set penalties at a later date if the offender misbehaves.

Within the discretion allowed by the code, various elements influence the decisions of judges. Social scientists believe that several factors influence the sentencing process: (1) the administrative context of the courts, (2) the attitudes and values of judges, (3) the presentence report, and (4) sentencing guidelines.

THE ADMINISTRATIVE CONTEXT OF THE COURTS

Judges are strongly influenced by the administrative context within which they impose sentences. As a result, differences are found, for example, between the assembly-line style of justice in misdemeanor courts and the more formal proceedings in felony courts.

Misdemeanor Courts: Assembly-Line Justice

Misdemeanor or lower courts have limited jurisdiction because they normally can impose only jail sentences of less than one year. These courts hear about 90 percent of criminal cases. Whereas felony cases are processed in lower courts only for arraignments and preliminary hearings, misdemeanor cases are processed completely in the lower courts. Only a minority of cases adjudicated in lower courts end in jail sentences. Most cases result in fines, probation, community service, restitution, or a combination of these.

Most lower courts are overloaded and allot minimal time to each case. Judicial decisions are mass produced because actors in the system share three assumptions. First, any person appearing before the court is guilty, because the police and prosecution have presumably filtered out doubtful cases. Second, the vast majority of defendants will plead guilty. Third, those charged with minor offenses will be processed in volume, with dozens of cases being decided in rapid succession within a single hour. The citation will be read by the clerk, a guilty plea entered, and the sentence pronounced by the judge for one defendant after another. See the box "Sentencing by Computer" for more on this rapid process.

Defendants whose cases are processed through the lower court's assembly line may appear to receive little or no punishment. However, people who get caught in the criminal justice system experience other punishments, whether or not

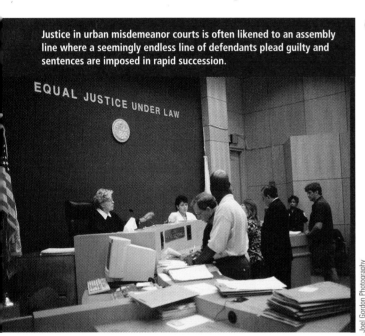

Justice in urban misdemeanor courts is often likened to an assembly line where a seemingly endless line of defendants plead guilty and sentences are imposed in rapid succession.

Joel Gordon Photography

TECHNOLOGY ISSUES IN CRIMINAL JUSTICE

Sentencing by Computer

The development of sentencing guidelines has reduced judges' discretion for determining appropriate sentences. Instead, judges add up points, based on the offense and the prior record, to determine the sentence range mandated by the legislature. In Michigan, private computer companies have developed software that will do sentencing calculations quickly for judges and for the probation officers who write presentence reports. Thus, with the push of a few keys, the computer produces the offender's sentence.

Advocates of sentencing software believe it will help speed up court processes. In addition, it may be useful during plea negotiations for exploring various sentencing options by quickly producing calculations based on different combinations of charges that the prosecution and defense are considering as part of a guilty plea.

Does relying on computer calculations pose any risks? Most basically, if incorrect numbers are included in the calculations, an improper sentence will be produced. For defendants with complex records, such as numerous arrests and probation violations, the person inputting the data could easily miscount arrests and reported probation violations in the score, even though the sentence is supposed to be based on the number of actual criminal convictions.

More importantly, does the software program diminish the image of justice, giving the impression that sentencing occurs by machine? State judges are supposed to represent the community, delivering messages about justice on the community's behalf as they make rulings. Does this technology tarnish the judge's role and image?

RESEARCHING THE INTERNET

To see an example of sentencing software, go to the corresponding site listed on the Cole/Smith Criminal Justice in America Companion Website: http://www.thomsonedu.com/criminaljustice/cole.

FOR CRITICAL ANALYSIS

What problems do you foresee if judges relied on computers for their sentencing decisions? Is justice served by this technology?

Sources: Drawn from Paul Egan, "Software Could Assist in Sentencing," *Lansing State Journal*, May 7, 1999, pp. 1A–2A. Reprinted by permission.

they are ultimately convicted. A person who is arrested but eventually released still incurs various tangible and intangible costs. Time spent in jail awaiting trial, the cost of a bail bond, and days of work lost create an immediate and concrete impact. Poor people may lose their jobs or be evicted from their homes if they fail to work and pay their bills for even a few days. For most people, simply being arrested is a devastating experience. It is impossible to measure the psychological and social price of being stigmatized, separated from family, and deprived of freedom.

Felony Courts   Felony cases are processed and felony offenders are sentenced in courts of general jurisdiction. Because of the seriousness of the crimes, the atmosphere is more formal and generally lacks the chaotic, assembly-line environment of misdemeanor courts. Caseload burdens can affect how much time individual cases receive. Exchange relationships among courtroom actors can facilitate plea bargains and shape the content of prosecutors' sentencing recommendations. Sentencing decisions are ultimately shaped, in part, by the relationships, negotiations, and agreements among the prosecutor, defense attorney, and judge. Table 10.3 shows the types of felony sentences imposed for conviction on different charges.

ATTITUDES AND VALUES OF JUDGES

All lawyers recognize that judges differ from one another in their sentencing decisions. Administrative pressures, the conflicting goals of criminal justice, and the influence of community values partly explain these differences. Sentencing decisions also depend on judges' attitudes concerning the offender's blameworthiness, the protection of the community, and the practical implications of the sentence (Steffensmeier and Demuth, 2001). For the public's attitudes about local sentencing practices, see "What Americans Think."

Blameworthiness concerns such factors as offense severity (such as violent crime or property crime), the offender's criminal history (such as recidivist or first timer), and role in commission of the crime (such as leader or follower). For example, a judge might impose a harsh sentence on a repeat offender who organized others to commit a serious crime.

Protection of the community hinges on similar factors, such as dangerousness, recidivism, and offense severity. However, it centers mostly on the need to incapacitate the offender or to deter would-be offenders.

Finally, the practical implications of a sentence can affect judges' decisions. For example, judges may take into account the offender's ability to "do time," as in the case of an elderly person. They may also consider the impact on the offender's family; a mother with children may require a different sentence than a single woman would. Finally, costs to the corrections system may play a role in sentencing, as judges consider probation officers' caseloads or prison crowding (Steffensmeier, Kramer, and Streifel, 1993).

PRESENTENCE REPORT

Even though sentencing is the judge's responsibility, the **presentence report** has become an important ingredient in the judicial mix. Usually a probation officer investigates the convicted person's background, criminal record, job status, and mental condition

presentence report A report, prepared by a probation officer, that presents a convicted offender's background and is used by the judge in selecting an appropriate sentence.

TABLE 10.3   Types of Felony Sentences Imposed by State Courts

Although a felony conviction is often equated with a sentence to prison, almost a third of felony offenders receive probation.

Most Serious Offense	Percentage of Felons Sentenced to		
	Prison	Jail	Probation
All offenses	41	28	31
Violent offenses	52	25	23
Murder	91	4	5
Sexual Assault	59	23	18
Rape	67	22	11
Other sexual assault	55	23	22
Robbery	71	15	14
Aggravated assault	42	29	29
Other violent	42	35	23
Property offenses	38	28	34
Burglary	46	26	28
Larceny	40	34	26
Motor vehicle theft	37	39	24
Fraud	31	28	41
Drug possession	39	27	34
Possession	34	28	38
Trafficking	42	26	32
Weapons offenses	45	28	27
Other offenses	35	35	30

Note: For persons receiving a combination of sanctions, the sentence designation came from the most severe penalty imposed—prison being the most severe, followed by jail and then probation.

Source: Matthew R. Durose and Patrick A. Langan, "Felony Sentences in State Courts, 2002," Bureau of Justice Statistics *Bulletin*, December 2004, p. 2.

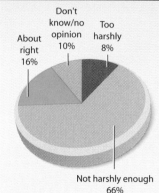
sentencing guidelines A mechanism to indicate to judges the expected sanction for certain offenses, in order to reduce disparities in sentencing.

to suggest a sentence that is in the interests of both the offender and society. Although the presentence report serves primarily to help the judge select the sentence, it also assists in the classification of probationers, prisoners, and parolees for treatment planning and risk assessment. In the report, the probation officer makes judgments about what information to include and what conclusions to draw from that information. In some states, however, probation officers present only factual material to the judge and make no sentencing recommendation. Because the probation officers do not necessarily follow evidentiary rules, they may include hearsay statements as well as firsthand information. The Close Up box gives an example of a presentence report.

In the federal court system, the presentence report is supplemented by an additional report written by a pretrial services officer (PSO). This report focuses on the defendant's behavior and compliance with conditions while out on bail—prior to trial or plea or between the date of conviction and the date of sentencing. The support staff within the courts are less visible and less familiar to the public than are many of the actors in law enforcement jobs. To learn more about a career as a PSO, read "Careers in Criminal Justice."

The presentence report is one means by which judges ease the strain of decision making. The report lets judges shift partial responsibility to the probation department. Because a substantial number of sentencing alternatives are open to judges, they often rely on the report for guidance. "A Question of Ethics" at the end of this chapter illustrates some of the difficulties faced by a judge who must impose a sentence with little more than the presentence report to consider.

SENTENCING GUIDELINES

Since the 1980s, **sentencing guidelines** have been established in the federal courts and in more than two dozen states. Such guidelines indicate to judges the expected sanction for particular types of offenses. They are intended to limit the sentencing discretion of judges and to reduce disparity among sentences given for similar offenses. Although statutes provide a variety of sentencing options for particular crimes, guidelines attempt to direct the judge to more-specific actions that should be taken. The range of sentencing options provided for most offenses centers on the seriousness of the crime and on the criminal history of an offender.

Legislatures and, in some states and the federal government, commissions construct sentencing guidelines as a grid of two scores (Tonry, 1993:140). As shown in Table 10.4 on page 281, one dimension relates to the seriousness of the offense, the other to the likelihood of offender recidivism. The offender score is obtained by totaling the points allocated to such factors as the number of juvenile, adult misdemeanor, and adult felony convictions; the number of times incarcerated; the status of the accused at the time of the last offense, whether on probation or parole or escaped from confinement; and employment status or educational achievement. Judges look at the grid to see what sentence should be imposed on a particular offender who has committed a specific offense. Judges may go outside the guidelines if aggravating or mitigating circumstances exist; however, they must provide a written explanation of their reasons for doing so (J. H. Kramer and Ulmer, 1996). See "Real-World Activity" at the end of the chapter to work with the Minnesota guidelines.

Sentencing guidelines are to be reviewed and modified periodically so that recent decisions will be included. Given that guidelines are constructed on the basis of past sentences, some critics argue that because the guidelines reflect only what has happened, they do not reform sentencing. Others question the choice of characteristics included in the offender scale and charge that some are used to mask racial criteria. Paula Krautt (2002:655) found differences in drug trafficking sentences among federal district and circuit courts. However, Lisa Stolzenberg and Stewart J. D'Alessio (1994) studied the Minnesota guidelines and found, compared with preguideline decisions, an 18 percent reduction in disparity for the prison/no-prison outcome and a 60 percent reduction in disparity of length of prison sentences.

Although guidelines make sentences more uniform, many judges object to having their discretion limited in this manner (Weinstein, 1992). However, Peter Rossi and

CLOSE UP

Sample Presentence Report

STATE OF NEW MEXICO
Corrections Department Field
Service Division

Santa Fe, New Mexico 87501
Date: March 4, 2006
To: The Honorable Manuel Baca
From: Presentence Unit, Officer Brian Gaines
Re: Richard Knight

EVALUATION

Appearing before Your Honor for sentencing is 20-year-old Richard Knight, who on November 10, 2005, pursuant to a Plea and Disposition Agreement, entered a plea of guilty to Aggravated Assault Upon a Peace Officer (Deadly Weapon) (Firearm Enhancement), as charged in Information Number 95-5736900. The terms of the agreement stipulate that the maximum period of incarceration be limited to one year, that restitution be made on all counts and charges whether dismissed or not, and that all remaining charges in the Indictment and DA Files 39780 be dismissed.

The defendant is an only child, born and raised in Albuquerque. He attended West Mesa High School until the eleventh grade, at which time he dropped out. Richard declared that he felt school was "too difficult" and that he decided that it would be more beneficial for him to obtain steady employment rather than to complete his education. The defendant further stated that he felt it was "too late for vocational training" because of the impending one-year prison sentence he faces, due to the Firearm Enhancement penalty for his offense.

The longest period of time the defendant has held a job has been for six months with Frank's Concrete Company. He has been employed with the Madrid Construction Company since August 2004 (verified). Richard lives with his parents, who provide most of his financial support. Conflicts between his mother and himself, the defendant claimed, precipitated his recent lawless actions by causing him to "not care about anything." He stressed the fact that he is now once again "getting along" with his mother. Although the defendant contended that he doesn't abuse drugs, he later contradicted himself by declaring that he "gets drunk every weekend." He noted that he was inebriated when he committed the present offense.

In regard to the present offense, the defendant recalled that other individuals at the party attempted to stab his friend and that he and his companion left and returned with a gun in order to settle the score. Richard claimed remorse for his offense and stated that his past family problems led him to spend most of his time on the streets, where he became more prone to violent conduct. The defendant admitted being a member of the 18th Street Gang.

RECOMMENDATION

It is respectfully recommended that the defendant be sentenced to three years incarceration and that the sentence be suspended. It is further recommended that the defendant be incarcerated for one year as to the mandatory Firearm Enhancement and then placed on three years probation under the following special conditions:

1. That restitution be made to Juan Lopez in the amount of $622.40.
2. That the defendant either maintain full-time employment or obtain his GED [general equivalency diploma].
3. That the defendant discontinue fraternizing with the 18th Street Gang members and terminate his own membership in the gang.

RESEARCHING THE INTERNET

You can see the actual forms that probation offers fill out in preparing a presentence report, at the corresponding website listed on the Cole/Smith Criminal Justice in America Companion Website: http://www.thomsonedu.com/criminaljustice/cole.

FOR CRITICAL ANALYSIS

Do you agree with Probation Officer Gaines's recommendation to Judge Baca? Do you see problems carrying out this sentence? For Richard Knight? For the Corrections Department?

Richard Berk (1997) found a fair amount of agreement between the sentences prescribed in the federal guidelines and those desired by the general public.

The future of sentencing guidelines is uncertain. In 2004 the U.S. Supreme Court decided that aspects of Washington State's sentencing guidelines violated the Sixth Amendment right to trial by jury, by giving judges too much authority to enhance sentences based on unproven factual determinations (*Blakely v. Washington*). One year later, the Supreme Court applied the *Blakely* precedent to the federal sentencing guidelines and found a similar violation of the Sixth Amendment when judges enhance sentences based on their own determinations (*United States v. Booker,* 2005). Observers anticipate that the U.S. Supreme Court will need to revisit this issue in order to provide guidance about how sentencing guidelines can be properly designed and applied.

WHO GETS THE HARSHEST PUNISHMENT?

Harsh, unjust punishments can occur because of sentencing disparities and wrongful convictions. The prison population in most states contains a higher proportion of African American and Hispanic men than appears in the general population. Are these disparities caused by racial prejudices and discrimination, or are other factors at work? Wrongful conviction occurs when people who are in fact innocent are

CAREERS IN CRIMINAL JUSTICE

U.S. Pretrial Services Officer (PSO)

NATURE OF THE WORK

U.S. pretrial services officers (PSO) are employees of the federal courts. They are not part of any federal law enforcement agency, such as the Department of Justice. Some PSOs may also have dual responsibilities as probation officers, depending on the staffing at a particular courthouse. They evaluate defendants in order to make recommendations about release on bail. They also monitor and supervise defendants who are granted pretrial release. In addition, they provide input on sentencing through reports to judges on the behavior of defendants during pretrial release. Most of their work takes place at the courthouse interviewing and evaluating defendants and keeping in contact with those who are out on bail. They must use professional judgment in writing reports and keeping accurate records. If a defendant actually skips bail, then U.S. marshals go out on the streets to apprehend the defendant.

REQUIRED QUALIFICATIONS

Applicants for positions as PSOs must have a four-year degree, preferably in criminal justice, psychology, or another social science field that provides knowledge of human behavior and law. They must undergo a medical exam, drug screening, and a background check. They also must be less than 37 years of age at the time of appointment. Experience with computers and fluency in Spanish are desirable. On being hired, PSOs attend a national training seminar and also receive on-the-job training for six months.

EARNINGS AND JOB OUTLOOK

Minimum salaries start at around $36,000 per year depending on the location of the court. Federal court employees who work in cities with a high cost of living receive slightly higher salaries. New PSOs with master's degrees or prior work experience in probation, correctional management, or substance abuse treatment may start at higher pay levels as well. Job openings will likely depend on the retirement of current PSOs or any congressionally authorized expansion of the court system as the nation's population grows. People interested in careers as PSOs should contact their local federal courthouse.

MORE INFORMATION

More information on a career as a PSO can be obtained from the website of the Administrative Office of the U.S. Courts and the "Who Does What?" link at the Federal Judicial Center's website. Both are listed on the Cole/Smith Criminal Justice in America Companion Website: http://www.thomsonedu.com/criminaljustice/cole.

---

nonetheless found guilty by plea or verdict. It also includes those cases in which the conviction of a truly guilty person is overturned on appeal because of due process errors.

Racial Disparities   Research on racial disparities in sentencing are inconclusive. Studies of sentencing in Pennsylvania, for example, found that there is a "high cost of being black, young (21–29 years), and male." Sentences given these offenders resulted in a higher proportion going to prison and incurring longer terms (Steffensmeier, Ulmer, and Kramer, 1998:789). While supporting the Pennsylvania results, research in Chicago, Kansas City, Missouri, and Miami found variation among the jurisdictions as to sentence length (Spohn and Holleran, 2000).

Do these disparities stem from the prejudicial attitudes of judges, police officers, and prosecutors? Are African Americans and Hispanics viewed as a "racial threat" when they commit crimes of violence and drug selling, which are thought to be spreading from the urban ghetto to the "previously safe places of the suburbs" (Crawford, Chiricos, and Kleck, 1998:484)? Are enforcement resources distributed so that certain groups are subject to closer scrutiny than are other groups?

Scholars have pointed out that the relationship between race and sentencing is complex and that judges consider many defendant and case characteristics. According to this view, judges assess not only the legally relevant factors of blameworthiness, dangerousness, and recidivism risk, but also race, gender, and age characteristics. The interconnectedness of these variables, not judges' negative attitudes, is what culminates in the disproportionately severe sentences given young black men.

TABLE 10.4   Minnesota Sentencing Guidelines Grid (Presumptive Sentence Length in Months)

The italicized numbers in the grid are the range within which a judge may sentence without the sentence departing from the guidelines. The criminal history score is computed by adding one point for each prior felony conviction, one-half point for each prior gross misdemeanor conviction, and one-quarter point for each prior misdemeanor conviction.

Less Serious ◄—————————————————————————————► More Serious

Severity of Offense (Illustrative Offenses)	Criminal History Score						
	0	1	2	3	4	5	6 or more
Sale of simulated controlled substance	12	12	12	13	15	17	19 *18–20*
Theft-related crimes ($2,500 or less) Check forgery ($200–$2,500)	12	12	13	15	17	19	21 *20–22*
Theft crimes ($2,500 or less)	12	13	15	17	19 *18–20*	22 *21–23*	25 *24–26*
Non-residential burglary theft crimes (more than $2,500)	12	15	18	21	25 *24–26*	32 *30–34*	41 *37–45*
Residential burglary simple robbery	18	25	27	30 *29–31*	38 *36–40*	46 *43–49*	54 *50–58*
Criminal sexual conduct, second degree	21	26	30	34 *33–35*	44 *42–46*	54 *50–58*	65 *60–70*
Aggravated robbery	48 *44–52*	58 *54–62*	68 *64–72*	78 *74–82*	88 *84–92*	98 *94–102*	108 *104–112*
Criminal sexual conduct, first degree Assault, first degree	86 *81–91*	98 *93–103*	110 *105–115*	122 *117–127*	134 *129–139*	146 *141–151*	158 *153–163*
Murder, third degree Murder, second degree (felony murder)	150 *144–156*	165 *159–171*	180 *174–186*	195 *189–201*	210 *204–216*	225 *219–231*	240 *234–246*
Murder, second degree (with intent)	306 *299–313*	326 *319–333*	346 *339–353*	366 *359–373*	386 *379–393*	406 *399–413*	426 *419–433*

☐ At the discretion of the judge, up to a year in jail and/or other nonjail sanctions can be imposed instead of prison sentences as conditions of probation for most of these offenses. If prison is imposed, the presumptive sentence is the number of months shown.

☐ Presumptive commitment to state prison for all offenses.

Note: First-degree murder is excluded from the guidelines by law and is punished by life imprisonment.

Source: *Seeking Justice: Crime and Punishment in America* (New York: Edna McConnell Clark Foundation, 1997), 24.

Wrongful Convictions   A serious dilemma for the criminal justice system concerns people who are falsely convicted and sentenced. Whereas the public expresses much concern over those who "beat the system" and go free, they pay comparatively little attention to those who are innocent yet convicted. Many of these people are wrongly convicted because victims and witnesses make mistakes in identifying alleged criminals from photographs and lineups.

The development of DNA technology has increased the number of people convicted of crimes and later exonerated by science. However, many cases do not have DNA evidence available. C. Ronald Huff notes that "because the great majority of cases do not produce biological material to be tested, one can only speculate about the error rate in those cases" (2002:2). Each year several cases of the conviction of innocent people come to national attention, yet there is no way to know how many more innocent people may be wrongly confined in prisons today.

Jeffrey Mark Deskovic greets his mother after serving 16 years of a life sentence for a murder he did not commit. Deskovic was freed after DNA evidence exonerated him. He became the 184th person nationwide since 1989 to be freed because of DNA evidence.

Suzanne DeChillo/The New York Times/Redux

Whether from racial discrimination or wrongful convictions, unjust punishments do not serve the ideals of justice. Such punishments raise fundamental questions about the criminal justice system and its links to the society it serves.

CHECKPOINT

6. What are the four factors thought to influence the sentencing behavior of judges?

Answers

6. The administrative context of the courts, the attitudes and values of judges, the presentence report, and sentencing guidelines.

A QUESTION OF ETHICS: WRITING ASSIGNMENT

Seated in her chambers, Judge Ruth Carroll read the presentence investigation report of the two young men she would sentence when court resumed. She had not heard these cases. As often happened in this very busy courthouse, the cases had been given to her only for sentencing. Judge Harold Krisch had handled the arraignment, plea, and trial.

The codefendants had held up a convenience store in the early morning hours, terrorizing the young manager and taking $47.50 from the till.

As she read the reports, Judge Carroll noticed that they looked pretty similar. Each offender had dropped out of high school, had held a series of low-wage jobs, and had one prior conviction for which probation had been imposed. Each had been convicted of Burglary 1, robbery at night with a gun.

Then she noticed the difference. David Bukowski had pleaded guilty to the charge in exchange for a promise of leniency. Richard Leach had been convicted on the same charge after a one-week trial. Judge Carroll pondered the decisions that she would soon have to make. Should Leach receive a stiffer sentence because he had taken the court's time and resources? Did she have an obligation to impose the light sentence recommended for Bukowski by the prosecutor and the defender?

There was a knock on the door. The bailiff stuck his head in. "Everything's ready, Your Honor."

"Okay, Ben, let's go."

WRITING ASSIGNMENT

Write a memo as if you are the judge and you must address the following questions: How should you decide? What factors should you weigh in your decision? How will you explain your decision?

REAL-WORLD ACTIVITY: AN APPLICATION

Standing before you for sentencing is William Arnette, who has been found guilty of the unauthorized use of a motor vehicle. Arnette has one prior felony conviction (simple robbery) and two prior misdemeanors (trespassing, shoplifting).

RESEARCHING THE INTERNET

Go to InfoTrac College edition and enter the keyword *sentencing guidelines*. Read the article entitled "Reforming Federal Sentencing Guidelines' Misguided Approach to Real-Offense Sentencing," by David Yellen, *Stanford Law Review*, 2005.

APPLICATION

Using the Minnesota guidelines (Table 10.4), what is the appropriate sentence for Arnette? Do you think that the sentence is appropriate and fair? Was enough information taken into consideration to create an appropriate sentence—or would you need to know more facts about each individual defendant and the circumstances of the crime?

SUMMARY

- In the United States, the four main goals of the criminal sanction are retribution, deterrence, incapacitation, and rehabilitation.

- Restoration (restorative justice), a new approach to punishment, has not become mainstream yet.

- The goals of the criminal sanction are carried out through incarceration, intermediate sanctions, probation, and death.

- Penal codes vary as to whether the permitted sentences are indeterminate, determinate, or mandatory. Each type of sentence makes certain assumptions about the goals of the criminal sanction.

- Good time allows correctional administrators to reduce the sentence of prisoners who live according to the rules and participate in various vocational, educational, and treatment programs.

- Capital punishment is allowed by the U.S. Supreme Court if the judge and jury take into account mitigating and aggravating circumstances.

- Judges have considerable discretion in fashioning sentences to take into account factors such as the seriousness of the crime, the offender's prior record, and mitigating and aggravating circumstances.

- The sentencing process is influenced by the administrative context of the courts, the attitudes and values of the judges, the presentence report, and sentencing guidelines.

QUESTIONS FOR REVIEW

1. What are the major differences among retribution, deterrence, incapacitation, and rehabilitation?

2. What is the main purpose of restoration (restorative justice)?

3. What are the forms of the criminal sanction?

4. What purposes do intermediate sanctions serve?

5. What has been the Supreme Court's position on the constitutionality of the death penalty?

6. Is there a link between sentences and race?

KEY TERMS AND CASES

determinate sentence (p. 264)
general deterrence (p. 259)
good time (p. 265)
incapacitation (p. 260)
indeterminate sentence (p. 264)
intermediate sanctions (p. 265)
mandatory sentence (p. 264)
presentence report (p. 277)

presumptive sentence (p. 264)
probation (p. 267)
rehabilitation (p. 261)
restorative justice (p. 261)
retribution (p. 258)
selective incapacitation (p. 260)
sentencing guidelines (p. 278)
shock probation (p. 267)

specific deterrence (p. 259)
Atkins v. Virginia (2002) (p. 269)
Furman v. Georgia (1972) (p. 267)
Gregg v. Georgia (1976) (p. 268)
McCleskey v. Kemp (1987) (p. 268)
Roper v. Simmons (2005) (p 270)
Witherspoon v. Illinois (1968) (p. 271)

GOING ONLINE

ThomsonNOW™

Maximize your study time by using ThomsonNOW's diagnostic study plan to help you review this chapter. The Study Plan will

- Help you identify areas on which you should concentrate

- Provide interactive exercises to help you master the chapter concepts

- Provide a posttest to confirm you are ready to move on to the next chapter

INSIDE THE CRIMINAL JUSTICE SYSTEM AND BEYOND: ONE MAN'S JOURNEY

Written by Chuck Terry

Prosecution, Adjudication, and Sentencing

Los Angeles County has the largest jail system in the country. On any given day it houses roughly 20,000 inmates. As I walked into the main jail I was so sick I could hardly stand. Once the chains were removed I was placed in a holding tank with other "new arrivals." Whereas getting booked at the city jail took less than an hour, here it took two days. Remember, I had yet to be formally charged and had not had contact with an attorney.

As time passed, more and more bodies were packed inside the tank. Before long we were standing shoulder to shoulder, butt to butt, like sardines in a can. My nightmare was at a high point. I felt like I wouldn't be able to do this much longer—like I might collapse or lose consciousness. Right then this guy looked at me and said, "Hey, brother, you're sick as hell aren't you?" When I said yes, he directed those around me to move over just enough so I could sit down. Never have I been so glad to sit.

We were eventually herded into a larger holding tank that had one seatless toilet and a sink for everyone. In this world privacy does not exist. Hours are spent in these concrete enclosures with others who are arrested for everything from public drunkenness to robbery. Most are addicts, skid-row winos, homeless people, or a mixture of all three. Many have mental problems. Within these rooms one hears a constant mixture of echoes from slamming cell doors, people yelling, wailing, vomiting, and laughing. Strange how, over time, I got used to it.

The next step of the journey involved being strip-searched. As our clothes were removed, the stench of body odor permeated the room. It took effort not to gag. After having every orifice of our naked bodies examined by deputies, we were steered to a shower area, given about thirty seconds to wash, and then sprayed with bug repellent. Next came jail clothing, a wool blanket, and a towel.

Before being assigned to a cell we were photographed, fingerprinted, and given receipts for our property. Finally, after nearly two days, I was led to a four-man cell—my next temporary home. There were already six men living there—two sleeping on the floor (these cells had enough space for two bunks, a toilet, a sink, and about thirty inches between the bunks). I, along with two of the others, slept on the concrete floor. Whereas they slept directly underneath each of the bunks, I took the space between them—and was glad to have it. No mattress. No pillow. But the blanket and the space sure were nice.

I welcomed the chance to rest. I still couldn't sleep, but it felt good to just lie there. Around 3:30 A.M. a guard came down the tier (the walkway in front of the rows of cells), waking up people whose names were on the daily court list. I was one of the fortunate few. Within a few minutes the cell door opened and I was guided to a holding tank where I waited with other court-bound men to be taken downstairs for breakfast. Once given food and seated, we had about three minutes to eat.

Our next stop was an area containing dozens of holding tanks—each acting as way stations for different courts. Deputies, reading names and court destinations from printouts, directed us to the appropriate tanks. I soon learned that I'd be going to the Torrance court. Before long we could hear the rattling of chains—a signal that we would soon be departing. As our names were called, we walked forward and placed our wrists in cuffs. After we were chained, we were led out of the jail into a parking lot where a huge fleet of black-and-white buses sat, waiting to take us to courts all over the county.

A jail bus ride can be an eventful occasion. For a short time you are almost in the world. Through steel-meshed windows you see cars, buildings, parks, streetlights, and people who are free—including women. Many of the men yell and joke about whatever crosses their mind. Others stare idly through the steel grillwork—silent and serious looking. Five days after my arrest I was finally going before a judge.

After arriving at the Torrance courthouse, we were taken to a basement holding tank and unchained. Because I didn't have money for a lawyer I was assigned a public defender (PD), whom I met through the bars of a holding cell located next to the courtroom. His name was Robert Harrison. Like every other lawyer I ever had, he was white.

He carried a briefcase packed with papers, had a suit on, and looked like he was in his late twenties. Although clearly hurried, he treated me with respect. After introducing himself he informed me that this would be my initial appearance and that I'd be back in two weeks for a preliminary hearing. Our meeting took about three minutes.

During the initial appearance I was arraigned in municipal court (the lower, or misdemeanor, court), which meant being legally charged, given a set amount of bail, and a date on which to return. The district attorney (DA) and public defender introduced themselves to the judge as participants in the case. The entire proceeding took less than a minute. Afterward, as bailiffs escorted me from the courtroom, my PD told me, "See you soon."

Two weeks later, still in jail and running on no sleep, I returned for my preliminary hearing—the phase of the process in which the district attorney tries to convince the court that a felony has been committed while the PD shoots for dismissal based on lack of evidence or an unlawful arrest. The woman who called the police testified that she had seen suspicious activity around my room—strangers coming and going. The police testified that I evaded arrest. The heroin, money, and other drugs taken from my pockets and room were used as evidence. My PD tried to get the case dismissed by arguing that the police searched me without probable cause. The DA said the search had been lawful. The court ruled against me, and I was bound over for arraignment in the superior court (felony court). After the hearing, my lawyer told me, "It doesn't look good." I asked him, "How much time do you think I'll have to do?" He said I'd "better plan on doing five" (that meant years and that meant prison).

Arraignment in the superior court came two weeks later. This time, as well as being told what I was charged with, I made a plea. In another brief meeting before the hearing, my lawyer told me, "When they ask you to plead, say 'Not guilty.' The judge will then set a trial date. Before that time arrives I hope to know more about what the DA wants from this case." I did as he suggested and a trial date was set. Within a few weeks my PD came to visit me in the county jail to tell me about a deal being offered by the district attorney. If I pled guilty to possession of a controlled substance (heroin), the rest of the charges would be dropped and I would be sent to the Southern California Regional Guidance Center at Chino—state prison, for a ninety-day evaluation, a process designed to assist the court at sentencing. He said, "Because of the evidence in this case I don't think we'd have a chance to win at trial. If you take the deal there is the possibility that a positive evaluation by the people at Chino might influence the judge to send you to a drug program. The worst-case scenario, though, is two to ten years for possession.

On the other hand, if you go to trial and lose, you will most likely get five to fifteen years for possession with the intent to sell."

I knew my situation was bleak. The court already had a presentence investigation (PSI) report from my last case, in which I received jail time and probation. I didn't think I had a chance of being found not guilty for my current charges. Plus I had heard about guys getting breaks after going to Chino. So the deal sounded good and I went for it.

To formally accept the deal I had to plead guilty in court to the charge of possession of heroin. My PD told me I needed to understand that doing so must be a decision I willingly made and that the judge possibly would not accept the deal. Finally, there were no guarantees as to what type of sentence I'd get. He said he'd recommend a drug program, but the chances were good that I'd have to do prison time, regardless of what type of evaluation I received from Chino.

When the court date arrived I appeared in Judge Barrett's courtroom. The district attorney told the judge that in exchange for a guilty plea to possession of a controlled substance, the people would agree to drop the rest of the charges. My PD said that we agreed. Then the judge said, "Mr. Terry, before accepting this plea I must ensure that you are doing so voluntarily. Has anyone coerced you in any way to plead guilty to this charge?" I said, "No." "Has anyone promised that you will receive a specific sentence if you plead guilty?" "No." "Do you understand that you do not have to make this plea and that you have a right to a trial by a jury of your peers?" "Yes." "And understanding all this, do you waive that right at this time?" By now I was wondering if I was making a mistake. It seemed as if the judge was trying to talk me out of it. I looked at my PD for assurance. He nodded his head, indicating it was OK. I said, "Yes." After accepting my plea of guilty the judge sent me to Chino as expected and said that sentencing would take place upon my return to court.

The "evaluation" from the ninety-day observation came from a twenty-minute interview by a counselor who recommended a drug program and a fifteen-minute interview by a psychologist (nicknamed San Quentin Sally) who said I was a threat to society and belonged in prison. Within three months I was back in the county jail awaiting my final court date.

Finally, five days after I returned from Chino, I was again taken before Judge Barrett for sentencing. Inside the courtroom, before the actual hearing took place, my PD showed me a copy of the evaluation from Chino that clearly indicated the likelihood of a prison sentence. San Quentin Sally not only recommended prison but also said I was a chronic liar with a dismal future. Once I read that I lost all hope for a drug program. Right then I also felt alone, isolated, like it was me against the world and I was definitely losing. I had no friends or family in the courtroom, I was surrounded by strangers dressed in suits and fancy dresses, and the only person who seemed to care about my well-being was my PD.

When the hearing began, the DA used my criminal history and the evaluation from Chino as justification for a prison sentence. My PD suggested a drug program because I had an extensive history of addiction and no arrests for violent crimes. He pointed out that this was also the conclusion of the counselor at Chino. Before imposing the sentence, the judge asked me if I had anything to say. I said no. Then he said, "After considering all sides of this matter I feel little choice but to send you to the department of corrections for the term prescribed by law. I understand you have a problem with drugs, but you've had your chances in the past. It is my hope that when you get to prison you do something to better yourself so when you get out you can live a normal, decent life. With this said, I sentence you to do not less than two but no more than ten years in the California Department of Corrections for possession of narcotics."

I felt good that day when they chained me up to take me back to the county jail. It had been a while since I got arrested, and I was finally headed for the last leg of my journey. I figured that with the time I had already spent in custody, plus good time, I would be out within eighteen months to two years.

Corrections

Anyone who pays any attention to public issues knows that the United States has a large and expanding prison population. With mass releases of prisoners in Russia, the United States has the highest incarceration rate in the developed world. For example, the United States has 10 times the population of Canada but about 35 times the prison population. The quadrupling of the prison population over the past three decades has raised the need to build new prisons, resulting in a construction boom and increased employment of correctional officers. Correctional budgets have climbed an average of 10 percent annually, and many states have diverted money from education, welfare, and health programs to meet the soaring needs of corrections.

Corrections refers to the great number of programs, services, facilities, and organizations responsible for the management of people accused or convicted of criminal offenses. In addition to prisons and jails, corrections includes probation, halfway houses, education and work release programs, parole supervision, counseling, and community service. Correctional programs operate in Salvation Army hostels, forest camps, medical clinics, and urban storefronts.

About 7.5 million adults and juveniles receive correctional supervision. An astounding 3.2 percent of U.S. adults (1 of every 15 men and 1 of every 100 women) are incarcerated or on probation or parole. Corrections is authorized by all levels of government, is administered by both public and private organizations, and costs $60 billion a year (BJS, 2004a:4). This chapter will examine (1) the history of corrections, (2) the organization of corrections, (3) the law of corrections, and (4) the policy trends in community corrections and incarceration.

QUESTIONS FOR INQUIRY

- How has the American system of corrections developed?
- What roles do federal, state, and local governments play in corrections?
- What is the law of corrections and how is it applied to offenders and correctional professionals?
- What is the direction of community corrections?
- Why has the prison population more than doubled in the last ten years?

corrections The variety of programs, services, facilities, and organizations responsible for the management of people who have been accused or convicted of criminal offenses.

Development of Corrections

How did corrections get where it is today? Why are offenders now placed on probation or incarcerated instead of being whipped or burned as in colonial times? Over the past two hundred years, ideas about punishment have moved like a pendulum from one far position to another (see Table 11.1). As we review the development of present-day policies, think about how future changes in society may lead to new forms of corrections.

INVENTION OF THE PENITENTIARY

Enlightenment A movement during the eighteenth century in England and France in which concepts of liberalism, rationalism, equality, and individualism dominated social and political thinking.

The late eighteenth century stands out as a remarkable period. At that time scholars and social reformers in Europe and America were rethinking the nature of society and the place of the individual in it. During the **Enlightenment**, as this period is known, philosophers and reformers challenged tradition with new ideas about the individual, about limitations on government, and about rationalism. Such thinking was the main intellectual force behind the American Revolution and laid the foundation of American values. The Enlightenment also affected the new nation's views on law and criminal justice. Reformers began to raise questions about the nature of criminal behavior and the methods of punishment.

Prior to 1800, Americans copied Europeans in using physical punishment such as flogging, branding, and maiming as the main criminal sanction. Yet, criminals were regularly sentenced to death for picking pockets, burglary, robbery, and horse stealing (Rothman, 1971:49). Jails existed throughout the country, but they served only to hold people awaiting trial or to punish people unable to pay their debts. As in England, the American colonies maintained houses of correction, where offenders were sentenced to terms of "hard labor" as a means of turning them from crime (Hirsch, 1992).

With the spread of Enlightenment ideas during the late eighteenth century, physical punishments began to wane. Gradually, "modern" penal systems emerged that emphasized fitting the punishment to the individual offender. The new goal was not to inflict pain on the offender's body (corporal punishment) but to change the individual and set him or her on the right path.

Many people promoted the reform of corrections, but John Howard (1726–1790), sheriff of Bedfordshire, England, was especially influential. His book, *The State of Prisons in England and Wales*, published in 1777, described the horrible conditions he observed in the prisons he visited (Howard, 1777/1929). Public response to the book resulted in Parliament's passing the Penitentiary Act of 1779, which called for the creation of a house

Until the early 1800s, Americans followed the European practice of relying on punishment that was physically brutal, such as death, flogging, and branding.

Photo by Time Life Pictures/Mansell/Time Life Pictures/Getty Images

TABLE 11.1 History of Corrections in America

Note the extent to which correctional policies have shifted from one era to the next and are influenced by societal factors.

	Correctional Model					
Colonial **(1600s–1790s)**	**Penitentiary** **(1790s–1860s)**	**Reformatory** **(1870s–1890s)**	**Progressive** **(1890s–1930s)**	**Medical** **(1930s–1960s)**	**Community** **(1960s–1970s)**	**Crime Control** **(1970s–2000s)**
Features						
Anglican Code	Separate confinement	Indeterminate sentences	Individual case approach	Rehabilitation as primary focus of incarceration	Reintegration into community	Determinate sentences
Capital and corporal punishment, fines	Reform of individual	Parole	Administrative discretion	Psychological testing and classification	Avoidance of incarceration	Mandatory sentences
	Power of isolation and labor	Classification by degree of individual reform	Broader probation and parole	Various types of treatment programs and institutions	Vocational and educational programs	Sentencing guidelines
	Penance	Rehabilitative programs	Juvenile courts			Risk management
	Disciplined routine	Separate treatment for juveniles				
	Punishment according to severity of crime					
Philosophical Basis						
Religious law	Enlightenment	National Prison Association Declaration of Principles	The Age of Reform	Biomedical science	Civil rights movement	Crime control
Doctrine of predestination	Declaration of Independence	Crime as moral disease	Positivist school	Psychiatry and psychology	Critique of prisons	Rising crime rates
	Human perfectibility and powers of reason	Criminals as "victims of social disorder"	Punishment according to needs of offender	Social work practice	Small is better	Political shift to the right
	Religious penitence		Focus on the offender	Crime as signal of personal "distress" or "failure"		New punitive agenda
	Power of reformation		Crime as an urban, immigrant ghetto problem			
	Focus on the act					
	Healing power of suffering					

of hard labor where offenders would be imprisoned for up to two years. The institution would be based on four principles:

1. A secure and sanitary building
2. Inspection to ensure that offenders followed the rules
3. Abolition of the fees charged offenders for their food
4. A reformatory regime

At night prisoners were to be confined to individual cells. During the day they were to work silently in common rooms. Prison life was to be strict and ordered. Influenced by his Quaker friends, Howard believed that the new institution should be a place of industry. More important, it should be a place that offered criminals opportunities for penitence (sorrow and shame for their wrongs) and repentance (willingness to change their ways). In short, the **penitentiary** served to punish and to reform.

Howard's idea of the penitentiary was not implemented in England until 1842, 50 years after his death. Although England was slow to act, the United States applied Howard's ideas much more quickly.

penitentiary An institution intended to punish criminals by isolating them from society and from one another so they can reflect on their past misdeeds, repent, and reform.

REFORM IN THE UNITED STATES

From 1776 to around 1830, a new revolution occurred in the American idea of criminal punishment. Although based on the work of English reformers, the new correctional philosophy reflected many ideas expressed in the Declaration of Independence, including an optimistic view of human nature and of individual perfectibility. Emphasis shifted from the assumption that deviance was part of human nature to a belief that crime resulted from environmental forces. The new nation's humane and optimistic ideas focused on reforming the criminal.

In the first decades of the nineteenth century, the creation of penitentiaries in Pennsylvania and New York attracted the attention of legislators in other states, as well as investigators from Europe. By the mid-1800s, the U.S. penitentiary had become world famous.

The Pennsylvania System   Several groups in the United States dedicated themselves to reforming the institutions and practices of criminal punishment. One of these groups was the Philadelphia Society for Alleviating the Miseries of Public Prisons, formed in 1787. This group, which included many Quakers, was inspired by Howard's ideas. They argued that criminals could best be reformed if they were placed in penitentiaries—isolated from one another and from society to consider their crimes, repent, and reform.

In 1790 the Pennsylvania legislature authorized the construction of two penitentiaries for the solitary confinement of "hardened and atrocious offenders." The first, created out of an existing three-story stone structure in Philadelphia, was the Walnut Street Jail. This 25-by-40-foot building had eight dark cells, each measuring 6 by 8 by 9 feet, on each floor. A yard was attached to the building. Only one inmate occupied each cell, and no communications of any kind were allowed. From a small, grated window high on the outside wall, prisoners "could perceive neither heaven nor earth."

From this limited beginning, the Pennsylvania system of **separate confinement** evolved. It was based on five principles:

1. Prisoners would not be treated vengefully but should be convinced that through hard and selective forms of suffering they could change their lives.

2. Solitary confinement would prevent further corruption inside prison.

3. In isolation, offenders would reflect on their transgressions and repent.

4. Solitary confinement would be punishment because humans are by nature social animals.

5. Solitary confinement would be economical because prisoners would not need a long time to repent, and so fewer keepers would be needed and the cost of clothing would be lower.

The opening of the Eastern Penitentiary near Philadelphia in 1829 culminated 42 years of reform activity by the Philadelphia Society. On October 25, 1829, the first prisoner, Charles Williams, arrived. He was an 18-year-old African American sentenced to two years for larceny. He was assigned to a 12-by-8-by-10-foot cell with an individual exercise yard 18 feet long. In the cell was a fold-up steel bed, a simple toilet, a wooden stool, a workbench, and eating utensils. Light came from an 8-inch window in the ceiling. Solitary labor, Bible reading, and reflection were the keys to the moral rehabilitation that was supposed to occur within the penitentiary.

> **separate confinement** A penitentiary system, developed in Pennsylvania, in which each inmate was held in isolation from other inmates. All activities, including craft work, took place in the cells.

Eastern State Penitentiary, located outside Philadelphia, became the model for the Pennsylvania system of "separate" confinement. The building was designed to ensure that each offender was separated from all human contact so that he could reflect upon his misdeeds.

The Library Company of Philadelphia

Although the cell was larger than most in use today, it was the only world the prisoner would see throughout the entire sentence. The only other human voice heard would be that of a clergyman who would visit on Sundays. Nothing was to distract the penitent prisoner from the path toward reform.

Within five years of its opening, Eastern endured the first of several outside investigations. The reports detailed the extent to which the goal of separate confinement was not fully observed, physical punishments were used to maintain discipline, and prisoners suffered mental breakdowns from isolation. Separate confinement had declined at Eastern by the 1860s, when crowding required doubling up in each cell, yet it was not abolished in Pennsylvania until 1913 (Teeters and Shearer, 1957: ch. 4).

The New York System   In 1819 New York opened a penitentiary in Auburn that evolved as a rival to Pennsylvania's concept of separate confinement. Under New York's **congregate system,** prisoners were held in isolation at night but worked with other prisoners in shops during the day. Working under a rule of silence, they were forbidden to exchange glances while on the job or at meals.

Auburn's warden, Elam Lynds, was convinced that convicts were incorrigible and that industrial efficiency should be the overriding purpose of the prison. He instituted a reign of discipline and obedience that included the lockstep and the wearing of prison stripes. He also started a **contract labor system.** By the 1840s Auburn was producing footwear, barrels, carpets, harnesses, furniture, and clothing. American reformers, seeing the New York approach as a great advance, copied it throughout the Northeast. Because the inmates produced goods for sale, advocates said operating costs would be covered.

During this period, advocates of the Pennsylvania and New York plans debated on public platforms and in the nation's periodicals. Advocates of both systems agreed that the prisoner must stay isolated from society and placed on a disciplined routine. In their view, criminality resulted from pervasive corruption that the family and the church did not sufficiently counterbalance. Only when offenders were removed from the temptations and influences of society and kept in a silent, disciplined environment could they reflect on their sins and offenses and become useful citizens. The convicts were not inherently depraved; rather, they were victims of a society that had not protected them from vice. While offenders were being punished, they would become penitent and motivated to place themselves on the right path. See Table 11.2 for a comparison of the Pennsylvania and New York systems.

Prisons in the South and West   Scholars tend to emphasize the nineteenth-century reforms in the populous Northeast, neglecting penal developments in the South and the West. Before 1817, four Southern states—Georgia, Kentucky, Maryland, and Virginia—had built prisons, some following the penitentiary model. Later prisons, such as the ones in Jackson, Mississippi (1842), and Huntsville, Texas (1848), followed the Auburn model. Further expansion ended with the Civil War, however. With the exception of San Quentin (1852), the sparse population of the West did not lend itself to the construction of many prisons until the latter part of the nineteenth century.

After the Civil War, southerners began to rebuild their communities and primarily agricultural economy. They lacked funds to build prisons but faced an increasing

congregate system A penitentiary system, developed in Auburn, New York, in which each inmate was held in isolation during the night but worked and ate with other prisoners during the day under a rule of silence.

contract labor system A system under which inmates' labor was sold on a contractual basis to private employers who provided the machinery and raw materials with which inmates made salable products in the institution.

TABLE 11.2   Comparison of Pennsylvania and New York (Auburn) Penitentiary Systems

	Goal	Implementation	Method	Activity
Pennsylvania (separate system)	Redemption of the offender through the well-ordered routine of the prison	Isolation, penance, contemplation, labor, silence	Inmates kept in their cells for eating, sleeping, and working	Bible reading, work on crafts in cell
New York (Auburn) (congregate system)	Redemption of the offender through the well-ordered routine of the prison	Strict discipline, obedience, labor, silence	Inmates sleep in their cells but come together to eat and work	Work together in shops making goods to be sold by the state

lease system A system under which inmates were leased to contractors who provided prisoners with food and clothing in exchange for their labor.

population of offenders. Given these challenges, a large African American inmate labor force, and the states' need for revenue, southern states developed the **lease system**. Businesses in need of workers negotiated with the state for the care of prisoners and their labor (logging, agriculture, mining, railroad construction). Because these entrepreneurs had no ownership interest in the prisoners, they exploited the prisoners worse than they had been as slaves (Rotman, 1995:176). The prisoner death rate soared.

Settlement in the West did not take off until the California gold rush of 1849. The prison ideologies of the East did not greatly influence corrections in the West, except in California. Prior to statehood, western prisoners were held in territorial facilities or federal military posts and prisons. Until Congress passed the Anticontract Law of 1887, restricting the employment of federal prisoners, leasing programs existed in California, Montana, Oregon, and Wyoming. In 1852 a lessee chose Point San Quentin and, using convict labor, built two prison buildings. In 1858, after reports of deaths, escapes, and brutal discipline, the state of California took over the facility. The Oregon territory had erected a log prison in the 1850s but soon leased it to a private company. On joining the Union in 1859, however, the state discontinued the lease system. In 1877 Oregon built a state prison on the Auburn plan, but with labor difficulties and an economic depression in the 1890s, the state turned it over to a lessee in 1895 (McKelvey, 1977:228).

REFORMATORY MOVEMENT

By the middle of the nineteenth century, reformers had become disillusioned with the penitentiary. Within 40 years of being built, penitentiaries had become overcrowded, understaffed, and minimally financed. Discipline was lax, brutality was common, and administrators were viewed as corrupt.

Cincinnati, 1870 The National Prison Association (the predecessor of today's American Correctional Association) at its 1870 meeting in Cincinnati embodied a new spirit of reform. In its famous Declaration of Principles, the association advocated a new design for penology: that prisons should operate according to a philosophy of inmate change, with reformation rewarded by release. Sentences of indeterminate length would replace fixed sentences, and proof of reformation—rather than mere lapse of time—would be required for a prisoner's release. Classification of prisoners on the basis of character and improvement would encourage the reformation program.

reformatory An institution for young offenders that emphasizes training, a mark system of classification, indeterminate sentences, and parole.

Elmira Reformatory The first **reformatory** took shape in 1876 at Elmira, New York, when Zebulon Brockway was appointed superintendent. Brockway believed that diagnosis and treatment were the keys to reform and rehabilitation. An interview with each new inmate resulted in an individualized work and education treatment program. Inmates followed a rigid schedule of work during the day, followed by courses in academic, vocational, and moral subjects during the evening. Inmates who did well achieved early release.

Designed for first-time felons aged 16–30, the approach at Elmira incorporated a mark system of classification, indeterminate sentences, and parole. Each offender entered the institution at grade 2, and if he earned nine marks a month for six months by working hard, completing school assignments, and causing no problems, he could be moved up to grade 1—necessary for release. If he failed to cooperate and violated the rules, he would be demoted to grade 3. Only after three months of satisfactory behavior could he reembark on the path toward eventual release. In sum, this system placed "the prisoner's fate, as far as possible, in his own hands" (Pisciotta, 1994:20).

mark system A point system in which prisoners can reduce their term of imprisonment and gain release by earning "marks" or points through labor, good behavior, and educational achievement.

By 1900 the reformatory movement had spread throughout the nation, yet by the outbreak of World War I in 1914, it was already in decline. In most institutions the architecture, the attitudes of the guards, and the emphasis on discipline differed little from those of the past. Too often, the educational and rehabilitative efforts took a back seat to the traditional emphasis on punishment. Yet the reformatory movement contributed the indeterminate sentence, rehabilitative programs, and parole.

The Cincinnati Principles and the reformatory movement set goals that inspired prison activists well into the twentieth century.

IMPROVING PRISON CONDITIONS FOR WOMEN

Until the beginning of the nineteenth century, female offenders in Europe and North America were treated no differently than men and were not separated from them when they were incarcerated. Only with John Howard's 1777 exposé of prison conditions in England and the development of the penitentiary in Philadelphia did attention begin to focus on the plight of the female offender. Among the English reformers, Elizabeth Gurney Fry, a middle-class Quaker, was the first person to press for changes. When she and other Quakers visited London's Newgate Prison in 1813, they were shocked by the conditions in which the female prisoners and their children were living (Zedner, 1995:333).

In the 1860s at Wethersfield Prison for Women, the inmates were trained for ironing, laundry work, and cooking; yet time was also spent learning such "ladylike" games as croquet.

News of Fry's efforts spread to the United States. The Women's Prison Association was formed in New York in 1844 with the goal of improving the treatment of female prisoners and separating them from men. Elizabeth Farnham, head matron of the women's wing at Sing Sing from 1844 to 1848, implemented Fry's ideas until male overseers and legislators thwarted her, forcing her to resign.

The Cincinnati Declaration of Principles did not address the problems of female offenders. It only endorsed the creation of separate treatment-oriented prisons for women. Although the House of Shelter, a reformatory for women, was created in Detroit following the Civil War, not until 1873 did the first independent female-run prison open in Indiana. Within 50 years, 13 other states had followed this lead.

Three principles guided female prison reform during this period: (1) the separation of female prisoners from men, (2) the provision of care in keeping with the needs of women, and (3) the management of women's prisons by female staff. "Operated by and for women, female reformatories were decidedly 'feminine' institutions"(Rafter, 1983:147).

As time passed, the original ideas of the reformers faltered. In 1927 the first federal prison for women opened in Alderson, West Virginia, with Mary Belle Harris as warden. Yet by 1935 the women's reformatory movement had "run its course, having largely achieved its objective (establishment of separate prisons run by women)" (Heffernan, 1972; Rafter, 1983:165).

REHABILITATION MODEL

In the first two decades of the twentieth century, reformers known as the Progressives attacked the excesses of big business and urban society and advocated government actions against the problems of slums, vice, and crime. The Progressives urged that knowledge from the social and behavioral sciences should replace religious and traditional moral wisdom as the guiding ideas of criminal rehabilitation. They pursued two main strategies: (1) improving conditions in social environments that seemed to be the breeding grounds of crime and (2) rehabilitating individual offenders. By the 1920s probation, indeterminate sentences, presentence reports, parole, and treatment programs were being promoted as a more scientific approach to criminality.

Although the Progressives were instrumental in advancing the new penal ideas, not until the 1930s did reformers attempt to implement fully what became known as the **rehabilitation model** of corrections. Taking advantage of the new prestige of the social sciences, penologists helped shift the emphasis of corrections. The new approach saw the social, intellectual, or biological deficiencies of criminals as causing

rehabilitation model A model of corrections that emphasizes the need to restore a convicted offender to a constructive place in society through some form of vocational or educational training or therapy.

their crimes. Because the essential elements of parole, probation, and the indeterminate sentence were already in place in most states, incorporating the rehabilitation model meant adding classification systems to diagnose offenders and treatment programs to rehabilitate them.

Because penologists likened the new correctional methods to those used by physicians in hospitals, this approach was often referred to as the **medical model.** Correctional institutions were to be staffed with people who could diagnose the causes of an individual's criminal behavior, prescribe a treatment program, and determine when the offender was cured and could be safely released to the community.

Following World War II, rehabilitation won new followers. Group therapy, behavior modification, counseling, and several other approaches became part of the "new penology." Yet even during the 1950s, when the medical model reached its height, only a small proportion of state correctional budgets went to rehabilitation. What frustrated many reformers was that, even though states adopted the rhetoric of the rehabilitation model, the institutions were still run with custody as the overriding goal.

Because the rehabilitation model failed to achieve its goals, it became discredited in the 1970s. According to critics of rehabilitation, its reportedly high recidivism rates prove its ineffectiveness. Robert Martinson undertook probably the most thorough analysis of research data from treatment programs. Using rigorous standards, he surveyed 231 studies of rehabilitation programs. Martinson summarized his findings by saying, "With few and isolated exceptions, the rehabilitative efforts that have been reported so far have had no appreciable effect on recidivism" (Martinson, 1974:25). The report had an immediate impact on legislators and policy makers, who took up the cry, "Nothing works!" As a result of dissatisfaction with the rehabilitation model, new reforms emerged.

COMMUNITY MODEL

The social and political values of particular periods have long influenced correctional goals. During the 1960s and early 1970s, U.S. society experienced the civil rights movement, the war on poverty, and resistance to the war in Vietnam. People challenged the conventional ways of government. In 1967 the U.S. President's Commission on Law Enforcement and Administration of Justice (1967:7) argued that the purpose of corrections should be to reintegrate the offender into the community.

Under this model of **community corrections,** the goal of corrections was to reintegrate the offender into the community. Proponents viewed prisons as artificial institutions that hindered offenders from finding a crime-free lifestyle. They argued that corrections should focus on providing psychological treatment and on increasing opportunities for offenders to succeed as citizens. Programs were supposed to help offenders find jobs and remain connected to their families and the community. Imprisonment was to be avoided, if possible, in favor of probation, so that offenders could seek education and vocational training that would help their adjustment. The small proportion of offenders who had to be incarcerated would spend a minimal amount of time in prison before release on parole. To promote reintegration, correctional workers were to serve as advocates for offenders in dealing with government agencies providing employment counseling, medical treatment, and financial assistance.

The community model dominated corrections until the late 1970s, when it gave way to a new punitiveness in criminal justice, in conjunction with the rebirth of the determinate sentence. Advocates of reintegration claim, as did advocates of previous reforms, that the idea was never adequately tested. Nevertheless, community corrections remains one of the significant ideas and practices in the recent history of corrections.

CRIME CONTROL MODEL

As the political climate changed in the 1970s and 1980s, legislators, judges, and officials responded with an emphasis on crime control through incarceration and risk containment. The critique of rehabilitation led to changes in the sentencing structures in more than half of the states and the abolition of parole release in many.

---

medical model A model of corrections based on the assumption that criminal behavior is caused by biological or psychological conditions that require treatment.

community corrections A model of corrections based on the goal of reintegrating the offender into the community.

Compared with the community model, this **crime control model of corrections** is more punitive and makes greater use of incarceration (especially for violent offenders and career criminals), longer sentences, mandatory sentences, and strict supervision of probationers and parolees.

The effect of these get-tough policies shows in the record number of people incarcerated, the long terms being served, the great number of parolees returned to prison, and the huge size of the probation population. In some states, the political fervor to be tough on criminals has resulted in the reinstitution of chain gangs and the removal of television sets, body-building equipment, and college courses from prisons. Some advocates point to the crime control policies as the reason for the fall of the crime rate. Others ask whether the crime control policies have really made a difference, considering the smaller number of men in the crime-prone age group and other changes in U.S. society.

The history of corrections in the United States reflects a series of swings from one model to another. The time may now be ripe for another look at correctional policy. The rhetoric used in criminal justice journals today differs markedly from that found in their pages 30 years ago. The optimism that once suffused corrections has waned. Researchers are now scrutinizing the financial and human costs of the retributive crime control policies of the 1990s. Are the costs of incarceration and surveillance justified? Has crime been reduced? Is society safer today than it was 25 years ago? Many researchers think not. Will corrections, then, find a new direction? If so, what will it be?

crime control model of corrections A model of corrections based on the assumption that criminal behavior can be controlled by more use of incarceration and other forms of strict supervision.

ThomsonNOW™

Improve your grade on the exam with Personalized Study! For reinforcement resources and a mastery check of Development of Corrections, go to www.thomsonedu.com/thomsonnow.

CHECKPOINT

Answers

1. What was the Enlightenment and how did it influence corrections?
→ 1. A period in the late eighteenth century when philosophers rethought the nature of society and the place of the individual in the world. The Enlightenment affected views on law and criminal justice; reformers began to raise questions about the nature of criminal behavior and the methods of punishment.

2. How did the Pennsylvania and New York systems differ?
→ 2. The Pennsylvania system of separate confinement held inmates in isolation from one another. The New York congregate system kept inmates in their cells at night, but they worked together in shops during the day.

3. What are the underlying assumptions of the rehabilitation, community, and crime control models of corrections?
→ 3. Rehabilitation model: criminal behavior is the result of a biological, psychological, or social deficiency; clinicians should diagnose the problem and prescribe treatment; when cured, the offender may be released. Community model: the goal of corrections is to reintegrate the offender into the community, so rehabilitation should be carried out in the community rather than in prison if possible; correctional workers should serve as advocates for offenders in their dealings with government agencies. Crime control model: criminal behavior can be controlled by greater use of incarceration and other forms of strict supervision.

Organization of Corrections in the United States

The organization of corrections in the United States is fragmented, with each level of government holding some responsibility for corrections. The federal government, the 50 states, the District of Columbia, the 3,047 counties, and most cities all have at least one correctional facility and many correctional programs. State and local governments pay about 95 percent of the cost of all correctional activities in the nation (BJS, 2004a:5).

FEDERAL CORRECTIONS SYSTEM

The correctional responsibilities of the federal government are divided between the Department of Justice, which operates prisons through the Federal Bureau of Prisons, and the Administrative Office of the United States Courts, which covers probation and parole supervision.

Federal Bureau of Prisons   The Federal Bureau of Prisons, created by Congress in 1930, now operates a system of prisons located throughout the nation and housing over 170,000 inmates, supervised by a staff of more than thirty thousand. Facilities and inmates are classified by security level, ranging from Level 1 (the least secure, camp-type settings such as the Federal Prison Camp in Tyndall, Florida) through Level 5 (the most secure, such as the supermax penitentiary in Florence, Colorado). Between these extremes are Levels 2 through 4 federal correctional institutions—other U.S. penitentiaries, administrative institutions, medical facilities, and specialized institutions for women and juveniles. The Bureau enters into contractual agreements with states, cities, and private agencies to provide community services such as halfway houses, prerelease programs, and electronic monitoring.

Federal Probation and Parole Supervision   Probation and parole supervision for federal offenders are provided by the Federal Probation and Pretrial Services System, a branch of the Administrative Office of the U.S. Courts. The federal judiciary appoints probation officers, who serve the court. The first full-time federal probation officer was appointed in 1927; today 4,560 are assigned to the judicial districts across the country. They assist with presentence investigations but focus primarily on supervising offenders on probation and those released either on parole or mandatory release.

STATE CORRECTIONS SYSTEMS

Although states vary considerably in how they organize corrections, in all states the administration of prisons falls under the executive branch of state government. This point is important because the judiciary often controls probation, parole may be separate from corrections, and in most states the county governments run the jails.

Community Corrections   States vary in how they carry out the community punishments of probation, intermediate sanctions, and parole. In many states, probation and intermediate sanctions are administered by the judiciary, often by county and municipal governments. By contrast, parole is a function of state government. The decision to release an offender from prison is made by the state parole board in those states with discretionary release. Parole boards are a part of either the department of corrections or an independent agency. In states with a mandatory system, the department of corrections makes the release. In all states, a state agency supervises the parolees.

State Prison Systems   A wide range of state correctional institutions, facilities, and programs exists for adult felons; these include prisons, reformatories, prison farms, forestry camps, and halfway houses. Because of the smaller female prisoner population, this variety does not exist for women.

State correctional institutions for men are usually classified by level of security: maximum, medium, and minimum. With changes in the number of prisoners and their characteristics, the distinction between maximum and medium security has disappeared in some systems. Crowding has forced administrators to house maximum-security inmates in medium-security facilities.

Thirty-eight states have created prisons that exceed maximum security. An estimated 20,000 men are currently kept in at least 57 of these "supermax" prisons. These institutions, such as California's Pelican Bay, hold the most disruptive, violent, and incorrigible offenders—the "toughest of the tough." In such institutions, inmates spend up to 23 hours a day in their cells. They are shackled whenever they are out of their cells—during recreation, showers, and telephone calls. All of these measures are designed to send a message to other inmates. Not surprisingly, supermax prisons generate controversy.

The maximum-security prison (holding about 36 percent of state inmates) is built like a fortress, usually surrounded by stone walls with guard towers and designed to prevent escape. New facilities are surrounded by double rows of chain-link fences with rolls of razor wire in between and along the tops of the fences. Inmates live in cells that include plumbing and sanitary facilities. Some facilities' barred doors

About 20,000 inmates are now held in at least 57 "supermax" prisons such as the Administrative Maximum Facility in Florence, Colorado, designed to house 400 of the most "predatory" convicts in the federal system. Critics charge that these facilities, designed to minimize human contact, violate human rights.

Stephen Ferry/Liaison/Getty Images

operate electronically so that an officer can confine all prisoners to their cells with the flick of a switch. The purposes of the maximum-security facility are custody and discipline. It maintains a military-style approach to order, with prisoners following a strict routine. Some of the most famous prisons, such as Attica (New York), Folsom (California), Stateville (Illinois), and Yuma (Arizona), are maximum-security facilities.

The medium-security prison (holding 48 percent of state inmates) externally resembles the maximum-security prison, but it is organized somewhat differently and its atmosphere is less rigid. Prisoners have more privileges and contact with the outside world through visitors, mail, and access to radio and television. The medium-security prison usually places greater emphasis on work and rehabilitative programs. Although the inmates may have committed serious crimes, they are not perceived as hardened criminals.

The minimum-security prison (with 16 percent of state inmates) houses the least-violent offenders, long-term felons with clean disciplinary records, and inmates who have nearly completed their term. The minimum-security prison lacks the guard towers and stone walls associated with correctional institutions. Often, chain-link fencing surrounds the buildings. Prisoners usually live in dormitories or even in small private rooms rather than in barred cells. There is more personal freedom: Inmates may have television sets, choose their own clothes, and move about casually within the buildings. The system relies on rehabilitation programs and offers opportunities for education and work release. It also provides reintegration programs and support to inmates preparing for release.

All prisoners face certain restrictions. See "Technology Issues in Criminal Justice" for a controversial new type of control that could affect prisoners at all levels.

State Institutions for Women   Only 7.3 percent (105,000) of the incarcerated population are women (BJS, 2005b:5). Although the ratio of arrests is approximately 6 men to 1 woman, the ratio in state and federal prisons is 14 men to 1 woman. A higher proportion of female defendants are sentenced to probation and intermediate punishments, partly as a result of male offenders' tendency to commit most of the violent crimes. However, the growth rate in number of incarcerated women has exceeded that for men since 1981. In fact, from 1995 to 2004 the annual growth of the female

TECHNOLOGY ISSUES IN CRIMINAL JUSTICE

Remote-Controlled Stun Belt

The transportation of prisoners presents a daily challenge for officials at courts, jails, and prisons. People in custody must be moved from jails and prisons to courts for hearings. They must be moved from jails to prisons and frequently among different prisons when they begin to serve their sentences. New technologies have been developed to help prevent prisoners from attempting to escape or otherwise misbehaving while being transported. The most controversial device is the remote-controlled stun belt that prisoners wear while being transported. The deputy or bailiff in control of the belt can deliver an excruciating 8-second, 50,000-volt jolt of electricity to prisoners. Americans became aware of the belts when a California prisoner who was zapped in a courtroom at the order of a judge filed a $50 million lawsuit. The prisoner had not attempted to escape or threaten anyone; he had merely talked too much when the judge had told him to be silent. The international human rights organization Amnesty International mounted a campaign to have the devices banned as torture. Although the New York Corrections Department canceled an order for the devices, 25 state corrections departments and one hundred county jails reportedly still use them.

Such devices may reduce the number of officers required to escort a prisoner, and they deter prisoners from misbehaving. However, such a jolt of electricity may kill some people if their heart rhythm is susceptible to disruption or if they hit their heads when they fall during the electric shock. Moreover, can officials be trusted to use these devices only in appropriate circumstances?

RESEARCHING THE INTERNET

To learn more about stun belts, go to the corresponding website listed on the Cole/Smith Criminal Justice in America Companion Website: http://www.thomsonedu.com/criminaljustice/cole. For opposition to the use of stun belts, see the website of Amnesty International, also listed on the Cole/Smith site.

FOR CRITICAL ANALYSIS

Is activation of a stun belt a form of torture that should be prohibited by the Eighth Amendment's ban on cruel and unusual punishment?

Sources: Drawn from Amnesty International, "Annual General Meeting Highlights USA Campaign," *Amnesty Action,* Summer 1999, p. 10; Minerva Canto, "Federal Government Investigates Use of Stun Belt," *Lansing State Journal,* August 7, 1998, p. 4A.

inmate population averaged 4.8 percent, higher than the 3.1 percent in male inmate population. The increase in the number of women prisoners seems driven by the war on drugs. The increased number of women in prison has significantly affected the delivery of programs, housing conditions, medical care, staffing, and security (BJS, 2005b:5).

Conditions in correctional facilities for women are more pleasant than those of similar institutions for men. Usually the buildings have no gun towers and barbed wire. Because of the small population, however, most states have only one facility, which is often located in a rural setting far removed from urban centers. Thus, women prisoners may be more isolated than men from their families and communities.

PRIVATE PRISONS

Corrections is a multibillion-dollar government-funded enterprise that purchases supplies and services from the private sector. Many jurisdictions have long contracted with private vendors to furnish food and medical services, educational and vocational training, maintenance, security, and the operation of aftercare facilities. All of this has been referred to as the "prison-commercial complex," which we discuss later in the chapter.

One response to prison and jail crowding and rising staff costs has come from private entrepreneurs who argue that they can build and run prisons at least as effectively, safely, and humanely as any level of government can, at a profit and at a lower cost to taxpayers. The management of entire institutions for adult felons under private contract is a relatively new approach in corrections that was launched in the 1980s.

At year end 2004, 34 states and the federal system reported a total of 98,901 inmates held in privately operated prisons. However, with the exception of New Jersey and Ohio, private facilities operate primarily in the South and West. Private prisons now hold 6.6 percent of the total adult inmate population (BJS, 2005b:7). The $1 billion-a-year private prison business is dominated by the Corrections Corporation of America and Wackenhut Corrections Corporation, which together hold more than three quarters of the market share of the private prison business (Thomas, 2002).

Advocates of privately operated prisons claim that they provide the same level of care as the states but do it more cheaply and flexibly. However, many of the "true costs" (fringe benefits, contracting supervision, federal grants) are not taken into consideration. In their analysis of 24 research studies, Travis Pratt and Jeff Maahs conclude that private prisons are no more cost-effective than public prisons (Pratt and Maahs, 1999). In cases where cost savings can be shown, such savings are fairly modest and result from reductions in staffing, fringe benefits, and other personnel-related costs (Austin and Coventry, 2001). Not surprisingly, correctional officers' unions continue to oppose private prisons.

Before corrections can become too heavily committed to the private ownership and operation of prisons, experts must examine the political, fiscal, ethical, and administrative issues. The political issues, including ethical questions concerning the delegation of social-control functions to people other than state employees, may be the most difficult to overcome. Some people believe that the administration of justice is a basic function of government that should not be delegated. They fear that private operations would skew correctional policy because contractors would use their political influence to continue programs not in the public interest. Joseph Hallinan describes the extent to which executives and shareholders of the Corrections Corporation of American and U.S. Corrections have funded political campaigns in Indiana, Kentucky, Oklahoma, and Tennessee (2001:168–70). Some experts also fear that the private corporations will press to maintain high occupancy and will be interested only in skimming off the best inmates, leaving the most troublesome ones to the public corrections system.

The fiscal value of private corrections cannot yet be demonstrated. However, labor unions have opposed these incursions into the public sector, pointing out that the salaries, benefits, and pensions of workers in other spheres such as private security are lower than in their public counterparts. Finally, questions have arisen about quality of services, accountability of service providers to corrections officials, and problems related to contract supervision. Opponents cite the many instances in which privately contracted services in group homes, day-care centers, hospitals, and schools have been terminated because of reports of corruption, brutality, or substandard services. Research shows that staff turnover, escapes, and drug use are problems in private prisons (S. D. Camp and G. G. Gales, 2002).

The idea of privately run correctional facilities has stimulated much interest among the general public and within the criminal justice community, but the future of this approach remains quite uncertain. The controversy about privatization has forced corrections to rethink some strongly held beliefs. In this regard, the possibility of competition from the private sector may have a positive impact on corrections. See "A Question of Ethics" at the end of this chapter for more on private prisons.

JAILS: DETENTION AND SHORT-TERM INCARCERATION

Most Americans do not distinguish between jails and prisons. A **prison** is a federal or state correctional institution that holds offenders who are sentenced to terms of more than one year. A **jail** is a local facility for the detention of people awaiting trial (about 50 percent of inmates) and sentenced misdemeanants. Jail also serves as a holding facility for social misfits—derelicts, junkies, prostitutes, the mentally ill, and disturbers of public order.

Of the 3,376 jails in the United States, 2,700 operate at the county level, with most administered by an elected sheriff. About 600 fall under municipal jurisdiction. Only in six states—Alaska, Connecticut, Delaware, Hawaii, Rhode Island, and Vermont—does the state administer jails for adults. There are also 13,500 police lockups (or drunk tanks) and similar holding facilities authorized to detain people for up to 48 hours. The Federal Bureau of Prisons operates 11 jails for detained prisoners only, holding a total of 11,000 inmates. Another 47 privately operated jails, under contract to state or local governments, house 2.4 percent of the total jail population (BJS, 2005e:96).

The capacity of jails varies greatly. The 50 largest jail jurisdictions hold 31 percent of the nation's jailed inmates (BJS, 2005a:9). The two jurisdictions with the most inmates, Los Angeles County and New York City, together hold approximately 32,400 inmates, nearly 5 percent of the national total (BJS, 2005a:9). Most jails, however, are much smaller, with 67 percent holding fewer than 50 people each (BJS, 1998:8). However, the number of these small facilities is dwindling because of new jail construction and the creation of regional, multicounty facilities.

Who Is in Jail?   With an estimated 11 million jail admissions per year, more people directly experience jails than experience prisons, mental hospitals, and halfway houses combined. Even if we consider that some of the people represented in this total are admitted more than once, probably at least six to seven million people are detained at some time during the year. Nationally, more than 700,000 people, both the convicted and the unconvicted, sit in jail on any one day. However, the number of people held at any one time in jail does not tell the complete story. Many are held for less than 24 hours; others may reside in jail as sentenced inmates for up to one year; a few may await their trial for more than a year. Compared with the American population as a whole, jails are disproportionately inhabited by men, minorities, the poorly educated, and people with low incomes (BJS, 2005a:8).

Managing Jails   Jail administrators face several problems that good management practices cannot always overcome. These problems include (1) the perceived role of the jail in the local criminal justice system, (2) the characteristics of the inmate population, and (3) fiscal problems.

ROLE OF THE JAIL   As facilities to detain accused people awaiting trial, jails customarily have been run by law enforcement agencies. Most of the 150,000 correctional officers in the jail system work under the direction of the county sheriff (see "Careers in Criminal Justice"). We might reasonably expect that the agency that arrests and transports defendants to court should also administer the facility that holds them. Typically, however, neither sheriffs nor deputies have much interest in corrections. Further, almost half the

prison An institution for the incarceration of people convicted of serious crimes, usually felonies.

jail An institution authorized to hold pretrial detainees and sentenced misdemeanants for periods longer than 48 hours.

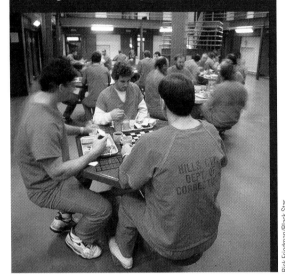

Direct supervision jails, like this one in Manchester, New Hampshire, are designed to increase the interaction of inmates with correctional officers. What are the advantages and disadvantages of this approach?

Rick Friedman/Black Star

jail inmates are sentenced offenders under correctional authority. Thus, many experts argue that jails have outgrown police administration.

INMATE CHARACTERISTICS The mixture of offenders of widely diverse ages and criminal histories is an often-cited problem in U.S. jails. Because criminal justice professionals view most inmates as temporary residents, they make little attempt to classify them for either security or treatment purposes. Horror stories of the mistreatment of young offenders by older, stronger, and more violent inmates occasionally come to public attention. The physical condition of most jails aggravates this situation, because most are old, overcrowded, and lacking in basic facilities. Many sentenced felons prefer to move on to state prison, where the conditions tend to be better.

Because inmate turnover is high and because local control provides an incentive to keep costs down, jails usually lack correctional services. They do not usually offer recreational facilities or treatment programs, and medical services are generally minimal. Such conditions add to the idleness and tensions of the inmates. Suicides and high levels of violence are hallmarks of many jails. In any one year, almost half the people who die while in jail have committed suicide. As discussed in "Real-World Activity" at the end of the chapter, direct supervision jails have been developed to improve the staff's ability to manage and interact with inmates and to provide service.

FISCAL PROBLEMS Jails help control crime but also drain local revenues. The tension between these two public interests often surfaces in debates over expenditures for jail construction and operation. Because revenues often fall short, many jails are overcrowded, lack programs, and do not have enough officers for effective supervision. In some areas multicounty jails serve an entire region as a means of operating facilities in a cost-efficient way.

CAREERS IN CRIMINAL JUSTICE

Correctional Officer—Local Jails

NATURE OF THE WORK

Officers must supervise individuals during the postarrest phase, when arrestees may be at their most stressed and violent. The constant turnover of the jail population presents an additional problem in terms of maintaining security and stability.

REQUIRED QUALIFICATIONS

Candidates for employment must be at least 18 to 21 years of age, be a U.S. citizen, and have a high school education, no felony convictions, and some work experience. They must be in good health and meet formal physical fitness, eyesight, and hearing standards. Some local departments provide training for officers according to criteria set by the American Jail Association. In some states, local correctional agencies have access to regional training academies. On-the-job training is a major resource for officer candidates.

EARNINGS AND JOB OUTLOOK

Job opportunities for correctional officers employed in county jails depend on local budgetary constraints, rather than on increases in the jail population. Salaries for entry-level officers vary greatly, with the highest being in the Northeast and the lowest in the rural South. Among all correctional officers, the lowest 10 percent earned less than $22,000 in 2003. The median annual earnings were $32,000.

MORE INFORMATION

See the website of the American Jail Association, listed on the Cole/Smith Criminal Justice in America Companion Website: http://www.thomsonedu.com/criminaljustice/cole. You can also contact local county government offices of human resources.

As criminal justice policy has become more punitive, jails, like prisons, have become crowded. Surveys have documented increases averaging 6 percent during each of the past five years. Even with new construction and with alternatives such as release on recognizance programs, diversion, intensive probation supervision, and house arrest with electronic monitoring, the jail population continues to rise. The $4.5 billion annual cost of operating jails heavily burdens local governments.

CHECKPOINT

Answers

4. What agencies of the U.S. government are responsible for prisons and probation?   ➡   **4.** The Federal Bureau of Prisons, which handles prisons, and the Administrative Office of the U.S. Courts, which handles probation.

5. What agencies of state government are responsible for prisons, probation, intermediate sanctions, and parole?   ➡   **5.** Prisons: department of corrections. Probation: judiciary or executive department. Intermediate sanctions: judiciary, probation department, department of corrections. Parole: executive agency.

6. What are the functions of jails?   ➡   **6.** Holding of offenders before trial and incarceration of offenders sentenced to short terms.

The Law of Corrections

Prior to the 1960s, most courts maintained a **hands-off policy** with respect to corrections. Only a few state courts had recognized rights for offenders. Most judges felt that prisoners and probationers did not have protected rights and that courts should not interfere in the operational agencies dealing with probation, prisons, and parole.

Since the 1960s, however, offenders have gained access to the courts to contest correctional officers' decisions and aspects of their punishment that they believe violate basic rights. Judicial decisions have defined and recognized the constitutional rights of probationers, prisoners, and parolees, as well as the need for policies and procedures that respect those rights.

hands-off policy Judges should not interfere with the administration of correctional institutions.

CONSTITUTIONAL RIGHTS OF PRISONERS

The U.S. Supreme Court decision in *Cooper v. Pate* (1964) signaled the end of the hands-off policy. The court said that through the Civil Rights Act of 1871 (referred to here as Section 1983), state prisoners were *persons* whose rights are protected by the Constitution. The act imposes *civil liability* on any official who violates someone's constitutional rights. It allows suits against state officials to be heard in the federal courts. Because of *Cooper v. Pate,* the federal courts now recognize that prisoners may sue state officials over such things as brutality by guards, inadequate nutrition and medical care, theft of personal property, and the denial of basic rights.

Cooper v. Pate (1964) Prisoners are entitled to the protection of the Civil Rights Act of 1871 and may challenge in federal courts the conditions of their confinement.

The first successful prisoners' rights cases involved the most excessive of prison abuses: brutality and inhumane physical conditions. Gradually, however, prison litigation has focused more directly on the daily activities of the institution, especially on the administrative rules that regulate inmates' conduct. This focus has resulted in a series of court decisions concerning the First, Fourth, Eighth, and Fourteenth Amendments to the Constitution. (See Chapter 3 for the full text of these amendments.)

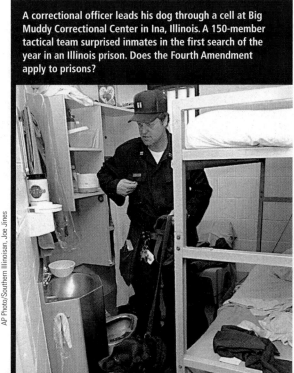

A correctional officer leads his dog through a cell at Big Muddy Correctional Center in Ina, Illinois. A 150-member tactical team surprised inmates in the first search of the year in an Illinois prison. Does the Fourth Amendment apply to prisons?

First Amendment The First Amendment guarantees freedom of speech, press, assembly, petition, and religion. In the courts, prisoners have successfully challenged many of the restrictions of prison life—access to reading materials, censorship of mail, and rules affecting some religious practices.

Since 1970, courts have extended the rights of freedom of speech and expression to prisoners. They have required correctional administrators to show why restrictions on these rights must be imposed. For example, in 1974 the Supreme Court ruled that

AP Photo/Southern Illinoisan, Joe Jines

censorship of mail was permissible only when officials could demonstrate a compelling government interest in maintaining security (*Procunier v. Martinez*). Communication between inmates and the outside world has since increased markedly. However, in *Turner v. Safley* (1987), the Court upheld a Missouri ban on correspondence between inmates in different institutions, as a means of combating gang violence and the communication of escape plans.

The First Amendment prevents Congress from making laws respecting the establishment of religion or prohibiting its free exercise. Cases concerning the free exercise of religion have caused the judiciary some problems, especially when the religious practice may interfere with prison routine and the maintenance of order.

The growth of the Black Muslim religion in prisons set the stage for suits demanding that this group be granted the same privileges as other faiths (special diets, access to clergy and religious publications, opportunities for group worship). Attorneys for the Muslims succeeded in winning several important cases that helped establish for prisoners the First Amendment right to free exercise of religion. These decisions also helped Native Americans, Orthodox Jews, and other prisoners to practice their religions. Court decisions have upheld prisoners' rights to be served meals consistent with religious dietary laws, to correspond with religious leaders, to possess religious literature, to wear a beard if their belief requires it, and to assemble for services. In sum, members of religious minorities have broken new legal ground on First Amendment issues.

Fourth Amendment

The Fourth Amendment prohibits *unreasonable* searches and seizures, but courts have not extended these protections much to prisoners. Thus, regulations viewed as reasonable to maintain security and order in an institution may be justified. For example, *Hudson v. Palmer* (1984) upheld the right of officials to search cells and confiscate any materials found.

The Supreme Court's opinions with regard to the Fourth Amendment reveal the fine balance between institutional need and the right to privacy. Body searches have been harder for administrators to justify than cell searches, for example. But body searches have been upheld when they advance policies clearly related to identifiable and legitimate institutional needs and when they are not intended to humiliate or degrade.

Hudson v. Palmer **(1984)** Prison officials have a right to search cells and confiscate any materials found.

Eighth Amendment

The Constitution's prohibition of cruel and unusual punishments has been tied to prisoners' needs for decent treatment and minimum health standards. The courts have applied three principal tests under the Eighth Amendment to determine whether conditions are unconstitutional: (1) whether the punishment shocks the conscience of a civilized society, (2) whether the punishment is unnecessarily cruel, and (3) whether the punishment goes beyond legitimate penal aims.

Federal courts have ruled that, although some aspects of prison life may be acceptable, the combination of various factors—the *totality of conditions*—may be such that life in the institution constitutes cruel and unusual punishment. When courts have found brutality, unsanitary facilities, overcrowding, and inadequate food, judges have used the Eighth Amendment to order sweeping changes and even, in some cases, to take over administration of entire prisons or corrections systems. In these cases judges have ordered wardens to follow specific internal procedures and to spend money on certain improvements.

Fourteenth Amendment

One word and two clauses of the Fourteenth Amendment are key to the question of prisoners' rights. The relevant word is *state*, which is found in several clauses of the Fourteen Amendment. It was not until the 1960s that the Supreme Court ruled that through the Fourteenth Amendment, the Bill of Rights restricts state government actions affecting criminal justice.

The first important clause concerns procedural due process, which requires that government officials treat all people fairly and justly and that official decisions be made according to procedures prescribed by law. The second important clause is the equal protection clause. Assertions that prisoners have been denied equal protection of the law are based on claims of racial, gender, or religious discrimination.

DUE PROCESS IN PRISON DISCIPLINE In *Wolff v. McDonnell* (1974), the Supreme Court ruled that basic procedural rights must be present when decisions are made about the disciplining of inmates. Specifically, prisoners have the right to receive notice of the complaint, to have a fair hearing, to confront witnesses, to get help in preparing for the hearing, and to be given a written statement of the decision. However, the Court also recognized special conditions of incarceration: It further stated that prisoners do not have the right to cross-examine witnesses and that the evidence presented by the offender shall not be unduly hazardous to institutional safety or correctional goals.

> **Wolff v. McDonnell (1974)** Basic elements of procedural due process must be present when decisions are made about the disciplining of an inmate.

LIBERTY

As a result of these Supreme Court decisions, prison officials have established rules that provide elements of due process in disciplinary and other proceedings. In many institutions, a disciplinary committee receives the charges, conducts hearings, and decides guilt and punishment. Even with these protections, prisoners remain powerless and may risk further punishment if they challenge the warden's decisions too vigorously.

EQUAL PROTECTION In 1968 the Supreme Court firmly established that racial discrimination may not be official policy within prison walls (*Lee v. Washington*). Segregation can be justified only as a temporary expedient during periods when violence between races is demonstrably imminent. The most recent cases concerning equal protection deal with issues concerning female offenders. Although the Supreme Court has yet to rule, state and lower federal courts have considered several cases. In *Pargo v. Elliott* (1995), female inmates in Iowa argued that their equal protection rights were violated because programs and services were not as good as those provided to male inmates. The court ruled that because of differences and needs, identical treatment is not required for men and women.

Impact of the Prisoners' Rights Movement

Although the Supreme Court in recent years has reduced its support of the expansion of prisoners' rights, some general positive changes in American corrections have occurred since the late 1970s. The most obvious are improvements in institutional living conditions and administrative practices. Law libraries and legal assistance are now generally available, communication with the outside is easier, religious practices are protected, inmate complaint procedures have been developed, and due process requirements are emphasized. Prisoners in solitary confinement undoubtedly suffer less neglect than they did before. Although overcrowding remains a major problem, many conditions have greatly improved and the most brutalizing elements of prison life have diminished. These changes did not entirely result from court orders, however. They also coincide with the growing influence of college-educated corrections professionals who have sought on their own to improve prisons.

LAW AND COMMUNITY CORRECTIONS

Although most correctional law concerns prisons and jails, two-thirds of adults under supervision live in the community on probation and parole. However, as with prisoners, offenders in the community have certain rights, and courts have addressed issues concerning due process and searches and seizures.

Probationers and parolees must live according to conditions specified at the time of their sentencing or parole release. These conditions may interfere with their constitutional rights. The conditions typically limit the right of free association by restricting offenders from contact with their crime partners or victims. However, courts have struck down conditions preventing parolees from exercising their First Amendment rights by giving public speeches and receiving publications.

The case of *Griffin v. Wisconsin* (1987) presents a good example of the clash between the Fourth Amendment and community corrections. Learning that Griffin might have a gun, probation officers searched his apartment without a warrant. Noting the practical problems of obtaining a search warrant while a probationer was under supervision, the Supreme Court said that the probation agency must be able to act before the offender damages himself or society. In Griffin's case the Court felt that the agency had satisfied the Fourth Amendment's reasonableness requirement.

When parole is revoked, prisoners are returned to prison to complete their sentences. Before that happens, a revocation hearing takes place. In a 1998 case,

Country musician Mindy McCready sits with her stepfather as they listen to her attorney file a motion to withdraw her guilty plea for a probation violation based on new evidence, during her sentencing hearing in Franklin, Tennessee. What legal rights do probationers have at revocation hearings?

AP Photo/John Russell

***Mempa v. Rhay* (1967)**
Probationers have the right to counsel at a combined revocation-sentencing hearing.

***Morrissey v. Brewer* (1972)** Due process rights require a prompt, informal, two-part inquiry before an impartial hearing officer before parole may be revoked. The parolee may present relevant information and confront witnesses.

***Gagnon v. Scarpelli* (1973)**
Before probation can be revoked, a two-stage hearing must be held and the offender provided with specific elements of due process. Requested counsel will be allowed on a case-by-case basis.

Pennsylvania Board of Pardons and Parole v. Scott, a closely divided Court ruled that evidence that would be barred from use in a criminal trial can be used in parole revocation hearings. Operating without a search warrant, officers found guns in the home of a paroled murderer who was barred from owning weapons. The Court upheld revocation of the offender's parole.

The Supreme Court has also addressed the question of due process when revocation is being considered. In *Mempa v. Rhay* (1967) the justices determined that a probationer had the right to counsel in revocation and sentencing hearings before a deferred prison sentence could be imposed. Similarly in *Morrissey v. Brewer* (1972) the court ruled that parolees facing revocation must be given a two-step hearing process. In the first stage, a hearing officer determines whether there is probable cause that a violation has occurred. Parolees have the right to be notified of the charges against them, to know the evidence against them, to be allowed to speak on their own behalf, to present witnesses, and to confront the witnesses against them. In the second stage, the revocation hearing, the parolee must receive a notice of charges and the evidence of a violation is disclosed, and he or she may cross-examine witnesses. The hearing body determines if the violation is sufficiently severe to warrant revocation. It must give the parolee a written statement outlining the evidence with reasons for the decision.

In the following year the Supreme Court applied the *Morrissey* procedures to probation revocation proceedings, in *Gagnon v. Scarpelli* (1973). But in *Gagnon* the Court also looked at the question of the right to counsel. It ruled that there was no absolute requirement but that in some cases probationers and parolees might request counsel, to be allowed on a case-by-case basis depending on the complexity of the issues, mitigating circumstances, and the competence of the offender.

LAW AND CORRECTIONAL PERSONNEL

Just as law governs relationships among inmates, probationers, and parolees, laws and regulations also define the relationships between correctional administrators and their staff. With the exception of those working for private, nonprofit organizations, correctional personnel are public employees. Here we consider two important aspects of correctional work. First, as public employees all correctional employees are governed by civil service rules and regulations. Second, correctional clients may sue state employees using Section 1983 of the United States Code.

Civil Service Laws   Civil service laws set the procedures for hiring, promoting, assigning, disciplining, and firing public employees. These laws protect public employees from arbitrary actions by their supervisors. Workplace rules also come to be developed through collective bargaining agreements between correctional-employee unions and the government. These agreements have the force of law and contain rules concerning assignments, working conditions, and grievance procedures.

Like their counterparts in the private sector, government employees are protected from discrimination. With the Civil Rights Act of 1964, Congress prohibited employment discrimination based on race, gender, national origin, and religion. Subsequent federal legislation prohibits some forms of age discrimination (Age Discrimination in Employment Act) and discrimination against people with disabilities (Americans with Disabilities Act). States have their own antidiscrimination laws. All these laws have increased the number of minorities and women who work in corrections.

Unlike many public employees, those who work in corrections operate from a difficult position. They must assert authority over persons who have shown that they lack self-control or have little regard for society's rules. Whether in prison, in a probationer's home, or on the street, this responsibility creates pressures and difficult—sometimes dangerous—situations.

Liability of Correctional Personnel   In *Cooper v. Pate* (1964) the Supreme Court said that Section 1983 provides a means for prisoners, but also probationers and parolees, to bring lawsuits against correctional officials. *Monell v. Department of Social Services of the City of New York* (1978) clarified the meaning of Section 1983. Individual public employees and their agency may be sued when a person's civil rights are violated by the agency's "customs and usages." Specifically, if an individual can show that harm was caused by employees whose wrongful acts were the result of these "customs, practices, and policies, including poor training and supervision," then the employees may be sued.

Although huge financial settlements make headlines, and the number of Section 1983 filings is large, few cases come to trial and very few correctional employees must personally pay financial awards to plaintiffs. However, no correctional employee wants to be involved in such legal situations.

ThomsonNOW
Improve your grade on the exam with Personalized Study! For reinforcement resources and a mastery check of The Law of Corrections, go to www.thomsonedu.com/thomsonnow.

CHECKPOINT

7. Why is the case of *Cooper v. Pate* important to the expansion of prisoners' rights?

8. Which two clauses of the Fourteenth Amendment have been interpreted by the Supreme Court to apply to prisoners' rights?

Answers

7. It allowed state prisoners to challenge the conditions of their confinement in the federal courts.

8. The due process and equal protection clauses.

Correctional Policy Trends

The United States has a large and expanding population under correctional supervision. Since the middle of the 1970s, the United States has fought a war on crime mainly by increasing the severity of sanctions against offenders. This has led to a 500 percent increase in correctional budgets, more than 4 million people on probation, 2 million incarcerated in prisons and jails, and 765,000 under parole supervision. These are staggering figures, especially considering that crime has been decreasing for the past decade. Figure 11.1 shows the tremendous growth in the correctional population since 1980.

FIGURE 11.1

Correctional populations in the United States, 1980–2004

Although the increase in prison populations receives the most publicity, a greater proportion of correctional growth has occurred in probation and parole.

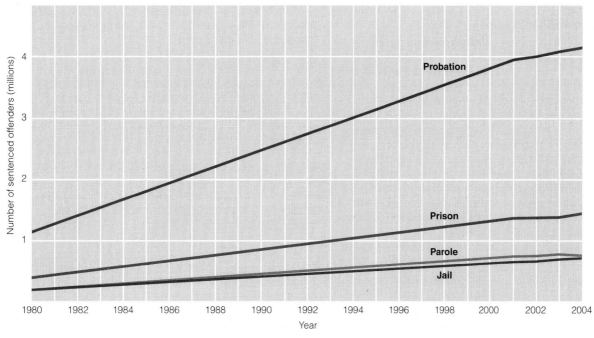

Source: Bureau of Justice Statistics, *Bulletin*, November 2005, p. 1.

Some observers believe that the drop in crime has resulted from harsher arrest and sentencing policies. Critics, however, say that the "lock 'em up" policies have had little impact on crime and that the fiscal and human costs of current policies severely damage families and communities. As mentioned earlier and discussed in "The Policy Debate," many believe that there now exists a prison-commercial complex that encourages increased spending on imprisonment regardless of need. We next examine community corrections and incarceration policies in order to understand current practices and future trends.

THE POLICY DEBATE

Is There a Prison-Commercial Complex?

Fifty years ago, President Dwight D. Eisenhower warned of the strong, unwarranted influence of the "military-industrial complex." He was concerned about the extent to which the armed forces of the United States and the manufacturers of military hardware shared an interest in the ever-expanding defense budget. Today critics point to a similar "prison-commercial complex" made up of bureaucratic, political, and economic interests that encourage increased spending on imprisonment, regardless of need.

One of the anomalies of the past decade is that, as crime rates have fallen, the prison population has continued to grow. Some have said that crime has fallen *because* of tough incarceration policies and that there is still too much violent and drug-related crime. Others believe that, with corrections costing more than $35 billion per year, many factors have encouraged expansion: the profits to be made in prison supplies and construction, the increased value of stock in corporations running private prisons, the greater number of correctional jobs, the expanded fiefdoms of prison bureaucrats, the growth of correctional officer labor unions, and the votes for politicians who pass "tough on crime" legislation.

Why are so many people in the United States locked up? Are government agencies and legislators merely responding to public demand for criminals to be isolated? Is there a prison-commercial complex that has influenced the upward spiral of the number of prisoners?

There Is a Prison-Commercial Complex

Those who believe that there is a prison-commercial complex argue that the "punishment industry" promotes high incarceration rates during a period of falling levels of crime. They say that corporations doing business with corrections have mutual interests with government agencies seeking to expand their domain and with legislators promoting tough crime policies.

People holding this view point to the 400 percent increase in correctional spending since 1979, the 600 percent increase in funds for prison construction, and the expectation that these allocations will continue to grow at an annual rate of 5 to 10 percent. They cite the spectacular growth of the private prison business and the billions of dollars spent to purchase goods and services. In addition to corporations, labor unions have also benefited from the rise in the number of prison employees, now set at more than 350,000. In many states, correctional officers have become a potent political force and have lobbied for expansion of the system.

The arguments supporting the existence of a prison-commercial complex that has promoted incarceration include these:

■ Spending for incarceration continues to rise and in most states exceeds appropriations for most government services.

■ There is a mutuality of interests among correctional agencies, businesses, and legislators that supports high incarceration.

■ Correctional workers and their unions support the hiring of more employees.

■ Legislators believe that voters expect them to be "tough on crime."

There Is No Prison-Commercial Complex

Many of those who support incarceration for offenders who have committed serious felonies say that there is no prison-commercial complex. They believe that prison expansion is driven by the need to provide space for the increased number of offenders incarcerated for longer terms and not by business interests hoping to profit from the crime problem.

Defenders also say that the growth of the prison population has helped reduce crime rates because so many offenders are no longer on the streets. They believe that treating criminals severely is just and that incarcerated felons deserve to be punished seriously. They argue that incarceration is expensive but to allow felons to live in society where they will continue their criminal ways costs much more.

The arguments against the existence of a prison-commercial complex include the following:

■ Increased incarceration rates are not being pushed by commercial interests but reflect current public policies.

■ Justice demands that serious offenders be incarcerated.

■ Incarceration policies have helped lower the crime rate.

■ The actions of Congress and the state legislatures reflect the public's support of incarceration policies.

What Should U.S. Policy Be?

Several questions about incarceration warrant serious attention. Does incarceration have an impact—one way or the other—on the crime rate? Is incarceration rising during a period of decreased criminality because it is being promoted by economic interests? Should imprisonment be used more sparingly, reserved for the worst offenders only?

RESEARCHING THE INTERNET

There are several websites concerning this issue, including two that are listed on the Cole/Smith Criminal Justice in America Companion Website: http://www.thomsonedu.com/criminaljustice/cole.

FOR CRITICAL ANALYSIS

What are the likely impacts of mass incarceration on urban neighborhoods? What major businesses might have an interest in increased incarceration? Which political interests might oppose increased incarceration?

COMMUNITY CORRECTIONS

Although escalating prison growth has captured the public's attention, the number of people on probation and parole has actually risen at a faster rate than the number of people incarcerated. Many factors may explain this growth, including more arrests and successful prosecutions, the lower costs of probation compared with incarceration, prison and jail crowding, and the great numbers of felons now being released from prison.

Probation   People on probation now make up 60 percent of the correctional population, yet budgets and staffing have not risen accordingly. In many urban areas, probation caseloads are growing well beyond reasonable management levels: 200- and even 300-person caseloads are no longer unusual. This has led to a deterioration in the quality of supervision. Yet the importance of probation for public safety has never been greater. For example, in one sample of large urban counties, up to 17 percent of felony arrests were of people on probation at the time of their alleged offense (Reaves and Hart, 1999). As a result, a renewed emphasis on public safety has arisen. Many agencies have seen a resurgence of intensive and structured supervision for selected offenders.

In many respects, then, probation finds itself at a crossroads. Although its credibility is probably as low as it has ever been, its workload is growing dramatically and, in view of the crowding in prison and jails, will probably continue to do so. Under the strain of this workload and on-again, off-again public support, probation faces a serious challenge. Can its methods of supervision and service be adapted successfully to high-risk offenders?

Parole   With the incarcerated population more than quadrupling during the past 30 years, the number of parolees has, not surprisingly, also grown. Currently over 650,000 felons gain release from prison each year. In 2004, 765,355 were under parole supervision, a threefold increase since 1980 (BJS, 2005c:1). With the massive incarcerations of the past decades, the number on parole will likely reach one million in the next five years.

Compared with parolees in 1990, today's parolees are older, were more likely to have been sentenced for drug violations, have served longer prison sentences, and have higher levels of substance abuse and mental illness (Beck, 2000). These characteristics increase reentry problems related to the renewal of family ties, obtaining a job, and living according to parole rules. Most parolees cannot obtain the assistance necessary to reenter the community successfully. (The reentry problem is extensively discussed in Chapter 14).

Further, increased numbers of offenders are being returned to prison as parole violators. Recent studies show that within three years of their release, 68 percent are arrested and 47 percent convicted for a new felony; 25 percent are returned to prison for their new crime. Taking revocations for new convictions and "technical violations" together, 52 percent of released prisoners are back in prison within three years. (BJS, 2002f:2). Alan Beck's analysis (1997:10) shows that the return of parolees accounts for much of the growth in total admissions to state prisons.

INCARCERATION

From 1940 until 1973, the number of people incarcerated in the United States remained fairly stable, with an incarceration rate of about 110 per 100,000 population. However, since 1973, when the overall crime rate started to fall, the incarceration rate has quadrupled, standing at 486 at the end of 2004 (BJS, 2005b:4). Compared with Canada and Europe, the United States has a higher incarceration rate than all but Russia, as seen in the Comparative Perspective box. The increase in the United States is difficult to understand in light of lower crime rates, state budgetary problems, and the easing of tough sentencing laws in some states.

Every June and December, the Bureau of Justice Statistics takes a census of the U.S. prison population. As shown in Figure 11.2, from the most recent low of 98 per 100,000 population in 1975, the incarceration rate has risen to a high of 486

COMPARATIVE PERSPECTIVE

Behind Bars in North America and Europe

Most Western countries have put more people behind bars in recent years, but in none has the incarceration rate risen higher than in the United States. The cause of the extraordinary American figure is not higher levels of crime, for the crime rates in the United States and in Western Europe are about the same (except for the rate of homicide, which is two to eight times greater in the United States, mostly because of the ready availability of guns).

The high U.S. rate—which rivals those of former Soviet nations—stems primarily from a shift in public attitudes toward crime that began about 30 years ago as apprehension about violence and drugs escalated. Politicians exploited the new attitudes with promises to get criminals off the streets. Congress and state legislatures, often at the prodding of presidents and governors, promoted "tough on crime" measures, including mandatory sentencing, three-strikes laws, longer sentences, and increased budgets for prison construction.

As a result, the length of sentences, already severe by Western European standards, became even more punitive. Consequently, the number of those locked up rose more than fivefold between 1972 and 2000 to more than two million. Most of those sentenced in recent years committed nonviolent crimes, such as drug possession, that other Western countries would not ordinarily punish by long prison terms.

Source: Roger Doyle, "By the Numbers," *Scientific American,* August 1999, p. 25.

in 2004. This corresponds to 1,433,793 men and women in state and federal prisons, or about one in every 112 adult male and one in every 1,724 adult female U.S. residents. An additional 713,990 were in local jails (BJS, 2005b:2).

Keep in mind that the size and growth of the prison population is not evenly distributed across the country. As Figure 11.3 shows, eight of the ten states with the highest incarceration rates are in the South. In 2004 the South incarcerated 540 people for each 100,000 inhabitants, a ratio much higher than the national average of 486 (BJS, 2004c:4). Arizona and Missouri are included in the top ten, so the South is not the only area with high incarceration rates.

FIGURE 11.2

Incarceration in federal and state prisons per 100,000 population, 1940–2004

Between 1940 and 1970, the incarceration rate was steady. From 1975 until the end of 2004, the incarceration rate continued to increase. The rate today is more than double what it was in 1985.

Source: Bureau of Justice Statistics, *Bulletin,* July, 2004, p. 1; October 2005, p. 2.

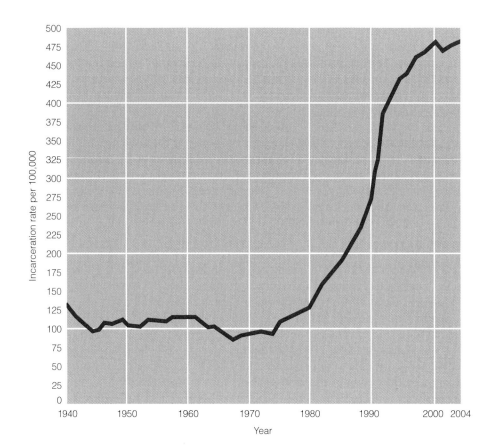

FIGURE 11.3
Sentenced prisoners in state institutions per 100,000 population, December 31, 2004

What can be said about the differences in incarceration rates among the states? There are not only regional differences but also differences between adjacent states that seem to have similar socioeconomic and crime characteristics.

Note: District of Columbia prisoners are now under the jurisdiction of the Federal Bureau of Prisons.

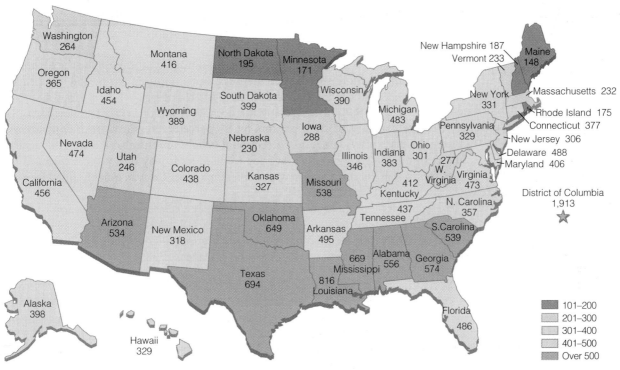

Source: Bureau of Justice Statistics, *Bulletin,* October 2005, p. 4

Why this increase? If little relationship exists between the crime rate and the incarceration rate, what factors explain the growth? Five reasons are often cited for the increase: (1) increased arrests and more likely incarceration, (2) tougher sentencing, (3) prison construction, (4) the war on drugs, and (5) state politics. None of these reasons should be viewed as a single explanation or as having more impact than the others.

Increased Arrests and More Likely Incarceration   Some analysts argue that the billions of dollars spent on the crime problem may be paying off. Not only have arrest rates increased, particularly for some offenses such as drug violations, aggravated assaults, and sexual assaults, but the probability of being sent to prison has also dramatically increased. In addition, the number of offenders returned to prison for parole violations has also increased. Between 1980 and 1998, the number of parolees sent back to prison—half of them for a technical violation, the others for a new felony conviction—increased by 54 percent (BJS, 2000a:11). In Texas, of the 77,000 offenders admitted to prison in 2004, 46 percent were parole or probation violators (Elliott and Murphy, 2005). Much of the growth in total admissions to state prisons can be attributed to increased arrests.

Tougher Sentencing Practices   Some observers think that a hardening of public attitudes toward criminals has resulted in longer sentences, in a smaller proportion of those convicted getting probation, and in fewer being released at the time of the first parole hearing.

In the past three decades, the states and the federal government have passed laws that increase sentences for most crimes. However, the tougher sentences do not seem to be the main factor keeping offenders in prison for longer periods; between 1990 and 1998 the mean sentence of new court commitments actually dropped. Rather, the 13 percent increase in the actual amount of time served is what has affected the total number of inmates (BJS, 2000a:12). The amount of time served is likely to increase further in the coming decade as the new truth-in-sentencing laws begin to make an impact and as the trend of parole boards being more restrictive continues.

Prison Construction   As the public in the 1970s began to favor harsher sentencing policies, the rate of incarceration grew. Prison crowding eventually reached crisis proportions, creating health and security issues. Many states attempted to build their way out of this problem—literally.

Large state budget surpluses during the booming economy of the 1990s made many legislatures willing to advance the huge sums required for prison expansion. Prison construction became a growth industry, producing 351 adult facilities that added more than 528,000 beds during the decade (BJS, 2001a:9). The new facilities increased the capacity of state prisons by 81 percent. Pressures from contractors, building material providers, and correctional officer unions also spurred expansion in many states. Yet many states that tried to build their way out of their crowded facilities found that, as soon as a new prison came on line, it was quickly filled (see the Close Up box).

The increased rate of incarceration may thus be related to the creation of additional space in the nation's prisons. As Joseph Davey notes, "The presence of empty state-of-the-art prison facilities can encourage a criminal court judge to incarcerate a defendant who may otherwise get probation" (Davey, 1998:84).

CLOSE UP

Prison Crowding Defies Easy Fixes

The problems facing Alabama's overcrowded and underfunded prisons are too big, too complex, and too long-lived to be fixed with any single solution, according to experts both inside and outside the system.

After Gov. Bob Riley pushed the early release of more than 4,000 inmates, Alabama's prisons remain nearly as overcrowded as they were when the governor launched the program almost two years ago. With 23,874 inmates jammed into state prisons, work release centers, and boot camps, the prison system has almost twice the 12,943 inmates it was designed to house.

A big reason Alabama's prisons are so overcrowded is that the state doles out harsher punishments than most other states. The state has the nation's fifth-highest incarceration rate and the 11th-longest sentences imposed. It ranks 14th in the country in actual time spent behind bars.

Statistics show that Alabama locks up a great many drug offenders. Of the states' current prisoners, 43.6 percent committed either a property or a drug offense. Crimes against individuals account for 51.6 percent of inmates. The most common felony for which prisoners are sentenced is drug possession.

It's not just crime that fuels Alabama's prison population. Many of the inmates who leave on parole are destined to return. About a third of those whose paroles have been revoked did not commit new crimes. They violated other terms of their parole.

In exchange for the privilege of parole, released prisoners must keep jobs, maintain contact with parole officers, and stay off drugs. Failure to comply with the rules can result in a parole revocation, sending the parolee back to prison to serve the balance of his original sentence. Reform advocates say the parole board members and officers should have much slower trigger fingers when dealing with these so-called "technical" violations.

Although the number of inmates paroled (4,174) over the last two years has jumped dramatically, new prisoners have arrived almost as fast. Since April 2003 the number of inmates has decreased only 1,083.

Prisons are the most expensive component of the criminal justice system. It is estimated that it would cost Alabama almost a billion dollars to build enough prisons to ensure a bed for every inmate. For a state prison system so short of funds that it doesn't supply napkins to its inmates, that's an almost unthinkable amount of cash, and Department of Corrections spokesman Brian Corbett noted that it doesn't include the money that would be needed to meet future needs.

"The reality is [that] not Dollar One has been budgeted for any new construction," he said. "You want to be tough on crime, and you want to incarcerate people, but you don't want to pay for it."

That leaves legislators and other policy makers to grapple with other options.

RESEARCHING THE INTERNET

For a different way of dealing with prison crowding, go to the North Carolina Sentencing Commission and Advisory Commission website and search for *commission*. This site is listed on the Cole/Smith Criminal Justice in America Companion Website: http://www.thomsonedu.com/criminaljustice/cole.

FOR CRITICAL ANALYSIS

If you were a member of the Alabama legislature, would you support the request for an additional 500-bed facility to relieve overcrowding? Why? Why not? What other options are available?

Source: Brendan Kirby, "Prison Crowding Defies Easy Fixes," *Mobile Register*, February 28, 2005, http://www.al.com/printer/printer.ssf?/base/news/1109587461986. Reprinted by permission.

The War on Drugs   Crusades against the use of drugs have recurred in U.S. politics since the late 1800s. The latest manifestation began in 1982, when President Ronald Reagan declared another "war on drugs" and asked Congress to set aside more money for drug enforcement personnel and for prison space. This came at a time when the country faced the frightening advent of crack cocaine, which ravaged many communities and increased the murder rate. In 1987 Congress imposed stiff mandatory minimum sentences for federal drug law violations, and many states copied these sentencing laws. The war continues today with each president urging Congress to appropriate billions more for an all-out law enforcement campaign against drugs.

The war on drugs succeeded on one front by packing the nation's prisons with drug law offenders, but many scholars think that is about all it has achieved. With additional resources and pressures for enforcement, the number of people sentenced to prison for drug offenses has increased steadily. In 1980 only 19,000 or about 6 percent of state prisoners had been convicted of drug offenses; by 2001 the number had risen to 246,100. Today, 21 percent of state prisoners are incarcerated for drug offenses, and in federal prisons the figure has reached 55 percent (BJS, 2005b:10). Furthermore, the average state drug sentence increased from 13 months in 1985 to 48 months in 2002 (BJS, 2004e:5).

State Politics   Incarceration rates vary among the regions and states, but why do states with similar characteristics differ in their use of prison? How much do local political factors influence correctional policies?

One might think that each state would show a certain association between crime rates and incarceration rates—the more crime, the more prisoners. Even when states have similar socioeconomic and demographic characteristics—poverty, unemployment, racial composition, drug arrests—unaccountable variations among their incarceration rates exist. For example, North Dakota and South Dakota share similar social characteristics and crime rates, yet the incarceration rate in South Dakota has risen 477 percent since 1978, compared with a rise of 133 percent in its neighbor (BJS, 2000c: Table 6.27; 2001a:3). One can even find similar and contiguous states such as Connecticut and Massachusetts, Arizona and New Mexico, or Minnesota and Wisconsin, where the state with the *higher* crime rate has the *lower* incarceration rate.

Since the 1970s most politicians have felt that the public has demanded that they be "tough on crime." Governors and legislators have pushed for tougher sentences and greater use of incarceration as a way of reducing crime. Joseph Davey found that seven states with "law-and-order" governors witnessed a "rapid increase in the rate of imprisonment without regard to changes in the crime rate." In contiguous states where governors advocated less punitive policies, imprisonment rates did not increase (Davey, 1998:111). With states now trying to deal with huge budget deficits, it will be interesting to see how incarceration rates are affected.

No one factor stands alone as the primary cause of the doubling of the incarceration rate during the past decade. Several plausible hypotheses exist. Given the general fear of crime, the current public attitudes toward crime and punishment, and the expansion of prison space, incarceration rates will likely remain high (see "What Americans Think"). Perhaps only when the costs of this form of punishment impinge more on the pockets of taxpayers will attitudes and policies shift, with a greater emphasis being placed on alternatives to incarceration.

WHAT AMERICANS THINK

Question: "Would you favor or oppose each of the following measures that have been suggested as ways to reduce prison crowding?"

Percentage Responding That They Favor

Shortening sentences
8%

Allowing prisoners early release for good behavior and participation in educational and work programs
64%

Developing local programs to keep more nonviolent and first-time offenders active and working in the community
90%

Giving the parole board more authority to release offenders early
21%

Increasing taxes to build more prisons
33%

Go to http://www.thomsonedu.com/criminaljustice/cole to compare your opinion on this issue with the opinions of other criminal justice students.

Source: Timothy J. Flanaghan, "Reform or Punish: Americans' Views of the Correctional System," in *Americans View Crime and Justice*, ed. Timothy J. Flanagan and Dennis R. Longmire (Thousand Oaks, CA: Sage, 1996), 88, 192. Reprinted by permission of Sage Publications, Inc.

ThomsonNOW

Improve your grade on the exam with Personalized Study! For reinforcement resources and a mastery check of Correctional Policy Trends, go to www.thomsonedu.com/thomsonnow.

CHECKPOINT

Answers

9. What are five explanations for the great increase in the incarcerated population? ⟶ **9.** Increased arrests and more likely incarceration, tougher sentencing, prison construction, the war on drugs, state politics.

10. Why might additional construction only aggravate the problem? ⟶ **10.** New prison beds will quickly become filled because judges will be less hesitant to sentence people to prison and because the correctional bureaucracy needs the space to be used.

A QUESTION OF ETHICS: WRITING ASSIGNMENT

You are a state senator. For the past 15 years your legislative district has benefited from the construction of two 500-bed facilities operated by American Prison Services (APS), Inc. Local residents of this poor, rural district have been hired as correctional officers, and merchants have profited by sales to the institution. With a downturn in the economy and the state facing a fiscal crisis, the governor has proposed that contract with APS be terminated and two prisons in your district be closed. He justifies this decision by pointing to the declining crime rate and the vacant beds in state-operated prisons.

As a member of the state legislature you have always stood for fiscal integrity—in fact, you supported construction of the prisons in your district by APS because they promised that operating expenses would be lower than at state facilities. The governor's budget for the department of corrections is now before the legislature.

Lobbyists for APS argue that their facilities should continue to operate as a hedge against future correctional needs. They also point to the benefits that have come to your district. Further, they remind you of the campaign contributions they made to help you get elected. The local chamber of commerce supports the APS position. Opposing APS, the union representing the state correctional officers say that their members shouldn't suffer because of a private company that is no longer needed. The governor is a member of your party and his operatives press you to support his budget. Finally, a major prison reform group argues that if the space is not needed, the private facilities should be closed. They say that to keep them open while there are vacancies in state institutions is another example of the "prison-commercial" complex.

WRITING ASSIGNMENT

Legislative debate on the future of the APS contract is strident. Each side puts forth strong arguments, putting intense pressure on you. How will you vote? Is this an ethical question? How will you explain your decision to your constituents or to your party's leadership? Writing as if you were the state senator, compose a short newsletter to your constituents explaining your vote on the APS contract.

REAL-WORLD ACTIVITY: AN APPLICATION

To deal with crowding, violence, and the inefficiency of old construction, many jurisdictions have turned toward the direct supervision jail. This type of jail involves a particular design and set of programs in an attempt to use the physical plant to improve the staff's ability to manage and interact with the inmate population and to provide services. Three general concepts are employed: podular design, space for interaction, and personal space.

The podular unit, which replaces the old cell blocks, provides a living area for a group of inmates. Twelve to 25 individual cells are organized into a unit (the pod) that serves as something like a self-contained minijail. Typically the cell doors open into a common living area where the inmates of the pod are allowed to congregate.

The direct supervision jail tends to reinforce interactions of various sorts. For example, inmates have greater freedom to interact socially and recreationally. Further, in traditional jails, bars and doors separate correctional officers from inmates; the direct supervision jail places them in the same rooms with inmates.

The new structure offers several advantages over older jails. First, its flexibility makes it more economical. When jail populations are low, whole pods can be temporarily shut down, saving operational and personnel costs. Second, minimum standards for recreation time and other nonlockup time can be met routinely without costly construction or renovation. Third, because staff have greater autonomy to manage their pods, supervising the staff is less demanding. Fourth, research indicates that direct supervision jails are 20 percent cheaper to construct, and they provide better inmate security and supervision. Finally, some evidence suggests that this new jail concept results in less violence and fewer inmate infractions, leaving staff feeling more secure in their work.

RESEARCHING THE INTERNET

Go to **InfoTrac** College Edition. Enter the keyword *direct supervision jail,* then read the article in *Corrections Today,* April 1993, to learn how the design of a facility can affect inmate behavior.

APPLICATION

What are the pros and cons of the direct supervision jail? If you were a correctional officer in one, what problems might you encounter?

SUMMARY

- From colonial days to the present, the methods of criminal sanctions that are considered appropriate have varied.

- The development of the penitentiary brought a shift away from corporal punishment.

- The Pennsylvania and New York systems were competing approaches to implementing the ideas of the penitentiary.

- The Declaration of Principles of 1870 contained the key elements for the reformatory and rehabilitation models of corrections.

- Three principles guided female prison reform during the nineteenth century: (1) separation from male prisoners, (2) care specialized to women's needs, and (3) management by female staff.

- Although based on the social sciences, the rehabilitative model failed to reduce recidivism.

- The community model of corrections tried to increase opportunities for offenders to be successful citizens and receive psychological treatment.

- The crime control model emphasized incarceration, long and mandatory sentencing, and strict supervision.

- The administration of corrections in the United States is fragmented in that various levels of government are involved.

- The correctional responsibilities of the federal government are divided between the Federal Bureau of Prisons (of the U.S. Department of Justice) and the Administrative Office of the U.S. Courts.

- In all states the administration of prisons falls under the executive branch of state government.

- Private prisons may or may not become accepted as a way to address overcrowding.

- Jails, which are administered by local government, hold people waiting trial and hold sentenced offenders.

- Jail administrators face several problems: (1) the perceived role of the jail in the local criminal justice system, (2) the inmate population, and (3) fiscal problems.

- Until the 1960s the courts held a hands-off policy with respect to corrections.

- The rights of offenders are found in the First, Fourth, Eighth, and Fourteenth Amendments to the U.S. Constitution.

- Through lawsuits in the federal courts, the prisoners' rights movement has brought many changes to the administration and conditions of U.S. prisons.

- Decisions of the Supreme Court have affected community corrections through rules governing probation and parole revocation.

- Prison populations have more than doubled during the past decade, accompanied by a great increase in facilities and staff to administer them.

QUESTIONS FOR REVIEW

1. What were the major differences between the New York and Pennsylvania systems in the nineteenth century?

2. What pressures do administrators of local jails face?

3. What types of correctional programs does your state support? What government agencies run them?

4. Why do some state legislators see private prisons as an attractive correctional option?

5. What Supreme Court decisions are the most significant to corrections today? What effect has each had on correctional institutions? On probation and parole?

6. What explanations might be given for the increased use of incarceration during the past two decades?

KEY TERMS AND CASES

community corrections (p. 294)
congregate system (p. 291)
contract labor system (p. 291)
corrections (p. 288)
crime control model of corrections (p. 295)
Enlightenment (p. 288)
hands-off policy (p. 301)

jail (p. 299)
lease system (p. 292)
mark system (p. 292)
medical model (p. 294)
penitentiary (p. 289)
prison (p. 299)
reformatory (p. 292)
rehabilitation model (p. 293)

separate confinement (p. 290)
Cooper v. Pate (1964) (p. 301)
Gagnon v. Scarpelli (1973) (p. 304)
Hudson v. Palmer (1984) (p. 302)
Mempa v. Rhay (1967) (p. 304)
Morrissey v. Brewer (1972) (p. 304)
Wolff v. McDonnell (1974) (p. 303)

GOING ONLINE

ThomsonNOW™

Maximize your study time by using ThomsonNOW's diagnostic study plan to help you review this chapter. The Study Plan will

- Help you identify areas on which you should concentrate

- Provide interactive exercises to help you master the chapter concepts

- Provide a posttest to confirm you are ready to move on to the next chapter

12

Community Corrections: Probation and Intermediate Sanctions

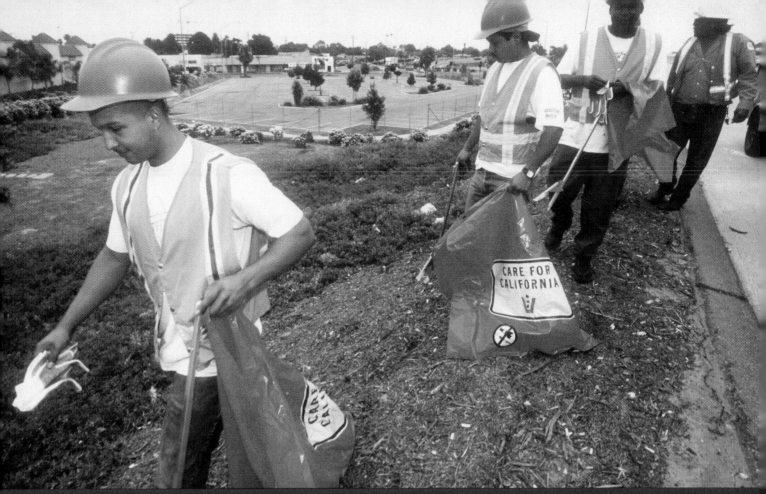

Photo by Gilles Mingasson/Liaison/Getty Images

Todd Harrison rakes his way across the littered lot as he and his coworkers move about in the Bayside, Florida, recreation area. He wears the "uniform" provided by the probation department—an orange hard hat and vest. He wears his own sunglasses and a T-shirt emblazoned "B.U.M." Harrison is one of ten probationers working under the watchful eye of Rich Clark, a community service supervisor employed by the nonprofit organization Upward Now, Inc. Two years before, Harrison was sentenced to 3 years on probation and 100 hours of community service for a larceny conviction. Because Todd was 19 at the time and had no prior record, the judge gave him a community sentence instead of sending him to prison—the usual sentence for more experienced criminals convicted of the same offense. Harrison lives with his mother, works the late shift at a convenience store, reports to his probation officer monthly, and spends five hours every Saturday under the supervision of Clark to complete his community service.

Things are looking up for Todd Harrison as he moves toward completion of his punishment.

Since the early nineteenth century, supervision in the community has been recognized as an appropriate punishment for some offenders. Probation was developed in the 1840s and parole followed in the 1870s. By the 1930s every state and the federal government used these forms of community corrections either to punish offenders without incarceration (probation) or to supervise offenders in the community after leaving prison (parole). Intermediate sanctions were developed in the 1980s when people saw the need for punishments that were less restrictive than prison but more restrictive than probation.

In years to come, community corrections will almost certainly play a much greater role in the criminal justice system. As shown in Figure 12.1, almost three-fourths of offenders are under correctional supervision in the community. This portion will likely increase as states try to deal with the high costs of incarceration. Many criminal justice experts consider probation and intermediate sanctions to be less expensive than imprisonment but just as effective.

QUESTIONS FOR INQUIRY

- What philosophical assumptions underlie community corrections?
- How did probation evolve, and how are probation sentences implemented today?
- What are the types of intermediate sanctions, and how are they administered?
- What key issues does community corrections face at the beginning of the twenty-first century?

Community Corrections: Assumptions

Community corrections seeks to keep offenders in the community by building ties to family, employment, and other normal sources of stability and success. This model of corrections assumes that the offender must change, but it also recognizes that factors within the community that might encourage criminal behavior (unemployment, for example) must also change.

Proponents usually cite four factors in support of community corrections:

1. Many offenders' criminal records and current offenses are not serious enough to warrant incarceration.
2. Community supervision is cheaper than incarceration.
3. Rates of **recidivism,** or returning to crime, for those under community supervision are no higher than for those who go to prison.
4. Ex-inmates require both support and supervision as they try to remake their lives in the community.

Community corrections is based on the goal of finding the "least restrictive alternative"—punishing the offender only as severely as needed to protect the community and to satisfy the public. Advocates call for programs to assist offenders in the community so they will have opportunities to succeed in law-abiding activities and to reduce their contact with the criminal world. Surveys have found the public supports community-based punishments for some types of offenders. (See "What Americans Think.")

FIGURE 12.1
Percentage of people in each category of correctional supervision
Although most people think of corrections as prisons and jails, in fact almost three-quarters of offenders are supervised within the community.

Source: Bureau of Justice Statistics, *Bulletin,* November 2005, p. 1.

recidivism A return to criminal behavior.

Probation: Correction without Incarceration

As we have seen, probation is the conditional release of the offender into the community, under the supervision of correctional officials. Although probationers live at home and work at regular jobs, they must report regularly to their probation officers. They must also abide by specific conditions, such as submitting to drug tests, obeying curfews, and staying away from certain people or parts of town. Although probation is used mainly for lesser offenses, states are increasingly using probation for more serious felonies, as shown in Figure 12.2.

Probation can be combined with other sanctions, such as fines, restitution, and community service. Fulfillment of these other sanctions may, in effect, become a condition for successful completion of probation. The sentencing court retains authority over the probationer, and if he or she violates the conditions or commits another crime, the judge can order the entire sentence to be served in prison.

The number of probationers now under supervision is at a record high and is still rising. Much has been written about overcrowded prisons, but the adult probation population has also been increasing—by an average of 2.8 percent a year since 1995, and up 50.8 percent since 1990 (BJS, 2005c:2). Today, although more than 4.1 million offenders are on probation, probation budgets in many states have been cut and caseloads increased as lawmakers divert greater resources to prisons.

Although probation offers many benefits over incarceration, the public often sees it as a "slap on the wrist" for offenders. With caseloads reaching three hundred in some urban areas, officers cannot provide the level of supervision necessary.

ORIGINS AND EVOLUTION OF PROBATION

Probation first developed in the United States when John Augustus, a Boston boot-maker, persuaded a judge in the Boston Police Court in 1841 to give him custody of a convicted offender for a brief period and then helped the man appear rehabilitated by the time of sentencing.

Massachusetts developed the first statewide probation system in 1880; by 1920, 21 other states had followed suit. The federal courts were authorized to hire probation officers in 1925. By the beginning of World War II, 44 states had probation systems.

Probation began as a humanitarian effort to allow first-time and minor offenders a second chance. Early probationers were expected not only to obey the law but also to behave in a morally acceptable fashion. Officers sought to provide moral leadership to help shape probationers' attitudes and behavior with respect to family, religion, employment, and free time.

By the 1940s the development of psychology led probation officers to shift their emphasis from moral leadership to therapeutic counseling. This shift brought three important changes. First, the officer no longer acted primarily as a community supervisor charged with enforcing a particular morality. Second, the officer became more of a clinical social worker who aimed at helping the offender solve psychological and social problems. Third, the offender was expected to become actively involved in the treatment. The pursuit of rehabilitation as the primary goal of probation gave the officer extensive discretion in defining and treating the offender's problems. Officers used their judgment to evaluate each offender and develop a treatment approach to the personal problems that presumably had led to crime.

During the 1960s, probation moved in another direction. Rather than counseling offenders, probation officers provided them with concrete social services such as assistance with employment, housing, finances, and education. This emphasis on reintegrating offenders and remedying the social problems they faced fit with federal efforts to wage a war on poverty. Instead of being a counselor or therapist, the probation officer served as an advocate, dealing with private and public institutions on the offender's behalf.

In the late 1970s the orientation of probation changed again as the goals of rehabilitation and reintegration gave way to "risk management." This approach, still dominant today, seeks to minimize the probability that an offender will commit a new offense. Risk management reflects two basic goals. First, in accord with the deserved-punishment ideal, the punishment should fit the offense, and correctional intervention should neither raise nor lower the level of punishment. Second, according to the community protection criterion, the risk that the probationer will return to crime determines the amount and type of supervision.

FIGURE 12.2
Felony sentences to probation in state courts

Although many people believe that probation is mainly used for those convicted of misdemeanors, 31 percent of convicted felons were sentenced to probation in 2004. Shown here are the percentages of felony offenders sentenced to probation, listed by the most serious charge for which they were convicted.

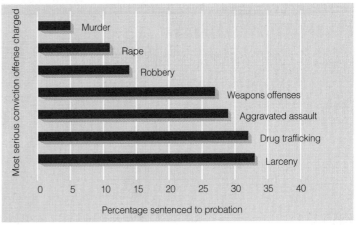

Source: Bureau of Justice Statistics, *Bulletin,* December 2004, p. 2.

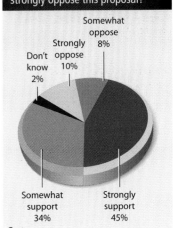

WHAT AMERICANS THINK

Question: "It has been proposed that nonviolent offenders be given community-based punishments rather than serve time in prison. Do you strongly support, somewhat support, somewhat oppose, or strongly oppose this proposal?"

Somewhat oppose 8%
Strongly oppose 10%
Don't know 2%
Somewhat support 34%
Strongly support 45%

Go to http://www.thomsonedu.com/criminaljustice/cole to compare your opinion on this issue with the opinions of other criminal justice students.

Source: Based on telephone interviews with a national adult sample conducted by Penn, Schoen and Berland Associates, June 10–13, 2000. Data provided by the Roper Center for Public Opinion Research, University of Connecticut.

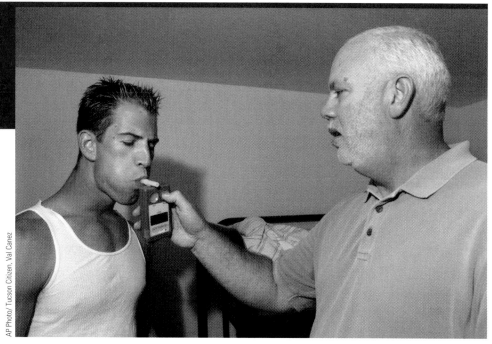

Jonathan Cady blows into a Breath-alyzer for probation officer Scott Greene in Cady's home in Tucson, Arizona. Frequent alcohol and drug testing is a condition of probation for many offenders. Administering these tests has become part of the officer's supervisory role.

AP Photo/ Tucson Citizen, Val Canez

ORGANIZATION OF PROBATION

As a form of corrections, probation falls under the executive branch, and people usually see it as a concern of state government. However, in about 25 percent of the states, probation falls to county and local governments. Further, in many states the judiciary administers it locally. The state sets the standards and provides financial support and training courses, but locally administered programs handle about two-thirds of all people under probation supervision.

In many jurisdictions, although the state is formally responsible for all probation services, the locally elected county judges are in charge. This seemingly odd arrangement produces benefits as well as problems. On the positive side, having probationers under the supervision of the court permits judges to keep closer tabs on them and to order incarceration if the conditions of probation are violated. On the negative side, some judges know little about the goals and methods of corrections, and the probation responsibility adds to the administrative duties of already overworked courts.

Judicially enforced probation seems to work best when the judge and the supervising officer have a close relationship. Proponents of this system say that judges need to work with probation officers whom they can trust, whose presentence reports they can accurately evaluate, and on whom they can rely to report on the success or failure of individual cases.

For the sake of their clients and the goals of the system, probation officers need direct access to corrections and other human services agencies. However, these agencies are located within the executive branch of government. Several states have combined probation and parole services in the same agency to coordinate resources and services better. Others point out, however, that probationers differ from parolees. Parolees already have served prison terms, frequently have been involved in more serious crimes, and often have been disconnected from mainstream society. By contrast, most probationers have not developed criminal lifestyles to the same degree and do not have the same problems of reintegration into the community.

PROBATION SERVICES

Probation officers play roles similar to both the police and social workers. In addition to assisting the judiciary with presentence investigations (see Chapter 10), probation officers supervise clients to keep them out of trouble and enforce the conditions of the sentence. This law enforcement role involves discretionary decisions about whether to report violations of probation conditions. Probation officers are also expected to act like social workers by helping clients obtain the housing, employment, and treatment services they need. The potential conflict between the roles is great. Not surprisingly, individual officers sometimes emphasize one role over the other. See "Careers in Criminal Justice" for more on the probation officer's job.

A continuing issue for probation officers is the size of their caseloads. How many clients can one officer effectively handle? In the 1930s the National Probation Association recommended a 50-unit caseload, and in 1967 the U.S. President's Commission on Law Enforcement and Administration of Justice reduced it to 35. However, today the national average for adult supervision is about 150, with some urban caseloads exceeding 300 (Petersilia, 1998). The oversized caseload is usually cited as one of the main obstacles to successful probation. Research indicates, however, that the caseload size matters less than the quality of the services and supervision (Petersilia and Turner, 1993). See "Real-World Activity" at the end of the chapter for further thought on heavy caseloads.

During the past decade, probation officials have developed methods of classifying clients according to their service needs, the element of risk they pose to the community, and the chance that they will commit another offense. Risk classification fits the deserved-punishment model of the criminal sanction in that the most serious cases receive the greatest restrictions and supervision. If probationers live according to the conditions of their sentence, the level of supervision is gradually reduced.

CAREERS IN CRIMINAL JUSTICE

Probation Officer—State, County

NATURE OF THE WORK

Probation officers supervise offenders in the community through personal contact with offenders and their families. They assist offenders with their treatment, housing, and employment needs. They monitor offenders to ensure that their behavior meets court-ordered requirements. Officers also spend much of their time working for the courts—investigating the background of offenders, preparing presentence reports, and making sentencing recommendations. Caseload size varies by agency, the needs of the offenders, and the risks they pose. Officers might handle a hundred or more active cases. Fieldwork can take the officer to high-crime areas that pose a risk of violence or communicable disease. Officers may have to remain on call 24 hours a day to supervise and assist offenders at any time.

REQUIRED QUALIFICATIONS

Background qualifications for probation officers vary by state, but a bachelor's degree in criminal justice, social work, or a related field from a four-year college or university is usually required. Some agencies require prior experience or graduate work. Candidates must be 21 years old, have never been convicted of a felony, and have familiarity with computer technology. Most probation officers receive formal training and typically work as a trainee for up to one year.

EARNINGS AND JOB OUTLOOK

The number of probation officers is expected to grow about as fast as other occupations during the next decade. The U.S. Department of Labor reports that this occupation is not attractive to some potential entrants, because of relatively low earnings, heavy workloads, and high levels of stress. However, many probation officers report a high level of personal satisfaction in helping offenders through their job. The median annual salary of a probation officer is about $40,000, with entry-level salaries under $25,000 in some regions.

MORE INFORMATION

Visit the website of the American Probation and Parole Association at the corresponding site listed on the Cole/Smith Criminal Justice in America Companion Website: http://www.thomsonedu.com/criminaljustice/cole. You can also obtain career information from your state or county probation office.

Several factors affect how much supervision serious cases actually receive. Consider the war on drugs. It has significantly increased probation levels in urban areas because large numbers of people convicted of drug sales or possession are placed on probation. Many of these offenders have committed violent acts and live in inner-city areas marked by drug dealing and turf battles to control drug markets. Under these conditions, direct supervision can place the probation officer in danger. In some urban areas, probationers are merely required to telephone or mail reports of their current residence and employment. In such cases, it is hard to see how any goal of the sanctions—deserved punishment, rehabilitation, deterrence, or incapacitation—is being realized. If none is of these objectives is being met, the offender is "getting off."

REVOCATION AND TERMINATION OF PROBATION

Probation ends in one of two ways: (1) the person successfully completes the period of probation, or (2) the probationary status is revoked because of misbehavior. In 2001 a national survey of probationers found that 60 percent of adults released from probation successfully completed their sentences, whereas only 13 percent had been reincarcerated (BJS, 2002b:4). Revocation of probation can occur for either a technical violation or a new arrest.

technical violation The probationer's failure to abide by the rules and conditions of probation (specified by the judge), resulting in revocation of probation.

Technical violations occur when a probationer fails to meet the conditions of a sentence by, for instance, violating curfew, failing a drug test, or using alcohol. Officers have discretion as to whether or not they bring this fact to the attention of the judge.

Probation officers and judges have widely varying notions of what constitutes grounds for revoking probation (see "A Question of Ethics" at the end of this chapter). Once the officer calls a violation to the attention of the court, the probationer may be arrested or summoned for a revocation hearing. Because of the contemporary emphasis on avoiding incarceration except for flagrant and continual violation of the conditions of probation, most revocations today occur because of a new arrest or conviction.

As discussed in Chapter 11, in two cases, *Mempa v. Rhay* (1967) and *Gagnon v. Scarpelli* (1973), the U.S. Supreme Court extended due process rights to probationers by ruling that before probation can be revoked, the offender is entitled to a preliminary and a final hearing and a right to counsel in some cases. When a probationer is taken into custody for violating the conditions of probation, a preliminary hearing must be held to determine whether probable cause exists to believe that the incident occurred. If there is a finding of probable cause, a final hearing, where the revocation decision is made, is mandatory. At these hearings the probationer has the right to cross-examine witnesses and to receive notice of the alleged violations and receive a written report of the proceedings. The Court ruled, though, that the probationer does not have an automatic right to counsel; this decision is to be made on a case-by-case basis. At the final hearing, the judge decides whether to continue probation or to impose tougher restrictions, such as incarceration.

For those who successfully complete probation, the sentence ends. Ordinarily the probationer is then a free citizen again, with obligation neither to the court nor to the probation department.

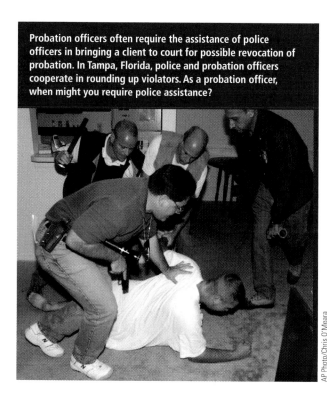

Probation officers often require the assistance of police officers in bringing a client to court for possible revocation of probation. In Tampa, Florida, police and probation officers cooperate in rounding up violators. As a probation officer, when might you require police assistance?

AP Photo/Chris O'Meara

ASSESSING PROBATION

Probation today stands at a crossroads. Some critics see it as nothing more than a slap on the wrist, an absence of punishment. Yet the importance of probation for public safety has never been greater: As of the end of 2004, 49 percent of probationers were convicted of a felony, yet three out of five felony probationers see their officer no more than once a month at best (BJS, 2005c:6). Joan Petersilia (1996) found that 60 percent of all Los Angeles probationers are tracked solely by computer and have no contact with officers. Although probation suffers from poor credibility in the public's eyes, its workload is growing dramatically and, in view of the crowding of prisons and jails, will probably continue to do so.

Although the recidivism rate for probationers is lower than the rate for those who have been incarcerated, researchers question whether this is a direct result of supervision or an indirect result of the maturing of the offenders. Most offenders placed on probation do not become career criminals, their criminal activity is short-lived, and they become stable citizens as they obtain jobs and get married. Most of those who are arrested a second time do not repeat their mistake again.

What rallies support for probation is its relatively low cost. Keeping an offender on probation instead of behind bars costs roughly $1,000 a year, a savings of more than $20,000 a year (Abadinsky, 1997). However, these savings might not satisfy community members who hear of a sex offender on probation who repeats his crime.

To offer a viable alternative to incarceration, probation services need the resources to supervise and assist their clients appropriately. The new demands on probation have brought calls for increased electronic monitoring and for risk-management systems that provide different levels of supervision for different kinds of offenders.

ThomsonNOW
Improve your grade on the exam with Personalized Study! For reinforcement resources and a mastery check of Probation: Correction without Incarceration, go to www.thomsonedu.com/thomsonnow.

CHECKPOINT

Answers

1. What are the four main assumptions underlying community corrections? ➡ 1. Many offenders' crimes and records do not warrant incarceration; community supervision is cheaper; recidivism rates for those supervised in the community are no higher than for those who serve prison time; incarceration is more destructive to the offender and society.

2. What are the major tasks of the probation officer? ➡ 2. To assist judges by preparing presentence reports and to provide assistance and supervision to offenders in the community.

3. What are the grounds for revocation of probation? ➡ 3. An arrest for a new offense or a technical violation of the conditions of probation that were set by the judge.

Intermediate Sanctions in the Community

Dissatisfaction with the traditional means of probation supervision, coupled with the crowding and high cost of prisons, has resulted in a call for intermediate sanctions. These are sanctions that restrict the offender more than does simple probation and that constitute actual punishment for more serious offenders.

Many experts have supported the case for intermediate sanctions. For example, Norval Morris and Michael Tonry relate, "Prison is used excessively; probation is used even more excessively; between the two is a near vacuum of purposive and enforced punishments" (1990:3). Sixty-nine percent of convicted felons are incarcerated, whereas 31 percent receive probation. Hence, all convicted felons receive either the severest or the most lenient of possible penalties (BJS, 2004e:2). Morris and Tonry urge that punishments be created that are more restrictive than probation yet match the severity of the offense and the characteristics of the offender, and that can be carried out while still protecting the community.

We can view intermediate sanctions as a continuum—a range of punishments that vary in levels of intrusiveness and control, as shown in Figure 12.3. Probation plus a fine or community service may be appropriate for minor offenses, whereas 6 weeks of boot camp followed by intensive probation supervision might be right for serious crimes. But some question whether offenders will be able to fulfill the conditions added to probation. Moreover, if prisons are overcrowded, is incarceration a believable threat if offenders fail to comply?

Corrections employs many types of intermediate sanctions. They can be divided into (1) those administered primarily by the judiciary (fines, restitution, and forfeiture),

FIGURE 12.3

Continuum of intermediate sanctions

Judges may use a range of intermediate sanctions, from those imposing a low level of control to those imposing a high level.

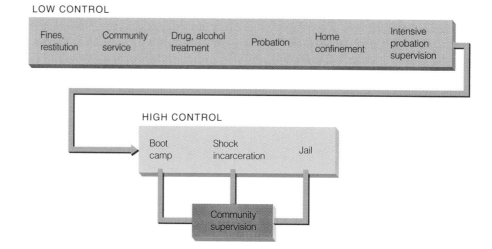

INTERMEDIATE SANCTIONS ADMINISTERED PRIMARILY BY THE JUDICIARY

(2) those administered primarily in the community with a supervision component (home confinement, community service, day reporting centers, and intensive probation supervision), and (3) those administered inside institutions and followed by community supervision (boot camp). Furthermore, sanctions may be imposed in combination—for example, a fine and probation, or boot camp with community service and probation.

The judiciary administers many kinds of intermediate sanctions. Here we discuss three of them—fines, restitution, and forfeiture. Because all three involve the transfer of money or property from the offender to the government or crime victim, the judiciary is considered the proper body not only to impose the sanction but also to collect what is due.

fine A sum of money to be paid to the state by a convicted person as punishment for an offense.

Fines   Fines are routinely imposed for offenses ranging from traffic violations to felonies. Studies have shown that the fine is used widely as a criminal sanction and that nationally well over $1 billion in fines has been collected annually. Yet, judges in the United States make little use of fines as the *sole* punishment for crimes more serious than motor vehicle violations. Instead, they typically use fines in conjunction with other sanctions, such as probation and incarceration; for example, two years of probation and a $500 fine.

Many judges cite the difficulty of collecting fines as the reason that they do not make greater use of this punishment. They note that offenders tend to be poor, and many judges fear that fines will be paid from the proceeds of additional illegal acts. Other judges are concerned that relying on fines as an alternative to incarceration will let affluent offenders "buy" their way out of jail while forcing the poor to serve time.

Fines are used extensively in Europe, are enforced, and are normally the sole sanction for a wide range of crimes. In Germany, 81 percent of all sentenced offenders must pay a fine, including 73 percent of those convicted of crimes of violence. In Sweden, fines are used in 91 percent of cases; in England, they are used in 47 percent of indictable offenses (roughly equivalent to an American felony) (Tonry, 1998:698). To deal with the concern that fines exact a heavier toll on the poor than on the wealthy, Sweden and Germany have developed the day fine, which bases the penalty on offender's income. The day fine has been tested in Arizona, Connecticut, Iowa, New York, and Washington.

restitution Repayment—in the form of money or service—by an offender to a victim who has suffered some loss from the offense.

Restitution   Restitution is repayment by an offender to a victim who has suffered some form of financial loss from the crime. It is *reparative* in that it seeks to repair the harm done. In the Middle Ages, restitution was a common way to settle a criminal case (Karmen, 2001:305). The offender was ordered to pay the victim or do the victim's work. The growth of the modern state saw the decline of such punishments based on "private" arrangements between offender and victim. Instead, the state prosecuted offenders, and punishments focused on the wrong the offender had done to society.

Though largely unpublicized, victim restitution has remained a part of the U.S. criminal justice system. In many instances, restitution derives from informal agreements between the police and offenders at the station, during plea bargaining, or in the prosecutor's sentence recommendation. Only since the late 1970s has restitution been institutionalized, usually as one of the conditions of probation.

As with fines, convicted offenders differ in their ability to pay restitution, and the conditions inevitably fall more harshly on less affluent offenders. Someone who has the "good fortune" to be victimized by an affluent criminal might receive full compensation, whereas someone victimized by a poor offender might never receive a penny.

Restitution is more easily imposed when the "damage" inflicted can be easily measured—value of property destroyed or stolen, or medical costs, for instance. But what should be the restitution for the terror of an attempted rape?

Forfeiture   With the passage of two laws in 1970—the Racketeer Influenced and Corrupt Organizations Act (RICO) and the Continuing Criminal Enterprise Act (CCE)—Congress resurrected forfeiture, a criminal sanction that had lain dormant since the American Revolution. Through amendments in 1984 and 1986, Congress improved ways to implement the law. Most states now have similar laws, particularly to deal with trafficking in controlled substances and with organized crime.

Forfeiture is government seizure of property and other assets derived from or used in criminal activity. Assets seized by federal and state agencies through forfeiture can be quite considerable. For example, the Drug Enforcement Administration alone annually seizes assets (including cash, real estate, vehicles, vessels, and airplanes) valued at more than a half billion dollars (BJS, 1999b:378).

forfeiture Government seizure of property and other assets derived from or used in criminal activity.

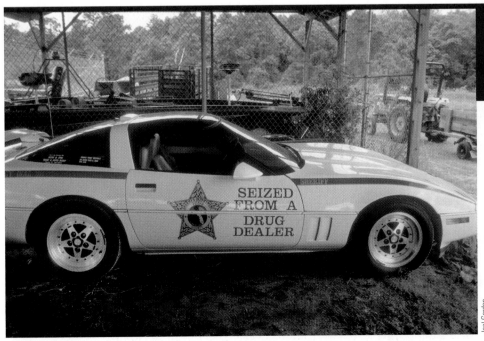

Vehicle seized in a drug bust by the Putnam County, Florida, Sheriff's Office under the asset forfeiture provisions of the Racketeer Influenced and Corrupt Organizations Act (RICO). The vehicle is now used in the DARE program.

Joel Gordon

Forfeiture is controversial. Critics argue that confiscating property without a court hearing violates citizens' constitutional rights. They have also raised concerns about the excessive use of this sanction, because forfeited assets often go into the budget of the law enforcement agency taking the action (Blumenson and Nilsen, 1998).

In a 1993 opinion, the Supreme Court ruled that the Eighth Amendment's ban on excessive fines requires that the seriousness of the offense be related to the property that is taken (*Austin v. United States*). The ruling places limits on the government's ability to seize property and invites the judiciary to monitor the government's forfeiture activities when convicted offenders challenge them.

Critics further argue that ownership of the seized property is often unclear. For example, in Hartford, Connecticut, a woman's home was seized because her grandson, unbeknownst to her, was using it as a base for selling drugs. Under a law passed by Congress in 2000, owners' property cannot be seized if they can demonstrate their innocence by a preponderance of evidence.

INTERMEDIATE SANCTIONS ADMINISTERED IN THE COMMUNITY

One basic argument for intermediate sanctions is that probation, as traditionally practiced, cannot accommodate the large numbers of offenders whom probation officers must supervise today. Probation leaders have responded to this criticism by developing new intermediate sanction programs and expanding old ones. Four of these are home confinement, community service, day reporting centers, and intensive supervision probation.

home confinement A sentence requiring the offender to remain inside his or her home during specified periods.

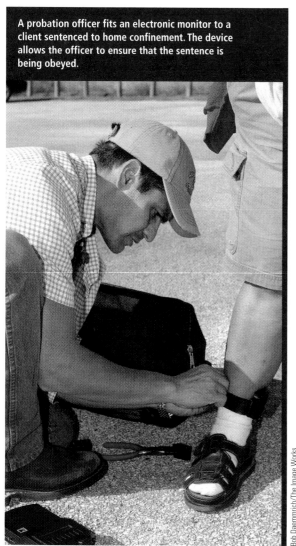

A probation officer fits an electronic monitor to a client sentenced to home confinement. The device allows the officer to ensure that the sentence is being obeyed.

Bob Daemmrich/The Image Works

Home Confinement   With technological innovations that provide for electronic monitoring, **home confinement,** in which offenders must remain at home during specific periods, has gained attention. Offenders under home confinement (often called "house arrest") may face other restrictions such as the usual probation rules against alcohol and drugs as well as strictly monitored curfews and check-in times.

Some offenders are allowed to go to a place of employment, education, or treatment during the day but must return to their homes by a specified hour. Those supervising home confinement may telephone offenders' homes at various times of the day or night to speak personally with offenders to make sure they are complying.

Home confinement offers a great deal of flexibility. It can be used as a sole sanction or in combination with other penalties. It can be imposed at almost any point in the criminal justice process: during the pretrial period, after a short term in jail or prison, or as a condition of probation or parole. In addition, home confinement relieves the government of the responsibility to provide the offender with food, clothing, and housing, as it must do in prisons. Home confinement programs have grown and proliferated.

The development of electronic monitoring equipment has made home confinement an enforceable sentencing option. The number of offenders currently being monitored is difficult to estimate, because the equipment manufacturers consider this confidential information. However, the best estimates say about 17 different companies provide electronic monitoring of nearly 100,000 offenders (Conway, 2001).

Two basic types of electronic monitoring devices exist. Passive monitors respond only to inquiries; most commonly, the offender receives an automated telephone call from the probation office and is told to place the device on a receiver attached to the phone. Active devices send continuous signals that a receiver picks up;

TECHNOLOGY ISSUES IN CRIMINAL JUSTICE

Stalker Trackers

The use of electronic monitoring technology has expanded to probationers who are permitted to walk the streets and go to work but whom authorities want to keep away from their victims. "Stalker trackers," one example, sound alarms and notify authorities if the offender comes too close to the victim's home. They are used frequently to protect stalking and domestic violence victims—people against whom the offenders may display a great deal of anger.

Many observers endorse the expansion of monitoring technology. Instead of merely notifying authorities, the devices warn potential victims about the presence of the offender. However, the devices remain susceptible to technical problems, and determined offenders may find ways to remove the devices.

 RESEARCHING THE INTERNET

The tracking-device industry is well represented on the Internet. One example can be found at the corresponding site listed on the Cole/Smith Criminal Justice in America Companion Website: http://www.thomsonedu.com/criminaljustice/cole.

FOR CRITICAL ANALYSIS

Can you think of other ways to use these devices effectively in community corrections settings? Can you envision other kinds of technological innovations that would serve beneficially as part of intermediate sanctions?

Source: Drawn from Paul Egan, "Stalker Trackers Popular New Tool," *Lansing State Journal*, February 15, 1999, pp. 1A, 5A.

---

a computer notes any break in the signal. See "Technology Issues in Criminal Justice" for a look at monitors called "stalker trackers."

Despite favorable publicity, home confinement with electronic monitoring poses certain legal, technical, and correctional issues that must be addressed before it can become a standard punishment. First, some criminal justice scholars question its constitutionality. Monitoring may violate the Fourth Amendment's protection against unreasonable searches and seizures. At issue is a clash between the constitutionally protected reasonable expectation of privacy and the invasion of one's home by surveillance devices. Second, the monitoring devices still have extensive technical problems, such as frequently giving erroneous reports that the offender is home. Third, offender failure rates may prove to be high. Being one's own warden is difficult, and visits by former criminal associates and other enticements may become problematic for many offenders. Anecdotal evidence suggests that four months of full-time monitoring is about the limit before a violation will occur. Furthermore, some crimes—such as child abuse, drug sales, and assaults—can be committed while the offender is at home.

Community Service   A **community service** sentence requires the offender to perform a certain amount of unpaid labor in the community. Community service can take a variety of forms, including assisting in social service agencies, cleaning parks and roadsides, or helping the poor. The sentence specifies the number of hours to be worked and usually requires supervision by a probation officer. Judges can tailor community service to the skills and abilities of offenders. For example, less educated offenders might pick up litter along the highway, whereas those with schooling might teach reading in evening literacy classes. Many judges order community service when an offender cannot pay a fine. The offender's effort to make reparation to the community harmed by the crime also serves a symbolic function.

Although community service has many supporters, some labor unions and workers criticize it for possibly taking jobs away from law-abiding citizens. In addition, some experts believe that if community service is the only sanction, it may be too mild a punishment, especially for upper-class and white-collar criminals.

Day Reporting Centers   Another intermediate sanction option is the **day reporting center**—a community correctional center to which the offender must report each day to carry out elements of the sentence. Designed to ensure that probationers follow the employment and treatment stipulations attached to their sentence, day reporting centers also increase the likelihood that offenders and the general public will consider probation supervision to be credible.

Most day reporting centers incorporate multiple correctional methods. For example, in some centers offenders must remain in the facility for eight hours or

community service A sentence requiring the offender to perform a certain amount of unpaid labor in the community.

day reporting center A community correctional center where an offender reports each day to comply with elements of a sentence.

Increasingly, nongovernmental organizations are administering community corrections programs. Talon, a 21-year-old recovering addict, looks out the window of his room during the second week of rehabilitation at Walden House in San Francisco. California has embarked on an ambitious experiment to divert drug offenders out of the prison system and into community treatment programs.

AP Photo/Jakub Mosur

intensive supervision probation (ISP) Probation granted under conditions of strict reporting to a probation officer with a limited caseload.

report for drug-related urine checks before going to work. Centers with a rehabilitation component carry out drug and alcohol treatment, literacy programs, and job searches. Others provide staff–offender contact levels equal to or greater than those in intensive supervision programs. However, one study found that offenders sentenced to day reporting plus intensive supervision probation were no more or less likely to recidivate than were those on intensive supervision alone (Marciniak, 2000:34).

The overall success or failure of these programs remains unclear. One study of New York City's program found that its stiff eligibility requirements resulted in few cases entering the center. A study of six day reporting centers in Massachusetts found that about 80 percent of offenders successfully completed the program (McDivitt and Miliano, 1992:160). Such success, however, depends at least in part on who is being treated. If such centers are used only for selected offenders with a low risk of returning to crime, knowing whether the centers themselves are effective will be difficult.

Intensive Supervision Probation (ISP)   Intensive supervision probation (ISP) is a means of dealing with offenders who need greater restrictions than traditional community-based programs can provide. Jurisdictions in every state have programs to intensively supervise such offenders. ISP uses probation as an intermediate form of punishment by imposing conditions of strict reporting to a probation officer who has a limited caseload.

There are two general types of ISP programs. *Probation diversion* puts under intensive surveillance those offenders thought to be too risky for routine supervision. *Institutional diversion* selects low-risk offenders sentenced to prison and provides supervision for them in the community. Daily contact between the probationer and the probation officer may cut rearrest rates. Such contact also gives the probationer greater access to the resources the officer can provide, such as treatment services in the community. Offenders have incentives to obey rules, knowing that they must meet with their probation officers daily and in some cases must speak with them even more frequently. Offenders often face additional restrictions as well, such as electronic monitoring, alcohol and drug testing, community service, and restitution.

ISP programs have been called "old-style" probation because each officer has only 20 clients and requires frequent face-to-face contact. Nonetheless, some people question how much of a difference constant surveillance can make to probationers with numerous problems. Such offenders frequently need help to get a job, counseling to deal with emotional and family situations, and a variety of supports to avoid drug or alcohol problems that may have contributed to their criminality. Yet ISP may be a way of getting the large number of drug-addicted felons into treatment.

Because it presents a "tough" image of community supervision and addresses the problem of prison crowding, ISP has become popular among probation administrators, judges, and prosecutors. Most ISP programs require a specific number of monthly contacts with officers, performance of community service, curfews, drug and alcohol testing, and referral to appropriate job-training, education, or treatment programs.

Some observers warn that ISP is not a "cure" for the rising costs and other problems facing corrections systems. Ironically, ISP can increase the number of probationers sent to prison. All evaluations of ISP find that, probably because of the closer contact with clients, probation officers uncover more violations of rules than they do in regular probation. Therefore, ISP programs often have higher failure rates than do regular probation, even though their clients produce fewer arrests (Tonry and Lynch, 1996:116).

Another surprising finding is that, when given the option of serving prison terms or participating in ISP, many offenders choose prison. In New Jersey, 15 percent of offenders withdrew their applications for ISP once they learned the conditions and requirements. Similarly, when offenders in Marion County, Oregon, were asked if they would participate in ISP, one-third chose prison instead (Petersilia, 1990). Apparently, some offenders would rather spend a short time in prison, where tough conditions may differ little from their accustomed life, than a longer period under demanding conditions in the community. To these offenders, ISP does not represent freedom, because it is so intrusive and the risk of revocation seems high.

Despite problems and continuing questions about its effectiveness, ISP has rejuvenated probation. These programs have carried out some of the most effective offender supervision. As with regular probation, the size of a probation officer's caseload, within reasonable limits, often matters less in preventing recidivism than does the quality of supervision and assistance provided to probationers. If properly implemented, ISP may improve the quality of supervision and services that foster success for more kinds of offenders.

INTERMEDIATE SANCTIONS ADMINISTERED IN INSTITUTIONS AND THE COMMUNITY

Among the most publicized intermediate sanctions are **boot camps.** Often referred to as *shock incarceration,* these programs vary; however, all stem from the belief that young offenders (usually 14- to 21-year-olds) can be "shocked" out of their criminal ways. Boot camps put offenders through a 30-to-90-day physical regimen designed to develop discipline and respect for authority. Like the Marine Corps, most programs emphasize a spit-and-polish environment and keep the offenders in a disciplined and demanding routine that seeks ultimately to build self-esteem. Most camps also include education, job-training programs, and other rehabilitation services. On successful completion of the program, offenders are released to the community. At this point probation officers take over, and the conditions of the sentence are imposed.

Boot camps proliferated in the 1980s. By 1995 some states and the Federal Bureau of Prisons operated 93 camps for adults and 30 for juveniles. At their peak, boot camps held more than 7,000 offenders. By 2000, however, about one-third of the camps had closed, and the decline in boot camp operations continues. In January 2005 the Federal Bureau of Prisons announced that it would phase out its remaining boot camps over six months. Further, the public uproar following the death of teenager Martin Anderson caused Florida to scrap its system of juvenile boot camps. Anderson died after being pummeled by a group of guards at a Panama City boot camp. He had been sent to the camp for joyriding in his grandmother's automobile (Caputo and Miller, 2006).

Evaluations of boot camp programs have reduced the initial optimism about such approaches. Critics suggest that the emphasis on physical training ignores young offenders' real problems. Some point out that, like the military, boot camp builds esprit de corps and solidarity, characteristics that can improve the leadership qualities of the young offender and therefore enhance a criminal career. In fact, follow-up studies of boot camp graduates show they do no better after release from the program than do other offenders. Research has also found that, like intensive supervision probation, boot camps do not automatically reduce prison crowding. A National Institute of Justice summary of the boot camp experiment notes that they fail to reduce recidivism or prison populations (NIJ, 2003).

Defenders of boot camps argue that the camps are accomplishing their goals; the failure lies in the lack of educational and employment opportunities in the participants' inner-city communities (see the Close Up box). A national study found that few boot camp graduates received any aftercare assistance on returning to their communities (Bourque, Han, and Hill, 1996). Because boot camps have been popular with the public, which imagines that strict discipline and harsh conditions will instill positive attitudes in young offenders, such camps will probably continue operating whether or not they are more effective than probation or prison.

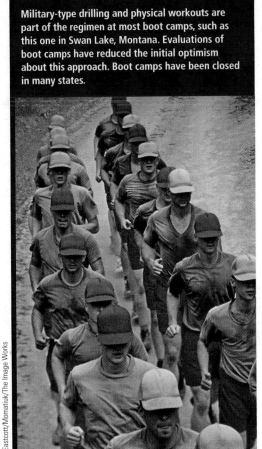

Military-type drilling and physical workouts are part of the regimen at most boot camps, such as this one in Swan Lake, Montana. Evaluations of boot camps have reduced the initial optimism about this approach. Boot camps have been closed in many states.

© Eastcott/Momatiuk/The Image Works

boot camp A short-term institutional sentence, usually followed by probation, that puts the offender through a physical regimen designed to develop discipline and respect for authority. Also referred to as *shock incarceration.*

CLOSE UP

After Boot Camp, a Harder Discipline

Nelson Colon misses waking up to the blast of reveille. He sometimes yearns for those 16-hour days filled with military drills and 9-mile runs. He even thinks fondly of the surly drill instructors who shouted in his face.

During his four months at New Jersey's boot camp, Mr. Colon adapted to the rigors of military life with little difficulty. He says it was a lot easier than what he faces now. He is back in his old neighborhood, trying to stay away from old friends and old ways.

So far, Colon, at age 18, has managed to stay out of trouble since he graduated with the camp's first class of 20 cadets in June. Yet each day, he said, he fears he will be pulled back onto the corner, only two blocks away, where he was first arrested for selling drugs at age 15.

A 10:00 P.M. curfew helps keep Colon off the streets. His parole officer checks in with him almost daily, sometimes stopping by at 11:00 to make sure he is inside. He is enrolling in night classes to help him earn his high school equivalency certificate, and he plans on attending Narcotics Anonymous meetings.

His biggest problems are the same ones that tens of thousands of Camden residents confront daily. Camden's unemployment rate exceeds 20 percent. There are few jobs in this troubled city, particularly for young men who have dropped out of high school. Colon has found work as a stock clerk in a sneaker store, but it is miles away at a shopping center on a busy highway, and he has no transportation there.

Selling drugs paid a lot more than stacking shoe boxes, and it did not require commuting. Mr. Colon says he pushes those thoughts of easy money out of his head and tries to remember what the boot camp's drill instructors told him over and over again.

"They used to tell us, 'It's up to you.' You have to have self-accountability. You have to be reliable for your own actions, not because some person wanted you to do it. They taught us not to follow, to lead. That was one of the most important things."

Mr. Colon said his immediate goal was to find a job that he could get to more easily, and then save enough to get as far away from Camden as possible. "I want to get out of here," he said.

"The people's mentality here is real petty. Life isn't nothing to them. The other night, they killed one of the guys I grew up with. They shot him a couple of times. My old friends came around and knocked on my door at one o'clock in the morning to tell me." He said it was his eighth childhood friend to die.

RESEARCHING THE INTERNET

For more on boot camps, use InfoTrac College Edition to access the article by Claire Souryal and Doris Layton MacKenzie, "Shock Therapy: Can Boot Camps Provide Effective Drug Treatment?" *Corrections Today,* February 1994.

FOR CRITICAL ANALYSIS

Do youthful offenders need special programs and services after they leave boot camp and return to their communities? If so, what do they need?

Source: Adapted from *New York Times,* September 3, 1995, p. B1.

IMPLEMENTING INTERMEDIATE SANCTIONS

Although the use of intermediate sanctions has spread rapidly, three major questions have emerged about their implementation: (1) Which agencies should implement the sanctions? (2) Which offenders should be admitted to these programs? (3) Will the "community corrections net" widen as a result of these policies so that more people will come under correctional supervision?

As in any public service organization, administrative politics play an ongoing role in corrections. In many states, agencies compete for the additional funding needed to run the programs. The traditional agencies of community corrections, such as probation offices, could receive the funding, or the new programs could be contracted out to nonprofit organizations. Probation organizations argue that they know the field, have the experienced staff, and—given the additional resources—could do an excellent job. They correctly point out that a great many offenders sentenced to intermediate sanctions are also on probation. Critics of giving this role to probation services argue that the established agencies are not receptive to innovation. They say that probation agencies place a high priority on the traditional supervision function and would not actively help clients solve their problems.

The different types of offenders who receive intermediate sanctions prompt a second issue in the implementation debate. One school of thought focuses on the seriousness of the offense; the other centers on the problems of the offender.

If categorized by the seriousness of their offense, offenders may receive such close supervision that they will not be able to abide by the sentence. Sanctions for serious offenders may accumulate to include, for example, probation, drug testing, addiction treatment, and home confinement. As the number of sentencing conditions increases, even the most willing probationers find fulfilling every one of them difficult.

Some agencies want to accept into their intermediate sanctions program only those offenders who *will* succeed. These agencies are concerned about their success ratio, especially because of threats to future funding if the program does not reduce recidivism. Critics point out that this strategy leads to "creaming," taking the most promising offenders and leaving those with worse problems to traditional sanctions.

The third issue concerns **net widening,** a process in which the new sanction increases the control over offenders' lives, rather than reducing it. This can occur when a judge imposes a more intrusive sentence than usual. For example, rather than merely giving an offender probation, the judge might also require that the offender perform community service. Critics of intermediate sanctions in this regard argue that they have created the following:

- *Wider nets.* Reforms increase the proportion of individuals in society whose behavior is regulated or controlled by the state.

- *Stronger nets.* By intensifying the state's intervention powers, reforms augment the state's capacity to control individuals.

- *Different nets.* Reforms transfer jurisdictional authority from one agency or control system to another.

Some have advocated intermediate sanctions as a less costly alternative to incarceration and a more effective alternative to probation. But how have they been working? Michael Tonry and Mary Lynch have discouraging news: "Few such programs have diverted large numbers of offenders from prison, saved public monies or prison beds, or reduced recidivism rates" (1996:99). With incarceration rates still at record highs and probation caseloads increasing, intermediate sanctions will probably play a major role in corrections through the first decade of this century. However, correctional reform has always had its limitations, and intermediate sanctions may not achieve the goals of their advocates.

net widening Process in which new sentencing options increase rather than reduce control over offenders' lives.

ThomsonNOW™
Improve your grade on the exam with Personalized Study! For reinforcement resources and a mastery check of Intermediate Sanctions in the Community, go to www.thomsonedu.com/thomsonnow.

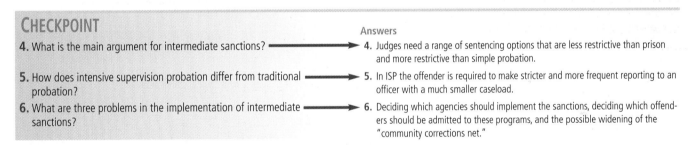

CHECKPOINT

Answers

4. What is the main argument for intermediate sanctions? ────────▶ 4. Judges need a range of sentencing options that are less restrictive than prison and more restrictive than simple probation.

5. How does intensive supervision probation differ from traditional ────────▶ 5. In ISP the offender is required to make stricter and more frequent reporting to an probation? officer with a much smaller caseload.

6. What are three problems in the implementation of intermediate ────────▶ 6. Deciding which agencies should implement the sanctions, deciding which offend-sanctions? ers should be admitted to these programs, and the possible widening of the "community corrections net."

The Future of Community Corrections

In 1995, 3.7 million Americans were under community supervision; by 2004, this figure had grown to 5 million (BJS, 2005d:1). Despite this tremendous growth, community corrections still lacks public support. Community corrections suffers from the image of being "soft on crime." As a result, some localities provide adequate resources for prisons and jails but not for community corrections.

Community corrections also faces the challenge that offenders today require closer supervision. The crimes, criminal records, and drug problems of these offenders are often worse than those of lawbreakers of earlier eras. Nationally, 31 percent of convicted felons are sentenced to probation with no jail or prison time, and about one-fourth of these have been found guilty of violent crimes (BJS, 2004e:2). Those people are supervised by probation officers whose caseloads number in the hundreds. Such officers, and their counterparts in parole, cannot provide effective supervision and services to all their clients.

Community corrections is burdened by even greater caseload pressures than in the past. With responsibility for about three-fourths of all offenders under correctional supervision, community corrections needs an infusion of additional resources.

For community corrections to succeed, the public must support it. However, such support will come only if citizens believe that offenders are receiving appropriate punishments.

Citizens must realize that policies designed to punish offenders in the community yield not mere "slaps on the wrists" but meaningful sanctions, even while these policies allow offenders to retain and reforge their ties to their families and society. Joan Petersilia argues that too many crime-control policies focus solely on the short term. She believes that long-term investments in community corrections will pay off for the offender and the community (Petersilia, 1996). Again, before new policies can be put in place, public opinion must shift toward support of community corrections.

A QUESTION OF ETHICS: WRITING ASSIGNMENT

As you look over the Recommendation for Revocation Report sent to you by Officer Sawyer, you are struck by the low-level technical violations used to justify sending James Ferguson, a minor drug offender, to prison. Sawyer cites Ferguson's failure to attend all the drug treatment sessions, to complete his community service, to pay a $500 fine. You call Sawyer in to discuss the report.

"Bill, I've looked over your report on Ferguson and I'm wondering what's going on here. Why isn't he fulfilling the conditions of his probation?"

"I'm really not sure, but it seems he just doesn't want to meet the conditions. I think he's got a bad attitude, and I don't like the guys he hangs around with. He's always mouthing off about the 'system' and says I'm on his case for no reason."

"Well, let's look at your report. You say that he works for Capital Services cleaning offices downtown from midnight till 8:00 A.M. yet has to go to the drug programs three mornings a week and put in ten hours a week at the Salvation Army Thrift Store. Is it that he isn't trying or does he have an impossible situation?"

"I think he could do it if he tried, but also, I think he's selling cocaine again. Perhaps he needs to get a taste of prison."

"That may be true, but do you really want to revoke his probation?"

WRITING ASSIGNMENT

What's going on here? Is Sawyer recommending revocation because of Ferguson's attitude and the suspicion that he is selling drugs again? Do the technical violations warrant prison? Analyze the information as presented and then make a choice: Write Officer Sawyer's report describing the reasons why Ferguson's probation should be revoked or write a memo as a judge who decides that probation revocation is not appropriate in this case.

REAL-WORLD ACTIVITY: AN APPLICATION

As a probation officer in Philadelphia, you are trying to manage a 300-person caseload. The probationers have committed a mixed range of offenses, many have been on probation before, and several have served jail or prison sentences. One-third of your clients have been on probation for less than six months, one-third for six months to a year, and one-third for more than one year.

 RESEARCHING THE INTERNET

Go to InfoTrac College Edition. Enter the keyword *probation caseload* and read the article entitled "Falling Crime Rates, Rising Caseload Numbers: Using

Police-Probation Partnerships," by Christopher Condon, *Corrections Today*, February 2003.

APPLICATION

What are some of the strategies that you will use to best meet the service and supervision needs of your clients?

SUMMARY

- Community supervision through probation and intermediate sanctions is a growing part of the criminal justice system.

- Probation is imposed on more than half of offenders. People with this sentence live in the community according to conditions set by the judge and under the supervision of a probation officer.

- Intermediate sanctions are designed as punishments that are more restrictive than probation and less restrictive than prison.

- The range of intermediate sanctions allows judges to design sentences that incorporate one or more of these punishments.

- Some intermediate sanctions are implemented by courts (fines, restitution, forfeiture), others in the community (home confinement, community service, day reporting centers, intensive supervision probation), and others in institutions and the community (boot camps).

- The use of community corrections is expected to grow in the twenty-first century, in spite of the problems of implementing them.

QUESTIONS FOR REVIEW

1. What is the aim of community corrections?

2. What is the nature of probation, and how is it organized?

3. What is the purpose of intermediate sanctions?

4. What are the primary forms of intermediate sanctions?

5. Why is net widening a concern?

KEY TERMS

boot camp (p. 327)
community service (p. 325)
day reporting center (p. 325)
fine (p. 323)

forfeiture (p. 323)
home confinement (p. 324)
intensive supervision
   probation (ISP) (p. 326)

net widening (p. 329)
recidivism (p. 316)
restitution (p. 323)
technical violation (p. 320)

GOING ONLINE

ThomsonNOW™

Maximize your study time by using ThomsonNOW's diagnostic study plan
to help you review this chapter. The Study Plan will

■ Help you identify areas on which you should concentrate

■ Provide interactive exercises to help you master the chapter concepts

■ Provide a posttest to confirm you are ready to move on to the next chapter.

13

Incarceration and Prison Society

PRISON

We're crowded into the department of corrections' bus, 40 convicts en route to the state prison. I'm handcuffed to two other men, the chains gleaming dully at wrists and ankles. The man on my right lifts his hand to smoke, the red eye of his cigarette burning through the darkness of the van. When he exhales, the man at my left coughs, the sound in his lungs suggesting that he's old, maybe sick. I want to ask what he's in for. But I don't speak, restrained by my fear, a feeling that rises cold up the back of my spine. For a long time no one else speaks either, each man locked in his own thoughts. It's someone up front, a kid, his voice brittle with fear, who speaks first. "What's it like down there—in the joint? Is it as bad as they say?"

"Worse," someone answers. "Cell blocks are dirty. Overcrowded. Lousy chow. Harassment. Stabbings."

"How do you live there?"

"You don't exactly live. You go through the motions. Eat, sleep, mind your own business. Do drugs when you can get them. Forget the world you came from."

This description of the "way in" was written by an inmate who was incarcerated in the Arizona penal system for seven years. It conveys much of the anxiety not only of the new "fish" but also of the old con. What is it like to be incarcerated? What does it mean to the inmates, the guards, and the administrators? Are the officers in charge or do the prisoners "rule the joint"? In the Close Up on page 335, Michael Santos describes his anxiety as a 24-year-old first-time offender entering the U.S. Federal Penitentiary in Atlanta.

Incarceration—what does it mean to the inmates, the officers, and the public? What goes on inside U.S. prisons? In this chapter we focus on such issues as the goals of incarceration, the challenges of management, and the inmate's experience. Discussion also centers on violence in prison and the policies and programs intended to keep correctional institutions from boiling over.

QUESTIONS FOR INQUIRY

- How do contemporary institutions differ from the old-style "big-house" prisons?
- What assumptions does each model of incarceration make?
- How is a prison organized?
- How is a prison governed?
- What is the role of correctional officers in a prison?
- What are the characteristics of the incarcerated population?
- What is prison like for men and for women?
- What programs and services are available to prisoners?
- What is the nature of prison violence?

The Modern Prison: Legacy of the Past

American correctional institutions have always been more varied than the way movies or novels portray them. Fictional depictions of prison life are typically set in a fortress, the "big house"—the maximum-security prisons where the inmates are tough and the guards are just as tough or tougher. Although big houses predominated in much of the country during the first half of the twentieth century, many prisons were built on another model. In the South, for instance, prisoners worked outside at farm labor, and the massive walled structures were not so common.

The typical big house of the 1940s and 1950s was a walled prison with large, tiered cell blocks, a yard, shops, and industrial workshops. About 2,500 prisoners served in each institution. They came from both urban and rural areas, were usually poor, and were predominantly white outside the South. The prison society was essentially isolated, with restricted access to visitors, mail, and other communication. Prisoners' days were strictly structured, with rules enforced by the guards. A basic division stood between inmates and staff; rank was observed and discipline maintained. In the big house, few treatment programs existed; custody stood as the primary goal.

During the 1960s and early 1970s, when the rehabilitation model prevailed, many states built new prisons and converted others into "correctional institutions." Treatment programs administered by counselors and teachers became a major part of prison life, although the institutions continued to give priority to the custody goals of security, discipline, and order.

During the past 30 years, as the population of the United States has changed, so has the prison population. The number of African American and Hispanic inmates has greatly increased. More inmates come from urban areas, and more have been convicted of drug-related and violent offenses. Former street gangs, often organized along racial lines, today regroup inside prisons; such gangs have raised the level of violence in many institutions.

Now the focus of corrections has shifted to crime control, which emphasizes the importance of incarceration. Not only has the number of people in prison greatly increased, but many states have removed educational and recreational amenities from institutions.

Although today's correctional administrators seek to provide humane incarceration, they must struggle with limited resources and shortages of cell space. Thus, the modern prison faces many of the difficult problems that confront other parts of the criminal justice system: racial conflicts, legal issues, limited resources, and growing

One Man's Walk through Atlanta's Jungle

MICHAEL G. SANTOS

I was not expecting to receive the southern hospitality for which Atlanta is famous when the bus turned into the penitentiary's large, circular drive, but neither did I expect to see a dozen uniformed prison guards—all carrying machine guns—surround the bus when it stopped. A month in transit already had passed by the time we made it to the U.S. Penitentiary (USP) in Atlanta, the institution that would hold me (along with over two thousand other felons) until we were transferred to other prisons, we were released, or we were dead.

I left the jail in Tacoma, Washington, on the first of August, but I didn't see the huge gray walls that surround USP Atlanta until the first of September. That month was spent in a bus operated by the U.S. Marshal Service as it moved across the country, picking up federal prisoners in local jails and dropping them off at various Bureau of Prison facilities.

As I crossed the country, I listened to tales from numerous prisoners who sat beside me on the bus. There wasn't much to discuss except what was to come. Each of us was chained at the hands and feet. There were neither magazines to read nor music playing. Mostly people spoke about a riot that had taken place behind USP Atlanta's walls a few months earlier. A lot of the men had been to prison before, and Atlanta would be nothing new. Those prisoners only talked about reuniting with old friends, explaining prison routine, or sat like stone-cold statues waiting for what was to come. I'd never been confined before, so it was hard to tune out the stories that others were telling. While I was listening, though, I remember telling myself that I *would* survive this sentence. No matter what it took, I *would* survive.

I was in my early 20s, younger than perhaps every other prisoner on the bus. Pimples spotted my face as I began my term, but I was certain my black hair would be white by the time I finished. I had been sentenced to forty-five years by a U.S. district court judge in Tacoma on charges related to cocaine trafficking. I was expected to serve close to thirty years before release. It was hard then—just as it is hard now—to believe the sentence was real. The best thing I could do, I reasoned, was to stay to myself. I'd heard the same rumors that every suburban kid hears about prison. I was anxious about what was to come, but I was determined to make it out alive and with my mind intact. Now it was all to begin!

After the bus stopped, the guards began calling us off by last name and prison number. It is not easy to walk with a twelve-inch chain connected to each ankle, and wrists bound to a chain that runs around the waist, but when my name was called, I managed to wobble through the bus's aisle, hop down the steps, and then begin the long march up the stairs leading to the fortress. As I was moving to the prison's doors, I remember glancing over my shoulder, knowing it would be the last time I'd see the world from the outside of prison walls for a long time.

Once inside the institution, the guards began unlocking my chains. About fifty other prisoners arrived with me that day, so the guards had plenty of chains to unlock, but their work didn't stop there. They also had to squeeze us through the dehumanizing admissions machine. The machine begins with photographs, fingerprints, and interrogations. Then comes the worst part, the strip search, where each prisoner stands before a prison official, naked, and responds to the scream: "Lift up your arms in the air! Let me see the back of your hands! Run your fingers through your hair! Open your mouth! Stick your tongue out! Lift your balls! Turn around! Bend over! Spread your ass! Wider! Lift the bottom of your feet! Move on!" The strip search, I later learned, is a ritual Atlanta's officers inflict on prisoners every time they have contact with anyone from outside the walls, and sometimes randomly as prisoners walk down the corridor.

There was a lot of hatred behind those walls. Walking through the prison must be something like walking through a jungle, I imagined, not knowing whether others perceive you as predator or prey, knowing that you must remain always alert, watching every step, knowing that the wrong step may be the one that sucks you into the quicksand. The tension is ever present; I felt it wrapped all over, under and around me. I remember it bothering me that I didn't have enough hatred, because not hating in the jungle is a weakness. As the serpents slither, they spot that lack of hatred and salivate over a potential target.

Every prisoner despises confinement, but each must decide how he or she is going to do the time. Most of the men run in packs. They want the other prisoners either to run with them or run away from them. I wasn't interested in doing either. Instead of scheming on how I could become king of the jungle, I thought about ways that I could advance my release date. Earning academic credentials, keeping a clean record, and initiating projects that would benefit the communities both inside and outside of prison walls seemed the most promising goals for me to achieve. Yet working toward such goals was more dangerous than running with the pack; it didn't take me long to learn that prisoners running in herds will put forth more energy to cause others to lose than they will to win themselves. Prison is a twisted world, a menagerie.

I found that a highly structured schedule would not only move me closer to my goals, but also would limit potential conflicts inside the prison. There is a pecking order in every prison, and prisoners vying for attention don't want to see others who are cutting their own path. I saw that bullies generally look for weaker targets, so I began an exercise routine that would keep me physically strong. If I were strong, I figured, others would be more reluctant to try me. Through discipline, I found, I could develop physical strength. Yet I've never figured out how to develop the look of a killer, or the hatred off which that look feeds.

I don't know whether the strategies I have developed for doing time are right for everyone. But they are working for me. Still, I know that I may spend many more years in prison. The only fear I have—and as I'm working on my eighth year, it's still here—is that someone will try me and drag me into an altercation that may jeopardize my spotless disciplinary record. I've been successful in avoiding the ever-present quicksand on my walk through the jungle so far, but I know that on any given day, something may throw me off balance, or I may take a wrong step. And one wrong step in this jungle can drown me in quicksand, sucking me into the abysmal world of prison forever. That wrong step also could mean the loss of life, mine or someone else's.

In prison, more than anywhere else I know, understanding that some things are beyond an individual's sphere of control is vital. No matter how much preparation is made, the steel and concrete jungle is a dangerous place in which to live.

RESEARCHING THE INTERNET

Michael Santos is now incarcerated at the Federal Prison Camp in Lompoc, California. While in prison he has completed bachelor's and master's degrees. He is the author of *About Prison* (Belmont, CA: Wadsworth, 2004) and *Inside: Life Behind Bars in America* (New York: St. Martin's Press, 2006). You can contact him at his website, listed on the Cole/Smith Criminal Justice in America Companion Website: http://www.thomsonedu.com/criminaljustice/cole.

Source: Written for this book by Michael G. Santos. In 1987 he was sentenced to 45 years in prison for drug trafficking. Because of his impeccable disciplinary record, he looks forward to his release in 2013.

populations. Despite these challenges, can prisons still achieve their objectives? The answer to this question depends, in part, on how we define the goals of incarceration.

Goals of Incarceration

Citing the nature of inmates and the need to protect staff and the community, most people consider security the dominant purpose of a prison. High walls, barbed-wire fences, searches, checkpoints, and regular counts of inmates serve the security function: Few inmates escape. More importantly, the features set the tone for the daily operations. Prisons stand as impersonal, quasi-military places where strict discipline, minimal amenities, and restrictions on freedom serve to punish criminals.

Three models of incarceration have predominated since the early 1940s: the custodial, rehabilitation, and reintegration models. Each is associated with one style of institutional organization.

custodial model A model of incarceration that emphasizes security, discipline, and order.

1. The **custodial model** assumes that prisoners have been incarcerated for the purpose of incapacitation, deterrence, or retribution. It emphasizes security, discipline, and order in subordinating the prisoner to the authority of the warden. Discipline is strict, and most aspects of behavior are regulated. Having prevailed in corrections before World War II, this model dominates most maximum-security institutions today.

2. The *rehabilitation model,* developed during the 1950s, emphasizes treatment programs designed to reform the offender. According to this model, security and housekeeping activities are viewed primarily as preconditions for rehabilitative efforts. Because all aspects of the organization should center on rehabilitation, professional treatment specialists carry a higher status than do other employees. Since the rethinking of the rehabilitation goal in the 1970s, treatment programs still exist in most institutions, but few prisons conform to this model today.

reintegration model A model of a correctional institution that emphasizes maintaining the offender's ties to family and community as a method of reform, recognizing that the offender will be returning to society.

3. The **reintegration model** is linked to the structures and goals of community corrections. Recognizing that prisoners will be returning to society, this model emphasizes maintaining the offenders' ties to family and community as a method of reform. Prisons following this model gradually give inmates greater freedom and responsibility during their confinement, moving them to halfway houses or work release programs before giving them community supervision.

Although one can find correctional institutions that conform to each of these models, most prisons are mainly custodial. Nevertheless, treatment programs do exist, and because almost all inmates return to society at some point, even the most custodial institutions must prepare them for their reintegration. See "What Americans Think" for a look at how the public views the goals of incarceration.

Much is asked of prisons. As Charles Logan notes, "We ask them to correct the incorrigible, rehabilitate the wretched, deter the determined, restrain the dangerous, and punish the wicked" (Logan, 1993:19). Because prisons are expected to pursue many different and often incompatible goals, they are almost doomed to fail as institutions. Logan believes that the mission of prisons is confinement. He argues that imprisonment serves primarily to punish offenders fairly and justly through lengths of confinement proportionate to the seriousness of their crimes. He summarizes the mission of prison as follows: "to keep prisoners—to keep them in, keep them safe, keep them in line, keep them healthy, and keep them busy—and to do it with fairness, without undue suffering, and as efficiently as possible" (Logan, 1993:21). If the purpose of prisons is punishment through confinement under fair and just conditions, what are the implications of this purpose for correctional managers?

CHECKPOINT

Answer

2. What three models of prison have predominated since the 1940s? ——————▶ **2.** The custodial, rehabilitation, and reintegration models.

Prison Organization

The prison's physical features and function set it apart from almost every other institution and organization in modern society. It is a place where a group of employees manage a group of captives. Prisoners must live according to the rules of their keepers, and their movements remain sharply restricted. Unlike managers of other government agencies, prison managers

- Cannot select their clients
- Have little or no control over the release of their clients
- Must deal with clients who are there against their will
- Must rely on clients to do most of the work in the daily operation of the institution—work they are forced to do and for which they are not paid
- Must depend on the maintenance of satisfactory relationships between clients and staff

Given these unique characteristics, how should a prison be run? What rules should guide administrators? As the description just given indicates, wardens and other key personnel are asked to perform a difficult job, one that requires skilled and dedicated managers.

Most prisons are expected to fulfill goals related to keeping (custody), using (working), and serving (treating) inmates. Because individual staff members are not equipped to perform all functions, separate lines of command organize the groups of employees that carry out these different tasks. One group is charged with maintaining custody over the prisoners, another group supervises them in their work activities, and a third group attempts to treat them.

The custodial employees are the most numerous. They are normally organized along military lines, from warden to captain to officer, with accompanying pay differentials down the chain of command. The professional personnel associated with the using and serving functions, such as industry supervisors, clinicians, and teachers, are not part of the custodial structure and have little in common with its staff. All employees are responsible to the warden, but the treatment personnel and the civilian supervisors of the workshops have their own salary scales and titles. Figure 13.1 presents the formal organization of staff responsibilities in a typical prison.

The multiple goals and separate lines of command often cause ambiguity and conflict in the administration of prisons. For example, the goals imposed on prisons are often contradictory and unclear. Conflict between different groups of staff (custodial versus treatment, for instance), as well as between staff and inmates, presents significant challenges for administrators.

How, then, do prisons function? How do prisoners and staff try to meet their own goals? Although the U.S. prison may not conform to the ideal goals of corrections and the formal organization may bear little resemblance to the ongoing reality of the informal relations, order *is* kept and a routine *is* followed.

WHAT AMERICANS THINK

Question: "We'd like to ask you about several aspects of the prison system in the United States. For each one, please say whether you think prisons are doing an excellent, good, only fair or poor job."

Excellent	Good	Fair	Poor	No Opinion
18%	49%	23%	8%	2%

Maintaining high security to keep prisoners from escaping

| 2% | 12% | 34% | 48% | 4% |

Rehabilitating inmates so they are less likely to commit crimes in the future

| 5% | 25% | 37% | 26% | 7% |

Maintaining a safe environment for inmates in prison

Go to http://www.thomsonedu.com/criminaljustice/cole to compare your opinion on this issue with the opinions of other criminal justice students.

Source: Based on telephone interviews of a national adult sample conducted by the Gallup Organization, August 29–September 5, 2000. Data provided by the Roper Center for Public Opinion Research, University of Connecticut.

CHECKPOINT

Answer

3. How do prisons differ from other organizations in society? ——————▶ **3.** It is a place where a group of workers manages a group of captives.

FIGURE 13.1
Formal organization of a prison for adult felons
Prison staff are divided into various sections consistent with the goals of the organization. Custodial employees are the most numerous.

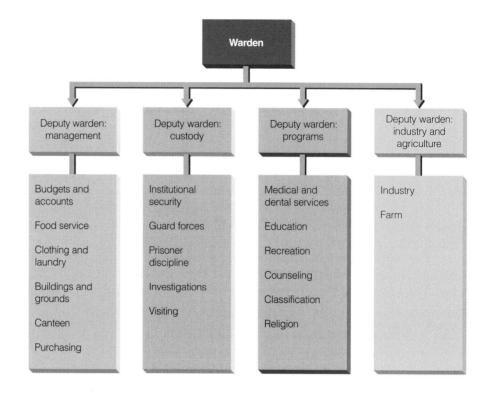

Governing a Society of Captives

Much of the public believes that prisons are operated in an authoritarian manner. In such a society, correctional officers give orders and inmates follow orders. Strictly enforced rules specify what the captives may and may not do. Staff members have the right to grant rewards and to inflict punishment. In theory, any inmate who does not follow the rules could be placed in solitary confinement. Because the officers have a monopoly on the legal means of enforcing rules and can call in the state police and the National Guard if necessary, many people believe that no question should arise as to how the prison is run.

But what quality of life should be maintained in prison? According to John DiIulio, a good prison is one that "provides as much order, amenity, and service as possible given the human and financial resources" (1987:12). *Order* is here defined as the absence of individual or group misconduct that threatens the safety of others—for example, assault, rapes, and other forms of violence or insult. *Amenities* include anything that enhances the comfort of the inmates, such as good food, clean cells, and recreational opportunities. *Service* includes programs designed to improve the lives of inmates: vocational training, remedial education, and work opportunities. Here, too, we expect inmates to be engaged in activities during incarceration that will make them better people and enhance their ability to lead crime-free lives upon release.

If we accept the premise that inmates, staff, and society need well-run prisons, what problems must correctional administrators address? The correctional literature points to four factors that make governing prisons different from administering other public institutions: (1) the defects of total power, (2) the limitation on the rewards and punishments officials can use, (3) the co-optation of correctional officers by inmates through exchange relationships, and (4) the strength of inmate leadership. After we review each of these research findings, we shall ask what kind of administrative systems and leadership styles ensure that prisons are safe and humane and serve inmates' needs.

THE DEFECTS OF TOTAL POWER

Imagine a prison society that comprises hostile and uncooperative inmates ruled by force. Prisoners can be legally isolated from one another, physically abused until they cooperate, and put under continuous surveillance. Although all of these things are possible, such practices would probably not be countenanced for long, because the public expects correctional institutions to be run humanely.

In reality, the power of officers is limited, because many prisoners have little to lose by misbehaving, and unarmed officers have only limited ability to force compliance with rules. Perhaps more important is the fact that forcing people to follow commands is an inefficient way to make them carry out complex tasks; efficiency further diminishes because of the ratio of inmates to officers (typically 40 to 1) and by the potential danger.

REWARDS AND PUNISHMENTS

Correctional officers often rely on rewards and punishments to gain cooperation. To maintain security and order among a large population in a confined space, they impose extensive rules of conduct. Instead of using force to ensure obedience, however, they reward compliance by granting privileges and punish rule violators by denying them.

To promote control, officers may follow any of several policies. One is to offer cooperative prisoners rewards such as choice job assignments, residence in the honor unit, and favorable parole reports. Inmates who do not break rules receive good time. Informers may also be rewarded, and administrators may ignore conflict among inmates on the assumption that it keeps prisoners from uniting against authorities.

Governing a society of captives is more complicated than the simplistic belief that officers give orders and inmates follow orders. Officer Perry Woods checks one of the dormitories at the Kilby Correctional Facility in Mount Meigs, Alabama. Woods is often outnumbered 386 to 1 as he attempts to keep order in this overcrowded prison. What tactics might he use to gain the cooperation of the inmates?

AP Photo/Jamie Martin

The system of rewards and punishments has some deficiencies. One is that the punishments for rule breaking do not represent a great departure from the prisoners' usual circumstances. Because inmates already lack many freedoms and valued goods—heterosexual relations, money, choice of clothing, and so on—not being allowed to attend, say, a recreational period does not carry much weight. Further, inmates receive authorized privileges at the start of the sentence and lose them if rules are broken, but officials authorize few rewards for progress or exceptional behavior. However, as an inmate approaches release, opportunities for furloughs, work release, or transfer to a halfway house can serve as incentives to obey rules.

GAINING COOPERATION: EXCHANGE RELATIONSHIPS

One way that correctional officers obtain inmate cooperation is by tolerating minor rule infractions in exchange for compliance with major aspects of the custodial regime. The correctional officer plays the key role in these exchange relationships. Officers and prisoners remain in close proximity both day and night—in the cell block, workshop, dining hall, recreation area, and so on. Although the formal rules require a social distance between officers and inmates, the physical closeness makes them aware that each relies on the other. The officers need the cooperation of the prisoners so that they will look good to their superiors, and the inmates count on the officers to relax the rules or occasionally look the other way. For example, officers in a Midwestern prison told researcher Stan Stojkovic that flexibility in rule enforcement especially mattered as it related to the ability of prisoners to cope with their environment. As one officer said, "Phone calls are really important to guys in this place. . . . You cut off their calls and they get pissed. So what I do is give them a little extra and they are good to me." Yet the officers also told Stojkovic that prison personnel would be crazy to intervene to stop illicit sex or drug use (Stojkovic, 1990:214).

Correctional officers must take care not to pay too high a price for the cooperation of their charges. Under pressure to work effectively with prisoners, officers may be blackmailed into doing illegitimate favors in return for cooperation. Officers who establish *sub-rosa,* or secret, relationships can be manipulated by prisoners into smuggling contraband or committing other illegal acts. At the end of the chapter, "A Question of Ethics" presents a dilemma that correctional officers frequently face.

INMATE LEADERSHIP

In the traditional prison of the big-house era, administrators enlisted the inmate leaders to help maintain order. Inmate leaders had been "tested" over time so that they were neither pushed around by other inmates nor distrusted as stool pigeons. Because the staff could rely on them, they served as the essential communications link between staff and inmates. Their ability to acquire inside information and gain access to higher officials brought inmate leaders the respect of other prisoners and special privileges from officials. In turn, they distributed these benefits to other prisoners, thus bolstering their own influence within the prison society.

Prisons seem to function more effectively now than they did in the recent past. Although prisons are more crowded, riots and reports of violence have declined. In many prisons, the inmate social system may have reorganized, so that correctional officers again can work through prisoners respected by fellow inmates. Yet, some observers contend that when wardens maintain order in this way, they enhance the positions of some prisoners at the expense of others. The leaders profit by receiving illicit privileges and favors, and they influence other prisoners by distributing benefits.

Further, descriptions of the contemporary maximum-security prison raise questions about administrators' ability to run institutions in this way. In most of today's institutions, prisoners are divided by race, ethnicity, age, and gang affiliation, so that no single leadership structure exists.

THE CHALLENGE OF GOVERNING PRISONS

The factors of total power, rewards and punishments, exchange relationships, and inmate leadership exist in every prison and must be managed. How they are managed greatly influences the quality of prison life. John DiIulio's research (1987) challenges the common assumption of many correctional administrators that "the cons run the joint." Instead, successful wardens have made their prisons function well by applying management principles within the context of their own style of leadership. Prisons can be governed, violence minimized, and services provided to the inmates if correctional executives and wardens exhibit leadership. Although governing prisons poses an extraordinary challenge, it can be and has been effectively accomplished.

ThomsonNOW
Improve your grade on the exam with Personalized Study! For reinforcement resources and a mastery check of Governing a Society of Captives, go to www.thomsonedu.com/thomsonnow.

CHECKPOINT

4. What four factors make governing prisons different from administering other public institutions? ➞

Answer

4. The defects of total power, a limited system of rewards and punishments, exchange relations between correctional officers and inmates, and the strength of inmate leadership.

Correctional Officers: The Linchpin of Management

A prison is simultaneously supposed to keep, use, and serve its inmates. The achievement of these goals depends heavily on the performance of its correctional officers. Their job is not easy. Not only do they work long and difficult hours with a hostile client population, but their superiors also expect them to do so with few resources or punishments at their disposal. Most of what they are expected to do must be accomplished by gaining and keeping the cooperation of the prisoners.

Much of the work of correctional officers involves searching and counting. Among such officers there is a saying, "We're all doing time together, except guards are doing it in eight-hour shifts."

THE OFFICER'S ROLE

Over the past 30 years, the correctional officer's role has changed greatly. No longer responsible merely for "guarding," the correctional officer now stands as a crucial professional who has the closest contact with the prisoners and performs a variety of tasks. Officers are expected to counsel, supervise, protect, and process the inmates under their care. But the officer also works as a member of a complex bureaucratic organization and is expected to deal with clients impersonally and to follow formal procedures. Fulfilling these contradictory role expectations is difficult in itself, and the physical closeness of the officer and inmate over long periods exacerbates this difficulty.

RECRUITMENT OF OFFICERS

Employment as a correctional officer is neither glamorous nor popular. The work is thought to be boring, the pay is low, and career advancement is minimal. Studies have shown that one of the primary incentives for becoming involved in correctional work is the security that civil service status provides. In addition, because most correctional facilities are located in rural areas, prison work often is better than other available employment. Because correctional officers are recruited locally, most of them are rural and white, in contrast to the majority of prisoners who come from urban areas and are often either African American or Hispanic (see Figure 13.2). Yet some correctional officers see their work as a way of helping people, often the people most in need in U.S. society.

Today, because they need more well-qualified correctional officers, most states recruit quality personnel. Salaries have been raised so that the average entry-level pay runs from $16,000 a year in some southern and rural states to over $30,000 in states such as Massachusetts and New Jersey (Editor, 2003). In addition to their salaries, most officers can earn overtime pay, supplementing base pay by up to 30 percent. However, low salaries in a competitive economy, the massive increase in the prison population, and a tougher, more violent class of prisoners have all probably contributed to a severe shortage of correctional officers in some states (Belluck, 2001). See "Careers in Criminal Justice" for a fuller description of the correctional officer's work at the state level.

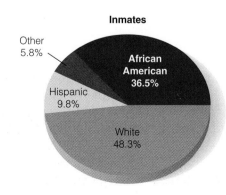

FIGURE 13.2
Racial/ethnic composition of correctional officers and inmates, adult systems, nationwide
Although the racial/ethnic composition of correctional officers does not equal that of the inmate population, the past quarter century has seen great strides toward equity.

Source: Camille Camp and George Camp, *Corrections Yearbook, 2002* (Middletown, CT: Criminal Justice Institute, 2003), 158. Includes both federal and state prisoners.

CAREERS IN CRIMINAL JUSTICE

Correctional Officer—State

NATURE OF THE WORK

There are 300,000 state correctional officers who work in the great array of reformatories, prisons, prison camps, and penitentiaries that compose American corrections. Regardless of the setting, they maintain order within the institution and enforce rules and regulations. To keep the facility secure, officers must often search inmates and their living quarters for contraband, settle disputes, enforce discipline, and communicate prisoner requests to higher levels. Officers may be assigned to housing units, perimeter patrols, or inmate work assignments. Correctional officers usually work an eight-hour day, five days a week, on rotating shifts.

REQUIRED QUALIFICATIONS

Correctional officers must be at least 18 to 21 years of age, be a U.S. citizen with no felony convictions, and have at least a high school education and some work experience. Most states require qualifying examinations, including personality screenings. Candidates must be in good health and meet fitness, eyesight, and hearing standards. The American Correctional Association sets training guidelines for recruits. Most states have training academies with instruction on legal restrictions, custody procedures, interpersonal relationships, use of firearms, and self-defense. After graduation from the academy, trainees typically receive several weeks or months of training in the job setting under the supervision of an experienced officer.

EARNINGS AND JOB OUTLOOK

As states have had to deal with the explosion of the prison population, the number of correctional officers has markedly increased during the past three decades. Although such expansion has slowed in recent years, in part because of budgetary constraints, turnover in the officer corps should provide future openings. With regional variation, the median annual earnings for state correctional officers are $34,000, with entry-level earnings of about $22,000.

MORE INFORMATION

See the American Correctional Association website, listed on the Cole/Smith Criminal Justice in America Companion Website: http://www.thomsonedu.com/criminaljustice/cole. You can also contact state departments of correction.

Correctional administrators have made special efforts to recruit women and minorities. Today approximately 30 percent of correctional officers belong to minority groups, and 23 percent are women (C. G. Camp, 2003:158). Female officers are no longer restricted to working with female offenders. For example, women represent 25 percent of Alabama's correctional officers, and 97 percent of these women work in male institutions (BJS, 1999a:81).

For most correctional workers, being a custodial officer is a dead-end job. Although officers who perform well may be promoted to higher ranks such as correctional counselor, few ever move into administrative positions. However, in some states and in the Federal Bureau of Prisons, people with college degrees can move up the career ladder to management positions.

USE OF FORCE

The use of force by correctional officers, as by the police, generates much controversy. Although corporal punishment and the excessive use of force are not permitted, correctional officers use force in many situations. They often confront inmates who challenge their authority or are attacking other inmates. Though unarmed and outnumbered, officers must maintain order and uphold institutional rules. Under these conditions they feel justified in using force.

All correctional agencies now have policies regarding the legitimate use of force. Officers violating these policies may face an inmate lawsuit and dismissal. There are five situations in which the use of force is legally acceptable:

1. *Self-defense*. If officers are threatened with physical attack, they may use a level of force that is reasonable to protect themselves from harm.

2. *Defense of third persons.* As in self-defense, an officer may use force to protect an inmate or another officer. Again, only reasonably necessary force may be used.

3. *Upholding prison rules.* If prisoners refuse to obey prison rules, officers may need to use force to maintain safety and security. For example, if an inmate refuses to return to his or her cell it may be necessary to use handcuffs and forcefully transfer the prisoner.

4. *Prevention of a crime.* Force may be used to stop a crime, such as theft or destruction of property, from being committed.

5. *Prevention of escapes.* Officers may use force to prevent escapes, because they threaten the well-being of society and order within correctional institutions. Although escape from a prison is a felony, officials may not shoot the fleeing inmate at will as in the past. Some agencies limit the use of deadly force to prisoners thought to be dangerous, whereas others require warning shots.

Correctional officers face challenges to self-control and professional decision making. Inmates often "push" officers in subtle ways such as moving slowly, or they use verbal abuse to provoke officers. Correctional officers are expected to run a "tight ship" and maintain order, often in situations where they are outnumbered and dealing with troubled people. In confrontational situations they must defuse hostility yet uphold the rules—a difficult task at best.

ThomsonNOW

Improve your grade on the exam with Personalized Study! For reinforcement resources and a mastery check of Correctional Officers: The Linchpin of Management, go to www.thomsonedu.com/thomsonnow.

CHECKPOINT

5. Name three of the five legally acceptable reasons for the use of force. ➡️

Answer

5. Self-defense, defense of third persons, upholding prison rules, prevention of crime, prevention of escapes.

Who Is in Prison?

The age, education, and criminal history of the inmate population influence how correctional institutions function. What are the characteristics of inmates in our nation's prisons? Do most offenders have long records of serious offenses, or are many of them first-time offenders who have committed minor crimes? Do some inmates have special needs that dictate their place in prison? These questions are crucial to understanding the work of wardens and correctional officers.

Data on the characteristics of prisoners are limited. The Bureau of Justice Statistics reports that a majority of prisoners are men, aged 25 to 44, and members of minority groups. Approximately 40 percent of state prisoners have not completed high school (see Figure 13.3).

Recidivists and those convicted of violent crimes make up an overwhelming portion of the prison population. Research shows that 44 percent of prisoners are rearrested within the first year after release. Within three years, approximately 25 percent of all released inmates will return to prison (BJS, 2002f:3). Most of today's prisoners have a history of persistent criminality. Four additional factors affect correctional operations: the increased number of elderly prisoners, the many prisoners with HIV/AIDS, the thousands of prisoners who are mentally ill, and the increase in long-term prisoners.

ELDERLY PRISONERS

Correctional officials have only recently become aware of the increasing number of inmates over age 55. In 2003 U.S. prisons held more than 60,000 offenders over 55 years old, an increase of 85 percent since 1995 (BJS, 2004d:8). One study projects a doubling of the elderly population in California prisons by 2020 (Auerhahn, 2002:373).

To some extent the prison population is growing older because it reflects the aging of the overall citizenry, but more so because sentencing practices have changed. Consecutive lengthy sentences for heinous crimes, long mandatory minimum sentences,

FIGURE 13.3
Sociodemographic and offense characteristics of state prison inmates
These data reflect the types of people found in state prisons. What do they indicate about the belief that many offenders do not "need" to be incarcerated?

Sources: Bureau of Justice Statistics [BJS], *Education and Correctional Population* (Washington, DC: U.S. Government Printing Office, January 2003), 2; BJS, *Bulletin*, July 2003, p. 10.

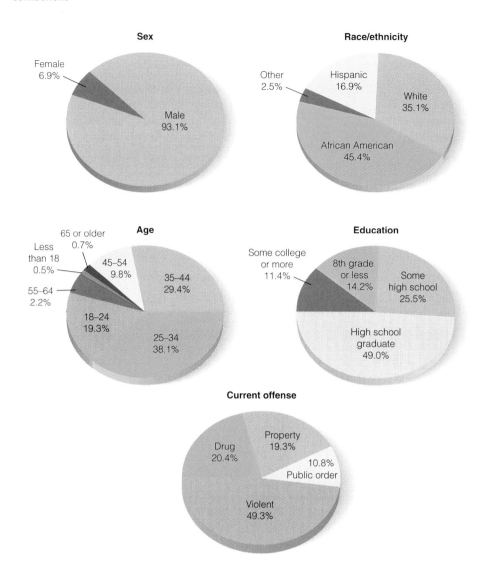

and life sentences without parole mean that more people who enter prison will spend most or all the rest of their lives behind bars.

Many security and medical needs of elderly prisoners differ from those of the average inmate. In many states, special sections of the institution have been designated for this older population so they will not have to mix with the younger, tougher inmates. Elderly prisoners are more likely to develop chronic illnesses such as heart disease, stroke, and cancer. The costs for maintaining an elderly inmate averages about $69,000 per year, triple the average cost for a younger inmate. Ironically, while in prison the offender will benefit from much better medical care and live a longer life than if he or she were discharged.

PRISONERS WITH HIV/AIDS

In the coming years, AIDS is expected to be the leading cause of death among men aged 35 and younger. With 57 percent of the adult inmate population under age 35, correctional officials must cope with the problem of HIV as well as AIDS and related health issues. In 2001 there were more than 24,000 HIV-positive inmates (1.9 percent of the prison population) and 6,200 offenders (0.5 percent) with AIDS. The number of HIV-positive inmates is undoubtedly low, because only 19 states conduct mandatory testing of inmates. Further, the rate of confirmed AIDS cases in state and federal prisons is much higher than in the total U.S. population. More than 250 inmates have been dying each year of AIDS, the second largest single cause of inmate death behind "illness" (BJS, 2005f:1). Because many inmates who are HIV infected remain undiagnosed, these numbers underestimate the scope of the problem.

To deal with offenders who have AIDS symptoms or who test positive for the virus, prison officials can develop policies on methods to prevent transmission of the disease, housing of those infected, and medical care for inmates with the full range of symptoms. However, administrators face a host of competing pressures as they decide what actions the institution should take. (See "Real-World Activity" at the end of the chapter.)

MENTALLY ILL PRISONERS

Mass closings of public hospitals for the mentally ill began in the 1960s. At the time, new antipsychotic drugs made treating patients in the community seem a more humane and less expensive alternative to long-term hospitalization. It soon became apparent, however, that community treatment works only if the drugs are taken and that clinics and halfway houses do not exist to assist the mentally ill. Mentally ill inmates tend to follow a revolving door from homelessness to incarceration and then back to the streets, with little treatment.

Currently far more mentally ill live in the nation's jails and prisons (191,000) than in state hospitals (62,000) (BJS, 2001b:3; *Ill-Equipped*, 2003:1). The incarceration rate of the mentally ill is four times that of the general population. The prison has become the largest psychiatric facility in some states. For example, New York City's Rikers Island houses three thousand mentally ill inmates (Winerip, 1999:42). In Los Angeles, 50 percent of those entering the county jail are identified as mentally ill (Butterfield, 1998b).

Correctional workers are usually unprepared to deal with the mentally ill. Cellblock officers, for instance, often do not know how to respond to disturbed inmates. Although most corrections systems have mental health units that segregate the ill, many inmates with psychiatric disorders live among other prisoners in the general population, where they are teased and otherwise exploited.

Nationally, 43 percent of state prisoners report mental illnesses. A schizophrenic prisoner sits among the general population in Nashville, Tennessee. Here, the mentally ill receive medication daily, but should they be placed in a separate mental health facility?

Photo by Stephen Ferry/Liaison/Getty

LONG-TERM PRISONERS

More prisoners in the United States serve longer sentences than do prisoners in other Western nations. A recent survey shows that nearly 310,000 prisoners are currently serving at least 20-year sentences. Of all inmates, about 10 percent are serving "natural life," which means there is no possibility that they will be paroled, a tripling since 1992. These long-term prisoners are often the same people who will become elderly offenders, with all their attendant problems.

Correctional administrators generally do not see long-term prisoners as control problems. Such prisoners face disciplinary infractions about half as often as do short-term inmates. They do, nonetheless, present challenges for administrators who must find ways of making long terms livable. Experts suggest that administrators follow three main principles: (1) maximize opportunities for the inmate to exercise choice in living circumstances, (2) create opportunities for meaningful living, and (3) help the inmate maintain contact with the outside world (Flanagan, 1995:256). Many long-term inmates will eventually be released after spending their prime years incarcerated. Will offenders be able to support themselves when they return to the community at age 50, 60, or 70?

The contemporary inmate population presents several challenges to correctional workers. Resources may not be available to provide rehabilitative programs for most inmates. Even if the resources exist, the goal of maintaining a safe and healthy

ThomsonNOW™
Improve your grade on the exam with Personalized Study! For reinforcement resources and a mastery check of Who Is in Prison, go to www.thomsonedu.com/thomsonnow.

environment may tax the staff's abilities. These difficulties are multiplied still further by AIDS and the increasing numbers of elderly and long-term prisoners. The contemporary corrections system must also deal with a different type of inmate, one who is more prone to violence, and with a prison society where racial tensions can soar. How well it meets this correctional challenge will greatly affect U.S. society.

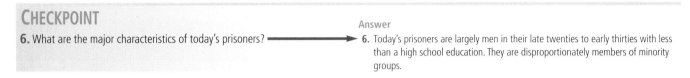

CHECKPOINT

6. What are the major characteristics of today's prisoners?

Answer

6. Today's prisoners are largely men in their late twenties to early thirties with less than a high school education. They are disproportionately members of minority groups.

The Convict World

Inmates of a maximum-security prison do not serve their time in isolation. Rather, prisoners form a society with its own traditions, norms, and leadership structure. Some choose to associate with only a few close friends; others form cliques along racial or "professional" lines. Still others serve as the politicians of the convict society; they attempt to represent convict interests and distribute valued goods in return for support. Just as the free world has a social culture, the "inside" has a prisoner subculture. Membership in a group provides mutual protection from theft and physical assault, the basis of wheeling and dealing activities, and a source of cultural identity (Irwin, 1980).

As any society does, the convict world has certain norms and values. Often described as the **inmate code,** these norms and values develop within the prison social system and help define the inmate's image of the model prisoner. As Robert Johnson notes, "The public culture of the prison has norms that dictate behavior 'on the yard' and in other public areas of the prison such as mess halls, gyms, and the larger program and work sites" (2002:100). Prison is an ultramasculine world. The culture breathes masculine toughness and insensitivity, impugning softness, and emphasizes the use of hostility and manipulation in one's relations with fellow inmates and staff. It makes caring and friendly behavior, especially with respect to the staff, look servile and silly (Sabo, Kupers, and London, 2001:7).

The code also emphasizes the solidarity of all inmates against the staff. For example, inmates should never inform on one another, pry into one another's affairs, "run off at the mouth," or put another inmate on the spot. They must be tough and trust neither the officers nor the principles for which the guards stand. Further, guards are "hacks" or "screws"; the officials are wrong and the prisoners are right.

Some sociologists believe that the code emerges within the institution as a way to lessen the pain of imprisonment (Sykes, 1958); others believe that it is part of the criminal subculture that prisoners bring with them (Irwin and Cressey, 1962). The inmate who follows the code enjoys a certain amount of admiration from other inmates as a "right guy" or a "real man." Those who break the code are labeled "rat" or "punk" and will probably spend their prison life at the bottom of the convict social structure, alienated from the rest of the population and targeted for abuse (Sykes, 1958:84).

A single, overriding inmate code probably does not exist in today's prisons. Instead, convict society has divided itself along racial lines (Carroll, 1974; Irwin, 1980). The level of adherence to the inmate code also differs among institutions, with greater modifications to local situations found in maximum-security prisons. Still, the core commandments described by Sykes almost 50 years ago remain.

inmate code The values and norms of the prison social system that define the inmates' idea of the model prisoner.

Contemporary prison society is divided along social, ethnic, and gang subgroups. There is no longer an inmate code to which all prisoners subscribe. As a correctional officer, how would you deal with these members of the white supremacist Aryan Brotherhood gang incarcerated in Ferguson Prison, Texas?

© Andrew Lichtenstein/Corbis

In a changing society that has no single code of behavior accepted by the entire population, the tasks of administrators become much more difficult. They must be aware of the different groups, recognize the norms and rules that members hold in each, and deal with the leaders of many cliques rather than with a few inmates who have risen to top positions in the inmate society.

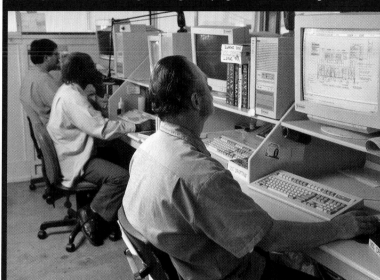

On entering prison, each inmate is confronted by the question "How am I going to do my time?" These gleaners at Deuel Vocational Institution in Tracy, California, are taking advantage of a program to learn drafting.

© Frank Pedrick/The Image Works

ADAPTIVE ROLES

On entering prison, a newcomer ("fish") is confronted by the question, "How am I going to do my time?" Some decide to withdraw and isolate. Others decide to become full participants in the convict social system. The choice, influenced by prisoners' values and experiences, helps determine strategies for survival and success.

Most male inmates use one of four basic role orientations to adapt to prison: "doing time," "gleaning," "jailing," and functioning as a "disorganized criminal" (Irwin, 1970:67).

Doing Time   Men "doing time" view their prison term as a brief, inevitable break in their criminal careers, a cost of doing business. They try to serve their terms with the least amount of suffering and the greatest amount of comfort. They avoid trouble by living by the inmate code, finding activities to fill their days, forming friendships with a few other convicts, and generally doing what they think is necessary to survive and to get out as soon as possible.

Gleaning   Inmates who are "gleaning" try to take advantage of prison programs to better themselves and improve their prospects for success after release. They use the resources at hand: libraries, correspondence courses, vocational training, schools. Some make a radical conversion away from a life of crime.

Jailing   "Jailing" is the choice of those who cut themselves off from the outside and try to construct a life within the prison. These are often "state-raised" youths who have spent much of their lives in institutional settings and who identify little with the values of free society. These are the inmates who seek power and influence in the prison society, often becoming key figures in the politics and economy of prison life.

Disorganized Criminal   A fourth role orientation—the "disorganized criminal"—describes inmates who cannot develop any of the other three orientations. They may be of low intelligence or afflicted with psychological or physical disabilities, and they find functioning in prison society difficult. They are "human putty" to be manipulated by others. These are also the inmates who cannot adjust to prison life and who develop emotional disorders, attempt suicide, and violate prison rules (K. Adams, 1992).

As these roles suggest, prisoners are not members of an undifferentiated mass. Individual convicts choose to play specific roles in prison society. The roles they choose reflect the physical and social environment they have experienced and also influence their relationships and interactions in prison. How do most prisoners serve their time? Although the media generally portray prisons as violent, chaotic places, research shows that most inmates want to get through their sentence without trouble. As journalist Pete Earley found in his study of Leavenworth, roughly 80 percent of inmates try to avoid trouble and do their time as easily as possible (1992:44).

THE PRISON ECONOMY

In prison, as outside, individuals want goods and services. Although the state feeds, clothes, and houses all prisoners, amenities remain sparse. Prisoners lack everything but bare necessities. Their diet and routine are monotonous and their recreational opportunities scarce. They experience a loss of identity (due to uniformity of treatment) and a lack of responsibility. In short, the prison is relatively unique in having been deliberately designed as "an island of poverty in the midst of a society of relative abundance" (V. Williams and Fish, 1974:40).

The number of items that a prisoner can purchase or receive through legitimate channels differs from state to state and from facility to facility. For example, prisoners in some state institutions may have televisions, civilian clothing, and hot plates. Not all prisoners enjoy these luxuries, nor do these amenities satisfy the lingering desire for a variety of other goods. Some state legislatures have decreed that amenities will be prohibited and that prisoners should return to Spartan living conditions.

Recognizing that prisoners do have some basic needs that are not met, prisons have a commissary or "store" from which inmates may, on a scheduled basis, purchase a limited number of items—toilet articles, tobacco, snacks, and other food products—in exchange for credits drawn on their "bank accounts." The size of a bank account depends on the amount of money deposited at the inmate's entrance, gifts sent by relatives, and amounts earned in the low-paying prison industries.

However, the peanut butter, soap, and cigarettes of the typical prison store in no way satisfy the consumer needs and desires of most prisoners. Consequently, an informal, underground economy acts as a major element in prison society. Many items taken for granted on the outside are inordinately valued on the inside. For example, talcum powder and deodorant become more important because of the limited bathing facilities. Goods and services that a prisoner would not have consumed at all outside prison can take on an exaggerated importance inside prison. For example, unable to get alcohol, offenders may seek a similar effect by sniffing glue. Or, to distinguish themselves from others, offenders may pay laundry workers to iron a shirt in a particular way, a modest version of conspicuous consumption.

Many studies point to the pervasiveness of this economy. The research shows that a market economy provides the goods (contraband) and services not available or not allowed by prison authorities. In many prisons inmates run private "stores." Food stolen from the kitchen for late-night snacks, homemade wine, and drugs such as marijuana are available.

As a principal feature of prison culture, this informal economy reinforces the norms and roles of the social system and influences the nature of interpersonal relationships. The extent of the underground economy and its ability to produce desired goods and services—food, drugs, alcohol, sex, preferred living conditions—vary according to the scope of official surveillance, the demands of the consumers, and the opportunities for entrepreneurship. Inmates' success as "hustlers" determines the luxuries and power they can enjoy.

Because real money is prohibited and a barter system is somewhat restrictive, the standard currency of the prison economy is cigarettes. They are not contraband, are easily transferable, have a stable and well-known standard of value, and come in "denominations" of singles, packs, and cartons. Furthermore they are in demand by smokers. Even those who do not smoke keep cigarettes for prison currency. As more prisons become "nonsmoking," cans of tuna fish, postage stamps, and soap have emerged as a new form of currency (Santos, 2004:120).

Certain positions in the prison society enhance opportunities for entrepreneurs. For example, inmates assigned to work in the kitchen, warehouse, and administrative office steal food, clothing, building materials, and even information to sell or trade to other prisoners. The goods may then become part of other market transactions. Thus, the exchange of a dozen eggs for two packs of cigarettes may result in the reselling of the eggs in the form of egg sandwiches made on a hot plate for five cigarettes each. Meanwhile, the kitchen worker who stole the eggs may use the income to get a laundry worker to starch his shirts, to get drugs from a hospital orderly, or to pay a "punk" for sexual favors.

Economic transactions can lead to violence when goods are stolen, debts are not paid, or agreements are violated. Disruptions of the economy can occur when officials conduct periodic "lockdowns" and inspections. Confiscation of contraband can result in temporary shortages and price readjustments, but gradually business returns. The prison economy, like that of the outside world, allocates goods and services, rewards and sanctions, and it is closely linked to the society it serves.

CHECKPOINT

Answers

7. Why is it unlikely that a single, overriding inmate code exists in today's prisons? ➡ **7.** The prison society is fragmented by racial and ethnic divisions.

8. What are the four role orientations found in adult male prisons? ➡ **8.** Doing time, gleaning, jailing, and functioning as a disorganized criminal.

9. Why does an underground economy exist in prison? ➡ **9.** To provide goods and services not available through regular channels.

Women in Prison

Most studies of prisons have focused on institutions for men. How do prisons for women differ, and what special problems do female inmates face?

Women constitute only 6.9 percent (about 101,000) of the entire U.S. prison population. However, the growth rate in the number of incarcerated women has exceeded that of men since 1981. In fact, since 1995 the population of men in state and federal prisons increased 29 percent, whereas that of women increased 48 percent. This growth is particularly acute in the federal system, which has absorbed an additional six thousand female inmates during the past 20 years, because of the war on drugs (BJS, 2004b:5). The increased number of women in prison has significantly affected the delivery of programs, housing conditions, medical care, staffing, and security.

Life in the nation's 98 confinement facilities for women and 93 coed facilities both differ from and resemble life in institutions for men alone. Women's prisons are smaller, with looser security and less structured relationships; the underground economy is not as well developed; and female prisoners seem less committed to the inmate code. Women also serve shorter sentences than do men, so their prison society is more fluid as new members join and others leave.

Many women's prisons have the outward appearance of a college campus, often seen as a group of "cottages" around a central administration/dining/program building. Generally these facilities lack the high walls, guard towers, and cyclone fences found at most prisons for men. In recent years, however, the trend has been to upgrade security for women's prisons by adding barbed wire, higher fences, and other devices to prevent escapes.

The characteristics of correctional facilities for women also include geographic remoteness and inmate heterogeneity. Few states operate more than one institution for women, so inmates generally live far from children, families, friends, and attorneys. In many institutions the small numbers of inmates limit the extent to which the needs of individual offenders can be recognized and treated. Housing classifications are often so broad that dangerous or mentally ill inmates are mixed with women who have committed minor offenses and have no psychological problems. Similarly, available rehabilitative programs are often not used to their full extent, because correctional departments fail to recognize women's problems and needs.

In most respects, we can see incarcerated women, like male prisoners, as disadvantaged losers in this complex and competitive society. However the two groups differ with regard to types of offenses and length of sentences, patterns of drug use, and criminal history. Thirty-two percent of female prisoners are sentenced for violent offenses, compared with 49 percent of male prisoners, and 30 percent for drug-related offenses, versus 20 percent of the men (BJS, 2003a:10). Overall, women receive shorter maximum sentences than do men. Half of the women have a maximum

FIGURE 13.4
Characteristics of female inmates in state prisons

Like their male counterparts, female prisoners typically are young, have little education, are members of minority groups, and are incarcerated for a serious offense.

Sources: Bureau of Justice Statistics [BJS], *Special Report,* December 1999; BJS, *Bulletin,* July 2003, p. 10.

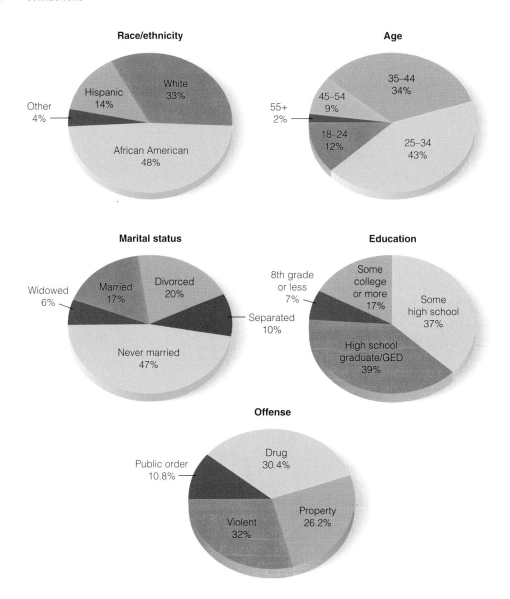

Race/ethnicity
White 33%
Hispanic 14%
Other 4%
African American 48%

Age
35–44 34%
45–54 9%
55+ 2%
18–24 12%
25–34 43%

Marital status
Divorced 20%
Married 17%
Widowed 6%
Separated 10%
Never married 47%

Education
8th grade or less 7%
Some college or more 17%
Some high school 37%
High school graduate/GED 39%

Offense
Drug 30.4%
Public order 10.8%
Property 26.2%
Violent 32%

sentence of 5 years or less, whereas half of the men have a sentence of 10 years or less (BJS, 2000a). Figure 13.4 summarizes some characteristics of female prisoners.

THE SUBCULTURE OF WOMEN'S PRISONS

Studies of the subculture of women's prisons have been less extensive than those of male convict society. Further, just as few ethnographic studies of men's prisons have taken place during the past two decades, very few of women's prisons exist.

Much early investigation of women's prisons focused on types of social relationships among female offenders. As in all types of penal institutions, same-sex relationships were found, but unlike in male prisons, such relationships among women appeared more voluntary than coerced. Perhaps more importantly, scholars reported that female inmates tended to form pseudofamilies in which they adopted various roles—father, mother, daughter, sister—and interacted as a unit, rather than identifying with the larger prisoner subculture (Girshick, 1999; Propper, 1982). Esther Hefferman views these "play" families as a "direct, conscious substitution for the family relationships broken by imprisonment, or . . . the development of roles that perhaps were not fulfilled in the actual home environment" (1972:41–42). She also notes the economic aspect of the play families and the extent to which they are formed to provide for their members. Such cooperative relationships help relieve the tensions of prison life, assist the socialization of new inmates, and permit individuals to act according to clearly defined roles and rules.

In discussing the available research on women in prison, we need to consider the most recent shifts in prison life. Just as the subculture of male prisons has changed since the pioneering research of the 1950s, the climate of female prisons has undoubtedly changed. Kimberly Greer (2000) found support for the idea that, compared with male prisons, prisons for women are less violent, involve less gang activity, and lack racial tension; however, the respondents indicated that their interpersonal relationships may be less stable and less familial than in the past. They reported higher levels of mistrust among women and greater economic manipulation.

In one of the few recent studies of prison culture, Barbara Owen (1998) found that the inmates at the Central California Women's Facility developed various styles of doing time. She observed that the vast majority wanted to avoid "the mix"—"behavior that can bring trouble and conflict with staff and other prisoners." A primary feature of "the mix" is anything for which one can lose "good time" or can result in being sent to administrative segregation. Being in "the mix" was related to "'homo-secting,' involvement in drugs, fights, and 'being messy,' that is being involved in conflict and trouble." Owen found most women want to do their time and go home, but some "are more at home in prison and do not seem to care if they 'lost time.'" (Owen, 1998:179).

MALE VERSUS FEMALE SUBCULTURES

Comparisons of male and female prisons are complicated by the nature of the research: Most studies have been conducted in single-sex institutions, and most follow theories and concepts first developed in male prisons. However, the following facts may explain the differences in subculture:

- Nearly half of male inmates but only a third of female inmates are serving time for violent offenses.

- There is less violence in prisons for women than in prisons for men.

- Women show greater responsiveness to prison programs.

- Men's prison populations are divided by security level, but most women serve time in facilities where the entire population is mixed.

- Men tend to segregate themselves by race; this is less true of women.

- Men rarely become intimate with their keepers, but many women share their lives with officers.

A major difference between the two types of prisons relates to interpersonal relationships. Male prisoners act for themselves and are evaluated by others according to how they adhere to subcultural norms. As James Fox (1982) notes in his comparative study of one women's prison and four men's prisons, men believe they must demonstrate physical strength and consciously avoid any mannerisms that might imply homosexuality. To gain recognition and status within the convict community, the male prisoner must strictly adhere to these values. Men form cliques, but not the family networks found in prisons for women. Male norms stress autonomy, self-sufficiency, and the ability to cope with one's own problems, and men are expected to "do their own time." Fox found little sharing in the men's prisons.

Women, on the other hand, place less emphasis on achieving status or recognition within the prisoner community. Fox writes that women are also less likely "to impose severe restrictions on the sexual (or emotional) conduct of other members" (1982:100). As noted previously, in prisons for women, close ties seem to exist among small groups akin to extended families. These family groups provide emotional support and share resources.

The differences between male and female prisoner subcultures have been ascribed to the nurturing, maternal qualities of women. Some critics charge that such an analysis stereotypes female behavior and imputes a biological basis to personality where none exists. Of importance as well is the issue of inmate–inmate violence in male and female institutions. The few data that exist indicate that women are less likely to engage in violent acts against other inmates than are men (Kruttschnitt and Krmpotich, 1990:371). In any case, it will be interesting to see whether such gender-specific differences continue

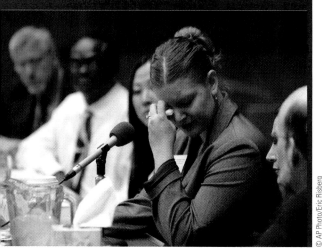

As the number of women prisoners has increased, cases of sexual misconduct by male correctional officers have escalated. At a public hearing before the National Prison Rape Elimination Commission, Hope Hernandez testifies how she was raped by a correctional officer while she was confined in a private jail. Sitting at the table are other rape victims. The commission was formed to set new policies to help prevent prison sexual assaults.

© AP Photo/Eric Risberg

to be found among prisoners as the feminist perspective gains influence among researchers and as society moves toward viewing women and men as equals.

ISSUES IN THE INCARCERATION OF WOMEN

As noted, the number of incarcerated women has greatly increased over the past ten years. Under pressures for equal opportunity, states seem to believe that they should run women's prisons as they do prisons for men, with the same policies and procedures. Joycelyn Pollock (1998) believes that when prisons emphasize parity, then use a male standard, women lose. She says that with the increased numbers of women in prison and more equality in programming, more security measures and more formalist approaches to supervision have also arisen.

Although correctional departments have been playing "catch up" to meet the challenges of the influx of women offenders, sexual misconduct by officers persists, along with women prisoners' demands for education and training, medical services, and methods for dealing with the problems of mothers and their children. We next examine each of these issues and the policy implications they pose for the future.

Sexual Misconduct   As the number of female prisoners has increased, cases of sexual misconduct by male correctional officers have escalated. After an investigation of sexual misconduct of officers in the women's prisons of five states—California, Georgia, Illinois, Michigan and New York—Human Rights Watch reported that male officers had raped, sexually assaulted, and abused female inmates. Guards had also "used their near total authority to provide or deny goods and privileges to female prisoners to compel them to have sex or, in other cases, to reward them for having done so" (New York Times, December 27, 1996, p. A18).

To deal with the problem of sexual abuse in prison, all but eight states have enacted statutes prohibiting sexual misconduct with correctional clients. Whereas some of these laws focus on correctional officers, several states are revising their statutes to include anyone who supervises offenders (*Criminal Justice Research Reports*, 2001). Beyond the new laws, corrections faces a great need for the implementation of effective sexual harassment policies, the training of officers, and tougher screening of recruits.

Educational and Vocational Training Programs   A major criticism of women's prisons is that they lack the variety of vocational and educational programs available in male institutions. Critics also charge that existing programs tend to conform to sexual stereotypes of "female" occupations—cosmetology, food service, housekeeping, sewing. Such training does not correspond to the wider employment opportunities available to women in today's world. Both men's and women's facilities usually offer educational programs so inmates can become literate and earn general equivalency diplomas (GEDs). Such programs matter a great deal, considering that upon release most women must support themselves, and many must support their children as well.

Merry Morash and her colleagues found that gender stereotypes shape vocational programs (Morash, Haarr, and Rucker, 1994). The American Correctional Association (1990) reports that the few work assignments available for incarcerated women do teach marketable job skills.

Medical Services   Women's prisons lack proper medical services. Yet, because of their socioeconomic status and limited access to preventive medical care, women usually have more serious health problems than do men. Compared with men, they have a higher incidence of asthma, drug abuse, diabetes, and heart disorders, and many women also have gynecological problems (Bershard, 1985; Yang, 1990). Although a higher percentage of women than men report receiving medical services in prison, women's institutions are less likely than men's to have a full-time medical staff or hospital facilities.

Saying that corrections must "defuse the time bomb," Leslie Acoca (1998) argues that failure to provide female inmates with basic preventive and medical treatments such as immunizations, breast cancer screenings, and management of chronic diseases "is resulting in the development of more serious health problems that are exponentially more expensive to treat." She says that poor medical care for the incarcerated merely shifts costs to overburdened community health care systems after release.

Mothers and Their Children   Of greatest concern to incarcerated women is the fate of their children. Over 65 percent of women inmates are mothers with, on average, two dependent children. Thus, on any given day, 167,000 American children—two-thirds of whom are under ten years old—have mothers who are in jail or prison. Roughly half of these children do not see their mothers the entire time they are in prison (BJS, 2000e:1).

Because about 65 percent of incarcerated mothers were single caretakers of minor children before they entered prison, they do not have partners to take care of their children. Relatives care for nearly 78 percent of these children, whereas 10 percent are in state-funded foster care (Acoca, 1997).

Imprisoned mothers have difficulty maintaining contact with their children. Because most states have only one or two prisons for women, mothers may be incarcerated 150 miles or more away. This makes transportation difficult, visits short and infrequent, and phone calls uncertain and irregular. When the children do visit the prison, they face strange and intimidating surroundings. In some institutions, children must conform to the rules governing adult visitations: strict time limits and no physical contact.

Other correctional facilities, however, seek ways to help mothers maintain links to their children. For example, the Dwight Correctional Center in Illinois schedules weekend retreats, similar to camping trips, for women and their children. In some states, children can meet with their mothers at almost any time, for extended periods, and in playrooms or nurseries where contact is possible. Some states transport children to visit their mothers; some institutions even let children stay overnight with their mothers. A few prisons have family visitation programs that let the inmate, her legal husband, and her children be together, often in a mobile home or apartment, for up to 72 hours.

The future of women's correctional institutions is hard to predict. More women are being sent to prison now, and more have committed the violent crimes and drug offenses that used to be more typical of male offenders. Will these changes affect the adaptive roles and social relationships that differentiate women's prisons from men's? Will women's prisons need to become more security conscious and to enforce rules through more formal relationships between inmates and staff? These important issues need further study.

ThomsonNOW
Improve your grade on the exam with Personalized Study! For reinforcement resources and a mastery check of Women in Prison, go to www.thomsonedu.com/thomsonnow.

CHECKPOINT

Answers

10. What accounts for the neglect of facilities and programs in women's prisons?

→ **10.** The small number of female inmates compared with the number of male inmates.

11. How do the social relationships among female prisoners differ from those among their male counterparts?

→ **11.** Men are more individualistic and their norms stress autonomy, self-sufficiency, and the ability to cope with one's own problems. Women are more sharing with one another.

12. What problems do female prisoners face in maintaining contact with their children?

→ **12.** The distance of prisons from homes, intermittent telephone privileges, and unnatural visiting environment.

classification The process of assigning an inmate to a category specifying his or her needs for security, treatment, education, work assignment, and readiness for release.

Prison Programs

Modern correctional institutions differ from those of the past in the number and variety of programs provided for inmates. Early penitentiaries included prison industries; educational, vocational, and treatment programs were added when rehabilitation goals became prevalent. During the last 35 years, as the public called for harsher punishment of criminals, legislators have gutted prison educational and treatment programs as "frills" that only "coddled" inmates. In addition, the great increase in the number of prisoners has limited access to those programs that are still available. Yet, a majority of respondents to one survey said that prisons do a poor or very poor job of rehabilitating prisoners (see "What Americans Think").

Administrators argue that programs help them deal with the problem of time on the prisoners' hands. They know that the more programs prisons offer, the less likely that inmate idleness will turn into hostility; the less cell time, the fewer tensions. Evidence suggests that inmate education and jobs may positively affect the running of prisons, as well as reducing recidivism.

CLASSIFICATION OF PRISONERS

Determining the appropriate program for an individual prisoner usually involves a process called **classification**. A committee—often comprising the heads of the security, treatment, education, and industry departments—evaluates the inmate's security level, treatment needs, work assignment, and eventually readiness for release.

Classification decisions are often based on the institution's needs rather than on those of the inmates. For example, inmates from the city may be assigned to farm work because that is where they are needed. Further, certain programs may remain limited, even though the demand for them is great. Thus, inmates may find that the few places in, for example, a computer course are filled and that there is a long waiting list. Prisoners often become angered and frustrated by the classification process and the limited availability of programs. Although release on parole can depend on a good record of participation in these programs, entrance for some inmates is blocked.

EDUCATIONAL PROGRAMS

Offenders constitute one of the most undereducated groups in the U.S. population. In many systems, all inmates who have not completed eighth grade are assigned full-time to prison school. Many programs provide remedial help in reading, English, and math. They also permit prisoners to earn their GED. Some institutions offer courses in cooperation with a college or university, although funding for such programs has come under attack. The Comprehensive Crime Control Act of 1994 bans federal funding to prisoners for postsecondary education (Buruma, I. 2005). Studies have shown that prisoners assigned to education programs tend to avoid committing crimes after release (Andrews and Bonta, 1994). However, it remains unclear whether education helps to rehabilitate these offenders or whether the types of prisoners ("gleaners") assigned to education programs tend to be those motivated to avoid further crimes.

VOCATIONAL EDUCATION

Vocational education programs attempt to teach offenders a marketable job skill. Unfortunately, too many programs train inmates for trades that already have an adequate labor supply or in which new methods have made the skills taught obsolete.

As the saying goes, "idle hands are the Devil's playground." Experienced administrators know that the more programs offered, the less likely inmates' boredom will translate into "mischief making."

AP Photo/Damian Dovarganes

Offenders often lack the attitudes necessary to obtain and keep a job—punctuality, accountability, deference to supervisors, cordiality to coworkers. Therefore, most prisoners need to learn not only a skill but also how to act in the work world.

Yet another problem is perhaps the toughest of all. In one state or another, the law bars ex-felons from practicing certain occupations, including nurse, beautician, barber, real estate salesperson, chauffeur, worker where alcoholic beverages are sold, cashier, and insurance salesperson. Unfortunately, some prison vocational programs actually train inmates for jobs they can never hold.

PRISON INDUSTRIES

Prison industries, which trace their roots to the early workshops of New York's Auburn Penitentiary, are intended to teach work habits and skills that will assist prisoners' reentry into the outside workforce. In practice, institutions rely on prison labor to provide basic food, maintenance, clerical, and other services. In addition, many prisons contain manufacturing facilities that produce goods, such as office furniture and clothing, used in correctional and other state institutions.

The prison industries system carries a checkered career. During the nineteenth century, factories were established in many prisons, and inmates manufactured items that were sold on the open market. With the rise of the labor movement, however, state legislatures and Congress passed laws restricting the sale of prison-made goods so that they would not compete with those made by free workers. In 1979 Congress lifted restrictions on the interstate sale of prison-made products and urged correctional administrators to explore with the private sector possible improvements for prison industry programs. Industrial programs would relieve idleness, allow inmates to earn wages that they could save until release, and reduce the costs of incarceration. The Federal Bureau of Prisons and some states have developed industries, but generally their products are not sold on the free market and the percentage of prisoners employed varies greatly. For example, in North Carolina and Utah more than 20 percent of prisoners work in prison industries, whereas in most states 5 percent or less do (C. G. Camp and Camp, 1999:96). Nonetheless, in 2002 about 3.5 percent of the prisoners in the United States produced goods and services worth $1.5 billion (Swarz, J. 2004).

Although the idea of employing inmates sounds attractive, the inefficiencies of prison work may offset its economic value. Turnover is great because many inmates are transferred among several institutions or released over a two-year period. Many prisoners have little education and lack steady work habits, making it difficult for them to perform many of the tasks of modern production. An additional cost to efficiency is the need to stop production periodically to count heads and to check that tools and materials have not been stolen.

REHABILITATIVE PROGRAMS

Rehabilitative programs seek to treat the personal defects thought to have brought about the inmate's criminality. Most people agree that rehabilitating offenders is a desirable goal, but they disagree a great deal on the amount of emphasis that these programs should receive.

Reports in the 1970s cast doubt on the ability of treatment programs to stem recidivism. They also questioned the ethics of requiring inmates to participate in rehabilitative programs in exchange for the promise of parole (Martinson, 1974). Supporters of treatment programs argue that certain programs, if properly run, work for certain offenders (Andrews et al., 1990; Palmer, 1992). A national survey found support for rehabilitative programs (see "What Americans Think").

Most corrections systems still offer a range of psychological, behavioral, and social services programs. How much they are used seems to vary according to the goals of the institution and the attitudes of the administrators. Nationally, little money is spent on treatment services, and these programs reach only 5 percent of the inmate population. Although rehabilitative programs remain a part of correctional institutions, then, their emphasis has diminished. Incarceration's current goal of humane custody implies no effort to change inmates.

WHAT AMERICANS THINK

Public support for rehabilitative programs (selective responses)

1. It is a good idea to provide treatment for offenders who are in prison?

Agree — 92%

5. Rehabilitative programs should be available even for offenders who have been involved in a lot of crime in their lives.

Agree — 69%

6. The best way to rehabilitate offenders is to give them an education.

Agree — 71%

7. The best way to rehabilitate offenders is to teach them a skill that they can use to get a job when they are released from prison.

Agree — 89%

9. It is important to try to rehabilitate adults who have committed crime and are now in the correctional system.

Agree — 88%

Go to http://www.thomsonedu.com/criminaljustice/cole to compare your opinion on this issue with the opinions of other criminal justice students.

Source: Francis T. Cullen, Jennifer A. Pealer, Bonnie S. Fisher, Brandon K. Applegate, and Shannon A. Santana, "Public Support for Correctional Rehabilitation in America: Change and Consistency?" in *Changing Attitudes to Punishment*, ed. Julian V. Roberts and Mike Hough (Cullompton, Devon, UK: Willan, 2002), 137.

MEDICAL SERVICES

Most prisons offer medical services through a full-time staff of nurses, augmented by part-time physicians under contract to the corrections system. Nurses take care of routine health care and dispense medicines from a secure in-prison pharmacy; regularly scheduled visits to the prison by doctors can enable prisoners to obtain checkups and diagnoses. For cases needing a specialist, surgery, or emergency medical assistance, prisoners must be transported to local hospitals, under close supervision by correctional staff. The aim is for the prison system to provide a range of medical assistance to meet the various needs of the population as a whole.

Although inmates' medical needs often echo those of the general population, prisoners pose two special needs, one due to poverty and the other to aging. Because prisoners as a group are very poor, they often bring to the prison years of neglect of their general health. Other consequences of being poor, such as an inadequate diet and poor hygiene, also affect the general health of the prison population.

CHECKPOINT

Answers

13. Why are prison programs important from the standpoint of prison administrators?

13. Programs keep prisoners busy and reduce security problems.

14. Why have legislators and the general public been so critical of educational and rehabilitative programs in prisons?

14. They are thought to "coddle" prisoners and give them resources not available to free citizens.

Violence in Prison

Prisons provide a perfect recipe for violence. They confine in cramped quarters a thousand men, some with histories of violent behavior. While incarcerated, these men are not allowed contact with women and live under highly restrictive conditions. Sometimes these conditions spark collective violence, as in the riots at Attica, New York (1971), Santa Fe, New Mexico (1980), Atlanta, Georgia (1987), and Lucasville, Ohio (1993).

Although prison riots are widely reported in the news, few people have witnessed the level of everyday interpersonal violence in U.S. prisons. For example, each year about 34,000 inmates are physically attacked by other inmates. In 2002, 48 assault victims died. An additional 168 prisoners committed suicide (BJS, 2005f:1). Great numbers of prisoners live in a state of constant uneasiness, always on the lookout for people who might demand sex, steal their few possessions, or otherwise hurt them. Some researchers suggest that the level of violence varies by offender age, institutional security designation, and administrative effectiveness (Maitland and Sluder, 1998:55).

ASSAULTIVE BEHAVIOR AND INMATE CHARACTERISTICS

For the person entering prison for the first time, the anxiety level and fear of violence run especially high. Gary, an inmate at Leavenworth, told Pete Earley, "Every convict has three choices, but only three. He can fight (kill someone), he can hit the fence (escape), or he can fuck (submit)" (1992:55).

Violent behavior in prisons is related to the characteristics of the inmates. Christopher Innes and Vicki Verdeyen suggest that violent offenders can be divided into those who (1) have learned to be violent, (2) cannot regulate their violence,

Preemptive strikes to rid prisons of drugs and weapons are one way to reduce violence. Here correctional officers prepare to enter the Maryland House of Corrections, a maximum security prison, to search every inmate and every cell.

AP Photo/Greg Nelson

because of mental disabilities, and (3) are violent and have severe personality disorders (1997:1). Three characteristics underlie these behavioral factors: age, attitudes, and race.

Age   Young men aged 16–24, both inside and outside prison, are more prone to violence than are their elders (L. M. S. Simon, 1993). Not surprisingly, 96 percent of adult prisoners are men, with an average age of 27 at time of admission.

Besides having greater physical strength than their elders, young men lack the commitments to career and family that can restrict antisocial behavior. In addition, many have difficulty defining their position in society. Thus, they interpret many things as challenges to their status.

Machismo, the concept of male honor and the sacredness of one's reputation as a man, requires physical retaliation against those who insult one's honor. Some inmates adopt a preventive strategy of trying to impress others with their bravado, which may result in counterchallenges and violence. The potential for violence among such prisoners is clear.

Attitudes   One sociological theory of crime suggests that a subculture of violence exists among certain socioeconomic, racial, and ethnic groups. In this subculture, found in the lower class and in its value system, violence is "tolerable, expected, or required" (Wolfgang and Ferracuti, 1967:263). Arguments are settled and decisions are made by the fist rather than by verbal persuasion. Many inmates bring these attitudes into prison with them.

Race   Race has become a major divisive factor in today's prisons. Racist attitudes, common in the larger society, have become part of the "convict code," or implicit rules of life. Forced association—having to live with people one would not likely associate with on the outside—exaggerates and amplifies racial conflict. Violence against members of another race may be how some inmates deal with the frustrations of their lives. The presence of gangs organized along racial lines contributes to violence in prison.

PRISONER–PRISONER VIOLENCE

Although prison folklore may attribute violence to brutal guards, most prison violence occurs between inmates. The Bureau of Justice Statistics reports that the rate of prisoner–prisoner assaults is 28 attacks per 1,000 inmates (BJS, 2003b:10). As Hans Toch has observed, the climate of violence in prisons has no free-world counterpart: "Inmates are terrorized by other inmates, and spend years in fear of harm. Some inmates request protective custody segregation, others lock themselves in, and some are hermits by choice" (1976:47–48).

Prison Gangs   Racial or ethnic gangs (also referred to as "security threat groups") are now linked to acts of violence in most prison systems. Gangs make it difficult for wardens to maintain control. By continuing their street wars inside prison, gangs make some prisons more dangerous than any American neighborhoods. Gangs are organized primarily to control an institution's drug, gambling, loan-sharking, prostitution, extortion, and debt-collection rackets. In addition, gangs protect their members from other gangs and instill a sense of macho camaraderie (Hunt et al., 1993:398).

Prison gangs exist in the institutions of most states and the federal system. In Illinois as much as 60 percent of the population belongs to gangs (Hallinan, 2001:95). The Florida Department of Corrections has identified 240 street gangs operating in their prisons (Davitz, 1998). A study by the American Correctional Association found more than 46,000 gang members in the federal system and in the prisons of at least 35 states (1994:21).

Many facilities segregate rival gangs by housing them in separate units of the prison or moving members to other facilities (Knox, 2000). Administrators have also set up intelligence units to gather information on gangs, particularly about illegal acts both in and outside of prison. In some prisons, however, these policies created a power vacuum within the convict society that newer groups with new codes of behavior soon filled (Hunt et al., 1993).

Protective Custody   For many victims of prison violence, protective custody offers the only way to escape further abuse. About 5,000 state prisoners are in protective custody (C. G. Camp and Camp, 2001:26). Life is not pleasant for these inmates. Often they are let out of their cells only briefly to exercise and shower (McGee, Warner, and Harlow, 1998). Inmates who ask to "lock up" have little chance of returning to the general prison population without being viewed as a weakling—a snitch or a punk—to be preyed on. Even when they are transferred to another institution, their reputations follow them through the grapevine.

PRISONER–OFFICER VIOLENCE

The mass media have focused on riots in which guards are taken hostage, injured, and killed. However, violence against officers typically occurs in specific situations and against certain individuals. Yearly, inmates assault more than 18,000 staff members (BJS, 2003b:10). Correctional officers do not carry weapons within the institution, because a prisoner might seize them. However, prisoners do manage to obtain lethal weapons and can use the element of surprise to injure an officer. In the course of a workaday an officer may encounter situations that require the use of physical force against an inmate—for instance, breaking up a fight or moving a prisoner to segregation. Because such situations are especially dangerous, officers may enlist others to help them minimize the risk of violence. The officer's greatest fear is unexpected attacks, such as a missile thrown from an upper tier or an officer's "accidental" fall down a flight of stairs. The need to watch constantly against personal attacks adds stress and keeps many officers at a distance from the inmates.

OFFICER–PRISONER VIOLENCE

A fact of life in many institutions is unauthorized physical violence by officers against inmates. Stories abound of guards giving individual prisoners "the treatment" when supervisors are not looking. Many guards view physical force as an everyday, legitimate procedure. In some institutions, authorized "goon squads" composed of physically powerful officers use their muscle to maintain order.

Correctional officers are expected to follow departmental rules in their dealings with prisoners, yet supervisors generally cannot observe staff–prisoner confrontations directly. Further, prisoner complaints about officer brutality are often not believed until the officer involved gains a reputation for harshness. Even in this case, wardens may feel they must support their officers in order to retain their support.

DECREASING PRISON VIOLENCE

Seven factors contribute to prison violence. Bowker (1982:64) outlines five: (1) inadequate supervision by staff members, (2) architectural design that promotes rather than inhibits victimization, (3) the easy availability of deadly weapons, (4) the housing of violence-prone prisoners near relatively defenseless people, and (5) a general high level of tension produced by close quarters. Two more factors are (6) the physical size and condition of the prison and (7) the relations between inmates and staff. We now discuss several of these, as they relate to the physical setting and management practices.

The Effect of Architecture and Size   The fortresslike prison certainly does not create an atmosphere for normal interpersonal relationships, and the size of the larger institutions can create management problems. The massive scale of the megaprison, which may hold up to 3,000 inmates, provides opportunities for aggressive inmates to hide weapons, dispense private "justice," and engage more or less freely in other illicit activities. The size of the population in a large prison may also result in some inmates' "falling through the cracks"—being misclassified and forced to live among more-violent offenders.

TECHNOLOGY ISSUES IN CRIMINAL JUSTICE

Scanning for Drugs

Prison officials are continually concerned about the risk of contraband entering the prison. During prisoners' visits with family and friends, officials typically observe prisoners closely and then conduct full strip searches before permitting them to return to their cells. Despite these careful measures, contraband still makes it through. For example, a girlfriend or boyfriend may pass a small quantity of drugs to the prisoner during a kiss which is then hidden under the prisoner's tongue. There is also a problem when corrupt corrections officers sneak drugs and other illegal items into prisons.

To combat prisoners' efforts to gain access to drugs, the Maryland prisons began using $55,000 scanners that look like handheld vacuum cleaners. The scanners detect traces of drugs more effectively than do drug-sniffing dogs. By moving the scanners past visitors and prisoners, officials can detect traces of drugs on their clothing or skin.

As this new technology is developed, criminal justice officials must be keenly aware of the devices' usefulness and limitations. For example, traces of a drug do not automatically prove possession or use. In addition, officials must be ready for unexpected consequences when the new technology is used.

 RESEARCHING THE INTERNET

There are many Internet sites dealing with the use of scanners. See two of them, listed on the Cole/Smith Criminal Justice in America Companion Website: http://www.thomsonedu.com/criminaljustice/cole.

FOR CRITICAL ANALYSIS

Although the scanners quite effectively detect particles from drugs, errors can occur. What if a visitor receives a $20 bill as change at a store without any way of knowing that the store had received it as part of a purchase by a drug user who had used the rolled up bill to snort cocaine? The bill, like a large amount of the currency circulating in the United States, would contain traces of the drug. If the scanner detected the drug, would the visitor be subjected to arrest? What if a correctional officer was the one who carried the tainted bill?

Source: Drawn from Ivan Penn, "Vacuum to Keep Prisons Drug-Free," *Lansing State Journal,* October 20, 1997.

The Role of Management The degree to which inmate leaders are allowed to take matters into their own hands can affect the level of violence among inmates. When administrators run a tight ship, security measures prevent sexual attacks in dark corners, the making of "shivs" and "shanks" (knives) in the metal shop, and open conflict among inmate groups. A prison must afford each inmate defensible space, and administrators should ensure that every inmate remains secure from physical attack.

Effective management can decrease the level of assaultive behavior by limiting opportunities for attacks. Wardens and correctional officers must therefore recognize the types of people with whom they are dealing, the role of prison gangs, and the structure of institutions. John DiIulio argues that no group of inmates is "unmanageable [and] no combination of political, social, budgetary, architectural, or other factors makes good management impossible" (DiIulio, 1991:12). He points to such varied institutions as the California Men's Colony, New York City's Tombs and Rikers Island, the Federal Bureau of Prisons, and the Texas Department of Corrections under the leadership of George Beto. At these institutions, good management practices have resulted in prisons and jails where inmates can "do time" without fearing for their personal safety. Wardens who exert leadership can manage their prisons effectively, so that problems do not fester and erupt into violent confrontations. As discussed in "Technology Issues in Criminal Justice," the use of scanning devices to discover contraband may help managers weed out problems.

In sum, prisons must be made safe. Because the state puts offenders there, it has a responsibility to prevent violence and maintain order. To exclude violence from prisons, officials may have to limit movement within institutions, contacts with the outside, and the right of inmates to choose their associates. Yet these measures may run counter to the goal of producing men and women who will be accountable when they return to society.

ThomsonNOW
Improve your grade on the exam with Personalized Study! For reinforcement resources and a mastery check of Violence in Prison, go to www.thomsonedu.com/thomsonnow.

CHECKPOINT

15. What five factors are thought to contribute to prison violence? ⟶

Answers

15. Inadequate supervision, architectural design, availability of weapons, housing of violence-prone inmates with the defenseless, and the high level of tension of people living in close quarters.

A QUESTION OF ETHICS: WRITING ASSIGNMENT

After three years of daily contact, correctional officer Bill MacLeod and Jack Douglas, who was serving a 3–5 year sentence, knew each other very well. They were both devoted to the Red Sox and the Celtics. Throughout the year they would chat about the fortunes of their teams and the outlook ahead. MacLeod got to know and like Douglas. They were about the same age and had come from similar backgrounds. Why they were now on opposite sides of the cell bars was something that MacLeod could not figure out.

One day Douglas called to MacLeod and said that he needed money because he had lost a bet gambling on the Red Sox. Douglas said that his wife would send him the money but that it couldn't come through the prison mail to him in cash. And a check or money order would show on his commissary account.

"The guy wants cash. If he doesn't get it, I'm dead." Douglas took a breath and then rushed on with his request. "Could you bring it in for me?

She'll mail the money to you at home. You could just drop the envelope on my bed."

"You know the rules. No gambling and no money," said MacLeod.

"But I'm scared shitless. It will be no big deal for you and it will make all the difference for me. Come on, we've gotten along well all these years. I think of you as being different from those other officers."

WRITING ASSIGNMENT

What should MacLeod do? Is this kind of request likely to be a one-time occurrence with Douglas? What if MacLeod's sergeant finds out? What if other inmates learn about it? In a short essay describe the conflict that MacLeod must face. How should he resolve this conflict?

REAL-WORLD ACTIVITY: AN APPLICATION

Although the numbers of prisoners with HIV/AIDS has decreased since its high point in 1995, the rate of occurrence remains higher than in the total U.S. population. Some believe that many inmates contact the HIV while incarcerated, but most evidence points out that engaging in "high risk" behaviors—intravenous drug use, needle sharing, and unprotected sex—prior to incarceration is at fault.

To deal with the HIV/AIDS crisis, correctional leaders have adopted policies to educate inmates in prevention techniques, have made testing for the virus a requirement, and, in some facilities, have imposed segregation of inmates with the disease. A host of legal, political, medical, budgetary, and attitudinal factors can complicate the implementation of these policies. For example, civil liberties groups have denounced the stigma that can be at-

tached to inmates who are given the AIDS label. Others say that the state has a responsibility to take measures to prevent the transmission of the disease and to provide medical care to the infected.

RESEARCHING THE INTERNET

Go to InfoTrac College Edition. Enter the keyword *AIDS prison* and read the editorial entitled "A Warning about AIDS in Prison," *New York Times*, July 24, 2006.

APPLICATION

If you were the commissioner of corrections, what policies would you implement to combat HIV/AIDS? What obstacles might you have to confront?

SUMMARY

- Three models of incarceration have predominated since the 1940s. (1) The custodial model emphasizes the maintenance of security. (2) The rehabilitation model views security and housekeeping activities as mainly a framework for treatment efforts. (3) The reintegration model recognizes that prisoners must be prepared for their return to society.

- The public's belief that the warden and officers have total power over the inmates is outdated.

- Good management through effective leadership can maintain the quality of prison life as measured by levels of order, amenities, and services.

- Most prisons are expected to fulfill goals related to keeping (custody), using (working), and serving (treating) inmates.

- Four factors make managing prisons different from administering other public institutions: defects of total power, limited use of rewards and punishments, exchange relationships, and strength of inmate leadership.

- Because they remain in close contact with the prisoners, correctional officers are the linchpins of the prison system. The effectiveness of the institution lies on their shoulders.

- Prison administrators must deal with the special needs of some groups, including elderly prisoners, prisoners with HIV/AIDS, mentally ill prisoners, and long-term prisoners.

- Inmates do not serve their time in isolation but are members of a subculture with its own traditions, norms, and leadership structure. Such norms are often described as the inmate code.

- Today's prisons, unlike those of the past, do not have a uniform inmate code but several, in part because of the influence of gangs.

- Inmates deal with the pain of incarceration by assuming an adaptive role and lifestyle.

- To meet their needs for goods and services not provided by the state, prisoners run an underground economy.

- Women make up only a small portion of the inmate population. This is cited as the reason for the limited programs and services available to female prisoners.

- Social relationships among female inmates differ from those of their male counterparts. Women tend to form pseudofamilies in prison. Many women experience the added stress of being responsible for their children on the outside.

- Educational, vocational, industrial, and treatment programs are available in prisons. Administrators believe these programs are important for maintaining order.

- Violence in prison depends on such things as administrative effectiveness, the architecture and size of prisons, and inmate characteristics such as age, attitudes, and race.

- Violence occurs between prisoners, often through gangs, and between prisoners and guards.

QUESTIONS FOR REVIEW

1. How do modern prisons differ from those in the past?

2. What characteristics of prisons distinguish them from other institutions?

3. What must a prison administrator do to ensure successful management?

4. What is meant by an adaptive role? Which roles are found in male prison society? In female prison society?

5. How does the convict society in institutions for women differ from that in institutions for men?

6. What are the main forms of prison programs, and what purposes do they serve?

7. What are forms and causes of prison violence?

KEY TERMS AND CASES

classification (p. 354)
custodial model (p. 336)

inmate code (p. 346)
reintegration model (p. 336)

GOING ONLINE

ThomsonNOW

Maximize your study time by using ThomsonNOW's diagnostic study plan to help you review this chapter. The Study Plan will

- Help you identify areas on which you should concentrate

- Provide interactive exercises to help you master the chapter concepts

- Provide a posttest to confirm you are ready to move on to the next chapter

14

Reentry into the Community

During his last night in the Texas State Prison at Huntsville, Angel Coronado could not sleep. Rather, he thought about the next morning, when he would be released from prison after three years, two years of which he had served in administrative segregation. Coronado, who was 20 years old and had a limited education, had been brought up in Donna, Texas, on the Mexican border. At age 12 he snorted cocaine, and as a teenager he soon fell in with a local gang. In 1999 he ran over a friend while driving drunk and was given a three-year prison sentence.

The next morning Coronado received a new set of clothes, $100 "gate money," instructions as to when he should report to his parole officer, and a bus ticket to Donna. Carrying his few belongings in a plastic bag, he joined about 20 other parolees on a Greyhound bus heading south. As the bus left Huntsville, some parolees cheered. There were high fives and some pointed their middle finger at the prison. Coronado remained quiet. He said that he hoped to land a job but knows that he lacks the skills to get more than minimum wage. He was also concerned about his first encounter with the gang members he left behind. As he said, "I may go out with them, but I know I must follow the parole rules. I can't go back to prison" (Johnson, 2002).

Angel Coronado is typical of the more than the 650,000 adult felons who leave state and federal prisons each year (about 1,780 daily). With the great expansion of incarceration during the past three decades, the number of offenders now returning to the community has increased dramatically.

Ex-prisoners are mostly male and unskilled, and 47 percent belong to minority groups. Many have alcohol and drug problems, and about one-third of state inmates have a physical or mental impairment (Maruschak and Beck, 2001:23). Some are "churners" who have already served terms for prior offenses and are being let out again. About two-thirds will return to a few metropolitan areas in their states where they will live in poor, inner-city neighborhoods (J. Lynch and Sabol, 2001:16). Some researchers believe that this leads to further instability in areas that already have high levels of crime, drug abuse, and other social problems (Clear et al., 2003). About 40 percent of parolees will return to prison, often within a year of their release.

In this chapter we examine the mechanisms by which prisoners are released from incarceration; we also look at their supervision in the community. Finally, we discuss the many problems facing parolees as they reenter society.

QUESTIONS FOR INQUIRY

- What is the "reentry problem"?
- What are the origins of parole, and how does it operate today?
- What are the mechanisms for the release of felons to the community?
- How are ex-offenders supervised in the community?
- What problems do parolees face during their reentry?

Prisoner Reentry

Prisoner reentry has become an important public issue. The sudden flood of offenders leaving prison and the fact that so many will return to prison either because of a new crime or a parole violation raise serious questions as to how the criminal justice system deals with the reentry of ex-felons (BJS, 2002a). What is the crux of this problem?

Jeremy Travis and Joan Petersilia point to several factors contributing to the reentry problem (2001). They argue that beginning in the 1970s the power of parole boards to make release decisions was abolished in mandatory release states and severely restricted in discretionary release states. This means that more inmates are automatically leaving prison, ready or not, when they meet the requirements of their sentence. It also means that there has been little or no prerelease planning to ensure that the new parolee has a job, housing, and a supportive family when he or she hits the streets.

A second factor they believe contributes to the reentry problem is the curtailment of prison education, job training, and other rehabilitation programs designed to prepare inmates for their return to the community.

Finally, Travis and Petersilia note that the profile of returning prisoners has changed in ways that pose new challenges to successful reentry. In particular the conviction offense and time served differ from what they were 20 years ago. Now, more than a third of prisoners released to parole are incarcerated for a drug offense—up from 12 percent in 1985. The average time served has also increased by almost a half year since 1990. Further, some drug and violence offenders are exiting prison after very long terms, perhaps 20 or more years. The longer time in prison means a longer period the prisoner has lived apart from family and friends.

Many have expressed concern regarding how the corrections system prepares prisoners to live as law-abiding citizens. Successful prisoner reentry requires that parole and services focus on linking offenders with community institutions—churches, families, self-help groups, and nonprofit programs. As emphasized by Joan Petersilia, "We must share the responsibility for transitioning offenders with the community." Ultimately, family and neighborhood stability and public safety depend on successful reentry (2003:3).

CHECKPOINT

1. What three factors have likely contributed to the reentry problem? →

Answers

1. Changes in the powers of parole boards, reduction in programs designed to assist ex-prisoners, and the changing profile of those being released from prison.

Release and Supervision

Except for the less than 4 percent of inmates who die in prison, all will eventually be released to live in the community. Currently about 77 percent of felons will be released on parole and will remain under correctional supervision for a specific period. About 19 percent will be released at the expiration of their sentence, having "maxed out" and earned the freedom to live in the community without supervision.

Parole is the *conditional* release of an offender from incarceration but not from the legal custody of the state. Thus, offenders who comply with parole conditions and do not further conflict with the law receive an absolute discharge from supervision at the end of their sentences. If a parolee breaks a rule, parole can be revoked and the person returned to a correctional facility. Parole rests on three concepts:

1. *Grace.* The prisoner could be kept incarcerated but the government extends the privilege of release.

2. *Contract.* The government enters into an agreement with the prisoner whereby the prisoner promises to abide by certain conditions in exchange for being released.

3. *Custody.* Even though the offender is released from prison, he or she remains a responsibility of the government. Parole is an extension of correctional programs into the community.

Only felons are released on parole; adult misdemeanants are usually released immediately after they have finished serving their sentences. Today about 766,000 people are under parole supervision, a threefold increase since 1980 (Travis and Petersilia, 2001; BJS, 2005c:1).

> **parole** The conditional release of an inmate from incarceration, under supervision, after part of the prison sentence has been served.

THE ORIGINS OF PAROLE

Parole in the United States evolved during the nineteenth century from the English, Australian, and Irish practices of conditional pardon, apprenticeship by indenture, transportation of criminals from one country to another, and the issuance of "tickets of leave." These were all methods of moving criminals out of prison as a response to overcrowding, unemployment, and the cost of incarceration.

A key figure in developing the concept of parole in the nineteenth century was Captain Alexander Maconochie, an administrator of British penal colonies in Tasmania and elsewhere in the South Pacific. A critic of definite prison terms, Maconochie devised a system of rewards for good conduct, labor, and study. Under his classification procedure, prisoners could pass through stages of increasing responsibility and freedom: (1) strict imprisonment, (2) labor on government chain gangs, (3) freedom within a limited area, (4) a ticket of leave or parole resulting in a conditional pardon, and (5) full restoration of liberty. Like modern correctional practices, this procedure assumed that prisoners should be prepared gradually for release. The roots of the American system of parole lie in the transition from imprisonment to conditional release to full freedom.

Maconochie's idea of requiring prisoners to earn their early release caught on first in Ireland. There, Sir Walter Crofton built on Maconochie's idea to link an offender's progress in prison to a ticket of leave. Prisoners who graduated through Crofton's three successive levels of treatment were released on parole under a series of conditions. Most significant was the requirement that parolees submit monthly reports to the police. In Dublin, a special civilian inspector helped releasees find jobs, visited them periodically, and supervised their activities.

THE DEVELOPMENT OF PAROLE IN THE UNITED STATES

In the United States, parole developed during the prison reform movement of the latter half of the nineteenth century. Relying on the ideas of Maconochie and Crofton, American reformers such as Zebulon Brockway of the Elmira State Reformatory in

New York began to experiment with the concept of parole. After New York adopted indeterminate sentences in 1876, Brockway started to release prisoners on parole. Under the new sentencing law, prisoners could be released when their conduct showed they were ready to return to society. This idea spread, so that 20 states had parole systems by 1900, and 44 states and the federal government had them by 1932 (Friedman, 1993:304). Today every state has some procedure for the release of offenders before the end of their sentences.

Although it has been used in the United States for more than a century, parole remains controversial. To many people, parole allows convicted offenders to avoid serving the full sentence they deserve. Public pressure to be tougher on criminals has led half the states and the federal government to restructure their sentencing laws and release mechanisms (Petersilia, 1999:479).

CHECKPOINT

2. In what countries did the concept of parole first develop? ——————→

Answers

2. England, Australia, Ireland.

Release Mechanisms

From 1920 to 1973 there was a nationwide sentencing and release policy. During this period all states and the federal government used indeterminate sentencing, authorized discretionary release by parole boards, and supervised prisoners after release, and they did this all in the interest of the rehabilitation of offenders.

With the 1970s came a critique of rehabilitation, the move to determinate sentencing, and the public's view that the system was "soft" on criminals. By 2003, 16 states and the federal government had abolished discretionary release by parole boards. Another five states had abolished discretionary parole for certain offenses (Petersilia, 2003:65). Further, in some of the states that kept discretionary release, parole boards have been reluctant to grant it.

There are now four basic mechanisms for people to be released from prison: (1) discretionary release, (2) mandatory release, (3) other conditional release, and (4) expiration release. Figure 14.1 shows the percentage of felons released by the various mechanisms.

Carolyn Aselton (left) is the sister of Hartford Police Officer Brian Aselton, who was murdered in 1999. Here, she reads a statement to the Connecticut Parole Board during a hearing for Jose Gonzalez (center left). The board unanimously rejected a request for early release for Gonzalez, who is serving an 8-year prison sentence for his part in the killing.

AP Photo/Douglas Healey

DISCRETIONARY RELEASE

States retaining indeterminate sentences allow **discretionary release** by the parole board within the boundaries set by the sentence and the penal law. This is a conditional release to parole supervision. This approach (illustrated in the Close Up box) lets the board members assess the prisoner's readiness for release within the minimum and maximum terms of the sentence. In reviewing the prisoner's file and asking questions, the parole board focuses on the nature of the offense, the inmate's behavior, and his or her participation in rehabilitative programs. This process places great faith in the ability of parole board members to predict the future behavior of offenders. See "A Question of Ethics" at the end of the chapter for more on parole boards.

MANDATORY RELEASE

Mandatory release occurs after an inmate has served time equal to the total sentence minus good time, if any, or to a certain percentage of the total sentence as specified by law. Mandatory release is found in federal jurisdictions and states with

FIGURE 14.1
Methods of release from state prison
Felons are released from prison to the community, usually under parole supervision, through various means depending upon the law.

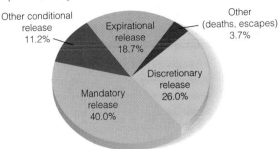

Other conditional release 11.2%
Expirational release 18.7%
Other (deaths, escapes) 3.7%
Discretionary release 26.0%
Mandatory release 40.0%

Source: Jeremy Travis and Joan Petersilia, "Reentry Reconsidered: A New Look at an Old Question." *Crime and Delinquency* 47 (July 2001): 295.

CLOSE UP

A Roomful of Strangers

After five years, three months, and four days in Stanhope Correctional Facility, Ben Brooks was ready to go before the Board of Parole. He woke with butterflies in his stomach, realizing that at nine o'clock he was to walk into the hearing room to confront a roomful of strangers. As he lay on his bunk he rehearsed the answers to the questions he thought the board members might ask: "How do you feel about the person you assaulted? What have you done with your time while incarcerated? Do you think you have learned anything here that will convince the board that you will follow a crime-free life in the community? What are your plans for employment and housing?" According to prison scuttlebutt, these were the types of questions asked, and you had to be prepared to answer that you were sorry for your past mistakes, had taken advantage of the prison programs, had a job waiting for you, and planned to live with your family. You had to "ring bells" with the board.

At breakfast, friends dropped by Ben's table to reassure him that he had it made. As one said, "Ben, you've done everything they've said to do. What else can they expect?" That was the problem—*What did they expect?*

At eight-thirty, Officer Kearney came by the cell. "Time to go, Ben." They walked out of the housing unit and down the long prison corridors to a group of chairs outside the hearing room. Other prisoners were already seated there. "Sit here, Ben. They'll call when they're ready. Good luck."

At ten minutes past nine the door opened and an officer called, "First case, Brooks." Ben got up, walked into the room. "Please take a seat, Mr. Brooks," said the African American seated in the center at the table. Ben knew he was Reverend Perry, a man known as being tough but fair. To his left was a white man, Mr. MacDonald, and to his right a Hispanic woman, Ms. Lopez. The white man led the questioning.

"Mr. Brooks. You were convicted of armed robbery and sentenced to a term of 6 to 10 years. Please tell the board what you have learned during your incarceration."

Ben paused and then answered hesitantly, "Well, I learned that to commit such a stupid act was a mistake. I was under a lot of pressure when I pulled the robbery and now am sorry for what I did."

"You severely injured the woman you held up. What might you tell her if she were sitting in this room today?"

"I would just have to say, I'm sorry. It will never happen again."

"But this is not the first time you have been convicted. What makes you think it will never happen again?"

"Well this is the first time I was sent to prison. You see things a lot differently from here."

Ms. Lopez spoke up. "You have a good prison record—member of the Toastmaster's Club, gotten your high school equivalency diploma, kept your nose clean. Tell the board about your future plans should you be released."

"My brother says I can live with him until I get on my feet, and there is a letter in my file telling you that I have a job waiting at a meat-processing plant. I will be living in my hometown but I don't intend to see my old buddies again. You can be sure that I am now on the straight and narrow."

"But you committed a heinous crime. That woman suffered a lot. Why should the board believe that you won't do it again?"

"All I can say is that I'm different now."

"Thank you, Mr. Brooks," said Reverend Perry. "You will hear from us by this evening." Ben got up and walked out of the room. It had only taken eight minutes, yet it seemed like hours. Eight minutes during which his future was being decided. Would it be back to the cell or out on the street? It would be about ten hours before he would receive word from the board as to his fate.

RESEARCHING THE INTERNET

For more on this subject, see the corresponding website listed on the Cole/Smith *Criminal Justice in America* Companion Website: http://www.thomsonedu.com/criminaljustice/cole.

FOR CRITICAL ANALYSIS

What is going on here? Analyze discretionary release from the standpoint of the inmate and the board members. What is each trying to accomplish?

discretionary release The release of an inmate from prison to conditional supervision at the discretion of the parole board within the boundaries set by the sentence and the penal law.

mandatory release The required release of an inmate from incarceration to community supervision upon the expiration of a certain period, as specified by a determinate-sentencing law or parole guidelines.

other conditional release A term used in some states to avoid the rigidity of mandatory release, by placing convicts in various community settings under supervision.

expiration release The release of an inmate from incarceration, without further correctional supervision; the inmate cannot be returned to prison for any remaining portion of the sentence for the current offense.

determinate sentences and good-time provisions (see Chapter 10). Without a parole board to make discretionary decisions, mandatory release is a matter of bookkeeping to check the correct amount of good time and other credits and make sure the sentence has been accurately interpreted. The prisoner is conditionally released to parole supervision for the rest of the sentence.

OTHER CONDITIONAL RELEASE

Because of the growth of prison populations, many states have devised ways to get around the rigidity of mandatory release, by placing inmates in the community through furloughs, home supervision, halfway houses, emergency release, and other programs (BJS, 2000b; Griset, 1995:307). These types of **other conditional release** also avoid the appearance of the politically sensitive label "discretionary parole."

EXPIRATION RELEASE

An increasing percentage of prisoners receive an **expiration release.** As noted earlier, such offenders have served the maximum court sentence, minus good time—they have "maxed out." These inmates are released from any further correctional supervision and cannot be returned to prison for their current offense.

IMPACT OF RELEASE MECHANISMS

Parole release mechanisms do more than simply determine the date at which a particular prisoner will be sent back into the community. Parole release also greatly affects other parts of the system, including sentencing, plea bargaining, and the size of prison populations.

One important effect of discretionary release is that an administrative body—the parole board—can shorten a sentence imposed by a judge. Even in states that have mandatory release, various potential reductions built into the sentence mean that the full sentence is rarely served. Good time, for example, can reduce punishment even if there is no eligibility for parole.

To understand the impact of release mechanisms on criminal punishment, we must compare the amount of time actually served in prison with the sentence specified by the judge. In most states good time and jail time are the main factors that

An increasing number of offenders are leaving prison at the expiration of their sentences. They have "maxed out" and leave without the requirement of parole supervision. What is their future?

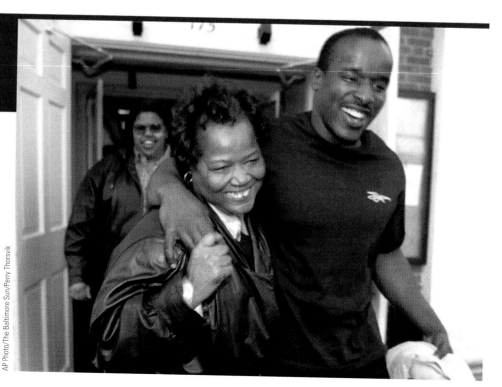

AP Photo/The Baltimore Sun/Perry Thorsvik

reduce the time actually served. On a national basis felony inmates serve an average of two and a half years before release. Figure 14.2 shows the average time served for selected offenses.

Supporters of discretion for the paroling authority argue that parole benefits the overall system. Discretionary release mitigates the harshness of the penal code. If the legislature must establish exceptionally strict punishments as a means of conveying a "tough on crime" image to frustrated and angry voters, parole can effectively permit sentence adjustments that make the punishment fit the crime. Not everyone convicted of larceny has done equivalent harm, yet some legislatively mandated sentencing schemes impose equally strict sentences. Early release on parole can be granted to an offender who is less deserving of strict punishment, such as someone who voluntarily makes restitution, cooperates with the police, or shows genuine regret.

FIGURE 14.2

Estimated time to be served (in months) by state prisoners for selected offenses

The data indicate that the average felony offender going to prison for the first time spends about two years in prison. How would you expect the public to react to that fact?

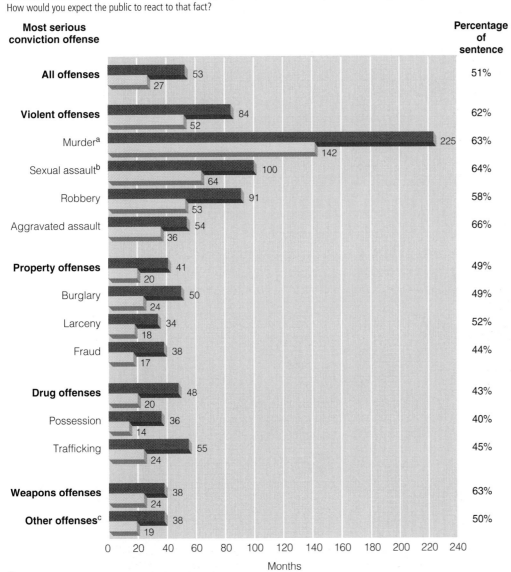

Most serious conviction offense		Percentage of sentence
All offenses	53 / 27	51%
Violent offenses	84 / 52	62%
Murder[a]	225 / 142	63%
Sexual assault[b]	100 / 64	64%
Robbery	91 / 53	58%
Aggravated assault	54 / 36	66%
Property offenses	41 / 20	49%
Burglary	50 / 24	49%
Larceny	34 / 18	52%
Fraud	38 / 17	44%
Drug offenses	48 / 20	43%
Possession	36 / 14	40%
Trafficking	55 / 24	45%
Weapons offenses	38 / 24	63%
Other offenses[c]	38 / 19	50%

Months (0 20 40 60 80 100 120 140 160 180 200 220 240)

[a]Includes nonnegligent manslaughter
[b]Includes rape
[c]Composed of nonviolent offenses such as receiving stolen property and vandalism

■ Mean prison sentence
■ Average time served

Source: Bureau of Justice Statistics, *Bulletin,* December 2005, p. 5.

A major criticism of discretionary release is that it shifts responsibility for many primary criminal justice decisions from a judge, who holds legal procedures uppermost, to an administrative board, where discretion rules. Judges know a great deal about constitutional rights and basic legal protections, but parole board members may not have such knowledge. In most states with discretionary release, parole hearings are secret, with only board members, the inmate, and correctional officers present. Often no published criteria guide decisions, and prisoners receive no reason for denial or granting of parole. However, an increasing number of states permit oral or written testimony by victims and by members of the offender's family.

CHECKPOINT

Answer

3. How does parole release affect the rest of the criminal justice system? ➔ 3. Parole release affects sentencing, encourages plea bargaining, relieves prison crowding, makes the sentence less harsh, and encourages good behavior in prison.

Parole Supervision in the Community

conditions of release Conduct restrictions that parolees must follow as a legally binding requirement of being released.

Parolees are released from prison on condition that they abide by laws and follow rules, known as **conditions of release,** designed to aid their readjustment to society and control their movement. As in probation, the parolee may be required to abstain from alcohol, keep away from undesirable associates, maintain good work habits, and not leave the state without permission (see "Technology Issues in Criminal Justice"). If they violate these conditions, they could be returned to prison to serve out the rest of their sentence. All states except Maine have some requirement for postprison supervision, and nearly 80 percent of released prisoners are subject to some form of conditional community supervision release (Petersilia, 1999:489).

The restrictions are justified on the ground that people who have been incarcerated must readjust to the community so that they will not fall back into preconviction habits and associations. The strict enforcement of these rules may create problems for parolees who cannot fulfill all the demands placed on them. For example, a parolee

TECHNOLOGY ISSUES IN CRIMINAL JUSTICE

Drug Testing

t is difficult to monitor parolees closely. How can authorities be sure that a parolee is not drinking alcohol or taking drugs? Periodic drug testing is sometimes ineffective because parole violators do such things as drink jugs of water to dilute their urine before taking a test. To increase the effectiveness of drug testing, a new drug patch with a high degree of sensitivity has been developed that continuously monitors the parolee's skin. The patch monitors the parolee's sweat for traces of banned substances. In some communities the patch is also used to monitor and test probationers and parents under investigation with respect to child custody.

Unfortunately, the high sensitivity of the patch offers both advantages and disadvantages. The patch makes it difficult for parolees to avoid detection if they use drugs. However, critics complain that the patch is so sensitive that it will reflect traces of drugs in the environment, such as in the air or on clothing, even when the parolee has done nothing wrong. As a result, parolees who have faithfully obeyed the rules risk being sent back to prison erroneously.

The controversy over the drug patch illustrates the problems involved in attempting to refine technology. When it works "too perfectly," does technology become a drawback? If a drug patch or other device can detect all drugs on a person's body, what assurances are there that it will only register drugs that the person has intentionally used? If you were a judge and had received reports that a drug patch can register drug traces from the environment, would you be willing to send a parolee back to prison for a "positive" reading from the patch?

RESEARCHING THE INTERNET

For more on drug testing as a civil liberties issue, go to the corresponding site listed on the Cole/Smith Criminal Justice in America Companion Website: http://www.thomsonedu.com/criminaljustice/cole.

FOR CRITICAL ANALYSIS

Do you see the use of drug tests of parolees as a privacy issue and a violation of civil liberties?

Source: Drawn from Vince Beiser, "Patchy Justice: Is a New Drug Test Too Error Prone?" *Mother Jones Magazine,* September–October 2000, p. 17.

may find it impossible to be tested for drugs, attend an Alcoholics Anonymous meeting, and work full-time while also meeting family obligations.

The day they come out of prison, parolees face a staggering array of problems. In most states, they receive only clothes, a token amount of money, a list of rules governing their conditional release, and the name and address of the parole officer to whom they must report within 24 hours. Although a promised job is often required for release, an actual job may be another matter. Most former convicts are unskilled or semiskilled, and the conditions of release may prevent them from moving to areas where they could find work. If the parolee is African American, male, and under 30, he joins the largest demographic group of unemployed people in the country.

Parolees bear the added handicap of former convict status. In most states, laws prevent former prisoners from working in certain types of establishments—where alcohol is sold, for example—thus ruling out many jobs. In many trades, workers must belong to a union, and unions often have restrictions on the admission of new members. Finally, many parolees, as well as other ex-convicts, face a significant dilemma. If they are truthful about their backgrounds, many employers will not hire them. If they are not truthful, they can be fired for lying if the employer ever learns about their conviction. Some problems that parolees encounter when they reenter the community are illustrated in the Close Up box. As you read about Jerome Washington's experience, ask yourself what problems you might encounter after a long term in "max."

Other reentry problems plague parolees. For many, the transition from the highly structured life in prison to open society is too difficult to manage. Many just do not have the social, psychological, and material resources to cope with the temptations and complications of modern life. For these parolees, freedom may be short-lived as they fall back into forbidden activities such as drinking, using drugs, and stealing.

COMMUNITY PROGRAMS FOLLOWING RELEASE

There are various programs to assist parolees. Some help prepare offenders for release while they are still in prison; others provide employment and housing assistance after release. Together, the programs are intended to help the offender progress steadily toward reintegration into the community. Almost all penologists agree that there should be pre- and postrelease programs to assist reentry, yet as Joan Petersilia notes, more than 90 percent of prisoners do not now participate in such programs (Petersilia, 2003:98). Although all states offer reentry programs, relatively few prisoners have access to them.

Among the many programs developed to help offenders return to the community, three are especially important: work and educational release, furloughs, and halfway houses. Although similar in many ways, each offers a specific approach to helping formerly incarcerated individuals reenter the community.

Work and Educational Release   Programs of **work and educational release,** in which inmates are released from correctional institutions during the day to work or attend school, were first established in Vermont in 1906. However, the Huber Act, passed by the Wisconsin legislature in 1913, is usually cited as the model on which such programs are based. By 1972 most states and the federal government had instituted these programs. Nonetheless, by 2002 only about one-third of prisons operated them for fewer than 3 percent of U.S. inmates (Petersilia, 2003:99).

Although most work and educational release programs are justifiable in terms of rehabilitation, many correctional administrators and legislators also like them because they cost relatively little. In some states a portion of the inmate's earnings from work outside may be deducted for room and board. One problem with these programs is that they allegedly take jobs from free citizens, a complaint often given by organized labor.

Furloughs   Isolation from loved ones is one of the pains of imprisonment. Although correctional programs in many countries include conjugal visits, only a few U.S. corrections systems have used them. Many penologists view the **furlough**—the

work and educational release
The daytime release of inmates from correctional institutions so they can work or attend school.

furlough The temporary release of an inmate from a correctional institution for a brief period, usually one to three days, for a visit home. Such programs help maintain family ties and prepare inmates for release on parole.

CLOSE UP

Returning to America

JEROME WASHINGTON

Returning to America after living in France, China, Swaziland, or the high Himalayas is one thing, but returning to America after serving sixteen years and three months in maximum security, mostly in Attica, is something altogether different.

In 1972 when I went to prison, Richard M. Nixon was president and politicians were still thought to be ethical; . . . the Supreme Court was reasonably balanced; the Vietnam War was winding down, but the weekly body count was still news. The HIV virus was unknown and free sex had more fans than the Super Bowl. Although everybody was not living the American Dream, and some people felt that life was hopeless, most were optimistic about their future and many had a strong commitment to social activism. People cared, and even the most disadvantaged could still dream without fear of having nightmares.

Soon after I got out I was with my brother Freddy. We were standing at Columbus Circle, a major hub, a New York City crossroads. Freddy was my guide. He asked where I'd like to go; what I'd like to do; what I'd like to see. Did I want to meet new people, or just hang out, drift from place to place? Suddenly, life was a smorgasbord, a cornucopia of enticements and alluring temptations. I didn't know where to start, what to do first. Prison was my immediate reference point and, there, decisions related to physical movement were made by the guards, not by me. "We can't stand here all day," my brother said, over and over.

"Go slow," I told myself as I recalled a number of prisoners who shortly after release returned to prison with new convictions, and new sentences. They tried to make everything happen at once, all at the same time. Like children, they wanted instant gratification. Played all their cards at the same time, swung before the ball got to the plate, struck out and found themselves back in a cell where their only landscape was the sun setting against the prison wall.

I decided to do life the same way I did prison. Nothing fancy. One step at a time, one day at a time, and most of all, don't forget to breathe.

Freddy was supportive and sensitive. He understood that I needed to relearn the rhythm of the streets, tune in on the city, explore my new freedom and tune out on prison. I had no preference which direction we'd walk, or which street we'd take. Freddy didn't seem to have any preference either. He just started off, leaving me to stay where I was or to catch up. I learned a

quick but important lesson. It was this kind of small, ordinary decision—often taken for granted and overlooked—that I missed most in prison. Now, by just walking off and letting me decide what to do, Freddy was tuning me in again to this level of free choice.

The morning after my release found me in Harlem. I was staying with Bert, a long-time family friend. I awoke at dawn. There was no excitement. No stage fright or butterflies to signal the first day of the rest of my life. Looking up from sleep I could have dreamed my release from prison the day before. The sky was as gray as a prison sky—the same sky I had seen for the past sixteen years and three months.

Not long after I went to prison, I woke in the middle of the night and sat up on the side of the bed. The cell was so quiet I could hear cockroaches foraging in my garbage.

"When I get out of prison," I said to myself, "sex can wait." Thinking of what I would most like to do, I said, "I'm going to eat strawberries! Big! Fresh! Red strawberries!" And that became my mantra for the rest of the time I was in prison.

On the day I was released, Kathrin, a friend, a sister, my confidante, came to pick me up. She was there with her camera, taking photos of me as I walked through the last gate to freedom. She drove me to the house where she lived with her husband and son, and fed me steamed shrimp, French champagne, and *strawberries!*

RESEARCHING THE INTERNET

To learn about reentry services offered to parolees, go to the corresponding website listed on the Cole/Smith Criminal Justice in America Companion Website: http://www.thomsonedu.com/criminaljustice/cole.

FOR CRITICAL ANALYSIS

Having overcome the initial shock of reentry, what are some of the problems that parolees such as Jerome Washington must face?

Note: Jerome Washington, a writer, is now discharged from parole supervision and is living in California.

Source: Jerome Washington, *Iron House: Stories from the Yard* (New York: Vintage, 1994), 155–63.

---

temporary release of an inmate from a correctional institution for a visit home—as a meaningful approach to inmate reintegration.

Furloughs are thought to offer an excellent means of testing an inmate's ability to cope with the larger society. Through home visits, the inmate can renew family ties and relieve the tensions of confinement. Most administrators also feel that furloughs increase prisoners' morale. The general public, however, does not always support the concept. Public outrage is inevitable if an offender on furlough commits another crime or fails to return. Correctional authorities are often nervous about using furloughs, because they fear being blamed for such incidents.

halfway house A correctional facility housing convicted felons who spend a portion of their day at work in the community but reside in the halfway house during nonworking hours.

Halfway Houses   As its name implies, the **halfway house** is a transitional facility for soon-to-be-released inmates that connects them to community services, resources, and support. Usually, felons work in the community but reside in the halfway house during nonworking hours. Halfway houses range from secure institutions in the community, with programs designed to assist inmates who are preparing for release on parole, to group homes where parolees, probationers, or others diverted from the system live with

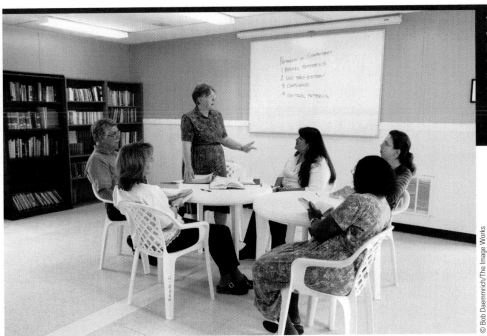

Transition from prison to the free world often takes place in a halfway house such as the Austin Transition Center in Del Valle, Texas. In many states parolees work in the community during the day but reside in a halfway house during nonworking hours. Halfway houses provide a range of services to assist former inmates.

minimal supervision and direction. Some halfway houses deliver special treatment services, such as programs designed to deal with alcohol, drug, or mental problems.

Residential programs have problems. Few neighborhoods want to host halfway houses or treatment centers for convicts. Community resistance has significantly impeded the development of community-based correctional facilities and has even forced some successful facilities to close. Many communities, often wealthier ones, have blocked the placement of halfway houses or treatment centers within their boundaries. One result of the NIMBY ("not in my backyard") attitude is that many centers are established in deteriorating neighborhoods inhabited by poor people, who lack the political power and resources to block unpopular programs.

In the 1970s, during the community corrections era, one could find halfway houses across the nation. However, a survey by the American Correctional Association (2000) recently found only 55 halfway houses being operated by ten state agencies. This means that such residential programs served fewer than 20,000 inmates. At a time when the need to assist offenders returning to their communities is great, lawmakers have deleted funding for residential support services from most state budgets.

PAROLE OFFICER: COP OR SOCIAL WORKER?

After release, a parolee's principal contact with the criminal justice system is the parole officer, who must provide both surveillance and assistance. Thus, parole officers are asked to play two different, some might say incompatible, roles: cop and social worker. Whereas parole was originally designed to help offenders make the transition from prison to the community, supervision has shifted ever more toward surveillance, drug testing, monitoring curfews, and collecting restitution. Safety and security have become major issues in parole services. (See "Careers in Criminal Justice" for information on the work requirements of parole officers.)

The Parole Officer as Cop   In their policing role, parole officers have the power to restrict many aspects of the parolee's life, to enforce the conditions of release, and to initiate revocation proceedings if parole conditions are violated. Like other officials in the criminal justice system, the parole officer has extensive discretion in low-visibility situations. In many states, parole officers have the authority to search the parolee's house without warning; to arrest him or her, without the possibility of bail, for suspected violations; and to suspend parole pending a hearing before the board.

CAREERS IN CRIMINAL JUSTICE

Parole Officer

NATURE OF THE WORK

Like their probation counterparts, parole officers supervise offenders in the community through personal contact with offenders and their families. Unlike probation officers, who are generally employed by the county, parole officers are employed by the state.

In most jurisdictions, they serve as armed peace officers with the power of arrest. As an essential ingredient in the reentry process, parole officers help offenders readjust to the community and find housing and employment. They monitor offenders' behavior to ensure that parole requirements are being met. If the conditions are not met or the offender commits another crime, the officer may recommend revocation of parole. Fieldwork may take the officer to high-crime areas that present a risk of violence.

REQUIRED QUALIFICATIONS

Background qualifications for parole officers vary by state, but a bachelor's degree in social work, criminal justice, or a related field is usually required. Some agencies require previous experience or graduate work. Candidates must be at least 21 years of age, have no felony convictions, and have no restrictions on their carrying a firearm. Most parole officers receive formal training and typically work as a trainee for up to one year.

EARNINGS AND JOB OUTLOOK

The number of parole officers is expected to grow as the number of inmates leaving prison increases during the next decade. Starting salaries for parole officers vary by region, with a range of $26,000 to $33,000 per year.

MORE INFORMATION

Visit the website of the American Probation and Parole Association at the corresponding site listed on the Cole/Smith Criminal Justice in America Companion Website: http://www.thomsonedu.com/criminaljustice/cole. You can also obtain career information from your state parole office.

This authoritarian component of the parole officer's role can give the ex-offender a sense of insecurity and hamper the development of mutual trust.

The parole officer is responsible for seeing that the parolee follows the conditions imposed by the parole board or department of corrections. Typically the conditions require the parolee to follow the parole officer's instructions; to permit the officer to visit the home and place of employment; to maintain employment; not to leave the state without permission; not to marry without permission; not to own a firearm; not to possess, use, or traffic in narcotics; not to consume alcohol to excess; and to comply with all laws and be a good citizen.

Parole officers are granted law enforcement powers in order to protect the community from offenders coming out of prison. However, because these powers diminish the possibility for the officer to develop a close relationship with the client, they can weaken the officer's ability to help the parolee adjust to the community.

The Parole Officer as Social Worker   Parole officers must act as social workers by helping the parolee find a job and restore family ties. Officers channel parolees to social agencies, such as psychiatric, drug, and alcohol clinics, where they can obtain help. As caseworkers, officers try to develop a relationship that allows parolees to confide their frustrations and concerns.

Because parolees are not likely to do this if they are constantly aware of the parole officer's ability to send them back to prison, some researchers have suggested that parole officers' conflicting responsibilities of cop and social worker should be separated. Parole officers could maintain the supervisory aspects of the position, and other personnel—perhaps a separate parole counselor—could perform the casework functions. Another option would be for parole officers to be charged solely with social work duties, while local police check for violations.

THE PAROLE BUREAUCRACY

Although parole officers have smaller caseloads than do probation officers, parolees require more extensive services. One reason is that parolees, by the very fact of their incarceration, have generally committed much more serious crimes. Another reason is that parolees must make a difficult transition from the highly structured prison environment to a society in which they have previously failed to live as law-abiding citizens. It is exceptionally difficult for a parole officer to monitor, control, and assist clients who may have little knowledge of or experience with living successfully within society's rules.

The parole officer works within a bureaucratic environment. Like most other human services organizations, parole agencies are short on resources and expertise. Because the difficulties faced by many parolees are so complex, the officer's job is almost impossible. As a result, parole officers frequently must classify parolees and give priority to those most in need. For example, most parole officers spend extra time with the newly released. As the officers gain greater confidence in the parolees, they can adjust their the level of supervision to "active" or "reduced" surveillance. Depending on how the parolees have functioned in the community, they may eventually be allowed to check in with their officers periodically instead of submitting to regular home visits, searches, and other intrusive monitoring.

ADJUSTMENT TO LIFE OUTSIDE PRISON

With little preparation, the ex-offender moves from the highly structured, authoritarian life of the institution into a world filled with temptations and complicated problems. Suddenly, ex-convicts who are unaccustomed to undertaking even simple tasks such as going to the store for groceries are expected to assume pressing, complex responsibilities. Finding a job and a place to live are not the only problems the newly released person faces. The parolee must also make significant social and psychological role adjustments. A male ex-convict, for example, must suddenly become not only a parolee but also an employee, a neighbor, a father, a husband, and a son. The expectations, norms, and social relations in the free world differ greatly from those learned in prison. The relatively predictable inmate code gives way to society's often unclear rules of behavior—rules that the offender had failed to cope with during his or her previous life in free society.

The problem of adjusting to life on the outside is well illustrated by the experience of Angel Coronado, whose release from the Texas State Prison was described in the opening section of this chapter. At that time Coronado vowed not to be returned to prison. However, since his release he has been mainly unemployed, has remained addicted to cocaine, and has served additional prison time for new crimes (Johnson, 2005).

In terms of living a crime-free life, today's parolees face even greater obstacles than did those released prior to 1990. Since that time Congress and many state legislatures have imposed new restrictions on ex-felons. These include denial of many things, including welfare benefits such as food stamps for those convicted of even minor drug crimes, access to public housing, receipt of student loans, and in some states voting rights. Studies have found that returning inmates often face so many restrictions after long periods of incarceration that the conditions amount to years of "invisible punishment" (Mauer and Chesney-Lind, 2002:1). As emphasized by Jeremy Travis (2002), the effects of these policies impact not only the individual parolee, but also their families and communities.

News accounts of brutal crimes committed by ex-offenders on parole fuel a public perception that parolees pose a threat to the community. The murder of 12-year-old Polly Klaas by a parolee and the rape and murder of 7-year-old Megan Kanka by a paroled sex offender spurred legislators across the nation to enact "sexual offender notification" laws. These laws require that the public be notified of the whereabouts of "potentially dangerous" sex offenders. In some states, paroled sex offenders must register with the police, whereas in others, the immediate neighbors must be

WHAT AMERICANS THINK

Question: "Some people think that if a person convicted of a crime serves his or her sentence and then does not violate the law for a period such as five years, government agencies SHOULD NOT make that criminal record available to employers or licensing agencies. Other people believe employers and licensing agencies SHOULD have access to such records and be able to consider the fact of a conviction in the hiring or licensing process. What do you think?"

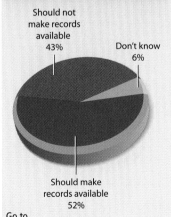

Should not make records available 43%

Don't know 6%

Should make records available 52%

Go to http://www.thomsonedu.com/criminaljustice/cole to compare your opinion on this issue with the opinions of other criminal justice students.

Source: Bureau of Justice Statistics, *Sourcebook of Criminal Justice Statistics, 2001* (Washington, DC: U.S. Government Printing Office, 2002), Table 2.55.

Sexual-offender registration laws have made it increasingly difficult for many parolees to adjust to the community. In Nueces County, Texas, District Court Judge Manuel Banales has ordered registered sex offenders to place signs in their yards and bumper stickers on their cars to make the public aware of who they are.

AP Photo/Corpus Christi Caller-Times, Paul Iverson

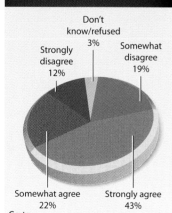

WHAT AMERICANS THINK

Question: "Please tell me if you agree or disagree with the following statement: 'People who are out of prison on parole and who fail a drug test, should be sent back to prison.'"

Don't know/refused 3%

Strongly disagree 12%

Somewhat disagree 19%

Somewhat agree 22%

Strongly agree 43%

Go to http://www.thomsonedu.com/criminaljustice/cole to compare your opinion on this issue with the opinions of other criminal justice students.

Source: Telephone interviews with a national adult sample by Beldon, Russonello, and Stewart, January 5–22, 2001. Data provided by the Roper Center for Public Opinion Research, University of Connecticut.

informed. Many states now have publicly accessible sex offender websites listing the names and addresses of those registered.

These laws have generated several unintended consequences. For example, parolees have been "hounded" from communities, the media have televised the parolees' homecomings, homes have been burned, parolees have been killed, and neighbors have assaulted parolees they erroneously thought were sex offenders. In some states, legislators wrote laws so broadly that statutory rape, consensual sodomy, and third-degree assault that might constitute inappropriate touching or sexual contact are included in the notification mandate. In 2006 two Maine parolees were shot by a man intent on killing registered sex offenders. One of those killed was on the list because, at age 19, he had been convicted of having consensual sex with his underage girlfriend. His murder heightened national debate as to whether the online registries put those listed at risk (G. Adams, 2006).

In any case, the fact of repeat violence fuels a public perception that parolees represent a continuing threat to the community. Although the new laws primarily center on people who have committed sex offenses against children, some fear that the community will eventually target all parolees. This preoccupation with potential parolee criminality makes it even more difficult for ex-offenders to reenter society successfully. "What Americans Think" on page 375 presents public attitudes on the availability of criminal records of ex-offenders. See also "Real-World Activity" at the end of this chapter.

REVOCATION OF PAROLE

The potential revocation of parole, for committing a new crime or violating the conditions of release, hangs constantly over the ex-inmate's head. The public tends to view the high number of revocations as a failure of parole. Corrections officials point to the great number of parolees who are required to be drug-free, be employed, and pay restitution—conditions that many find difficult to fulfill. Yet, as shown in "What Americans Think," there is strong support for sending back to prison those parolees who fail a drug test.

As discussed in Chapter 11, the Supreme Court ruled in *Morrissey v. Brewer* (1972) that if the parole officer alleges a technical violation, a two-step revocation proceeding is required. In the first stage a hearing determines whether there is probable cause to believe the conditions have been violated. The parolee has the right to be notified of the charges, to be informed of the evidence, to present witnesses, and to confront the witnesses. In the second stage the parole authority decides if the violation is severe enough to warrant return to prison.

Despite the increase in the number of parolees supervised, the percentage of those who are returned to prison because of a technical violation or conviction for a new offense has remained at about 40 percent (BJS, 2005c:9). However, the percentage of violators returned to prison varies by state, accounting for more than half of prison admissions in California (67 percent), Utah (55 percent), and Louisiana (53 percent) but less than 10 percent in Alabama and Florida. The percentage of parolees returned for technical violations also varies. For example, 17 percent of California's prison population consists of inmates who were returned for a technical violation, where in the State of Washington, only 1 percent were (Austin, 2001:319). As shown in Table 14.1, of those returned to prison, 70 percent had been arrested or convicted of a new offense.

TABLE 14.1   Reasons for Revocation among Parole Violators in State Prison

An increasing number of parolees are being returned to prison because of new arrests or technical violations. What factors might be causing this increase?

Reason for Revocation	
Arrest/conviction for new offense	69.9%
Drug-related violations	16.1
Positive test for drug use	7.9
Possession of drugs	6.6
Failure to report for drug testing	2.3
Failure to report for drug treatment	1.7
Absconders	22.3%
Failure to report/absconded	18.6
Left jurisdiction without permission	5.6
Other reasons	17.8%
Possession of gun(s)	3.5
Failure to report for counseling	2.4
Failure to meet financial obligations	2.3
Failure to maintain employment	1.2
Maintained contact with known offenders	1.2

Source: Bureau of Justice Statistics, *Special Report,* October 2001, p. 14.

CHECKPOINT

Answers

4. What are three programs designed to ease the reentry of offenders into the community?

→ 4. Work and educational release programs, furlough programs, and halfway houses.

5. What are the major tasks of parole officers?

→ 5. Surveillance and assistance.

6. What two conditions can result in the revocation of parole?

→ 6. Arrest for a new crime, or a technical violation of one or more of the conditions of parole.

The Future of Prisoner Reentry

The rising number of offenders returning to the community has only recently come to the attention of policy makers. One underrecognized impact of the incarceration policies of the 1980s was that "more prisoners in prison means that, eventually, more prisoners will be let out" (Butterfield, 2000). Corrections today faces a sudden flood of offenders leaving prison—about 650,000 per year—with about a third of these returning to prison, often within a year of their release. The recidivism rate demonstrates a failure of the criminal justice system to deal with the reentry problems of ex-felons. What is at the crux of this problem?

As you read earlier, Travis and Petersilia (2001) point to several factors that seem to have contributed to the reentry problem. First, the decline of parole boards, from mandatory release and other measures, means that more inmates must leave when their time is up—regardless of whether they have been prepared for the outside world of work, family, and other responsibilities. The percentage of releasees who have "maxed out" has also increased. Second, with the curtailment of rehabilitation and prerelease programs, parolees now have fewer prison programs preparing them for reentry into society and thus may be more vulnerable to returning to prison. Finally, the changing profile of returning prisoners has also affected reentry. Over a third of parolees were in prison for drug offenses, almost three times the percentage of 30 years ago. These prisoners may be at risk of slipping back into substance abuse. Prison terms also tend to be longer, so that parolees have a harder time of adjusting to life on the "outside" because they have been away for so long.

Thomson NOW

Improve your grade on the exam with Personalized Study! For reinforcement resources and a mastery check of The Future of Prisoner Reentry, go to www.thomsonedu.com/thomsonnow.

As prison populations rise, demands that felons be allowed to serve part of their time in the community will undoubtedly mount. These demands will not come from the public, which typically believes that all offenders should serve their full sentences. Instead, they will come from legislators and correctional officials who recognize that government lacks the money and facilities to incarcerate all offenders for the complete terms of their sentences. Although many offenders are not successfully integrated into the community, most will end up back in free society whether or not they serve their full sentences. Parole and community programs represent an effort to address the inevitability of their return. Even if such programs do not prevent all offenders from leaving a life of crime, they do help some to turn their lives around.

A QUESTION OF ETHICS: WRITING ASSIGNMENT

The five members of the parole board questioned Jim Allen, an offender with a long history of sex offenses involving teenage boys. Now approaching age 45 and having met the eligibility requirement for a hearing, Allen respectfully answered the board members.

Toward the end of the hearing, Richard Edwards, a dentist who had recently been appointed to the board, spoke up: "Your institutional record is good, you have a parole plan, a job has been promised, and your sister says she will help you. All of that looks good, but I just can't vote for your parole. You haven't attended the behavior modification program for sex offenders. I think you're going to repeat your crime. I have a 13-year-old son, and I don't want him or other boys to run the risk of meeting your kind."

Allen looked shocked. The other members had seemed ready to grant his release.

"But I'm ready for parole. I won't do that stuff again. I didn't go to that program because electroshock to my private area is not going to help me. I've

been here five years of the seven-year max and have stayed out of trouble. The judge didn't say I was to be further punished in prison by therapy."

After Jim Allen left the room, the board discussed his case. "You know, Rich, he has a point. He has been a model prisoner and has served a good portion of his sentence," said Brian Lynch, a long-term board member. "Besides we don't know if Dr. Hankin's program works."

"I know, but can we really let someone like that out on the streets?"

WRITING ASSIGNMENT

Are the results of the behavior-modification program for sex offenders relevant to the parole board's decision? Is the purpose of the sentence to punish Allen for what he *did* or for what he *might* do in the future? Would you vote for his release on parole? Prepare a statement for the parole board describing your response to these questions.

REAL-WORLD ACTIVITY: AN APPLICATION

Carl DeFlumer has spent 42 of his 62 years in prison for killing a boy when he was 14 and sodomizing another 29 years later. In 1994 the New York State Board of Parole granted his release to live with his sister. Word of DeFlumer's impending release caused a howl of protest in Bethlehem, the rural community where his sister lives. Residents expressed fear for the safety of their children. As one said, "You need a building permit to put a fence in your yard. But they can put one of these guys next door and not even tell you."

RESEARCHING THE INTERNET

Go to **InfoTrac** College Edition. Enter the keyword *parole neighborhood* and read the article entitled "Residents Hope to Fend Off a Neighborhood Parole Office," *New York Times*, March 12, 2000.

APPLICATION

Should residents be allowed to determine if parolees can live in their community? What should happen to offenders who complete their sentence and have no place to reside?

SUMMARY

- The successful reentry of ex-prisoners to the community has become a pressing problem.

- Conditional release from prison on parole is the primary method by which inmates return to society. While on parole they remain under correctional supervision.

- There are four types of release: discretionary, mandatory, other conditional release, and expiration release.

- Parole boards exercise the discretion to consider various factors in making the decision to release.

- Parolees gain release from prison on the condition that they do not again violate the law and that they live according to rules designed both to help them adjust to society and to control their movements.

- Parole officers are assigned to assist ex-inmates making the transition to society and to ensure that they follow the conditions of their release.

- Upon release, offenders face many problems: They must find housing and employment and renew relationships with family and friends.

- Community corrections assumes that reentry should be a gradual process through which parolees should be assisted. Work and educational release, furloughs, and halfway houses are geared to ease the transition.

- Parole may be revoked for commission of a crime or for violating the rules governing supervision.

QUESTIONS FOR REVIEW

1. What are the basic assumptions of parole?

2. How do mandatory release, discretionary release, and unconditional release differ?

3. What roles does the parole officer play?

4. What problems confront parolees upon their release?

KEY TERMS AND CASES

conditions of release (p. 370)
discretionary release (p. 367)
expiration release (p. 368)

furlough (p. 373)
halfway house (p. 373)
mandatory release (p. 368)

other conditional release (p. 368)
parole (p. 365)
work and educational release (p. 372)

GOING ONLINE

ThomsonNOW™

Maximize your study time by using ThomsonNOW's diagnostic study plan to help you review this chapter. The Study Plan will

- Help you identify areas on which you should concentrate

- Provide interactive exercises to help you master the chapter concepts

- Provide a posttest to confirm you are ready to move on to the next chapter

INSIDE THE CRIMINAL JUSTICE SYSTEM AND BEYOND: ONE MAN'S JOURNEY

Written by Chuck Terry

Prison

The trip from the county jail to prison, a bus ride known among prisoners as "the chain," can be an unsettling experience. On this particular trip I was accompanied by about thirty other inmates. The scenery we saw outside the grilled windows changed as we headed southeast out of Los Angeles. Freeways, business districts, and suburban neighborhoods were left behind and replaced by small towns, farms, and livestock. During the ride I thought about all I would be missing out there, all the things I wouldn't be able to do wherever I was going, and wondered what my future would bring. For first-termers "the chain" can be as scary as hell. For others it may be routine. Most probably wonder if they'll get out alive. I always did.

Once again, my destination was the Regional Guidance Center at Chino. Only this time, rather than coming for a ninety-day evaluation, I would be classified as a "new commitment." Instead of being "evaluated," I would be processed and sent to another facility somewhere within the state. As we approached the institution I saw the familiar-looking guard towers, chain-link fences covered with barbed razor wire, and the outside windows of the cell blocks. Once we arrived, the bus passed through an electronically operated gate. Our entrance was monitored by armed guards. It was here that I experienced that fleeting sense of impending doom, the feeling that I might never get out of prison again. After the bus stopped we sat for several minutes, chained together and relatively quiet, until the guards came and escorted us inside.

After entering the guidance center I was again booked—fingerprinted, photographed, searched—and told where to live. Given that I had just come from here, being new wasn't that big a deal. Besides, I was getting used to these places. Yet the time I spent inside in the years to come unquestionably affected my sense of identity and ideas about life. After two months of processing, including psychological and physical examinations, I was sent to the California Correctional Center at Lassen, a facility more commonly known as "Susanville," the town in which it is located.

In prison I learned to hate and to do whatever I could to use drugs without compromising my integrity. All myths aside, drugs are hard to get in prison. I learned what it's like to be a minority. Mostly, I learned to see myself and the world from the perspective of a convict.

Life inside is extremely monotonous, although life-threatening situations can arise in a heartbeat. Prison is a world in which you can never show weakness, where you adapt to survive, and where race and "fitting in" are very important. In prison it's not so much what crime you did (except for heinous crimes such as sex offenses or crimes against children—those offenders get no respect), but who you are within that world that determines how you are seen and treated both by fellow inmates and prison workers. And who you are is gauged by the people you run with, how you carry yourself, and your character. And it all takes place within a structure of nearly total control and oppression.

People often ask me what it is really like in prison. The answer depends on historical context, where you are doing time, and who you are. It is different now than it was twenty years ago. It will vary and depend on political ideology, level of custody (maximum or minimum), what color you are (and how that matches with the racial composition of the prison), how old you are, how much experience you have within the system, and, of course, the perspectives you bring with you into the institution. But the degrading, dehumanizing effects of prison are usually similar because they stem from the same structural roots.

Prisoners are, by definition, a threat to society and in need of control. Therefore, we (I include myself here because I am writing from the perspective of a convict) must be confined, observed, and kept in our place. To achieve these goals our keepers tell us where and when to eat, sleep, go to the bathroom, exercise, and work. What we see, hear, smell, touch, and do on a daily basis depends on them. We are deprived of privacy, heterosexual relationships, education, employment (except at the most menial levels), and the ability to attain material things. Adding to these effects is the contempt with which we are often treated by prison officials.

Sadly, most of the hate and anger generated from the structure of prisons are directed toward other inmates. We seldom focus our attention on changing the conditions and people who bind us. For the most part, we accept our situation as being "the way it is." Perhaps we do this because we believe we deserve it. After all, we are in prison and the guards are just doing their jobs. But sometimes the veils we hide behind are ripped apart as the harsh realities of life become impossible to deny, often as a result of institutionalized violence.

One day, during my months at Susanville, a friend told me that everyone was getting together to have a work strike. Once in the yard I saw something that I never saw before or since: all the races (brown, white, black) were participating in a single act of defiance against the conditions of the prison. Leaders from each race acted as representatives, spoke openly about our needs, and emphasized that this was to be a nonviolent strike. We would simply not go to work until our demands were met.

Within fifteen minutes of this gathering, we heard "Yard recall, yard recall, all men return to your dorms" over the loudspeakers. To establish more control than was possible from the gun towers, extra guards armed with rifles appeared at strategic locations on the roofs of our housing units. We were herded inside our dorms, placed on lockdown status, and fed sack lunches (two baloney sandwiches and an apple) twice a day.

On the afternoon of the fourth day we heard bullets ricocheting against the bricks that made up the lower part of the dorm walls. Above the bricks were windows, out of which we could see the yard, the gun towers, and the guards on the roofs. The bullets made a loud pinging sound like you hear in movies. A friend of mine, five feet away, turned toward me and said, "They're poppin' caps out there [shooting bullets]!" Someone else said, "Those ain't real bullets," as if it weren't possible for such a thing to happen. Next thing I know, my friend fell to the ground and said, "I'm hit." Thinking he was joking, I told him, "Quit bullshitting, get up." But I quickly saw blood coming from his groin area. He really had been shot.

With reality becoming obvious and the bullets still pinging, we all dropped to the floor. I grabbed my friend (who was moaning in agony), dragged him under my bunk for safety, put a tourniquet on his wound, and tried to calm him until the guards came and took him out of there. That evening, after things had settled down, we saw the "goon squad," a row of twelve guards, three in each row, dressed in full battle gear with helmets and clubs, coming across the yard toward our end of the prison. For a few minutes we lost sight of the "gooners," but before long we saw all the men from an upstairs dorm running across the yard, the goon squad right behind them.

Over the course of that long night every man in the prison was "guided" to what is called a "classification hearing," a legal procedure that must take place before a body can be transferred to another institution. Until the early hours of the following day, many inmates were openly beaten during their journeys to the hearing. It was like watching a live version of the Rodney King beating, right in front of our eyes. At classification we were asked, "Are you ready to work?" Those who said no were shipped to another prison.

Of the more than one thousand inmates housed in that prison, over 120 were transferred that night. Three were shot and many more seriously hurt. Interestingly, television newscasters reported that "inmates were violently rioting" (a lie) in the local prison but were now "back under control."

After the strike was "resolved," I went back to my clerk job in "Receiving and Release" (the place where inmates enter and leave the prison). After seeing my friend shot and all the beatings that had taken place, I had to ask my boss (a sergeant) why the guards had to hurt so many people that night. He answered, "They just want you guys to know who is running this joint."

Over the next several months the story about what happened got out. People from the state capital came to investigate. About 200 inmates took lie detector tests to validate their stories. Not one guard would agree to do the same. And nobody forced the issue. To my knowledge, nothing was ever done to rectify the damage that had been done that day. It is as if it never happened.

Similarly, the harsh reality of living in prison is seldom acknowledged. Does anyone deserve to live in such an environment? Does it matter if one is convicted for murder or possession of drugs? Apparently not. Why you are sentenced to prison makes little difference once you're on the inside.

After being in prison for twelve months I appeared before a parole board that consisted of two men who talked to me as if I were some kind of dog. Their comments were based on my "history," which they had in front of them in a file: rap sheet, prior presentence investigations, police reports, and the results from the ninety-day evaluation. For the most part they harassed and belittled me with questions about my past. The only thing I said was yes when they asked me if I understood them. After they'd had their say, I was asked to step outside the room while they made a decision. They told me they decided to give me a total of twenty-six months (from the time of arrest until release), which was about what I'd expected. They also told me that if I didn't start acting right, the next time they saw me would be at Folsom Prison and they would bury me so deep I'd never see daylight again. As I left the room I felt great. Many people I knew didn't get a "date" at all and had to wait another year just to appear.

In my final years in prison, the perception I had about myself and the world took a dramatic shift, largely as the result of attending two years of college classes. Learning was exciting. It opened my eyes to things I never knew and helped me see that there were other, more important things to do besides using heroin. In 1992 I was discharged from parole.

Coming Home

Getting released from prison is like coming home from a war. The more time you do the greater the shock. From a world where great meaning comes from the color of your skin, whom you hang out with, which bench you sit on in the yard, and where you eat in the chow hall, you find yourself out here. Choices. Kids. Shopping. Women. Asshole car drivers. Pets. Around people who define themselves based on their jobs, how many "things" they have, or their political affiliation. Life inside was structured. You clearly knew your place—count time, chow line, yard line, sick line. Out here it's really different.

I was assigned to a parole officer known as "Lock-'em-up Tom." Like my old probation officer, Tom told me he didn't think I had a chance of making it. He said I would have to regularly test for drugs and attend Twelve-Step meetings at least three times a week. When I informed him that I no longer had a drug problem, he smiled and said, "Well, Chuck, that might be true. But you also don't know how to live out here. Its kinda like the first time you went to jail—it was something new. You had to learn about it and adapt in order to survive. As I see it, that's what you need to do now—only in reverse. By getting involved with other clean addicts you might just learn how." Tom never did lock me up. He spied on me, tested me, and always talked down to me. Yet his ideas about what I'd have to do to make it were definitely grounded in reality. In many ways I am still learning how to live out here.

15

Juvenile Justice

On the night of October 12, 2001, 14-year-old Devin Lyman and three friends—Andrew Anderson, aged 16, and two other juveniles, aged 11 and 13, sneaked out of their homes and wandered around downtown Canaan, Connecticut, a community of two thousand located in the Litchfield Hills. Around 1:30 A.M., the boys set fire to leaves under a wooden platform near Keilty's Depot, a popular restaurant in the 130-year-old Canaan Railroad Station. As the fire spread to the building, the boys fled. The two younger boys wanted to call 911 from a nearby pay phone, but Anderson and Lyman talked them out of it. The blaze consumed the historic landmark, caused more than $2 million in damage, wrecked several businesses, and cost dozens of jobs.

In the police investigation, suspicion focused on the four juveniles. Under questioning, Lyman made up a false alibi but later confessed. Because he and Armstrong were older than 14 at the time of the incident, the juvenile court judge waived jurisdiction and they were indicted in the adult court. The 11- and 13-year-old boys were dealt with in juvenile court; their names have not been released.

In May 2002 Devin Lyman pleaded guilty to third-degree arson and first-degree criminal mischief. In a June court appearance before Judge Alexandra DiPentima, Lyman said that he didn't mean to burn down the building: "I can't describe the sorrow I feel toward these people (the victims). I hope they somehow can forgive." Lyman's mother pointed out that her son had never been in trouble before and that he was only six months too old for protection by the juvenile justice system. Defense attorney Michael Sconyers argued that Lyman was only one of four boys and wasn't the instigator. "Devin is only 15, he's an unformed human being. Devin is not a criminal."

Judge DiPentima disagreed with Sconyers. "Punishment must fit the criminal as well as the crime. And while attorney Sconyers has indicated Devin is not a criminal, he indeed is." She then sentenced Devin to a 10-year prison term to be suspended after eight months, followed by

5 years of probation, 800 hours of community service, and payment of symbolic restitution of $8,000. Addressing the offender, she said, "What you did and didn't do changed people's lives in a permanent and devastating way. Your parents and teachers support you. Don't let them down again, and more importantly, don't let yourself down" (*Hartford Courant,* June 27, 2002, p. A1).

At the same time that society confronts the frightening fact that young offenders can commit terrible acts, no consensus has been reached on how to solve this problem. Should juveniles continue to be treated differently from adults when they commit crimes, assuming that juveniles can be taught to change their ways? Or should society treat all criminals alike, by being tough on everyone who commits violent crimes? Separate institutions and processes have developed to handle crimes by juveniles.

The juvenile justice system is a separate but interrelated part of the broader criminal justice system. The formal processes of juvenile justice differ from those in the adult system, but the greatest differences concern emphasis. One cannot separate the problems of youth from the activities and concerns of policing, courts, or corrections. With juveniles committing a significant portion of criminal offenses, we need to pay serious attention to this system.

QUESTIONS FOR INQUIRY

1. What is the extent of youth crime in the United States?
2. How did the juvenile justice system develop, and what assumptions was it based on?
3. What determines the jurisdiction of the juvenile justice system?
4. How does the juvenile justice system operate?
5. What are some of the problems facing the American system of juvenile justice?

Youth Crime in the United States

Dramatic criminal acts by youths make headlines: In Denver a child visiting the zoo was hit by a bullet intended by one teenager for another. A 17-year-old Salt Lake City boy was kicked and then shot to death by a group of his fellow high school students.

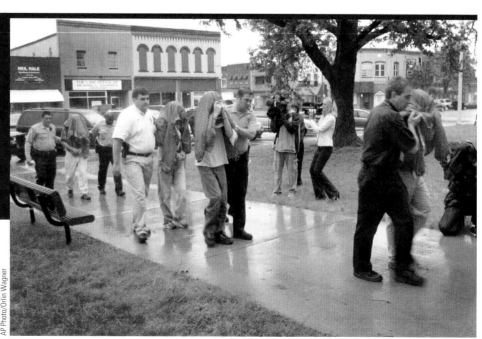

Four of five Riverton High School students suspected in a school-shooting plot are led to a hearing at the Cherokee County Courthouse in Columbus, Kansas, on April 24, 2006. Sheriff's deputies found guns, ammunition, knives, and coded messages in the bedroom of one suspect and documents about firearms and references to Armageddon in two suspects' school lockers. It is alleged that the students planned the rampage to coincide with the anniversary of the Columbine High School shootings.

AP Photo/Orlin Wagner

FIGURE 15.1
Percentage of arrests of people under 18 years old (rounded)
Juveniles are arrested for a wide range of offenses. For some offenses—such as arson, vandalism, motor vehicle theft, and burglary—juveniles account for a larger proportion of arrests than the percentage of juveniles in the general population would suggest.

Source: Federal Bureau of Investigation, *Uniform Crime Reports* (Washington, DC: U.S. Government Printing Office, 2005), Table 41.

Percentage of arrests involving juveniles:

Category	Percentage
All arrests	16%
Violent Crime Index	15%
Property Crime Index	32%
Arson	51%
Vandalism	39%
Disorderly conduct	30%
Burglary	29%
Larceny-theft	28%
Robbery	24%
Weapons	23%
Liquor laws	22%
Sex offense	20%
Stolen property	19%
Other assault	19%
Forcible rape	16%
Aggravated assault	14%
Drug abuse	12%
Murder	9%
Fraud	3%
Prostitution	2%
Driving under the influence	1%

A British tourist was killed while at a rest stop; a 13-year-old boy was one of the suspects. Are these only isolated incidents, or is the United States facing a major increase in youth crime?

The juvenile crime incidents just described are rare. In a nation with 70 million people under 18, about 1.5 million arrests of juveniles take place each year, 96,000 (4 percent) of which are for violent crimes. After rising from 1988 to 1994, the juvenile violent crime rate has now returned to 1985 levels (FBI, 2005b: Table 41). Yet when American high school seniors are asked to identify the two or three most serious problems they worry about, they cite crime and drugs, as shown in "What Americans Think." *STATUS OFFENSE*

Youth crimes range from UCR index crimes (for example murder, rape, robbery, assault) to "youthful crimes" such as curfew violations, loitering, and being a runaway (see Figure 15.1). About 1 in 20 people in the under-18 cohort is taken into police custody each year, and nearly a million are processed by juvenile courts. Most juvenile crimes are committed by young men; only 28 percent of arrestees under age 18 are female (OJJDP, 2002). Some researchers have estimated that one boy in three will be arrested by the police at some point before his 18th birthday.

Criminologists have tried to explain the rise of the "epidemic" of violent youth crime that erupted in the mid-1980s, reaching its peak in 1993. The general rise in

WHAT AMERICANS THINK

Question: "Of all the problems facing the nation today, how often do you worry about each of the following?"

Percentage of high school seniors responding "often" or "sometimes".

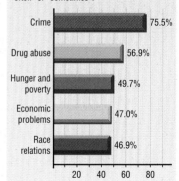

Problem	Percentage
Crime	75.5%
Drug abuse	56.9%
Hunger and poverty	49.7%
Economic problems	47.0%
Race relations	46.9%

Go to http://www.thomsonedu.com/criminaljustice/cole to compare your opinion on this issue with the opinions of other criminal justice students.

Source: Bureau of Justice Statistics, *Sourcebook of Criminal Justice Statistics, 2003* (Washington, DC: U.S. Government Printing Office, 2004), Table 2.69.

TECHNOLOGY ISSUES IN CRIMINAL JUSTICE

Impact of Entertainment Technology on Behavior

The development of technology can provide new tools to combat crime. New inventions offer a greater capacity to investigate crimes, combat criminals with new weapons, and monitor offenders. While new technology may help with respect to the crime problem, can technology also be a cause of crime? For example, a significant debate centers on the role of violent entertainment in influencing the behavior of juveniles. Cable television, video rentals, and DVD rentals permit young people to gain access to shows containing violence and sex. Rock music and rap songs sometimes include lyrics that glorify violence. Some experts assert that such exposure can desensitize viewers to the wrongfulness of violence and the suffering endured by victims. Other experts claim that the existing evidence does not show that violent entertainment encourages violent behavior.

Violent shows and music lyrics have fueled the debate for two decades, but recent years have brought a proliferation of ultrarealistic and extremely bloody video games. Children can experience the "thrill" of shooting, killing, and mutilating realistic video characters. Moreover, players must be skilled and successful in video violence to win the game. Will concerns mount with the expansion of "virtual reality" devices in which consumers look through viewfinders attached to a headset to make them feel as if they are really participating in a battle scene?

In September 2000 the Federal Trade Commission released a report on violent entertainment marketed to children. For example, the federal agency examined 118 electronic games with a Mature rating for violence and found that 70 percent of those games were promoted for players under age 17. The marketing plans for most of these games expressly sought to attract juvenile buyers, and the rest were advertised in magazines and television shows with a substantial audience of children. The report, which also criticized the promotion to children of violent movies and music with objectionable lyrics, led to calls in Congress for greater regulation of the entertainment industry.

RESEARCHING THE INTERNET

The website of the American Psychology Association has much information on the links between television violence and behavior. Also look at the National Institute of Mental Health website. Both are listed on the Cole/Smith Criminal Justice in America Companion Website: http://www.thomsonedu.com/criminaljustice/cole.

FOR CRITICAL ANALYSIS

Do you think that video games and other technology-based forms of entertainment (for example, CDs, DVDs, and videos) teach young people inappropriate values or otherwise encourage crime and violence? If so, what should society do to respond to this problem? Are there ways that technology could be used to teach positive values (for example, computer software and the Internet)?

Sources: Drawn from Federal Trade Commission, "FTC Releases Report on the Marketing of Violent Entertainment to Children," press release, September 11, 2000; Richard Rhodes, "Hollow Claims about Fantasy Violence," *New York Times*, September 17, 2000, p. 19.

violence among youths has led some to consider the impact of entertainment technology on behavior (see "Technology Issues in Criminal Justice"). Scholars also point more specifically to the drug trade, especially crack cocaine and the related increase in gun carrying and use by youths. Alfred Blumstein (1996) suggests that as more juveniles, particularly inner-city minority male youths, were recruited into the drug trade, they armed themselves with guns and used those firearms in battles over market turf.

Youth gangs have become another dangerous presence in most American cities. Gangs such as the Black P Stone Nation, CRIPS (Common Revolution in Progress), and Bloods first came to police attention in the 1970s. The National Youth Gang Survey estimates that there are now more than 21,500 gangs with 731,500 members (OJJDP, 2004:1). See "Real-World Activity" for more on gangs.

Juvenile delinquency, neglect, and dependency have been concerns since the beginning of the Republic, yet not until the early twentieth century did a separate system to deal with these problems evolve. The contemporary juvenile justice system has gone through a major shift of emphasis as well. The rest of the chapter explores the history of juvenile justice, the process it follows today, and some of the problems associated with it.

ThomsonNOW
Improve your grade on the exam with Personalized Study! For reinforcement resources and a mastery check of Youth Crime in the United States, go to www.thomsonedu.com/thomsonnow.

CHECKPOINT

Answers

1. What might explain the "epidemic" of violent crime committed by juveniles in the 1990s? ⟶ 1. Juveniles, armed with guns, recruited into the inner-city drug trade.

The Development of Juvenile Justice

The system and philosophy of juvenile justice that began in the United States during the social reform period of the late nineteenth century was based on the idea that the state should act as would a parent in the interest of the child. This view remained unchallenged until the 1960s, when the Supreme Court ushered in the juvenile rights period. With the rise in juvenile crime in the 1980s, the juvenile justice system shifted again to one focusing on the problem of controlling youth crime. Today, people are yet again reexamining the philosophy and processes of the juvenile justice system.

The idea that children should be treated differently from adults originated in the common law and in the chancery courts of England. The common law had long prescribed that children under seven years of age were incapable of felonious intent and were therefore not criminally responsible. Children aged 7 to 14 could be held accountable only if it could be shown that they understood the consequences of their actions.

The English chancery courts, established during the Middle Ages, heard only civil cases, mainly concerning property. However, under the doctrine of *parens patriae,* which held the king to be the father of the realm, the chancery courts exercised protective jurisdiction over all children, particularly those involved in questions of dependency, neglect, and property. At this time the criminal courts, not a separate juvenile court, dealt with juvenile offenders. In legitimizing the actions of the state on behalf of the child, however, the concept of *parens patriae* laid the groundwork for the development of juvenile justice.

Table 15.1 outlines the shifts in how the United States has dealt with the problems of youth. These shifts fall into five periods of American juvenile justice history. Each was characterized by changes in juvenile justice that reflected the social, intellectual, and political currents of the time. During the past two hundred years, population shifts from rural to urban areas, immigration, developments in the social sciences, political reform movements, and the continuing problem of youth crime have all influenced how Americans have treated juveniles.

parens patriae The state as parent; the state as guardian and protector of all citizens (such as juveniles) who cannot protect themselves.

THE PURITAN PERIOD (1646–1824)

The English procedures were maintained in the American colonies and continued into the nineteenth century. The earliest attempt by a colony to deal with problem children was passage of the Massachusetts Stubborn Child Law in 1646. With this law, the Puritans of the Massachusetts Bay Colony imposed the view that the child was evil and they emphasized the need of the family to discipline and raise youths. The law dealt with those who would not obey their parents.

THE REFUGE PERIOD (1824–1899)

As the population of American cities began to grow during the early 1800s, the problem of youth crime and neglect became a concern for reformers. Just as the Quakers of Philadelphia were instrumental during the same period in reforming correctional practices, other groups supported changes toward the education and protection of youths. These reformers focused their efforts primarily on the urban immigrant poor, seeking to have parents declared "unfit" if their children roamed the streets and were apparently "out of control." Although not all such children engaged in criminal acts, the reformers believed that children whose parents did not discipline and train them to abide by the rules of society

During the nineteenth century, reformers such as Denver's Judge Ben Lindsey were alarmed by the living conditions of inner-city youth. One result was development of juvenile court in cities such as Denver and Chicago.

© Corbis

TABLE 15.1 Juvenile Justice Developments in the United States

Period	Major Developments	Causes and Influences	Juvenile Justice System
Puritan (1646–1824)	Massachusetts Stubborn Child Law (1646).	• Puritan view of child as evil • Economically marginal agrarian society	Law provides • Symbolic standard of maturity • Support for family as economic unit
Refuge (1824–1899)	Institutionalization of deviants; House of Refuge in New York established (1825) for delinquent and dependent children.	• Enlightenment • Immigration and industrialization	Child seen as helpless, in need of state intervention
Juvenile Court (1899–1960)	Establishment of separate legal system for juveniles; Illinois Juvenile Court Act (1899).	• Reformism and rehabilitative ideology • Increased immigration, urbanization, large-scale industrialization	Juvenile court institutionalized legal irresponsibility of child.
Juvenile Rights (1960–1980)	Increased "legalization" of juvenile law; *Gault* decision (1967); Juvenile Justice and Delinquency Prevention Act (1974) calls for deinstitutionalization of status offenders.	• Criticism of juvenile justice system on humane grounds • Civil rights movement by disadvantaged groups	Movement to define and protect rights as well as to provide services to children.
Crime Control (1980–present)	Concern for victims, punishment for serious offenders, transfer to adult court of serious offenders, protection of children from physical and sexual abuse	• More-conservative public attitudes and policies • Focus on serious crimes by repeat offenders	System more formal, restrictive, punitive; increased percentage of police referrals to court; incarcerated youths stay longer periods.

Sources: Adapted from Barry Krisberg, Ira M. Schwartz, Paul Litsky, and James Austin, "The Watershed of Juvenile Justice Reform," *Crime and Delinquency* 32 (January 1986): 5–38; U.S. Department of Justice, *A Preliminary National Assessment of the Status Offender and the Juvenile Justice System* (Washington, DC: U.S. Government Printing Office, 1980), 29.

would end up in prison. The state's power was to be used to prevent delinquency. The solution was to create institutions where these children could learn good work and study habits, live in a disciplined and healthy environment, and develop "character."

The first of these institutions was the House of Refuge in New York, which opened in 1825. This half-prison, half-school housed destitute and orphaned children as well as those convicted of crime (Friedman, 1993:164). Similar facilities followed in Boston, Philadelphia, and Baltimore. Children were placed in these homes by court order, usually because of neglect or vagrancy. They often stayed until they were old enough to be legally regarded as adults. The houses were run according to a strict program of work, study, and discipline.

Some states created "reform schools" to provide the discipline and education needed by wayward youth in a "homelike" atmosphere, usually in rural areas. The first, the Lyman School for Boys, opened in Westboro, Massachusetts, in 1848. A similar Massachusetts reform school for girls opened in 1855 for "the instruction . . . and reformation, of exposed, helpless, evil disposed and vicious girls" (Friedman, 1993:164). Institutional programs began in New York in 1849, Ohio in 1850, and Maine, Rhode Island, and Michigan in 1906.

Despite these reforms, children could still be arrested, detained, tried, and imprisoned. Even in states that had institutions for juveniles, the criminal justice process for children was the same as that for adults.

THE JUVENILE COURT PERIOD (1899–1960)

With most states providing services to neglected youth by the end of the nineteenth century, the problem of juvenile criminality became the focus of attention. Progressive reformers pushed for the state to provide individualized care and treatment to deviants of all kinds—adult criminals, the mentally ill, juvenile delinquents. They urged adoption of probation, treatment, indeterminate sentences, and parole for adult offenders and succeeded in establishing similar programs for juveniles.

Referred to as the "child savers," these upper-middle-class reformers sought to use the power of the state to "save" children from a life of crime (Platt, 1977). They shared a concern about the role of environmental factors on behavior and a belief that benevolent state action could solve social problems. They also believed the claim of the new social sciences that they could treat the problems underlying deviance.

Reformers wanted a separate juvenile court system that could address the problems of individual youths by using flexible procedures that, as one reformer said, "banish entirely all thought of crime and punishment" (Rothman, 1980:213). They put their idea into action with the creation of the juvenile court.

Passage of the Juvenile Court Act by Illinois in 1899 established the first comprehensive system of juvenile justice. The act placed under one jurisdiction cases of dependency, neglect, and delinquency ("incorrigibles and children threatened by immoral associations as well as criminal lawbreakers") for children under 16. The act had four major elements:

- A separate court for delinquent, dependent, and neglected children.
- Special legal procedures that were less adversarial than those in the adult system.
- Separation of children from adults in all portions of the justice system.
- Programs of probation to assist the courts in deciding what best served the interests of the state and the child.

Activists such as Jane Addams and Julia Lathrop, both of the settlement house movement; Henry Thurston, a social work educator; and the National Congress of Mothers successfully promoted the juvenile court concept. By 1904, ten states had implemented procedures similar to those of Illinois. By 1917, all but three states provided for a juvenile court.

The philosophy of the juvenile court derived from the idea that the state should deal with a child who broke the law much as a wise parent would deal with a wayward child. The doctrine of *parens patriae* again helped legitimize the system. Procedures would be informal and private, records would be confidential, children would be detained apart from adults, and probation and social workers would be appointed. Even the vocabulary and physical setting of the juvenile system were changed to emphasize diagnosis and treatment instead of findings of guilt. The term *criminal behavior* was replaced by *delinquent behavior* when it referred to the acts of children. The terminology reflected the underlying belief that these children could be "cured" and returned to society as law-abiding citizens.

Because procedures were not to be adversarial, lawyers were unnecessary. Psychologists and social workers, who could determine the juvenile's underlying behavioral problem, became the main professionals attached to the system. But these reforms took place in a system in which children lacked the due process rights held by adults.

THE JUVENILE RIGHTS PERIOD (1960–1980)

Until the early 1960s few questioned the sweeping powers of juvenile justice officials. When the U.S. Supreme Court expanded the rights of adult defendants, however, lawyers and scholars began to criticize the extensive discretion given to juvenile justice officials. In a series of decisions (see Figure 15.2), the U.S. Supreme Court expanded the rights of juveniles.

In the first of these cases, *Kent v. United States* (1966), the Supreme Court ruled that juveniles had the right to counsel at a hearing at which a juvenile judge may waive jurisdiction and pass the case to the adult court.

In re Gault (1967) extended due process rights to juveniles. Fifteen-year-old Gerald Gault had been sentenced to six years in a state training school for making a prank phone call. Had he been an adult, the maximum punishment for making such a call would have been a fine of $5 to $50 or imprisonment for two months at most. Gault was convicted and sentenced in an informal proceeding without being represented by counsel. The justices held that a child in a delinquency hearing must receive

In re Gault (1967) Juveniles have the right to have counsel, to confront and examine accusers, to be protected against self-incrimination, and to have adequate notice of charges when confinement is a possible punishment.

FIGURE 15.2
Major decisions by the U.S. Supreme Court regarding the rights of juveniles

Since the mid-1960s the Supreme Court has gradually expanded the rights of juveniles but has continued to recognize that the logic of the separate system for juvenile offenders justifies differences from some adult rights.

Note: For discussion of death penalty cases, see Chapter 10.

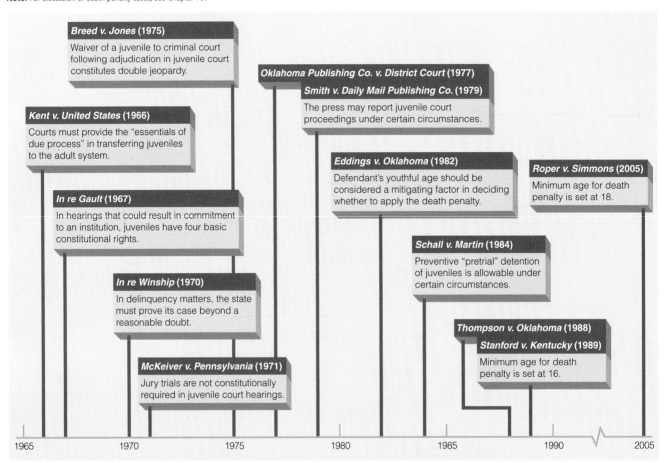

Source: Office of Juvenile Justice and Delinquency Prevention, *1999 National Report* (Washington, DC: U.S. Government Printing Office, 1999), 90–91.

In re Winship (1970) The standard of proof beyond a reasonable doubt applies to juvenile delinquency proceedings.

McKeiver v. Pennsylvania (1971) Juveniles do not have a constitutional right to a trial by jury.

Breed v. Jones (1975) Juveniles cannot be found delinquent in juvenile court and then transferred to adult court without a hearing on the transfer; to do so violates the protection against double jeopardy.

status offense Any act committed by a juvenile that is considered unacceptable for a child, such as truancy or running away from home, but that would not be a crime if it were committed by an adult.

certain procedural rights, including notice of the charges, right to counsel, right to confront and cross-examine witnesses, and protection against self-incrimination. They did not extend to juveniles the right of trial by jury. Writing for the majority, Justice Abe Fortas emphasized that due process rights and procedures have a place in juvenile justice: "Under our Constitution the condition of being a boy does not justify a kangaroo court."

Shortly after the precedent-setting *Gault* decision, a series of cases further defined the rights of juveniles. In the case of *In re Winship* (1970), the Court held that proof must be established "beyond a reasonable doubt" and not on "a preponderance of the evidence" before a juvenile may be classified as a delinquent for committing an act that would be a crime if committed by an adult. The Court was not willing to give juveniles every due process right, however: It held in *McKeiver v. Pennsylvania* (1971) that "trial by jury in the juvenile court's adjudicative stage is not a constitutional requirement." But in *Breed v. Jones* (1975), the Court extended the protection against double jeopardy to juveniles by requiring that, before a case is adjudicated in juvenile court, a hearing must be held to determine if it should be transferred to the adult court.

Another area of change concerned **status offenses**—acts that are not illegal if committed by an adult; these include skipping school, running away from home, or living a "wayward, idle or dissolute life" (Feld, 1993:203). In 1974 Congress passed the Juvenile Justice and Delinquency Prevention Act, which included provisions for taking status offenders out of correctional institutions. Since then, people have worked on diverting such children out of the system, on reducing the possibility of incarceration, and on rewriting status offense laws.

As juvenile crime rates continued to rise during the 1970s, the public began calling for tougher approaches to dealing with delinquents. In the 1980s, at the same time that adult offenders faced stricter sanctions, juvenile justice policies shifted to crime control.

THE CRIME CONTROL PERIOD (1980–PRESENT)

Since 1980 the public has demanded a "crackdown on crime." Legislators have responded in part by changing the juvenile system. Greater attention is now being focused on repeat offenders, with policy makers calling for harsher punishment for juveniles who commit crimes.

In *Schall v. Martin* (1984), the Supreme Court significantly departed from the trend toward increased juvenile rights. The Court confirmed that the general notion of *parens patriae* was a primary basis for the juvenile court, equal in importance to the Court's desire to protect the community from crime. Thus, juveniles may be held in preventive detention before trial if they are deemed a "risk" to the community.

> **Schall v. Martin (1984)** Juveniles can be held in preventive detention if there is concern that they may commit additional crimes while awaiting court action.

The *Schall* decision reflects the ambivalence permeating the juvenile justice system. On one side are the liberal reformers, who call for increased procedural and substantive legal protections for juveniles accused of crime. On the other side are conservatives devoted to crime control policies and alarmed by the rise in juvenile crime.

The present crime control policy has brought many more juveniles to be tried in adult courts. As noted by Alex Kotlowitz, "The crackdown on children has gone well beyond those accused of violent crimes" (1994:40). Delinquency cases adjudicated in the adult criminal courts have increased 47 percent since 1987 (OJJDP, 1999:170).

In spite of the increasingly tough policies directed at juvenile offenders, changes that occurred during the juvenile rights period continue to affect the system profoundly. Lawyers are now routinely present at court hearings and other stages of the process, adding a note of formality that was not present 20 years ago. Status offenders seldom end up in secure, punitive environments such as training schools. The juvenile justice system looks more like the adult justice system than it did, but it remains less formal. Its stated intention is also less harsh: to keep juveniles in the community whenever possible.

> **Thomson**NOW™
> Improve your grade on the exam with Personalized Study! For reinforcement resources and a mastery check of The Development of Juvenile Justice, go to www.thomsonedu.com/thomsonnow.

Public support for a get-tough stance toward older juveniles seems to be growing. The juvenile court, where the use of discretion and the desire to rehabilitate were traditionally uppermost, has become a system of rules and procedures similar to adult courts. With deserved punishment more prominent as a correctional goal, juveniles

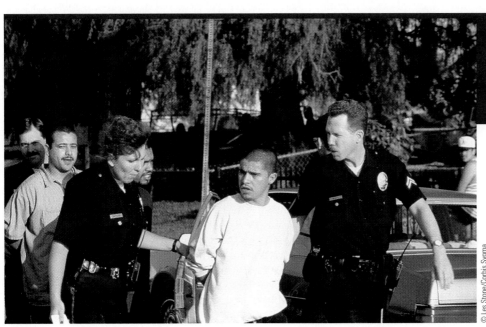

Since the 1980s the police and courts have followed crime control policies on juvenile crime. Even though violations committed by juveniles have fallen to 1989 levels, legislators continue to argue for tougher policies to deal with delinquents.

© Les Stone/Corbis Sygma

COMPARATIVE PERSPECTIVE

The Hidden Juvenile Justice System in Norway

There is no punishment for crimes in Norway for a child who is under fifteen. Thus, there are no special courts to try criminal cases against juvenile offenders. Older teenagers may be tried in ordinary courts and sentenced to prison. However, most sentences consist of only a suspended sentence or probation or several months in an open prison.

In practice, the prosecutor transfers the juvenile case directly to a division of the "social office," the *barnevern*—literally, child protection. After a trial the judge may also refer the child to this office. Police evidence is turned over to the social workers, not for prosecution, but for "treatment."

The usual first step in treatment is that the *barnevern* takes emergency custody of the child and places the child in a youth home. If the parents or guardians do not give consent, the child welfare committee will consider arguments against placement. Here the question is the appropriate treatment for the child.

The *barnevern* is most often associated in the public mind with handling of cases of child abuse and neglect. In such a case, the board will turn over custody of the child to the social workers for placement in a foster home or youth home. Once the custody is removed from the parents, the burden of proof is on the parents to retain custody. Social workers are well aware of numerous such cases of recovering alcoholics who, even after recovery, have been unable to retain custody of their children.

In contrast to the U.S. juvenile court, the Norwegian model is wholly dominated by the social worker. The function of the judge is to preside over the hearing and to maintain proper legal protocol, but the child welfare office presents the evidence and directs the case. The five laypeople who constitute the [social welfare committee] are advised by the child welfare office well before the hearing of the "facts" of the case. Before the hearing, the youth will have been placed in a youth home or mental institution "on an emergency basis"; the parents' rights to custody will have already been terminated.

The hearing is thus a mere formality after the fact. There is overwhelming unanimity among members of the board and between the board and social worker administrators. The arguments of the clients and of their lawyers seem to "fall on deaf ears."

Proof of guilt brought before the committee will generally consist of a copy of the police report of the offenses admitted by the accused and a school report written by the principal after he or she has been informed of the lawbreaking. Reports by the *barnevern*-appointed psychologist and social worker are also included. The *barnevern*, in its statement, has summarized the reports from the point of view of its arguments (usually for placement). Otherwise, the reports are ignored.

The hearing itself is a far cry from standard courtroom procedure. The youth and his or her parents may address the board briefly. The attorney sums up the case for a return to the home. Expert witnesses may be called and questioned by the board concerning, for instance, their treatment recommendations.

Following the departure of the parties, the *barnevern* office presents what amounts to "the case for the prosecution." There is no opportunity to rebut the testimony and no opportunity for cross-examination.

Placement in an institution is typically for an indefinite period. No notice of the disposition of the matter is given to the press. This absence of public accountability may serve more to protect the social office than the child.

Children receive far harsher treatments than do adults for similar offenses. For instance, for a young adult first offender the typical penalty for thievery is a suspended sentence. A child, however, may languish in an institution for years for the same offense.

A *barnevern*'s first work ought to be to create the best possible childhood. However, the *barnevern* also has a control function in relation to both the parents and the child, and the controller often feels a stronger duty to the community than to the parents and child. The institutionalization of children with behavioral problems clearly reflects this social control function. Approximately half of the children under care of the child welfare committee were placed outside the home and the other half placed under protective watch.

The system of justice for children accused of crimes is therefore often very harsh. This is in sharp contrast to the criminal justice system for adults, which is strikingly lenient. Where punishment is called *treatment,* however, the right of the state can almost become absolute. The fact that the state is represented by social work administrators creates a sharp ethical conflict for those whose first duty is to the client.

What we see in Norway is a process of juvenile justice that has not changed substantially since the 1950s. Due to flaws within the system, including the lack of external controls, the best intentions of social workers "have gone awry." Where care and protection were intended, power and secrecy have prevailed. Juvenile justice in Norway today is the justice of America yesterday.

Source: Condensed from Katherine Van Wormer, "The Hidden Juvenile Justice System in Norway: A Journey Back in Time," *Federal Probation,* March 1990, pp. 57–61.

who are repeat offenders are receiving severer sentences. Read the Comparative Perspective to examine how Norway deals with youth crime.

CHECKPOINT

Answers

2. What were the major elements of the Illinois Juvenile Court Act of 1899? ➔ 2. A separate court for delinquent, dependent, and neglected children; special legal procedures that were less adversarial than in the adult system; separation of children from adults throughout the system; programs of probation to assist judges in deciding what is in the best interest of the state and the child.

3. What was the main point of the decision in *In re Gault?* ➔ 3. Procedural rights for juveniles, including notice of charges, right to counsel, right to confront and cross-examine witnesses, and protection against self-incrimination.

The Juvenile Justice System

Juvenile justice operates through a variety of procedures in different states; even different counties within the same states vary. Because the offenses committed by juveniles are mostly violations of state laws, there is little federal involvement in the juvenile justice system. Despite internal differences, the juvenile justice system is characterized by two key factors: (1) the age of clients and (2) the categories of cases under juvenile instead of adult court jurisdiction.

AGE OF CLIENTS

Age normally determines whether a person is processed through the juvenile or adult justice system. The upper age limit for a juvenile varies from 16 to 18. In 38 states and the District of Columbia, it is the 18th birthday; in 8 states, the 17th; and in the remainder, the 16th. In 49 states, judges have the discretion to transfer juveniles to adult courts through a waiver hearing. Figure 15.3 shows the age at which juveniles can be transferred to adult court.

CATEGORIES OF CASES

Four types of cases fall under the jurisdiction of the juvenile justice system: delinquency, status offenses, neglect, and dependency. Mixing together young criminals and children who suffer from their parents' inadequacies dates from the earliest years of juvenile justice.

Delinquent children have committed acts that if committed by an adult would be criminal—for example, auto theft, robbery, or assault. Juvenile courts handle about 1.8 million delinquency cases each year, 77 percent involving male delinquents and

delinquent A child who has committed an act that if committed by an adult would be criminal.

FIGURE 15.3

The youngest age at which juveniles may be transferred to adult criminal court by waiver of juvenile jurisdiction

The waiver provisions of states vary greatly, and no clear regional or other factor explains the differences.

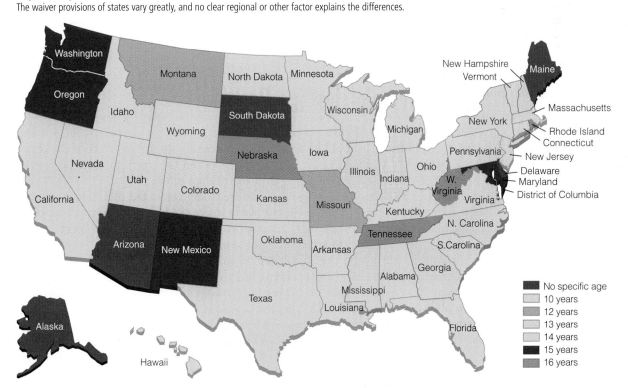

Legend:
- No specific age
- 10 years
- 12 years
- 13 years
- 14 years
- 15 years
- 16 years

Source: Office of Juvenile Justice and Delinquency Prevention, *Trying Juveniles as Adults in Criminal Court* (Washington, DC: U.S. Government Printing Office, 1998), 14–15.

29 percent involving African Americans. Among the criminal charges brought before the juvenile court, 23 percent are for crimes against the person, 45 percent for property offenses, 11 percent for drug law violations, and 21 percent for public order offenses (Sickmund, 2003:12).

Recall that status offenses are acts that are illegal only if they are committed by juveniles. Status offenders have not violated a penal code; instead they are charged with being ungovernable or incorrigible: as runaways, truants, or **PINS** (persons in need of supervision). Status offenders make up about 10 percent of the juvenile court caseload. Although female offenders account for only 15 percent of delinquency cases, they are involved in 42 percent of the status offense cases.

Juvenile justice also deals with problems of neglect and dependency—situations in which children are viewed as being hurt through no fault of their own because their parents have failed to provide a proper environment for them. People see the state's proper role as acting as a parent to a child whose own parents are unable or unwilling to provide proper care. Illinois, for example, defines a **neglected child** as one who, because of some action or inaction of his or her parents, is not receiving proper care. This may include not being sent to school, not receiving medical care, being abandoned, living in an injurious environment, or not receiving some other care necessary for the child's well-being. A **dependent child** either has no parent or guardian or is receiving improper care because of the physical or mental disability of the parent. The law governing neglected and dependent children is broad and includes situations in which the child is viewed as a victim of adult behavior.

Nationally about 75 percent of the cases referred to the juvenile courts are delinquency cases, 20 percent of which are status offenses. Twenty percent are dependency and neglect cases, and about 5 percent involve special proceedings, such as adoption. The system, then, deals with both criminal and noncriminal cases. Often juveniles who have done nothing wrong are categorized, either officially or in the public mind, as delinquents. In some states little effort is made in pre-judicial detention facilities or in social service agencies to separate the classes of juveniles.

PINS Acronym for "person(s) in need of supervision," a term that designates juveniles who are either status offenders or thought to be on the verge of trouble.

neglected child A child who is not receiving proper care, because of some action or inaction of his or her parents.

dependent child A child who has no parent or guardian or whose parents cannot give proper care.

CHECKPOINT

4. What are the jurisdictional criteria for the juvenile court? ⟶

Answers

4. The age of the juvenile, usually under 16 or 18, and the type of case: delinquency, status offense, neglect, or dependency.

The Juvenile Justice Process

Underlying the juvenile justice system is the philosophy that the police, judges, and correctional officials should be primarily concerned with the interests of the child. Prevention of delinquency is the system's justification for intervening in the lives of juveniles who are involved in either status or criminal offenses.

In theory at least, juvenile proceedings are to be conducted in a nonadversarial environment, and the juvenile court is a place where the judge, social workers, clinicians, and probation officers work together to diagnose the child's problem and select a treatment program to attack that problem.

Juvenile justice is a bureaucracy based on an ideology of social work and is staffed primarily by people who think of themselves as members of the helping professions. Not even the recent emphasis on crime control and punishment has removed the treatment philosophy from most juvenile justice arenas. However, political pressures and limits on resources may stymie the implementation of this philosophy by focusing on the punishment of offenders rather than the prevention of delinquency.

Like the adult system, juvenile justice functions within a context of exchange relationships between officials of various government and private agencies that influence decisions. The juvenile court must deal not only with children and their parents, but also with patrol officers, probation officers, welfare officials, social workers,

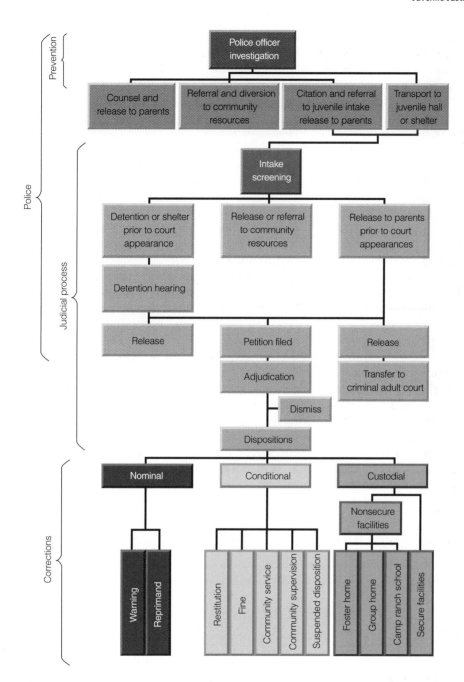

FIGURE 15.4
The juvenile justice system
Decision makers have more options for the disposition of juvenile offenders, compared with options in the criminal justice system for adults.

Source: National Advisory Commission on Criminal Justice Standards and Goals, *Report of the Task Force on Juvenile Justice and Delinquency Prevention* (Washington, DC: Law Enforcement Assistance Administration, 1976).

psychologists, and the heads of treatment institutions—all of whom have their own goals, perceptions of delinquency, and concepts of treatment.

Figure 15.4 outlines the sequence of steps taken from police investigation to correctional disposition. As you examine this figure, compare the procedures with those of the criminal justice system for adults. Note the various options available to decision makers and the extensive discretion that they may exercise.

POLICE INTERFACE

Many police departments, especially in cities, have special juvenile units. The juvenile officer is often selected and trained to relate to youths, knows much about relevant legal issues, and is sensitive to the special needs of young offenders. This officer also serves as an important link between the police and other community institutions, such as schools and other organizations serving young people. Some communities hire *resource officers* who provide a counseling and security presence in school buildings.

Police in Pinellas County, Florida, talk to Joshua Heldreth, who was caught trespassing on the grounds of a medical facility that religious groups had targeted for protests. When dealing with juveniles who violate the law, police officers use their discretion to decide whether to turn the youth over to his or her parents or to begin the formal processes of the juvenile court system by taking the child into custody.

AP Photo/Chris O'Meara

Most complaints against juveniles are brought by the police, although an injured party, school officials, and even the parents can initiate them as well. The police must make three major decisions with regard to the processing of juveniles:

1. Whether to take the child into custody

2. Whether to request that the child be detained following apprehension

3. Whether to refer the child to court

The police exercise enormous discretion in these decisions. They do extensive screening and make informal adjustments in the street and at the stationhouse. In communities and neighborhoods where the police have developed close relationships with the residents or where policy dictates, the police may deal with violations by giving warnings to the juveniles and notifying their parents. Figure 15.5 shows the disposition of juveniles taken into police custody.

Initial decisions about what to do with a suspected offender are influenced by such factors as the predominant attitude of the community; the officer's attitude toward the juvenile, the juvenile's family, the offense, and the court; and the officer's conception of his or her own role. The disposition of juvenile cases at the arrest stage also relies on the seriousness of the offense, the child's prior record, and his or her demeanor.

Although young people commit many serious crimes, the juvenile function of police work centers largely on order maintenance. In most incidents of this sort, the law is ambiguous, and blame cannot easily be assigned. Many offenses committed by juveniles that involve physical or monetary damage are minor infractions: breaking windows, hanging around the business district, disturbing the peace, displaying sexual behavior in public, and shoplifting. Here the function of the investigating officer is not so much to solve crimes as to handle the often legally uncertain complaints involving juveniles. The officer seeks both to satisfy the complainant and to keep the youth from future trouble. Given this emphasis on settling cases within the community—instead of strictly enforcing the law—the police power to arrest can be used to deter juveniles from criminal activity and to encourage them to conform to the law.

INTAKE SCREENING AT THE COURT

The juvenile court processing of delinquency cases begins with a referral in the form of a *petition*, not an arrest warrant as in the adult system. When a petition is filed, an *intake hearing* is held, over which a hearing officer presides. During this stage, the officer determines whether the alleged facts are sufficient for the juvenile court to take jurisdiction or whether some other action would be in the child's best interest.

Nationally, 45 percent of all referrals are disposed of at this stage, without formal processing by a judge. **Diversion** is the process of screening children out of the system without a decision by the court. In 47 percent of these cases, the charges are dismissed; another one-third or so are diverted to an informal probation, 6 percent placed in a mental health facility or other treatment facility, and 21 percent dealt with through some agreed-on alternative sanction (Sickmund, 2003:2).

PRETRIAL PROCEDURES

When a decision is made to refer the case to the court (55 percent of cases), the court holds an initial hearing. Here, the

FIGURE 15.5
Disposition of juveniles taken into police custody
The police have discretion in the disposition of juvenile arrest cases. What factors can influence how a case is disposed?

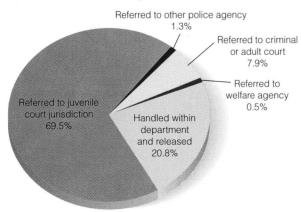

Referred to other police agency
1.3%

Referred to criminal or adult court
7.9%

Referred to welfare agency
0.5%

Referred to juvenile court jurisdiction
69.5%

Handled within department and released
20.8%

Source: Bureau of Justice Statistics, *Sourcebook of Criminal Justice Statistics,* May 2006, Table 4.25, http://www.albany.edu/sourcebook/tost_4.html#4_ab.

juveniles are informed of their rights and told that if a plea is given it must be voluntary.

If the juvenile is to be detained pending trial, most states require a **detention hearing,** which determines if the youth is to be released to a parent or guardian or to be held in a detention facility until adjudication. Some children are detained to keep them from committing other crimes while awaiting trial. Others are held to protect them from the possibility of harm from gang members or parents. Still others are held because if released they will likely not appear in court as required. Juveniles do not have the option of bail. Nationally, about 19 percent of all delinquency cases involve detention during the time between referral to the juvenile court and disposition of the case (Sickmund, 2003:18).

The conditions in many detention facilities are poor; abuse is often reported. In some rural areas juveniles continue to be detained in adult jails even though the federal government has pressed states to hold youths in separate facilities. Although much attention centers on the adjudication processes of the juvenile court and the sanctions imposed by judges, many more children are punished through confinement in detention centers and jails before any court action has taken place than are punished by the courts.

TRANSFER TO ADULT COURT

One of the first decisions to be made is whether a case should be transferred to the criminal (adult) justice system. In 49 states, juvenile court judges may **waive** their jurisdiction. This means that after considering the seriousness of the charge, the age of the juvenile, and the prospects of rehabilitation, the judge can transfer the case to adult court. In 26 states, certain violent crimes such as murder, rape, and armed robbery are excluded by law from the jurisdiction of the juvenile courts (NIJ, 1997). In 13 states, prosecutors have the authority to file a case directly with the adult court (Sickmund, 2003:18). Critics question whether prosecutors will "make better informed and more appropriate 'criminal adulthood' decisions than would judges in an adversarial waiver hearing" (Feld, 2004:599). See " What Americans Think" for a look at public attitudes about transferring juveniles to adult court.

Since a "tougher" approach to juvenile crime took hold in the 1970s, the number of cases transferred has increased dramatically. However, waived cases represent less than 1 percent (about 8,000) of delinquency cases (OJJDP, 2001). The likelihood of waiver varies by offense, offender age, and offender race. A study of 40 large urban

diversion The process of screening children out of the juvenile justice system without a decision by the court.

detention hearing A hearing by the juvenile court to determine if a juvenile is to be detained or released prior to adjudication.

waiver Procedure by which the juvenile court relinquishes its jurisdiction and transfers a juvenile case to the adult criminal court.

When 12-year-olds Jake Eakin and Evan Savoie were charged with the slaying of 13-year-old Craig Sorger, they were among the youngest youths to have their case decided in adult court. Eakin, shown in the Grant County Superior Court in Ephrata, Washington, pleaded guilty to second-degree murder, testified against Savoie, and was sentenced to 14 years in prison. Savoie was found guilty of first-degree murder and received the maximum sentence of 26 years. Critics contend that juveniles should never be treated as adults.

AP Photo/The Wenatchee World, Kelly Gilli

counties found that nearly two-thirds of juvenile felony defendants in adult court were charged with a violent crime, compared with only one-quarter of adults. Forty percent were 17 to 18 years of age, and 62 percent were African American (BJS, 2003c:1).

Many states now place on the youth the burden of proving that he or she is amenable to treatment in the juvenile instead of the adult court. Transferring juveniles to be tried in the adult criminal courts remains controversial, as outlined in "The Policy Debate."

ADJUDICATION

Juvenile courts deal with almost 1.8 million delinquency cases a year (Sickmund, 2003:12). *Adjudication* is the trial stage of the juvenile justice process. If the child has not admitted to the charges and the case has not been transferred to the adult court, an adjudication hearing is held to determine the facts in the case and, if appropriate, label the juvenile "delinquent."

The Supreme Court's decision in *Gault* (1967) and other due process rulings mandated changes in criminal proceedings that have changed the philosophy and actions of

---

THE POLICY DEBATE

Should Juvenile Offenders Be Tried as Adults?

Arrests of juveniles for violent crimes more than doubled between 1988 and 1994. Since their peak in 1994, juvenile violent crime arrests have declined, yet cases still come up that are so serious that the public demands severe punishment. Youths are also the primary victims of violent crime. Experts cite the availability of guns, the prevalence of urban youth gangs, and the problem of drugs as the causes of violent youth crimes.

In the face of crimes such as the school yard shootings of the late 1990s, the public has loudly called for "getting tough with these young hoods." Politicians and criminal justice planners have urged that steps be taken to ensure that juveniles accused of serious crimes be dealt with in the adult courts.

For Trying Juveniles as Adults

Those who want to make trying juveniles as adults easier point not only to the continuing high levels of violence but also to the heinous nature of some crimes committed by youths. They see the juvenile courts as "coddling" these young predators. Often, only when a youth is transferred to the adult system is his or her long record of felonies revealed—felonies for which the juvenile court ordered little punishment. The current level of violence by juveniles requires that offenders be dealt with swiftly and quickly so as to deter the upcoming generation from following in the footsteps of their older siblings.

The arguments for trying serious juvenile offenders in the adult criminal justice system include these:

- Violence by juveniles is a serious problem and must be dealt with in a swift and certain manner.

- Juvenile courts have not been effective in stemming the tide of violence by young people.

- Procedures for waiving juvenile jurisdiction are cumbersome in many states.

- Justice demands that heinous crimes, regardless of the age of the accused, be dealt with to the full extent the law provides.

Against Trying Juveniles as Adults

Although they recognize that serious youth crime is a problem, many experts believe that trying juveniles as adults only makes things worse. They point

out that treating adolescents as adults ignores the fact that they are at a different stage of social and emotional development. They argue that children should not be held to the same standards as adults. In an increasingly violent world, children need help to navigate the temptations and threats of adolescence.

The arguments against trying serious juvenile offenders in the adult criminal justice system include these:

- The juvenile justice system is better able to deal with the social and emotional problems of young offenders.

- The basic foundations of criminal law recognize that children carry diminished responsibility for their acts.

- Punishing juveniles in adult institutions robs them of their childhood and threatens their future.

- The problem of violent crime by juveniles must be dealt with by changing the environment within which they live.

What Should U.S. Policy Be?

Under pressure to "do something" about violent juvenile crime, legislators have proposed that the age of adulthood be lowered and that the cases of serious offenders be tried in the adult criminal justice system. Is this the best way to protect community safety—to punish youthful offenders in the adult criminal justice system? Is the juvenile corrections system equipped to treat and guide juvenile offenders in a way that will return them to their communities as productive people?

RESEARCHING THE INTERNET

You can find the article "Delinquents or Criminals: Policy Options for Young Offenders" at the corresponding website listed on the Cole/Smith Criminal Justice in America Companion Website: http://www.thomsonedu.com/criminaljustice/cole.

FOR CRITICAL ANALYSIS

What are the likely consequences of trying juveniles as adults? What are the likely consequences of trying these offenders in the juvenile courts?

the juvenile court. Contemporary juvenile proceedings are more formal than those of the past, although still more informal than adult courts. The parents and child must receive copies of petitions with specific charges; counsel may be present, and free counsel can be appointed if the juvenile cannot pay; witnesses can be cross-examined; and a transcript of the proceedings must be kept.

As with other Supreme Court decisions, local practice may differ sharply from the procedures spelled out in the high court's rulings. Juveniles and their parents often waive their rights in response to suggestions from the judge or probation officer. The lower social status of the offender's parents, the intimidating atmosphere of the court, and judicial hints that the outcome will be more favorable if a lawyer is not present are reasons the procedures outlined in *Gault* may not be followed. The litany of "getting treatment," "doing what's right for the child," and "working out a just solution" may sound enticing, especially to people who are unfamiliar with the intricacies of formal legal procedures. In practice, then, juveniles still lack many of the protections given to adult offenders. Table 15.2 lists some of the differences between the juvenile and adult criminal justice systems.

The concept of restorative justice has been extended to juveniles. At the Red Hook Youth Court in New York, a 15-year-old arrested for spraying graffiti sits before a jury of his peers and a 16-year-old judge. The court deals with minor offenses, often where formal charges have not yet been brought. Officials say that 85 percent of the offenders complete restitution, ranging from community service to letters of apology.

Joe Tabacca

TABLE 15.2   The Adult and Juvenile Criminal Justice Systems Compared

Compare the basic elements of the adult and juvenile systems. To what extent does a juvenile have the same rights as an adult? Are the different decision-making processes necessary because a juvenile is involved?

	Adult System	Juvenile System
Philosophical Assumptions	Decisions made as result of adversarial system in context of due process rights	Decisions made as result of inquiry into needs of juvenile within context of some due process elements
Jurisdiction	Violations of criminal law	Violations of criminal law, status offenses, neglect, dependency
Primary Sanctioning Goals	Retribution, deterrence, rehabilitation	Retribution, rehabilitation
Official Discretion	Widespread	Widespread
Entrance	Official action of arrest, summons, or citation	Official action, plus referral by school, parents, other sources
Role of Prosecuting and Defense Attorneys	Required and formalized	Sometimes required; less structured; poor role definition
Adjudication	Procedural rules of evidence in public jury trial required	Less formal structure to rules of evidence and conduct of trial; no right to public trial or jury in most states
Treatment Programs	Run primarily by public agencies	Broad use of private and public agencies
Application of Bill of Rights Amendments		
Fourth: Unreasonable searches and seizures	Applicable	Applicable
Fifth: Double jeopardy	Applicable	Applicable (re: waiver to adult court)
Self-incrimination	Applicable (*Miranda* warnings)	Applicable
Sixth: Right to counsel	Applicable	Applicable
Public trial	Applicable	Applicable in less than half of states
Trial by jury	Applicable	Applicable in less than half of states
Fourteenth: Right to treatment	Not applicable	Applicable

The increased concern about crime has given prosecuting attorneys a more prominent part in the system. In keeping with the traditional child-saver philosophy, prosecuting attorneys rarely appeared in juvenile court prior to the *Gault* decision. Now that a defense attorney is present, the state often retains legal counsel as well. In many jurisdictions, certain prosecutors deal specifically with juvenile cases. They advise the intake officer, administer diversion programs, negotiate pleas, and act as an advocate during judicial proceedings.

Juvenile proceedings and court records have traditionally remained closed to the public to protect the child's privacy and potential for rehabilitation. However, judges in the adult courts may not have access to juvenile records. This means that people who have already served time on juvenile probation or in institutions are erroneously perceived to be first offenders when they are processed for crimes as adults. Some people argue that adult courts should have access to juvenile records and that young criminals should be treated more severely than adults to deter them from future illegal activity.

DISPOSITION

If the court makes a finding of delinquency, the judge will schedule a dispositional hearing to decide what action should be taken. Typically, before passing sentence the judge receives a *predispositional report* prepared by a probation officer. Similar to a presentence report, it serves to assist the judge in deciding on a disposition that serves the best interests of the child and is consistent with the treatment plan developed by the probation officer.

At trial, the court finds few juveniles to be not delinquent, because the intake and pretrial processes normally filter out cases in which a law violation cannot be proved. Besides dismissal, four other choices are available: probation, alternative dispositions, custodial care, and community treatment.

Juvenile court advocates have traditionally believed that rehabilitation is the only goal of the sanction imposed on young people. For most of the twentieth century, judges sentenced juveniles to indeterminate sentences so that correctional administrators could decide when release was appropriate. As in the adult criminal justice system, indeterminate sentences and unbridled discretion in juvenile justice have faced harsh criticism during the last three decades. Several states have tightened the sentencing discretion of judges, especially with regard to serious offenses. The State of Washington, for example, has adopted a determinate-sentencing law for juveniles. In other states, youths can be transferred more readily to the adult court for adjudication and sentencing. Jurisdictions such as the District of Columbia, Colorado, Florida, and Virginia have passed laws requiring mandatory sentences for certain offenses committed by juveniles. As can be seen by the Gallup Poll presented in "What Americans Think," those interviewed did not distinguish juveniles from adults when the case involves punishment for a violent crime.

CORRECTIONS

Many aspects of juvenile corrections resemble those of adult corrections. Both systems, for example, mix rehabilitative and retributive sanctions. However, juvenile corrections differs in many respects from the adult system. Some of the differences flow from the *parens patriae* concept and the youthful, seemingly innocent people with whom the system deals. At times, the differences appear in formal operational policies, such as contracting for residential treatment. At other times, the differences show only in the style and culture of an operation, as they do in juvenile probation.

One predominant aim of juvenile corrections is to avoid unnecessary incarceration. When children are removed from their homes, they are inevitably damaged emotionally, even when the home life is harsh and abusive, for they are forced to abandon the only environment they know. Further, placing children in institutions may cause labeling; the children begin to perceive themselves as "bad" because they have received punitive treatment, and children who see themselves as bad are likely to behave that way. Finally, treatment is believed to be more effective when the child is living in a normal, supportive home environment. For these reasons, noninstitutional forms of corrections are seen as highly desirable in juvenile justice and have proliferated in recent years.

Probation   In 58 percent of cases, the juvenile delinquent is placed on probation and released to the custody of a parent or guardian. Often the judge orders that the delinquent undergo some form of education or counseling. The judge can also require the delinquent to pay a fine or make restitution while on probation.

Juvenile probation operates in much the same way that adult probation does; sometimes the same agency carries it out. In two respects, however, juvenile probation can differ markedly from adult probation. First, juvenile probation officers have smaller caseloads. Second, the juvenile probation officer is often infused with the sense that the offender is worthwhile and can change and that the job is valuable and enjoyable. Such attitudes make for greater creativity than adult probation officers usually express. For example, a young offender can be paired with a "big brother" or "big sister" from the community. See "Careers in Criminal Justice" for information about the work of probation officers for juveniles.

Intermediate Sanctions   Although probation and commitment to an institution are the system's two main dispositional options, intermediate sanctions served in the community account today for 15 percent of adjudicated juvenile cases. Judges have wide discretion to warn, fine, arrange for restitution, refer a juvenile for treatment at either a public or a private community agency, or withhold judgment.

Judges sometimes suspend judgment—that is, continue a case without a finding—when they wish to put a youth under supervision but are reluctant to apply the label "delinquent." The judge holds off on giving a definitive judgment but can give one should a youth misbehave while under the informal supervision of a probation officer or parents.

Custodial Care   Of those juveniles declared delinquent, 29 percent are placed in public or private residential facilities. The national incarceration rate per 100,000

WHAT AMERICANS THINK

Question: "In your view, how should juveniles between the ages of 14 and 17 who commit violent crimes be treated in the criminal justice system—should they be treated the same as adults, or should they be given more lenient treatment in a juvenile court?"

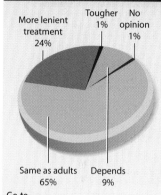

More lenient treatment 24%

Tougher 1%

No opinion 1%

Same as adults 65%

Depends 9%

Go to http://www.thomsonedu.com/criminaljustice/cole to compare your opinion on this issue with the opinions of other criminal justice students.

Source: Conducted by the Gallup Organization, August 29–September 5, 2000. Data provided by the Roper Center for Public Opinion Research, University of Connecticut.

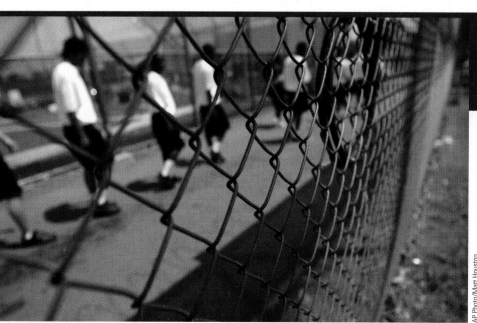

Juvenile offenders file in for lunch at the Cheltenham Youth Facility in Maryland. Nationally more than 130,000 youths under the age of 18 spend time in juvenile or adult correctional facilities.

AP Photo/Matt Houston

Rehabilitation: Do you think the main emphasis in juvenile prison should be to try and rehabilitate the adolescent so that he or she might return to society as a productive citizen?

63.3%

Punishment: Do you think the main emphasis in juvenile prison should be to punish the adolescent covicted of a crime?

18.7%

Protection: Do you think the main emphasis in juvenile prison should be to protect society from future crime he or she might commit?

11.2%

Not sure

6.7%

Go to http://www.thomsonedu.com/criminaljustice/cole to compare your opinion on this issue with the opinions of other criminal justice students.

Source: Melissa M. Moon, Jody L. Sundt, Francis T. Cullent, and John Paul Wright, "Is Child Saving Dead? Public Support for Juvenile Rehabilitation," *Crime and Delinquency* 46 (June 2000): 46.

FIGURE 15.6

Juveniles in public facilities: Types of offenses and nondelinquent reasons for placement.

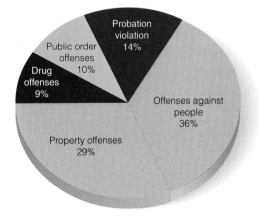

Source: M. Sickmund, "Juveniles in Corrections," in *National Report Series Bulletin* (Washington, DC: Office of Juvenile Justice and Delinquency Prevention, June 2004), 6.

juveniles aged 10–18 is 371. Like the adult incarceration rates, these rates vary widely among the states; the highest is in South Dakota (632) and the lowest in Hawaii and Vermont (71). Nationally, 74 percent of incarcerated juveniles are held in public facilities, with the remainder in private facilities (Sickmund, 2004:8). In addition approximately 2,500 inmates under age 18 do time in state and federal prisons for adults (BJS, 2005a:5). See "What Americans Think" for a picture of attitudes toward prisons for juveniles.

Policy makers are concerned about the overrepresentation of incarcerated African American juveniles. One study found that the disproportionate confinement of minority juveniles often stems from disparity at the early stages of case processing (Sickmund, 2004:12). Thus, if more African Americans are detained than others, more of them will likely be adjudicated in juvenile court, and more placed in residential facilities.

Institutions for juvenile offenders are classified as either nonsecure or secure facilities. Nonsecure placements (foster homes, group homes, camps, ranches, or schools) include a significant number of nonoffenders—youths referred for abuse, neglect, or emotional disturbance. Secure facilities, such as reform schools and training schools, deal with juveniles who have committed serious violations of the law and have serious personal problems. Most secure juvenile facilities are small, designed to hold 40 or fewer residents. However, many states have at least one facility holding two hundred or more hard-core delinquents who receive limited freedom. Because the residents are younger and somewhat more volatile than adults, behavioral control is often an everyday issue, and fights and aggression are common. Poor management practices, such as those described in "A Question of Ethics" at the end of this chapter, can lead to difficult situations.

Boot camps for juvenile offenders saw a spurt of growth in the early 1990s. By 1997 more than 27,000 teenagers were passing through 54 camps in 34 states annually. However, as with boot camps for adults, the results have not been promising. A national study showed that recidivism among boot camp attendees ranged from 64 percent to 75 percent, slightly higher than for youths sentenced to adult prisons (*New York Times,* January 2, 2000, p. WK3). States are rethinking their policies, with many closing their programs.

A national survey of public custodial institutions showed that 36 percent of juveniles were incarcerated for violent offenses, 60 percent used drugs regularly, and 50 percent said that a family member had been in prison at some time in the past. Also, 88 percent of the residents were male, only 30 percent had grown up in a household with both parents, and the percentages of African Americans (40 percent) and Hispanics (18 percent) were greater than the percentage of those groups in the general population (OJJDP, 1999:195). The Close Up on page 404 tells the story of Fernando, whose background matches this profile. Figure 15.6 shows the types of offenses and nondelinquent reasons for the placement of juveniles in public correctional facilities.

Institutional Programs Because of the emphasis on rehabilitation that has dominated juvenile justice for much of the past 50 years, a wide variety of treatment programs have been used. The juvenile correctional programs of most states include counseling, education, vocational training, and an assortment of psychotherapeutic methods. Unfortunately, research has raised many questions about the effectiveness of rehabilitation programs in the juvenile corrections setting. For example, incarceration in a juvenile training institution primarily seems to prepare many offenders for entry into adult corrections. John Irwin's concept of the state-raised youth is a useful way of looking at children who come in contact with institutional life at an early age, lack family relationships and structure, become accustomed to living in a correctional facility, and cannot function in other environments (Irwin, 1970).

CAREERS IN CRIMINAL JUSTICE

Probation Officer—Juveniles

NATURE OF THE WORK

Juvenile probation officers are responsible for the supervision and guidance of youth who have been referred to them by the court, police, or social service agencies. Through the development of close ties with offenders' families, school authorities, and health agencies, probation officers help juvenile offenders meet their educational and treatment needs. They also monitor their behavior to ensure that court-ordered requirements are met. Caseload size varies by agency, by the needs of the offenders, and by the risks they pose. Caseloads for juveniles tend to be lower than those for adult probationers. Officers may be on call 24 hours a day to supervise and assist offenders.

REQUIRED QUALIFICATIONS

Background qualifications for juvenile probation officers vary by state, but a bachelor's degree in social work, criminal justice, or a related field from a four-year college or university is usually required. Some agencies require graduate work or pre-

vious experience with youths. Candidates must be 21 years of age and have no felony convictions. Most juvenile probation officers receive both formal and on-the-job training.

EARNINGS AND JOB OUTLOOK

The number of probation officers for juveniles is expected to grow about as fast as other occupations during the next decade. Probation officers handling a juvenile caseload report a high level of personal satisfaction in their work. Juvenile probation officers earn about $40,000 a year, with entry-level salaries under $25,000 in many regions.

MORE INFORMATION

Visit the website of the American Probation and Parole Association at the corresponding site listed on the Cole/Smith Criminal Justice in America Companion Website: http://www.thomsonedu.com/criminaljustice/cole. Career information can also be obtained from your state, juvenile court, or probation office.

Aftercare   The juvenile equivalent of parole supervision is known as **aftercare.** Upon release the offender is placed under the supervision of a juvenile parole officer who assists with educational, counseling, and treatment services. As with the adult system, juveniles may be returned to custodial care should they violate the conditions of their parole.

> **aftercare** Juvenile justice equivalent of parole, in which a delinquent is released from a custodial sentence and supervised in the community.

Community Treatment   In the past decade, treatment in community-based facilities has become much more common. Today many private, nonprofit agencies have contracts with states to provide services for troubled youths. Community-based options include foster homes in which juvenile offenders live with families, usually for a short period, and group homes, often privately run facilities for groups of 12–20 juvenile offenders. Each group home has several staff personnel who work as counselors or houseparents during 8- or 24-hour shifts. Group home placements can allow juveniles to attend local schools; they can also provide individual and group counseling, as well as offer a more structured life than most of the residents received in their own homes. However, critics suggest that group homes often are mismanaged and may do little more than "warehouse" youths.

ThomsonNOW™
Improve your grade on the exam with Personalized Study! For reinforcement resources and a mastery check of The Juvenile Justice Process, go to www.thomsonedu.com/thomsonnow.

CHECKPOINT

Answers

5. What three discretionary decisions do the police make with regard to processing juveniles?

6. What is the purpose of diversion?

7. What are five sentencing dispositions available to the judge?

5. (1) Whether to take the child into custody, (2) whether to request that the child be detained, (3) whether to refer the child to court.

6. To avoid formal proceedings when the child's best interests can be served by treatment in the community.

7. Suspended judgment, probation, community treatment, institutional care, judicial waiver to an adult court.

CLOSE UP

Fernando, 16, Finds a Sanctuary in Crime

Fernando Morales was glad to discuss his life as a 16-year-old drug dealer. He had recently escaped from Long Lane School, a [Connecticut] correctional institution that became his home after he was caught with $1,100 worth of heroin known as P.

"The Five-O caught me right here with the bundles of P," he said, referring to a police officer, as he stood in front of a boarded-up house on Bridgeport's East Side. "They sentenced me to eighteen months, but I jetted after four. Three of us got out a bathroom window. We ran through the woods and stole a car. Then we got back here and the Five-O's came to my apartment, and I had to jump out the side window on the second floor."

WHAT FUTURE?

Since his escape, Fernando has been on the run for weeks. He still went to the weekly meetings of his gang, but he was afraid to go back to his apartment, afraid even to go to a friend's place to pick up the three guns he had stashed away. "I would love to get my baby Uzi, but it's too hot now."

"Could you bring a photographer here?" he asked. "I want my picture in the newspaper. I'd love to have me holding a bundle right there on the front page so the cops can see it. They're going to bug out."

The other dealers on the corner looked on with a certain admiration. They realized that a publicity campaign might not be the smartest long-term career move for a fugitive drug dealer—"Man, you be the one bugging out," another dealer told him—but they also recognized the logic in Fernando's attitude. He was living his life according to a common assumption on these streets: There is no future.

When you ask the Hispanic teenagers selling drugs here what they expect to be doing in five years, you tend to get a lot of bored shrugs. Occasionally they'll talk about being back in school or being a retired drug dealer in a Porsche. But the most common answer is the one that Fernando gave without hesitation or emotion: "Dead or in jail."

The story of how Fernando got that way is a particularly sad one, but the basic elements are fairly typical in the lives of drug dealers and gang members in any urban ghetto. He has grown up amid tenements, housing projects, torched buildings, and abandoned factories. His role models have been adults who use "the city" and "the state" primarily as terms for the different types of welfare checks. His neighborhood is a place where 13-year-olds know by heart the visiting hours at local prisons.

THE FAMILY: A MOTHER LEAVES, A FATHER DRINKS

Fernando Morales was born in Bridgeport, Connecticut, and a few months after his birth his mother moved out. Since then he has occasionally run into her on the street. Neither he nor his relatives can say exactly why she left—or why she didn't take Fernando and her other son with her—but the general assumption is that she was tired of being hit by their father.

The father, Bernabe Morales, who was 24 years old and had emigrated from Puerto Rico as a teenager, moved the two boys in with his mother at the P. T. Barnum public housing project. Fernando lived there until the age of 8, when his grandmother died. . . .

After that Fernando and his brother Bernard lived sometimes with their father and his current girlfriend, sometimes with relatives in Bridgeport or Puerto Rico. They eventually settled with their father's cousin, Monserrate Bruno, who already had ten children living in her two-bedroom apartment. . . .

His father, by all accounts, was a charming, generous man when sober but something else altogether when drinking or doing drugs. He was arrested more than two dozen times, usually for fighting or drugs, and spent five years in jail while Fernando was growing up. He lived on welfare, odd jobs, and money from selling drugs, a trade that was taken up by both his sons.

THE "INDUSTRY": MOVING UP IN THE DRUG TRADE

Fernando's school days ended two years ago, when he dropped out of ninth grade. "School was corny," he explained. "I was smart, I learned quick, but I got bored. I was just learning things when I could be out making money."

Problems and Perspectives

Much of the criticism of juvenile justice has emphasized the disparity between the treatment ideal and the institutionalized practices of an ongoing bureaucratic system. Commentators focus on how the language of social reformers disguises the day-to-day operations that lack the elements of due process and in which custodial incarceration is all too frequent. Other criticisms claim that the juvenile justice system does not control juvenile crime.

The juvenile court, in both theory and practice, is a remarkably complex institution that must perform a wide variety of functions. The juvenile justice system must play such a range of roles that goals and values will inevitably collide. In many states the same judges, probation officers, and social workers are asked to deal with both neglected children and young criminals. Although departments of social services usually deal primarily with cases of neglect, the distinction between the criminal and the neglected child is often not maintained.

In addition to recognizing that the juvenile system has organizational problems, society must acknowledge that research has revealed little about the causes of delinquency and its prevention or treatment. Over the years, people have advanced

Fernando might have found other opportunities—he had relatives working in fast-food restaurants and repair shops, and one cousin tried to interest him in a job distributing bread that might pay $700 a week—but nothing with such quick rewards as the drug business flourishing on the East Side.

He had friends and relatives in the business, and he started as one of the runners on the street corner making sales or directing buyers to another runner holding the marijuana, cocaine, crack, or heroin. The runners on each block buy their drugs—paying, for instance, $200 for fifty bags of crack that sell for $250—from the block's lieutenant, who supervises them and takes the money to the absentee dealer called the owner of the block.

By this winter Fernando had moved up slightly on the corporate ladder. "I'm not the block lieutenant yet, but I have some runners selling for me," he explained as he sat in a bar near the block. Another teenager came in with money for him, which he proudly added to a thick wad in his pocket. "You see? I make money while they work for me."

Fernando still worked the block himself, too, standing on the corner watching for cars slowing down, shouting "You want P?" or responding to veteran customers for crack who asked, "Got any slab, man?" Fernando said he usually made between $100 and $300 a day, and that the money usually went as quickly as it came.

He had recently bought a car for $500 and wrecked it making a fast turn into a telephone pole. He spent money on gold chains with crucifixes, rings, Nike sneakers, Timberland boots, an assortment of Russell hooded sweatshirts called hoodies, gang dues, trips to New York City and his 23-year-old girlfriend.

His dream was to get out of Bridgeport. "I'd be living fat somewhere. I'd go to somewhere hot, Florida or Puerto Rico or somewhere, buy me a house, get six blazing girls with dope bodies." In the meantime, he tried not to think about what his product was doing to his customers.

"Sometimes it bothers me. But see, I'm a hustler. I got to look out for myself. I got to be making money. Forget them. If you put that in your head, you're going to be caught out. You going to be a sucker. You going to be like them." He said he had used marijuana, cocaine, and angel dust himself, but made a point of never using crack or heroin, the drugs that plagued the last years of his father's life. . . .

THE GANGS: "LIKE A FAMILY" OF DRUG DEALERS

"I cried a little, that's it," was all that Fernando would say about his father's death. But he did allow that it had something to do with his subsequent decision to join a Hispanic gang named Neta. He went with friends to a meeting, answered questions during an initiation ceremony, and began wearing its colors, a necklace of red, white, and blue beads.

"It's like a family, and you need that if you've lost your own family," he said. "At the meetings we talk about having heart, trust, and all that. We don't disrespect nobody. If we need money, we get it. If I need anything they're right there to help me."

Neta is allied with Bridgeport's most notorious gang, the Latin Kings, and both claim to be peaceful Hispanic cultural organizations opposed to drug use. But they are financed at least indirectly by the drug trade, because many members like Fernando work independently in drug operations, and the drug dealers' disputes can turn into gang wars. . . .

"I like guns, I like stealing cars, I like selling drugs, and I like money," he said. "I got to go to the block. That's where I get my spirit at. When I die, my spirit's going to be at the block, still making money. Booming." . . .

"I'll be selling till I get my act together. I'm just a little kid. Nothing runs through my head. All I think about is doing crazy things. But when I be big, I know I need education. If I get caught and do a couple of years, I'll come out and go back to school. But I don't have that in my head yet. I'll have my little fun while I'm out."

RESEARCHING THE INTERNET

Using InfoTrac College Edition, enter the keyword *youth gangs*. Access the article "Understanding and Responding to Youth Gangs: A Juvenile Corrections Approach," *Corrections Today*, August 1999.

FOR CRITICAL ANALYSIS

What are the roots of gang affiliations such as Fernando's? What policies might be developed to deal with the gang problem?

Source: John Tierney, *New York Times,* April 13, 1993, pp. Al, B6. Copyright © 1993 by The New York Times Company. Reprinted by permission.

---

various social and behavioral theories to explain delinquency. One generation looked to slum conditions as the cause of juvenile crime, and another pointed to the affluence of the suburbs. Psychologists sometimes point to masculine insecurity in a matriarchal family structure, and some sociologists note the peer group pressures of the gang. This array of theories has led to an array of proposed—and often contradictory—treatments. In such confusion, those interested in the problems of youth may despair. What is clear is that we need additional research on the causes of delinquency and the treatment of juvenile offenders.

What trends may foretell the future of juvenile justice? The conservative crime-control policies that have hit the adult criminal justice system—with their emphasis on deterrence, retribution, and getting tough—have apparently also influenced juvenile justice. One can point to growing levels of overcrowding in juvenile institutions, increased litigation challenging the abuse of children in training schools and detention centers, and higher rates of minority youth incarceration. All of these problems have emerged during a period of declining youth populations and fewer arrests of juveniles. With the demographic trend now reversing and the concern about drugs increasing, one can see a surge of adolescents going through their criminally high-risk years in a system and community that simply cannot cope with them.

A QUESTION OF ETHICS: WRITING ASSIGNMENT

Residents of the Lovelock Home had been committed by the juvenile court because they were either delinquent or neglected. All 25 boys, aged 12 to 16, were streetwise, tough, and interested only in getting out. The institution had a staff of social services professionals who tried to deal with the educational and psychological needs of the residents. Because state funding was short, these services looked better in the annual report than to an observer visiting Lovelock. Most of the time the residents watched television, played basketball in the backyard, or just hung out in one another's rooms.

Joe Klegg, the night supervisor, was tired from the eight-hour shift that he had just completed on his "second job" as a daytime convenience-store manager. The boys were watching television when he arrived at seven. Everything seemed calm. It should have been, because Joe had placed a tough

15-year-old, Randy Marshall, in charge. Joe had told Randy to keep the younger boys in line. Randy used his muscle and physical presence to intimidate the other residents. He knew that if the home was quiet and there was no trouble, he would be rewarded with special privileges such as a "pass" to see his girlfriend. Joe wanted no hassles and a quiet house so that he could doze off when the boys went to sleep.

WRITING ASSIGNMENT

Does the situation at Lovelock Home raise ethical questions, or does it merely raise questions of poor management practices? What are the potential consequences for the residents? For Joe Klegg? What is the state's responsibility? Write a short essay addressing these questions.

REAL-WORLD ACTIVITY: AN APPLICATION

Police and juvenile probation officers in Boston have developed Operation Cease Fire, a coordinated attempt to end gang gun violence. The program is based on the knowledge that a few offenders account for a substantial proportion of all crime and that these offenders are often concentrated in particular neighborhoods.

Operation Cease Fire uses two strategies. First, interagency collaboration identifies individuals and gangs at risk for committing violence. A task force of federal, state, and municipal criminal justice and social service agencies regularly meets to share information, identify gang members to be targeted, discuss tactics to increase investigation effectiveness, and develop a repertoire of interventions and strategies.

A second strategy is aimed at increasing deterrence through swift and certain sanctioning. When a violent act is committed, the various agencies can at their discretion not only arrest suspects, but also shut down drug markets, strictly enforce probation restrictions, make disorder arrests, deal more strictly with cases in adjudication, deploy federal enforcement power, and so on.

RESEARCHING THE INTERNET

Go to InfoTrac College Edition. Enter the keyword *Operation Cease Fire* and read the article entitled "Attention, Oakland Troublemakers: The Police Are Keeping a Close Eye on You," by Jesse McKinley, *New York Times,* August 22, 2006.

APPLICATION

Operation Cease Fire develops in gang members a new set of expectations regarding violent behavior. When gang members seek rehabilitative services, the program assists them. But when they persist in violent activity, the coordinated agencies hit them with undesirable sanctions until the violence stops. Would this approach work in your city? What problems might you foresee in effectively reducing gang violence with a program such as Operation Cease Fire?

SUMMARY

- Crimes committed by juveniles rose in the early 1990s and remain an issue of serious concern.

- The history of juvenile justice comprises five periods: Puritan, Refuge, juvenile court, juvenile rights, and crime control.

- Creation of the juvenile court in 1899 established a separate juvenile justice system for dealing with delinquency, neglected children, and dependent children.

- The *In re Gault* decision by the U.S. Supreme Court in 1967 brought due process to the juvenile justice system.

- Decisions by police officers and juvenile intake officers dispose of a large portion of cases that are never referred to the court.

- In juvenile court most cases are settled through a plea agreement.

- After conviction or plea, a disposition hearing is held. The judge reviews the offense and the juvenile's social history before passing sentence.

- Possible dispositions of a juvenile case include suspended judgment, probation, community treatment, and institutional care.

- Juvenile court jurisdiction is increasingly being waived so that youths can be tried in the adult criminal justice system.

- Options for juvenile corrections include probation, intermediate sanctions, custodial care, institutional programs, aftercare, and community treatment.

QUESTIONS FOR REVIEW

1. What are the major historical periods of juvenile justice in the United States?

2. What is the jurisdiction of the juvenile court system?

3. What are the major processes in the juvenile justice system?

4. What are the sentencing and institutional alternatives for juveniles who are judged delinquent?

5. What due process rights do juveniles have?

KEY TERMS AND CASES

aftercare (p. 403)
delinquent (p. 393)
dependent child (p. 394)
detention hearing (p. 397)
diversion (p. 397)
neglected child (p. 394)

parens patriae (p. 387)
PINS (p. 394)
status offense (p. 390)
waiver (p. 397)
Breed v. Jones (1975) (p. 390)
In re Gault (1967) (p. 389)

In re Winship (1970) (p. 390)
McKeiver v. Pennsylvania (1971) (p. 390)
Schall v. Martin (1984) (p. 391)

GOING ONLINE

ThomsonNOW™

Maximize your study time by using ThomsonNOW's diagnostic study plan to help you review this chapter. The Study Plan will

- Help you identify areas on which you should concentrate

- Provide interactive exercises to help you master the chapter concepts

- Provide a posttest to confirm you are ready to move on to the next chapter

INSIDE THE CRIMINAL JUSTICE SYSTEM AND BEYOND: ONE MAN'S JOURNEY

Written by Chuck Terry

Reflections

The other day, while stopped at a red light, I suddenly thought about all the years I spent in "those places." Cells, segregated chow halls, racial tension, monotony, overcrowded conditions. All the years spent being ordered around by judges, guards, and parole officers. And then I thought about all the people who are there right now. Not only are there many more people doing it than before, but they are doing it for extensively longer periods of time. The thought chilled me to the bone. It hasn't always been like this.

People used to consider rehabilitation as a valid justification for imprisonment. Those who broke the law were seen as less fortunate and in need of help. This was when societal goals included using the law to even up the socioeconomic playing field for women and minorities, when social programs designed to fight poverty were being implemented rather than cut, and when popular enemies included communists and crooked politicians. Now many dwell on the harm created by "single-parent families," "illegal immigrants," "welfare dependency," and the evils of affirmative action. And now we have the perfect scapegoat, someone everyone can hate—the criminal.

Today "criminals" are depicted as inherently "bad" people. They are blamed for, among other things, our economic problems, fear of going out at night, dilapidated schools, rundown neighborhoods, and our children's unhappiness. Prisons and all the things that go along with "protecting" the public (alarm systems, more prisons, gated communities, increased budgets for policing, new laws) are "sold" and "bought" as essential mechanisms of control. By keeping "these people" in their place "we" can live "normal," safe lives.

Our aim now is to punish instead of rehabilitate. Increasing levels of formal social control are the means by which crime is "fought." We seldom address crime-generating factors like our market mentality, which revolves around the need to have, to get, and to have yet more; the increasing economic gap between the "haves" and "have-nots"; capital flight; racism; child abuse; homophobia; chronic unemployment; rampant inequality; economic insecurity; and the desperation that leads to drug addiction and other social ills. Instead, our attention is diverted toward individuals. We seem to blindly accept the sanity of draconian sentencing policies such as mandatory minimum laws that require prison time for selling crack cocaine, even for first-time offenders. Or the "Three Strikes and You're Out Law" in California that, though designed to imprison violent offenders, has been twisted and reshaped so that today roughly 70 percent of those going to prison under this law do so for a nonviolent crime. After spending so many years in "those places," I find what I see today difficult to accept.

Today I find myself around academics and "experts" in the field of criminal justice. I hope that we can learn from each other. I am given the opportunity to write papers like this and speak in front of hundreds of students in undergraduate classes. I feel fortunate to be doing all this, and more than grateful to be free from the grips of addiction and the criminal justice system.

Yet the story is far from over. The nightmare continues. "Those places" are being jammed with bodies faster than they can be built. Prisons and jails become home to the unemployable, addicts, the underprivileged, and outcasts of society. And rather than help, or even punish, doing time on such a massive scale will likely have disastrous effects on individuals, families, and communities that will last lifetimes and beyond. Can it be that we are crippling or incapacitating "those people"? After being oppressed, controlled, and degraded (especially for long periods of time), inmates turn into angry, fearful human beings who are unable to cope with things that people out here deal with all the time. The difficulty of participating in interpersonal relationships, finding and retaining employment, controlling anger, and "fitting in," to name a few, can become insurmountable obstacles. Yet most of our efforts to do anything about the situation only worsens it.

Efforts to improve sophisticated techniques of identifying, labeling, and monitoring parolees, "gang" members, and other "miscreants" are continually being developed. The school I attended inside no longer offers college classes—funding was pulled. Lifting weights—a positive, healthy way to release energy—is no longer allowed in many prisons: can't let "them" get too strong.

Today I have a friend in the county jail facing sixty years to life under California's three-strikes law for possession of less than a gram of cocaine. He is an addict, 48 years old, and if convicted will probably never get out. His first two strikes were for burglaries in the 1970s. Over the last few years he has battled with his addiction and, at one time, made it nearly two years without using. If the laws would have been the way they are today before I got clean, I would have been "striked out" myself. Is there anything wrong with all this?

My hope is that we are entering a new era, one in which we work on replacing blame and increasing levels of social control with understanding and compassion. An era in which we acknowledge the reality of contemporary life, its horrors, and its injustices as well as its joys. And I hope we can begin to alter the way we view those we perceive as being different from ourselves. All of us have fears. All of us need to belong and fit in somewhere. Oppression, hatred, and blame do not build better lives for anyone. We all need hope.

Reducing violence and crime requires lessening the harm we do to one another—including criminals. I know that, for me, the way I lived for so many years in "those places" affected my self-image, outlook, and actions in such a way that I had become almost completely alienated from everything in the outside world. Luckily, education and my motivation to learn gave me a new perspective and some hope. It helped me see more clearly. I was lucky to make it. Maybe it's time that people out here begin to imagine what it's like to be locked up. What it's like to be pushed into a life of crime, addiction, desperation, and hopelessness. Maybe by taking a closer look at the real factors associated with crime, and by changing the way we "see" those who get caught up in the criminal justice system, we can begin to end the nightmare.

Glossary

accusatory process The series of events from the arrest of a suspect to the filing of a formal charge (through an indictment or information) with the court.

adjudication The process of determining whether the defendant is guilty.

adversary process Court process employed in the United States and other former British colonies in which lawyers for each side represent their clients' best interests in presenting evidence and formulating arguments as a means to discover the truth and protect the rights of defendants.

affidavit Written statement of fact, supported by oath or affirmation, submitted to judicial officers to fulfill the requirements of probable cause for obtaining a warrant.

aftercare Juvenile justice equivalent of parole, in which a delinquent is released from a custodial sentence and supervised in the community.

aggressive patrol A patrol strategy designed to maximize the number of police interventions and observations in the community.

anomie A breakdown or disappearance of the rules of social behavior.

appeal A request to a higher court that it review actions taken in a trial court.

appellate courts Courts that do not try criminal cases but hear appeals of decisions of lower courts.

arraignment The court appearance of an accused person in which the charges are read and the accused, advised by a lawyer, pleads guilty or not guilty.

arrest The physical taking of a person into custody on the grounds that there is reason to believe that he or she has committed a criminal offense. Police may use only reasonable physical force in making an arrest. The purpose of the arrest is to hold the accused for a court proceeding.

assigned counsel An attorney in private practice assigned by a court to represent an indigent. The attorney's fee is paid by the government with jurisdiction over the case.

Atkins v. Virginia (2002) Execution of the mentally retarded is unconstitutional.

bail An amount of money, specified by a judge, to be paid as a condition of pretrial release to ensure that the accused will appear in court as required.

Barron v. Baltimore (1833) The protections of the Bill of Rights apply only to actions of the federal government.

bench trials Trials conducted by a judge who acts as fact finder and determines issues of law. No jury participates.

Bill of Rights The first ten amendments added to the U.S. Constitution to provide specific rights for individuals, including criminal justice rights concerning searches, trials, and punishments.

biological explanations Explanations of crime that emphasize physiological and neurological factors that may predispose a person to commit crimes.

boot camp A short-term institutional sentence, usually followed by probation, that puts the offender through a physical regimen designed to develop discipline and respect for authority. Also referred to as *shock incarceration.*

Bordenkircher v. Hayes (1978) A defendant's rights were not violated by a prosecutor who warned that refusing to enter a guilty plea would result in a harsher sentence.

Boykin v. Alabama (1969) Defendants must state that they are voluntarily making a plea of guilty before a judge may accept the plea.

Breed v. Jones (1975) Juveniles cannot be found delinquent in juvenile court and then transferred to adult court without a hearing on the transfer; to do so violates the protection against double jeopardy.

challenge for cause Removal of a prospective juror by showing that he or she has some bias or some other legal disability. The number of such challenges available to attorneys is unlimited.

Chimel v. California (1969) Supreme Court decision that endorsed warrantless searches for weapons and evidence in the immediate vicinity of people who are lawfully arrested.

circumstantial evidence Evidence provided by a witness from which a jury must infer a fact.

citation A written order or summons, issued by a law enforcement officer, directing an alleged offender to appear in court at a specific time to answer a criminal charge.

civil law Law regulating the relationships between or among individuals, usually involving property, contracts, or business disputes.

classical criminology A school of criminology that views behavior as stemming from free will, demands responsibility and accountability of all perpetrators, and stresses the need for punishments severe enough to deter others.

classification The process of assigning an inmate to a category specifying his or her needs for security, treatment, education, work assignment, and readiness for release.

clearance rate The percentage of crimes known to the police that they believe they have solved through an arrest; a statistic used to measure a police department's productivity.

community corrections A model of corrections based on the goal of reintegrating the offender into the community.

community service A sentence requiring the offender to perform a certain amount of unpaid labor in the community.

conditions of release Conduct restrictions that parolees must follow as a legally binding requirement of being released.

congregate system A penitentiary system, developed in Auburn, New York, in which each inmate was held in isolation during the night but worked and ate with other prisoners during the day under a rule of silence.

continuance An adjournment of a scheduled case until a later date.

contract counsel An attorney in private practice who contracts with the government to represent all indigent defendants in a county during a set period of time and for a specified dollar amount.

contract labor system A system under which inmates' labor was sold on a contractual basis to private employers who provided the machinery and raw materials with which inmates made salable products in the institution.

control theories Theories holding that criminal behavior occurs when the bonds that tie an individual to society are broken or weakened.

Cooper v. Pate (1964) Prisoners are entitled to the protection of the Civil Rights Act of 1871 and may challenge in federal courts the conditions of their confinement.

corrections The variety of programs, services, facilities, and organizations responsible for the management of people who have been accused or convicted of criminal offenses.

count Each separate offense of which a person is accused in an indictment or an information.

crime control model A model of the criminal justice system that assumes freedom is so important that every effort must be made to repress crime; it emphasizes efficiency, speed, finality, and the capacity to apprehend, try, convict, and dispose of a high proportion of offenders.

crime control model of corrections A model of corrections based on the assumption that criminal behavior can be controlled by more use of incarceration and other forms of strict supervision.

crimes without victims Offenses involving a willing and private exchange of illegal goods or services that are in strong demand. Participants do not feel they are being harmed, but these crimes are prosecuted on the ground that society as a whole is being injured.

criminogenic Having factors thought to bring about criminal behavior in an individual.

custodial model A model of incarceration that emphasizes security, discipline, and order.

cyber crimes Offenses that involve the use of one or more computers.

dark figure of crime A metaphor that emphasizes the dangerous dimension of crime that is never reported to the police.

day reporting center A community correctional center where an offender reports each day to comply with elements of a sentence.

defense attorney The lawyer who represents accused offenders and convicted offenders in their dealings with criminal justice.

delinquent A child who has committed an act that if committed by an adult would be criminal.

demonstrative evidence Evidence that is not based on witness testimony but that demonstrates information relevant to the crime, such as maps, X-rays, and photographs; includes real evidence involved in the crime.

dependent child A child who has no parent or guardian or whose parents cannot give proper care.

detention hearing A hearing by the juvenile court to determine if a juvenile is to be detained or released prior to adjudication.

determinate sentence A sentence that fixes the term of imprisonment at a specific period.

differential response A patrol strategy that assigns priorities to calls for service and chooses the appropriate response.

direct evidence Eyewitness accounts.

directed patrol A proactive form of patrolling that directs resources to known high-crime areas.

discovery A prosecutor's pretrial disclosure to the defense of facts and evidence to be introduced at trial.

discretion The authority to make decisions without reference to specific rules or facts, using instead one's own judgment; allows for individualization and informality in the administration of justice.

discretionary release The release of an inmate from prison to conditional supervision at the discretion of the parole board within the boundaries set by the sentence and the penal law.

discrimination Differential treatment of individuals or groups based on race, ethnicity, gender, sexual orientation, or economic status, instead of on their behavior or qualifications.

disparity A difference between groups that may either be explained by legitimate factors or indicate discrimination.

diversion The process of screening children out of the juvenile justice system without a decision by the court.

double jeopardy The subjecting of a person to prosecution more than once in the same jurisdiction for the same offense; prohibited by the Fifth Amendment.

dual court system A system consisting of a separate judicial structure for each state in addition to a national structure. Each case is tried in a court of the same jurisdiction as that of the law or laws broken.

due process model A model of the criminal justice system that assumes freedom is so important that every effort must be made to ensure that criminal justice decisions are based on reliable information; it emphasizes the adversarial process, the rights of defendants, and formal decision-making procedures.

Enlightenment A movement during the eighteenth century in England and France in which concepts of liberalism, rationalism, equality, and individualism dominated social and political thinking.

entrapment The defense that the individual was induced by the police to commit the criminal act.

exchange A mutual transfer of resources: a balance of benefits and deficits that flow from behavior based on decisions about the values and costs of alternatives.

exclusionary rule The principle that illegally obtained evidence must be excluded from trial.

exigent circumstances When there is an immediate threat to public safety or the risk that evidence will be destroyed, officers may search, arrest, or question suspects without obtaining a warrant or following other usual rules of criminal procedure.

expiration release The release of an inmate from incarceration, without further correctional supervision; the inmate cannot be returned to prison for any remaining portion of the sentence for the current offense.

federalism A system of government in which power is divided between a central (national) government and regional (state) governments.

felonies Serious crimes usually carrying a penalty of death or incarceration for more than one year.

filtering process A screening operation; a process by which criminal justice officials screen out some cases while advancing others to the next level of decision making.

fine A sum of money to be paid to the state by a convicted person as punishment for an offense.

forfeiture Government seizure of property and other assets derived from or used in criminal activity.

frankpledge A system in old English law in which members of a *tithing* (a group of ten families) pledged to be responsible for keeping order and bringing violators of the law to court.

fundamental fairness A legal doctrine supporting the idea that so long as a state's conduct maintains basic standards of fairness, the Constitution has not been violated.

furlough The temporary release of an inmate from a correctional institution for a brief period, usually one to three days, for a visit home. Such programs help maintain family ties and prepare inmates for release on parole.

Furman v. Georgia (1972) The death penalty, as administered, constitutes cruel and unusual punishment.

Gagnon v. Scarpelli (1973) Before probation can be revoked, a two-stage hearing must be held and the offender provided with specific elements of due process. Requested counsel will be allowed on a case-by-case basis.

general deterrence Punishment of criminals that is intended to be an example to the general public and to discourage the commission of offenses.

Gideon v. Wainwright (1963) Indigent defendants have a right to counsel when charged with serious crimes for which they could face six or more months of incarceration.

going rate Local court officials' shared view of the appropriate sentence, given the offense, the defendant's prior record, and other case characteristics.

"good faith" exception Exception to the exclusionary rule that permits the use of improperly obtained evidence when police officers acted in honest reliance on a defective statute, a warrant improperly issued by a magistrate, or a consent to search by someone who lacked authority to give such permission.

good time A reduction of an inmate's prison sentence, at the discretion of the prison administrator, for good behavior or participation in vocational, educational, or treatment programs.

grand jury Body of citizens drawn from the community to hear evidence presented by the prosecutor in order to decide whether enough evidence existence to file charges against a defendant.

Gregg v. Georgia (1976) Death penalty laws are constitutional if they require the judge and jury to consider certain mitigating and aggravating circumstances in deciding which convicted murderers should be sentenced to death. Proceedings must be also be divided into a trial phase and a punishment phase, and there must be opportunities for appeal.

habeas corpus A writ or judicial order requesting the release of a person being detained in a jail, prison, or mental hospital. If a judge finds the person is being held improperly, the writ may be granted and the person released.

halfway house A correctional facility housing convicted felons who spend a portion of their day at work in the community but reside in the halfway house during nonworking hours.

hands-off policy Judges should not interfere with the administration of correctional institutions.

home confinement A sentence requiring the offender to remain inside his or her home during specified periods.

Hudson v. Palmer (1984) Prison officials have a right to search cells and confiscate any materials found.

In re Gault (1967) Juveniles have the right to have counsel, to confront and examine accusers, to be protected against self-incrimination, and to have adequate notice of charges when confinement is a possible punishment.

In re Winship (1970) The standard of proof beyond a reasonable doubt applies to juvenile delinquency proceedings.

incapacitation Depriving an offender of the ability to commit crimes against society, usually by detaining the offender in prison.

inchoate offense Conduct that is criminal even though the harm that the law seeks to prevent has not been done but merely planned or attempted.

incident-driven policing Policing in which calls for service are the primary instigators of action.

incorporation The extension of the due process clause of the Fourteenth Amendment to make binding on state governments the rights guaranteed in the first ten amendments to the U.S. Constitution (the Bill of Rights).

indeterminate sentence A period, set by a judge, that specifies a minimum and a maximum time to be served in prison. Sometime after the minimum, the offender may be eligible for parole. Because it is based on the idea that the time necessary for treatment cannot be set, the indeterminate sentence is closely associated with rehabilitation.

indictment A document returned by a grand jury as a "true bill" charging an individual with a specific crime on the basis of a determination of probable cause as presented by a prosecuting attorney.

inevitable discovery rule Supreme Court ruling that improperly obtained evidence can be used when it would later have been inevitably discovered by the police.

information A document charging an individual with a specific crime. It is prepared by a prosecuting attorney and presented to a court at a preliminary hearing.

inmate code The values and norms of the prison social system that define the inmates' idea of the model prisoner.

inquisitorial process Court process employed in most countries of the world in which the judge takes an active role in investigating the case and examining evidence by, for example, questioning witnesses.

intensive supervision probation (ISP) Probation granted under conditions of strict reporting to a probation officer with a limited caseload.

intermediate sanctions A variety of punishments that are more restrictive than traditional probation but less severe and costly than incarceration.

internal affairs unit A branch of a police department that receives and investigates complaints alleging violation of rules and policies on the part of officers.

jail An institution authorized to hold pretrial detainees and sentenced misdemeanants for periods longer than 48 hours.

jurisdiction The geographic territory or legal boundaries within which control may be exercised; the range of a court's authority.

jury A panel of citizens selected according to law and sworn to determine matters of fact in a criminal case and to deliver a verdict of guilty or not guilty.

labeling theories Theories emphasizing that the causes of criminal behavior are not found in the individual but in the social process that labels certain acts as deviant or criminal.

law enforcement The police function of controlling crime by intervening in situations in which the law has clearly been violated and the police need to identify and apprehend the guilty person.

law enforcement intelligence Information collected and analyzed by law enforcement officials concerning criminal activities and organizations, such as terror groups, gangs, drug traffickers, and organized crime.

learning theories Theories that see criminal behavior as learned, just as legal behavior is learned.

lease system A system under which inmates were leased to contractors who provided prisoners with food and clothing in exchange for their labor.

legal responsibility The accountability of an individual for a crime because of the perpetrator's behavior and the circumstances of the illegal act.

less-lethal weapons Weapons such as pepper spray and air-fired beanbags or nets that are used in an effort to incapacitate a suspect without inflicting serious injuries.

life course theories Theories that identify factors affecting the start, duration, nature, and end of criminal behavior over the life of an offender.

line functions Police components that directly perform field operations and carry out the basic functions of patrol, investigation, traffic, vice, juvenile, and so on.

local legal culture Norms shared by members of a court community as to how cases should be handled and how a participant should behave in the judicial process.

mala in se Offenses that are wrong by their very nature.

mala prohibita Offenses prohibited by law but not wrong in themselves.

mandatory release The required release of an inmate from incarceration to community supervision upon the expiration of a certain period, as specified by a determinate-sentencing law or parole guidelines.

mandatory sentence A sentence determined by statutes and requiring that a certain penalty be imposed and carried out for convicted offenders who meet certain criteria.

mark system A point system in which prisoners can reduce their term of imprisonment and gain release by earning "marks" or points through labor, good behavior, and educational achievement.

McCleskey v. Kemp (**1987**) The Supreme Court rejects a challenge of Georgia's death penalty on grounds of racial discrimination.

McKeiver v. Pennsylvania (**1971**) Juveniles do not have a constitutional right to a trial by jury.

medical model A model of corrections based on the assumption that criminal behavior is caused by biological or psychological conditions that require treatment.

Mempa v. Rhay (**1967**) Probationers have the right to counsel at a combined revocation-sentencing hearing.

mens rea "Guilty mind" or blameworthy state of mind, necessary for legal responsibility for a criminal offense; criminal intent, as distinguished from innocent intent.

merit selection A reform plan by which judges are nominated by a commission and appointed by the governor for a given period. When the term expires, the voters approve or disapprove the judge for a succeeding term. If the judge is disapproved, the committee nominates a successor for the governor's appointment.

Miranda v. Arizona (**1966**) U.S. Supreme Court decision declaring that suspects in custody must be informed of their rights to remain silent and be represented during questioning.

misdemeanors Offenses less serious than felonies and usually punishable by incarceration of no more than a year, probation, or intermediate sanction.

money laundering Moving the proceeds of criminal activities through a maze of businesses, banks, and brokerage accounts so as to disguise their origin.

Morrissey v. Brewer (**1972**) Due process rights require a prompt, informal, two-part inquiry before an impartial hearing officer before parole may be revoked. The parolee may present relevant information and confront witnesses.

motion An application to a court requesting that an order be issued to bring about a specific action.

National Crime Victimization Surveys (NCVS) Interviews of samples of the U.S. population conducted by the Bureau of Justice Statistics to determine the number and types of criminal victimizations and thus the extent of unreported as well as reported crime.

National Incident-Based Reporting System (NIBRS) A reporting system in which the police describe each offense in a crime incident, together with data describing the offender, victim, and property.

neglected child A child who is not receiving proper care, because of some action or inaction of his or her parents.

net widening Process in which new sentencing options increase rather than reduce control over offenders' lives.

Nix v. Williams (**1984**) Legal decision in which the Supreme Court created the inevitable discovery exception to the exclusionary rule.

nolle prosequi An entry, made by a prosecutor on the record of a case and announced in court, indicating that the charges specified will not be prosecuted. In effect, the charges are thereby dismissed.

nonpartisan election An election in which candidates' party affiliations are not listed on the ballot.

North Carolina v. Alford (**1970**) A plea of guilty by a defendant who maintains his or her innocence may be accepted for the purpose of a lesser sentence.

occupational crimes Criminal offenses committed through opportunities created in a legal business or occupation.

open fields doctrine Supreme Court doctrine under which property owners have no reasonable expectation of privacy in open fields on and around their property.

order maintenance The police function of preventing behavior that disturbs or threatens to disturb the public peace or that involves face-to-face conflict among two or more people. In such situations the police exercise discretion in deciding whether a law has been broken.

organized crime A framework for the perpetuation of criminal acts—usually in fields such as gambling, drugs, and prostitution—providing illegal services that are in great demand.

other conditional release A term used in some states to avoid the rigidity of mandatory release, by placing convicts in various community settings under supervision.

parens patriae The state as parent; the state as guardian and protector of all citizens (such as juveniles) who cannot protect themselves.

parole The conditional release of an inmate from incarceration, under supervision, after part of the prison sentence has been served.

partisan election An election in which candidates openly endorsed by political parties are presented to voters for selection.

penitentiary An institution intended to punish criminals by isolating them from society and from one another so they can reflect on their past misdeeds, repent, and reform.

percentage bail Defendants may deposit a percentage (usually 10 percent) of the full bail with the court. The full amount of the bail is required if the defendant fails to appear. The percentage of bail is returned after disposition of the case, although the court often retains 1 percent for administrative costs.

peremptory challenge Removal of a prospective juror without giving any reason. Attorneys are allowed a limited number of such challenges.

PINS Acronym for "person(s) in need of supervision," a term that designates juveniles who are either status offenders or thought to be on the verge of trouble.

plain view doctrine Officers may examine and use as evidence, without a warrant, contraband or evidence that is in open view at a location where they are legally permitted to be.

plea bargain A defendant's plea of guilty to a criminal charge with the reasonable expectation of receiving some consideration from the state for doing so, usually a reduction of the charge. The defendant's ultimate goal is a penalty lighter than the one formally warranted by the charged offense.

political crime An act, usually done for ideological purposes, that constitutes a threat against the state (such as treason, sedition, or espionage); also describes a criminal act by the state.

positivist criminology A school of criminology that views behavior as stemming from social, biological, and psychological factors. It argues that punishment should be tailored to the individual needs of the offender.

Powell v. Alabama (1932) An attorney must be provided to a poor defendant facing the death penalty.

presentence report A report, prepared by a probation officer, that presents a convicted offender's background and is used by the judge in selecting an appropriate sentence.

presumptive sentence A sentence for which the legislature or a commission sets a minimum and maximum range of months or years. Judges are to fix the length of the sentence within that range, allowing for special circumstances.

preventive detention Holding a defendant for trial, based on a judge's finding that, if the defendant were released on bail, he or she would endanger the safety of any other person and the community or would flee.

preventive patrol Making the police presence known, to deter crime and to make officers available to respond quickly to calls.

prison An institution for the incarceration of people convicted of serious crimes, usually felonies.

proactive Acting in anticipation, such as an active search for potential offenders that is initiated by the police without waiting for a crime to be reported. Arrests for crimes without victims are usually proactive.

probable cause An amount of reliable information indicating that it is more likely than not that evidence will be found in a specific location or that a specific person is guilty of a crime.

probation A sentence that the offender is allowed to serve under supervision in the community.

problem-oriented policing An approach to policing in which officers routinely seek to identify, analyze, and respond to the circumstances underlying the incidents that prompt citizens to call the police.

procedural criminal law Law defining the procedures that criminal justice officials must follow in enforcement, adjudication, and corrections.

prosecuting attorney A legal representative of the state with sole responsibility for bringing criminal charges. In some states this person is referred to as the district attorney, state's attorney, or county attorney.

psychological explanations Explanations of crime that emphasize mental processes and behavior.

public defender An attorney employed on a full-time, salaried basis by a public or private nonprofit organization to represent indigents.

"public safety" exception Exception to *Miranda* requirements that permits police to immediately question a suspect in custody without providing any warnings, when public safety would be jeopardized by taking the time to supply the warnings.

reactive Occurring in response, such as police activity in response to notification that a crime has been committed.

real evidence Physical evidence—such as a weapons, records, fingerprints, and stolen property—involved in the crime.

reasonable doubt The standard used by a jury to decide if the prosecution has provided enough evidence for conviction.

reasonable expectation of privacy The objective standard developed by courts for determining whether a government intrusion into an individual's person or property constitutes a search because it interferes with the individual's interests that are normally protected from government examination.

reasonable suspicion A police officer's belief based on articulable facts that would be recognized by others in a similar situation as indicating that criminal activity is afoot and necessitates further investigation that will intrude on an individual's reasonable expectation of privacy.

recidivism A return to criminal behavior.

reformatory An institution for young offenders that emphasizes training, a mark system of classification, indeterminate sentences, and parole.

rehabilitation The goal of restoring a convicted offender to a constructive place in society through some form of vocational or educational training or therapy.

rehabilitation model A model of corrections that emphasizes the need to restore a convicted offender to a constructive place in society through some form of vocational or educational training or therapy.

reintegration model A model of a correctional institutions that emphasizes maintaining the offender's ties to family and community as a method of reform, recognizing that the offender will be returning to society.

release on recognizance (ROR) Pretrial release granted, on the defendant's promise to appear in court, because the judge believes that the defendant's ties to the community guarantee that he or she will appear.

restitution Repayment—in the form of money or service—by an offender to a victim who has suffered some loss from the offense.

restorative justice Punishment designed to repair the damage done to the victim and community by an offender's criminal act.

retribution Punishment inflicted on a person who has infringed on the rights of others and so deserves to be penalized.

Ricketts v. Adamson (1987) Defendants must uphold the plea agreement or suffer the consequences.

Roper v. Simmons (2005) Execution of offenders for crimes committed while under the age of 18 is unconstitutional.

Santobello v. New York (1971) When a guilty plea rests on a promise of a prosecutor, the promise must be fulfilled.

Schall v. Martin (1984) Juveniles can be held in preventive detention if there is concern that they may commit additional crimes while awaiting court action.

search Government officials' examination of and hunt for evidence in or on a person or place in a manner that intrudes on reasonable expectations of privacy.

seizure Situations in which police officers use their authority to deprive people of their liberty or property and which must not be "unreasonable" according to the Fourth Amendment.

selective incapacitation Making the best use of expensive and limited prison space by targeting for incarceration those individuals whose incapacity will do the most to reduce crime in society.

self-incrimination The act of exposing oneself to prosecution by being forced to respond to questions whose answers may reveal that one has committed a crime. The Fifth Amendment protects defendants against self-incrimination.

sentencing guidelines A mechanism to indicate to judges the expected sanction for certain offenses, in order to reduce disparities in sentencing.

separate confinement A penitentiary system, developed in Pennsylvania, in which each inmate was held in isolation from other inmates. All activities, including craft work, took place in the cells.

service The police function of providing assistance to the public, usually in matters unrelated to crime.

shock probation A sentence in which the offender is released after a short incarceration and resentenced to probation.

social conflict theories Theories that assume criminal law and the criminal justice system are primarily a means of controlling the poor and the have-nots.

social process theories Theories that see criminality as normal behavior. Everyone has the potential to become a criminal, depending on (1) the influences that impel one toward or away from crime and (2) how one is regarded by others.

social structure theories Theories that blame crime on the existence of a powerless lower class that lives with poverty and deprivation and often turns to crime in response.

socialization The process by which the rules, symbols, and values of a group or subculture are learned by its members.

sociological explanations Explanations of crime that emphasize as causes of criminal behavior the social conditions that bear on the individual.

specific deterrence Punishment inflicted on criminals to discourage them from committing future crimes.

state attorney general Chief legal officer of a state, responsible for both civil and criminal matters.

status offense Any act committed by a juvenile that is considered unacceptable for a child, such as truancy or running away from home, but that would not be a crime if it were committed by an adult.

stop Government officials' interference with an individual's freedom of movement for a duration that typically lasts less than one hour and only rarely extends for as long as several hours.

stop-and-frisk search Limited search approved by the Supreme Court in *Terry v. Ohio* that permits police officers to pat down the clothing of people on the streets if there is reasonable suspicion of dangerous criminal activity.

subculture The symbols, beliefs, values, and attitudes shared by members of a subgroup of the larger society.

substantive criminal law Law that defines acts subject to punishment and specifies the punishments for such offenses.

sworn officers Police employees who have taken an oath and been given powers by the state to make arrests and use necessary force, in accordance with their duties.

system A complex whole consisting of interdependent parts whose actions are directed toward goals and are influenced by the environment within which they function.

technical violation The probationer's failure to abide by the rules and conditions of probation (specified by the judge), resulting in revocation of probation.

Tennessee v. Garner (1985) Deadly force may not be used against an unarmed and fleeing suspect unless necessary to prevent the escape and unless the officer has probable cause to believe that the suspect poses a significant threat of death or serious injury to the officers or others.

Terry v. Ohio (1968) Supreme Court decision endorsing police officers' authority to stop and frisk suspects on the streets when there is reasonable suspicion that they are armed and involved in criminal activity.

testimony Oral evidence provided by a legally competent witness.

theory of differential association The theory that people become criminals because they encounter more influences that view criminal behavior as normal and acceptable than influences that are hostile to criminal behavior.

totality of circumstances Flexible test established by the Supreme Court for identifying whether probable cause exists to justify a judge's issuance of a warrant.

trial courts of general jurisdiction Criminal courts with jurisdiction over all offenses, including felonies. In some states these courts also hear appeals.

trial courts of limited jurisdiction Criminal courts with trial jurisdiction over misdemeanor cases and preliminary matters in felony cases. Sometimes these courts hold felony trials that may result in penalties below a specific limit.

Uniform Crime Reports (UCR) An annually published statistical summary of crimes reported to the police, based on voluntary reports to the FBI by local, state, and federal law enforcement agencies.

United States attorneys Officials responsible for the prosecution of crimes that violate the laws of the United States. Appointed by the president and assigned to a U.S. district court jurisdiction.

United States v. Drayton (2002) Legal decision declaring that police officers are not required to inform people of their right to decline to be searched when police ask for consent to search.

United States v. Salerno and Cafero (1987) Preventive detention provisions of the Bail Reform Act of 1984 are upheld as a legitimate use of government power designed to prevent people from committing crimes while on bail.

USA Patriot Act A federal statute passed in the aftermath of the terrorist attacks of September 11 that broadens government authority to conduct searches and wiretaps and that expands the definitions of crimes involving terrorism.

victimology A field of criminology that examines the role the victim plays in precipitating a criminal incident and also examines the impact of crimes on victims.

visible crime An offense against persons or property, committed primarily by members of the lower class. Often referred to as "street crime" or "ordinary crime," this type of offense is the one most upsetting to the public.

voir dire A questioning of prospective jurors to screen out people the attorneys think might be biased or otherwise incapable of delivering a fair verdict.

waiver Procedure by which the juvenile court relinquishes its jurisdiction and transfers a juvenile case to the adult criminal court.

warrant A court order authorizing police officers to take certain actions, for example, to arrest suspects or to search premises.

Williams v. Florida (1970) Juries of fewer than 12 members are constitutional.

Witherspoon v. Illinois (1968) Potential jurors who object to the death penalty cannot be automatically excluded from service; however, during voir dire those who feel so strongly about capital punishment that they could not give an impartial verdict may be excluded.

Wolff v. McDonnell (1974) Basic elements of procedural due process must be present when decisions are made about the disciplining of an inmate.

work and educational release The daytime release of inmates from correctional institutions so they can work or attend school.

workgroup A collection of individuals who interact in the workplace on a continuing basis, share goals, develop norms regarding how activities should be carried out, and eventually establish a network of roles that differentiates the group from others and that facilitates cooperation.

working personality A set of emotional and behavioral characteristics developed by members of an occupational group in response to the work situation and environmental influences.

References

Abadinsky, H. 1997. *Probation and Parole.* 6th ed. Upper Saddle River, NJ: Prentice-Hall.

Abbe, O. G., and P. S. Herrnson. 2002. "How Judicial Election Campaigns Have Changed." *Judicature* 85:286–95.

Abwender, D. A., and K. Hough. 2001. "Interactive Effects of Characteristics of Defendant and Mock Juror on U.S. Participants' Judgment and Sentencing Recommendations." *Journal of Social Psychology* 141:603–16.

Acoca, L. 1997. "Hearts on the Ground: Violent Victimization and Other Themes in the Lives of Women Prisoners." *Corrections Management Quarterly* 1 (Spring): 44–55.

———. 1998. "Defusing the Time Bomb: Understanding and Meeting the Growing Health Care Needs of Incarcerated Women in America." *Crime and Delinquency* 44 (January): 49–69.

"Actor Tom Sizemore Gets Jail Time." 2005. March 25. http://www.cbsnews.com/stories/2005/03/25/entertainment.

Adams, G. 2006. "Sex Offenders' Killer Studied States' Lists." http://www.boston.com.

Adams, K. 1992. "Adjusting to Prison Life." In *Crime and Justice: A Review of Research,* vol. 16, ed. M. Tonry. Chicago: University of Chicago Press, 275–359.

———. 1999. "What We Know about Police Use of Force." In *Use of Force by Police: Overview of National and Local Data.* Washington, DC: U.S. Government Printing Office.

Adler, F. 1975. *Sisters in Crime: The Rise of the New Female Criminal.* New York: McGraw-Hill.

Adler, S. J. 1994. *The Jury: Disorder in the Court.* New York: Doubleday.

Alexander, R., Jr. 1993. "The Demise of State Prisoners' Access to Federal Habeas Corpus." *Criminal Justice Policy Review* 6:55–70.

Alley, M. E., E. M. Bonello, and J. A. Schafer. 2002. "Dual Responsibilities: A Model for Immersing Midlevel Managers in Community Policing." In *The Move to Community Policing: Making Change Happen,* ed. M. Morash and J. Ford. Thousand Oaks, CA: Sage, 112–25.

Amar, A. R. 1997. *The Constitution and Criminal Procedure: First Principles.* New Haven, CT: Yale University Press.

American Correctional Association. 1990. *The Female Offender: What Does the Future Hold?* Alexandria, VA: Kirby Lithographic Company.

———. 1994. *Gangs in Correctional Facilities: A National Assessment.* Laurel, MD: American Correctional Association.

———. 2000. *Vital Statistics in Corrections.* Lanham, MD: American Correctional Association.

Anderson, G., R. Litzenberger, and D. Plecas. 2002. "Physical Evidence of Police Officer Stress." *Policing* 25:399–420.

Andrews, D. A., and J. Bonta. 1994. *The Psychology of Criminal Behavior.* Cincinnati, OH: Anderson.

Andrews, D. A., I. Zinger, R. D. Hoge, J. Bonta, P. Gendreau, and F. T. Cullen. 1990. "Does Correctional Treatment Work? A Clinically Relevant and Psychologically Informed Meta-Analysis." *Criminology* 28:369–404.

Archibold, R. 2006. "Border Patrol Draws Scrutiny as Its Role Grows." *New York Times,* June 4. http://www.nytimes.com.

Armstrong, K., and S. Mills. 1999. "Death Row Justice Derailed." *Chicago Tribune,* November 14 and 15, p. 1.

Associated Press. 2005. "Deputies Will Be Disciplined for Wild Shootout." *Pasadena Star News,* June 9. http://www.pasadenastarnews.com.

Association of Certified Fraud Examiners. 2004. *Report to the Nation on Occupational Fraud and Abuse.* Austin, TX: Association of Certified Fraud Examiners.

Auerhahn, K. 1999. "Selective Incapacitation and the Problem of Prediction." *Criminology* 37:703–34.

———. 2002. "Selective Incapacitation, Three Strikes, and the Problem of Aging Prison Population: Using Simulation Modeling to See the Future." *Criminology and Public Policy* 1:353–88.

Austin, J. 2001. "Prisoner Reentry: Current Trends, Practices, and Issues." *Crime and Delinquency* 47 (July): 314–33.

Austin, J., and G. Coventry. 2001. " Emerging Issues in Privatizing Prisons." *Corrections Forum* 10 (December): 11.

Axtman, K. 2005a. "A New Motion to Make Jury Service More Attractive." *Christian Science Monitor,* May 23, pp. 2–3.

———. 2005b. "Houston Grapples with Gang Resurgence." *Christian Science Monitor,* April 29, pp. 2–3.

Baldus, D. C., G. Woodworth, and C. A. Pulaski. 1994. *Equal Justice and the Death Penalty: A Legal and Empirical Analysis.* Boston: Northeastern University Press.

Bandy, D. 1991. "$1.2 Million to Be Paid in Stray-Bullet Death." *Akron Beacon Journal,* December 3, p. B6.

Basemore, G., and M. S. Umbreit. 1994. Foreword to *Balanced and Restorative Justice: Program Summary.* Washington, DC: Office of Juvenile Justice and Delinquency Prevention, U.S. Government Printing Office.

Baum, D. 2006. "Deluged: When Katrina Hit, Where Were the Police?" *New Yorker,* January 9. http://www.thenewyorker.com.

Bayley, D. H. 1994. *Police for the Future.* New York: Oxford University Press.

———. 1998. *What Works in Policing?* New York: Oxford University Press.

Beck, A. 1997. "Growth, Change, and Stability in the U.S. Prison Population, 1980–1995." *Corrections Management Quarterly* 8 (January): 1–14.

———. 2000. "State and Federal Prisoners Returning to the Community: Findings from the Bureau of Justice Statistics." Paper presented at the First Reentry Courts Initiative Cluster Meeting, Washington, DC, April 13.

Beck, A. J., J. C. Karberg, and P. M. Harrison. 2002. "Prison and Jail Inmates at Mid-Year 2001." Bureau of Justice Statistics *Bulletin,* April.

Becker, H. S. 1963. *Outsiders: Studies in the Sociology of Deviance.* New York: Free Press.

Beckett, K., K. Nyrop, and L. Pfingst. 2006. "Race, Drugs, and Policing: Understanding Disparities in Drug Delivery Arrests." *Criminology* 44:105–37.

Bell, D. 1967. *The End of Ideology.* 2nd rev. ed. New York: Collier.

Belluck, P. 2001. "Desperate for Prison Guards, Some States Even Rob Cradles." *New York Times,* April 21, p. A1.

Berenson, A. 2006. "The Safety of Tasers Is Questioned Again." *New York Times,* May 25. http://www.nytimes.com.

Bernstein, N. 2006. "Magistrate Rules That Government Must Reveal Monitoring." *New York Times,* May 31. http://www.nytimes.com.

Bershard, L. 1985. "Discriminatory Treatment of the Female Offender in the Criminal Justice System." *Boston College Law Review* 26:389–438.

BJS (Bureau of Justice Statistics). 1997. *Police Use of Force.* Washington, DC: U.S. Government Printing Office.

———. 1998. *Bulletin,* January.

———. 1999a. *Sourcebook of Criminal Justice Statistics, 1998.* Washington, DC: U.S. Government Printing Office.

———. 1999b. *Special Report,* July.

———. 2000a. *Bulletin,* August.

———. 2000b. *Correctional Populations in the United States, 1997.* Washington, DC: U.S. Government Printing Office.

———. 2000c. *Sourcebook of Criminal Justice Statistics, 1999.* Washington, DC: U.S. Government Printing Office.

———. 2000d. *Special Report,* May.

———. 2000e. *Special Report,* August.

———. 2001a. *Bulletin,* August.

———. 2001b. *Special Report,* July.

———. 2002a. *Bulletin,* June.

———. 2002b. *Bulletin,* August.

———. 2002c. *Bulletin,* September.

———. 2002d. *Sourcebook of Criminal Justice Statistics, 2001.* Washington, DC: U.S. Government Printing Office.

———. 2002e. *Special Report,* May.

———. 2002f. *Special Report,* June.

———. 2003a. *Bulletin,* July.

———. 2003b. *Census of State and Federal Correctional Facilities, 2000.* Washington, DC: U.S. Government Printing Office.

———. 2003c. *Special Report,* May.

———. 2004a. *Bulletin,* May.

———. 2004b. *Bulletin,* July.

———. 2004c. *Bulletin,* October.

———. 2004d. *Bulletin,* November.

———. 2004e. *Bulletin,* December.

———. 2004f. *Sourcebook of Criminal Justice Statistics, 2003.* Washington, DC: U.S. Government Printing Office.

———. 2005a. *Bulletin,* April.

———. 2005b. *Bulletin,* October.

———. 2005c. *Bulletin,* November.

———. 2005d. *Bulletin,* December.

———. 2005e. *Sourcebook of Criminal Justice Statistics, 2004.* Washington, DC: U.S. Government Printing Office.

———. 2005f. *Special Report,* August.

———. 2006. *Criminal Victimization in the United States, 2004.* Washington, DC: U.S. Government Printing Office.

Bloch, P., and D. Anderson. 1974. *Policewomen on Patrol: First Report.* Washington, DC: Police Foundation.

Blumberg, M. 1989. "Controlling Police Use of Deadly Force: Assessing Two Decades of Progress." In *Critical Issues in Policing,* ed. G. Dunham and G. Alpert. Prospect Heights, IL: Waveland Press.

Blumenson, E., and E. Nilsen. 1998. "The Drug War's Hidden Economic Agenda." *The Nation,* March 9, p. 11.

Blumstein, A. 1996. "Youth Violence, Guns, and Illicit Drug Markets." In *NIJ Research Preview.* Washington, DC: National Institute of Justice, U.S. Government Printing Office.

Boland, B. 2001. *Community Prosecution in Washington, D.C.: The U.S. Attorney's Fifth District Pilot Project.* Washington, DC: National Institute of Justice, U.S. Government Printing Office.

Boland, B., E. Brady, H. Tyson, and J. Bassler. 1983. *The Prosecution of Felony Arrests.*

Washington, DC: Bureau of Justice Statistics, U.S. Government Printing Office.

Bonczar, T. P., and T. L. Snell. 2004. "Capital Punishment, 2003." Bureau of Justice Statistics *Bulletin,* November.

Bonne, J. 2001. "Meth's Deadly Buzz." *MSNBC News Special Report.* February. http://www.msnbc.msn.com.

Bourque, B. B., M. Han, and S. M. Hill. 1996. "A National Survey of Aftercare Provisions for Boot Camp Graduates." In *Research in Brief.* Washington, DC: National Institute of Justice, U.S. Government Printing Office.

Bowers, F. 2002. "The Intelligence Divide: Can It Be Bridged?" *Christian Science Monitor,* October 8, p. 2.

Bowker, L. H. 1982. "Victimizers and Victims in American Correctional Institutions." In *Pains of Imprisonment,* ed. R. Johnson and H. Toch. Beverly Hills, CA: Sage.

Bradley, C. 1992. "Reforming the Criminal Trial." *Indiana Law Journal* 68:659–64.

Braga, A. A. 1999. "Problem-oriented Policing in Violent Crime Places: A Randomized Controlled Experiment." *Criminology* 37: 541–80.

Brandl, S., and Frank, J. 1994. "The Relationship between Evidence, Detective Effort, and the Disposition of Burglary and Robbery Investigations." *American Journal of Police,* 13:149–68.

Bray, K. 1992. "Reaching the Final Chapter in the Story of Peremptory Challenges." *U.C.L.A. Law Review* 40:517–55.

Brennan, P. A., S. A. Mednick, and J. Volavka. 1995. "Biomedical Factors in Crime." In *Crime,* ed. J. Q. Wilson and J. Petersilia. San Francisco: ICS Press.

Bright, S. B. 1994. "Counsel for the Poor: The Death Sentence Not for the Worst Crime but for the Worst Lawyer." *Yale Law Journal* 103:1850.

Britt, C. 2000. "Social Context and Racial Disparities in Punishment Decisions." *Justice Quarterly* 17:707–32.

Broeder, D. W. 1959. "The University of Chicago Jury Project." *Nebraska Law Review* 38:774–803.

Bruce, M. 2003. "Contextual Complexity and Violent Delinquency among Black and White Males." *Journal of Black Studies* 35:65–98.

Bureau of Labor Statistics. 2005. "Labor Force Statistics from the Current Population Survey." U.S. Department of Labor. http://www.bls.gov/cps/home.htm.

Buruma, I. 2005. "What Teaching a College-Level Class at a Maximum Security Correctional Facility Did for the Inmates—and for Me." *The New York Times Magazine,* February 20, pp. 36–41.

Bushway, S. D., and A. M. Piehl. 2001. "Judging Judicial Discretion: Legal Factors and Racial Discrimination in Sentencing." *Law and Society Review* 35:733–64.

Business Wire. 2001. "WorldNet Technologies, Creators of a State of the Art Weapons Detection System, Signs Consulting Deal with NuQuest." November 27 (available on Lexis-Nexis).

Butterfield, F. 1995. "More Blacks in Their 20's Have Trouble with the Law." *New York Times,* October 5, p. A18.

———. 1996. "Three Strikes Rarely Invoked in Courtrooms." *New York Times,* September 10, p. A1.

———. 1998a. "Decline in Violent Crimes Is Linked to Crack Market." *New York Times,* December 18, p. A16.

———. 1998b. "Prisons Replace Hospitals for the Nation's Mentally Ill." *New York Times,* March 5, p. A26.

———. 2000. "Often, Parole Is One Stop on the Way Back to Prison." *New York Times,* November 29, p. A1.

Bynum, T., and S. Varano. 2002. "The Anti-Gang Initiative in Detroit: An Aggressive Enforcement Approach to Gangs." In *Policing Gangs and Youth Violence,* ed. S. H. Decker. Belmont, CA: Wadsworth, 214–38.

Calhoun, F. 1990. *The Lawmen.* Washington, DC: Smithsonian Institution.

Callahan, L. A., M. A. McGreevy, C. Cirincione, and H. J. Steadman. 1992. "Measuring the Effects of the Guilty But Mentally Ill (GBMI) Verdict." *Law and Human Behavior* 16:447–62.

Callahan, R. 2002. "Scientists: Liars Are Betrayed by Their Faces." Associated Press Wire Service, January 2.

Camp, C. G. 2003. *Corrections Yearbook, 2002.* Middletown, CT: Criminal Justice Institute.

Camp, C. G., and G. M. Camp. 1999. *Corrections Yearbook, 1999.* Middletown, CT: Criminal Justice Institute.

———. 2001. *Corrections Yearbook, 2000.* Middletown, CT: Criminal Justice Institute.

Camp, D. D. 1993. "Out of the Quagmire: After *Jacobson v. United States:* Toward a More Balanced Entrapment Standard." *Journal of Criminal Law and Criminology* 83:1055–97.

Camp, S. D., and G. G. Gales. 2002. "Growth and Quality of U.S. Private Prisons: Evidence from a National Survey." *Criminology and Public Policy* 1:427–50.

Cancino, J. M., and R. Enriquez. 2004. "A Qualitative Analysis of Officer Peer Retaliation: Preserving the Police Culture." *Policing: International Journal of Police Strategies and Management* 27:320–40.

Caputo, M., and C. M. Miller. 2006. "In Wake of Death, Juvenile Boot Camp System is Scrapped." *Miami Herald,* April 27. http://www.miami.com/miamiherald/14438114.htm.

Carlson, T. 1995. "Safety, Inc." *Policy Review,* Summer, pp. 67–73.

Carr, J. G. 1993. "Bail Bondsmen and the Federal Courts." *Federal Probation* 57 (March): 9–14.

Carroll, L. 1974. *Hacks, Blacks, and Cons: Race Relations in a Maximum Security Prison.* Lexington, MA: Lexington Books.

Casey, M. 1999. "Defense Lawyers for Poor Clients May Get Pay Raise." *New York Times,* April 11, p. 5.

Catalano, S. M. 2005. "Criminal Victimization, 2004." Bureau of Justice Statistics

National Crime Victimization Survey. September. NCJ 210674.

Cauffman, E. L., L. Steinberg, and A. R. Piquero. 2005. "Psychological, Neuropsychological, and Physiological Correlates of Serious Antisocial Behavior in Adolescence: The Role of Self-Control." *Criminology* 43:133–76.

Chaddock, G. R. 2002. "Sniper Revives Prospects for Gun-Tracking Moves." *Christian Science Monitor,* October 17, p. 1.

Champagne, A., and K. Cheek. 1996. "PACs and Judicial Politics in Texas." *Judicature* 80:26–29.

Champion, D. J. 1989. "Private Counsels and Public Defenders: A Look at Weak Cases, Prior Records, and Leniency in Plea Bargaining." *Journal of Criminal Justice* 17:253–63.

Chapman, S. G. 1970. *Police Patrol Readings.* 2nd ed. Springfield, IL: Thomas.

Chapper, J. A., and R. A. Hanson. 1989. *Understanding Reversible Error in Criminal Appeals.* Williamsburg, VA: National Center for State Courts.

"Charging Common Criminals under Terrorism Laws Doesn't Fit in America's Justice Values." 2003. *Asheville Citizen-Times,* July 23. http://www.citizentimes.com.

Chavez, P. 2005. "Shooting Raises Racial Tension in L.A." *Sacramento Union,* February 21. http://www.sacunion.com.

Chermak, S., and E. McGarrell. 2004. "Problem-Solving Approaches to Homicide: An Evaluation of Indianapolis Violence Reduction Partnership." *Criminal Justice Policy Review* 15:161–92.

Chiricos, T., K. Padgett, and M. Gertz. 2000. "Fear, TV News, and the Reality of Crime." *Criminology* 38:755–85.

Christopher, R. L. 1994. "Mistake of Fact in the Objective Theory of Justification." *Journal of Criminal Law and Criminology* 85:295–332.

Church, T. W. 1985. "Examining Local Legal Culture." *American Bar Foundation Research Journal* 1985 (Summer): 449.

Clear, T. R. 1994. *Harm in American Penology.* Albany: State University of New York Press.

Clear, T. R., G. F. Cole, and M. D. Reisig. 2006. *American Corrections.* 7th ed. Belmont, CA: Thomson Wadsworth.

Clear, T. R., and D. R. Karp. 1999. *Community Justice: Preventing Crime and Achieving Justice.* New York: Westview Press.

Clear, T. R., D. R. Rose, E. Waring, and K. Scully. 2003. "Coercive Mobility and Crime: A Preliminary Examination of Concentrated Incarceration and Social Disorganization." *Justice Quarterly* 20 (March): 33–63.

CNN. 2004. "Boston Police Accept 'Full Responsibility' in Death of Red Sox Fan." October 22. http://www.cnn.com.

———. 2005a. "Autopsy: Toddler Hit Twice by LAPD." August 3. http://www.cnn.com.

———. 2005b. "BTK Sentenced to 10 Life Terms." August 18. http://www.cnn.com.

———. 2005c. "Radar Details How He Killed 10 People." June 28. http://www.cnn.com.

———. 2005d. "Rapper Lil' Kim Gets 366 Days in Prison." July 6. http://www.cnn.com.

Cohen, L. E., and M. Felson. 1979. "Social Change and Crime Rates: A Routine Activity Approach." *American Sociological Review* 44:588–608.

Cohen, M., T. R. Miller, and S. B. Rossman. 1990. "The Costs and Consequences of Violent Behavior in the United States." Paper prepared for the Panel on the Understanding and Control of Violent Behavior, National Research Council, National Academy of Sciences, Washington, DC.

Cohen, T. H., and B. A. Reaves. 2006. *Felony Defendants in Large Urban Counties, 2002.* Washington, DC: U.S. Government Printing Office.

Cole, D. 1999. *No Equal Justice: Race and Class in the American Criminal Justice System.* New York: The New Press.

Collins, J. 2005. *Preventing Identity Theft in Your Business: How to Protect Your Business, Customers, and Employees.* New York: Wiley.

Commission on Accreditation for Law Enforcement Agencies. 1989. *Standards for Law Enforcement Accreditation.* Fairfax, VA: Author.

"Concern Mounts over Anti-Terrorism Law." 2005. *Michigan Daily.* April 7. http://www.michigandaily.com.

Connors, E., T. Lundregan, N. Miller, and T. McEwen. 1996. *Convicted by Juries, Exonerated by Science: Case Studies in the Use of DNA Evidence to Establish Innocence after Trial.* Washington, DC: National Institute of Justice, U.S. Government Printing Office.

Conway, P. 2001. "The 2001 Electronic Monitoring Survey." *Journal of Electronic Monitoring* 14 (Winter–Spring): 7–9.

Cooney, M. 1994. "Evidence as Partisanship." *Law and Society Review* 28:833–58.

Costanzo, M. 1997. *Just Revenge.* New York: St. Martin's Press.

Crawford, C., T. Chiricos, and G. Kleck. 1998. "Race, Racial Threat, and Sentencing of Habitual Offenders." *Criminology* 36 (August): 481–512.

Criminal Justice Research Reports. 2001. July–August, p. 87.

Cullen, F. T., L. Cao, J. Frank, R. H. Langworthy, S. L. Browning, R. Kopache, and T. J. Stevenson. 1996. "'Stop or I'll Shoot': Racial Differences in Support for Police Use of Deadly Force on Fleeing Felons." *American Behavioral Scientist* 39 (February): 449–60.

Cullen, F. T., T. Leming, B. Link, and J. Wozniak. 1985. "The Impact of Social Supports in Police Stress." *Criminology* 23:503–22.

Cunningham, W. C., J. J. Strauchs, and C. W. Van Meter. 1990. *Private Security Trends, 1970 to the Year 2000.* Boston: Butterworth-Heinemann.

Daly, K. 1998. "Gender, Crime, and Criminology." In *The Handbook of Crime and Punishment,* ed. M. Tonry. New York: Oxford University Press, 85–108.

Daly, K., and M. Chesney-Lind. 1988. "Feminism and Criminology." *Justice Quarterly* 5:497–538.

Davey, J. D. 1998. *The Politics of Prison Expansion: Winning Elections by Waging War on Crime.* Westport, CT: Praeger.

Davies, T. Y. 1983. "A Hard Look at What We Know (and Still Need to Learn) about the 'Costs' of the Exclusionary Rule: The NIJ Study and Other Studies of 'Lost' Arrests." *American Bar Foundation Research Journal* 1983:611–90.

Davis, M., R. Lundman, and R. Martinez, Jr. 1991. "Private Corporate Justice: Store Police, Shoplifters, and Civil Recovery." *Social Problems* 38:395–408.

Davitz, T. 1998. "The Gangs Behind Bars." *Insight on the News,* September 28.

Dawson, M., and R. Dinovitzer. 2001. "Victim Cooperation and the Prosecution of Domestic Violence in a Specialized Court." *Justice Quarterly* 18:593–622.

DeFrances, C. J. 2002. "Prosecutors in State Courts, 2001." Bureau of Justice Statistics *Bulletin,* May.

DeFrances, C. J., and J. Litras. 2000. "Indigent Defense Services in Large Counties, 1999." Bureau of Justice Statistics *Bulletin,* November.

DeJong, C., S. Mastrofski, and R. Parks. 2001. "Patrol Officers and Problem Solving: An Application of Expectancy Theory." *Justice Quarterly* 18:31–61.

Dewan, S., and B. Meier. 2005. "Boy Who Took Antidepressants Is Convicted in Killings." *New York Times,* February 15. http://www.nytimes.com.

DiIulio, J. J., Jr. 1987. *Governing Prisons.* New York: Free Press.

———. 1991. *No Escape: The Future of American Corrections.* New York: Basic Books.

———. 1993. "Rethinking the Criminal Justice System: Toward a New Paradigm." In *Performance Measures for the Criminal Justice System.* Washington, DC: Bureau of Justice Statistics, U.S. Government Printing Office.

Dill, F. 1975. "Discretion, Exchange, and Social Control: Bail Bondsmen in Criminal Courts." *Law and Society Review* 9:644–74.

Dillehay, R. C., and M. R. Sandys. 1996. "Life under *Wainwright v. Witt:* Juror Dispositions and Death Qualification." *Law and Human Behavior* 20:147–65.

Dodge, J., and M. Pogrebin. 2001. "African-American Policewomen: An Exploration of Professional Relationships." *Policing* 24: 550–52.

Donziger, S. R., ed. 1996. *The Real War on Crime: The Report of the National Criminal Justice Commission.* New York: HarperCollins.

Dority, B. 2005. "The USA Patriot Act Has Decimated Many Civil Liberties." In *Homeland Security: Current Controversies,* ed. A. Nakaya. Detroit: Thomson/Gale, 130–36.

Durose, M. R., E. L. Schmitt, and P. Langan. 2005. *Contacts between Police and Public: Findings from the 2002 National Survey.* Washington, DC: Bureau of Justice Statistics, U.S. Government Printing Office, April.

Earley, P. 1992. *The Hot House: Life inside Leavenworth Prison.* New York: Bantam Books.

Editor, 2003. "Wages and Benefits Paid to Correctional Employees." *Correctional Compendium,* January 28, pp. 8–26.

Egan, T. 1999. "A Drug Ran Its Course, Then Hid with Its Users." *New York Times,* September 19, p. A1.

Eisenberg, T., P. Hannaford-Agor, V. P. Hans, N. L. Mott, G. T. Munsterman, S. J. Schwab, and M. T. Wells. 2005. "Judge-Jury Agreement in Criminal Cases: A Partial Replication of Kalven and Zeisel's The American Jury." *Journal of Empirical Legal Studies* 2:171–206.

Eisenstein, J., R. B. Flemming, and P. F. Nardulli. 1988. *The Contours of Justice: Communities and Their Courts.* Boston: Little, Brown.

Elliott, J., and B. Murphy. 2005. "Parole, Probation Violators Add to Crowding." *Houston Chronicle,* January 20. http://www.chron.com/ca/CDA/printstory.mpl/metropolitan/3000503.

Emmelman, D. S. 1996. "Trial by Plea Bargain: Case Settlement as a Product of Recursive Decisionmaking." *Law and Society Review* 30:335–60.

Engber, D. 2005. "Does the FBI Have Your Fingerprints?" *Slate,* April 22. http://www.slate.msn.com/id/2117226.

Engel, R. S., and J. M. Calnon. 2004. "Examining the Influence of Drivers' Characteristics during Traffic Stops with Police: Results from a National Survey." *Justice Quarterly* 21:49–90.

Engel, R. S., J. M. Calnon, and T. J. Bernard. 2002. "Theory and Racial Profiling: Shortcomings and Future Directions in Research." *Justice Quarterly* 19:249–73.

FBI (Federal Bureau of Investigation). 2005a. *Crime in the United States, 2004.* Washington, DC: U.S. Government Printing Office. http://www.fbi.gov.

———. 2005b. *Uniform Crime Reports.* Washington, DC: U.S. Government Printing Office.

———. 2006a. *Preliminary Annual Uniform Crime Report, 2005.* June. http://www.fbi.gov.

———. 2006b. *2005 FBI Computer Crime Survey.* Washington, DC: U.S. Government Printing Office.

Felch, J. 2003. "How a 'Calm but Aggravated' Teenager Died on East Thrill Place." *Denver Post,* July 11. http://www.denverpost.com.

Feld, B. C. 1993. "Criminalizing the American Juvenile Court." In *Crime and Justice: A Review of Research,* vol. 17, ed. M. Tonry. Chicago: University of Chicago Press, 197–280.

———. 2004. "Editorial Introduction: Juvenile Transfers." *Criminology and Public Policy* 3 (November): 599–603.

Felice, J. D., and J. C. Kilwein. 1992. "Strike One, Strike Two . . .: The History and Prospect for Judicial Reform in Ohio." *Judicature* 75:193–200.

Feuer, A. 2006. "For Ex-F.B.I. Agent Accused in Murders, a Case of What Might Have Been." *New York Times,* April 15. http://www.nytimes.com.

Fishbein, D. H. 1990. "Biological Perspectives in Criminology." *Criminology* 28:27–72.

Fitzgerald, J. 2005. "Martha Stewart Arrives Home, with Media Horde." *USA Today,* March 4. http://www.usatoday.com.

Flanagan, T. J., ed. 1995. *Long-Term Imprisonment.* Thousand Oaks, CA: Sage.

Flango, V. E. 1994. *Habeas Corpus in State and Federal Courts.* Williamsburg, VA: National Center for State Courts.

Flynn, K. 1999. "Record Payout in Settlements against Police." *New York Times,* October 1. http://www.nytimes.com.

Fox, J. G. 1982. *Organizational and Racial Conflict in Maximum Security Prisons.* Lexington, MA: Lexington Books.

Frank, J., S. G. Brandl, F. T. Cullen, and A. Stichman. 1996. "Reassessing the Impact of Race on Citizens' Attitudes toward the Police: A Research Note." *Justice Quarterly* 13 (June): 320–34.

Fridell, L. 1990. "Decision Making of the District Attorney: Diverting or Prosecuting Intrafamilial Child Sexual Abuse Offenders." *Criminal Justice Policy Review* 4:249–67.

Friedman, L. M. 1993. *Crime and Punishment in American History.* New York: Basic Books.

Frohmann, L. 1997. "Convictability and Discordant Locales: Reproducing Race, Class, and Gender Ideologies in Prosecutorial Decisionmaking." *Law and Society Review* 31:531–56.

Fukurai, H. 1996. "Race, Social Class, and Jury Participation: New Dimensions for Evaluating Discrimination in Jury Service and Jury Selection." *Journal of Criminal Justice* 24:71–88.

Fyfe, J. 1993. "Police Use of Deadly Force: Research and Reform." In *Criminal Justice: Law and Politics,* 6th ed., ed. G. F. Cole. Belmont, CA: Wadsworth.

Garcia, M. 2005. "N.Y. Using Terrorism Law to Prosecute Street Gang." *Washington Post,* February 1, p. A3.

Garner, J., and E. Clemmer. 1986. *Danger to Police in Domestic Disturbances—A New Look.* Washington, DC: Bureau of Justice Statistics, U.S. Government Printing Office.

Garner, J. H., and C. D. Maxwell. 1999. "Measuring the Amount of Force by and against the Police in Six Jurisdictions." In *Use of Force by the Police.* Washington, DC: National Institute of Justice, U.S. Government Printing Office.

Garner, J. H., C. D. Maxwell, and C. G. Heraux. 2002. "Characteristics Associated with the Prevalence and Severity of Force Used by the Police." *Justice Quarterly* 19:705–46.

Garner J., T. Schade, J. Hepburn, and J. Buchanan. 1995. "Measuring the Continuum of Forced Used by and against the Police." *Criminal Justice Review* 20 (Autumn): 146–68.

Garvey, C. 2002. "Risk Assessment: Looking for Chinks in the Armor." In *Readings in Security Management,* ed. R. McCrie. New York: ASIS International, 99–104.

Gest, T. 2001. *Crime and Politics: Big Government's Erratic Campaign for Law and Order.* New York: Oxford University Press.

Girshick, L. B. 1999. *No Safe Haven: Stories of Women in Prison.* Boston: Northeastern University Press.

Glueck, S., and E. Glueck. 1950. *Unraveling Juvenile Delinquency.* New York: Commonwealth Fund.

Gold, J. 2006. "Appeals Court OKs Jayson Williams Retrial." *Houston Chronicle,* April 21. http://www.chron.com.

Goldfarb, R. L. 1965. *Ransom: A Critique of the American Bail System.* New York: Harper & Row.

Goldman, J. 2002. "Skakel Is Found Guilty of 1975 Moxley Murder." *Los Angeles Times,* June 8. http://www.latimes.com.

Goldschmidt, J., and J. M. Shaman. 1996. "Judicial Disqualifications: What Do Judges Think?" *Judicature* 80:68–72.

Goldstein, H. 1979. "Improving Policing: A Problem-oriented Approach." *Crime and Delinquency* 25:236–57.

———. 1990. *Problem-oriented Policing.* New York: McGraw-Hill.

Goodman, J. 1994. *Stories of Scottsboro.* New York: Random House.

Goolkasian, G. A., R. W. Geddes, and W. DeJong. 1989. "Coping with Police Stress." In *Critical Issues in Policing,* ed. R. G. Dunham and G. P. Alpert. Prospect Heights, IL: Waveland Press, 489–507.

Gordon, J. 2005. "In Patriots' Cradle, the Patriot Act Faces Scrutiny." *New York Times,* April 24. http://www.nytimes.com.

Gorman, S. 2003. "Analysts Worry Budget Short on Homeland Security Funds." *Government Executive Magazine,* February 11. http://www.Govexec.com.

Gottfredson, M., and T. Hirschi. 1990. *A General Theory of Crime.* Stanford, CA: Stanford University Press.

Governor's Office on Drug Control Policy. 2006. *Iowa's Drug Control Strategy, 2006.* http://www.state.ia.us/odcp/docs/Strategy_06.pdf.

Graham, B. L. 1995. "Judicial Recruitment and Racial Diversity on State Courts." In *Courts and Justice,* ed. G. L. Mays and P. R. Gregware. Prospect Heights, IL: Waveland Press.

Greene, J. A. 1999. "Zero Tolerance: A Case Study of Police Policies and Practices in New York City." *Crime and Delinquency* 45 (April): 171–87.

Greenwood, P., J. M. Chaiken, and J. Petersilia. 1977. *Criminal Investigation Process.* Lexington, MA: Lexington Books.

Greer, K. R. 2000. "The Changing Nature of Interpersonal Relationships in a Women's Prison." *Prison Journal* 80 (December): 442–68.

Grennan, S. A. 1987. "Findings on the Role of Officer Gender in Violent Encounters with Citizens." *Journal of Police Science and Administration* 15:78–85.

Griset, P. L. 1993. "Determinate Sentencing and the High Cost of Overblown Rhetoric: The New York Experience." *Crime and Delinquency* 39 (April): 552.

———. 1995. "The Politics and Economics of Increased Correctional Discretion over Time Served: A New York Case Study." *Justice Quarterly* 12 (June): 307–23.

Haarr, R. N., and M. Morash. 1999. "Gender, Race and Strategies of Coping with Occupational Stress in Policing." *Justice Quarterly* 16:303–36.

Hackett, D. P., and J. M. Violanti, eds. 2003. *Police Suicide: Tactics for Prevention.* Springfield, IL: Thomas.

Hagan, F. E. 1997. *Political Crime: Ideology and Criminality.* Needham Heights, MA: Allyn and Bacon.

Hagan, J., and R. D. Peterson. 1995. "Criminal Inequality in America: Patterns and Consequences." In *Crime and Inequality,* ed. J. Hagan and R. D. Peterson. Stanford, CA: Stanford University Press, 14–36.

Hails, J., and R. Borum. 2003. "Police Training and Specialized Approaches to Respond to People with Mental Illness." *Crime and Delinquency* 49:52–61.

Hall, J. 1947. *General Principles of Criminal Law.* 2nd ed. Indianapolis: Bobbs-Merrill.

Hall, M. G. 1995. "Justices as Representatives: Elections and Judicial Politics in the United States." *American Politics Quarterly* 23: 485–503.

Hallinan, J. T. 2001. *Going Up the River: Travels in a Prison Nation.* New York: Random House.

Hambling, D. 2005. "Police Toy with 'Less Lethal' Weapons." April 30. http://www.newscientist.com.

Hans, V., and N. Vidmar. 1986. *Judging the Jury.* New York: Plenum Press.

Hanson, R. A., and J. Chapper. 1991. *Indigent Defense Systems.* Williamsburg, VA: National Center for State Courts.

Hanson, R. A., and H. W. K. Daley. 1995. *Challenging the Conditions of Prisons and Jails: A Report on Section 1983 Litigation.* Washington, DC: Bureau of Justice Statistics, U.S. Government Printing Office.

Harcourt, B. E., and J. Ludwig. 2006. "Broken Windows: New Evidence from New York City and a Five-City Social Experiment." *University of Chicago Law Review* 73:271–320.

Harkin, T. 2005. "Confronting the Meth Crisis." Press release, February 7. http://www.harkin.senate.gov.

Harlow, C. 2000. "Defense Counsel in Criminal Cases." Bureau of Justice Statistics *Bulletin,* November.

Hastie, R., S. Penrod, and N. Pennington. 1983. *Inside the Jury.* Cambridge, MA: Harvard University Press.

Hathaway, W. 2002. "A Clue to Antisocial Behavior: Study Finds Gene Marker for Which Abused Children May Become Troubled Adults." *Hartford Courant,* August 2, p. A17.

Hawdon, J., and J. Ryan. 2003. "Police-Resident Interactions and Satisfaction with Police: An Empirical Test of Community Policing Assertions." *Criminal Justice Policy Review* 14:55–74.

Heffernan, E. 1972. *Making It in Prison.* New York: Wiley.

Hegsted, M. 2005. "Sniper's Conviction Upheld." *Potomac News,* April 23. http://www.potomacnews.com.

Henning, P. J. 1993. "Precedents in a Vacuum: The Supreme Court Continues to Tinker with Double Jeopardy." *American Criminal Law Review* 31:1–72.

Herbert, S. 1996. "Morality in Law Enforcement: Chasing 'Bad Guys' with the Los Angeles Police Department." *Law and Society Review* 30:799–818.

Hickey, T. J. 1995. "A Double Jeopardy Analysis of the Medgar Evers Murder Case." *Journal of Criminal Justice* 23:41–51.

Hickman, M. J., and B. A. Reaves. 2001. *Local Police Departments, 1999.* Washington, DC: Bureau of Justice Statistics, U.S. Government Printing Office.

———. 2003. *Local Police Departments, 2000.* Washington, DC: Bureau of Justice Statistics, U.S. Government Printing Office.

———. 2006a. *Local Police Departments, 2003.* Washington, DC: Bureau of Justice Statistics, U.S. Government Printing Office.

———. 2006b. *Sheriffs' Offices, 2003.* Washington, DC: Bureau of Justice Statistics, U.S. Government Printing Office.

Hicks, N. 2005. "Bill Aims to Gut Police Liability in High-Speed Chases." *Lincoln Journal Star,* February 6. http://www.journalstar.com.

Hicks, W. 2003. "Police Vehicular Pursuits: An Overview of Research and Legal Conceptualizations for Police Administrators." *Criminal Justice Policy Review* 14:75–95.

Hinduja, S. 2004. "Perceptions of Local and State Law Enforcement Concerning the Role of Computer Crime Investigative Teams." *Policing* 27:341–57.

Hinton, H. L., Jr. 2002. "Considerations for Investing Resources in Chemical and Biological Preparedness." In *Terrorism: Are We Ready?* ed. D. Miller. Huntington, NY: Nova Science, 21–31.

Hirsch, A. J. 1992. *The Rise of the Penitentiary.* New Haven, CT: Yale University Press.

Hirschel, D., and I. Hutchinson. 2003. "The Voices of Domestic Violence Victims: Predictors of Victim Preference for Arrest and the Relationship between Preference for Arrest and Revictimization." *Crime and Delinquency* 49:313–36.

Hirschi, T. 1969. *Causes of Delinquency.* Berkeley: University of California Press.

Ho, N. T. 2000. "Domestic Violence in a Southern City: The Effects of a Mandatory Arrest Policy on Male-Versus-Female Aggravated Assault Incidents." *American Journal of Criminal Justice* 25:107–18.

Hoctor, M. 1997. "Domestic Violence as a Crime against the State." *California Law Review* 85 (May): 643–700.

Hoffman, M. 1999. "Abolish Peremptory Challenges." *Judicature* 82:202–4.

Holmes, M. D. 2000. "Minority Threat and Police Brutality: Determinants of Civil Rights Criminal Complaints in U.S. Municipalities." *Criminology* 38:343–67.

Holmes, M. D., H. M. Hosch, H. C. Daudistel, D. A. Perez, and J. B. Graves. 1996. "Ethnicity, Legal Resources, and Felony Dispositions in Two Southwestern Jurisdictions." *Justice Quarterly* 13:11–29.

Houston, B., and J. Ewing. 1991. "Justice Jailed." *Hartford Courant,* June 16, p. A1.

Howard, J. 1929. *The State of Prisons in England and Wales.* London: J. M. Dent. (Original work published in 1777)

Howlett, D. 2004. "Chicago Plans Advanced Surveillance." *USA Today,* September 9. http://www.usatoday.com.

Huff, C. R. 2002. "Wrongful Conviction and Public Policy: The American Society of Criminology 2001 Presidential Address." *Criminology* 40:1–18.

Hunt, G., S. Riegel, T. Morales, and D. Waldorf. 1993. "Changes in Prison Culture: Prison Gangs and the Case of the Pepsi Generation." *Social Problems* 40:398–409.

Hurtado, P. 2005. "Lil' Kim Takes the Stand, Denies Perjury Charges." *Newsday,* March 11, p. A18.

Ill-Equipped: U.S. Prisons and Offenders with Mental Illness. 2003. New York: Human Rights Watch.

Innes, C. A., and V. D. Verdeyen. 1997. "Conceptualizing the Management of Violent Inmates." *Corrections Management Quarterly* 1 (Fall): 1–9.

International Association of Chiefs of Police. 1998. *The Future of Women in Policing: Mandates for Action.* Alexandria, VA: Author.

Iribarren, C. J., J. H. Markovitz, D. R. Jacobs, P. J. Schreiner, M. Daviglus, and J. R. Hibbeln. 2004. "Dietary Intake of n-3, n-6 Fatty Acids and Fish: Relationship with Hostility in Young Adults—the CARDIA Study." *European Journal of Clinical Nutrition* 58:24–31.

Irwin, J. 1970. *The Felon.* Englewood Cliffs, NJ: Prentice-Hall.

———. 1980. *Prisons in Turmoil.* Boston: Little, Brown.

Irwin, J., and D. Cressey. 1962. "Thieves, Convicts, and the Inmate Culture." *Social Problems* 10:142–55.

Ith, I. 2001. "Taser Fails to Halt Man with Knife; Seattle Officer Kills 23-Year-Old." *Seattle Times,* November 28, p. A1.

Jackman, T. 2006. "Fairfax Gunman's Home Yields More Weapons." *Washington Post,* May 11, p. B1.

Jackman, T., and C. W. Barr. 2006. "Fairfax Killer Had Fled Psychiatric Center." *Washington Post,* May 10, p. A1.

Jacob, H. 1973. *Urban Justice.* Boston: Little, Brown.

Jacobs, J. B., and C. Panarella. 1998. "Organized Crime." In *The Handbook of Crime and Punishment,* ed. M. Tonry. New York: Oxford University Press, 159–77.

Jenkins, S. 2005. "By Hook or Crook, Surviving Storm." *Washington Post,* September 19. http://www.washingtonpost.com.

Johnson, K. 2002. "From Extreme Isolation, Waves of Felons are Freed." *USA Today,* December 12, p. 1A.

———. 2005. "After Years of Solitary, Freedom Hard to Grasp." *USA Today,* June 9. http://www.usatoday.com.

Johnson, R. 2002. *Hard Time: Understanding and Reforming the Prison.* 3rd ed. Belmont, CA: Wadsworth.

Jordan, J. 2002. "Will Any Woman Do? Police, Gender and Rape Victims." *Policing* 25:319–44.

Kaczor, B. 2002. "King Brothers Will Return to Courtroom in 2003." *Naples* (FL) *Daily News,* December 27. http://www.naplesnews.com.

Kampeas, R. 2001. "Terror Attacks Bring Profound Changes in FBI Focus, Challenges for New Director." Associated Press News Service, October 27.

Kane, R. J. 2002. "The Social Ecology of Police Misconduct." *Criminology* 40:867–96.

Karmen, A. 2001. *Crime Victims.* 4th ed. Belmont, CA: Wadsworth.

Kassebaum, G., and D. Okamoto. 2001. "The Drug Court as a Sentencing Model." *Journal of Contemporary Criminal Justice* 17:89–104.

Kates, B. 2003. "We Get $5-a-Head for Security." *New York Daily News,* November 24. http://www.nydailynews.com.

Kelling, G. L. 1985. "Order Maintenance, the Quality of Urban Life, and Police: A Line of Argument." In *Police Leadership in America,* ed. W. A. Geller. New York: Praeger.

———. 1991. *Foot Patrol.* Washington, DC: National Institute of Justice, U.S. Government Printing Office.

Kelling, G. L., and C. M. Coles. 1996. *Fixing Broken Windows: Restoring and Reducing Crime in Our Communities.* New York: Free Press.

Kelling, G. L., and M. Moore. 1988. "The Evolving Strategy of Policing." In *Perspectives on Policing,* no. 13. Washington, DC: National Institute of Justice, U.S. Government Printing Office.

Kelling, G. L., T. Pate, D. Dieckman, and C. E. Brown. 1974. *The Kansas City Preventive Patrol Experiments: A Summary Report.* Washington, DC: Police Foundation.

Kennedy, R. 1997. *Race, Crime, and the Law.* New York: Pantheon.

Kenney, D. J., and J. O. Finckenauer. 1995. *Organized Crime in America.* Belmont, CA: Wadsworth.

Kerlikowske, R. G. 2004. "The End of Community Policing: Remembering the Lessons Learned," *FBI Law Enforcement Bulletin* 73:6–11.

Kettler, S. 2005. "Young Killer David Harris Sentenced." WCPO.COM, February 22. http//www.wcpo.com/news/2005/local/02/22/harrissentenced.html.

Kingsnorth, R., R. MacIntosh, and S. Sutherland. 2002. "Criminal Charge or Probation Violation? Prosecutorial Discretion and Implications for Research in Criminal Court Processing." *Criminology* 40:553–77.

Kirkpatrick, D. D. 2005. "In Secretly Taped Conversations, Glimpses of the Future President." *New York Times,* February 20. http://www.nytimes.com.

Kleinknecht, W. 1996. *The New Ethnic Mobs: The Changing Face of Organized Crime in America.* New York: Free Press.

Klockars, C. B. 1985. "Order Maintenance, the Quality of Urban Life, and Police: A Different Line of Argument." *Police Leadership in America,* ed. W. A. Geller. New York: Praeger.

Klofas, J., and J. Yandrasits. 1989. "'Guilty but Mentally Ill' and the Jury Trial: A Case Study." *Criminal Law Bulletin* 24:423–43.

Knox, G. W. 2000. "A National Assessment of Gangs and Security Threat Groups (STGs) in Adult Correctional Institutions: Results of the 1999 Adult Corrections Survey." *Journal of Gang Research* 7:1–45.

Kolbert, E. 1999. "The Perils of Safety." *New Yorker,* March 22, p. 50.

Kotlowitz, A. 1994. "Their Crimes Don't Make Them Adults." *The New York Times Magazine,* February 13, p. 40.

Kramer, G. P., and D. M. Koenig. 1990. "Do Jurors Understand Criminal Justice Instructions? Analyzing the Results of the Michigan Juror Comprehension Project." *University of Michigan Journal of Law Reform* 23:401–37.

Kramer, J. H., and J. T. Ulmer. 1996. "Sentencing Disparity and Departures from Guidelines." *Justice Quarterly* 13 (March): 81.

Krane, J. 2003. "Concerns about Citizen Privacy Grow as States Create MATRIX Database." *Boston Globe,* September 24. http://www.boston.com.

Krautt, P. 2002. "Location, Location, Location: Interdistrict and Intercircuit Variation in Sentencing Outputs for Federal Drug-Trafficking Offenses." *Justice Quarterly* 19 (December): 633–71.

Kridler, C. 1999. "Sergeant Friday, Where Are You?" *Newsweek,* May 17, p. 14.

Krimmel, J. T. 1996. "The Performance of College-Educated Police: A Study of Self-Rated Performance Measures." *American Journal of Policing* 15:85–96.

Kristof, N. D. 2005. "When Rapists Walk Free." *New York Times,* March 5. http://www.nytimes.com.

Kruttschnitt, C., and S. Krmopotich. 1990. "Aggressive Behavior among Female Inmates: An Exploratory Study." *Justice Quarterly* 7 (June): 371–89.

Kurbrin, C. E., and E. A. Stewart. 2006. "Predicting Who Reoffends: The Neglected Role of Neighborhood Context in Recidivism Studies." *Criminology* 44:165–97.

Laffey, M. 1998. "Cop Diary." *New Yorker,* August 10, pp. 36–39.

Langworthy, R. H., T. Hughes, and B. Sanders. 1995. *Law Enforcement Recruitment Selection and Training: A Survey of Major Police Departments.* Highland Heights, IL: Academy of Criminal Justice Sciences.

Laub, J. H., and R. J. Sampson. 2003. *Shared Beginnings, Divergent Lives: Delinquent Boys to Age 70.* Cambridge, MA: Harvard University Press.

Lauritsen, J., J. Laub, and R. Sampson. 1992. "Conventional and Delinquent Activities: Implications for the Prevention of Violent Victimization among Adolescents." *Violence and Victims* 7:91–102.

Lauritsen, J., and N. White. 2001. "Putting Violence in Its Place: The Influence of Race, Ethnicity, Gender, and Place on the Risk for Violence." *Criminology and Public Policy* 1:37–59.

Lave, T. R. 1998. "Equal before the Law." *Newsweek,* July 13, p. 14.

Lawal, L. 2006. "Online Scams Create 'Yahoo! Millionaires.'" June 1. http://www.cnn money.com.

Lear, E. T. 1995. "Contemplating the Successive Prosecution Phenomenon in the Federal System." *Journal of Criminal Law and Criminology* 85:625–75.

Lee, M. S., and J. T. Ulmer. 2000. "Fear of Crime among Korean Americans in Chicago Communities." *Criminology* 38:1173–206.

Leo, R. A. 1996. "*Miranda's* Revenge: Police Interrogation as a Confidence Game." *Law and Society Review* 30:259–88.

Leonard, J. 2002. "Dropping 'Nonlethal' Beanbags as Too Dangerous." *Los Angeles Times,* June 3, p. 1.

Leovy, J., and N. Lee. 2005. "Grieving Police Provide Account of Fatal Standoff." *Los Angeles Times,* July 12. http://www.latimes.com.

Lersch, K. M. 2002. "Are Citizen Complaints Just Another Measure of Officer Productivity? An Analysis of Citizen Complaints and Officer Activity Measures." *Police Practices and Research* 3:135–47.

Lersch, K. M., and L. Kunzman. 2001. "Misconduct Allegations and Higher Education in a Southern Sheriff's Department." *American Journal of Criminal Justice* 25:161–72.

Levine, J. P. 1992. *Juries and Politics.* Belmont, CA: Wadsworth.

Lichtblau, E., and J. Risen. 2006. "Top Aide Defends Domestic Spying." *New York Times,* February 7. http://www.nytimes.com.

Liptak, A. 2003. "County Says It's Too Poor to Defend the Poor." *New York Times,* April 15. http://www.nytimes.com.

Lipton, E. 2006. "Security Cuts for New York and Washington." *New York Times,* June 1. http://www.nytimes.com.

Liska, A. E., and S. F. Messner. 1999. *Perspectives on Crime and Deviance.* 3rd ed. Upper Saddle River, NJ: Prentice-Hall.

Lithwick, D., and J. Turner. 2003. "A Guide to the Patriot Act, Part 4." *Slate,* September 11. http://www.slate.msn.com.

Llana, S. M. 2006. "What's at Root of Boston's Rise in Murders?" *Christian Science Monitor,* May 10. http://www.csmonitor.com.

Lochner, T. 2002. "Strategic Behavior and Prosecutorial Agenda Setting in the United States Attorneys' Office." *Justice System Journal* 23:271–94.

Logan, C. 1993. "Criminal Justice Performance Measures in Prisons." In *Performance Measures for the Criminal Justice System.* Washington, DC: Bureau of Justice Statistics, U.S. Government Printing Office, 19–60.

Lombroso, C. 1968. *Crime: Its Causes and Remedies.* Montclair, NJ: Patterson Smith. (Original work published in 1912)

Lord, V. B., and P. Friday. 2003. "Choosing a Career in Police Work: A Comparative Study between Applications for Employment with a Large Police Department and Public High School Seniors." *Police Practices and Research* 4:63–78.

Lorentzen, A. 2002. "Trooper Who Had Stopped Bank Suspect Kills Self." *Seattle Times,* September 28. http://www.seattletimes.com.

Loviglio, J. 2002. "Judge Reverses Himself, Will Allow Fingerprint-Analysis Testimony."

Associated Press Wire Service, March 13 (available on Lexis-Nexis).

Luginbuhl, J., and M. Burkhead. 1994. "Sources of Bias and Arbitrariness in the Capital Trial." *Journal of Social Issues* 7:103–12.

Lumb, R. C., and R. Breazeale. 2003. "Police Officer Attitudes and Community Policing Implementation: Developing Strategies for Durable Organizational Change." *Policing and Society* 13:91–106.

Lundman, R., and R. Kaufman. 2003. "Driving While Black: Effects of Race, Ethnicity, and Gender on Citizen Self-Reports of Traffic Stops and Police Actions." *Criminology* 41:195–220.

Lynch, D. 1999. "Perceived Judicial Hostility to Criminal Trials: Effects on Public Defenders in General and on Their Relationships with Clients and Prosecutors in Particular." *Criminal Justice and Behavior* 26:217–34.

Lynch, J., and W. J. Sabol. 2001. *Prisoner Reentry in Perspective.* Washington, DC: Urban Institute.

Lynem, J. N. 2002. "Guards Call for Higher Wages, More Training: Industry Faces Annual Staff Turnover Rate of up to 300%." *San Francisco Chronicle*, August 22, p. B3.

Maitland, A. S., and R. D. Sluder. 1998. "Victimization and Youthful Prison Inmates: An Empirical Analysis." *Prison Journal* 78:55–73.

Mann, C. R. 1993. *Unequal Justice: A Question of Color.* Bloomington: Indiana University Press.

Manning, P. K. 1977. *Police Work.* Cambridge, MA: MIT Press.

Marciniak, L. M. 2000. "The Addition of Day Reporting Centers to Intensive Probation Supervision: A Comparison of Recidivism Rates." *Federal Probation* 58 (December): 34–39.

Margasak, L. 2006. "Security Agency's Security Hit." *Boston Globe*, March 7. http://www.boston.com.

Marsh, J. R. 1994. "Performing Pretrial Services: A Challenge in the Federal Criminal Justice System." *Federal Probation* 58 (December): 3–10.

"Martha Stewart's House Arrest Is Extended." 2005. *New York Times*, August 4. http://www.nytimes.com.

"Martha's Prison Time Nearly Over." 2005. CBS News, March 2. http://www.cbsnews.com.

Martin, S. E. 1991. "The Effectiveness of Affirmative Action." *Justice Quarterly* 8:489–504.

———. 2005. "Women Officers on the Move." In *Critical Issues in Policing*, 5th ed., ed. R. G. Dunham and G. P. Alpert. Long Grove, IL: Waveland Press, 350–71.

Martinson, R. 1974. "What Works? Questions and Answers about Prison Reform." *The Public Interest*, Spring, p. 25.

Maruschak, L., and A. J. Beck. 2001. *Medical Problems of Inmates, 1997.* Washington, DC: Bureau of Justice Statistics, U.S. Government Printing Office.

Maschke, K. J. 1995. "Prosecutors as Crime Creators: The Case of Prenatal Drug Use." *Criminal Justice Review* 20:21–33.

Mastrofski, S. D., M. D. Reisig, and J. D. McCluskey. 2002. "Police Disrespect toward the Public: An Encounter-Based Analysis." *Criminology* 40:519–52.

Mastrofski, S. D., J. J. Willis, and J. B. Snipes. 2002. "Styles of Patrol in a Community Policing Context." In *The Move to Community Policing: Making Change Happen*, ed. M. Morash and J. Ford. Thousand Oaks, CA: Sage, 81–111.

Mauer, M., and M. Chesney-Lind, eds. 2002. *Invisible Punishment: The Collateral Consequences of Mass Imprisonment.* New York: The New Press.

Maxwell, S. R. 1999. "Examining the Congruence between Predictors of ROR and Failures to Appear." *Journal of Criminal Justice* 27:127–41.

Maxwell, S. R., and C. Maxwell. 2000. "Examining the 'Criminal Careers' of Prostitutes within the Nexus of Drug Use, Drug Selling, and Other Illicit Activities." *Criminology* 38:787–809.

Mazerolle, L. D., D. Rogan, J. Frank, C. Famega, and J. Eck. 2003. "Managing Citizen Calls to the Police: The Impact of Baltimore's 3-1-1 Call System." *Criminology and Public Policy* 2:97–124.

McCoy, C. 1986. "Policing the Homeless." *Criminal Law Bulletin* 22 (May–June): 263.

———. 1993. *Politics and Plea Bargaining: Victims' Rights in California.* Philadelphia: University of Pennsylvania Press.

———. 1995. "Is the Trial Penalty Inevitable?" Paper presented at the annual meeting of the Law and Society Association, Phoenix, AZ, June.

McDivitt, J., and R. Miliano. 1992. "Day Reporting Centers: An Innovative Concept in Intermediate Sanctions." In *Smart Sentencing: The Emergence of Intermediate Sanctions*, ed. J. M. Byrne, A. J. Lurigio, and J. Petersilia. Newbury Park, CA: Sage, 152–65.

McGarrell, E., S. Chermak, A. Weiss, and J. Wilson. 2001. "Reducing Firearms Violence through Directed Patrol." *Criminology and Public Policy* 1:119–48.

McGee, R. A., G. Warner, and N. Harlow. 1998. "The Special Management Inmate." In *Incarcerating Criminals*, ed. T. J. Flanagan, J. W. Marquart, and K. G. Adams. New York: Oxford University Press, 99–106.

McGuire, D. 2004. "Study: Online Crime Costs Rising." *Washington Post*, May 25. http://www.washingtonpost.com.

McKelvey, B. 1977. *American Prisons.* Montclair, NJ: Patterson Smith.

McNulty, T. L., and P. E. Bellair. 2003. "Explaining Racial and Ethnic Differences in Adolescent Violence: Structural Disadvantage, Family, Well-Being, and Social Capital." *Justice Quarterly* 20:1–31.

"Meet the Hackers." 2006. *Business Week Online*, May 29. http://www.businessweekcom.

Meier, B. 2004. "A Drug on Trial: Justice and Science; Boy's Murder Case Entangled in Fight over Antidepressants." *New York Times*, August 23. http://www.nytimes.com.

Meier, R. F., and T. D. Miethe. 1993. "Understanding Theories of Criminal Victimization." In *Crime and Justice: A Review of Research*, ed. M. Tonry. Chicago: University of Chicago Press.

Melekian, B. 1990. "Police and the Homeless." *FBI Law Enforcement Bulletin* 59:1–7.

Menard, S. 2000. "The 'Normality' of Repeat Victimization from Adolescence through Early Adulthood." *Criminology* 17:541–74.

Mentzer, A. 1996. "Policing in Indian Country: Understanding State Jurisdiction and Authority." *Law and Order* 44 (June): 24–29.

Messner, S. F., and R. Rosenfeld. 1994. *Crime and the American Dream.* Belmont, CA: Wadsworth.

Meyer, C., and T. Gorman. 2001. "Criminal Faces in the Crowd Still Elude Hidden ID Camera Security." *Los Angeles Times*, February 2, p. 1.

"Michigan State Police Drop Out of Anti-Terrorism Network." 2005. *Detroit Free Press*, March 7. http://www.freep.com.

Miethe, T. D. 1995. "Fear and Withdrawal from Urban Life." *Annals of the American Academy of Political and Social Science* 539 (May): 14–27.

Miller, L. 2006. "They Seek Kids for Sex: Pedophiles Take Advantage of Younger, Trusting Individuals." *Louisiana Weekly*, April 24. http://www.louisianaweekly.com.

Miller, M., and M. Guggenheim. 1990. "Pretrial Detention and Punishment." *Minnesota Law Review* 75:335–426.

Monkkonen, E. H. 1981. *Police in Urban America, 1869–1920.* Cambridge, England: Cambridge University Press.

———. 1992. "History of the Urban Police." In *Modern Policing*, ed. M. Tonry and N. Morris. Chicago: University of Chicago Press, 547–80.

Moore, M. 1992. "Problem-Solving and Community Policing." In *Modern Policing*, ed. M. Tonry and N. Morris. Chicago: University of Chicago Press, 99–158.

Moore, M., and G. L. Kelling. 1983. "To Serve and to Protect: Learning from Police History." *The Public Interest*, Winter, p. 55.

Moran, R. 2002. *Executioner's Current: Thomas Edison, George Westinghouse, and the Invention of the Electric Chair.* New York: Knopf.

Morash, M., and J. K. Ford, eds. 2002. *The Move to Community Policing: Making Change Happen.* Thousand Oaks, CA: Sage.

Morash, M., J. K. Ford, J. P. White, and J. G. Boles. 2002. "Directing the Future of Community-Policing Initiatives." In *The Move to Community Policing: Making Change Happen*, ed. M. Morash and J. Ford. Thousand Oaks, CA: Sage, 277–88.

Morash, M., R. N. Haarr, and L. Rucker. 1994. "A Comparison of Programming for Women and Men in the U.S. Prisons in the 1980s." *Crime and Delinquency* 40 (April): 197–221.

Morris, N., and M. Tonry. 1990. *Between Prison and Probation: Intermediate Punishments in a Rational Sentencing System.* New York: Oxford University Press.

Moses, P. 2005. "Corruption? It Figures: NY Police Department's Crime Stats and the Art of Manipulation." *Village Voice*, March 29. http://www.villagevoice.com.

Mosher, C., T. Miethe, and D. Phillips. 2002. *The Mismeasure of Crime*. Thousand Oaks, CA: Sage.

Munadi, S., and C. Hauser. 2006. "Afghan Convert to Christianity Is Released, Officials Say." *New York Times*, March 28. http://www.nytimes.com.

Murphy, P. V. 1992. "Organizing for Community Policing." In *Issues in Policing: New Perspectives*, ed. J. W. Bizzack. Lexington, KY: Autumn Press, 113–28.

Nadelmann, E. A. 1993. *Cops across Borders: The Internationalization of U.S. Criminal Law Enforcement*. University Park: Pennsylvania State University Press.

Nagin, D. S. 1998. "Criminal Deterrence Research at the Outset of the Twenty-first Century." In *Crime and Justice*, vol. 23, ed. M. Tonry. Chicago: University of Chicago Press, 1–42.

Nalla, M. 2002. "Common Practices and Functions of Corporate Security: A Comparison of Chemical, Financial, Manufacturing, Service, and Utility Industries." *Journal of Security Administration* 25:33–46.

National Legal Aid and Defender Association. 1999. "Full-Court Press on Federal CJA Rate Increase." Press release, April 21.

National White Collar Crime Center and the FBI. 2006. *IC3 2005 Internet Crime Report*. Washington, DC: U.S. Government Printing Office.

NBC4 News. 2005. "Mother of Girl Shot by Police Surprised at Cocaine Report." August 4. http://www.nbc4.tv.news.

New York Times. 2003. "Some Members of Congress Concerned over F.B.I. Shifts in Priorities." June 18. http://www.nytimes.com.

Newman, T. C. 1996. "Fair Cross-Section and Good Intention: Representation in Federal Juries." *Justice System Journal* 18:211–32.

Niesse, M. 2004. "Audit: Atlanta Hedged Crimes in '96 Bid." *Washington Post*, February 20. http://www.washingtonpost.com.

NIJ (National Institute of Justice). 1996. *Victim Costs and Consequences: A New Look*. Washington, DC: U.S. Government Printing Office.

———. 1997. *Research in Brief*, January.

———. 2003. *Correctional Boot Camps: Lessons from a Decade of Research*. Washington, DC: U.S. Government Printing Office.

Novak, V. 1999. "The Cost of Poor Advice." *Time*, July 5, p. 38.

Ogletree, C. J., Jr., M. Prosser, A. Smith, and W. Talley, Jr. 1995. *Beyond the Rodney King Story: An Investigation of Police Misconduct in Minority Communities*. Boston: Northeastern University Press.

OJJDP (Office of Juvenile Justice and Delinquency Prevention). 1999. *Juvenile Offenders and Victims: 1999 National Report*. Washington, DC: U.S. Government Printing Office.

———. 2001. *Delinquency Cases Waived to Criminal Court, 1989–1998*. Washington, DC: U.S. Government Printing Office.

———. 2002. http://www.ojjdp.ncjrs.org/ojstatbb/html.

———. 2004. *Fact Sheet*, April.

Oliver, W. M. 2002. "9–11, Federal Crime Control Policy, and Unintended Consequences." *ACJS Today* 22 (September–October): 1–6.

Otto M., J. Adang, and J. Mensink. 2004. "Pepper Spray: An Unreasonable Response to Suspect Verbal Resistance." *Policing* 27: 206–19.

Owen, B. 1998. *"In the Mix": Struggle and Survival in a Woman's Prison*. Albany: State University of New York Press.

Packer, H. L. 1968. *The Limits of the Criminal Sanction*. Stanford, CA: Stanford University Press.

Palmer, T. 1992. *The Re-Emergence of Correctional Intervention*. Newbury Park, CA: Sage.

Peoples, J. M. 1995. "Helping Pretrial Services Clients Find Jobs." *Federal Probation* 59 (March): 14–18.

Perkins, D. B., and J. D. Jamieson. 1995. "Judicial Probable Cause Determinations after *County of Riverside v. McLaughlin*." *Criminal Law Bulletin* 31:534–46.

Petersilia, J. 1990. "When Probation Becomes More Dreaded Than Prison." *Federal Probation*, March, p. 24.

———. 1996. "A Crime Control Rationale for Reinvesting in Community Corrections." *Perspectives* 20 (Spring): 21–29.

———. 1998. "Probation and Parole." In *The Handbook of Crime and Punishment*, ed. M. Tonry. New York: Oxford University Press, 563–88.

———. 1999. "Parole and Prisoner Reentry in the United States." In *Prisons*, ed. M. Tonry and J. Petersilia. Chicago: University of Chicago Press.

———. 2003. *When Prisoners Come Home: Parole and Prisoner Reentry*. New York: Oxford University Press.

Petersilia, J., and S. Turner. 1993. "Intensive Probation and Parole." In *Crime and Justice*, vol. 17, ed. M. Tonry. Chicago: University of Chicago Press.

Peterson, J. L., and M. J. Hickman. 2005. "Census of Publicly Funded Forensic Crime Laboratories, 2002." Bureau of Justice Statistics *Bulletin*, February, p. 1.

Phillips, S. 1977. *No Heroes, No Villains*. New York: Random House.

Pisciotta, A. W. 1994. *Benevolent Repression: Social Control and the American Reformatory-Prison Movement*. New York: New York University Press.

Platt, A. 1977. *The Child Savers*. 2nd ed. Chicago: University of Chicago Press.

Pollock, J. M. 1998. *Counseling Women in Prison*. Thousand Oaks, CA: Sage.

PR Newswire. 2001. "Ion Track Instruments Unveils New Technology to Aid in Fight against Terrorism and Drug Trafficking." March 22 (available on Lexis-Nexis).

———. 2002. "As Homeland Security Bill Approaches House Vote, It Still Neglects Problems with Massive Private Security Industry." July 24 (available on Lexis-Nexis).

Pratt, T., and J. Maahs. 1999. "Are Private Prisons More Cost Effective than Public Prisons? A Meta-Analysis of Evaluation Research

Studies." *Crime and Delinquency* 45 (July): 358–71.

Priehs, R. 1999. "Appointed Counsel for Indigent Criminal Appellants: Does Compensation Influence Effort?" *Justice System Journal* 21:57–79.

Propper, A. 1982. "Make Believe Families and Homosexuality among Imprisoned Girls." *Criminology* 20:127–39.

Provine, D. M. 1996. "Courts in the Political Process in France." In *Courts, Law, and Politics in Comparative Perspective*, ed. H. Jacob, E. Blankenburg, H. Kritzer, D. M. Provine, and J. Sanders. New Haven, CT: Yale University Press, 177–248.

Prussel, D., and K. Lonsway. 2001. "Recruiting Women Police Officers." *Law and Order* 49 (July): 91–96.

Purser, B. 2005. "Houston County, Georgia E-911 Able to Pinpoint Cell Phones." *Macon (GA) Telegraph*, February 10, p. 6.

Radelet, M. L. 2004. "Post-*Furman* Botched Executions." http://www.deathpenaltyinfor.org/article.php?scid=8&did=478.

Radelet, M. L., H. A. Bedau, and C. E. Putnam. 1992. *In Spite of Innocence*. Boston: Northeastern University Press.

Radelet, M. L., W. S. Lofquist, and H. A. Bedau. 1996. "Prisoners Released from Death Rows Since 1970 Because of Doubts about Their Guilt." *Thomas M. Cooley Law Review* 13: 907–66.

Rafter, N. H. 1983. "Prisons for Women, 1790–1980." In *Crime and Justice*, 5th ed., ed. M. Tonry and N. Morris. Chicago: University of Chicago Press.

Randolph, E. D. 2001. "Inland Police Like New Weaponry." *Riverside (CA) Press-Enterprise*, November 24, p. B4.

Reaves, B. A. 1992. *State and Local Police Departments, 1990*. Washington, DC: Bureau of Justice Statistics, U.S. Government Printing Office.

Reaves, B. A., and A. L. Goldberg. 2000. *Local Police Departments, 1997*. Washington, DC: Bureau of Justice Statistics, U.S. Government Printing Office.

Reaves, B. A., and T. C. Hart. 1999. *Felony Defendants in Large Urban Counties, 1996: State Court Case Processing Statistics*. Washington, DC: Bureau of Justice Statistics, U.S. Government Printing Office.

———. 2000. *Law Enforcement Management and Administrative Statistics, 1999*. Washington, DC: Bureau of Justice Statistics, U.S. Government Printing Office.

Reaves, B. A., and M. J. Hickman. 2002. "Police Departments in Large Cities, 1999–2000." Bureau of Justice Statistics *Special Report*, May.

Redfern, C. 2004. "Man Found Innocent of Attempted Murder." *Santa Cruz (CA) Sentinel*, April 24. http://www.baumhedlundlaw.com/SSRIs/Zoloft%20%20Santa%20Cruz%20man%20acquitted.htm.

Regoli, R. M., and J. D. Hewitt. 1994. *Criminal Justice*. Englewood Cliffs, NJ: Prentice-Hall.

Reibstein, L. 1997. "NYPD Black and Blue." *Newsweek*, June 2, p. 66.

Reichers, L. M., and R. R. Roberg. 1990. "Community Policing: A Critical Review of Underlying Assumptions." *Journal of Police Science and Administration* 17:105–14.

Reid, T. R. 2004. "Rape Case against Bryant Is Dropped." *Washington Post*, September 2. http://www.washingtonpost.com.

Reid, T. V. 1996. "PAC Participation in North Carolina Supreme Court Elections." *Judicature* 80:21–25.

———. 2000. "The Politicization of Judicial Retention Elections: The Defeat of Justices Lamphier and White." In *Research on Judicial Selection 1999*. Chicago: American Judicature Society, 45–72.

Reilly, M. 2004a. "Ex-Net Convicted of Cover-Up of Shooting." *Newark Star-Ledger*, May 1. http://www.nj.com.

———. 2004b. "Prosecutor: We'll Retry Williams on Key Charge." *Newark Star-Ledger*, May 22. http://www.nj.com.

Reisig, M. D. 2002. "Citizen Input and Police Service: Moving beyond the 'Feel Good' Community Survey." In *The Move to Community Policing: Making Change Happen*, ed. M. Morash and J. Ford. Thousand Oaks, CA: Sage, 43–60.

Reisig, M. D., J. D. McCluskey, S. D. Mastrofski, and W. Terrill. 2004. "Suspect Disrespect toward the Police." *Justice Quarterly* 21: 241–68.

Reiss, A. J., Jr. 1971. *The Police and the Public*. New Haven, CT: Yale University Press.

———. 1992. "Police Organization in the Twentieth Century." In *Crime and Justice: A Review of Research*, vol. 15, ed. M. Tonry and N. Morris. Chicago: University of Chicago Press, 51–97.

Richey, W. 2003. "Florida Fights over Death-Row Lawyers." *Christian Science Monitor*, February 20, p. 2.

Richtel, M. 2002. "Credit Card Theft Thrives Online as Global Market." *New York Times*, May 13. http://www.nytimes.com.

Ring, W. 2005. "Backlogs in Labs Undercut DNA's Crime-Solving Value." *Lansing (MI) State Journal*, April 28, p. A3.

Robinson, A. L. 2000. "The Effect of a Domestic Violence Policy Change on Police Officers' Schemata." *Criminal Justice and Behavior* 27:600–24.

Rosen, L. 1995. "The Creation of the Uniform Crime Report: The Role of Social Science." *Social Science History* 19 (Summer): 215–38.

Rossi, P. H., and R. A. Berk. 1997. *Just Punishments: Federal Guidelines and Public Views Compared*. New York: Aldine DeGruyter.

Rothman, D. J. 1971. *The Discovery of the Asylum: Social Order and Disorder in the New Republic*. Boston: Little, Brown.

———. 1980. *Conscience and Convenience*. Boston: Little, Brown.

Rotman, E. 1995. "The Failure of Reform." In *Oxford History of the Prison*, ed. N. Morris and D. J. Rothman. New York: Oxford University Press.

Rousey, D. C. 1984. "Cops and Guns: Police Use of Deadly Force in Nineteenth-Century New Orleans." *American Journal of Legal History* 28:41–66.

Ryan, H. 2004. "Williams Cleared of Aggravated Manslaughter in Driver's Shooting." COURT-TV, April 30. http://www.courttv.com.

Sabo, D., T. A. Kupers, and W. London. 2001. "Gender and the Politics of Punishment." In *Prison Masculinities*, ed. D. Sabo, T. A. Kupers, and W. London. Philadelphia: Temple University Press.

Sampson, R. J., and J. H. Laub. 1993. *Crime in the Making: Pathways and Turning Points through Life*. Cambridge, MA: Harvard University Press.

Sampson, R., and S. Raudenbush. 2001. "Disorder in Urban Neighborhoods: Does It Lead to Crime?" National Institute of Justice *Research in Brief*, February, pp. 1–6.

Sampson, R. J., and W. J. Wilson. 1995. "Toward a Theory of Race, Crime and Urban Inequality." In *Crime and Inequality*, ed. J. Hagan and R. Peterson. Palo Alto, CA: Stanford University Press.

Sandoval, G. 2006. "Teens Arrested in My-Space Extortion Scam." CNET News.com, May 26. http://www.news.com.

Santos, M. 2004. *About Prison*. Belmont, CA: Wadsworth.

Sarche, J. 2005. "Kobe Case Settled." *Pasadena Star-News*, March 2. http://www.pasadenastarnews.com.

Scalia, J. 2002. "Prisoners Petitions Filed in U.S. District Courts, 2000, with Trends 1980–2000." Bureau of Justice Statistics *Special Report*, January.

Schafer, J. A. 2002. "The Challenge of Effective Organizational Change: Lessons Learned in Community-Policing Implementation." In *The Move to Community Policing: Making Change Happen*, ed. M. Morash and J. Ford. Thousand Oaks, CA: Sage, 243–63.

Scheingold, S. A. 1995. *Politics, Public Policy, and Street Crime*. Philadelphia: Temple University Press.

Schultz, D. 2000. "No Joy in Mudville Tonight: The Impact of Three Strikes' Laws on State and Federal Corrections Policy, Resources, and Crime Control." *Cornell Journal of Law and Public Policy* 9:557–83.

Schwartz, J. 2003. "Acquitted Man Says Virus Put Pornography on Computer." *New York Times*, August 11. http://www.nytimes.com.

Security Industry Association. 2000. "Economic Crime Cost Reaches $200 Billion in 2000." *Research Update*, January, p. 1.

Shane, S., and E. Lichtblau. 2006. "Cheney Pushed U.S. to Widen Eavesdropping." *New York Times*, May 14. http://www.nytimes.com.

Shapiro, B. 1997. "Sleeping Lawyer Syndrome." *The Nation*, April 7, pp. 27–29.

Sherman, L. W. 1995. "The Police." In *Crime*, ed. J. Q. Wilson and J. Petersilia. San Francisco: ICS Press, 327–48.

———. 1998. "Police." In *Handbook of Crime and Punishment*, ed. M. Tonry. New York: Oxford University Press, 429–56.

Sherman, L. W., and R. A. Berk. 1984. "The Specific Effects of Arrest for Domestic Assault." *American Sociological Review* 49:261–72.

Sherman, L. W., and E. G. Cohn. 1986. "Citizens Killed by Big City Police: 1970–84." Unpublished manuscript, Crime Control Institute, Washington, DC, October.

Sherman, L. W., P. R. Gartin, and M. E. Buerger. 1989. "Hot Spots of Predatory Crime: Routine Activities and the Criminology of Place." *Criminology* 27:27–55.

Sherman, L. W., J. D. Schmidt, D. P. Rogan, P. R. Gartin, E. G. Cohn, D. J. Collins, and A. R. Bacich. 1991. "From Initial Deterrence to Long-Term Escalation: Short Custody Arrest for Poverty Ghetto Domestic Violence." *Criminology* 29: 821–50.

Sherman, L. W., and D. A. Weisburd. 1995. "General Deterrent Effects of Police Patrol in Crime 'Hot Spots': A Randomized Controlled Trial." *Justice Quarterly* 12 (December): 625–48.

Sichel, J. 1978. *Women on Patrol*. Washington, DC: U.S. Government Printing Office.

Sickmund, M. 2003. "Juveniles in Court." In *National Report Series Bulletin*. Washington, DC: Office of Juvenile Justice and Delinquency Prevention, June.

———. 2004. "Juveniles in Corrections." In *National Report Series Bulletin*. Washington, DC: Office of Juvenile Justice and Delinquency Prevention, June.

Silverman, E. 1999. *NYPD Battles Crime*. Boston: Northeastern University Press.

Simon, L. M. S. 1993. "Prison Behavior and the Victim–Offender Relationships among Violent Offenders." *Justice Quarterly* 10 (September): 489–506.

Simon, R. 1975. *Women and Crime*. Lexington, MA: D.C. Heath.

Sims, B., B. Yost, and C. Abbott. 2005. "Use and Nonuse of Victim Services Programs: Implications from a Statewide Survey of Crime Victims." *Criminology and Public Policy* 4:361–84.

Skogan, W. G. 1990. *Disorder and Decline: Crime and the Spiral of Decay in America*. New York: Free Press.

———. 1995. "Crime and Racial Fears of White Americans." *Annals of the American Academy of Political and Social Science* 539 (May): 59–71.

Skolnick, J. H. 1966. *Justice without Trial: Law Enforcement in a Democratic Society*. New York: Wiley.

Skolnick, J. H., and D. H. Bayley. 1986. *The New Blue Line*. New York: Free Press.

Skolnick, J. H., and J. J. Fyfe. 1993. *Above the Law: Police and Excessive Use of Force*. New York: Free Press.

Slater, H. P., and M. Reiser. 1988. "A Comparative Study of Factors Influencing Police Recruitment." *Journal of Police Science and Administration* 16:160–75.

Smith, C. E. 1990. *United States Magistrates in the Federal Courts: Subordinate Judges*. New York: Praeger.

———. 1994. "Imagery, Politics, and Jury Reform." *Akron Law Review* 28:77–95.

———. 1995a. "The Constitution and Criminal Punishment: The Emerging Visions of Justices Scalia and Thomas." *Drake Law Review* 43:593–613.

———. 1995b. "Federal Habeas Corpus Reform: The State's Perspective." *Justice System Journal* 18:1–11.

———. 1995c. "Judicial Policy Making and Habeas Corpus Reform." *Criminal Justice Policy Review* 7:91–114.

———. 1997. *Courts, Politics, and the Judicial Process*. 2nd ed. Belmont, CA: Wadsworth.

———. 1999. "Criminal Justice and the 1997–98 U.S. Supreme Court Term." *Southern Illinois University Law Review* 23:443–67.

———. 2000. *Law and Contemporary Corrections*. Belmont, CA: Wadsworth.

———. 2003. *Criminal Procedure*. Belmont, CA: Wadsworth.

Smith, C. E., and J. A. Baugh. 2000. *The Real Clarence Thomas: Confirmation Veracity Meets Performance Reality*. New York: Peter Lang.

Smith, C. E., and H. Feldman. 2001. "Burdens of the Bench: State Supreme Courts' Non-Judicial Tasks." *Judicature* 84:304–9.

Smith, C. E., and J. Hurst. 1996. "Law and Police Agencies' Policies: Perceptions of the Relative Impact of Constitutional Law Decisions and Civil Liabilities Decisions." Paper given at the annual meeting of the American Society of Criminology, Chicago.

Smith, C. E., and M. McCall. 2002. "Constitutional Rights and Technological Innovation in Criminal Justice." *Southern Illinois Law Journal* 27:103–27.

Smith, C. E., M. McCall, and C. Perez McCluskey. 2005. *Law and Criminal Justice: Emerging Issues in the Twenty-First Century*. New York: Peter Lang.

Smith, C. E., and R. Ochoa. 1996. "The Peremptory Challenge in the Eyes of the Trial Judge." *Judicature* 79:185–89.

Smith, S. K., and C. J. DeFrances. 1996. "Indigent Defense." *Bureau of Justice Statistics Bulletin*, February.

Sorensen, J. R., J. M. Marquart, and D. E. Brock. 1993. "Factors Related to Killings of Felons by Police Officers: A Test of the Community Violence and Conflict Hypotheses." *Justice Quarterly* 10:417–40.

Sorensen, J. R., and D. H. Wallace. 1999. "Prosecutorial Discretion in Seeking Death: An Analysis of Racial Disparity in the Pretrial Stages of Case Processing in a Midwestern County." *Justice Quarterly* 16:561–78.

Spangenberg, R. L., and M. L. Beeman. 1995. "Indigent Defense Systems in the United States." *Law and Contemporary Problems* 58:31–49.

Sparrow, M. K., M. H. Moore, and D. M. Kennedy. 1990. *Beyond 911: A New Era for Policing*. New York: Basic Books.

Spears, J. W., and C. C. Spohn. 1997. "The Effect of Evidence Factors and Victim Characteristics on Prosecutors' Charging Decisions in Sexual Assault Cases." *Justice Quarterly* 14:501–24.

Spelman, W. G., and D. K. Brown. 1984. *Calling the Police: Citizen Reporting of Serious Crime*. Washington, DC: Police Executive Research Forum.

Spencer, C. 2000. "Nonlethal Weapons Aid Lawmen: Police Turn to Beanbag Guns, Pepper Spray to Save Lives of Defiant Suspects." *Arkansas Democrat-Gazette*, November 6, p. B1.

Spitzer, S. 1975. "Toward a Marxian Theory of Deviance." *Social Problems* 22:638–51.

Spohn, C. 1992. "An Analysis of the 'Jury Trial Penalty' and Its Effect on Black and White Offenders." *The Justice Professional* 7:93–97.

Spohn, C., and D. Holleran. 2000. "The Imprisonment Penalty Paid by Young, Unemployed Black and Hispanic Male Offenders." *Criminology* 38:281–306.

———. 2001. "Prosecuting Sexual Assault: A Comparison of Charging Decisions in Sexual Assault Cases Involving Strangers, Acquaintances, and Intimate Partners." *Justice Quarterly* 18:651–85.

Stafford, M. C., and M. Warr. 1993. "A Reconceptualization of General and Specific Deterrence." *Journal of Research in Crime and Delinquency* 30 (May): 123–35.

Stanford, M. R., and B. L. Mowry. 1990. "Domestic Disturbance Danger Rate." *Journal of Police Science and Administration* 17: 244–49.

Stanko, E. 1988. "The Impact of Victim Assessment on Prosecutors' Screening Decisions: The Case of the New York District Attorney's Office." In *Criminal Justice: Law and Politics*, 5th ed., ed. G. F. Cole. Pacific Grove, CA: Brooks/Cole.

Steffensmeier, D., and S. Demuth. 2001. "Ethnicity and Judges' Sentencing Decisions: Hispanic-Black-White Comparisons." *Criminology* 39:145–78.

Steffensmeier, D., J. Kramer, and C. Streifel. 1993. "Gender and Imprisonment Decisions." *Criminology* 31:411–46.

Steffensmeier, D., J. Ulmer, and J. Kramer. 1998. "The Interaction of Race, Gender, and Age in Criminal Sentencing: The Punishment Cost of Being Young, Black, and Male." *Criminology* 36:763–97.

Steinberg, J. 1999. "The Coming Crime Wave Is Washed Up." *New York Times*, January 3, p. 4WK.

Steury, E., and N. Frank. 1990. "Gender Bias and Pretrial Release: More Pieces of the Puzzle." *Journal of Criminal Justice* 18:417–32.

Steward, D., and M. Totman. 2005. *Racial Profiling: Don't Mind If I Take a Look, Do Ya? An Examination of Consent Searches and Contraband Hits at Texas Traffic Stops*. Austin: Texas Justice Coalition.

Stoddard, E. R. 1968. "The Informal 'Code' of Police Deviancy: A Group Approach to Blue-Coat Crime." *Journal of Criminal Law, Criminology, and Police Science* 59: 204–11.

Stojkovic, S. 1990. "Accounts of Prison Work: Corrections Officers' Portrayals of Their Work Worlds." *Perspectives on Social Problems* 2:211–30.

Stolzenberg, L., and S. J. D'Alessio. 1994. "Sentencing and Unwarranted Disparity: An Empirical Assessment of the Long-Term Impact of Sentencing Guidelines in Minnesota." *Criminology* 32:301–10.

———. 1997. "Three Strikes and You're Out: The Impact of California's New Mandatory Sentencing Law on Serious Crime Rates." *Crime and Delinquency* 43:457–69.

Strodtbeck, F., R. James, and G. Hawkins. 1957. "Social Status in Jury Deliberations." *American Sociological Review* 22:713–19.

Stroshine, M. S. 2005. "Information Technology Innovations in Policing." In *Critical Issues in Policing*, 5th ed., ed. R. G. Dunham and G. P. Alpert. Long Grove, IL: Waveland Press, 172–83.

Sullivan, K. M. 2003. "Under a Watchful Eye: Incursions on Personal Privacy." In *The War on Our Freedoms: Civil Liberties in an Age of Terrorism*," ed. R. C. Leone and G. Anrig, Jr. New York: Public Affairs, 128–46.

Sutherland, E. H. 1947. *Criminology*. 4th ed. Philadelphia: Lippincott.

Swarz, J. 2004. "Inmates vs. Outsourcing." *USA Today*, July 6, p. 1.

Sykes, G. M. 1958. *The Society of Captives*. Princeton, NJ: Princeton University Press.

Taifa, N. 2002. Testimony on Behalf of American Civil Liberties Union of the National Capital Area Concerning Proposed Use of Surveillance Cameras, before the Joint Public Oversight Hearing Committee on the Judiciary, Council of the District of Columbia, June 13. http://www.dcwatch.com.

Teeters, N. K., and J. D. Shearer. 1957. *The Prison at Philadelphia's Cherry Hill*. New York: Columbia University Press.

Thomas, C. W. 2002. "A 'Real Time' Statistical Profile of Private Prisons for Adults." http://web.crim.ufl.edu/pcp/census.

Thompson, R. A. 2001. "Police Use of Force against Drug Suspects: Understanding the Legal Need for Policy Development." *American Journal of Criminal Justice* 25:173–97.

Thurman, Q., J. Zhao, and A. Giacomazzi. 2001. *Community Policing in a Community Era*. Los Angeles: Roxbury.

Toch, H. 1976. *Peacekeeping: Police, Prisons, and Violence*. Lexington, MA: Lexington Books.

Tonry, M. 1993. "Sentencing Commissions and Their Guidelines." In *Crime and Justice*, vol. 17, ed. M. Tonry. Chicago: University of Chicago Press.

———. 1995. *Malign Neglect: Race, Crime, and Punishment in America*. New York: Oxford University Press.

———. 1998. "Intermediate Sanctions." In *Handbook of Crime and Punishment*, ed. M. Tonry. New York: Oxford University Press, 683–711.

Tonry, M., and M. Lynch. 1996. "Intermediate Sanctions." In *Crime and Justice*, vol. 20, ed. M. Tonry. Chicago: University of Chicago Press, 99–144.

Travis, J. 2002. "Invisible Punishment: An Instrument of Social Exclusion." In *Invisible Punishment: The Collateral Consequences of*

Mass Imprisonment, ed. M. Bauer and M. Chesney-Lind. New York: The New Press, 15–36.

Travis, J., and J. Petersilia. 2001. "Reentry Reconsidered: A New Look at an Old Question." *Crime and Delinquency* 47 (July): 291–313.

"The Trial." 2004. *Newark Star-Ledger*, February 8. http://www.nj.com.

Trulson, C. R. 2005. "Victims' Rights and Services: Eligibility, Exclusion, and Victim Worth." *Criminology and Public Policy* 4:399–414.

Turley, J. 2002. "Detaining Liberty." *Lansing State Journal*, August 18, p. 11A.

"2005 Economics of Law Practice Survey." 2005. *Wisconsin Lawyer* 78 (12). http://www.wisbar.org.

Uchida, C. 2005. "The Development of the American Police: An Historical Overview." In *Critical Issues in Policing*, ed. R. G. Dunham and G. P. Alpert. Long Grove, IL: Waveland Press, 20–40.

Uchida, C., and T. Bynum. 1991. "Search Warrants, Motions to Suppress and 'Lost Cases': The Effects of the Exclusionary Rule in Seven Jurisdictions." *Journal of Criminal Law and Criminology* 81:1034–66.

Ugwuegbu, D. 1999. "Racial and Evidential Factors in Juror Attributions of Legal Responsibility." In *The Social Organization of Law*, 2nd ed., ed. M. P. Baumgartner. San Diego, CA: Academic Press.

U.S. Department of Health and Human Services. 2005. *Results from the 2004 National Survey on Drug Use and Health: National Findings*. Washington, DC: Substance Abuse and Mental Health Services Administration, U.S. Government Printing Office.

U.S. Department of State. 2004. *Country Reports on Human Rights Practices*. http://www.state.gov.

U.S. President's Commission on Law Enforcement and Administration of Justice. 1967. *The Challenge of Crime in a Free Society*. Washington, DC: U.S. Government Printing Office.

University of Pittsburgh Medical Center. 2005. "Lead in Environment Causes Violent Crime, Reports University of Pittsburgh Researcher at AAAS." *UPMC News Release*, February 18. http://newsbureau.upmc.com.

Utz, P. 1978. *Settling the Facts*. Lexington, MA: Lexington Books.

Varano, S. P., J. D. McCluskey, J. W. Patchin, and T. S. Bynum. 2004. "Exploring the Drug-Homicide Connection." *Journal of Contemporary Criminal Justice* 20:369–92.

Vaughn, M. S. 2001. "Assessing the Legal Liabilities in Law Enforcement: Chiefs' Views." *Crime and Delinquency* 47:3–27.

Vicenti, C. N. 1995. "The Reemergence of Tribal Society and Traditional Justice Systems." *Judicature* 79:134–41.

Vila, B., and D. J. Kenney. 2002. "Tired Cops: The Prevalence and Potential Consequences of Police Fatigue." *National Institute of Justice Journal* 248:16–21.

von Hirsch, A. 1976. *Doing Justice*. New York: Hill and Wang.

Walker, P. 1998. "Felony and Misdemeanor Defendants Filed in the U.S. District Courts during Fiscal Years 1990–95: An Analysis of the Filings of Each Offense Level." *Journal of Criminal Justice* 26:503–11.

Walker, S. 1984. "'Broken Windows' and Fractured History: The Use and Misuse of History in Recent Police Patrol Analysis." *Justice Quarterly* 1 (March): 88.

———. 1999. *The Police in America*. 3rd ed. New York: McGraw-Hill.

———. 2001. *Sense and Nonsense about Crime and Drugs: A Policy Guide*. 5th ed. Belmont, CA: Wadsworth.

Walker, S., C. Spohn, and M. DeLeone. 2003. *The Color of Justice: Race, Ethnicity and Crime in America*. 3rd ed. Belmont, CA: Wadsworth.

Walker, S., and K. B. Turner. 1992. "A Decade of Modest Progress: Employment of Black and Hispanic Police Officers, 1983–1992." Omaha: Department of Criminal Justice, University of Nebraska at Omaha.

Walker, S., and B. Wright. 1995. "Citizen Review of the Police, 1994: A National Survey." In *Fresh Perspectives*. Washington, DC: Police Executive Research Forum.

Walsh, W. 1989. "Private/Public Police Stereotypes: A Different Perspective." *Security Journal* 1:21–27.

Walsh, W. F., and G. F. Vito. 2004. "The Meaning of Compstat." *Journal of Contemporary Criminal Justice* 20:51–69.

Wasby, S. 2003. "The Work of the Circuit's Chief Judge." *Justice System Journal* 24:63–90.

Wasserman, D. T. 1990. *A Sword for the Convicted: Representing Indigent Defendants on Appeal*. New York: Greenwood Press.

Watson, A., P. Hanrahan, D. Luchins, and A. Lurigio. 2001. "Mental Health Courts and the Complex Issue of Mentally Ill Offenders." *Psychiatric Services* 52:477–81.

Weinstein, J. B. 1992. "A Trial Judge's Second Impression of the Federal Sentencing Guidelines." *Southern California Law Review* 66:357.

Weisburd, D., S. D. Mastrofski, A. M. McNally, R. Greenspan, and J. J. Willis. 2003. "Reforming to Preserve: Compstat and Strategic Problem Solving in American Policing." *Criminology and Public Policy* 2:421–56.

Weitzer, R. 2002. "Incidents of Police Misconduct and Public Opinion." *Journal of Criminal Justice* 30:397–408.

Welch, M. 1994. "Jail Overcrowding: Social Sanitation and the Warehousing of the Urban Underclass." In *Critical Issues in Crime and Justice*, ed. A. Roberts. Thousand Oaks, CA: Sage, 249–74.

"What Was She Thinking?" 2005. *XXL Magazine*, July. http://xxlmag.com/Features/2005/july/lil-kim/.

White, J. 2004. *Defending the Homeland*. Belmont, CA: Thomson/Wadsworth.

White, M. D., J. Fyfe, S. Campbell, and J. Goldkamp. 2003. "The Police Role in Preventing Homicide: Considering the Impact of Problem-oriented Policing on the Prevalence of Murder." *Journal of Research in Crime and Delinquency* 40:194–225.

White, M. S. 1995. "The Nonverbal Behaviors in Jury Selection." *Criminal Law Bulletin* 31:414–45.

Wilbanks, W. 1987. *The Myth of a Racist Criminal Justice System*. Pacific Grove, CA: Brooks/Cole.

Williams, E. J. 2003. "Structuring in Community Policing: Institutionalizing Innovative Change." *Police Practice and Research* 4: 119–29.

Williams, H., and P. V. Murphy. 1990. "The Evolving Strategy of Police: A Minority View." In *Perspectives on Policing*, no. 13. Washington, DC: National Institute of Justice, U.S. Government Printing Office.

Williams, H., and A. M. Pate. 1987. "Returning to First Principles: Reducing the Fear of Crime in Newark." *Crime and Delinquency* 33 (January): 53–59.

Williams, V., and M. Fish. 1974. *Convicts, Codes, and Contraband*. Cambridge, MA: Ballinger.

Willing, R. 2006. "FBI Cases Drop as It Focuses on Terror." *USA Today*, April 13. http://www.usatoday.com.

Willis, J. J., S. D. Mastrofski, and D. Weisbrud. 2004. "Compstat and Bureaucracy: A Case Study of Challenges and Opportunities for Change." *Justice Quarterly* 21:463–96.

Wilson, J. Q. 1968. *Varieties of Police Behavior*. Cambridge, MA: Harvard University Press.

Wilson, J. Q., and R. Herrnstein. 1985. *Crime and Human Nature*. New York: Simon & Schuster.

Wilson, J. Q., and G. L. Kelling. 1982. "Broken Windows: The Police and Neighborhood Safety." *Atlantic Monthly*, March, pp. 29–38.

Winerip, M. 1999. "Bedlam in the Streets." *The New York Times Sunday Magazine*, May 23, p. 42.

Winkeljohn, M. 2002. "A Random Act of Hate: Duckett's Attack Linked to Racism." *Atlanta Journal and Constitution*, August 4, p. E1.

Wolfgang, M. E., and F. Ferracuti. 1967. *The Subculture of Violence*. London: Tavistock.

Worden, A. P. 1993. "The Attitudes of Women and Men in Policing: Testing Conventional and Contemporary Wisdom." *Criminology* 31 (May): 203–24.

———. 1994. "Counsel for the Poor: An Evaluation of Contracting for Indigent Criminal Defense." *Justice Quarterly* 10:613–37.

———. 1995. "The Judge's Role in Plea Bargaining: An Analysis of Judges' Agreement with Prosecutors' Sentencing Recommendations." *Justice Quarterly* 12:257–78.

Worth, R. F. 2001. "73 Tied to Genovese Family Are Indicted, Officials Say." *New York Times*, December 6, p. A27.

Yang, S. S. 1990. "The Unique Treatment Needs of Female Substance Abusers: The Obligation of the Criminal Justice System to Provide Parity Services." *Medicine and Law* 9:1018–27.

Zagaris, B. 1998. "U.S. International Cooperation against Transnational Organized Crime." *Wayne Law Review* 44 (Fall): 1401–64.

Zedner, L. 1995. "Wayward Sisters." In *The Oxford History of Prisons*, ed. N. Morris and D. J. Rothman. New York: Oxford University Press, 329–61.

Zhao, J., C. Gibson, N. Lovrich, and M. Gaffney. 2002. "Participation in Community Crime Prevention: Are Volunteers More or Less Fearful of Crime?" *Journal of Crime and Justice* 25:41–61.

Zhao, J. S., N. P. He, N. Loverich, and J. Cancino. 2003. "Marital Status and Police Occupational Stress." *Journal of Crime and Justice* 26:23–46.

Zhao, J., M. Scheider, and Q. Thurman. 2003. "Funding Community Policing to Reduce Crime: Have COPS Grants Made a Difference?" *Criminology and Public Policy* 2:7–32.

Cases Cited

Adams v. Williams, 407 U.S. 143 (1972).
Argersinger v. Hamlin, 407 U.S. 25 (1972).
Atkins v. Virginia, 122 S.Ct. 2242 (2002).
Austin v. United States, 61 LW 4811 (1993).
Barron v. Baltimore, 32 U.S. 243 (1833).
Batson v. Kentucky, 476 U.S. 79 (1986).
Blackledge v. Allison, 431 U.S. 71 (1976).
Blake v. Los Angeles, 595 F.2d 1367 (1979).
Blakely v. Washington, 124 S.Ct. 2531 (2004).
Bond v. United States, 529 U.S. 334 (2000).
Bordenkircher v. Hayes, 343 U.S. 357 (1978).
Boykin v. Alabama, 395 U.S. 238 (1969).
Breed v. Jones, 421 U.S. 519 (1975).
Brigham City, Utah v. Stuart, 126 S.Ct. 1943 (2006).
Brewer v. Williams, 430 U.S. 387 (1977).
Brown v. Mississippi, 297 U.S. 281 (1936).
Bumper v. North Carolina, 391 U.S. 543 (1968).
Burch v. Louisiana, 441 U.S. 130 (1979).
California v. Acevedo, 500 U.S. 565 (1991).
Carroll v. United States, 267 U.S. 132 (1925).
Chimel v. California, 395 U.S. 752 (1969).
City of Indianapolis v. Edmond, 531 U.S. 32 (2000).
Coolidge v. New Hampshire, 403 U.S. 443 (1971).
Cooper v. Pate, 378 U.S. 546 (1964).
Cupp v. Murphy, 412 U.S. 291 (1973).
Dawson v. State, 274 Ga. 327 (2001).
Deck v. Missouri, 125 S.Ct. 2007 (2005).
Delaware v. Prouse, 440 U.S. 648 (1979).
Dickerson v. United States, 530 U.S. 428 (2000).
Douglas v. California, 372 U.S. 353 (1963).
Durham v. United States, 214 F.2d 862 (D.C. Cir. 1954).
Eddings v. Oklahoma, 455 U.S. 104 (1982).
Escobedo v. Illinois, 378 U.S. 478 (1964).
Ewing v. California, No. 01–6978 (2003).
Fierro v. Gomez, 865 F.Supp. 1387 (N.D. Cal. 1994).

Flippo v. West Virginia, 528 U.S. 11 (1999).
Florida v. J. L., 529 U.S. 266 (2000).
Ford v. Wainwright, 477 U.S. 399 (1986).
Foster v. Florida, 537 U.S. 990 (2002).
Furman v. Georgia, 408 U.S. 238 (1972).
Gagnon v. Scarpelli, 411 U.S. 778 (1973).
Georgia v. Randolph, 126 S.Ct. 1515 (2006).
Gideon v. Wainwright, 372 U.S. 335 (1963).
Graham v. Connor, 490 U.S. 396 (1989).
Gregg v. Georgia, 428 U.S. 153 (1976).
Griggs v. Duke Power Company, 401 U.S. 424 (1971).
Griffin v. Wisconsin, 483 U.S. 868 (1987).
Hamdi v. Rumsfeld, 542 U.S. 507 (2004).
Heath v. Alabama, 474 U.S. 82 (1985).
Hester v. United States, 265 U.S. 57 (1924).
Hill v. McDonough, 126 S.Ct. 2096 (2006).
Hudson v. Palmer, 52 L.W. 5052 (1984).
Illinois v. Caballes, 125 S.Ct. 834 (2005).
Illinois v. Gates, 462 U.S. 213 (1983).
Illinois v. Lidster, 540 U.S. 419 (2004).
Illinois v. Wardlow, 528 U.S. 119 (2000).
In re Gault, 387 U.S. 9 (1967).
In re Winship, 397 U.S. 358 (1970).
Johnson v. Zerbst, 304 U.S. 458 (1938).
Kansas v. Hendricks, 117 S.Ct. 2072 (1997).
Kent v. United States, 383 U.S. 541 (1966).
Knowles v. Iowa, 525 U.S. 113 (1998).
Lawrence v. Texas, 539 U.S. 558 (2003).
Lee v. Washington, 390 U.S. 333 (1968).
Lockhart v. McCree, 476 U.S. 162 (1986).
Lockyer, Attorney General of California v. Andrade, 538 U.S. 63 (2003).
Mapp v. Ohio, 367 U.S. 643 (1961).
Maryland v. Wilson, 519 U.S. 408 (1997).
Massiah v. United States, 377 U.S. 201 (1964).
McCleskey v. Kemp, 478 U.S. 1019 (1987).
McKeiver v. Pennsylvania, 403 U.S. 528 (1971).
Medellin v. Dretke, 125 S.Ct. 2088 (2005).
Mempa v. Rhay, 389 U.S. 128 (1967).
Michigan Department of State Police v. Sitz, 496 U.S. 440 (1990).
Michigan v. Long, 463 U.S. 1032 (1983).
Minnesota v. Dickerson, 508 U.S. 366 (1993).
Miranda v. Arizona, 384 U.S. 436 (1966).
Missouri v. Seibert, 542 U.S. 600 (2004).
M'Naghten's Case, 8 Eng. Rep. 718 (1843).
Monell v. Department of Social Services of the City of New York, 436 U.S. 658 (1978).
Montana v. Egelhoff, 116 S.Ct. 2013 (1996).
Moran v. Burbine, 475 U.S. 412 (1986).
Morrissey v. Brewer, 408 U.S. 471 (1972).
Murray v. Giarratano, 492 U.S. 1 (1989).
Nelson v. Campbell, 124 S.Ct. 2117 (2004).
New York v. Belton, 453 U.S. 454 (1981).
New York v. Class, 475 U.S. 321 (1986).
New York v. Quarles, 467 U.S. 649 (1984).
Nix v. Williams, 467 U.S. 431 (1984).
North Carolina v. Alford, 400 U.S. 25 (1970).
Oklahoma Publishing Co. v. District Court, 430 U.S. 308 (1977).

Oliver v. United States, 466 U.S. 170 (1984).
Pargo v. Elliott, 69 F.3d 280 (8th Cir. 1995).
Pennsylvania Board of Pardons and Parole v. Scott, 524 U.S. 357 (1998).
People v. LaValle, 3 NY3d 88 (2004).
Powell v. Alabama, 287 U.S. 45 (1932).
Procunier v. Martinez, 416 U.S. 396 (1974).
The Queen v. Dudley and Stephens, 14 Q.B.D. 273 (1884).
R.A.V. v. City of St. Paul, 112 S.Ct. 2538 (1992).
Ricketts v. Adamson, 481 U.S. 1 (1987).
Ring v. Arizona, 122 S.Ct. 2428 (2002).
Robinson v. California, 370 U.S. 660 (1962).
Roe v. Wade, 410 U.S. 113 (1973).
Roper v. Simmons, 125 S.Ct. 1183 (2005).
Ross v. Moffitt, 417 U.S. 660 (1974).
Santobello v. New York, 404 U.S. 260 (1971).
Schall v. Martin, 467 U.S. 253 (1984).
Scott v. Illinois, 440 U.S. 367 (1979).
Skinner v. Oklahoma, 316 U.S. 535 (1942).
Smith v. Daily Mail Publishing Co., 443 U.S. 97 (1979).
South Dakota v. Opperman, 428 U.S. 364 (1976).
Stanford v. Kentucky, 492 U.S. 361 (1989).
Strickland v. Washington, 466 U.S. 686 (1984).
Tennessee v. Garner, 471 U.S. 1 (1985).
Terry v. Ohio, 392 U.S. 1 (1968).
Thompson v. Oklahoma, 108 S.Ct. 1687 (1988).
Trop v. Dulles, 356 U.S. 86 (1958).
Turner v. Safley, 482 U.S. 78 (1987).
United States v. Bajakajian, 118 S.Ct. 2028 (1998).
United States v. Booker, 125 S.Ct. 738 (2005).
United States v. Brawner, 471 F.2d 969 (D.C. Cir. 1972).
United States v. Drayton, 122 S.Ct. 2105 (2002).
United States v. Jacobson, 503 U.S. 540 (1992).
United States v. Leon, 468 U.S. 897 (1984).
United States v. Robinson, 414 U.S. 218 (1973).
United States v. Salerno and Cafero, 481 U.S. 739 (1987).
United States v. Ursery, 116 S.Ct. 2135 (1996).
United States v. Wade, 388 U.S. 218 (1967).
Virginia v. Black, 538 U.S. 343 (2003).
Warden v. Hayden, 387 U.S. 294 (1967).
Weeks v. United States, 232 U.S. 383 (1914).
Whren v. United States, 517 U.S. 806 (1996).
Wiggins v. Smith, 539 U.S. 510 (2003).
Williams v. Florida, 399 U.S. 78 (1970).
Wisconsin v. Mitchell, 113 S.Ct. 2194 (1993).
Witherspoon v. Illinois, 391 U.S. 510 (1968).
Wolf v. Colorado, 338 U.S. 25 (1949).
Wolff v. McDonnell, 418 U.S. 539 (1974).
Wyoming v. Houghton, 526 U.S. 295 (1999).

Name Index

Subject Index

Note: Page numbers in **boldface** type indicate pages on which terms are defined.

Photo Credits

Part and chapter openers, Technology Issues in Criminal Justice box: © Chad Baker/ Getty Images
Careers in Criminal Justice box: Don Farrall/Getty Images
Close Up box: Jason Reed/Getty Images
The Policy Debate box: Jeremy Woodhouse/Getty Images
Comparative Perspective box: Ryan McVay/Getty Images
The Criminal Justice Process: The State of Michigan versus Christopher Jones: Nick Koudis/Getty Images

Chapter 1: p. 3, AP Photo/Louis Lanzano; p.5, AP Photo/Susan Walsh; p. 7, Photo by Gary Tramontina/Getty Images; p. 11, AP Photo/THE NEWS & OBSERVER/Chuck Liddy; p. 14, AP Photo/Michael Kim; p.15, Chronicle photo by Penni Gladstone; p. 20, AP Photo/Carlo Allegri, Pool; p. 23, Bob Daemmerich/Stock, Boston

Chapter 2: p. 33, Bo Rader-Pool/Getty Images; p. 36, REUTERS/Richard Carson/ Landov; p. 38, Lynsey Addario/Corbis; p. 39, AP Photo/Scott Audette; p. 47, AP Photo/ Kevork Djansezian; p. 49, Courtesy of Community Coalition on Family Violence, Knoxville TN.; p. 54, © Bettmann/Corbis; p. 58, AP Photo/Paul Vernon

Chapter 3: p.62, Associated Press, COURT TV.COM; p. 66, Archive Photos; p. 68, © George Frey/Getty Images; p. 69, AP Photo/Arizona Daily Sun, Greg Bryan; p. 76, Time Life Pictures/Mansell/Getty Images; p. 79, Joel Nito/APF/Getty Images; p. 83, main photo and inset, Courtesy of California Dept. of Corrections and Rehabilitation

Chapter 4: p. 89, Photo by Marko Georgiev/Getty Images; p. 93, Culver Pictures; p. 94, Photo by David McNew/Getty Images; p. 95, © Andrew Lichtenstein/The Image Works; p. 99, © Syracuse Newspapers /Dennis Nett/The Image Works; p. 103, © Joel Gordon; p. 104, Mark Richards/PhotoEdit; p. 110, © Viviane Moos/Corbis; p. 112, AP Photo/ Nick Ut

Chapter 5: p. 117, © Gerald Martineau-The Washington Post; p.122, © REUTERS/ Chip East/Landov; p. 123, Michael Nagle/The New York Times/Redux; p. 124, Bob Daemmrich/The Image Works; p. 128, John Klicker/The New York Times/Redux; p. 131, AP Photo/Erik S. Lesser; p. 134, © Karen Kasmauski/Corbis; p. 139, © Royalty-Free/Corbis; p. 140, © Lou Dematteis/The Image Works

Chapter 6: p. 147, main photo, © Eric Micheletti, The Military Picture Library/Corbis, inset, AP Photo/Ric Francis; p. 149, AP Photo/Peter Dejong; p. 152, Joe Rodriguez/Black Star; p. 157, Scott Audette/Reuters/Landov; p. 158, © Brooks Kraft/Corbis; p. 160, AP Photo/Daily Inter Lake, Karen Nichols; p. 162, © Ken Cedeno/Corbis; p. 164, Shawn Moore/DOL; p. 171, © Ed Kashi/Corbis; p. 173, © Syracuse Newspapers/Li-Hua Lan/ The Image Works

Chapter 7: p. 177, Doug Menuez/Getty Images; p. 181, Photo by Bill Pugliano/Getty Images; p. 182, A. Ramey/PhotoEdit; p. 184, Photo by Joe Raedle/Getty Images; p. 186, AP Photo/Gregory Bull; p. 189, AP Photo/Rich Pedroncelli; p. 191, © Mark Richards/ PhotoEdit; p. 195, AP Photo/The Oklahoman, Steve Sisney

TO THE OWNER OF THIS BOOK:

We hope that you have found *Criminal Justice in America,* Fifth Edition useful. So that this book can be improved in a future edition, would you take the time to complete this sheet and return it? Thank you.

School and address: _____

_____

Department: _____

Instructor's name: _____

1. What I like most about this book is: _____

_____

_____

2. What I like least about this book is: _____

_____

_____

3. My general reaction to this book is: _____

_____

_____

4. The name of the course in which I used this book is: _____

_____

5. Were all of the chapters of the book assigned for you to read? _____

   If not, which ones weren't? _____

6. In the space below, or on a separate sheet of paper, please write specific suggestions for improving this book and anything else you'd care to share about your experience in using this book.

_____

_____

_____

_____

_____

_____

A LIFE FOR A
LIFE LIFE IMPNN
FOLD HERE

JAMES A. PALUCH, JR.
ED. BY THOMAS BERNARD
+ ROBERT JOHNSON

BUSINESS REPLY MAIL
FIRST-CLASS MAIL   PERMIT NO. 34   BELMONT CA

POSTAGE WILL BE PAID BY ADDRESSEE

AMERICA'S
OTHER
DEATH
PENALTY

L.A. CA.

Attn: Carolyn Henderson Meier,
Criminal Justice Editor

2004

Wadsworth/Thomson Learning

10 Davis Dr

Belmont CA 94002-9801

ISBN 1-931719-37-3
ROXBURY PUBLISHING

NO POSTAGE
NECESSARY
IF MAILED
IN THE
UNITED STATES

E-MAIL ROXBURY@ROXBURY.NET
OPTIONAL: WWW.ROXBURY.NET

Your name: _____ Date: _____

May we quote you, either in promotion for *Criminal Justice in America,* Fifth Edition, or in future publishing ventures?

Yes: _____ No: _____

Sincerely yours,

George F. Cole and Christopher E. Smith